Handbook
for Bible
Teachers
and
Preachers

Handbook
for Bible
Teachers
and
Preachers

APPLICATIONS TO LIFE FROM
EVERY BOOK OF THE BIBLE

G. CAMPBELL
MORGAN

BAKER BOOK HOUSE
Grand Rapids, Michigan 49506

Originally published in four volumes
by Fleming H. Revell Company, 1912

One-volume edition, with revised outlines,
copyright 1982 by
Baker Book House Company

Formerly published under the title
Living Messages of the Books of the Bible

ISBN: 0-8010-6190-3

Seventh printing, October 1993

Printed in the United States of America

Contents

Introduction

WITH regard to the Scriptures of the Old Testament, Paul wrote, "Whatsoever things were written aforetime were written for our learning, that through patience and through comfort of the Scriptures we might have hope."

He thus clearly revealed the true mission of these sacred writings in our day, as he declared that they "were written for our learning, that . . we might have hope." Their mission is that of teaching, in order to the inspiration of hope.

This view of the value of the Old Testament Scriptures reveals a most important conception of their nature. The apostle did not suggest that the writers of olden times wrote with the men of later ages in their thought. They wrote for their own age, and for the men by whom they were surrounded. Nevertheless the apostle declared that these things were written for us. It is evident, therefore, that he believed that behind the authors there was an Author; that encompassing the minds of the men who wrote in different places, and at different times, was one master Mind; and that this Author had in view not only the age in which these things were written, but all successive ages.

The peculiar value of these ancient writings for the present time is that they inspire hope in those who read. Hope is an attitude of mind in the midst of conflict, danger, and difficulty. In the age of God's ultimate victory, hope will be changed into sight and possession. What a man sees, he no longer hopes for. The sacred writings of the Hebrew people contain the stories of men in the midst of conflict and peril, reveal the confidences that filled them with hope, tell of the victories they won, of the defeats they suffered; and the supreme value of these Scriptures is that they create hope for those who are still upon the pilgrimage, who are still in the thick of the battle, who are still

carrying on the work of building. The words and works of God in ancient times, the victories men won, and the defeats they suffered, all serve to fill the heart with hope, as they reveal the way of victory, and utter the word of warning.

The apostle with equal clearness revealed the method by which the Scriptures of the old economy fulfilled this mission. This is indicated by the words *patience and comfort*, which with equal accuracy might be rendered *endurance and encouragement*.

The meaning of *endurance* is perhaps best illustrated for us by the eleventh chapter of the letter to the Hebrews. To read that chapter is to pass in review the whole of the Old Testament Scriptures. The great outstanding names are mentioned, and others are referred to, whose names are not given. Throughout the whole chapter, faith is revealed as the principle of victory. All these men are seen passing through circumstances of difficulty and of danger, with their eyes set upon an ultimate purpose, which they supremely desired to be accomplished. None of them reached the ultimate goal, but they died contented, having seen it from afar, and having endured, in their movement towards it, "as seeing Him Who is invisible." The final declaration of the chapter shows that the men of faith to-day are in the same process. Referring to those named, the writer said, "These all, having had witness borne to them through their faith, received not the promise, God having provided some better thing concerning us, that apart from us they should not be made perfect." Thus the things written aforetime produce in the minds of those who are continuing the conflict the quality of endurance.

The word *encouragement* is perhaps even more full of suggestiveness. It is closely allied to the word in the New Testament which is used of the Holy Spirit, the word Paraclete. All the spacious value of the word Paraclete, as used of the Holy Spirit, is contained in the word *encouragement* when used in reference to the Scriptures of truth. It suggests appeal and advocacy. The things written aforetime make their perpetual appeal to men as they advocate the true principle of life in the midst of conflict.

To summarize, the Scriptures of the Old Testament were written by many men in varied circumstances. These men were thinking in all probability, for the most part, of their own age. They wrote songs of their own sorrows and aspirations. They wrote the history of their own times, declaring the faults and sins of the people, as well as their victories. These things they wrote for their own age. That, however, is not all the story. Encompassing them, teaching, guiding, instructing, was the One Who knew all the ages, and saw the long process clearly to the consummation ; and therefore they contain living messages to us. In these writings of the old economy the final message is not to be found, " God, having of old time spoken unto the fathers in the prophets by divers portions and in divers manners, hath at the end of these days spoken unto us in His Son." The final message is the word of the Son, and in it all those of the past merge into perfect harmony ; yet these things written aforetime help us to understand more perfectly the all-inclusive message of the Son.

From this general study we may now make certain deductions which will have a direct bearing upon this series of studies in the messages of the Old Testament.

As to origin we believe the Old Testament Scriptures to be human in workmanship, but Divine in compulsion. The holy men of old wrote with perfect naturalness things of their own age, but they wrote better and more comprehensively than they knew. Any careful study of the New Testament will show how these writers perpetually quoted from the Old in such a manner as to show that its statements were more full of meaning than the men who wrote them knew. The quotation immediately preceding the passage which we have been considering is a remarkable illustration of this fact. " The reproaches of them that reproached thee fell upon me " was a human statement describing a then present experience. Yet the writer was guided, perhaps all unconsciously, by the great master Mind, in order that ultimately the final and supreme suffering should be more perfectly understood. Wherever there is Divine compulsion behind human workmanship, that workmanship becomes more than human ; it is Divine.

As to history, we believe the Old Testament to be accurate in statement and faithful in presentation. Again, to take one illustration, we believe that the Hebrew race, which, having lost its nationality, has never been overwhelmed by, or absorbed into, other races, sprang from that one man who was the friend of God, and who at His call went forth from his own land a pilgrim of faith. We moreover believe that the present " scattered and peeled " condition of that race is the direct outcome of the sins and failures chronicled accurately and faithfully in the Old Testament.

As to religion, we believe the Old Testament to be a foreshadowing of, and process towards, the ultimate revelation which is contained in the New Testament. Christ Himself is the Goal towards which all the religious thinking of the Old Testament Scriptures moves. Finality in religion is not found in the things written aforetime. The symbolism of the ancient worship is a foreshadowing of that which is to come after. The messages of the prophets and psalmists are whispers which merge into perfect music only when the Son Who is in the bosom of the Father declares the God Who has never been seen. All the highways through the centuries lead on towards the city, but the city itself, the city of God, can only be built by the King Himself. From the darkness, through the twilight, men moved towards the perfect light. Through all the ages God followed His perpetual method, line upon line, precept upon precept, here a little and there a little. Through all the centuries He said in effect to men what Christ actually said to His disciples : " I have yet many things to say unto you, but ye cannot bear them now." Thus, quietly and surely, if slowly, God moved on to the final Word, Who was made flesh. We do not go back to the Old Testament to find the religion of to-day. We do go to it to discover the highways which led to finality in religion.

As to value, we therefore believe the Old Testament Scriptures to be a revelation of God and man preparatory to the final revelation of the New. To read the Old Testament writings from Genesis to Malachi, and to have no acquaintance with the New, is still to be imperfectly acquainted with God and man.

At the heart of the Old Testament may be found the insignificant " What is man ? " At the heart of the New is the great exclamation, " Behold the Man." Yet the Old is of value as it reveals clearly the true principle of human life, the real reason of human sorrow, all the highways that lead towards human redemption.

So also the revelation of God in the Old Testament is valuable, but incomplete. He is introduced by the simple statement of His infinite Majesty as Creator. In the presence of that first statement man stands a submissive worshipper, but yet without any intimate knowledge of God. The Word must become flesh, must be seen, be looked upon, be handled, be touched, ere man will know God.

The chief value of the revelation of man and of God in the Old Testament is that it makes perfectly clear man's need for God, and God's method with man. Yet it leaves us crying with Job for a " Daysman " able to put His hand upon man in his helplessness, and upon God in His holiness, and make them both one.

Recognizing these values and limitations of the Old Testament Scriptures, we proceed to our study, upon the assumption that every book has some direct and living message having application not to its own age merely, but to every succeeding one. The principles abide ; their applications vary with the varying ages. We desire, then, in our new series to discover in each book the central truth, and to make application of it to the age in which we live. The method to be followed, therefore, will be that of stating the permanent values, and from these deducing the living message.

Genesis

THE PERMANENT VALUES	THE LIVING MESSAGE
I. Theology—the science of God. II. Cosmogony—the science of the universe. III. Anthropology—the science of man. IV. Sociology—the science of society. V. Hamartiology—the science of sin. VI. Ethnology—the science of races. VII. Soteriology—the science of salvation. Note: These subjects are dealt with in Genesis fundamentally, and not finally.	I. **God and man are intimately related.** A. God created man in His own image. B. God governs man for man's own good. C. God loves man. II. **Man realizes his own life by faith in God.** A. Faith is the simple law of life. B. Failure in faith is failure in life. C. Faith may differ in expression. 1. Abraham—obedient. 2. Isaac—passive. 3. Jacob—restless. Note: Faith is the basis upon which God can work out His will in man, and man can work out his salvation from God.

IT is perpetually being asked to-day whether there are any permanent values in the book of Genesis. In the light of later revelation is there any reason for retaining this book, except, perhaps, that of interest in an ancient writing which has yet no vital relationship to our own times? In answer to that enquiry it may at once be stated that the whole system of the Christian religion depends upon the accuracy of certain statements made in this book. Without them that system is an erection without a foundation, conclusions without premises. These declarations, at once the simplest and the profoundest in the book, constitute its permanent values, not merely because all subsequent Scripture depends upon them; but also because if there were no other writings, these statements supply us with answers to questions which must arise to the thinking mind.

The permanent values may be stated briefly and concisely, in order that the living message may be deduced therefrom. There can be little doubt that there are very many people who have no particular desire to destroy the book of Gene-sis, who are interested in it as a collection of stories, having been familiar with it from child-hood, who have, nevertheless, never realized of what vital importance it is, and how much it contains of supreme value.

Its values may thus be technically tabulated. The book contains the foundation truths of theology, cosmogony, anthropology, sociology, hamartiology, ethnology, soteriology. These words are used with the express purpose of indicating the profound conviction that Genesis is preëminently a scientific book. None of these subjects are dealt with finally, but all are presented fundamentally. Genesis supplies men with the rudiments of the science of God. It offers a theory of the origin of the universe. It says the first thing concerning the science of man. It lays the foundations of the science of society. It reveals the simplest matters of the science of sin. It introduces the study of the science of races. Finally, it presents the initial truths concerning the science of salvation.

The essential value of the book is the fundamental character of its teaching on all these mat-

1

ters. Its declarations meet us at the point where knowledge, proceeding along the line of investigation, fails; and present truths undiscovered by investigation. Investigation is a perfectly proper exercise of the human mind. All that men are doing in their attempt to discover the underlying secrets of nature and life is in harmony with the purpose of God in the creation of human intellect. It is nevertheless conceded that man ever arrives at a point beyond which he is unable to go. It is at this point that Genesis speaks in the terms of revelations made to man, rather than a record of discoveries made by man. Processes and consummations will be dealt with in subsequent revelation, or discovered by further investigation. To possess the book of Genesis alone is not to be acquainted with the final truth on any of the subjects named. It is to have the initial word which no subsequent discoveries contradict, and without which all later declarations are meaningless. In order to illustrate this let us pass over the ground in briefest statement by enquiring what the book supplies in each department, and what are the things lacking.

As to theology. Genesis presents God as Creator, King, and determined Redeemer; and upon these fundamental facts all Christian theology depends. The nature of God is not revealed. His methods are not declared. His ultimate purpose is not stated.

As to cosmogony. Genesis declares that the whole universe has come into being by the will and act of God. The hall-mark of the Divine handiwork is upon every blade of grass and upon every flaming constellation. Nothing is stated in detail concerning the process of creation, or the period occupied, or the ultimate purpose.

As to anthropology. Genesis teaches that man is a mingling of dust and Deity by the will and act of God; a being placed under authority, and having dominion over all things beneath him: a being responsible, therefore, to God. Nothing is said concerning the laws which regulate the interaction of the physical and the psychical. Nothing is declared concerning man's ultimate destiny.

As to sociology. Genesis reveals the truth that the first circle of society is the family, based upon the marriage relationship; and that the true nation is made up of families which rec-

ognize their inter-responsibility under the Divine government. The application of these principles to varied and complex conditions is not to be found in this book.

As to hamartiology. Genesis affirms that sin in the case of man is failure of faith in the goodness of God, and consequent rebellion against His government. The ultimate issues of sin in individual destiny are not declared.

As to ethnology. Genesis records the break-up of the unity of the race, following upon an attempted confederacy of godlessness. The ultimate issue in its scattering is not described.

As to soteriology. Genesis makes it perfectly plain that human salvation must come from God, and through man. In whispers and symbols and shadows, man is taught that having sinned, his only hope is that God will be his Redeemer. Nothing is distinctly said concerning the method or finality.

To deny the accuracy of these fundamental statements is to lose the meaning of all subsequent teaching. If God is not Creator, King, and Redeemer, there is no resting place for man other than the restlessness of agnosticism. On the way to agnosticism, human speculations may retain the name of religion; but the logical outcome of the denial of these fundamental assertions concerning God is denial of the existence of God.

To deny what this book teaches concerning the origin of the universe is to be compelled to attempt to account for the things seen by some undefined action and interaction within the universe, which has behind it no personality.

To deny that man is a mysterious mingling of dust and Deity by the will and act of God is necessarily to be compelled to think of him as the last product of animal evolution; and therefore as himself an animal, and nothing more.

If the teaching be denied that human society is founded on the family, and based upon the marriage relationship, then sociology becomes chaotic, and spurious socialism denies the sanctity of or necessity for the marriage relationship.

If the teaching be incorrect that sin is rebellion against God, based upon unbelief, then necessarily the terms in which it has been described by the Christian faith must be modified, until eventually it is declared to be non-existent, none other than the under side of good.

Failure to accept the teaching that national divisions are finally the outcome of a false attempt at unity, based upon self-sufficient rebellion against God, must ultimately result in affirming those divisions to be good which, nevertheless, have been productive of all wars and kindred evils.

To deny the suggestions concerning human salvation as possible only through the intervention of God is ultimately to abandon the idea of salvation as either unnecessary or altogether impossible.

There is a sense in which these things do not constitute the message of this book to our own age, although they do constitute its permanent values. For the sake of argument, let us suppose that this book is the only inspired word ever given to man. What is its ultimate message? It teaches with unvarying definiteness first, the immediate relation between God and man; and secondly, that the great principle for the realization of human life is such faith in God as expresses itself in obedience to His throne.

This book of first things declares the immediate relation between God and man. It is perfectly true that subsequent books state this more fully, and deal with it more explicitly. When we pass from the sublime stateliness of these original statements, through the giving of the law, the establishing of worship; through the thunder of the prophets, and the wailing minor threnody of their pleadings with humanity; and still on to the matchless and final splendour of the brief words spoken by the Man of Galilee; through the unveiling of the meaning of these words by the Spirit, in the apostolic writings, we find this truth wrought out in greater detail and with mightier force. Nevertheless, all that the law indicated, all that the prophets enforced, all that Jesus said, and all that the apostles expounded, depend absolutely for accuracy upon the teaching of this truth as contained in this book. If that first fact of man's relationship to God is not established, then everything that followed was false dreaming, mistaken enthusiasm, or mischievous vapouring.

Remembering the three main divisions of the book, as indicated in the study of its content, Generation, Degeneration, Regeneration, it is at once evident that the supreme message every-where is that God has to do with man; man has to do with God. In the first division we see the story of creation, tracing everything from the material order to man, and then describing man as to his nature and office; and behind all the processes of creation suggested, God is declared; and immediately presiding over the final movement by which man appears, God is seen. That is the first great truth. Man is related to God, for He created him, and He alone perfectly understands him, and consequently He only can govern him. The message of Genesis to our own age is, first of all, that of man's immediate relation to God. We need Genesis because it is difficult sometimes to believe that any such relation exists. We look into the faces of men and women, the flotsam and jetsam of our great cities, at both ends of the social scale, and there seems to be no trace of Deity. If in that statement there seems to be something of personal satisfaction, it is by no means intended. Therefore let a personal word be spoken. To look into one's own heart is to find it most difficult to believe that man is "offspring of God." Nevertheless, when this book affirms that God said, "Let us make man in our image, after our likeness," and that He made him to have dominion; that He placed him in circumstances where he should be reminded of his relation to God, and called upon to respond thereto; I know that I am reading the deepest truth of my own life. This conception of the relation between man and God creates that consciousness of what sin is, which fills the soul with fear. The determined prostitution of powers which are akin to God, to purposes of evil, is terrible indeed; and this message concerning the true nature of man must create a profound conviction of the awfulness of sin. It is, nevertheless, a message of hope, for it suggests the possibility of renewal. To be without God is indeed to be without hope. To believe the truth that man is related to God is to know the renewal of hope. In this first message then, there is thunder, but in it there are also tears. It is because man loses his sense of essential relation to God that sin and sorrow continue. If we could say to the men of this age, In His image, after His likeness, as we ought, there would necessarily follow the profoundest and deepest conviction of sin, and the most genuine return to Him; and therefore to holiness of character, and righteousness of life.

The second message is an inevitable sequence of the first. It is. indeed, a corollary, something which is inseparable therefrom. As man is related to God by creation and government, it follows that the true secret for the realization of his life is that of faith, which expresses itself in obedience. This is at once taught as we pass into the second division of the book, that dealing with Degeneration. Man's confidence in God was first shaken when the enemy said, " Yea, hath God said, Ye shall not eat of any tree of the garden ? " and declared, " Ye shall not surely die." He called in question the goodness and truth of God, and thereby attacked the confidence of a human being. When faith wavered, through listening to a slander upon God, the issue was an act of 'disobedience. Faith and obedience are always joined together.

> " Trust and obey,
> For there's no other way "

may be so simple a statement as to be considered doggerel rather than poetry. It is, nevertheless, the philosophy of Genesis, and of the Christian religion. When trust failed, obedience ceased ; and immediately there passed over all life a blasting and a mildew, and humanity failed to realize itself. Thus the fundamental truth is taught that man can only realize his own God-created life by trusting God, and walking in the way of His commandment.

In the final division of the book, that dealing with the beginnings of Regeneration, the principal subject is that of the life stories of individual and representative men, Abraham, Isaac, Jacob. Throughout all these the supreme revelation is that of God seeking to restore men to obedience by restoring them to the main principle of human life, that of faith in Himself. Faith is seen having different methods of expression. In the case of Abraham, seven communications were made to him, and his faith was always obedient without questioning. Two communications were

made to Isaac, whose faith was passive. To him God spoke merely by way of ratification. Five communications were made to Jacob, whose faith was restless ; and these always came after a period of wandering, in order to restore him. The one principle is found in all ; in Abraham obedient, in Isaac passive, in Jacob restless ; and because that principle was present, God was able to work for the remaking of these men, and they were able to find their way back into conscious relationship with Him.

Thus the book reveals the fact that faith is the basis upon which God can work His will in man, and upon which man can realize the will of God. All this is carried out in greater detail in subsequent books of the Bible, but this is the simple and almost overwhelming message of Genesis to the men of this age. First, that man is not wholly of the dust, but that between him and God there is immediateness of relationship ; and secondly, that man only finds himself, and realizes the true meaning of his own life as he places his confidence in God, and obeys Him with unquestioning loyalty.

Hear, then, the final message of the book. Oh, man, thou art of God. Thou canst only enter into thine own life and realize it as thy confidence is reposed in Him, and thy obedience is yielded to Him. That is the truth which this book utters to all men as a philosophy of life. To those who have fallen, and are excluded from their own life because they are out of fellowship with God, it declares that as they return to the principle of faith in God, they will find their feet placed again upon the highway that leads them home. Not that they will be able to rebuild the ruined temple, or reconstruct the wasted years, but He will be able to do these things when they trust and obey. The book of Genesis declares that the just shall live by faith. Without faith it is impossible to please God. These principles underlie every story, and constitute the living message of the whole book.

Exodus

THE PERMANENT VALUES	THE LIVING MESSAGE

I. **The divine method with the race and the responsibility of the race.**
  A. The method.
    1. The creation of a testimony.
    2. The guarding of the testimony.
  B. The responsibility.
    1. Created by the testimony.
    2. Limited by the testimony.
II. **The divine method with the instrument and the responsibility of the instrument.**
  A. The method.
    1. A progressive revelation of Himself.
    2. A direct and minute administration of affairs.
  B. The responsibilities.
    1. Worship.
    2. Obedience.
III. **The divine method with the individual and the responsibility of the individual.**
  A. The method.
    1. Opportunities for choice.
    2. Ratification of choice.
  B. The responsibilities.
    1. Choice.
    2. Creation of destiny.
	I. **The sovereignty of God.**
	  A. His righteousness.
	    1. In purpose.
	    2. In plan.
	  B. His judgment.
	    1. Wisdom.
	    2. Power.
	II. **The salvation of man.**
	  A. Worship.
	    1. God at centre.
	    2. Life concentric.
	  B. Obedience.
	    1. Simple and complete.
	    2. Against opposition.

IN the book of Exodus nothing is commenced, nothing is finished. To read it, having no acquaintance with the book preceding it, or with those following, would be to be conscious of incompleteness. The first word "Now" might with equal accuracy be translated "And"; which immediately suggests relation to something which has gone before. The last phrase, "Throughout all their journeys," connects with what is to follow, for the book contains no account of the journeys referred to.

These facts help us to understand the message of the book. It is a part of a larger whole, and its supreme value is its revelation of the procedure of God in human history. There are two ways in which we may consider the story it tells. We may think of it as a record of the doings of men, or as the record of the doings of God. To adopt the former method is to be impressed with the sense of failure. The story of Moses is one of failure and weakness, save when he was victorious and strong as the result of his relationship to God. The greatness of the man can only be accounted for in that illuminative word of the psalmist, "Thy gentleness hath made me great." Aaron is a perpetual revelation of weakness. The story of the people is one of unceasing failure, caused by their inability to rise to the height of the revelations they received, and manifest in their eager haste to confess themselves able to keep the commandments of God, and their equally eager haste to break those commandments.

To take the other standpoint, that of the Divine procedure, is to discover the line of progress, and to observe the method by which God was moving forward towards the accomplishment of an ultimate purpose. Thus the chief value of the book is its revelation of the fact that human progress has ever been the result of the grace and the patience of God. Its permanent values, then, are its revelations of the methods of God, and the responsibilities of man. Let us consider these values, and from them deduce the living message of the book.

The principles of the Divine procedure are eternally the same. His methods change as they follow the law of adaptation to new ages, and consequently new requirements. In this book we are observing these methods in their earliest stages; and we shall notice them in three particulars which may thus be stated. The Divine method with the race, and the responsibility of the race in the light thereof. The Divine method with the instrument, and the responsibility of that instrument. The Divine method with the individual, and the responsibility of the individual.

As to the Divine method with the race. This book is the story of the nation. In our analysis it has been termed The emergence of the nation. In the final division of Genesis, that of Regeneration, we have the account of the calling of a man, the creation of a family, and the multiplication of the families; until at its close we see a multitude of people in the land of Goshen, their moral fibre being tempered by suffering; as yet without national consciousness or national power. In Exodus the story of the emergence of this multitude into a nation is told. Its first division reveals a people in bondage; its second tells the story of deliverance from bondage, by the hand of God; and its last gives an account of their organization into national life. It is important that we should understand the meaning of the creation of this nation. It cannot be too often emphasized that it was not the election of a nation from among others in order that upon that nation God might lavish His love while He

abandoned the others. The purpose of God was far wider than that of the creation of this nation; it was that of the creation of a testimony through this nation, for the sake of the others. The Divine intention was the creation of a people who under His government should reveal in the world the breadth and beauty and beneficence of that government; a people who, gathered in their national life about His throne and His altar, obeying His commands and worshipping Him, should reveal to outside nations the meaning of the Kingship of God. It was not the selection of a pet, but the creation of a pattern. The story, then, of the nation is that of the creation of a testimony, and the Divine ensurance of its proclamation through both the failure and the success of the people. The method is to human seeming a long and tedious one, but it is the only one possible. It is that which God has ever followed. He constantly embodies a truth in an instrument; either a man, a society, or a nation; in order that other men, other societies, other nations may understand it. The responsibilities of the races, in the midst of which the testimony is borne, are created and limited by that testimony.

The method of God with the instrument was that of progressive revelation of Himself. That movement is clearly marked in this book of Exodus. The first distinct revelation was that made to a man by the mystery of the burning bush and the declaration, "I AM"; the vision of a bush ablaze with fire, and yet not consumed: a voice declaring essential being, and giving no explanation. A little further on there was a further unveiling of the meaning of the first word, "I AM," in the exposition of the values of the name Jehovah. That great name had been known as a name, but its intention had not been understood. This truth was revealed to Moses in a passage full of beauty, which opens and closes with the simple declaration, "I am Jehovah"; and in its course affirms His power to lead His people out, and to bring them in. That is to say, the name was explained as revealing the fact of God's ability to become to His people whatever their need demanded. For a clear statement of the values of the name Jehovah the student may with profit turn to the article in the Emphasized Bible by Mr. Rotherham. This was the second stage of Divine Self-revelation to this people. The "I AM" of the burning bush, full of infinite majesty, in the presence of which man could only worship, was now seen to be the One who becomes what His people need, the One who enters into all their circumstances with them, in strong ability. Later on, after the deliverance, and as the work of organization was about to commence, God revealed Himself to them as the God of grace in His declaration, "Ye shall be a peculiar treasure unto Me from among all the peoples . . . and ye shall be unto Me a kingdom of priests, and an holy nation." Almost immediately following, and with startling suddenness there is a further revelation as He manifested Himself as the God of law. The people imagined they were able to keep the covenant He proposed to make with them. They did not know their own weakness, and consequently, almost immediately after He had spoken of making them His own peculiar treasure, the word went forth which commanded that they should not be allowed to touch the mountain from the midst of which the thunder of His law was to be uttered. Yet again, Moses and the elders were permitted to go into the very presence of God. There is perhaps no more wonderful chapter in the whole book than that which gives the account of how these men saw God while "He laid not His hand" upon them. There is no description of what they saw, but they saw Him. Thus they came one step further along the line of revelation, and discovered that the infinite mystery of the Being of the burning bush was also personal, in some such way that they might see and eat in His presence, while they were unable to describe what they had seen. The personality of God was not there fully unveiled. All its deepest meaning was not yet revealed; but the fact was declared and made real to the consciousness. Still later to Moses, on behalf of the people, Jehovah proclaimed the glory of His essential nature, in that matchless passage: "Jehovah, Jehovah, a God full of compassion and gracious, slow to anger, and plenteous in mercy and truth; keeping mercy for thousands, forgiving iniquity and transgression and sin; and that will by no means clear the guilty: visiting the iniquity of the fathers upon the children, and upon the children's children, upon the third and fourth generation." Finally, the overwhelming and stupendous fact of the glory of God was demonstrated in the hour when, the tabernacle having been reared according to pattern, the Divine presence filled it, and the priests were unable to stand and minister in His presence.

This rapid survey helps us to see that while all the details, such as the technicalities of the legal code, and the minutiæ of the instructions concerning the construction of the tabernacle, are important, the supreme method of God in dealing with the instrument through which He should reveal Himself among the nations was that of unveiling the truth concerning Himself to them, ever leading them a little deeper into the mystery, giving them some new gleam of its light, offering them fresh unveilings, and so conducting them into higher realms of spiritual apprehension.

Side by side with this unveiling of Himself, His method is seen to be that of direct and minute administration of the affairs of their lives.

The responsibility of the instrument may now be stated in the briefest way as twofold; that, namely, of worship and obedience.

Finally, Exodus reveals the Divine method with, and the consequent responsibility of, the individual. There are two notable illustrations—Pharaoh and Moses. God's method with each was the same, while the issue was different.

The case of Pharaoh is that of a man strong, acute, but rebellious—a man who acted wholly by sight and upon the basis of policy. God's attitude towards him was that of giving him every opportunity to make his own choice, and work it out into destiny.

His method with Moses was the same. He was a man strong, capable, and obedient. Instead of acting by sight, and on the basis of policy, he "endured as seeing Him who is invisible," and thus lived and triumphed by faith. With him the dealings of God were ever those of a great patience as He led him on, step by step, until His gentleness had made him great. God's patience condemned Pharaoh. God's patience crowned Moses. The Divine method with these two representative men, both of them notable leaders, was that of giving each man his opportunity of choice; not leaving him wholly to the dictates of his own lust and desire, but attempting, by patience and persuasion, to direct his choice. Therefore human responsibility is clearly revealed to be that of choice, and ultimately, therefore, that of the creation of destiny. The history of these two men is indeed a remarkable revelation of abiding truth. One faulty, failing, sometimes even cowardly, rose into a strange dignity and nobleness of character, because he chose to submit to the government of God. The other strong, astute, moved with determination towards destruction, not because God elected him to destruction, but because he refused God's ministry and patience, and the prolonged opportunity which was given to him.

The living message of Exodus is twofold. It reveals the fact of the sovereignty of God, and the true method for the saving of men. In Genesis we found the fundamental revelation of man's immediate relationship to God, and the declaration that faith is the one principle by which man may realize his life. These same truths are in Exodus, but with a changed emphasis. The God to whom man is related is declared to be Sovereign. Man in his failure is taught that his faith must express itself in worship and obedience.

The whole truth concerning God revealed in the book of Exodus may be expressed concisely in the stately language of the psalmist:

" Clouds and darkness are round about Him :
   Righteousness and judgment are the foundation of His
      throne."

The two words by the use of which the psalmist describes the throne of God are most suggestive—" righteousness and judgment." These are the two elements in the method of God with His people which are clearly revealed in the book of Exodus, and which in combination constitute the foundation of His throne. The meaning of righteousness is so apparent as to need little explanation. Perhaps its value in this connection may be more clearly seen by abbreviating the word. To omit the central syllable is to have the word, rightness ; and once again, to drop the final one is to have the simple word, right. As a matter of fact, this is the simple and essential meaning of the Hebrew word. Right, then, is one element in the strength of the foundation of the throne of God. This whole book delivers that message with unvarying insistence. The government of God is right, in purpose and in method. In its operation there is no deviation from that which is strictly, absolutely, eternally essentially right.

The other word " judgment " helps to an understanding of the word right. We are in perpetual danger of misinterpreting the meaning of judgment by emphasizing only one of its values. The Hebrew word translated " judgment " literally means verdict. That by no means expresses all the values which by use it came to represent. It does, however, suggest the root principle that lies within it—that, namely, of discrimination. This particular word signifying verdict comes from another which means to judge, to come to a decision, to find a verdict, to pronounce sentence. For our understanding of the intention of the great declaration we may with advantage make use of a word which at first seems to be entirely foreign, but which in reality catches the very heart of the meaning—the word method. Righteousness and method are the foundation of His throne. We all use the word judgment in that sense in regard to our fellow men, and in so doing are more true to its real intention than we are when we use it in regard to God, as though it simply indicated His punishment of man. Of some man whom we hold in high esteem we say that he is a man of rare judgment. That is the true use of the word. We do not mean by that that his one characteristic is that of visiting evil with punishment, although we do know that the man of true judgment will be angry with wrong. The fact that God is a God of judgment does most certainly include within it the truth that He is angry in the presence of wrong ; and moreover, that He will visit upon sin His hot indignation. The supreme demonstration of this truth, as of all others, is to be found in Christ, who was capable of saying, " Depart, ye cursed," as surely as " Come, ye blessed." Judgment, however, means that, and infinitely more. Taken in conjunction with righteousness, it shows that in His government all His activity is that of method, based upon right. As the God of judgment He led and exalted Moses, and led and cast down Pharaoh.

In this book of Exodus we see the government of God based upon righteousness and judgment, illustrated in His dealing with His people. His government is that of wisdom. This is revealed in His selection of time, places, and instruments. In the first five verses of Exodus is a list of names of those who went into

Egypt with Jacob, followed by these words, " And Joseph was in Egypt already." It is perfectly true that he was there through the hatred and crime of his brethren, but this book reveals the deeper reason of his being there ; and God is seen seated high upon His throne of righteous method, selecting a man, and a time, and a place. This surely was Joseph's understanding of all the painful story, for when his brethren came eventually into his presence, he said, " It was not you that sent me hither, but God." Throughout the whole of this book it is manifest that no contingencies surprise Him, no exigencies find Him unprepared; but that in all circumstances and in all conditions, He is perfect in wisdom and in power ; and that in His operation the largest and smallest things are taken account of, and pressed into service.

One illustration of this will suffice. Ere the people could become a nation it was necessary that their moral fibre should be stiffened. For this God was strong and patient enough to wait four centuries. The hour approaching for their deliverance, He opened a door through the cry of a baby, as that cry touched a woman's heart, and admitted a Hebrew to the court of Pharaoh. This God is the God we adore, manipulating ages and events, and compelling them to minister to things of a moment; and at the same time, touching the tiniest and simplest things of life, and compelling them to issues which include centuries.

As to the saving of man, Exodus teaches that faith expresses itself in worship and obedience. This is not a haphazard choosing of words. Thou shalt worship and obey is the all-inclusive command of the sovereign God. Worship consists in putting God at the centre of the life ; and service in seeing to it that all the life is centred in Him. That was the supreme revelation to the men of this nation. At its centre there was an ark. The nations knew eventually that there was something strange and mystic connected with that ark ; and attempted to capture it, with what difficulty and trouble to themselves subsequent books reveal. It was only an ark, but it was the symbol of the truth that at the centre of human life God must be enthroned. That is worship in its first movement. It is not, however, completed until it expresses itself in obedience. To place

the ark beneath the curtains at the centre of the encampment, and then to go away to break the law is not worship ; it is blasphemy. The ark being placed there, and God being recognized, He must be obeyed in every department and activity of the life. To study the ethical code of this book is to discover that in all the minutest matters of food and raiment and habits and friendship, the will of God must be discovered and obeyed. Moreover, the story teaches that obedience must be persistent even against opposition. This is perhaps most remarkably revealed in the story of how Moses persisted in his determination to obey the command of God in spite of the opposition raised by Pharaoh. Pharaoh attempted to prevent their going away to worship. He first declared they should not go. Then under compulsion, in effect he said, You may worship in your own way, but you must do it in the land. The answer of Moses declared their determination to go three days' journey, according to the Divine command. Then Pharaoh suggested compromise as he urged that if they must go outside his land, they should not go far away. Again the answer was one which insisted upon the three days' journey. Yet again Pharaoh proposed that if they must go themselves they should leave their children behind. To this they refused to give one moment's attention, and again the declaration was made, " We and our children." Finally, Pharaoh's last appeal was made, to leave their cattle ; and to that the ultimate answer was given, " There shall not an hoof be left behind."

This story is indeed a living message to our own age revealing the necessity for absolute and uttermost obedience. The call of God is to separation, and the world urges us to remain in the land, and be neighbourly. It is ours to reply that friendship with the world is enmity against God. Then we are told that if we insist upon being peculiar it is not necessary to compel our children to be so. God grant that our answer may ever be, " We and our children." The last suggestion of the enemy is that we should leave our cattle, that it is necessary for us to conduct our business according to the spirit of the age. The final answer of the Christian is ever that which declares that not a hoof shall be left behind.

Leviticus

THE PERMANENT VALUES	THE LIVING MESSAGE

I. Recognition of sin and revelation of its nature—man and his need.
A. The fact of sin recognized by the whole book.
  1. Offerings.
  2. Priests.
  3. People.
  4. Feasts.
  5. Signs.
B. The nature of sin revealed, in that all these things indicate a relationship between God and man, and thus reveal that by sin man is excluded from: nearness.
                knowledge.
                communion.
C. The revealing light, the holiness of God (the Hebrew word used 159 times).
II. Recognition of redemption and revelation of its nature—God and His provision.
A. The fact of redemption, the key to the whole book.
B. The nature of redemption revealed in the method.
  1. Substitution.
  2. Imputation.
  3. Death.
C. The unnamed love revealed.
	I. Concerning sin.
	A. Sin is unlikeness to God.
	B. Sin is distance from God.
	C. Sin is wrong done to God.
	II. Concerning redemption.
	A. Redemption is founded on righteousness.
	B. Redemption therefore is only possible by blood—by life poured out.
	C. Redemption is in order to holiness.

THE opening words of Leviticus reveal the necessity for acquaintance with the book of Exodus. " And Jehovah called unto Moses, and spake unto him out of the tent of meeting." If we had read this statement without such acquaintance we should at once enquire, Who is Jehovah? Who is Moses? What is the tent of meeting? Having read Exodus, we have no need to ask these questions.

The book of Exodus ends with the story of the covering cloud; and there is really no break between the close of that book, and the beginning of Leviticus.

The book of Leviticus deals with the first half of the second part of the message of Exodus, having to do wholly with worship. In common with the books already considered, Leviticus has no final teaching. Its instructions leave us unable to worship in the way in which it declares we ought to worship. It reveals the underlying necessities of the case, and thus prepares the way for all that fuller unfolding of the true method of worship, which came in the fullness of time by the mission of Christ.

We shall follow the method adopted in dealing with Genesis and Exodus, and ask first, what are the permanent values of the book; and from these deduce its living message to our own age.

There are two supreme values. First, a recognition of sin, and a revelation of its nature;

and secondly, a recognition of redemption, and a revelation of its nature; or, more briefly, sin and redemption, the fundamental matters concerning man and his need, and God and His provision.

On the subject of sin there is much with which Leviticus does not deal. Indeed, there are mysteries connected therewith which the Bible does not attempt to explain. We have no final teaching in the Scriptures of Truth concerning the genesis of sin in the universe. I use the word sin rather than evil, because it indicates a moral wrong, whereas evil includes not only the moral wrong, but all suffering and sorrow resulting therefrom. The Bible makes it perfectly clear that suffering and sorrow are the result of sin. It gives us, however, no explicit teaching concerning the origin of sin. Neither does the Bible enter into any details concerning the ultimate issues of the presence of sin in the universe. We do find, however, all that it is necessary for man to know, and the simplest thing stands revealed upon the pages of this book of Leviticus. The fact of sin is recognized from beginning to end. If there be no such thing as culpable moral perversion, then this book is a farrago of nonsense. To pass in review its five divisions is to be conscious of sin. The offerings described were rendered necessary by the sin of those who were commanded to bring them. The mediation of the priests as between the soul and God was called for as the result of sin. The laws of separation recognized the sin from which the people must be separated, in order that their separation from God might be cancelled. The feasts of consecration emphasize the benefits gained as the result of escape from sin.

The nature of sin is revealed in that in all these things the fundamental relationship between God and man is taken for granted; and yet the necessity for man's redemption and restoration to God is revealed. Sin is, therefore, so far as man's experience is concerned, exclusion from nearness to God, from knowledge of God, from communion with God. In the light of the New Testament we know far more of these matters than the book of Leviticus reveals; but in this book they are stated in their first simplicity, and fundamental values. The whole economy of worship, as herein set forth, emphasized the fact of the distance of God from man, because of sin; and of man's consequent need of some proc-

ess by which he might be brought back to God. The creation of a way of entrance indicates the necessity for its making. The necessity for its making reveals the fact that sin separates between man and God.

The truth stands out in clear and awful relief by virtue of another fact. The revealing light throughout the book of Leviticus is that of the holiness of God. The awful word is stamped upon its page, occurring more often in this than in any other book of the Divine Library, either in the Old or the New Testament. The Hebrew word, translated "holy" more often than in any other way, but sometimes by other words, occurs over one hundred and fifty times in the course of the twenty-seven chapters. This is a mechanical and technical suggestion, but if the word be marked in the reading of the book with a blue pencil, it will be seen how the thought is interwoven with the texture from first to last. The superlative instance of its use occurs in the midst of the commandments which have to do with the ordinary and every-day cleanliness of the people. In connection with matters so apparently prosaic, the great word is spoken, "Be ye holy; for I am holy." The holiness of God shines like a white, fearful light upon the whole book. It is in contrast with that holiness that the sin of man is seen and understood. Because of the absolute holiness of God, man in his sin is excluded from His presence. According to the teaching of this book, sin is fundamentally, essentially, wrong done to God.

This recognition of the fact of sin, and revelation of its nature, constitutes the background which throws up into clear relief the teaching concerning redemption. The whole scheme of worship as set forth in Leviticus serves to place before the mind of humanity, first, the idea of redemption, as existing in the purpose and economy of God; and secondly, that in process of time it would be wrought out into visibility and actuality in the history of man. The supreme value of the book, therefore, is its revelation to man of the Divine purpose of redemption. The offerings constituted provision for approach. The mediation of the priest was the method for the appropriation of the provision. The laws of separation revealed the conditions upon which such appropriation might be made. The feasts of consecration revealed the benefits of approach;

and the symbols of ratification were the signs of restored relation. The thought running throughout the whole economy is that of man, who has sinned, and so been excluded from God, being brought back to Him.

The offerings indicated the provision of a method by which man might be brought back into nearness to, and knowledge of, and communion with God. The first three revealed the ideal relationship; the burnt, speaking of complete devotion; the meal, of established communion; and the peace, of the experience growing therefrom. The final two suggested the method by which those away from communion might be restored; both the sin and the trespass offerings in different applications teaching the possibility of the cancelling of sin, and the restoration of the soul to God. Whether our interpretation of the individual significance of the offerings agrees or not, we shall all agree that the underlying teaching is that of the possibility of restored approach to God. The priesthood was that by which it was possible for man to appropriate the provision. No man was permitted to bring his own offering to God. It was necessary that there should be one to stand between the sinner and God, and present the offering. The thought is still that of the possibility; and the fact that a mediating ministry is created, by which the provision for approach can be appropriated, is a revelation of the purpose of God. The same underlying thought is discoverable in the conditions laid down, upon which conditions man might avail himself of the mediation of the priests; and also in the feasts which symbolized restored relationship, and the signs which ratified the same. It is of the utmost importance that this one unifying revelation of the book of Leviticus should never be lost sight of. While there is great value in a minute and detailed examination of all the ancient economy of worship, we need to be most careful that, while attending to details, we do not lose sight of the consistent revelation of the fact of redemption as provided by God, existing in His purpose, and wrought out in His plan.

A general survey of the book with that unifying truth in mind will reveal the nature of that redemption by which sinning man is brought back to God. Three words indicate the consistent method. They are, substitution, imputation,

death. For the moment I am not discussing the question as to whether this is the true method of human redemption, but am simply endeavouring to emphasize what this book suggests. The first thought is undoubtedly that of substitution. Every sacrifice was that of a life standing in the place of another. In order to the restoration of a sinning man to God, some one must take his place as a sinning man. This substitution is closely associated with imputation. In the ceremonies of this ancient ritual there were constantly included acts which suggested the transference of the guilt of man to the life which stood in his place. Finally, the one substituted, and to whom the guilt was imputed, must die. That was the one and only way of redemption suggested by all the economy of the Hebrew worship.

It is well that we should remember that all the sacrifice of animals was that of sinless life. No animal has ever sinned. It is moreover true, and to be considered most carefully, that all the consciousness of the animals who died through the long years of the Hebrew observance of these religious rites was, in the last analysis, consciousness homed in God. No animal feels pain of which God is unconscious. "The whole creation groaneth and travaileth in pain together until now. . . . The Spirit Himself maketh intercession for us with groanings which cannot be uttered." To put God away from His universe, as distant from it, and unconscious of it, and then blame Him for asking for the slaughter of animals, is to break in upon the teaching of unity obtaining in the universe. Of all the suffering of sinless life God was more conscious than the life that suffered, or the men who watched the suffering. Whether the devout souls of those bygone days were conscious of it or not, through all that ancient economy there was a revelation of the awful truth of the passion of God in the presence of human sin, which had its final manifestation and method in the suffering and death of Christ.

Therefore, in this book of Leviticus there is most evidently present, though unnamed, a recognition of the love out of which the work of redemption proceeds. It is unnamed, for the word love does not occur in the book; but it is present, for the whole economy is evidence thereof. The only sufficient reason for redemption, and the only sufficient impulse for suffering, is love. I am aware that this is a theological question, and that other reasons have been assigned for God's work of redemption. I am only able to state that which is the profound conviction of my own heart, that the final explanation of the Divine provision of redemption is to be found in the all-inclusive statement of the New Testament, "God is love." The holiness of God might have been vindicated, and the last demand of His righteousness satisfied, by the absolute annihilation of everything that had failed. The deepest meaning in the mystery of redemption, as shadowed in the book of Leviticus, is expressed by the prophet Hosea, "How shall I give thee up, Ephraim?" Though love is not mentioned in Leviticus, if I study it until I am overawed by the white light of infinite holiness, overwhelmed by the insistence upon righteousness, indicated by the blood and suffering, by fire and ashes, I am being taught that God's heart of love compelled Him to make a way back to His home and heart for sinning man, even though the process was one of infinite cost.

The living message of the book is already declared, in some senses, when its permanent values are recognized. This book speaks to us of sin and of redemption. Concerning sin it has a threefold declaration. Sin is unlikeness to God. Sin is distance from God. Sin is wrong done to God.

Sin is unlikeness to God. That is taught in Leviticus by all the economy of worship, which insists first of all upon the fact that God may only be thought of as distanced from man. While we have already declared that the supreme teaching of Leviticus is that of God's determination to bring man near to Himself, it is perfectly evident that such determination is in itself an evidence of existing distance. The ceremony which commenced with the erection of the tabernacle, and continued through all the ritual, is one that emphasizes the fact that God is unlike man. God is thought of as within the holy of holies, protected from the approach of man by veils, and by laws so stringent, that any violation of them has the death penalty attached to it. Man is thus excluded from God, because of the dissimilarity in character between them. Man made in the image and the likeness of God is a being on whom the image is defaced, and in whom the likeness is unrecognizable.

Sin is distance from God. We have dwelt on the one aspect of that truth in emphasizing the teaching of the book concerning the distance of God from man, by the unlikeness of man to God. There is another side to this, however, that, namely, of man's distance from God in experience. Because he is excluded from intimate fellowship he does not know God, does not love God, does not serve God. All this, moreover, is a condition out of which it is impossible for him to rise, save by the way of redemption, according to the purpose and power of God.

Sin is wrong done to God. This is the supreme message of the book of Leviticus concerning sin. The sinfulness of sin is always emphasized in its aspect of relation between man and God. While it is perfectly true that it is difficult for the finite mind to comprehend the fact that wrong can be done to God, it is nevertheless true that the whole teaching of the Hebrew economy of worship emphasizes the fact that wrong done to man is ultimately wrong done to God. Thus sin is wrong done to God in Himself, and in His creatures. If it be held that sin consists only in wrong done to our fellow men, it will inevitably ultimately weaken the sense of sin, and its degree will be decided by the character of the man wronged. The only way in which the keen sense of the heinousness of sin against our brother can be kept alive in the heart is by the perpetual recognition of the fact that he also belongs to God. If upon every face is seen the impress of the Divine relationship as revealed in Genesis; and if, therefore, it is perpetually remembered that to hurt my brother is to harm God, the sinfulness of sin against man will be recognized. On the other hand, if this be lost sight of, men will be seen everywhere as separated units; and distinctions will be made as between sin against one man, and sin against another. To recognize the truth of what Leviticus teaches, that sin is finally wrong done to God, will be to get the only sense of its awfulness, which has in it anything calculated to produce repentance in the presence of wrong done, and a motive for the doing of right. The whole truth was ultimately summarized by Christ in His epitome of the law and the prophets, by quotation from the ancient writings, "Thou shalt love the Lord thy God with all thy heart, and with all thy soul, and with all thy mind. And . . . thou shalt love thy neighbour as thyself." The book of Leviticus says little about wrong to the neighbour; not that it is forgotten, but that its true meaning is only recognized, as sin is known as wrong done to God. The psalmist saw deeply into the true meaning of sin when he said, " Against Thee, Thee only have I sinned." It was that fundamental conviction of the meaning of sin which created his keen consciousness of the wrong he had done to Bathsheba and to Uriah. Take away from the heart of man the sense that when he sins it is against God, and he will grow careless about Bathsheba and Uriah.

The message of Leviticus concerning redemption is naturally connected with this message concerning sin. This also is threefold. Redemption is founded upon righteousness. Redemption is only possible by blood—that is, by life poured out. Redemption is in order to holiness.

Redemption is founded upon righteousness. It is not the operation of a pity which says that sin is of no consequence. There can be no restoration of man to God, save upon the basis of right; and the activity of tenderness is always that of the severity of righteousness.

Redemption is only possible by blood. The writer of the letter to the Hebrews gathered up the whole message of the Levitical economy in the words, " Apart from shedding of blood there is no remission." The shedding of blood is life given up. It is necessary to make this statement emphatically, because it is now sometimes asked whether it is not permissible to say that we are saved by life, rather than by blood, seeing that the old economy declared that " the blood is the life"? While that is perfectly true, it would still be utterly false to say that the teaching of Levit-

icus is that a man is saved by life. It teaches rather that he can only be saved by life given up, given up through suffering—not by blood, but by blood-shedding. The ancient symbolism was indeed awful and appalling, but the final weight of awe and horror ought to be that of the sin which made such symbolism necessary, in order to teach its real meaning to God. There are those who speak of the doctrine of salvation by the shedding of blood as being objectionable and vulgar. The shedding of blood is objectionable; it is awful, it is dastardly; but it is the ultimate expression of the activity of sin; and the whole meaning of the appalling truth is that sin, in the universe, touches the very life of God with wounding.

I know the book of Leviticus is terrible reading; it is a tragic story of blood and fire. It is time that this living message was heard anew, that sin smites God in the face, and wounds Him in the heart; and that redemption is the outcome of the tender compassion, which receives the wounding, and bends over the sinner, pardoning him by virtue of that infinite and unfathomable mystery of which the shedding of blood is the only equivalent symbolism.

Redemption is in order to holiness. The final note of the message of Leviticus is that redemption does not excuse man from holiness, but that it is the method by which man is made holy. To fulfill all the requirements of the external ritual, and yet continue in sin, would be to commit the most heinous sin of all.

Leviticus speaks forevermore of the awfulness of sin in the light of the holiness of God, of the plenteous redemption springing from the love of God, and of the possibility of holiness of life, created by communion with God.

Numbers

THE PERMANENT VALUES	THE LIVING MESSAGE

I. Warning—the paralysis of doubt.
  A. The facts.
    1. Discontent due to lack of confidence in God.
    2. Disaster due to distorted vision of circumstances and God.
  B. The secrets.
    1. Mixed motives.
    2. Mixed multitudes.
  C. The results.
    1. A narrowed outlook produced discontent.
    2. The judgment of sight produced panic.
II. Comfort—the patience of Jehovah.
  A. Provision.
    1. Order arranged.
    2. Purity demanded.
    3. Worship provided for.
    4. Movement ordered.
  B. Patience.
    1. The methods.
    2. The fact.
  C. Persistence.
    1. Back to Kadesh-Barnea.
    2. The whole process to Messiah assured.
	I. Of comfort.
	  A. God cannot be defeated.
	  B. God's methods are perfect.
	  C. God's provisions are sufficient.
	II. Of warning.
	  A. The crisis of Kadesh-Barnea comes.
	    1. To the individual.
	    2. To the church.
	  B. Everything depends upon our attitude toward God.
	  C. Our attitudes toward the opportunity reveal our attitude toward God.
	  D. If we are failing, why?
	    1. Mixed motives.
	    2. Mixed multitudes.

AGAIN it is necessary to draw attention to the close connection between this book and those which have preceded it. The story is a continuation of that which has gone before. In order to see this clearly, let us read two verses in close connection, the former being the seventeenth verse of the fortieth chapter of Exodus, and the latter the first verse of the first chapter in Numbers.

"And it came to pass, in the first month in the second year, on the first day of the month, that the tabernacle was reared up."

"And the Lord spake unto Moses in the wilderness of Sinai, in the tent of meeting, on the first day of the second month, in the second year after they were come out of the land of Egypt."

The tabernacle was finished, and the glory of the Lord descended and filled it on the first day of the first month of the second year; and the command to Moses to number the people with a view to their passing over into possession of the land was given in the same year in the second month on the first day. Thus there was a month between the story with which Exodus ends and that with which Numbers begins.

The book of Numbers opens and closes in the same region geographically. In the opening part of the book we find the Israelites on the margin of the land. At the close of the book we find them again on the margin of the land. In the first part of the story they were perfectly prepared, so far as organization was concerned, for passing into the land. At the close of the book they are seen perfectly prepared, so far as organization is concerned, for passing into the land. Between the beginning and the end of the book there is an interval of about forty years. These were years of arrested progress in the history of the nation, and of definite progress in the Divine Self-revelation; and therefore in the Divine process.

Let us carefully note the connection of this book of Numbers, not merely as to its record of historic facts, but in its relation to the process of revelation.

Genesis teaches two principal truths; first, the essential relation between God and man; secondly, that faith is the principle upon which man lives, for the pleasing of God, and the realization of his own life.

Exodus takes up that principle of faith, and expounds it more fully; giving us a vision of God in government, and of those human attitudes to that government which are inclusively expressed in the word "faith." Divine government is seen as proceeding upon the foundation of righteousness and judgment. The human attitudes of the life of faith are those of worship and obedience.

The book of Leviticus deals with worship, revealing, first, the fact of sin as constituting the need of man; and finally, the fact of redemption as constituting the provision of God for meeting that need. Thus, while Exodus reveals the human attitudes of worship and obedience, Leviticus deals with worship, and Numbers with obedience.

While Numbers tells a sad story of disobedience, its message is one concerning the importance of obedience. It shows how, under the government of God, disobedience was overruled to obedience by discipline. The message of Numbers we shall endeavour to discover, as on previous occasions, by dwelling first upon the permanent values of the book, which consist in its revelations of the paralysis of doubt, and the patience of Jehovah. It is a book of warning, as it deals with the former; and a book of comfort, as it reveals the latter.

In considering the warning of the book, we begin with the second division, which consists of the story of exclusion and wandering. The first fact recorded is that of the incipient discontent existing among the people. One month after the filling of the tabernacle with the glory of God, that marvellous revelation of His actual presence

amongst them, Jehovah heard their murmuring. At first there was no definite statement of complaint. The unrest had not broken out into organized manifestation. That came later. There was wide-spread discontent due to doubt, which was really lack of confidence in God. We must not underestimate the difficulty of the position those people occupied. The process of organizing a disorganized people into national consciousness is never an easy one to the people themselves. There is a freedom in slavery which men miss when they emerge into the freedom which abolishes slavery. When the slaves were set free in the United States of America, the Government had to face a problem which they have not solved until this moment. The negroes came out of slavery, in which there was freedom—evil freedom, pernicious freedom, freedom from the necessity for thought, or planning, or organization—into a liberty in which there was necessity for organization and order. The process is not an easy one, and the work is not yet accomplished. So the Israelites had been slaves in the land of Goshen; their tasks were appointed, and their taskmasters compelled their obedience. Their difficulties had been great, their bondage cruel, but they were free from the necessity for thought and arrangement. Having escaped from the taskmaster, they imagined that freedom meant escape from rule. They had been taught in the year of their encampment under the shadow of the mountain that they had to submit to law, and it was irksome to them, and they became discontented. This discontent resulted from lack of perfect confidence in God.

Then follows the story of Kadesh-Barnea and the disaster that overtook them there. The spies were sent, the minority and majority reports were submitted; and as is almost invariably the case, the minority report was the true one. The majority declared the land to be fair and beautiful, but impossible of possession, because of the giants and the walled cities. The men of the minority also saw the giants, and the walled cities, but they saw God. The majority had lost the clear vision of God, and therefore were filled with fear by the Anakim and the walled cities. With the loss of clear vision there was the loss of perfect confidence.

The secrets of this failure were mixed motives and mixed multitudes. Murmuring is the expression of selfishness. Selfishness is due to a lack of singleness of motive. Had these people perfectly appreciated the fact that they were being created a nation to fulfill the purpose of God in the world, and had they been utterly abandoned to that as the one single motive, there had been no murmuring. When they murmured, it was for the fleshpots, for "the leeks and the onions and the garlic." They attempted compromise between being a nation of Jehovah, and a people seeking their own comfort. These mixed motives issued in murmuring.

There were not only mixed motives, there were mixed multitudes. They are found first in Exodus, and last in Nehemiah. When coming out of Egypt, the Israelites were accompanied by mixed multitudes. In Leviticus we find one graphic picture of the result, a mixed marriage between an Israelitish woman and an Egyptian man, with offspring which violated the law of God, and brought fresh punishment in consequence. These mixed multitudes fell to murmuring. The results were a narrowed outlook producing discontent, and the judgment of sight producing panic. Such is the first permanent value of the book of Numbers. It reveals to us the fact that when men lose their vision of God, doubt produces discontent and disaster.

When we turn to the other side of the story, we find the comfort of the patience of Jehovah. That is an all-inclusive definition. Notice first the provision that Jehovah made for these people, as recorded in the first ten chapters. Notice next the patience of Jehovah, as revealed in chapters eleven to twenty-five. Notice finally the persistence of Jehovah, as manifested in chapters twenty-six to thirty-six.

The provision of Jehovah consisted in the order of the camp arranged; the purity of the camp demanded; the worship of the camp provided for; and the movement of the camp ordered, immediately under Divine guidance by the cloud.

The patience of God is the supreme revelation of the book. This patience is not incompetent carelessness, but powerful carefulness. Its methods are many. He punished the people for wrong-doing, but always towards the realization of purpose. He placed them in circumstances which developed the facts of their inner life, until they knew them for themselves. That is the meaning of the forty years in the wilderness.

They were not years in which God had withdrawn Himself from the people and refused to have anything to do with them. Every year was necessary for the teaching of a lesson, and the revealing of a truth. As Moses declared to them, "Thou shalt remember all the way which the Lord thy God hath led thee these forty years in the wilderness, that He might humble thee, to prove thee, to know what was in thine heart, whether thou wouldest keep His commandments or no."

His method was also that of the adaptation of laws to new surroundings. The story of the daughters of Zelophehad illustrates this. God listened to the complaint of these women, and made provision for them, adapting His laws—do not misunderstand that phrase, never lowering the standard of righteousness—adapting His laws to meet the requirements of the people, as they passed on their way.

Finally, His patience was evidenced by the supernatural protection of these people. The resources of God were all at their disposal. Whatever they needed, He supplied. Thus through all the years we see the overruling of the patient God; not patient in the self-centred method of abandoning a failing people, leaving them, if possible, to work out their own salvation; but with the patience that refused to abandon them, and thus enabled them to work out their own salvation.

The patience of God was persistent. He led them back finally to Kadesh-Barnea; and thus the whole process necessary to the ultimate coming of the Messiah, and the full realization of the Divine purpose, was assured.

Thus we find, as we read the book of Numbers, two things forever sounding in our ears—the paralysis of doubt, and the patience of Jehovah.

From these I deduce the living message of the book to our own age. I begin with the last first. Numbers speaks to this age a threefold message of comfort. It declares that God cannot ultimately be defeated. It reveals the fact that His methods are perfect. It says to all trusting souls that His provisions are sufficient, if they will but appropriate them.

It declares that God cannot be defeated. We saw in Exodus that God cannot be defeated by the opposition of enemies, as we studied His majestic procedure against the obstinacy of Pharaoh. There are those who believe this, but who are not quite sure that He cannot be defeated by the failure of His instruments. The book of Numbers corrects this false impression. It is the story of a failing people. At the very outset, one month from the descent of the glory, they murmured through lack of faith. Was the purpose of God defeated? By no means. There are senses in which those who bear His name, and deliver His message may—measuring always by human standards—postpone the issue ; but they can never finally prevent it. As I read this book, I watch the movements of God, and my heart sings a song of joy as I see that He cannot ultimately be defeated.

It teaches me, in the next place, that God's methods are perfect. Note some of the emphases of that revelation. God will not spoil the result even by sparing Moses. There is no greater comfort than that to be derived from the conviction that God will never allow His love to interfere with His absolute loyalty to the principles of His own Being. It is, however, equally true that He will not fail to recognize fidelity in the midst of infidelity. The men who bore the majority report died in the wilderness ; but Caleb and Joshua were preserved, and finally entered the land. Yet again, God will not cast off the frailest, while there remains any opportunity for bringing them into harmony with His mind and will. While there is the remotest chance of my remaking, He waits for me, and bears with me in tender love through the processes of pain, by which He works to purge me from dross, and realize in me that upon which His heart is set.

God ordinarily works through natural processes, but interferes by supernatural means whenever it is necessary for Him to do so. It is the fashion of the hour to deny the stories of past supernatural interventions, on the ground that there are no such operations of God to-day. It would be more correct to say that men are so blind that they do not see the goings of God. We still speak of remarkable coincidences which, if we did but view from the true height, we should discover were remarkable interpositions of God.

The final note of comfort is the revelation of the book that God's provisions are sufficient for the fulfillment of all the needs of life and service. He has always proved Himself sufficient in resource for such souls as have really put their trust in Him, for the needs of their own life, and the demands of their service.

Turning to the warning message of the book of Numbers, the first point of emphasis must be that the crisis at Kadesh-Barnea always comes to the individual, and to the Church of God. Personally I think we are justified in carrying that statement further, and saying that it comes also to the nation, and that Russell Lowell was right when he sang,

> " Once to every man and nation
> Comes the moment to decide."

We, however, will confine ourselves to its application to the individual, and to the Church. With regard to the individual, I only pause to say that the crisis inevitably comes when faith is confronted by walled cities and Anakim, and is called upon to proceed against them in simple confidence in God. What we do in the crisis always depends upon whether we see the difficulties in the light of God, or God in the shadow of the difficulties.

The crisis comes over and over again to the Church of God. In the past she has sometimes passed into possession, but too often has passed back to the beggarly experiences of the wilderness. At this hour the whole Church is at Kadesh-Barnea. God is calling her to go out and possess the nations in the name of the Christ, with a new urgency, created by the opening of all the doors of opportunity. At this moment in very deed the whole land is before us. What are we going to do? Everything depends upon whether we see the walled cities and the giants, or God. Nothing less than a triumphant faith, born of a clear vision of God Himself, will enable us to go forward. It is only faith which can co-operate towards infinite issues. Sight can do small things. Faith alone is equal to infinite things. Sight can build a coffee-tavern in a slum, and perhaps it is worth doing; but to suggest to sight the building of the city of God is to fill it with panic in the presence of all the difficulties. The question of the hour for the Church is one as to her relationship to God. The question of the hour in foreign missions is not a question of finance ; it is not a question of men. It is only whether the Church is prepared to obey in faith. If we listen to the reports of men who judge by sight, we shall do nothing. We shall be told that the task of evangelizing Japan is hopeless, because the ethic of its own religion is sufficient for its need. We shall be told that it is a perilous thing to enter China, because revolt is incipient everywhere, and presently will manifest itself in rebellion. We shall be told of unrest in India, and that missionaries ought not to imperil their lives by going there. In brief, we shall hear only of the walled cities and the Anakim.

Oh, for Calebs and Joshuas, who are prepared to say, Anakim, yes; walled cities, certainly; hindrance upon hindrance; but these all in the light of God. Oh, for the spirit of Paul, who wrote: "I will tarry at Ephesus until Pentecost, for a great door and effectual is opened unto me, and there are many adversaries." He saw the open door, and the adversaries; and both of them combined to constitute the reason of his determined tarrying at the post of duty.

The living message of this book of Numbers is that everything depends upon our attitude towards God. Let that, however, be stated, for the purpose of heart investigation, in another way. Our attitude towards opportunities reveals our attitude towards God. Are we murmuring and discontented with the method of the "Divine government? Let us beware lest the fire of God break forth upon us in anger. Are we afraid in the presence of the problems at home, and the tremendous opportunities abroad? Then

let us remember that our fear is born of our lack of faith. The man discontented with all that the life of faith means looks back to the land of bondage, and sighs for the leeks and onions and garlic. His lust for these is evidence of his lack of fellowship with God. The man who is looking at the lands to be possessed, and recognizing all the glory of the fruitage, and the beauty of the pasture, but will not go up because of the difficulties, has lost his vision of God.

They were discontented and afraid—why? The answer of Numbers is the answer of to-day. False attitudes are created by mixed motives and mixed multitudes.

Mixed motives. I speak, as God is my witness, to my own heart. Art thou afraid of the toilsome pathway, and the weary battle, and the bruising? Then it is because selfishness is still dominant. When the eye is single, the heart undivided, and love unified upon the one principle of winning God's victory, there is no halting, no turning back. The old Hebrew phrase, "a pure heart," more truly translated, is "an undivided heart." In order to do God's work in the world, we need the undivided heart.

Turning from the individual to the Church; the reason of her halting is the mixed multitudes. We shall always be paralyzed as long as we consent to be patronized by worldliness inside the Church. We shall never be strong while into the assemblies, where we consider our missionary obligation, we admit the counsel of men of sight.

God is ready. Are we?

Deuteronomy

THE PERMANENT VALUES	THE LIVING MESSAGE

I. **God's love of man is the motive of His government**. (This is the burden of the retrospective and prospective sections of the book.)
  A. The retrospective sections.
    1. History—4:37.
    2. Law—10:12-15.
  B. The prospective sections.
    1. The song.
    2. The blessing.
II. **Man's love of God is the motive of his obedience.** (This is emphasized in the retrospective sections as to law; and in the introspective sections as to covenant-keeping.)
  A. Law—5:10—quoted from Exodus.
    6:5—the comprehensive statement.
    10:12—relation to the love of God.
    11:1, 13, 22
    13:3 } "Thou shalt love."
    19:9
  B. Covenant—30:6—the circumcised heart.
    30:15, 16, 19, 20—the principle of choice.
	I. **The affirmations.**
	  A. God's laws are the expression of His love.
	    1. Necessarily.
	    2. Perfectly.
	  B. Man's love is demonstrated by obedience.
	    1. Only love will submit to their severity.
	    2. Obedience is the final proof of confidence.
	II. **The arguments.**
	  A. The revelations of history.
	  B. The issues of law.
	III. **The appeal.**
	  A. Know God.
	  B. Love God.
	  C. Obey God.

THE opening and closing statements of Deuteronomy constitute the boundaries of the book, and give us the key to its interpretation. Its opening words are: "These be the words which Moses spake unto all Israel, beyond Jordan in the wilderness, in the Arabah over against Suph, between Paran, and Tophel, and Laban, and Hazeroth, and Di-zahab." Its closing declaration, written in all probability by the hand of Joshua, is, "There hath not arisen a prophet since in Israel like unto Moses, whom Jehovah knew face to face; in all the signs and the wonders, which Jehovah sent him to do in the land of Egypt, to Pharaoh, and to all his servants, and to all his land; and in all the mighty hand, and in all the great terror, which Moses wrought in the sight of all Israel."

The book contains the final words of Moses to the chosen people, and they are words resulting from his "face to face" friendship with Jehovah. This friendship, with its intimate knowledge of God—a knowledge which gleams through all these final words—was the result of the process and progress of revelation. Moses could not have delivered these prophecies on the day after he had escaped from Egypt. He had much to learn. The messages recorded in Deuteronomy repeat things already said, but with a new tone and a new emphasis, and there is felt a new atmosphere in their utterance. The tone, emphasis, and atmosphere are due to the fact that progressively Moses had come to such full knowledge of God that the man who wrote the last page of the book of Deuteronomy had to say of him that he was a prophet who knew God "face to face." It would be an interesting theme to trace carefully the development, and to notice the progress of Moses' knowledge of God. I shall content myself with two or three brief sentences, indicating not so much his progress, as the processes which resulted therein.

When three months old, the child was committed to the Nile, by faith in God, as the writer of the letter to the Hebrews tells us. By sweet art the mother contrived to nurse the boy. How long that continued, we do not know. Quite long enough, in all probability, for her to have soothed him to sleep with stories of his own people, and to have implanted in his mind thoughts of God which could never be obliterated. His training in the Egyptian court played no unimportant part in his discovery of truth concerning God. It was training by contrast. In the Mosaic economy the influence of Egyptian forms of worship is to be discovered. For instance, Egypt in its religious rites made use of sacred arks, but they contained a piece of stone, a serpent, water from the Nile, or something material, and often base. In the loneliness of the wilderness God taught His servant that in all these things there were the form, the possibility, the principle; but that they needed to be corrected at the centre. When he constructed the sacred ark according to pattern, it received holy things, the symbols of a holy God, who could only be approached by sacrifice. Thus at the court of Pharaoh, he was prepared for the contrasts which were to follow.

Then came the forty years in the wilderness. I do not sympathize with those who pity Moses as he left the court of Egypt, and went down into the wilderness. There was far more grandeur in the rough, rugged mountains, and God's overarching sky, than in anything Egypt possessed. In the quiet meditation of those forty years he came nearer to God, gazing upon the wonders of nature, touching the fringes of His force, and baring his soul to the influences of His majesty. Next in order came the more direct visions and revelations which were necessary for his work. First, that at the burning bush, and the uttering of the unutterable fact, "I AM THAT I AM." For forty years he had been in the presence of God, had seen His might diffused through mountains and plains, in storms and calms, in stars and stones, until at last, in one solitary scrub bush in the wilderness, there gleamed the Glory that he had never seen—a Presence spoke, and the voice said: "I AM THAT I AM."

A little later the word "I am" was linked with the great name of Jehovah. Then Moses discovered that the God, the fringes of whose garments he had touched for forty years, and whose glory had burned in the bush, and whose voice he had heard out of the mystic splendour, was a God ready to *become* everything His people needed.

After a while he longed for a fuller revelation, and cried out of the depth of his heart hunger, "Show me, I pray Thee, Thy glory," and God answered, "I will make all My *goodness* pass before thee." Then he learned that God's glory is His goodness.

Then followed another forty years of wilderness wandering, during which he discovered that the foundation of the throne of God was righteousness and judgment, saw the goodness of God, marked His patience, learned His heart; and finally, out of that full knowledge, delivered his last messages to his people.

These discourses constitute a survey of the whole economy of God in relation to His people. There are six of them, falling into three groups. The first two are retrospective; the second two are introspective; the last two are prospective. Through all, there runs a new note of love. The former facts are repeated; the sovereignty of God is insisted upon; the obedience of man is called for; but these facts are now set in relation to love. This is no mere piece of imagination. The word love, as indicating relationship between God and man, occurs only once in Exodus, when God declares that He shows "mercy unto thousands of them that love Me and keep My commandments"; and as indicating relationship between man and man, once in Leviticus: "Thou shalt love thy neighbour as thyself." The word love is a lonely stranger in the first four books.

Everything is changed in the book of Deuteronomy. Its supreme and overwhelming message is that of love. To understand this will enable us to state the permanent values, and to deduce the living message.

The permanent values are two; first, that God's love of man is the motive of His government; and secondly, that man's love of God is the motive of his obedience.

God's love of man is the motive of His government. This is the special burden of the retrospective and prospective sections. In the close of the first discourse, which was a retrospect of the history of the people, Moses declared: " Because He loved thy fathers, therefore He chose their seed after them, and brought thee out with His Presence, with His great power, out of Egypt." By that statement he revealed his conviction that the inspiration of God's government was His love.

The next discourse was a résumé of laws, in which there was no lowering of the standard of righteous requirement, but remarkable interpretation of the meaning of the laws upon which He still insisted: "And now, Israel, what doth the Lord thy God require of thee, but to fear the Lord thy God, to walk in all His ways, and to love Him, and to serve the Lord thy God with all thy heart and with all thy soul, to keep the commandments of the Lord, and His statutes, which I command thee this day for thy good? Behold, unto the Lord thy God belongeth the heaven, and the heaven of heavens, the earth, with all that therein is. Only the Lord had a delight in thy fathers to love them, and He chose their seed after them, even you above all peoples, as at this day." Insisting upon the necessity for their obedience to the laws which he had reviewed, he declared that they were the outcome of the love of God.

Thus, as he looked back over the history, he said that it was a history of the government of love; and as he recapitulated the laws, he declared that they were the outcome of love.

The last two discourses consist of the song and the blessing. In that song, love is never mentioned; but it breathes the spirit of love from beginning to end. It is a song of God's triumph over unfaithfulness. Pæan and dirge alternate throughout; the story of the Divine faithfulness, and of human unfaithfulness. Is there any love song ever sung so mighty as that which tells of love, which triumphs over the unfaithfulness of the loved one? That is the deepest truth about

God, and Moses celebrated it in his final song. These people were to be dispersed, and Moses foretold the dispersion; and then, at the command of God, wrote the song, and taught it to the people. A song will linger in the heart long after a code of ethics has been forgotten. Many a man who has broken all the laws of his country and his God, in some distant land, has been wooed back to mother and to God by some old song. So Moses wrote the song of a love that through pain, if necessary, will proceed towards the fulfillment of its own high purpose.

The last words of Moses were of blessing only. His eyes were fixed upon the far distant day when the tribes should be restored, and fulfill the first Divine ideal. In the midst of the blessing is a great declaration," He loveth the peoples." Thus, whether it be a review of history, a résumé of laws, a song for the future, or a foretelling of restoration, the last great message of the man who knew God "face to face" was that God's love was the motive of His government.

The other fact is equally true, and equally manifest. Man's love of God is the motive of his obedience. This is emphasized in the retrospective and introspective divisions of the book; and in each case in one discourse preëminently. Man's love of God as the motive of obedience is declared in the repetition of laws, " Showing mercy unto thousands of them that love Me and keep My commandments. . . . Thou shalt love the Lord thy God with all thine heart, and with all thy soul, and with all thy might. And these words, which I command thee this day, shall be upon thine heart." The tremendous truth which Israel was destined to teach the world was that of the unity of God: " Hear, O Israel, the Lord our God is one Lord." The outcome of that truth of the unity of God is the command, " Thou shalt love the Lord thy God with all thine heart, and with all thy soul, and with all thy might." The nation and the individual were to be unified by the love of one God. Further on in this discourse promises are made, and the condition was ever, "If ye shall . . . love the Lord your God." The expression of love is obedience to law. Man's love of God is the only sufficient motive for his obedience to the laws of God.

In dealing with the covenant, Moses declared " The Lord thy God will circumcise thine heart, and the heart of thy seed, to love the Lord thy God with all thine heart, and with all thy soul, that thou mayest live," and so revealed the secret of its keeping. Then in his last prophetic utterance he again insisted upon the fact that the only motive sufficiently strong to enable a man to keep the law of God is that of love to God.

The permanent values in this case constitute the living message. To repeat the values is to utter the message. God's love of man is the motive of His government. Man's love of God is the motive of his obedience. In order to emphasize these truths, let us hear again the affirmations of this book, listen to its arguments, and attend to its appeal.

What, then, are the affirmations? The first is that God's laws are the expressions of His love, and that for two reasons. Because God is love, He cannot make a law that is not an expression of His love; and because man needs law, God, being love, must provide it. To make man and put him down in the world without government, would be to leave him to work out his own ruin. He needs law because he is finite, and infinite issues lie all about him; and it is necessary that he should know the laws of the infinite in order to obey them. Love, then, is the inspiration of God's government of a nation, or of a man.

The affirmation of the book, on the other side, is that man's love of God is the motive of his obedience. Nothing but love will submit to the severity of God's law. It is a severe law. It besets me behind and before, and will not allow me to escape.

> " O Love, that will not let me go."

There is a stern ring in that word as well as a tender tone. So severe is the law of God that nothing but love will submit to it. Obedience is the final demonstration of confidence; and confidence is never perfect unless it is the confidence of absolute love. So that obedience to law on the part of man is demonstration of his love of God; and the love of God is the motive of his obedience.

The arguments of this book are those of all human history. The historian needs an interpreter. The singers are the interpreters of history. In this song Moses argued for the love of God by reviewing His methods. In our own times, Browning has the same great theme:

" I have gone the whole round of Creation : I saw and I spoke !
I, a work of God's hand for that purpose, received in my brain
And pronounced on the rest of His handiwork—returned Him again
His creation's approval or censure; I spoke as I saw.
I report, as a man may of God's work—all's love, yet all's law !
Now I lay down the judgeship He lent me. Each faculty tasked
To perceive Him has gained an abyss where a dewdrop was asked,
Have I knowledge ? Confounded, it shrivels at wisdom laid bare.
Have I forethought ? How purblind, how blank, to the Infinite care !
Do I task any faculty highest to image success?
I but open my eyes—and perfection, no more and no less,
In the kind I imagined, full-fronts me, and God is seen God
In the star, in the stone, in the flesh, in the soul and the clod.
And thus, looking within and around me, I ever renew
(With that stoop of the soul which, in bending, upraises it too)
The submission of Man's nothing-perfect to God's All-Complete,
As by each new obeisance in spirit I climb to His feet."

All's love, but all's law. The seers are always the singers. I have already referred to one of George Matheson's hymns. Let us not miss the strength of that hymn, while we glory in its tenderness.

> " O Love, that will not let me go."

Do not let us sing that as though love only knew the method of a tender caress. We must sing all the hymn if we would know what the first line means.

> " O Love, that will not let me go,
> I rest my weary soul in Thee;
> I give Thee back the life I owe,
> That in Thine ocean's depths its flow
> May richer, fuller be.
>
> " O Light, that followest all my way,
> I yield my flickering torch to Thee;
> My heart restores its borrowed ray,
> That in Thy sunshine's blaze its day
> May brighter, fairer be.
>
> " O Joy, that seekest me through pain,
> I cannot close my heart to Thee;
> I trace the rainbow through the rain,
> And feel the promise is not vain
> That morn shall tearless be.

> " O Cross, that liftest up my head,
> I dare not ask to fly from Thee ;
> I lay in dust life's glory dead,
> And from the ground there blossoms red
> Life that shall endless be."

Love, then, is law gripping me, binding me to the cross, compelling me to lay life's glory in the dust of death, and so ensuring the blossoming of red life.

The first appeal of the book is to love of God. It is objected that love cannot be commanded. That is true. Love is born when least expected. We love, because He first loved. On the other hand, love can be refused. We may not love, even though He first loves. The message then is, "Harden not your heart." Do not blind yourself to God's love. Detect it in the rainbow and in the rain, in the cross and in the red life that blossoms from the ground. Having detected it, answer it. The final appeal of Deuteronomy shows how love is answered. It is by obedience. In answer to love, and in the power of love, obey. There is a reflex action in this sacred matter. To obey in answer to love is to come to love the One obeyed ; and so more perfectly to obey, out of more perfect love.

Joshua

THE PERMANENT VALUES	THE LIVING MESSAGE

I. "Jehovah is a Man of War."
  A. Its Reason: His perpetual war with sin.
    1. The extermination of the Canaanites.
      a. After probation—Gen. 15:16; 18, 19.
      b. Because of corruption—Lev. 18:24, 25, 27.
    2. His dealing with His own.
  B. Its instruments.
    1. Men loyal to Him.
    2. The forces of the universe.
  C. Its methods.
    1. Restraint of natural powers, within the bounds of His government.
    2. Restraint of the lust of a conquering army.
II. "The just shall live by faith."
  A. Acceptance of the standard of God's holiness.
  B. Abandonment to the government of God's will.
  C. Achievement in the strength of God's might.
	I. "Jehovah is a Man of War." He is the foe of sin today as ever.
	  A. Personal.
	  B. Social.
	  C. Civic.
	  D. National.
	II. "The just shall live by faith."
	  A. Personally.
	  B. Relatively.
	    (To exercise righteous influence and produce the result of righteous conditions, faith is necessary.

THE second division of the Hebrew Scriptures, designated The Prophets, fell into two sections. The first was called The Earlier Prophets, and comprised Joshua, Judges, I. and II., Samuel, and I. and II. Kings. In some arrangements the book of Ruth was included with that of Joshua. In others it was counted as one of the five rolls constituting the Hagiographa, or book of Psalms. The placing of the historical books of the Old Testament in the division known as The Prophets indicated the fact that they were considered to be prophetic in the full sense of the word. History is prophetic in that it has a teaching value. To read from the true standpoint is to observe the method of God, and to learn the principles of human life.

The book of Joshua is a link between the death of Moses and the death of Joshua, and covers a period of from forty-five to fifty years in the history of the ancient people. Joshua was born in slavery, and the first years of his life were spent in the midst of the hard and terrible conditions in which his people lived in Egypt. He was about forty years of age at the time of the exodus and was one of the minority who brought the true report of the land, when the spies were sent forth. The book bearing his name tells the story of the coming of the chosen people into the land and their settlement therein.

In order to the discovery of its permanent values, we must again presuppose acquaintance with its content, and proceed to enquire what are the impressions which as a whole it makes upon the mind. It is a book crowded with incident, and there are general impressions inevitably resulting from its study which I propose to indicate by two quotations, one taken from an earlier book, and the other from a later one. The first is from the song the Israelites sang on the borders of the Red Sea, after they had crossed, "Jehovah is a Man of war." The other is from the prophecy of Habakkuk, "The just shall live by his faith."

In the song sung upon the banks of the Red Sea by the delivered people, there emerges into definite statement a great truth, never lost sight of through the whole Bible, " Jehovah is a Man of war." In the prophecy of Habakkuk, the truth which emerged as a principle in Genesis is crystallized into a definite statement. The permanent values of the book of Joshua, then, are that it illustrates these two truths, thus impressing them upon the mind, and revealing the intimate relationship between them.

Let us take the first of these statements and examine it carefully. This book is criticized by those who declare that its teaching concerning the attitude of Joshua, and the activity of the people under his command, are out of harmony with the truth concerning God revealed by our Lord Jesus Christ. It is hardly necessary for me to say that I join issue with that conclusion altogether. I hold, on the contrary, that this book, rightly read, interprets the meaning of that side of truth concerning Jehovah which we sometimes find it difficult to understand.

Let it first be recognized that this conception of God runs through the whole Bible. It emerges into clear statement in the song after the crossing of the Red Sea. It is manifest in all the history of the Hebrew people, as written for us in this book, and in the book of Judges, in I. and II. Samuel, in I. and II. Kings, and in that priestly repetition of the story of the Kings which we have in I. and II. Chronicles. The people were commanded to battle, led in battle, punished in battle, under the direct government of God. This conception of God is celebrated by the Old Testament writers. One supreme instance is found in that matchless twenty-fourth psalm,

" Jehovah strong and mighty,
Jehovah mighty in battle."

It was held, moreover, by the prophet Isaiah, who declared, " By fire will Jehovah plead, and by His sword, with all flesh." The thought runs through the new Testament in spiritual fervour, though material forms of expression are absent. The underlying fact is manifested in the anger of Jesus, and suggested in the phrase " the wrath of God." The same conception obtains in the last book of the Bible, when material symbolism and spiritual truth so wonderfully merge in the passage, " I saw the heaven opened ; and behold, a white horse, and He that sat thereon, called Faithful and True ; and in righteousness He doth

judge and make war. And His eyes are a flame of fire, and upon His head are many diadems ; and He hath a name written, which no one knoweth but He Himself. And He is arrayed in a garment sprinkled with blood : and His name is called The Word of God. And the armies which are in heaven followed Him upon white horses, clothed in fine linen, white and pure. And out of His mouth proceedeth a sharp sword, that with it He should smite the nations : and He shall rule them with a rod of iron : and He treadeth the winepress of the fierceness of the wrath of Almighty God."

This conception of God as a warlike One, a God of battles, capable of anger, moving forth ever and anon in definite punishment by the sword, runs through all the Bible. It has been questioned and criticized, always through partial, and consequently false views of God. It is affirmed that this conception of God is out of harmony with the truth declared emphatically by the revelation of Jesus Christ, and in the words " God is love." I affirm, on the contrary, that if this conception be inaccurate, if in certain given circumstances, and in the presence of certain conditions, God is not a God of war, then He cannot be a God of love. All the references to Him as a God of war in the Bible, and all the activities attributed to Him, spring from one simple fountainhead ; and that is the eternal and undying love of His heart. In this book of Joshua that supreme fact is clearly manifest and explained.

God is perpetually at war with sin. That is the whole explanation of the extermination of the Canaanites. The story of that extermination must be read in connection with the things chronicled in previous books, and in the light of the actual facts as to the condition of the people in Canaan. In a vision recorded in Genesis, Abraham was told of the captivity of his descendants, and that they should suffer hardship in a strange land for four hundred years, and then be brought back into the land to possess it. In the course of that declaration it was said, " The iniquity of the Amorite is not yet full." In that incidental word we have the key to the situation. The people who dwelt in Canaan, when Joshua led God's people in, had filled to the full the cup of iniquity. Their corruption is revealed in Leviticus, in the warnings uttered to the Hebrews against the evil things they would find in the land; "Defile not ye yourselves in any of these things: for in all these the nations are defiled which I cast out from before you: and the land is defiled: therefore do I visit the iniquity thereof upon it, and the land vomiteth out her inhabitants." And again, in a parenthesis which flashes its light upon the whole story, ("For all these abominations have the men of the land done, which were before you, and the land is defiled"). These are distinct declarations of God, that the people were to be exterminated because of the evils existing in the land. There was absolute immorality and atrocious cruelty. The Assyrian records, which have comparatively recently been brought to light, reveal the condition of Phœnicia. The whole truth concerning the purging of the land by the Hebrew people under the command of God is stated by Dr. Moorhead thus, "It was terrible surgery this; but it was surgery and not murder—the excision of the cancer that the healthy part might remain." That exactly explains what happened when the Hebrew people dispossessed the corrupt peoples who occupied the land of Canaan.

Then it must be remembered that this was not done until after long probation. The land had not been without definite teaching and warning. Melchizedek had lived in Canaan, king of righteousness and king of Salem. Abraham had dwelt there. Solemn warning had been given in the destruction of Sodom and Gomorrah, the fame of which had spread through the length and breadth of the land. Blind to the light, deaf to the voice, these people had persisted in sin, until they had become absolutely immoral and atrociously cruel; and for the sake of succeeding generations and the surrounding nations, it was necessary to excise the cancer, and give the opportunity of healthy life.

God is seen in this book of Joshua as a warlike One proceeding to battle, not for a capricious purpose, not for the enlargement of territory, for the whole earth is His; but in order to change and end the corrupt condition of affairs in the larger interests of the oncoming centuries, and of the whole human race. It was a conflict as between truth and liberty on the one hand, and lying and licentiousness on the other. One or the other had to go down in the struggle, and

God moved forward as a warlike One, using these people as His scourge to purify the land, and to plant in that little strip of country a people who, whatever their faults were, should yet become the depository of the truth which should at last permeate the world, and give men everywhere the opportunity for life, which it was necessary they should have.

Moreover, it must be observed that God was not merely clearing a land in order to find a home for people upon whom He had set His heart. Solemn warnings were given to the Israelites perpetually by word and by deed, that if they turned to the sins of the people they had exterminated, they in their turn should be cast out. That is precisely what happened. They did turn, in spite of the law, in spite of the leading of God, to the abominations which they found in the land, failed to bear the testimony which they were created to bear, and consequently to-day are a people "scattered and peeled." God was as surely against Israel as against Canaan when, in the person of one member of the nation, she turned with lusting eyes to the things of evil. That solemn halt and awful defeat at Ai teach the lesson of the meaning of God's warlike nature as surely as did the stories of the sweeping out of the men who were already in the land. As a matter of fact, the dealing of God with His own is almost severer than His dealing with the Canaanites. One man had coveted a Babylonish garment and a wedge of gold, had grasped something of the spoil for the enrichment of himself, and had hidden it in his tent; and the whole march of Israelites was halted by defeat; and until the evil thing was found and destroyed, and the sinning man had expiated his offense by the very death that the Hebrew people were inflicting upon the sinners of the land, there could be no going forward. God is the terrible foe of sin, refusing to make truce with it, after probation and long patience visiting in judgment corrupt peoples, and punishing with severity the very instrument raised up for the carrying out of His work, whenever it becomes contaminated by sin. God's rule is ever the expression of His righteousness, impulsed by love. Supposing these people had been allowed to remain and retain their power; supposing there had never been brought into existence the people who were to receive the oracles of revelation, what would have been the history of the world by now? By that very purging, by those drastic measures of wrath against iniquity persisted in after long probation, God gave the race its new opportunity, as He prepared the way for the coming of the One in whom His love was to be incarnate, and His anger to be most perfectly manifest.

God used as His instruments men so far as they were loyal to Him. He also pressed into service the forces of the universe, in so far as they were necessary for the carrying out of His purpose; the restraint of a river while His hosts crossed over, the trembling of the earth until the walls of the city fell, the lengthening of the day until the battle was won. It may be said that God does not to-day divide rivers, or cause mountains to tremble, or stay the sun in his going. These interventions were but representative of a method. God does not repeat Himself unless there be absolute necessity for it. Yet who shall say that the earthquake is not still His minister, the lightning His sword, and the hurricane His chariot. Is it not possible that, if we had the illuminated eye, we should discover that the things we describe as catastrophes are but evidences of the goings of God in supernatural strength, for the accomplishment of some far-off purpose upon which His heart of love is set?

Once more, notice the methods which are remarkable in relation to these people. Notice the peculiar restraint of the natural force of His appointed soldiers, within the bounds of His government. Is it possible to conceive of anything much more foolish than attempting to take a city by the blowing of rams' horns and the marching of men? Yet that is not the way to state the case. Let us rather enquire whether it is possible to conceive of anything more heroic than the ability to walk seven days round a city, without striking a blow, after having won a battle by the sword on the other side of Jordan? I cannot laugh at the story as being unlikely. I am rather amazed at the picture of the restrained soldiers of God, content to do His bidding, while leaving to Him the issues. When at last the walls trembled, no one imagined that the blast of the rams' horns had shaken them, no one imagined that the tramp of feet round them had made them tremble. They knew, and we know, that these men were being taught that God

operates for the accomplishment of His purposes through the obedient and heroic faith of men who will obey Him, however foolhardy their action may appear in the eyes of men. The restraint of the lust of a conquering army is equally remarkable. Compare the Assyrian records, to which we have already made reference, and see what the men of that very district did in the day of victory, how they treated their captives. The contrast is almost startling. Jehovah is a Man of war. His purpose is righteous. His instruments are controlled by righteousness. His methods are righteous. I see Him in this book of Joshua moving in resistless fury against sin, in the interests of the nations, of the race at large, and of the unborn centuries, in order that truth might have its opportunity in the world, in the interests of man.

The other truth that " the just shall live by his faith " has become patent by this statement of the first permanent value of the book. This truth emerged in Genesis, was expressed in clear statement by Habakkuk, and enforced by threefold citation in the apostolic writings. The declaration means that the power of the righteous life is faith. It is by faith in God that the righteous lives. With a fine sense of accuracy the writer of the letter to the Hebrews has rendered the passage " My righteous one shall live by faith " —that is, he shall live the righteous life, by faith. The power of righteousness is faith. The book of Joshua is a remarkable interpretation of this fact, and it is especially valuable to notice the interpretation of faith which this book offers. The writer of the letter to the Hebrews declares " By faith the walls of Jericho fell down," and that statement touches the keystone of the victories of Joshua. The first strategic battle was won at Jericho. Beyond that, the whole land stretched out before them. This being granted, carefully observe what this history of the conquest of the land teaches concerning faith. Faith is the acceptance of God's standard of holiness. Faith is abandonment to the government of God's will. Faith is achievement in the strength of God's might.

It is first acceptance of God's standard of holiness. In the first words of Joshua addressed to these people, he warned them of the perils which awaited them in the land to which they came, and charged them that they must be pure and strong. In his last discourse the same passionate abandonment to the standard of God's holiness is manifest. That is faith. Faith is not an attitude which asks for mercy, and professes to receive it, while careless about holiness. Faith finds the grip of its anchorage in the holiness of God. That is the underlying secret of the strength and victories of Joshua.

Faith is also abandonment to the government of God's will. We have already referred to this, as revealed in the story of the taking of Jericho. The men who were content to do such things as they did were men of faith. In the stirring days of the evangelical revival, when the Wesleys and Whitefield were passing like flames of fire through the country, they sang:

> " Fools and madmen let us be,
> Yet is our sure trust in Thee."

That is faith; to be willing to do things at which the wisdom of the world scoffs, if God command. In that way God's victories are won, and in no other.

Faith finally, therefore, is achievement in the strength of God's might. All the victories of righteousness through the centuries testify to this fact.

The permanent values of the book of Joshua constitute its living message, and therefore I need but repeat them in a few final sentences.

To-day " Jehovah is a Man of war." At this hour He is the foe of sin in personal, social, civic, and national life. At this moment, in this individual life of mine and in the world at large, He is moving forward in unabated, undeviating, unceasing hostility to sin. Blessed be His name! Thank God that He will not make peace with sin in my heart. How I have tried to evade some issue with Him, to plead the excuse, " The fathers have eaten sour grapes, and the children's teeth are set on edge "; to urge the difficulty of the circumstances in which I am; to plead my infirmity. All the while God is a Man of war, smiting sin, refusing to make truce with it, accepting no white flag of surrender offered to Him, except that of the abandonment of sin, and all because He loves me. The moment you can persuade me that God Almighty will excuse sin in my life, I cease to believe in His love. He is the foe of sin in me, in London, in England, in the world. If in these days His methods are not exactly the methods of the past, let it never be forgotten that even to-day every army that marches is under His control; that He girds Cyrus outside the covenant as surely now as in the days of old. I bless His name for the thunder of His authority, and for the profound conviction that He is fierce and furious in His anger against sin, wherever it manifests itself.

To-day also, as in the ancient days, " My righteous one shall live by faith." Personally that is true. If a man is to have the victory of the righteous life he must win it by faith, by accepting God's standard of holiness, by abandoning the life to the government of God's will. Then and then only, will he achieve victory in God's power. It is equally true relatively. To exercise a righteous influence, and to produce the result of righteous conditions, we must have faith in God. Blot God out of your propaganda, refuse to have His name and the name of His Christ mentioned, when you gather together to discuss the amelioration of social conditions, and confusion is written across your assembly. It is only as God is recognized in His holiness, and obeyed in His law, that righteous conditions can obtain in personal, or social, or national life. May we hear the message, and answer it with all our hearts to the glory of His name.

Judges

THE PERMANENT VALUES	THE LIVING MESSAGE

I. The deterioration of a nation.
  A. Its manifestation.
    1. Cause—religious apostasy.
    2. Course—political disorganization.
    3. Curse—social chaos.
  B. Its characteristics.
    1. Blindness—religious.
    2. Folly—political.
    3. Immorality—social.
II. The administration of God.
  A. Its methods.
    1. Punishment.
    2. Mercy.
    3. Deliverance.
  B. Its purpose.
    1. The last statement—21:25.
      (Earlier statements: 17:6; 18:1;
      19:1)
    2. The next book.
    3. Its ultimate—David.
        Jesus.
	I. As to the nation—a warning.
	  A. The process of deterioration.
	  B. The process of restoration.
	II. As to the administration of God—a message of hope.
	  A. He forever moves towards purpose.
	  B. His methods are still the same.
	    1. Punishment.
	    2. Mercy.
	    3. Deliverance.

THE central division in the lecture on the content of this book gives the history of the Hebrew people from Joshua to Samson, in a series of seven cycles. Each one runs the same course—of sin, of punishment, of deliverance.

The permanent values must be deduced from this division. That is not to undervalue the introduction or the appendix. These are necessary for the complete picture, but for our present purpose we shall confine ourselves to these seven cycles.

The permanent values may be summarized under two heads. The book reveals to us first, the deterioration of the nation; and secondly, the administration of God.

In considering the book of Joshua, we found that its first revelation was summarized in that ancient declaration "Jehovah is a Man of war," and we saw God in perpetual conflict with sin; while its second value was expressed in the statement "the just shall live by faith," faith being the acceptance of God's standard of holiness, abandonment to the government of God's will, and achievement in the strength of God's might. In dealing with the first of these values, we saw that the hostility of God to sin was manifested not only to the sin of the people who were to be exterminated, but also to the sin of the people who were to be the instruments of that extermination. That fact is brought out into clear relief in this book. Here we see God in constant conflict with the sin of these people, and yet as constantly working for their deliverance.

The lessons of this book, then, may be summarized by the quotation of two Scriptures,

> "Righteousness exalteth a nation :
> But sin is a reproach to any people,"

and,   "Jehovah executeth righteous acts,
> And judgments for all that are oppressed."

Take the first, "Righteousness exalteth a nation: But sin is a reproach to any people." The meaning of the first half of the verse is plain— "Righteousness exalteth," lifteth up, setteth on high. The meaning of the second part has been somewhat obscured by the use of the word "reproach." The Hebrew word is nowhere else so translated. Its usual translation seems to suggest no possible connection with reproach. In the refrain of Psalm cxxxvi., "His mercy endureth forever," the word "mercy" is the same as that translated "reproach" in this text. I am not suggesting that we should read this text "Righteousness exalteth a nation: but sin is a mercy to any people." I have rather drawn attention to the peculiarity of the word in order to say that I believe there is the profoundest significance in its use. The word is derived from a root which means to bow or bend the neck. It is a pictorial word, and its meaning must always be interpreted by the setting in which it is found. The neck may be bent in condescension, the bending of superiority to inferiority. It may be done in courtesy, the bending of a friend to a friend. It may be done in submission, the bending of a slave to the yoke. I believe that when this word was written by Solomon, he employed it for its root value, rather than for its generally accepted value. The thought then would be, Righteousness exalteth a nation, but sin bends the neck of any people. Thus the word stands in direct contrast to the word "exalteth." Righteousness makes erect; sin bows the neck. Some may object that one word can have two opposite meanings. I will tell you a story. A boy said to his father, "Father, what does cleave mean?" "To cleave means to cut into two," replied the father. "Why, father," exclaimed the boy, "I thought that a man must cleave to his wife!" Forgive the homely illustration of the fact that this word must be interpreted by the context. To cleave is either to make one of two, or to make two of one.

The other text reveals the truth that fills our heart with hope, "Jehovah executeth righteous acts, And judgments for all that are oppressed." I place the emphasis for my present purpose upon the word "executeth." God is an Administrator as well as a Lawgiver.

The seven cycles of this book show how sin bows the neck of a nation, as they reveal the cause, the course, and the curse of deterioration. The cause of deterioration was religious apostasy. Its course was political disorganization. Its curse was social chaos and crime.

The first movement of religious apostasy was toleration of things that were out of harmony with the holiness of God. In the earlier chapters the declaration is made five or six times, "they drave them not out." They tolerated the presence in the land of the corrupt peoples, whom they had been commanded to exterminate. That was the first evidence of religious apostasy. It always is. Religious apostasy never begins with intellectual questioning. I have the profoundest respect for the man who is face to face with intellectual doubt and difficulty. Let him alone. If he be true, he will "beat his music out," and "find a stronger faith his own." Religious apostasy begins with toleration for the things that are out of harmony with the holiness of God. This was followed by admiration of the things tolerated, until admiration became conformity; and in that strip of land which ought to have been swept clean of corruption, altars to Baal, and idol places of worship were erected by the people raised up to end these very abominations.

Religious apostasy is always the first movement in national deterioration, and it is inevitably followed by political disorganization. This manifested itself in the case of Israel almost immediately. After the passing of Joshua they ceased to act as one people. They began to live in their own small territory and to fight for their own selfish ends. Civil war almost exterminated the tribe of Benjamin. The nation was broken up into factions, and so was no longer able to act in perfect unity of thought and purpose; and consequently was weak in the presence of enemies, and suffered defeat.

The curse was experienced in internal lawlessness. One graphic touch tells how the highways were deserted, and men walked along the byways, which means that lawlessness was so rampant that men had to find their way by stealth to evade the highway robbers who filled the land. Crimes were committed everywhere, while stubbornness of heart characterized the people.

Mark their strange blindness. One of the most startling things in the book of Judges is the speed with which they forgot. They seem to have forgotten the taking of Jericho, and the victory on the other side of the Jordan. They seem, moreover, to have forgotten their earlier history, the deliverance from Egypt, and the wonderful years in the wilderness in which they were taught that the throne of God must be recognized as the centre of their life. They were blind, moreover, to the present activity of God, hardly recognizing the hand of His judgments. This blindness and their religious apostasy were related to each other, as effect to cause.

Mark the folly of these people. This was evidenced by their limited survey, and by their selfishness. Religious apostasy is always limited survey. To have a home policy and a foreign policy which leave God out of the reckoning is to be blind indeed. The outcome of such blindness is selfishness. These people sought their own personal aggrandizement when they forgot God.

Finally mark the immorality, which was the inevitable outcome of their blindness and folly, and to which we have referred in speaking of the curse of social chaos

Thank God, however, there is something more in the book of Judges than all this, or it would be a heart-breaking picture. The administration of God is revealed throughout, and concerning it there are three matters to be specially noted; punishment, mercy, and deliverance.

This is one of the books of the Bible which we must burn and fling away if we deny that God does directly, immediately, and definitely punish sin. It nevertheless reveals matters of supreme importance, in order to a correct appreciation of the method and purpose of punishment. The punishment of God is poetic. That which fell upon these people was the necessary result of their own sin. They bent the neck to low ideals of religion, and were compelled to bend the neck to the rule of the people to whose immorality they had stooped. The people they ought to have driven out, but whom they tolerated and admired, and to whom they conformed themselves, became their tyrants. God visited them by bringing upon them the scourge of an idolatrous people, because they had stooped to idolatry.

The punishment of God is severe. During the years before Gideon was raised up, these people with so great a birthright were compelled to take

refuge in caves, not daring to show themselves, being hunted upon the mountains of their own land, and having to hide their heads for very fear. That is an illustration of the severity of God's punishment.

Yes, but there is another word to be uttered. Not only was the punishment poetic and severe, it was remedial. It always aimed at bringing the people back to a consciousness of sin and of God.

Through all these processes Jehovah is seen watching and waiting in mercy for His people, hearing them the moment they cry to Him, and answering them immediately with deliverance.

That brings us to the final matter in the administration of God—His deliverance. Deliverance was wrought at the right moment, by the right instrument, to the right issue. I do not pause to dwell upon the fact that it was wrought at the right moment, for we have already seen that He acted, directly the people turned to Him in penitence. It is intensely interesting, however, to notice how the deliverance was wrought by the right instrument. To look at the conditions in the midst of which the judges were raised up is ever to see how the right man was found for the accomplishment of the work.

The story of Shamgar is told in one verse. He was a rough, rugged hero, fitted to his times, accomplishing revolution, and so correcting the people.

Then there was the wonderful alliance between Deborah and Barak in an age which lacked enthusiasm and enterprise. Deborah was a woman of poetry and flame, and with a fine scorn laid a whip of scorpions round the men who skulked, when they ought to have been fighting. Barak was a strategist and adviser. Deborah without Barak would have kindled enthusiasm, but would have accomplished nothing. Barak would have done absolutely nothing without Deborah.

Then came Gideon in the most strenuous hour of all the period, and proved his heroism first by his fear. Never criticize Gideon for demanding proof on proof. He was a man so afraid of himself, that he must have proof on proof; but so sure of God, that he was content with three hundred men, and lamps and pitchers and trumpets, to lead an attack upon a great host.

The story of Jephthah is full of power. I am always sorry for Jephthah. He was a man with the iron in his soul, born into the world not in the proper way, and therefore despised by his legitimate brethren, he had become a freebooter and an outlaw. Yet he was a man of remarkable, honest, rugged strength. When God wanted a leader in those days of lawlessness, He took this man, whom his brothers had despised, and made him the instrument of deliverance.

The story of Samson is full of sadness, as it reveals a nation utterly deteriorated, and a man unable to deliver. A most significant word is written concerning him, " He shall *begin* to save Israel." He never succeeded. One of the most tragic things in the Bible is written of him, a statement that makes the soul blanch with fear as nothing else does, " He wist not that the Lord was departed from him." Oh, the tragedy of it. It may come to you, it may come to me, if we play with evil things, when we ought to be fighting the Lord's battles.

We should not have looked for any one of these men where God looked for them. They who wear soft raiment are in kings' palaces. When God wants a prophet, He takes a herdman ; when a leader, He finds a shepherd ; when apostles, He calls fishermen.

In order to see the purpose of the administration of God, look at the last verse in the book of Judges, " Every man did that which was right in his own eyes." The same thing is written four times in the appendix. It is said that this reveals nothing more than that the book of Judges was written in the time of the kings ; and that the writer, looking back, accounted for the chaos by the fact that there was no king. That is truly the human side of it ; but there is the Divine side of it.

" Every man did that which was right in his own eyes " ; that is, religious apostasy, political disorganization, social chaos. The book of Ruth follows that of Judges, and may be described as the idyll of the king. How does it end? With David the king. What is its issue? Jesus, far off down the centuries. So at last there came a King, and no man is any longer to do that which is right in his own eyes, but is to crown Him and obey Him. That is the ending of religious apostasy, of political disorganization, and of social chaos. So the lines run out from this book of Judges, through the idyll of the king, to the coming of the King.

Again, the permanent values constitute the living message. The book of Judges is full of teaching for this day, and for this nation. It first of all utters a warning, revealing to us, if we have eyes to see, and ears to hear, and hearts to understand, the process of deterioration. It is as true of our own nation as of Israel, that if there is religious apostasy, there must be political disorganization, and this issues in social chaos. In other words, social failure is rooted in religious apostasy. Therefore the process of restoration must begin with the cause, and so change the course, and remove the curse. When I am told that I am to leave my pulpit, and give myself to social propapanda, I say, No, I have no time and no right, however much my heart may break in the presence of social conditions, to waste time and energy fooling with the fringe of things. It is for the Christian preacher and the Christian Church to cry aloud, Back to God, and so back to political emancipation, and to social order.

Then there is in this book a message full of hope as to the administration of God. He is forever moving towards the ultimate goal, and never loses sight thereof. His methods are still the same. He still punishes by war, catastrophe, reaction. Take up the newspaper to-day, and read the sad and awful story of suicide after suicide on the other side of the sea. What does it mean? The nemesis of impure commercial methods. God is surely abroad in the world, making men their own executioners, when there is no other way of checking the floods of vice. Yet He is forevermore a God ready to pardon. If this nation could but be turned back to Him, He would visit us again with His own salvation.

Finally, let us remember that God always finds the providential man at the right moment. When the punishment has done its work, and the discipline has wrought a sense of wrong in the heart of the people, He finds the deliverer. We cannot produce him. Let us be careful lest we stone him when he comes, for he will not appear where we are looking, but from some unexpected quarter.

Ruth

THE PERMANENT VALUES	THE LIVING MESSAGE

I. The secrets of saintship—God, the sufficiency of the trusting.
  A. The difficulties.
    1. Ruth.
      a. A Moabitess.
      b. Seeing God's people in circumstances of suffering and want.
      c. Coming in poverty to a hostile people.
    2. Boaz.
      a. Living in times of degeneracy.
      b. "A mighty man of wealth."
      c. Legal difficulties threatening love for Ruth.
  B. The characters.
    1. Ruth—a woman in all the grace and beauty of womanhood.
    2. Boaz—a man in all the strength and glory of manhood.
  C. The secret.
    1. Ruth.
      a. An open mind.
      b. A personal choice.
      c. Loyalty—in spite of difficulties.
    2. Boaz.
      a. Loyalty—in the midst of difficulties.
      b. His relation to God and his fellowmen.
      c. Caution and courage.
II. The values of saintship—the trusting, instruments of God: Boaz and Ruth (Obed, Jesse, David).
	I. Circumstances neither make nor mar saints.
	II. The one principle of victory is faith. The laws of faith are:
	  A. An open mind.
	  B. A personal decision.
	  C. Practical application.
	  D. Persistent courage.
	III. The value of one life to God is only known in the fuller life beyond.

NEVER measure the value of a book by its bulk. This little brochure of a few pages is one of the rarest and most beautiful idylls in literature, even after translation. In seeking for its living message it is most necessary that we should have in mind a well-defined outline of the picture it represents.

The background is revealed in the opening words, "And it came to pass in the days when the judges judged." That places the story in that period in the history of the Hebrew people which we considered in our lecture on the book of Judges. The events chronicled transpired in troublous, stormy, and difficult times; in the midst of religious apostasy, political disorganization, and social chaos. That in itself is suggestive, reminding us that God has never left Himself without witness. In the darkest days, the light has never been totally extinguished.

The subsidiary foreground of the book presents the persons of Elimelech and Naomi, Mahlon and Chilion, and Orpah; and the events of famine, emigration, and the sorrows following; the return of only one of those who had departed, accompanied by a stranger to the land; and finally the story of the wooing and the wedding.

In the immediate foreground two figures stand

out in bold relief, Ruth and Boaz. The picture is of the Rosa Bonheur type, only a few lines, strong, clear, definite ; yet full of light and shade. To think of the book of Ruth is to think of Ruth and Boaz. Ultimately, observing the historic movement and the processes of God, it is seen that these two in their union constituted a highway for God, through perils, for the accomplishment of purpose.

Taking the book thus, there are two permanent values which I shall suggest. First, the book teaches the secrets of saintship ; God is the sufficiency of trusting souls. Secondly, it teaches the values of saintship ; trusting souls are the instruments of God.

I must not be tempted into a long discussion of what is meant by saintship, but content myself with a simple yet inclusive definition. A saint is a person separated to the will of God. Ruth and Boaz lived the life of saintship in circumstances of the utmost difficulty, finding their sufficiency for such life in God.

Ruth was a Moabitess, of an accursed race, who according to the law of Moses was not allowed to enter the congregation of the covenant. While this story finally teaches that no such disability remains when faith in God is exercised, we must not forget the difficulty as it existed for Ruth ; how the people would be likely to look at her, how she herself, as she came into contact with the religion of the Hebrew people, would realize the greatness of her distance. Again, there was nothing calculated to allure her, from the standpoint of material prosperity. Those she had known of the people of Jehovah had been compelled to leave their land on account of famine. From them she knew of the perils of those who had remained in the land, and all the sadness of their condition. She came back with Naomi into poverty, and to people who in all probability were hostile to them both. Thus the saintship of Ruth was in spite of difficulties, and flourished amid circumstances calculated to discourage her.

Boaz lived amid people of privilege in times of degeneracy. Perhaps there are no circumstances in which it is harder to live the life of the saint. It is to-day easier to live a godly life in the midst of worldly men and women, than in the midst of worldly Christians. Then again, he was a mighty man of wealth, and consequently able to procure whatever would contribute to the ease of his material existence. That condition is always perilous to the life of faith. It is to-day easier to live an out-and-out Christian life in circumstances of stress and strain, than in those of ease and luxury.

Once more notice carefully the legal difficulties threatening his love for Ruth. There was a nearer kinsman than he, who had first right; and appeal must be made to him ere Boaz could claim Ruth. There is a fine loyalty to principle manifested in this man's dealings in this particular. How easy it would have been for him to sacrifice principle in order to win.

Thus both Ruth the Moabitess, and Boaz the man of Judah were saints, in spite of difficulties peculiar to each.

How full of beauty they were. Ruth was a woman capable of love, characterized by modesty, of fine gentleness, of splendid courage; a woman in all the grace and beauty of womanhood. Boaz was a man of integrity, of courtesy, of tender passion, of courage ; a man in all the strength and glory of manhood.

The secret in each case was that of the sufficiency of God for such as trust Him. In the case of Ruth three things are clearly manifest. First, she was a woman of an open mind, willing to receive the teaching of Naomi. Secondly, she was a woman who at a crisis made her own choice against all the prejudices of her nationality, against the persuasion of Naomi, to whom she owed the very light of her religion ; separating herself of her own free will from Moab, and transferring herself to Judah and to Jehovah. Finally, she was persistently, patiently, and definitely loyal to her choice. She turned her back upon the land of her birth and childhood, with all its associations and acquaintances, and followed Naomi until she had put the waters of Jordan between herself and Moab. To this woman of open mind, God revealed Himself; and she, answering in obedient faith, found Him sufficient through all dangers and difficulties, and lived the life of a saint, full of beauty.

In the case of Boaz also three things are worthy of notice. First, his loyalty to God in the midst of difficulties. In the hour when men took the name of God upon their lips, while their lives were out of harmony with their profession, here was a man absolutely loyal ; a man true in the midst of untruth; a man of faith in the midst of an age of faithlessness. Secondly, he was a man who made application of his relation to God in his relation to his fellow men. He greeted the men who worked for him in terms which disclosed his relation to God. Yet he was neither a slovenly nor a careless man. He saw immediately the stranger in his fields. He took personal oversight of all his affairs, yet he lived a life so godly as to be able to greet his workmen in terms which revealed his relationship to God. Finally, he was a man of caution and of courage. The two things are never far apart. Caution is the very soul of courage. Courage is the true expression of caution. All these things reveal the fact that, trusting God, Boaz found Him sufficient to enable him to live a godly life in circumstances of difficulty. Thus the secret of the grace and beauty of Ruth, and the strength and manliness of Boaz lie in the fact that in differing circumstances, they both lived upon the same principle of simple yet sublime faith in God.

Such souls as these are the instruments through which God is ever able to move towards the accomplishment of His purposes. The story of the ultimate values of the faith of Ruth and Boaz is told in the ending of this book. Boaz and Ruth, Obed, Jesse, David. So we see the very footsteps of Almighty God. Boaz the Hebrew, and Ruth the Moabitess in union, become the highway for God towards the ultimate realization of His purposes.

The living message may be stated in three propositions. First, circumstances neither make nor mar saints. The difficulty of the life of saintship to the wealthy man is answered by the story of Boaz. The difficulty of the life of faith to a poor woman is answered by the story of Ruth.

The difficulty of living a godly life when the early training has been in the atmosphere of godliness is often affirmed, and that with a great amount of reason. There have been hours when I have envied the loyalty, the devotion, the splendour of the Christian life of some man whose conversion was a volcanic eruption, after which he left behind him forever the vulgarities of the old life, and entered into the graces of the new with surprising fullness of experience. It is possible to have been brought up in the atmosphere of Christianity and so to lack the reason

for that ceaseless watchfulness which exists in the case of those who have lacked such training. How shall we answer those who urge this difficulty? By telling the story of Boaz.

Some, on the other hand, urge quite another reason, that of irreligious training. They lack the advantages that others had. They were never sung to sleep in infancy with songs of the Christ. After conversion they came into a strange atmosphere, and have to learn the way, and therefore so much cannot be expected from them as from others. How shall we answer those who thus speak? By telling the story of Ruth. The difficulties of privilege in the case of Boaz. The difficulties of limitation in the case of Ruth. Yet by faith they were non-existent, they were cancelled, they did not obtain. The privileged man shines with the lustre of sainthood; the woman lacking all such privilege, flashes in the beauty and glory of saintship. Why? Because God is the mightiest environment of any human life Because God is an inheritance, possessing which all poverty is cancelled, and all other wealth is made as of no account. So I repeat my first proposition. Circumstances can neither make nor mar saints. If we cannot begin our saintship in the land of Moab, we shall never be saints in the land of Judah. If a man cannot be a saint as a wealthy man, though he lose all his wealth, poverty will not make a saint of him. If a man cannot be a saint as a poor man, wealth, if it comes to him, will in all probability damn him.

Therefore as a necessary sequence to the first proposition, I make the second. The principle of victory is faith. "Faith is the assurance of things hoped for, the proving of things not seen." Faith is the principle that takes hold upon God, and appropriates all His resources. Faith takes hold of that in God which man needs, and enables God to take hold of that in man which He needs. From both of these people I learn something of the laws of faith. An open mind; a personal decision; direct application of the things believed to the details of every-day life; persistent courage in the face of all difficulty. Faith is not a sentiment about which we sing. It is an attitude of life, based upon the conviction of the soul.

Finally the book teaches the value to God of that life, which makes the great surrender, and follows Him in faith. The value of such a life can never be known until we pass within the veil. Remember again the sequence with which this book closes ; Obed, Jesse, David. Boaz and Ruth had passed into the light ere David came, the king for whom the nation was waiting, yet the sequence did not end with David. A little later a prophet from some height of vision broke into a great song. " Thou, Bethlehem Ephrathah, which art little to be among the thousands of Judah, out of thee shall One come forth unto Me that is to be ruler in Israel." Far down the centuries there shone a light at midnight, and songs were heard, and in the direct line of the man of Judah and of privilege, and the woman of Moab and of limitation, to Bethlehem came the King. They did not see the issues. They did not live to reap the ultimate harvest of their fidelity, but God found foothold in the man and woman of faith, and in their united lives. That is the principle of which I think we need to be reminded, in order to encourage our hearts in the midst of work. We talk about results. If all the results of my ministry can be statistically stated, it is a dire failure.

Paul was a saint, cribbed, cabined and confined in prison. It is impossible to read his letters without being conscious of a certain amount of restlessness as he made appeal to his loved ones, " remember my bonds." A man whose motto was, The Regions Beyond, whose piercing eye saw the far distances, and who was profoundly conscious of the value of the evangel, who knew and wrote " I am debtor . . . I am ready ; " was yet imprisoned, and had to content himself with writing letters. To-day those letters are of greater value than all his work. He did not know that presently they would be gathered together, and would constitute the great exposition of the evangelical faith for all the centuries.

Robert Morrison wrote in his diary, " This day I entered with Mr. Laidler to learn Latin. I paid ten shillings and sixpence, and am to pay one guinea per quarter. I know not what may be the end. God only knows." That ten shillings and sixpence was the beginning of that linguistic education which made Morrison the translator of the Bible, and opened the way for all the work which has been done in China during the past century.

These are but instances, yet take the comfort of them. May this be my last word. Remember that of the work you do to-day you cannot see the issue, if it is work wrought by faith in God. It may be in the great city of London, or in some hidden hamlet among the hills that your life will be lived, small, unknown, never published, never noticed either in the religious or irreligious press, and yet you may be God's foothold for things of which you cannot dream, which if told you now you would not possibly believe. The one cry of my heart and of thy heart, comrade of faith, according to this book, should be a cry for out-and-out abandonment to Him, in order that by our loyalty He may win the victories of His royalty.

I Samuel

THE PERMANENT VALUES	THE LIVING MESSAGE

I. **Jehovah reigning by adaptation and advance.**
  A. Samuel.
    1: Hannah—her faith (Jehovah's foothold) and her song (Jehovah's interpretation).
    2. The new order—the prophet.
    3. His work—preparation, reformation, and foundation of the Kingdom.
  B. Saul.
    1. The man—physical strength (fitful and failing), mental acumen (moods and madness), and spiritual life (torpor and death).
    2. The Kingdom—disaster.
  C. David.
    1. The training as shepherd in the fields, a courtier at the palace, and an outlaw in exile.
    2. The progress.
II. **Man co-operating by failure and by loyalty.**
  A. Samuel.
    1. Opportunity—parentage, call, and appointment.
    2. Response—loyal.
    3. Issues—messages of God delivered and work of God advanced.
  B. Saul.
    1. Opportunity—call, anointing, friendship for Samuel, popularity, and personal equipment.
    2. Response—vacillation, self-will, and disobedience.
    3. Issues—his failure a revelation and his death a warning.
  C. David.
    1. Opportunity—his call and anointing, waiting and suffering, and the crisis of battle with Amalek.
    2. Response—obedience, patience, and action.
    3. Issues—an instrument in Jehovah's progress.
	I. **The absolutism of God.**
	  A. Revealed.
	    1. No territory out of His jurisdiction.
	    2. No persons beyond His control.
	    3. No event escaping His overruling.
	  B. Interpreted.
	    1. Operating towards accomplishment.
	    2. Including adverse forces and facts.
	    3. Creating its own agents.
	II. **The relation of man.**
	  A. The ultimate victory of God is independent of the attitudes of individuals or peoples towards Him.
	  B. The place of individuals or peoples in that ultimate victory is dependent upon their attitude towards Him.

THE two books of Samuel constitute one story. The first gives the history of the transition from Theocracy to Monarchy. The inwardness of that transition is revealed by a paragraph in the eighth chapter " Then all the elders of Israel gathered themselves together, and came to Samuel unto Ramah : and they said unto him, Behold, thou art old, and thy sons walk not in thy ways : now make us a king to judge us like all the nations. But the thing displeased Samuel, when they said, Give us a king to judge us. And Samuel prayed unto the Lord. And the Lord said unto Samuel, Hearken unto the voice of the people in all that they say unto thee : for they have not rejected thee, but they have rejected Me, that I should not be King over them." Two brief statements from that passage, " Make us a king to judge us like all the nations," and "They have rejected Me, that I should not be King over them," tell the story of the transition, as to the human desire which produced it, and as to the Divine attitude towards it. The nation asked for "a king to judge us like all the nations." The reason for their existence as a nation was that they should be unlike the nations. The unlikeness consisted in the fact that this nation had as its only King Jehovah. The real meaning of their request is therefore interpreted by the language of Jehovah to Samuel, " They have rejected Me, that I should not be King over them." The days of the judges were days of religious apostasy, political disorganization, and social chaos ; and religious apostasy in the case of these people meant that they refused to obey the King eternal, immortal, invisible. This attitude expressed itself in the request they brought to Samuel, " Make us a king to judge us like all the nations." Sin ever issues in an attempt to substitute the false for the true. That is the history of idolatry. Every idol is witness to man's need of God. The lack of God creates the necessity for putting something in His place. These men, turning from God as King, desired a king like the nations. The first book of Samuel tells the story of the immediate issues of this desire.

The permanent values of the book may be exclusively expressed in two statements. Its supreme revelation is that of Jehovah reigning by adaptation, in order to advance. Its second value is that it reveals the fact that, under this government of God, men coöperate with Him towards the final issues, either by failure or by loyalty. It would appear as though the first of these statements—namely, that Jehovah reigns by adaptation in order to advance—contradicts His declaration concerning the people, " They have rejected Me, that I should not be King over them," and yet it is by no means a contradiction. It is one thing to reject Jehovah, but it is quite another to dethrone Him. The first is possible. The second is impossible. This is the supreme lesson of the book. The people, chosen to exhibit the breadth, the beauty, and the beneficence of His government, rejected Him from being King, but they did not dethrone Him. As I watch the movement of this story, gathering around the three central figures, Samuel, Saul and David, the supreme revelation is not of these men, but of Jehovah reigning by the adaptation of His method to the requirements of the hour, and so through disobedience or obedience, through success or failure, through men loyal or rebellious, moving quietly, steadily, and surely on. As our analysis of the book suggests, the whole movement gathers round three personalities, and centring our attention upon them for the purpose of this study, we must yet keep in mind the prevailing conditions.

The story of Samuel is introduced by that of Hannah. Hannah was a woman whose faith became Jehovah's foothold, and whose song became Jehovah's interpretation. While it is the glad thanksgiving of a woman whose prayer has been heard and answered, it is infinitely more. All the values of the book are gathered up into this song of the God who reigns, and concerning whom she affirms :

> " The Lord killeth, and maketh alive :
> He bringeth down to the grave, and bringeth up.
> The Lord maketh poor, and maketh rich :
> He bringeth low, He also lifteth up.
> He raiseth up the poor out of the dust,
> He lifteth up the needy from the dunghill,
> To make them sit with princes,
> And inherit the throne of glory."

The song moves on :

> " They that strive with the Lord shall be broken to pieces ;
> Against them shall He thunder in heaven :
> The Lord shall judge the ends of the earth ;
> And He shall give strength unto His king,
> And exalt the horn of His anointed."

Samuel was a prophet. Peter, speaking in the presence of the assembled multitude in Jerusalem, said, " The prophets from Samuel and them that followed after." In that reference he included the whole of the Hebrew prophets, beginning with Samuel. There is a sense in which there had been prophets before him ; indeed, Moses himself was a prophet of whom it is said there never arose another like him. Yet, in one particular respect, Samuel was the first of the prophetic order. The kings were never mediators between God and man. The people rejected Jehovah from being King, and so passed out of close communion and intimate relationship with Him ; and He consented in order to the fulfilling of His purpose, but He never recognized the king as standing between Himself and them. He chose their kings for them, He allowed the lust for a king to work itself out in the ultimate disaster of the centuries, but He never spoke to men through the king, but always through the prophets.

With Samuel, then, the prophet emerges as the authoritative representative of Jehovah. Samuel, as prophet, became the king-maker, finding Saul, and anointing him; finding David, and anointing him; and henceforward, when a Divine message had to be delivered to the people, it did not come directly from God to the king, but to the king and all the people, through the prophet. In the economy of God, the prophet's office was always superior to that of the king. Thus, when Jehovah was rejected by the will of the people, and they clamoured for a king like the other nations, He took this man, the child of a woman's simple faith, trained him through quiet days in the temple courts, called him while yet a boy, and gave him a strange message to deliver, and made him at last the one to anoint Saul a king after the people's own heart, and David a king after God's own heart. The prophets became the mediators, the messengers, the interpreters of the law. They stood between God and the people. Thus Jehovah reigned; and adapting His methods, found Samuel, equipped him for his work, and delivered His message through him.

The history of Saul is one of the most tragic recorded in the Bible, full of fascination and of tremendous power in its appeal to individual life. In placing this man upon the throne, God answered the prayer of the people's rebellion. "Make us a king to judge us like all the nations." Consequently, in the economy of God, Saul became a revelation, an interpretation, and a discipline. The meaning of the psalmist's word is revealed in the method,

> "He gave them their request;
> But sent leanness into their soul."

Saul stands out upon the page of Israel's history, an object lesson in the real meaning of their choice. He was a man of enormous physical strength, yet fitful and failing from first to last; a man of undoubted mental acumen, yet a man of moods, who presently became a madman; a man as to spiritual life characterized from the very beginning by torpor and slowness, and at last, so devoid of spiritual illumination and power, that he turned his back upon Jehovah, and consulted a witch who muttered and worked incantations. He was a revelation to the people of what the possession of a king like the nations really meant.

Then look at the kingdom under Saul. After he was chosen, for a time they were practically without a king. He manifested his weakness by hiding among the stuff when he ought immediately to have taken hold of the sceptre. I am perfectly well aware that others interpret that story differently. They affirm that Saul was a man of such extreme modesty that after he was appointed he went back to work in quietness, without taking the kingdom. Such modesty is sin. It is as great a sin to urge modesty, and keep in the background when God calls to the foreground as it is to go to the front, when God's appointment is in the rear. Then came the period of the wars—wars ending ultimately in the most terrible disaster. Under Saul's reign the kingdom became disorganized.

When we come to David again we see adaptation and advance. Once again God gave His people a king, but this time a man after His own heart. The king of God's choosing was a shepherd, whose youthful days had been spent in the fields; a courtier who, passing from the fields to the palace, became Saul's son-in-law; an outlaw for long years, to use his own graphic description, hunted like "a partridge in the mountains." Through all these processes God was preparing him for a kingdom, not merely to reign over it, but to realize it. As a shepherd, he loved the sheep under his care, and rescued them from the paw of the lion and the bear. In the king's palace he became accustomed to courtly ways. As an outlaw he was prepared through discipline, and created a new type for the future strength of the kingdom. Thus God was remaking the kingdom in a cave, while the nation was going to pieces round the king after their own heart. The kingdom itself was thus being prepared for renewal through disaster. The special note in all this is that of Jehovah reigning, moving definitely forward, pressing into the service of His own progress, towards the fulfillment of His purpose, Samuel, Saul, David; governing by adaptation; taking hold of the child of faith and making him a prophet; taking hold of physical magnificence, and by its failures making it a revelation of the sin that had been committed; taking hold of the shepherd lad, and by processes making him king. Thus God ever sits high enthroned, and moves in victory across disaster towards ultimate purpose.

The second value of this book is but the obverse side of the first, teaching that man coöperates with God by failure, and by loyalty. Again our examination centres round the three personalities, and its purpose is not so much to show the result of their attitude as the process of God.

Samuel found his opportunity in his parentage, his call, his appointment. He responded to his opportunity by loyalty. The issues were that the messages of God were delivered to the people, and the work of God was advanced.

Saul found his opportunity in his call and anointing, in Samuel's friendship for him, and in his popularity and personal equipment. He responded by vacillation, by self-will, by disobedience. The issues were the revelation of his failure and the warning of his death.

David's opportunities were his call and anointing, his long waiting and suffering, and finally the crisis of the battle with Amalek in the hour of Saul's death. He responded by obedience and patience, and at the decisive moment by definite action. The issues were that he became the instrument of Jehovah's progress, a man through whom God moved forward towards ultimate realization.

That rapid survey shows that each man had his opportunity; each man made his response thereto; two of them the response of obedience, one that of disobedience; but whether by failure or by loyalty, men coöperate with God towards the final winning of His victory. If a man does not coöperate with God loyally, he is compelled by the supremacy of His throne, by the sovereignty of His government, to coöperate even through his own disaster and defeat.

I may quite briefly state the living message of this book. The permanent values constitute that living message. Let me state them in other terms. In this book I see the absolutism of God, and the relation of man to that absolutism. It first reveals the absolutism of God. There is no territory outside His jurisdiction; no person beyond His control, or who finally escapes His government; no event outside His consciousness, or beyond His overruling. This book not only reveals these things, it interprets them. It shows that this absolutism of God is operating towards accomplishment, includes in its operation all adverse facts and forces, and creates its own agents whenever it is necessary so to do. It is this living message that we need supremely today.

What, then, is the relation of man to this absolutism of God? The ultimate victory is independent of the attitudes of individuals or peoples towards Him. Through Samuel, Saul and David, He moved right on towards the Anointed and the ultimate Kingdom. The ultimate destiny of individuals is dependent upon their attitude towards Him. Samuel was obedient, and was used and saved. Saul was disobedient, and was used and destroyed. David was obedient, and was used and saved. It does not at all matter what my attitude towards God is, as to His ultimate victory. It matters everything as to my ultimate destiny. Everything depends upon me as to my own destiny. Nothing depends upon me ultimately as to His victory. He will press into His service for His final victory all souls who are loyal to Him, and they will share in the rapture of His victory. He will press into the service of His ultimate victory all souls in rebellion, and they will share in the wrath of His victory. So my responsibility must be, so far as my own destiny is concerned, the responsibility of obedience. This book inspires a great song, which can best be uttered in the words of the psalmist, "The Lord reigneth; let the earth rejoice."

II Samuel

THE PERMANENT VALUES	THE LIVING MESSAGE

I. God's opportunity is created by the attitude of man towards Him.
  A. The statement of the principle—22:26-28.
  B. The illustration.
    1. The attitudes of David.
      a. Conception of supremacy—22:1-16.
      b. Conviction of righteousness—22:17-27.
      c. Confidence in mercy—22:28-46.
      d. Conformity of desire—22:47-51.
    2. The answers of God.
      a. The exercise of sovereignty—22:1-3.
      b. The exercise of righteousness—22:21-28.
      c. The exercise of mercy—22:35-36.
      d. The exercise of salvation—22:51.
  C. All the resources of God operative in the life of a man in the right attitude. Thus the man becomes the instrument of God.
II. Man's opportunity is created by the attitude of God toward him.
  A. The statement of the principle.
  B. The illustration.
    1. The attitudes of Jehovah.
      a. Purpose—23:1.
      b. Power—23:2.
      c. Principle—23:3-4.
      d. Persistence—23:5.
    2. The answers of David.
      a. Consent.
      b. Cooperation.
      c. Conformity.
      d. Confidence.
  C. All the possibilities of man realized, because of the attitude of God. Thus God is able to operate through him.
	I. The lesson of I Samuel recognized: that the ultimate victory of God is independent of the attitudes of individuals or peoples towards God.
	
	II. The supreme matter for service is the attitude of the soul.
	
	III. The triumph of a man is the triumph of God over him.

THE first book of Samuel closes with the introduction of David. We saw him in preparation for his life-work; in the fields as shepherd; in the palace as musician and courtier; in the wilderness as outlaw. He was fitted for the position to which he was appointed, and for which he had been anointed. In the second book, we have the history of his specific contribution to the purpose of God. The question of preliminary preparation for service is not in view here, but rather the service resulting therefrom. We have already seen the threefold process of preparation in the fields, in the palace, in exile. In the fields, the essential spirit of a king, that of the shepherd, had its training. In the palace, the incidentals of kingliness were cultivated. In the exile, fibre was toughened, and the king was prepared for government. All these values are in this story. David is here the shepherd of his people, the centre of his court, and the strong ruler. The story of the book begins with the crisis that brought David into his specific work. Our attention, then, is fixed upon him fulfilling the office of king under the direct government of God, and from that standpoint there are two permanent values in the study. The book teaches us first that God's opportunity is created by the attitude of man towards Him; and secondly, that man's opportunity is created by the attitude of God towards him.

In the appendix to this book are two psalms which are of great use, as they state the principles which the story illustrates. As in the first book of Samuel the whole of its values are suggested in Hannah's song, with which it opens; so in the second book the values are crystallized in David's songs, with which it closes.

Let us begin with the first statement, that God's opportunity is created by the attitude of man towards Him. That principle emerges into clear declaration in the first of the two psalms:

" With the merciful Thou wilt show Thyself merciful,
With the perfect man Thou wilt show Thyself perfect;
With the pure Thou wilt show Thyself pure;
And with the perverse Thou wilt show Thyself froward.
And the afflicted people Thou wilt save :
But Thine eyes are upon the haughty, that Thou mayest bring them down."

All of which means that God is to a man what the man is to God. That is the principle. The story of David perfectly illustrates it. The attitude of David towards God is revealed as fourfold. There is manifested first, his conception of the supremacy of God; secondly, his conviction of the righteousness of God; thirdly, his confidence in the mercy of God; and finally, his conformity of desire to the will of God. There were times when faith faltered, and he did foolish things, when his passion mastered him, when he fell into fearful sin; but underneath the faltering faith I find faith which never faltered; deeper than the passion was the passionate desire for holiness; profounder than any sin, however heinous, was the attitude of soul which could say, "My soul followeth hard after God."

David's conception of the Divine supremacy I need not stay to illustrate. It may be stated superlatively. There is no instance recorded in which he called in question the crown rights of Jehovah. His conviction of the righteousness of God never wavered. Foolish things he did, aw-ful sins he committed, but he never doubted the righteousness of God's dealing with him. Charged with sin by the prophet of God, he confessed it, and bent himself to the stroke of God, convinced of the absolute rightness of the Divine character and method. He had perfect confidence in God's mercy. If there is one demonstration of confidence in mercy more powerful than another, it is willingness to be punished. " Let us now fall into the hand of the Lord; for His mercies are great: and let me not fall into the hand of man." That submission to the stroke of God is the finest revelation of his confidence in the tenderness of the Divine heart. His deepest desire perpetually was for conformity to the will of God. A man of passion, he fell into dark deeds of crime; yet through all the long processes of punishment, through the sin of his children, and the breaking of his heart in consequence, he never murmured against the stroke of God, but in perfect confidence in His mercy, and unceasing conformity of desire after His will, he endured.

That attitude created the Divine opportunity. Over a man who had a conception of His supremacy, God was able to exercise His sovereignty, taking him up, setting him upon the throne, and leading him in the administration of his kingdom. Towards the man convinced of His righteousness, it was possible for God to exercise that rightness in all His dealing with him. To the man with desire conformed to aspiration after Himself, God was able to come as Saviour. Thus all the forces of God are seen operating in the life of a man in right attitude towards Him, and so this man became the instrument of God through whom He accomplished His wider purpose. How I thank God that it was written of David that he was a man after God's own heart. There are men in the Bible of whom had it been written, it could never have helped me as it does when I see it written of David—a man who did so fall and fail and stoop to sin. Why does it help me? Because it excuses sin? A thousand times no! but because it shows me that God's measurement of a man, and God's ability to deal with a man, depend upon the deepest aspiration in that man's heart; and that God takes the measurement of a man by what he wills to be, and not by the faltering and failing of the moment. Even David could look up into the face of God, and say, "The Lord will perfect that which concerneth me." This is the first great revelation of the book, that God's opportunity to make me and use me is created by the deep, underlying, positive attitude of my life towards Him.

Now we may turn to the other side. Whence came these attitudes of David towards God? How is it that they came to be such, as I have attempted to epitomize as a conception of supremacy, a conviction of righteousness, a confidence in mercy, a conformity of desire. The attitude of God towards David created David's attitude towards God. This attitude David described in the second of the two psalms already referred to. Let us rapidly survey it. It first declares the purpose of God:

> " David, the son of Jesse, saith,
> And the man who was raised on high saith,
> The anointed of the God of Jacob,
> And the sweet psalmist of Israel."

It then reveals a secret of power:

> " The Spirit of the Lord spake by me,
> And His word was upon my tongue."

It then affirms a principle of kingship:

> " The God of Israel said,
> The Rock of Israel spake to me:
> One that ruleth over men righteously,
> That ruleth in the fear of God,
>
> He shall be as the light of the morning, when the
>   sun riseth,
> A morning without clouds ;
> When the tender grass springeth out of the earth,
> Through clear shining after rain."

It finally declares the Divine persistence:

> " Verily my house is not so with God ;
> Yet He hath made with me an everlasting covenant,
> Ordered in all things, and sure:
> For it is all my salvation, and all my desire,
> Although He maketh it not to grow."

These are the attitudes of God towards David as he understood them—purpose, power, principle and persistence, and they created his attitude towards God.

The purpose of God as manifested. The singer evidently recognized that his appointment to kingship was Divine, and poetically he describes that, both as to the man upon whom the choice

of God rested, and the ultimate issue of the choice. He did not sing of the anointed of the God of Israel, but of the anointed of the God of Jacob ; that is, the God of the man Jacob in all his meanness chose David to be king ; and in the fact as stated there is a suggestion of his consciousness of his own unworthiness. The man so anointed became not the sweet psalmist of Jacob, for songs cannot proceed out of meanness, but the sweet psalmist of Israel, for God can change Jacob to Israel, and so make possible all songs. That was the Divine purpose, and David's assurance of it created his attitude towards God.

The power of God as known. The statement " The Spirit of the Lord spake by me, and His word was upon my tongue," is poetically true to his previous description of himself as " the sweet psalmist of Israel," but it contains the whole philosophy of godly life. It is not merely a statement that he was inspired when he sang his song, but that the inspiration of his life was that of the Spirit of the Lord, and the expression of it was the word spoken. The New Testament equivalent of the verse is, " Work out your own salvation with fear and trembling ; for it is God which worketh in you both to will and to work, for His good pleasure." Thus the singer was assured, in the second place, that God's power was commensurate with all His purpose.

The principle of God for his guidance. The king who rules righteously and in the fear of God is a benediction to his people ; the benediction of the rising sun in the morning, when there are no clouds. The king who rules his people righteously is like sunlight after rain. It is somewhat difficult in this country to appreciate the beauty of the figure. In the country of David all the land is parched and burned and brown after the summer drought. Then there comes a day of sweet, silent rain, followed by clear shining ; and suddenly, like a flash of emerald, all the earth is green. This was the singer's picture of the result of the exercise of kingship in the fear of God, and in righteousness. This does not seem to help us, yet the principle is applicable to all. When God would prepare David for the exercise of kingship, He did so by giving him a picture of the final King ;

and whatever He wills that we should be, and do for Him, He reveals to us the pattern in His Son.

The persistence of God. Notwithstanding this threefold revelation of purpose, power, and principle, David was compelled to say, " My house is not so with God ; yet ——" Thank God for that " yet " ! There is all the Gospel in it for my heart ! " Yet He hath made with me an everlasting covenant, ordered in all things and sure." Thus David affirmed finally his confidence in the persistence of Jehovah.

How did he answer these attitudes of God, which created his opportunity? He heard the purpose, and consented to it. Saul the anointed king hid behind the stuff. David the anointed king moved right on with his eye upon the goal, never turning back. Conscious of the Divine power, he answered it, and coöperated with it. He felt the power, and responded to it. " The Spirit of the Lord spake by me, and His word was upon my tongue." Mark well the intimate relationship between these things. Whittier sang beautifully of men who die with all their music in them. I do not criticize Whittier. There are people who die with all their music in them, who never had their chance to sing. But if we have music in us, and can express it, we have no business to die with it in us. " It is God which worketh in you . . . work out." That is the principle of salvation.

The principle of kingship is revealed, and while David certainly failed, he yet conformed thereto. Think of the condition of the kingdom when he came to it ; then see it as he left it. From utter political and social chaos he had brought it to its highest realization. Solomon stands out upon the page of Bible history in lonely and wonderful splendour in certain directions ; but as king he was a disastrous failure, so much so that when he died the kingdom was rent in twain. Solomon was the Lorenzo de Medici of Hebrew history, solacing the people for lack of liberty with shows and pageantry ; and God help the people when they are so seduced. David lifted Israel to its heroic age, to its finest and its best. He was imperfect, and his kingdom was imperfect, but by comparison he answered the revelation of that principle so that it was fulfilled in measure in his history.

His answer to the persistence of God was that of his perfect confidence in it. It was that confidence which made him write his penitential psalms. When we speak of David's sins let us in all fairness speak also of his penitence. When we would know how deep his penitence was, let us hear his declaration, " Against Thee, Thee only, have I sinned." That is the language of a man dealing with the profoundest things of life. Of course, if men deal with the surface ripples only, they will say that God is not harmed by human sin ; but to know God is finally to exclaim of every sin, " Against Thee, Thee only, have I sinned." Yet such a confession demonstrates the consciousness of the persistence of God in mercy. I would be overwhelmed by my sin, and by my sin made careless of sin, and ultimately by my sin made to continue in sin, were it not that I know the infinite goodness of God is set upon delivering me, if I will but stand in right attitude towards Him. Thus God was able to operate through David, His opportunity being created by David's attitude towards Him ; yet that attitude of David towards God was the result of His attitude towards David. The deepest truth of all in this revelation of inter-relationship is that of God's attitude towards a man. Man's responsibility is created thereby. His responsibility is that of his attitude, and that in turn decides the Divine action.

The living message of this book is patent. In order to understand it, one of the lessons of the first book of Samuel must be remembered, namely, that the ultimate victory of God is independent of the attitude of individuals or peoples towards Him. With that clearly in mind, it will be recognized that the supreme matter for coöperation in service is the attitude of the soul towards God. Fitness for service is created by the conformity of the life to the will of God. Conformity of the life depends wholly upon the attitude of the soul towards God. The conformity of my life to the will of God does not depend upon my ability, but upon my abandonment ; not upon my persuading God to do something, but upon my allowing myself to be persuaded by God to be something. The attitude of conformity is that of being willing to know, to be, to do His will. By that attitude God measures a man, and through that attitude acts with a man.

That doctrine is a two-edged sword. God is

measuring me not as man would measure me. I am prone to measure a man by the last sin he has committed. God never does. He measures by the attitude of his soul. This doctrine is full of comfort, but it is awful in its severity. What is my attitude towards God? Have I lived a clean life? Would I, if I had had the chance to live a filthy one? That is the question. Half the purity in which some men boast is a question of birth and of environment. We talk of other men living in the underworld. The question is, would we live there if we could? If so, God measures us as in the underworld. This is fire. It scorches, it burns. God have mercy on me, a sinner.

Yes, but are you down? Have you committed a sin? Are your Christian friends not quite so friendly as they were, in consequence; yet all the while do you want to go right? Then that attitude of your soul is God's measurement of you.

Yes, but do not let us slip out by that door, if all the while we want to do the evil thing. Let us be careful. God help us to discriminate. We need supremely to guard against disproportionate excuse or accusing.

Now do you not see the sin of the priestcraft? Who is to come in between the soul and God? I am only an interpreter of principles. I dare not bare my soul to you, and would not have you bare yours to me. David was a man after God's own heart, because of the posture of his soul; and God at last fulfilled the underlying desire of his heart. The triumph of a man is the triumph of God over him, and man only wins when he yields to Him.

I Kings

THE PERMANENT VALUES	THE LIVING MESSAGE

I. The failing government of man.
  A. Two thrones (see chart).
  B. The successive methods.
    1. Solomon—material magnificence.
    2. Rehoboam—autocracy.
    3. Jeroboam—democracy.
    4. Judah—succession and policy.
    5. Israel—intrigues, murders, and rebellion.
  C. Disruption, Disintegration, and Disaster.
II. The unfailing government of God.
  A. The prophetic voices.
    1. Ahijah—11:26-29.
    2. Shemaiah—12:21-24.
    3. "The man of God"—13:1-10.
    4. Ahijah—14:4-16.
    5. Jehu—16:1-4.
    6. Elijah—17–21.
    7. Micaiah—22:8-28.
  B. The direct interference.
    1. Appearances to Solomon and building of the temple.
    2. Adversaries raised up against Solomon.
    3. Death of Abijah.
    4. Withdrawal of rain and the consequent famine.
    5. Carmel and fire.
    6. Appearance to Elijah in the earthquake.
    7. Spirit of lying in prophets to entice Ahab to battle.
	I. As to human government—if God be out of count, every method ends in disaster.
	II. As to divine government.
	  A. The abandonment of the thrones of earth.
	  B. The witness of truth.
	  C. Direct interference.

THIS book is bounded by death. Opening with the death of David, and closing with the death of Ahab, it covers a period of a little more than a century and a half. The story which it tells is that of a nation passing from affluence and influence to poverty and paralysis. In order to discover the permanent values of this book we must keep before the mind two thrones—that on earth with its succession of kings, and that in the heavens with its one King. In looking at the former we see the failing government of men, and in looking at the latter we see the unfailing government of God.

In order that we may see the two thrones let us glance at a very simple chart:

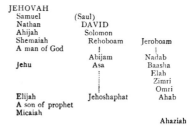

There Jehovah stands for the one Throne and the abiding King. Deflected from the Throne is the throne set up on earth, with the names of the succeeding kings as far as Ahab, where our present book ends. Beneath the name of Jehovah are the names of the prophets through whom

He delivered His messages, and maintained His connection with the people through this period in which, to use His own words, the nation had rejected Him from being King.

Turning our attention first to the throne on the earth, we observe the succession of kings. Jehovah first gave them Saul, a king after their own heart. Then with David, the man after God's own heart, commenced the succession which reached the point of supreme darkness in Ahab. This is a story of disruption, disintegration, and disaster.

On the other hand, in fixing our attention upon the Throne in the heavens, we see the one King maintaining His rule ; and, through the prophets, from Samuel to Elijah, declaring His message. This is a story of government, grace, and guidance.

In this order let us consider the teaching of the two thrones.

Looking first at the earthly throne, we notice the successive methods of government. In some senses there is only one, that of monarchy ; but monarchs have different methods. Our English government to-day is described as a monarchy ; so also is the Russian ; but no one will suggest that their methods are the same. As a matter of fact, the King of England has nothing like the executive power of the President of the United States of America. While in this book we have the story of kings, their methods are quite different. As we look at these methods we shall see a nation, having rejected Jehovah from being King, attempting to govern itself. The people named the name of Jehovah, built His temple, sang His songs, and offered His sacrifices ; but men may do all these, and be infidel. This nation still used the terminology, and observed the ceremonial of the worship of Jehovah, but attempted to govern itself.

The story of David occupied our attention in our last lecture. In observing the successive methods, therefore, we commence with Solomon. His method was that of material magnificence. There may be some senses in which that description may seem incomplete, yet I think it includes the whole story. Let the facts be recalled. First there was the organization of the kingdom, and the building of the temple. Through both these processes there was the multiplication of riches, and the manifestation of display. The

failure of Solomon began long before it became outward, patent, manifest. From the beginning there may be detected the activity of that sensual nature which issued in such inevitable and disastrous ruin. He was called Solomon the Magnificent, the Wise, the Peaceful ; but the true story of his reign is told in one brief, almost startling sentence, when " all the congregation of Israel came, and spake unto Rehoboam, saying, *Thy father made our yoke grievous.*" For something like a parallel to the reign of Solomon, we may go to Italy and look at Florence under the sway of Lorenzo de Medici. Lorenzo was also a magnificent man, a philosopher and a scholar ; but in cruel despotism he robbed the people of Florence of their liberty, silencing and solacing them with pageantry, shows, and pomp. Mrs. Oliphant describes the condition of affairs in graphic words when she writes, " Fair Florence lying in bonds or, rather, dancing in them, with smear of blood upon her garments and loathsome song upon her lips." It was against that condition of affairs that Savonarola raised his voice in protest. That is very largely the story also of Solomon's reign. All that Samuel had told the people concerning the effect of kingship was fulfilled in even more marked degree under Solomon than under Saul. He attempted to govern the people by magnificent display and material grandeur ; and failure is seen in the disruption of the kingdom, following upon long continued disaffection, immediately Solomon was removed.

To Rehoboam the people gathered in discontent, saying, " Thy father made our yoke grievous." To their complaint he replied, " My little finger is thicker than my father's loins. And now whereas my father did lade you with a heavy yoke, I will add to your yoke : my father chastised you with whips, but I will chastise you with scorpions." Here a new method of government emerges, that of autocracy. Rehoboam's language was essentially that of the autocrat, and he was the almost necessary offspring of Solomon.

In Jeroboam another method is seen. Of course, it must be remembered that he was Divinely called. God distinctly announced to him by the prophet that He would rend the kingdom in twain, because of the corruption of the reign of Solomon ; that He would leave one tribe for Rehoboam that a lamp might be maintained for the house of David ; and that the rest of the people should gather to him, and he should reign over them. Nevertheless, he immediately turned aside from allegiance to Jehovah, and attempted to govern on other lines. His first act was that of political accommodation in the realm of religion. " Whereupon the king took counsel, and made two calves of gold ; and he said unto them, It is too much for you to go up to Jerusalem : behold thy gods, O Israel, which brought thee up out of the land of Egypt." This is a revelation of his constant method of appeal to democracy. Rehoboam was an autocrat, who believed that the people should trust in princes. Jeroboam was a democrat, who believed that princes should trust in the people. Neither of them trusted in Jehovah, and they failed equally. The result of Rehoboam's autocracy was that the people said, " What portion have we in David ? . . . To your tents, O Israel." The issue of Jeroboam's democracy was that the people had their religion made easy, were content with calves, and became corrupt.

As to the rest. In Judah, Abijam, Asa, and Jehoshaphat constituted a succession of kings reigning by policy, with God largely shut out of their thoughts. Asa's reign was in many respects better than that of Abijam, yet there was manifest ultimately a fear and cowardice, which led him to a base act of compromise. Jehoshaphat walked timidly in paths of right, failing to act with thoroughness, and finally entered into an unholy alliance with the king of Israel. The story of those kings of Judah is that of government by policy.

Turning to Israel we find even more terrible failure in a succession of men who cared nothing for the welfare of the kingdom, and esteemed the throne only as a prize for personal possession. There was succession by intrigue and murder of men who absolutely ignored the Throne of Jehovah, and led the people further and further into evil. With Omri, a man elected by popular acclaim, there was a new beginning, but it was a new beginning of the old sin and folly. Then we come to Ahab and Jezebel, a marvellous combination of strength and wit ; in both, tremendous force of character was prostituted to base purposes, and the whole nation groaned under the dominion, and was en-slaved by it. At last Ahaziah succeeded, but the story of sin and folly, of idolatry and disaster ran on.

Government by man means disruption, disintegration, and disaster. He cannot govern himself. Whether by material magnificence, or by the assumption of autocratic power, or by appeal to democratic desire, or in any other way, all government of man by man is a disastrous failure. This is the story writ large upon the page of the first book of Kings.

Turning to the Throne in the heavens we observe the unfailing government of God. This is manifest first in the voices of prophecy which break in upon the confused babel with suddenness, in distinct proclamations. Ahijah declared that after the death of Solomon the kingdom would be rent in twain, and later foretold the death of the son of Jeroboam. Shemaiah warned Rehoboam not to fight against Jeroboam. A nameless man of God appeared suddenly to Jeroboam, and prophesied against the altar. Jehu pronounced the doom to fall upon Baasha. Elijah, in the hour when the darkness was deepest, appeared suddenly as a flash of lightning at midnight. He proclaimed Jehovah in tones of thunder ; and vindicated Him at Carmel, and in the matter of Naboth's vineyard. A son of the prophets rebuked Ahab for allowing Benhadad to escape. Micaiah, in spite of all that was done to prevent him, declared the coming scattering of Israel upon the mountains. In these appearances of the prophets, and their testimony borne, I see Jehovah governing independently of the throne of earth, when that throne was occupied by men who forgot Him.

The government of Jehovah was more than that of testimony. It operated in direct interferences. He appeared to Solomon, and the building of the temple resulted therefrom. The story of Solomon's punishment begins with the declaration, " The Lord raised up an adversary unto Solomon." In the withdrawal of rain and the consequent famine, and in the awe-inspiring scenes on Carmel, Jehovah declared Himself by direct interference in the affairs of the sinning people.

Thus, high lifted above the forces of battle, pressing into His service spirits of evil as well as forces of good, bringing men from distant lands as adversaries, manipulating history even while men in history had rejected Him, is seen the One enthroned Jehovah. The throne on earth never rightly filled, occupied by a succession of men who attempted all methods of government, each in succession disastrously failing; the Throne in heaven filled, and never shaken. Over all the chaos God reigned towards order.

The living message of this book is not about the temple in its structure, interesting though that story is. It is not merely a history of the Hebrew nation. That also is interesting and important in some senses. This book has something to say to us about human government and about Divine government, which it is well for us to hear and heed. Concerning human government it declares one thing. If God be out of count, every method ends in disaster. In the earlier part of Solomon's reign attention was given to religious forms and ceremonies, to internal development, to commercial treaties, to intellectual attainment. Yet all failed because God was out of count. Religious forms and ceremonies are grave-cloths if the spirit be not right with God. A nation cannot be governed by insisting that it shall adopt religious forms or ceremonies. Neither can a nation be governed by internal development, or commercial treaties, or ships which ply to Tarshish bringing back apes and peacocks, and with them disaster and ruin. Government based upon human autocracy must end in revolution sooner or later, when the people, oppressed by one of their number who does not understand them, and cannot govern them in their own interests but only in his own, begin to straighten themselves in the power of an inherent relationship to Deity. Shut God out of the question, and democracy will be the most awful tyranny the world has ever seen. We are to-day dealing with forces we hardly understand. Socialism that is godless will be a reign of terror indeed. Once teach men to consolidate and combine for their own interests, without reference to the Throne of God, and the result will be the utmost disaster. Man cannot govern himself, for he does not know himself. How then can he govern others of whom he knows so much less, or how can two govern a third, or a multitude govern itself? It cannot be. There are forces and facts in one human being that defy the government of all human beings. If man put God out of count, I care not whether his method

of government be autocracy or democracy, whether it be individualism or socialism, it will fail disastrously.

On the other hand, the book of Kings has a living message concerning Divine government. Of course it cannot tell all the glorious issue of such government, because it is in itself a story of failure. We have to come a good deal further on before we see the issue. The world has never yet seen it realized, but it will see it. It is because we believe that, some of us love to revel amid the mystic mysteries of the Apocalypse, even though we do not profess to understand all its suggestiveness. One man, the seer of the Galilean lake, on the lonely island of Patmos, its shores washed by waters, looked and saw the city of God coming down out of heaven from God, and heard the greatest chorus that poets have ever sung, "Behold, the tabernacle of God is with men, and He shall dwell with them, and they shall be His peoples, and God Himself shall be with them, and be their God."

This book of Kings does not give us that vision of the ultimate, but it does reveal God's method in the midst of failure. It is first that of abandonment of the throne of earth. He acted in separation from it. This abandonment was not capricious. So long as the kings were in rebellion, so long as they forgot Him and His Throne, and sought to establish government without Him, He abandoned them in order that their evil choice might work itself out into manifestation. This book, moreover, teaches us that God bears perpetual witness to truth in the midst of falsehood, and ever causes some measure of light to shine in the midst of darkness.

Forgive me if I try to impress that final lesson upon your memory in the simplest way. My story constitutes a small picture, but it is a microcosm of the problem. I knew a case of a woman bereaved of her husband in the midst of the battle of life. The outlook to her was that of utter and absolute disaster. Full of despair, she passed days in silence and in weeping, until her girlie about seven years old came one day to her side, and looking into the tear-dimmed eyes said, Mother, is God dead? Putting her arms about the child, the woman said, Darling, you are His messenger to me. "The Lord reigneth." Do not let us forget, however dark the outlook may be, God is not dead. "The Lord reigneth."

II Kings

THE PERMANENT VALUES	THE LIVING MESSAGE

I. The failure of man.
  A. Its cause: the lost sense of Jehovah.
    1. Illustrated in their kings.
    2. Manifested in their idolatries and alliances.
    3. Evident in their inability to detect the hand of Jehovah.
  B. Its manifestations: the lost ideal of nationality.
    1. Righteousness undervalued.
    2. Sin lightly esteemed.
    3. Pride of nationality.
  C. Its hopelessness: the lost sensitiveness of conscience.
    1. The prophetic period—"Who hath believed . . . ?"
    2. The reformation—superficial.
    3. The religious order—neglected.
  D. Its issue: the lost vision.
    1. Conquered.
    2. Captive.
    3. Castaway.
II. The victory of God.
  A. Its cause: His purpose.
  B. Its method: His persistence.
  C. Its hopefulness: His principles.
  D. Its issues: His power.
	I. "**Where there is no vision the people cast off restraint**"—Prov. 29:18; the lost vision of God.
	  A. Degraded ideals.
	  B. Deadened conscience.
	  C. Defeated purposes.
	II. "**He shall not fall nor be discouraged**"—Isa. 42:4; the enthroned Jehovah.
	  A. Power.
	  B. Knowledge.
	  C. Activity.

AS we have already said, the two books of Kings appear in the Hebrew Bible as one, and tell a continuous story. Our second book, therefore, forms a sequel to the first. In the first we have the history of about a century and a half, and in the second of about three centuries.

Once again the two thrones are in view. The first—steadfast, immovable, always abounding in activity and in progress; the second—trembling, failing, and at last abolished. The early part of the history of this period, contained in the first book of Kings, emphasizes the facts of the failing government of man, and the unfailing government of God. The latter part, contained in the second book, emphasizes the results issuing in each case. The permanent values of the second book, then, are its revelations of the failure of man, and the victory of God.

I confess to the difficulty of an embarrassment of riches in approaching this study. This was the period of the prophets. All the great prophetic messages preserved for us were delivered during this period. That fact creates the difficulty of interpreting the message of this book. Read the book apart from the prophecies, and it is disappointing indeed. Read the book as the background of the prophecies, and then we see in the background man's failure, and in the foreground God's great and overwhelming victory.

Let us notice what this book teaches concerning the failure of man, as to its cause, its manifestations, its hopelessness, and its issue.

The cause of human failure was the lost sense of Jehovah; its manifestation was the lost ideal of nationality; its hopelessness was the lost sensitiveness of conscience; and its issue was the lost vocation.

The fact of the people's lost sense of Jehovah is illustrated in their kings. There were exceptions. Joash, Amaziah, Jotham, Hoshea served the Lord; but even of them it is written, "not like David," or that "the high places were not taken away." These did not utterly fail, yet failed partially, either by compromise, or some measure of backsliding. Two names stand out as the names of kings who followed the Lord— those of Hezekiah and Josiah; yet even they failed in some degree. Apart from these, the story of the kings is that of men who had no vision of God. They persisted in courses of evil. They turned their back upon the principles of righteousness. They multiplied transgression through the length and breadth of the land. Men occupied the throne on earth, who had lost their vision of the Throne in the heavens.

This lost sense of Jehovah was manifested also in the idolatries and alliances of the people. No man who has a clear vision of God turns to an idol. An idol is always a substitute for something else, an attempt to fill a vacuum. There is a sense in which idolatry is a perpetual proof of man's capacity for God. That is not to excuse idolatry. It is rather to show the heinousness of its sin. At the back of every sin there lies a possibility of good. That does not mean that sin is something to be pitied, petted, pampered. If man prostitutes something that is good, hell is the proper result. Idolatry is a demonstration of the capacity for God; but when a man turns to an idol, it is because he has lost his vision of God. Hosea spoke of Ephraim as "a silly dove," "a cake not turned," but he declared that Ephraim would get back to God, and then would say, "What have I to do any more with idols?" That is always the language of the man who sees God. The groves and the Baalim, the worshippers of Moloch and the children passing through the fire, all mean that the people had lost their vision of Jehovah.

Once again, the fact that the cause of the failure was a lost sense of Jehovah is evident in the inability of the people to detect the hand of God as it fell upon them in punishment. Isaiah declared that God had laid His hand upon them, until they were a mass of bruises and sores, and enquired, "Why will ye be still stricken?"

The second fact grows immediately out of the first. The result of the lost vision of God is the lost ideal of national life; righteousness is undervalued, sin is lightly esteemed, and a false pride of nationality exists. Jonah, the son of Amittai, was a prophet to the people of God. One brief verse tells of the fact that he prophesied. The burden of the prophecy is not given. That of Jonah which lives is not the prophecy he delivered, but the story he wrote of his prophetic vision to Nineveh. It was not written for the sake of Nineveh, but for the sake of Israel. It was written for Israel in a time when she was characterized by two contradictory attitudes. The first was that of a false exclusiveness; she did not believe there could be any pity or mercy in the heart of God for any other than herself. The second was that of failure to be exclusive as God meant her to be; she was forming alliances with other nations, contrary to the Divine command and will. The story of Jonah and Nineveh is the condemnation of exclusiveness. These people had lost the true ideal of nationality; the ideal given by God to Abraham in His first covenant; the ideal repeated when the nation emerged into national life; the ideal constantly kept before the mind by all the religious economy and prophetic utterances; the ideal which was expressed in the words, " I will bless thee and make thy name great; *and be thou a blessing.*" When these people lost their clear vision of God, they lost their understanding of the meaning of their own national life.

Then look at the hopelessness of the situation. Remember that this was the great prophetic period. In order that we may see this I have prepared a simple chart.

The two thrones are suggested and the two processes are seen. On the one side a line of prophets, on the other a succession of kings. On that of the kings—Saul, David, Solomon, the division under Rehoboam and Jeroboam, and then through Kings of Israel and Judah to the captivity in each case. That is the throne on the earth.

Now turn to the other side, and see the Throne in the heavens. God dealt with His people through the prophets. In the inner column are the names of the prophets mentioned in the books of Kings. They are Samuel,

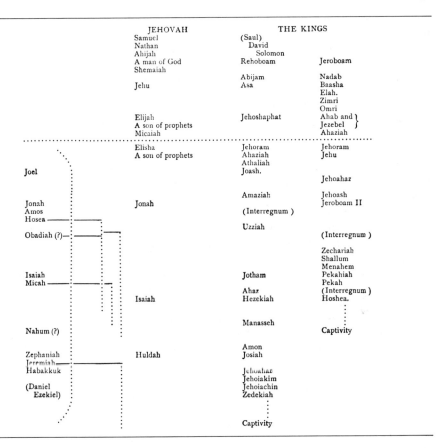

JEHOVAH	THE KINGS	
Samuel	(Saul)	
Nathan	David	
Ahijah	Solomon	
A man of God	Rehoboam	Jeroboam
Shemaiah		
	Abijam	Nadab
Jehu	Asa	Baasha
		Elah.
		Zimri
		Omri
Elijah	Jehoshaphat	Ahab and }
A son of prophets		Jezebel }
Micaiah		Ahaziah

. . . .

	Elisha	Jehoram	Jehoram
	A son of prophets	Ahaziah	Jehu
		Athaliah	
Joel		Joash.	
			Jehoahaz
		Amaziah	Jehoash
Jonah	Jonah		Jeroboam II
Amos		(Interregnum)	
Hosea —————			
Obadiah (?)—		Uzziah	
			(Interregnum)
			Zechariah
			Shallum
			Menahem
Isaiah		Jotham	Pekahiah
Micah —————			Pekah
		Ahaz	(Interregnum)
	Isaiah	Hezekiah	Hoshea.
		Manasseh	
Nahum (?)			Captivity
		Amon	
Zephaniah	Huldah	Josiah	
Jeremiah—			
Habakkuk		Jehoahaz	
		Jehoiakim	
(Daniel		Jehoiachin	
Ezekiel)		Zedekiah	
		Captivity	

Nathan, Ahijah, a man of God, Shemaiah, Jehu, Elijah, a son of prophets, Micaiah, Elisha, a son of prophets, Jonah, Isaiah, and the prophetess Huldah.

The outer column begins with the second book of the Kings, and contains the names of men who were speaking during the period, but who are not named in the text: Joel, Jonah, Amos, Hosea, Isaiah, Obadiah, Nahum, Zephaniah, Jeremiah, Habakkuk; and in exile, Daniel and Ezekiel. The immediate result of the ministry of these men was almost nothing. Isaiah, in that part of his prophecy in which he described the result of his own preaching, enquired—and it is the story of all the prophetic ministry— "Who hath believed our report? and to whom hath the arm of the Lord been revealed?" Mark the hopelessness of the case, the lost sensitiveness of conscience that could listen to such messages as these, and yet continue in the sin of rebellion and in forgetfulness of God.

Think of another fact. The reformations were all superficial. Immediately Hezekiah had passed away, the people returned to their old ways of evil. Josiah conducted a remarkable reformation, and yet it is a significant fact that Zephaniah never referred to it. The reason is to be found in the story of Huldah the prophetess. When the reformation was proceeding, and the book of the law was discovered, they sent to Huldah, and she, inspired of God to deliver her message, said in effect that there was no real value in the reformation; that the king meant well, and would be rewarded, but that the people were not following God. The condition of the religious life of the period is seen more clearly in Chronicles, the two books that deal with the life of the people from the Temple standpoint. When Hezekiah began his reformation he commenced with the Temple, and before anything else could be done it took the whole company of priests and Levites sixteen days to carry rubbish therefrom, which simply means that the Temple had become a lumber store. In the days when Josiah carried out his reformation, the book of the law was found. Mark the significance of this fact, that it had to be found! Moreover, its teaching so astonished Josiah that he halted in the middle of his work to enquire from the prophetess Huldah. The people had so forgotten the law of their God that, when it was found, they were absolutely unfamiliar with it.

Finally the issue of the failure was that of the loss by the nation of its vocation. I cannot tell the story in detail, but three words sum it up— conquered, captive, castaway! Is there a sadder story in all the history of the world than that?

But look at the other side, that of the victory of God. The secret of that victory is discovered by going back to the beginnings. When God promised Abraham that He would bless him and make him a blessing, and that through his seed the whole world should be blessed, "*He sware by Himself.*" We have a light upon that ancient declaration in the letter to the Hebrews, when the writer declared " He could sware by none greater, He sware by Himself . . . that by two immutable things, in which it is impossible for God to lie, we may have a strong encouragement," God entered into a covenant with Abraham. He will fulfill His covenant. He will be true to Himself. He will·allow nothing ultimately to thwart the purpose of His love. He remembered His covenant throughout the whole of the process.

Then notice the method of God. " The Lord testified . . . by the hand of every prophet, and of every seer." In that method there was included His judgments, the awful visitations which these people never seem to have understood ; and His tender mercy, directly the people turned to Him, He turned to them, and was ready to receive them.

The principle of the Divine activity was its perpetual hopefulness. In the prophecy of Hosea this is clearly revealed. In the wonderful love song of Jehovah we touch the hidden spring of everything, " How shall I give thee up, Ephraim ? " That is the inspiration of God's victory. It is that determination of love, and that hopefulness of God, which issue in His victory.

Finally observe the issues. The national ideal was preserved in captivity, and is preserved until this hour. There is no study more fascinating than that of the Hebrew people. Scattered over the face of the earth, and neutralized among strange people, their nationality cannot be destroyed. God preserves them wherever they go. They are still His, and His mark is upon them. Even in captivity the national ideal was preserved. He preserved the seed for the fulfillment of His purpose, until at last the promise to Abraham was fulfilled.

The prophetic utterances constitute a literature for the ages. There are senses in which the Hebrew prophets have a more living message to this age than the Christian apostles have. The apostolic writings are for the Church. The prophets speak still to the nations—Joel, with his far-flung vision of the Day of the Lord ; Jonah, with his condemnation of exclusiveness ; Amos, the herdman of Tekoah, who thundered concerning national accountability; Hosea, who interpreted the sin of the God-forgetting people as spiritual adultery ; Obadiah, with his curse on cowardice ; Isaiah, the prophet of the Theocracy ; Micah, dealing with authority, false and true ; Nahum, with his vindication of Jehovah's vengeance ; Zephaniah, with the message of the severity and goodness of God ; Jeremiah, the prophet of failure ; Habakkuk, with his problems of faith. These constitute a literature for all time, and it was made in the age when these people so signally failed.

Let me state briefly what seem to me to be the living messages of this book. I do so by two quotations that come right out of the period. This is the first, " Where there is no vision the people cast off restraint." The second is, " He shall not fail nor be discouraged." Let us see the setting of these two quotations. The first one is found in the Proverbs of Solomon, not in the collection of proverbs which he collected himself, but in the second collection which the men of Hezekiah, King of Judah, copied out. Mark the suggestiveness of this. Solomon, the man by whom all the seeds of disruption were sown, wrote down as a proverb, " Where there is no vision the people cast off restraint." Go to the beginning of the period in the first book of Samuel, " The word of the Lord was precious in those days"—that is, it was rare in those days; " *there was no open vision.*" That is how the period began. There was no vision of God.

Come to the end, the last period, the Lamentations of Jeremiah : " Her prophets find no vision from Jehovah." That is the story of it all.

What, then, is the message of the book? If the vision of God be lost, the issue must be degraded ideals, deadened consciences, defeated purposes. That is the national teaching of the book. " Where there is no vision the people cast off restraint," abandon observance of the Sabbath, abandon themselves to their own appetites, until a nation like our own becomes drugged with drink, while it does not know that it is drunk.

Thank God the book has another message. Isaiah, the greatest prophet of the period, declared of Jehovah, " He shall not fail nor be discouraged." The man who said this was the man whose writing commences, " The *vision* of Isaiah, the son of Amos." This man could make this declaration in the midst of all the decadence of his age, because, to use his own words, " In the year that King Uzziah died I saw the Lord sitting upon a throne." That vision ultimately enabled him to say : " Why sayest thou, O Jacob, and speakest, O Israel, My way is hid from the Lord, and my judgment is passed away from my God? Hast thou not known? hast thou not heard ? the everlasting God, the Lord, the Creator of the ends of the earth fainteth not, neither is weary." That is power. " There is no searching of His understanding." That is knowledge. " He giveth power to the faint ; and to him that hath no might He increaseth strength. Even the youths,"—who seem as though one never can tire them,—" shall faint and be weary, and the young men shall utterly fall : but they that wait upon the Lord shall renew their strength ; they shall mount up with wings as eagles ; they shall run, and not be weary ; they shall walk, and not faint." Nothing finer than that was ever written, and it was written in that awful period of human failure by the man who saw the throne and Jehovah. That is the living message of the hour. " The Lord . . fainteth not, neither is weary." " He shall not fail nor be discouraged." If we are to serve our age, we must see God ; and seeing Him, we shall ever be inspired by the certainty of the ultimate victory.

I Chronicles

THE PERMANENT VALUES	THE LIVING MESSAGE

The condemnation of rationalism—the revelation of the supreme importance of the recognition of God in the national life of the chosen people.
 	
I. **The demonstration of the genealogies.**
  A. The elections of God.
  B. Their principles.
    1. Of exclusion.
    2. Of inclusion.
  C. Their purpose.
    1. The ultimate in view.
    2. All details toward the ultimate.
 	
II. **The illustration of David.**
  A. David presented in his strength.
    1. The national crowning.
    2. The capture of Jebus.
    3. The mighty men.
    4. The gathering of the people.
  B. David's deepest life.
    1. His master passion.
      a. Care for the Ark.
      b. Desire to build.
    2. His submission.
      a. The method of God.
      b. The answer of David.
    3. His service.
      a. The gathering of treasure.
      b. The arrangements.
	The importance of the recognition of God in the life of a nation.
	
	I. **Because of the fact of the divine activity.**
	  A. That is a reason.
	  B. That is a hope.
	
	II. **Because of the effect upon the national life.**
	  A. Moral standards.
	  B. Character of individuals.
	  C. Conception of social relationships.

IN order that we may understand this book, and discover its permanent value and living message, it is important that we should know when it was written, for in the discovery of the when, we shall in all probability find the answer to the why. There is internal evidence that it was written in close association with the time of Ezra and Nehemiah. In the section at the commencement which deals with the genealogies, names occur which clearly indicate this. In the sixth chapter it is written: "Azariah begat Seraiah, and Seraiah begat Jehozadak; and Jehozadak went into captivity, when the Lord carried away Judah and Jerusalem by the hand of Nebuchadnezzar." This was evidently written by one looking back upon the captivity. If that is borne in mind, we shall begin to see the reason of the peculiarities of both this book and the one which follows it. There is the closest connection between the story contained in Chronicles and that told in the books of Ezra and Nehemiah; a much closer connection than that between Kings and Ezra and Nehemiah. II. Chronicles ends with a proclamation of Cyrus, King of Persia, which made possible the rebuilding of the house of God in Jerusalem. That proclamation is the commencement of the book of Ezra. There can be little doubt that the story in Chronicles was written at the return from captivity, in order to encourage the people to build the house of God, for its central subject is the temple of God. Thus we find the key to these two books of Chronicles. Notice the peculiarities without entering into details. In the books of Chronicles, Israel, the Northern Kingdom, is out of sight. There are references to it, but only when it is absolutely necessary to show relationship to Judah. Judah is in view, only to fix attention upon David. David is the central personality. Judah the nation ; David the personality. Yet the purpose of the writer was not that of dealing with Judah or with David, but of dealing with the temple of God. David is referred to in order that there may be brought into clear vision the master passion of his life, the building of the temple.

It has sometimes been said that the books of Kings are of prophetic origin, because of their prophetic outlook ; and that the books of Chronicles are of priestly origin, because of their priestly outlook. That is quite true, but it is only a secondary truth. The deeper truth is that in Kings we have history simply, while in Chronicles we see the relation of the nation to religious life ; the writer's one object being to bring into prominence all the facts concerning the temple, in order to show how absolutely important was that temple to the life of the people. The sub-titles, which I suggested in our previous study of the contents of the books, suggest this ; the Temple desired and approached ; and the Temple possessed and abandoned.

The first book has one preëminent value. It reveals the supreme importance of the recognition of God in the national life of the chosen people. Other books have taught the fact of the relation of God and the nation, but this book reveals the importance of the recognition of that fact by the people.

We shall notice first how the genealogies demonstrate the importance of recognizing God ; and secondly, how the story of David illustrates the same truth.

If we take the first ten chapters, and consider them carefully, we see that their value does not consist in the stringing together of names. Through all there is evidence of a Divine movement, persistent and startling, which compels us to pause and enquire. They begin with Adam and end with Nehemiah ; and there is constant selection, election, choice ; the turning aside of the current ; the starting of a new movement. Beginning with Adam, we remember the names of his sons, Cain, Abel, Seth. Of these, neither Cain nor Abel is mentioned. There is selection, and the name chosen is that of Seth. From him the Divine procedure moves through Enoch to Noah ; then on through Shem to Abram and Isaac ; then through Judah to Jesse and David ; then Solomon and Rehoboam, to captivity. Among the tribes of Levi there is distinct selection to purpose. Three sons of Levi, Kohath, Gershon, Merari, are chosen.

From Adam to Zedekiah the writer reveals the fact that God made successive selections, ever starting the stream on a new course by choosing individuals. The principle of inclusion was always that of character, based upon obedience ; and wherever there was such character based upon obedience, all disability was cancelled. The principle of exclusion was that all rights and privileges are cancelled by disobedience. Privileges of descent, of relationship, never count in the economy of God. The one thing that counts is obedience, and the character that grows out of it. The purpose of selection, as revealed in these genealogies, is that from the beginning the ultimate is in view. It is perfectly evident as one studies at all carefully these new beginnings and new developments, that the apparently crooked way is yet the straight way to the goal. The straight way would have followed the inheritance through the first-born, and that would often have been the straight way to failure and defeat. Whenever God made a new selection, setting aside rights and privileges in which men made their boast, choosing men who were not in the line of ordinary human expectation, He did so because His mind was set upon the ultimate goal. All the details of Divine selection led to the ultimate goal.

All this demonstrates the necessity for the recognition of God in the national life. To gather up the history suggested in the genealogies is to see confusion, disaster, failure. It is a picture that fills the heart with heaviness, and the spirit with sorrow. To look higher, and see how through all, God is moving ; selecting, changing, making perpetual progress towards His goal, is to see that the ultimate fact in all the centuries is the fact of God ; and these genealogies show that the way of permanence for human life, and the way of stability for national life, is the way of recognition of Him. God moved onward in spite of human failure. Men were ruined or made, in proportion as they recognized Him. Thus, before the story of the king in whose heart was a passion for the temple is told, there is this strange and almost weird section of ten chapters, filled with names. Through all the generations of men, through century after century, God is seen selecting, changing, interfering, moving quietly onward towards the ultimate goal.

Turn from this demonstration of the fact of the Divine interference and government to the illustration afforded by the story of David. The king is presented in all his strength. There are four pictures of him. The first is that of the national crowning. All the story of the preparation has been told—the shepherd life, the period at the court of Saul, the long, weary exile as outlaw hiding in Adullam, the seven preparatory years reigning over the Southern Kingdom of Judah. Now at Hebron all Israel crowns him.

The next picture is that of the capture of Jebus. David takes a stronghold which was thought to be impregnable, and makes it forevermore the earthly centre of Hebrew national life and aspiration.

The third picture is that of the mighty men, in which is revealed David's influence on personal character. He had gathered to Adullam men in debt, in danger, discontented ; and when we read the story of the mighty men in Chronicles, we see the mightier man, David, who made them what they were.

The last picture is that of the multitudes as they march to the standard of the new king. They were men who " could use both the right hand and the left," which speaks of the careful training they had received. They were "mighty men of valour, men trained for war," which suggests disciplined strength. They were men who " could handle shield and spear," which means they were experts in offensive and defensive warfare. This is the picture of people influenced by a great and mighty king. The book is not so much dealing with the greatness of the people in itself, as revealing it in order that the greatness of David may be seen.

All this has been told in order to lead to something else. Beginning with the story of the ark, there is revealed David's attitude towards the temple. There we touch the deepest thing in his life. He was a king, a warrior, a poet ; but none of these tells the story of the deepest thing in his heart, or reveals its master passion. Notice his care for the ark of God. Notice his desire to build the temple of God. These are not the master passions of his life, but they are expressions thereof. The master passion of this king, warrior, shepherd is that of a profound recognition of the relation of the nation to God, and of the necessity that it should never forget God. That is why he cared for the ark. That is why he desired to build the temple.

The strength of that master passion is revealed in his submission to God. When he said it was in his heart to build a house for God, Nathan the prophet said, " Do all that is in thine heart." But neither King David, nor Prophet Nathan, great as was their desire for the temple, understood the full meaning thereof. God forbade his building, but revealed anew to him how he had been led by God.

Immediately David began to do something for God, and the very thing he wanted to do, even though he did not build the temple. The actual last work was, in the wisdom of God, committed to Solomon, but from that moment David was at the work he longed to do. His willingness not to begin the building was a revelation of his recognition of the importance of his work, and of his absolute abandonment to the will of God. Yet he worked in gathering treasure, in making arrangements, in choosing the site, in appointing the Levites, in setting in order the service of song, in appointing the porters, and the keepers of the treasure.

Ezra, or whomsoever the author of this book may have been, wanted to show the importance of that of which the temple was but the outward symbol—the nation's recognition of God. David became for the moment in his eyes the embodiment of the national idea, the national purpose. The master passion of David was that of recognizing God, and expressing the recognition. Paul summarized the whole story of David's life in the sentence so often quoted, " He . . . in his own generation served the counsel of God." He was shepherd, warrior, poet ; but in all these things he answered the master passion. As king he reigned always under the conviction of the throne of God, and the supremacy of Jehovah. He was a warrior, carrying out the Divine purpose. He was a poet, and "The Lord reigneth" is the very key-note of his poetry. Because he knew the national importance of this recognition, he cared for the ark, and desired the temple.

The living message of this book is quite patent if we have discovered its permanent value. With no uncertain sound it speaks to us to-day of the absolute importance of the recognition of God in the life of the nation. If you are inclined to say that this book is applicable to the Hebrew nation, and to no other, I pray you think again of the wonderful prophecy of Amos. The mistake Israel made was that of thinking that God governed the Hebrew nation, and had no care for others. The message of Amos was that of national accountability; and ere he delivered his message to Judah and Israel, he swept the ever-decreasing circles around them, beginning with all the distant nations, and showing how God governed them also. If that be true of the nations long ago, it is equally true to-day.

It is important that the nation should recognize God, because of the fact of the Divine activity. Begin wherever you will, and look at the centuries, and you discover the same principle at work in all human history, God choosing, selecting, lifting up, casting down. The great word of the prophet of old is the word of to-day. Speaking to Cyrus, the man outside the covenant, He said, "I will gird thee, though thou hast not known Me." That is the story of all human history. God is lifting up and casting down. Another word of one of the old Hebrew prophets declared, "I will overturn, overturn, overturn . . . until He come whose right it is." God has not given up overturning. The Divine hand is at work now as surely as in the first ten chapters of Chronicles, selecting a new man and making a new start; and if he fails, selecting another, and again moving forward. If the first-born son in the proper succession is not ready for the work, he is flung aside; and if the man of privilege does not answer his opportunity, he is cast away upon the scrap-heap, and God finds an obscure man, and marches on towards the ultimate. That is a gospel to my heart. That is comfort to my soul. That is the thing that cures the heart of its panic. God is still choosing, selecting, guiding, controlling. That is why the nation should recognize Him. Oh, the madness of trying to arrange without Him, of shutting Him out of view.

It is important that the nation should recognize God, not merely because of the fact of His government, but because of the effect of the recognition of God upon national life. Take God out of the national life, and the national thinking, and what will happen? You will have no moral standard at all. Talking quite recently to one of the responsible Ministers of the Crown on the subject of the teaching in the Day Schools of this country, speaking not from the standard of a Christian man, but from the standpoint of a statesman, he said: "If there is no Bible, where is your text-book of morals? There is the supreme difficulty. We must teach morals, and there is no text-book or standard in the world if we take the Bible away."

When the nation has lost its moral standard, it has lost the strength of individual character; it has lost its conception of social relationships. It is useless to talk of a new social order unless at its very basis is the conviction and the consciousness of the throne of God and the government of God. That is the supreme message of this book.

The thing of importance in any nation is the building of the temple, the creation of the opportunity for the people to deal with God. The political propaganda which begins by attacking or neglecting God, and a national recognition of Him, is absolutely pernicious. The man who worships is the true patriot, whether he be a king, a statesman, or a commoner. The man who loves his nation and serves it, is the man who serves God.

II Chronicles

THE PERMANENT VALUES	THE LIVING MESSAGE
The condemnation of rationalism—the revelation of the absolute importance of the recognition of God which was merely formal in the life of the chosen people.	The importance of formal religion in the life of a nation.
I. The demonstration by contrast—Solomon.	I. The discovery of the point of application— cf. II Chron. 5:13-14 and Acts 2:1-4.
A. Solomon's inheritance.	
1. The conditions.	
2. The supreme inheritance.	
B. Solomon's greatness.	II. The manifestation of formalism.
1. In relation to God.	
2. In relation to the people.	
C. Solomon's service.	III. The disaster of formalism—therefore, "strengthen the things that remain."
1. The temple built.	
2. Administration from that centre.	
D. Solomon's failure.	
1. Its cause.	
2. Its course.	
II. The illustration in history—the kings of Judah (Rehoboam to Zedekiah).	
A. The rending of the kingdom.	
1. Jeroboam—substitution of false form.	
2. Rehoboam—retention of the true form.	
B. The degeneracies.	
1. Observance of the form and neglect of the facts.	
2. Growing neglect of the forms.	
C. The reformations.	
1. Always beginning at the House of God.	
2. The appalling revelations of each beginning.	
D. The ultimate disaster.	
1. The house burned with fire.	
2. The people carried away.	

THE general atmosphere of the second book of Chronicles is the same as that of the first. The temple of Solomon had long been in ruins. At the time of writing, the temple of Zerubbabel was about to be erected. The books give one continuous story; yet in the two we have two phases of one great truth. In the first we have the revelation of the importance of the temple to the national life. In the second we have the revelation of how absolutely useless the temple was. That is a paradox, a contradiction; and to recognize it is to be able to understand the permanent value of this book.

The first book of Chronicles is the condemnation of rationalism in national life. The second book is the condemnation of ritualism in national life. In the first book I see the necessity for a nation's remembrance of God, and recognition of His government in all its affairs. In the second book I have a revelation of the absolute folly and failure of the nation which recognizes God formally, but does not answer the symbolism of its recognition by the actuality of its conduct and character. That is the difference between rationalism and ritualism. Rationalism says, We can manage without God. Ritualism says,

We must adopt the terminology which suggests God, and having done that, it is careless of that actual dealing with Him, which is vital to national life.

In the first division of the book we have the story of Solomon, and it constitutes a demonstration by contrast of the impotence and uselessness of formal religion. In the second division which gives us the history of the Kings of Judah, we have illustration in history. Take first this demonstration by contrast. In looking at the details we notice four things: Solomon's inheritance, his greatness, his service, his failure.

As to Solomon's inheritance. A superficial statement is that he came to the throne and the kingdom. That is perfectly correct so far as it goes. The throne and the kingdom created his opportunity for fulfilling the supreme purpose of his life. Solomon's supreme inheritance was that of the work of building the temple, for the recognition of God on the part of the nation. He came to be king over a people recognizing the supremacy of the throne of Jehovah.

His father David had prepared for the building of the temple, the master passion of his life having been that of the recognition of the relation of national strength to submission to the throne of God. The government of the people from the beginning of their national existence was closely associated with the formulæ of worship. Moses was the lawgiver. His first work was the building of the tabernacle, and the setting in the centre of the nation of all the symbols of its relation to God. When Solomon commenced to reign he did not offer his first sacrifice at the place where the ark was, the temporary tent which David had erected, but at the old tabernacle, long neglected. That action of Solomon was significant. The tabernacle had symbolized the people's relationship to God, and by going to it he expressed his conviction that their national greatness and strength depended upon their relation to the throne of God. His temple was to be the successor of Moses' tabernacle. Solomon's inheritance, then, was the opportunity, right, and privilege, of building that temple which was to remind the people of their relation to God.

Then as to Solomon's greatness. The beginning was a wonderful one. The greatness of the man is revealed in the simplicity of his heart as he made his plea for wisdom. It is seen, moreover, in the fact that, as a king, he bore his people on his heart in intercession before God.

His service consisted of the building of the temple; and then in the administration of his kingdom from that centre. That we need not stay to describe. All the details are simply set forth by the chronicler.

His failure was disastrous, and was caused by the violation, in his own self-centred life, of the truth the temple expressed. Even in the days of prosperity there are evidences of weakness, as a man of sensual passion is seen playing upon the edge of the awful things that ultimately ruined him. The whole failure of Solomon was due to the fact that he answered the cry of his own self-life, and in doing so violated the principle of Divine government, to which the temple he had erected bore witness before himself and his people.

The temple became, in the case of Solomon, a form and nothing more. Consequently, it became not merely of no use, but a paralysis in the life of the king, and a poison in the life of the nation.

Turn to the second division of the book. It tells the story of Judah from Rehoboam to Zedekiah. The sin of Jeroboam in Israel consisted of the substitution of a false form of worship for the true. Rehoboam retained the true form in Judah. Throughout the history there is the observance of the form, and the neglect of the fact. This issued in growing neglect of the form. We never find nations or men long observe a form when it becomes devoid of power. Mere formalism must die sooner or later. The issue is irreligion, infidelity. It was so here. All the reformations began at the house of God. Asa renewed the altar, and restored the dedicated vessels to their place. Jehoshaphat instituted a series of special missions all through the country, sending men to read and explain the book of the law through the towns and villages. Joash restored the house after Athaliah's destruction of it. Hezekiah opened the doors, and assembled the people for worship. Josiah repaired the house of the Lord.

In each case the revelations of the beginnings of the reformations are appalling. Asa renewed the altar, and restored the dedicated vessels. That implies a broken altar and desecrated vessels. Jehoshaphat felt it necessary to send special prophetic messengers through the country to interpret the book of the law, which reveals the prevailing ignorance of the law. Joash restored the house of the Lord after Athaliah's destruction. That means that the house had been destroyed. Hezekiah opened the doors, which means that while the house still stood, the people had become so utterly weary of formalism, that the doors had been closed. Mark the marvel of the story of Josiah. In the midst of a reformation that must have been very partial, they found the book of the law; and finding it, and reading in it, the king was so startled at the awful condition of his people that he halted the whole reformation, in order to find out from the prophetess Huldah the meaning of this law, and the effect likely to be produced by his reformation. Thus all through the story we see the people getting lower, in spite of the fact that at the commencement of this period of history the temple was built and established, and became the central symbol of their religious life.

Finally there came the ultimate disaster. The house was burned with fire, and the people were carried away into captivity. In the first book the story is told of the passionate desire of the man after God's own heart to build the temple, knowing as he did the importance of the recognition by the nation of the fact of God. In the second book the aspiration of David becomes the achievement of Solomon. The passionate desire of the old man becomes the actual deed of the young man. I stand in the earlier chapters almost amazed at the splendour and beauty of the temple, and I listen to the songs of the singers, and watch the worship of the worshippers, and I thank God with David that the house is built. Yet immediately I see the nation beginning to fall, and gradually, stage after stage, sinking lower, until the house is burned and the chosen nation is cast away. If the first book teaches that it was necessary that these people should recognize God, the second teaches us that when the recognition was that of form and ceremony, it was worse than useless. That to me is the permanent value of this book, which thrills and throbs through all its history, and upon all its pages.

The living message of the book is that of the impotence of formal religion in the life of a na-

tion. Let us first discover the point of application. In the thirteenth verse of the fifth chapter I read, " It came even to pass, when the trumpeters and singers were as one, to make one sound to be heard in praising and thanking the Lord; and when they lifted up their voice with the trumpets and cymbals and instruments of music, and praised the Lord, saying, For He is good: for His mercy endureth forever: that then the house was filled with a cloud, even the house of the Lord." It was a great moment. The temple finished, its worship of song perfected, all the notes of the instruments and voices merged into one great ascription of praise. Then the glory filled the house. In the Acts I read, " When the day of Pentecost was now come, they were all together in one place. And suddenly there came from heaven a sound as of the rushing of a mighty wind, and it filled all the house where they were sitting. And there appeared unto them tongues parting asunder, like as of fire; and it sat upon each one of them." The connection between these two passages is evident. Doubtless there is disparity, but there is also similarity. The two temples; the first was natural, the last spiritual. The temple in the olden days, made according to the pattern of God, in the unity of worship crowned with the glory of God, and filled with His presence; the symbol in the centre of the nation of the presence and government of God. That is the Old Testament picture. Observe the New Testament picture. Again the temple, no longer of material things, but of living stones, merged into the habitation of God by the baptism of the Spirit, a perfect unity.

As the temple in Chronicles was the centre and criterion of national life, so the Church of God is the centre and criterion of national life, if she do but understand her vocation, and fill her position. The application of the first book of Chronicles is to the nation. The message delivered to the nation was this, If you think by policy and diplomacy to maintain your strength without recognizing God, you are doomed to disaster. Now the message is to the Church. It is a warning to the spiritual Church lest she should become formal, and so fail to establish the nation. I have no desire to use any phrase in a controversial sense here, but I am bound, in the interpretation of truth as I see it in the Bible, to say this, the Bible knows nothing of the establishment of the Church by the State, but it teaches forevermore that the Church must establish the nation. In order to do this, formal religion is infinitely worse than none. By formal religion I mean high Church doctrine without full Church life. I mean Puritan philosophy without Puritan experience. I mean a Nonconformist conscience without conduct conformed to Christ. These things are the essence of ritualism.

What is high Church doctrine without full Church life? The doctrine of the Church that is forevermore arguing for the correctness of its views, and cursing the man who does not share them! That is a formalism which curses a nation.

What is Puritan philosophy without Puritan experience? There are some who think the Puritan philosophy consisted in a passion for destroying buildings. Nothing of the kind. The Puritan philosophy is that man is spiritual, and has the right of access to God who is Spirit, without the intervention of man or ceremony. Oh, the dignity of it! But if that is our philosophy, and we do not go to God, our philosophy becomes paralysis instead of power. Sometimes I am a little tired of hearing about the Puritanism of the Free Churches. I want to see it in the life of those who know what it is to have commerce with God. What do I care about the accidentals in the Puritan movements of long ago—the speech, the dress, the iconoclasm? If a man looks at these things only, he has never seen the Puritan movement. The Puritan movement was that of strenuous saints, who refused to let any one come between themselves and God. Hold that philosophy to be a fine one, and live six days a week as though there were no God, and that is a ritualism which is a peril to a nation.

What is a Nonconformist conscience without Christian conduct? The presence of the crowd at the platform meeting when we show our superiority to other people, and its absence from the service of worship, and its neglect of the worship of work. We need the conscience sensitive to the call of Christ; the conscience that

worships, and then strips itself to serve. If I am forevermore talking about my conscience, and boasting in my freedom, and fighting merely for the shibboleths of freedom; that is ritualism, and I have no room to criticize the man who is a ritualist in some other section of the Church.

The disaster of formalism. What is it? It is not merely that the Church is a failure. That, of course, is a disaster. I am not, however, prepared to shed tears over the failure of a system. I am prepared to shed them over the fact that when the system fails, the work is not done. That is the supreme and final agony. If the Church of God is not what it ought to be, we have a nation without salt and without light, a nation rushing headlong to Godlessness, characterized by base ideals and ignoble conduct; by cowardice in the presence of a wrong, and carelessness about the importance of right. If that be the national condition, the blame is with the Church of God. I do not say the churches, but the Church, the Catholic Church, which is the Temple of God. If she were instinct with the life of Christ, and allowed that life to fill and flood and flow through her, the nation could no longer be careless.

I go back to the creation of the temple, and what followed in Jerusalem. The multitudes were amazed, perplexed, critical. The tragedy of the hour is that the Church does not amaze London, does not perplex London, does not make London critical. Why not? Because of her formalism. The world has done with formalism. Whether it be her theatres, her public houses, or anything else, she means business; and a world that means business is never going to be influenced by a Church that is playing. What we need is the Church, the Temple, filled with the Presence, flaming in its glory, flashing in its light, communicating its fire. Then we shall be able to say to the evil statesman, You dare not! We shall be able to say to vested interests, Disgorge! We shall cast out devils in the name of Christ. But formalism can do none of these things. What then is the message of the second book of Chronicles? What is the living word? "Strengthen the things that remain."

Ezra

THE PERMANENT VALUES	THE LIVING MESSAGE

The potter in his activity. "He made it again another vessel."
 	
I. Jehovah's instruments.
  A. Outside the covenant.
    1. Cyrus.
    2. Darius.
    3. Artaxerxes.
  B. Within the covenant.
    1. Zerubbabel and Joshua.
    2. Ezra.
II. Jehovah's might.
  A. Constructive.
    1. Inspiring the edicts.
    2. Qualifying His workers.
    3. Gathering His people.
  B. Destructive—overcoming opposition.
III. Jehovah's people.
  A. A remnant composed of members of all the tribes.
  B. A testimony to one truth, the unity of God.
IV. Jehovah's work.
  A. The things lost.
    1. National independence.
    2. National influence.
  B. The things gained.
    1. A place.
    2. A race.
	I. Concerning God, the living message is that of the permanent value.
	  A. The ultimate word in sovereignty.
	  B. The revelation of the inspiration of sovereignty.
	  C. Sovereignty the strength of hope.
	II. To man, the living message consists of the things resulting—Hag. 2:4.
	  A. Conviction in place of carelessness.
	  B. Consecration in place of comfort.
	  C. Courage in place of cowardice.
	  D. Confidence in place of contempt.

THE book of Ezra cannot be considered alone. In order that we may study it, and its message, it is necessary that we should first recognize the connection between it and the two following books. The three deal with the history of the period in which one of the prophecies of Jeremiah was fulfilled. Let us read from Jeremiah, first, in the twenty-fifth chapter, verses eleven to fourteen :

"This whole land shall be a desolation, and an astonishment ; and these nations shall serve the king of Babylon seventy years. And it shall come to pass, when seventy years are accomplished, that I will punish the king of Babylon, and that nation, saith the Lord, for their iniquity, and the land of the Chaldeans ; and I will make it desolate forever. And I will bring upon that land all My words which I have pronounced against it, even all that is written in this book, which Jeremiah hath prophesied against all the nations. For many nations and great kings shall serve themselves of them, even of them : and I will recompense them according to their deeds, and according to the work of their hands."

Again in the twenty-ninth chapter, verses ten to fourteen :

"Thus saith the Lord, After seventy years be accomplished for Babylon, I will visit you, and perform My good word towards you, in causing you to return to this place. For I know the thoughts that I think towards you, saith the Lord, thoughts of peace, and not of evil, to give you hope in your latter end. And ye shall call upon Me, and ye shall go and pray unto Me, and I will hearken unto you. And ye shall seek Me, and find Me, when ye shall search for Me with all your heart. And I will be found of you, saith the Lord, and I will turn again your captivity, and I will gather you from all the nations, and from all the places whither I have driven you, saith the Lord ; and I will bring you again unto the place whence I caused you to be carried away captive."

These words are taken from the prophecies which were delivered before the fall of Jerusalem, and on the occasion of Jeremiah's visit to Zedekiah. The king of Babylon and his army were threatening Jerusalem ; and Jeremiah suffered because he persistently declared that they would successfully take the city, carry away the king, and destroy the people.

Seventy years had elapsed from the fall of Jerusalem. The power of Babylon had been broken, and that forever. Cyrus the Elamite was on the throne ; king of Persia, though not a native of Persia, taking that name because Persia was the strongest of the countries he had mastered ; king of Babylon, because he had broken the power of Babylon, in exact fulfillment of Jeremiah's prophecy, after seventy years. Thus, Persia had become the ruling power.

We now come to the story of the events, the first of which the two books of Chronicles were written to inspire. The permanent value of the three books lies in their revelation of the Divine activity overruling human failure.

Before the messages actually delivered to Zedekiah, Jeremiah had uttered two on the supremacy of Jehovah ; the first describing a visit to the potter's house, and the second dealing with the vessel broken. The first of these opens thus, " The word which came to Jeremiah from the Lord, saying, Arise, and go down to the potter's house, and there I will cause thee to hear My words. Then I went down to the potter's house, and, behold, he wrought his work on the wheels. And when the vessel that he made of the clay was marred in the hand of the potter, he made it again another vessel, as

seemed good to the potter to make it."

That is the picture Jeremiah saw in the house of the potter. He then applied it in these words :

" Then the word of the Lord came to me, saying, O house of Israel, cannot I do with you as this potter? saith the Lord. Behold, as the clay in the potter's hand, so are ye in Mine hand, O house of Israel." The house of Israel is the clay. God is the Potter. He wrought His work on the wheels ; the vessel was marred in the hands of the Potter. That is the history of everything from Abraham to the Captivity. What next? " He made it again another vessel." Ezra, Nehemiah, and Esther are the books that tell us the story of how God began to make again the vessel that had been marred in His own hand. God has not finished that work yet. He will finish it. Israel is not cast off forever. God has yet His work to do in this world through His ancient people. In Ezra, Nehemiah, and Esther I see God's new beginning. We are tempted to think that the work is slow. Never let us descend to the vulgarity of measuring God by almanacs.

In the light of what I have attempted to say of its relation, we may consider the book of Ezra. Let us first pass over it and notice four things ; Jehovah's instruments ; Jehovah's might ; Jehovah's people ; Jehovah's work.

First, then, Jehovah's instruments. These were found both outside and inside the covenant people. The hour had come when the vessel was so marred and spoiled that God began again, but He began with the same piece of clay. The instruments outside were Cyrus, Darius, Artaxerxes, each one of whom issued a decree which was inspired of God, as surely as were the messages of Isaiah. God laid the constraint of His mighty power upon the heart of kings. He girded Cyrus, although Cyrus had not known Him. He took this man outside the covenant, and pressed him into the accomplishment of His own purpose. So also with Darius and Artaxerxes. God was beginning a new thing, and He took hold of mighty kings and warriors, and made the very marching of their armies part of His progress, and used the sighing of captives under their control to touch their heart and drive their will, so that they coöperated with Him.

He found His instruments inside also; Zerubbabel, the man with the Babylonish name, a grandson of Jehoiachim, and a prince of Judah in the Davidic line; and Joshua, the son of Jehozadak. These two embodied the twofold principle that had been manifest in all His dealings with the people, that of the king and the priest. These He placed in the midst of ruin and degradation, and they began to inspire other hearts, and so the new movement commenced. Then Ezra also, "A ready scribe in the law of Moses," which does not mean merely that he was a man who was able to write clearly and accurately. This is the first place in which the word "scribe" occurs in the Bible in the sense in which we perpetually find it in the New Testament. Jesus used the word at the close of His parables concerning the Kingdom, when He said: "Every scribe who hath been made a disciple to the Kingdom of heaven is like unto a man that is a householder, which bringeth forth out of his treasure things new and old." The scribe was the interpreter, the teacher, the unfolder of the meaning of the will of God. In that sense Ezra was "a ready scribe in the law of Moses."

Thus God laid His hand upon Cyrus, Darius, and Artaxerxes outside the covenant; and upon Zerubbabel, Joshua, and Ezra within the covenant. The principle revealed is that God presses into His service men who do not know Him, and who are unconscious that they are carrying out His will; and inspires men who do know Him, and compels them to constructive activity. We cannot study the three edicts, recognizing that they were the edicts of pagan kings, without recognizing them as inspired of God. His might was manifested, moreover, in the way in which He qualified His workers for the work they had to do; gathered His people from far and near—not merely Judah, all the tribes of Israel being represented.

That leads us to Jehovah's people, the clay, the remnant composed of members of all the tribes. "So the priests, and the Levites, and some of the people, and the singers, and the porters, and the Nethinim, dwelt in their cities, and all Israel in their cities." "And the children of Israel, the priests and the Levites, and the rest of the children of the captivity, kept the dedication of this house of God with joy. And they offered at the dedication of this house of God an hundred bullocks, two hundred rams, four hundred lambs; and for a sin offering for all Israel, twelve he-goats, according to the number of the tribes of Israel." God, in remaking, did not merely take two tribes, but representatives of all the twelve.

When He brought them back from captivity, He established one great truth in the world, and in the midst of human history; that of the unity of Deity. They came back, having learned only the first thing, but they never forgot it again. The great word of Moses was, "The Lord thy God is one Lord." The unity of Deity produces the unification of humanity in the worship of the one God. Believe that, and there can be no idolatry. But they turned to idolatry, until Israel was driven into captivity, and Judah also. Seventy years passed over their heads, and they came back, and never set up an idol again. Ephraim said, "What have I to do any more with idols?" They had a great deal more to learn; but from the hour in which they came back under Zerubbabel, until this hour, call them Jews, Hebrews or Israelites, as you will, this one thing is certain; they have never set up an idol. They became a people, poor in many respects, failing in many respects; yet through crushing, bruising, and discipline, a people who in human history embody the truth that there is one God.

Finally, notice Jehovah's work. When these people gathered back they had lost their national influence. Never again did they so stand alone, as to be able to bear their distinctive testimony, in such a way as to produce conviction. Yet there was gain in that hour when the remnant came back. They began building, and built with some interruptions for twenty years; then stopped, and for sixty years nothing was done. But God was at work. He had found a place for them, and as Jeremiah said, it was the place from which He drove them out. They were back at the geographical centre. Not merely had He found a place. He had saved that peculiar people and race from extinction by absorption. The Pharisees were born in this period, and as a result of the Divine movement. The Pharisees were first of all men who set themselves against anything in the nature of intermixture with the nations around. At last that exclusiveness became a bondage and a curse, as every good thing does if it is not allowed to expand and to express itself in new forms. Pharisaism was a true thing in its inception, being an endeavour to keep the race distinct until He should come through it, and of it, after the flesh, who by His coming was able to proceed to the larger things of which these people had been the foreshadowing. God had begun to make it again another vessel.

If that be the permanent value, what is the living message of the book? Its living message concerning God is the permanent value. "He made it again." That is the ultimate word in sovereignty. It is so different from anything men had ever dreamed or done. The ultimate word of sovereignty as man has misunderstood it, and misinterpreted it in his own government, is that if you have had an opportunity and failed, sovereignty smites and crushes you and flings you out. The last word of God's sovereignty is, "He made it again." That helps me. The same truth is found in the story of Jonah, "The word of the Lord came unto Jonah the second time." The clay is in the hand of the Potter, but the vessel is marred, the ideal is not realized, the clay that might have been a shape of exquisite beauty is crushed. God's sovereignty says, I will begin again. If that be the ultimate word of sovereignty, it reveals the fact that its inspiration is His love, His compassion, His pity. Of course, if a man will not have it so, his blood is upon his own head. If a nation will not have it so, then its dust and ashes are of its own creation. But the very inspiration of Divine sovereignty is expressed there, "He made it again."

Therefore, the sovereignty of God is the strength of hope on the darkest day that ever comes. "He made it again." How it helps me about my own life. How it helps me about the things of my service, which are so poor and so broken. How it helps me when I see the cause of the peoples I serve falling to pieces in dis-

aster, when I see the chosen instruments of Jehovah failing in the day of catastrophe. When I feel that which is most hopeful is blighted by frost, then there is an anthem in my heart, "He made it again." Take God off His throne, and my song ceases, the blossom of my hope withers, and my heart is broken.

The living message of the book, therefore, consists in the appeal consequent upon the fact of the Divine government and sovereignty, and is expressed in the word of Haggai: "Be strong, O Zerubbabel, saith the Lord; and be strong, O Joshua, son of Jehozadak, the high priest; and be strong, all ye people of the land, saith the Lord, and work: for I am with you, saith the Lord of hosts." That is the message. Be strong, because I am with you, says Jehovah, I am still on the throne. God is still able to gird Cyrus. Change your names. God still holds in His hand the German Emperor, the Russian Emperor, King George the Fifth. Do not get back into these old centuries and miss the living message. Do not imagine that God manipulated Cyrus, and leaves the kings of to-day alone. They are all within the hand of God.

Because I am with you, "Be strong . . . and work." That is the message. Take the book of Haggai, which is so intimately related to Ezra. How were these people to be strong, and work? They were to have conviction of the throne of God in place of carelessness; consecration in place of despair; courage in place of cowardice; confidence in God's ultimate, instead of contempt for the poverty of the day in which they lived and served.

"God's in His heaven, all's right with the world"; but I must be strong, and work. There must be the song in my heart that tells, "He will make it again"; but there must be agony in my heart, travail in my life, the cross in my service, so that I may march right onward to the goal.

Nehemiah

THE PERMANENT VALUES	THE LIVING MESSAGE
The clay in its attitude. "My righteous one shall live by faith."	Stated in Hab. 2:4 and Isa. 50:10.
I. The attitude.	I. The darkness.
A. Concern—expressed in enquiry and sorrow (1:2, 4).	A. The prophecy of Malachi.
B. Confidence—expressed in prayer and sorrow (1:5—2:4, 4:9).	B. The indifferent multitudes.
C. Cooperation—expressed in activity.	C. The widespread dis-loyalty to truth.
II. The activity.	D. The lack of enthusiasm.
A. Caution.	II. The life of faith.
1. The secret examination.	A. Is sure of God.
2. The arrangements for division of labour.	B. Acts with Him, and for Him.
B. Courage.	C. Declines all compromise.
1. The single-handed start.	D. Trusts God.
2. The invincible determination.	
C. No compromise.	
1. With those outside.	
a. Contempt.	
b. Conspiracy.	
c. Cunning.	
2. With those inside.	
a. The nobles.	
b. Those disloyal.	
III. The achievement.	
A. The city walls and the people.	
B. The law expounded and enforced.	
C. The purpose—a highway flung up.	

THERE is a very special interest attaching to this book, from the fact that it is the last fragment of inspired Hebrew history. Both in the Hebrew Scriptures, and in all the earlier manuscripts of the Christian Scriptures, Ezra and Nehemiah appear as one book. Subsequently they appear as two, under the titles, the first and second books of Ezra. The name Nehemiah was first given to the second part of this one book in the writings of Jerome. In the Wycliffe translation they are called the first and second books of Esdras. In the Miles Coverdale translation they are entitled, the first book of Esdras, and the second book of Esdras, otherwise called Nehemias. In the Geneva Bible, published in 1560, they first appeared, named as we have them in our Bibles, the books of Ezra and Nehemiah. One story is commenced in the book of Ezra, and completed in this book of Nehemiah. The period covered by the two books was about one hundred and ten years. Under Zerubbabel and Ezra, inspired and influenced by the prophesying of Haggai and Zechariah, the temple was rebuilt. We have the story of the beginning, the delay and the resumption of the work, the whole period covering about twenty-one years. Then an interval of sixty years was followed by the reformation under Ezra. Another interval of thirteen years, and then Nehemiah and Ezra together built the walls. Yet another interval of twelve years followed, of which we have no details, and then Nehemiah instituted the final reformation. The book ends as incompletely and as unsatisfactorily in some senses as does the book of the Acts. That is not to say that the book is incomplete and unsatisfactory, but just when we would like to know a great deal more it ceases. Enough, however, is chronicled for the purpose for which the book was written.

Now let us look at the history as seen in the light of the Divine economy. As history merely, it is the history of a decadent people, the story of a ruined economy. It is pitiful in the light of the former things; their making; that triumphal deliverance, by which they emerged from a mob into an organized people: the conquests under Joshua; and the kingdom under David. All that is left is a poor remnant, paying tribute; rebuilding the temple, frightened in the midst of the work, leaving it for long years, taking it up again and bringing it to such completion that the old men wept as they remembered the former glory; passing away into formalism and backsliding, until a new reformation called them to return. Then a long, long period of silence; presently Nehemiah and the rebuilding of the wall, a wonderful piece of work; then a relapse, until we see a new reformation made necessary by the fact that they are failing to support the Levites, are neglecting the Sabbath, and are not bringing tithes to the house of God. It is a dark and sorry page of human history.

If, however, we look at this history as in the light of the Divine economy, there are three points of supreme interest. First, the People; secondly, the Purpose; and, finally, the Potter.

Look first, then, at the people. In the book of Nehemiah they are seen without any conscious national influence; and it is a very interesting and almost startling fact that in the books of Ezra and Nehemiah and Esther there is no reference at all to any Messianic hope. Through all the former books there have been references. Malachi prophesied a century later than Nehemiah, and in his message there is the clearest Messianic reference; but there is no fragment in these books to show that these people had any Messianic hope at all. Nehemiah has consolidated a remnant in a city with walls. Long centuries before, a man living in a city was discontented with it, having had a vision of the City of God. He turned his back upon Ur of

the Chaldees, because it was a city of men, with all the characteristics of cities which men build, and set himself out upon a pilgrimage to find the City of God. The centuries have run their course, and, in the last piece of inspired history, the people coming from his loins, having been governed by God, guided by God, and guarded by God, are seen in a city. Is that Abraham's hope? Is that the ultimate?

When they began to rebuild the temple, in order to inspire them, Haggai and Zechariah prophesied, and one of the visions of the prophecy of Zechariah had reference to a city. A young man is seen going to measure the city in ruins, and he is warned that he cannot measure the ultimate city which will be without walls, not needing material defense, too large to be enclosed within walls. Now I see the city with the walls completed, a great victory for the time being, for the shutting out of certain enemies, and the creation of a sense of citizenship and nationality in the hearts of this poor remnant of people. That is the last picture. Yet though Nehemiah has built walls to exclude enemies, the worst enemies cannot be excluded. They are still inside. Somewhere between fifty and one hundred years later Malachi came, and we read his prophecy to know the things inside the walls, the evil, failure and disaster that Nehemiah could not exclude.

Thus, with all the background in long perspective, of victory after victory, deliverance after deliverance, glory after glory, we see this city that Nehemiah flings the wall around. It is so poor a city that one of his enemies laughed at his walls, and said a fox could break through them.

Now what does all this mean? In the letter to the Hebrews we find the answer. "That which is becoming old and waxeth aged is nigh unto vanishing away." The writer of the letter was quoting the prophecy of Jeremiah, the predictions of which are so closely associated with the period at which we are looking, although he prophesied at least one hundred and thirty years before Nehemiah. Jeremiah had declared that in seventy years there should be restoration. At the end of the seventy years, Zerubbabel and Joshua led back the remnant. In the midst of the prophecy of Jeremiah there are grouped the prophecies of hope, in which he declared that at last there should be a new covenant, not external, but internal, written upon the heart. The writer of the letter quoted that prophecy, and then proceeded to show why there was need for a new covenant, "That which is becoming old and waxeth aged is nigh unto vanishing away." That is the picture that the book of Nehemiah gives of the people in the economy of God.

Now let us turn to the purpose of God in this period of Nehemiah. The central section of the book tells the story of the reading of the law. Following the reading of the law, the great prayer of the Levites. Following the prayer of the Levites, the covenant made with the remnant. Malachi, from fifty to a hundred years afterwards, uttered the last injunction to these people, before the coming of John the Baptist and Christ: "Remember ye the law of Moses My servant, which I commanded unto him in Horeb for all Israel, even statutes and judgments." The last injunction of the last prophet spoken to these people, spoken to the very conditions described in the book of Nehemiah, was: "Remember ye the law." Once again I turn to my New Testament, and, in Paul's Galatian letter, read: "Before faith came, we were kept in ward under the law, shut up unto the faith which should afterwards be revealed. So that the law hath been our tutor to bring us unto Christ, that we might be justified by faith." That is the key to the history which begins with the reading of the law under Nehemiah. That is what the law was doing in Nehemiah's day, and continued to do for four hundred years. "The law hath been our tutor." Tutor is a better word than schoolmaster, but it is faulty. We have taken the Greek word and Anglicized it, and we speak of a pedagogue and pedagogy; but the pedagogue was not the teacher in Greece, and the law was not a teacher in Judaism. The pedagogue was the man who saw to it that the boy went to school, not the man who taught him. Paul used the word correctly. He says we were kept in ward by the law. He does not say the law is our schoolmaster or tutor, but the law is our jailer. So that we might read "the law hath been our policeman to bring us unto Christ." Policeman may not be a perfect translation, but it is far

nearer the thought than either tutor or schoolmaster.

Now, mark what was happening in the city under Nehemiah. The civil reformation as a secondary thing to that wonderful reading of the law. These people had utterly failed, in spite of priest and prophet. The law was left, and that law was enunciated among the broken remnant, and became their custodian. It held them in ward, kept them all the prisoners of God through four hundred years, notwithstanding their frivolity and triviality. When Christ came there were no priests worthy the name; no king, save one who paid tribute, and was himself corrupt; no prophet, save His own immediate herald; but the law was there. The Divine purpose, as seen in Nehemiah, was that of putting the people under law, locking them up, until the faith should come. That is the Divine movement which is manifest in this book.

The last matter is that of the Potter Himself—God—still at work putting His hand upon His people, making them again in spite of themselves. I need not enlarge upon that. I should feel that we had disastrously failed in our attempt to glean the messages of these books if that truth of the overruling, reigning God had not been clearly seen. What I do ask you to notice is the instrument of the Potter. Nehemiah was not a king, was not a priest, was not a prophet. The three great orders through which God had reigned and ruled are absent. They have all failed. I think it is quite likely that Nehemiah was of the royal line of David, but he was neither king nor prince. He was a cupbearer at the court of an alien. He did not reign over these people as king. He was not a priest offering sacrifices. He was not a prophet, so far as the Hebrew people were concerned. He was a citizen, one of themselves, and withal one into whose blood the iron of the captivity had entered, one into whose heart the sorrows of his people's failures had come. The king had failed and was set aside. The prophet I will not say had failed as the king had failed, for he had delivered his message, but it had not been persuasive. The priest was corrupt, though still in the midst. Then God took a common man, and made him neither king, nor priest, nor prophet, but a plain, blunt man, who went right on and flung up a wall in seven weeks, and made a chance for the law to be read and expounded.

It is evident that the supreme interest centres in Nehemiah. The nation had failed ; prophet, priest and king had failed ; but here was a man, and this man embodied the supreme principle.

The permanent value of the book is its illustration of the truth, " My righteous one shall live by faith." That is to return to the book of Joshua, the first in the present series. Joshua was neither king nor prophet nor priest, and the lesson of his history is, " My righteous one shall live by faith." The last fragment of the historic portion of the Hebrew Bible has that as its supreme message also, through Nehemiah; but the circumstances are different. They may be described by a quotation from Isaiah : " Who is among you that feareth the Lord, that obeyeth the voice of His servant ? He that walketh in darkness, and hath no light, let him trust in the name of the Lord, and stay upon his God."

Nehemiah is a most radiant revelation of the fulfillment of that charge. Nehemiah feared the Lord, obeyed the voice of His servant, walked in circumstances of darkness where there was no light, yet trusted in the name of Jehovah, and stayed upon his God. That is to say, " My righteous one shall live by faith." In one man the great principle is revealed. Notice, then, in the midst of circumstances of darkness the attitude of faith, the activity of faith, and the achievement of faith.

The attitude of faith was that of perfect confidence in God. From first to last Nehemiah's faith in God never wavered. It was, moreover, that of concern about the purpose of God. Hear these brief words, " I asked . . . concerning the Jews and Jerusalem." Hear these briefer words, " I sat down and wept." Finally, it was that of coöperation with God. That is clearly revealed in our next consideration.

The activity of faith as illustrated in the case of Nehemiah was, first, that of extreme caution. He went up alone. He did not tell any one what he was doing, but went silently round to see where the wall needed the most attention, and in order to obtain at first hand all the facts of the case. Then when he did declare himself and began his building, with fine discriminative caution, he divided the work among the people, so that every man built over against his own

house. After caution, courage. A single-handed start to build a ruined wall and restore a lost order, and invincible determination. The book thrills and throbs and pulsates with the tremendous force of this man's will. Caution and courage. The two things we revealed together in one brief statement. Caution, " I consulted with myself." Courage, " I contended with the nobles."

In the activity of faith as here illustrated there was not only caution and courage, but no compromise. No compromise with the foes without. The story of the opposition against Nehemiah from without can be told in three words : Contempt, Conspiracy, Cunning. They spoke of his work with contempt. He declared, in reply, that the work would be done, but they would not be allowed to help. Then they tried to hinder him by conspiracy, but he proved himself to be a man of keen eyes ! Finally, they tried to catch him with cunning, and he replied with fine satire, I am doing a great work. Why should I come down to you ? No compromise with foes within. He found foes within, for the nobles were exacting usury from the poorer people. It was then he said, " I consulted with myself," and " I contended with the nobles." There came an hour when a priest allowed the enemy lodging room in the temple, and Nehemiah flung his furniture out, and he " contended with them, and cursed them, and plucked off their hair." No compromise. That is the final fact in faith's activity.

And once more, a glance at faith's achievement. The wall was built in seven weeks. He gathered his people, and if some of them were loath to go up to Jerusalem because of the difficulty he compelled them ; others he scattered through the towns and villages. Then followed the greatest achievement, the exposition of the law.

In the last analysis, Nehemiah's achievement was that he flung up a highway for God, provided Him with vantage ground on which to stand and wait, until, to quote Paul's great word, " the faith," should come. It is a fine ending to inspired history.

If that be the permanent value, the living message is stated in two quotations I have already made : " My righteous one shall live by faith," and " Who is among you that feareth the Lord, that obeyeth the voice of His servant ? He that walketh in darkness, and hath no light, let him trust in the name of the Lord and stay upon his God." The book of Nehemiah brings this message to every period of darkness. I will not stay to apply it to personal life, but to larger life. Is this an hour of dark outlook? I am afraid in all honesty I must say to you that it does so seem to me. I could certainly, so far as I am concerned, take the prophecy of Malachi, and preach it as it stands to this day and generation. I think there is a wonderful and almost tragic similarity between the last condition of the Hebrew people and the hour in which we live. All about us are indifferent multitudes. Far more widespread than some of us think, is incipient, and sometimes open disloyalty to the Truth of God. On the other hand, there is a lack of enthusiasm about the things of Christ—languishing foreign Missionary Societies. It is not my ordinary custom to speak thus of the age. I do it now to reveal why I do not very often do it. The true attitude of faith, in any hour of darkness, hour of peril, such as I believe we are in at the present moment, is, first, that it is sure of God. It has no hopeless dirge to chant upon the sunless air. In the second place, faith acts with God, and for God, in strenuous endeavour. The man who nurses his orthodoxy, and does nothing for God, is a liar and a hypocrite. If you believe in evangelical faith, you are out upon the evangelistic path; whether it be at home or abroad matters nothing. The man who is evangelical believes in the doctrines of sin and grace, believes that men will be lost, and lost irrevocably unless saved through the Cross. If we believe these things we must put blood and sweat into the business of saving men. Faith is first sure of God. It then acts with God and for God. Finally, it declines all compromise with foes outside or inside. Faith trusts God as Nehemiah did, does its own day's work, and leaves all the future to Him. In the presence of this study, I have only one thing to say: "Lord, I believe, help Thou mine unbelief."

Esther

THE PERMANENT VALUES	THE LIVING MESSAGE

God acting in providence.
I. The method.
  A. Hidden but active.
    1. Ruling to issues (10:3).
    2. Using the trivialities.
      a. Before the peril.
      b. In the midst of the peril.
  B. Inclusive—an all-pervading atmosphere.
    1. The individuals.
    2. The events.
II. The principles.
  A. Perfect knowledge.
  B. Undeviating righteousness.
  C. Absolute power.
III. The issues.
  A. To those recognizing them—confidence and courage.
  B. To those in rebellion—panic and punishment.
  C. Historic issue—progress.
	I. The truth.
	  A. God is.
	  B. God acts in providence.
	  C. God is touching life at every point.
	II. The application.
	  A. Reckon with Him.
	  B. Trust Him.
	  C. Act with Him.

THE events recorded in the book of Esther took place in the sixty years between the work of Zerubbabel and that of Ezra, of which we have no account save that thus supplied. We can only speculate as to the condition of affairs in Jerusalem. The reformation under Ezra, particulars of which are given in the second part of the book bearing his name, show how far the people had wandered from allegiance to Jehovah in that period. During those years there was no king, and no prophet.

The story told in Esther, however, has nothing to do with Jerusalem, or with those who had returned there under Zerubbabel and Joshua, but with those who had refused to return. The name Mordecai occurs in the lists given in the book of Ezra, but it is not possible that this should be the man bearing that name whose story is told in the present book

Among the great visions of Zechariah, the first was that of the myrtle trees in the shady place. It symbolized the condition into which the chosen people were about to come. Israel in the period of her degeneracy was foreshadowed in that first vision of Zechariah. Believing that Israel is still there, I nevertheless quite clearly see that the description was partially fulfilled in that period of sixty years. The symbolism of the myrtle tree in Scripture is a very interesting one. Isaiah was the first one who made use of it. The probability is that the tree had never been grown in Palestine until it was brought from Babylon. Then Isaiah seized upon it as symbolic of the nation. No longer the tall cedar, but the myrtle, with its beautiful star-like flower. It is an interesting thing, though I do not desire to base anything like a dogmatic interpretation upon it, that Esther's original name was Hadassah, which means myrtle, while Esther is a Persian name which means " star," suggestive of the form of flower that the myrtle tree bears. The beautiful daughter of the Hebrew race at the court of a Persian king, born in captivity, was called Myrtle. In all likelihood her father named her Hadassah, because the myrtle tree had become the sign and symbol of the race. The Persians called her Star, to indicate that she was the flower of the myrtle tree, full of beauty, full of grace.

There are peculiarities in this story which have raised doubts as to whether it ought to have any place in the canon of Scripture. The name of God is never mentioned. There is found no reference to the Hebrew religion. The temple never appears. No ceremonial of the Hebrew worship is referred to. No requirement of the law is named from beginning to end. There is one reference to Jerusalem in the second chapter and sixth verse. That merely accounts for Mordecai, and shows whence these people had come. There is one reference to a fast, and one to a feast, showing that the religious habit of the Hebrews obtained among the Jews, but nothing else from beginning to end. Perhaps the book is a fragment of profane history captured for sacred purposes ; perchance copied bodily from Persian history and incorporated in the ancient Hebrew Scriptures. While there is no name of God, and no reference to the Hebrew religion anywhere, no one reads this book without being conscious of God. Its permanent value is that it is a revelation of God acting in providence.

Now providence is a sadly abused word. Christian people talk about providence, and special providences, in a way that reveals lamentable ignorance. The root meaning of providence is foresight; and the acquired meaning is activity resulting from foresight. In *Hamlet*, when the King is discussing the madness of Hamlet, he says,

" Alas, how shall this bloody deed be answered ?
It will be laid to us, whose *providence*
Should have kept short, restrained, and out of haunt,
This mad young man."

There the meaning of the word is revealed, " whose providence," that is our foresight, and the activity resulting from foresight, ought to have restrained this mad young man. If providence radically means foresight, and by usage the activity resulting from foresight, it is evident that providence can never perfectly be postulated of man, but only of God. Man has no foresight. No man knows what a day will bring forth.

God alone foresees, and He alone is able to act upon the basis of foreknowledge. In the introductory section of " Paradise Lost," when Milton is writing the great argument, and is attempting to prepare his own soul for the tremendous task he has set himself, he says :

" What in me is dark
Illumine, what is low raise and support,
That to the height of this great argument
I may assert eternal *providence*,
And justify the ways of God to men."

That is a profound use of the word providence. The doctrine of Divine providence is that God both possesses and exercises absolute power over all the works of His hands. If I want the supreme Bible passage on providence, I find it in the eleventh Psalm. The advice given to David was, Flee, man, flee as a bird to the mountains, the wicked are bending their bow, men are against thee, the foundations are destroyed, and when the foundations are destroyed, what can the righteous man do? To which he replied, Why do you tell me to flee? The foundations are not destroyed. The Lord is in His temple, His eyes behold, His eyelids try the children of men. He will try the righteous and He will rain brimstone upon the wicked. In effect he said, The things you call foundations are scaffolding. The foundation has never been moved. I am not going to run away. I believe in the Divine providence.

Esther is the book of pictures, and the teaching of pictures is that of the Divine providence. God amid the shadows, but at work. God hidden, unrecognized by the vast majority, undetected, but at work. The book then reveals the method of Divine providence, the principles of Divine providence, and some of the issues of Divine providence.

The book reveals first, the method of providence. It shows that God hidden is still active, and that His activity is always the ruling event towards an issue. At the end of the book of Esther, these words are written, " Mordecai, the Jew, was next unto the King Ahasuerus, and great among the Jews, and accepted of the multitude of his brethren ; seeking the good of his people, and speaking peace to all his seed." That is not the final issue, but the issue so far as these pictures are concerned. Notice carefully the contrast of that condition of affairs, with the condition obtaining when the book opens. Then the head man at the court of Ahasuerus was Haman, and in the heart of Haman there was enmity against Mordecai, and against the Jews; so that the whole of these people were in peril. At the end of the book, the man in authority is Mordecai, and he is seeking the good of his people, and speaking peace to his seed. Between the opening peril, incipient if not manifest, and the closing safety, clearly manifest, you have all the story of the book, and it is the story of " God within the shadow keeping watch above His own"; preventing and providing; taking care of His people; watching over them; moving quietly and surely on, until the peril is past and the people are brought to the place of safety and peace.

Now notice the method of His activity while hidden. He is seen using trivialities. Before the peril becomes imminent, while it is still incipient in the heart of Haman, the king's carousal issues in the removal of Vashti, and the introduction of Esther. Here we need to make a careful discrimination. God did not make Ahasuerus drunk, and God did not put into his heart the unholy desire that Vashti should be presented to his drunken lords; but God is in the shadow while Ahasuerus and his crowd of lords indulge in their carousal, while Vashti declines to yield to the whim of the king; and He uses Esther for the deliverance. A little while later, the peril is not merely incipient, it is imminent. Then the sleepless king is God's method. The king could not sleep, and when he could not sleep, he commanded that the records should be brought and read to him, and when they were read in the loneliness of the night, an entry was found of a service which one Mordecai had rendered, which the king had forgotten, and he asked about him, and took counsel with Haman as to what should be done to any man whom the king delighted to honour. Almost immediately Mordecai, who had been in a place of peril, was raised to a place of power. Infidelity will say it happened that the king could not sleep, and it happened that he had the records read to him, and it happened that Mordecai's name was discovered in the reading. Far simpler is the explanation, " Standeth God within the shadow, keeping watch above His own." There was a day when the Hebrew Psalmist said, " Thou holdest mine eyes waking."

He charged his sleeplessness upon God, and perhaps he was right. What is certain is that through the sleeplessness of the king God moved for the safety of His people.

Once again the method of the Divine providence is all-inclusive. God is an all-pervading atmosphere. There is no individual presented but that lives, moves, and has being in God. Ahasuerus, Vashti, Mordecai, Esther, and Haman are all in this atmosphere. The Divine presence enwrapping all their being, they are compelled to work out into manifestation the deep facts of their inward life; and all the while they are compelled as they work these things out into manifestation to coöperate in the Divine purpose and Divine intention, as it works carefully for the preservation of His people, and quietly forward to yet larger issues. Not individuals only are in this all-pervading atmosphere, but events also; royal carousals and banquets, royal proclamations; the small family interests in the life of Mordecai and Esther; personal ambitions, such as that of Haman; all these things are seen in this Divine atmosphere, in one case scorching, blasting, destruction, and in another healing, helping, deliverance. The principles, as well as the method of the Divine providence, are clearly revealed. God proceeds upon the basis of perfect knowledge. "His eyes behold. . . . His eyelids try." The Hebrew Psalms are pictorial. God is spoken of under the figure of a man, "His eyes behold." That is the idea of intense looking. "His eyelids try." That is the idea of close scrutiny and penetration. determination to see everything. That is the first principle of providence. It is based upon intimate, accurate, absolute knowledge.

The second principle is that of the undeviating righteousness of God. First, loyalty to man's free will. One of the supreme values of this book is that the name of God is left out of it, although He is close at hand. Ahasuerus sent out his invitations and entertained the aristocracy of the nation for one hundred and eighty days, and the democracy for seven days, which is about the usual proportion. He did just as he liked about it. He was not compelled to do this, that, or the other. Haman entered into all his own intrigues, made his own arrangements, built his own gallows. No one compelled Haman to build the gallows; he wrought out of his own free will. Mordecai did his own piece of political manœuvering when he placed Esther in the Court. They all went their own way, and had their own will. They were left absolutely to work out their own purposes. Yet, while they were absolutely free to work out their own will, the sphere of the operations of will is God, and they could not escape Him. Ahasuerus got drunk amid his lords, and followed out his drunken mania to its issue, and then at the right moment the great hand of God interfered. Haman built his gallows, but at last God hung him on it. In this tremendous revelation of providence I see the undeviating righteousness of God in His loyalty to man's free will, and this issues in poetic justice. All the way through the punishment fits the crime.

Another principle of providence revealed is that of the absolute power of God. Mark the marvel of these revelations of the fact that human freedom is made contributory to Divine purpose. That is a matter we can never understand entirely. Whenever we try to compress the God of the Bible into a philosophy we break down at that point. Nevertheless, it is actually, simply, and entirely true to human experience. It is seen not only in the book of Esther. It is equally evident in our own lives. We look back. We have wrought out our own will, yet in the larger outlook we have wrought out in perfect freedom of activity the purpose of God. There is no possibility of escape.

Finally, look at the issues of providence. To those recognizing this providence, this overruling activity of God, there come a great confidence and a great courage. To those in rebellion against it, who do not recognize it and who deny it, there are panic and punishment.

The historic issue of providence is the progress of God towards the ultimate goal. Of this the book of Esther is but one illustration in the midst of others. All the way through the Bible we see the same mighty, sure, onward movement.

If this book of Esther illustrates—I have tried to use that word carefully, I do not say it declares it as a theory but it illustrates—the providence of God, what is its living message? First, it is the illustration of a truth, demanding an application. The truth is that of the existence of God. There are many arguments for the existence of God, but the argument of providence is not the least weighty. I know it is the fashion to-day in theological circles, and in Christian evidence work, to say that the argument from design is played out. It has never been answered, and when lifted on to its highest level, and the evidence of human history, mental, moral, and spiritual, is taken, one of the supremest arguments for God is the marvellous harmony of human events. Things that seem to be far apart and even contradictory as we watch them, are yet seen to contribute to the same onward movement, to the reaching of the same great goal. I say that the supreme message of this book is that God is, and that God acts. I have more than once quoted a couplet from James Russell Lowell. Let me now quote two verses out of the poem in the midst of which the couplet occurs :

" Careless seems the great Avenger; history's pages but record
One death-grapple in the darkness 'twixt old systems and the word ;
Truth forever on the scaffold, Wrong forever on the throne —
Yet that scaffold sways the future and, behind the dim unknown,
Standeth God within the shadow, keeping watch above His own.

" We see dimly in the present what is small and what is great,
Slow of faith how weak an arm may turn the iron helm of fate,
But the soul is still oracular ; amid the market's din,
List the ominous stern whisper from the Delphic cave within —
' They enslave their children's children who make compromise with sin.' "

That final word of these two verses is based upon Lowell's tremendous conviction that God stands " within the shadow, keeping watch above His own." He stands there to-day just as much as He did in the olden days. The Court of Ahasuerus characterized by ostentation and voluptuousness was in the atmosphere of God. So is every Court in Europe and the world to-day. While men drink and forget Him, like an all-pervasive atmosphere He is moulding, governing ; burning or healing ; saving or damning ; according to what man is, in his attitude towards Him. "Who among us can dwell amid the everlasting burnings?" was the great question of Isaiah, and it was a recognition of the fiery presence of God from which men cannot escape, and of the activity of God in every human life. Let us make this personal, pertinent, immediate—no man escapes God for half an hour. We can change our destiny, but we cannot escape God. We may make God a blasting force, or a healing one, according to our attitude towards Him. That is providence. Providence is not a sweet sensational method, by which God juggles to take care of a few eccentric people. That is what I meant at the beginning by saying that providence is God's foresight and God's activity based upon His foresight. We are all hemmed in by it. "In whom we live and move and have our being." That is providence. "The God in whose hand thy breath is, and whose are all thy ways, hast thou not glorified." That is providence. I cannot escape His influence. He is touching my life at every point.

The application of a story like this is not declared in its words, not even enunciated, but it glows in letters of flaming fire upon all the pages of the book. Reckon with God. Trust in God. Coöperate with God.

Reckon with God. I put it so. You remember the Authorized Version read as a man "thinketh within himself, so is he." The Revised Version renders, as a man "reckoneth within himself, so is he." At first it seems a little disappointing, but weigh it out and think out the enormous force of it, as a man "reckoneth within himself, so is he." Reckon with God; take Him into account, is the message of the book of Esther to the court of the king, to the palaces of the nobles, to the assemblies of the people, to the rulers, to the nation. That is the message of Esther to every man and woman. Reckon with God, for He stands within the shadow and no man can miss His fire or escape His hand. When you have decided to reckon with Him, know this, that as Cowper declared:

> " Behind a frowning providence
> He hides a smiling face."

At the back of all is the infinite love.

Then trust Him, and trusting Him act with Him, and so demonstrate at last the truth of the supremest word about providence in the New Testament, "To them that love God all things work together for good."

Job

THE PERMANENT VALUES	THE LIVING MESSAGE
A revelation of experience in fallen human nature. I. The central figure: Job. II. The central fact: Job stripped. 　A. Of wealth. 　B. Of children. 　C. Of health. 　D. Of the partner of his love in faith. 　E. Of his friends. 　F. Of the sense of the greatness of personality. 　G. Of the sense of relation to deity. 　H. Of the sense of the government of God over good and evil. III. The central value: Job's consciousness. 　A. The need—9:2, 3, 32, 33. 　B. The enquiry—14:14, 15. 　C. The cry—16:19-21. 　D. The confidence—19:25-27a. 　E. The quest—23:3-9. 　F. The challenge—31:35-37. 　G. The awakening—40:4, 5. 　H. The attitude—42:1-6.	I. The need of fallen humanity. 　A. Intermediation. 　B. Light on immortality. 　C. An advocate in God. 　D. A vindicator. 　E. A judge. 　F. An indictment. 　G. A true sense of self. 　H. A vision producing repentance. II. The answers of Jesus. 　A. Meet the need. 　B. Answer the enquirer. 　C. Fulfill the meaning.

IN order to make a discovery of the permanent value and the living message of the book of Job, it is preëminently necessary that we should breathe its atmosphere, the qualities of which may perhaps be expressed by three words—sin, sorrow, silence.

It is not a book of solutions; it is rather a revelation of human experience. The central figure is Job. The central fact of the history is that of his being deprived of everything. The central value is the revelation of his experiences resulting from the process.

Job is not an ideal man. He is real. The circumstances in the midst of which we find him are not perfect circumstances. They are the ordinary circumstances of human life, those of sin, of sorrow, and of silence. The experiences, then, are those of a real man, in such circumstances as we are all familiar with in greater or less degree.

In our attempt to discover the living message of the book we shall first observe the process of the stripping of this man to the nakedness of his spiritual being. Secondly, we shall examine the central words that he uttered as expressive of his experiences. Finally we shall show that the only answers to Job are given by Jesus.

First, then, let us recall the process of the stripping of this man to the nakedness of his spiritual being. Gradually he was divested of all the things that clothe the spirit of a man; or to change the figure, all the things upon which a man leans for help and strength were removed, until we have the tremendous and awful spectacle of a soul naked and alone in the universe of God. First he lost his wealth. In a few brief hours, or days at the most, he passed from wealth to poverty, from plenty to penury. All the material things upon which he had leaned were swept away. The second stage in the stripping was that of the loss of his children. Then he lost his health. After that he lost the partnership of love in the exercise of faith. Out of love for him, and in order to make a way of escape out of the tragedy of his pain, his wife said, "Renounce God and die." There had existed the partnership of faith between husband and wife, but that ended, and Job was left to an awful loneliness. The next event in the stripping was that of the loss of his friends. His acquaintances had already departed with the loss of his property. Eliphaz, Bildad, and Zophar proved the sincerity of their friendship first, by the fact that they came to see him in his sorrow; secondly, by the fact that they remained in silent sympathy with him for seven days; and thirdly, because when they spoke, they said everything directly to him. He lost the comfort of their friendship, however, because they misunderstood him, and imputed to him sins of which he would not confess himself guilty.

But we must look a little more closely for the discovery of the last movements in the process of stripping. At the end of the first and second stages, when he had lost his wealth and his children, he said, "Naked came I out of my mother's womb, and naked shall I return thither." Notice very carefully the majesty of that declaration. Even though he had lost wealth, acquaintances, and children, he had not yet lost the sense of the dignity and greatness of his own personality. He still recognized that he was more than all he possessed. When his friends arrived, he poured out in their listening ears all the lamentation of his soul. As I read that lamentation I find that this sense of the greatness of personality was weakened by the overwhelming agony of the suffering through which he had passed. It is evident that he was beginning to doubt the dignity of his own being, and when a little later we come to his reply to the first address of Eliphaz, not only is that sense of the greatness of personality weakened, it is lost. He cursed the day he was born, and cried out for the darkness and desolation of the grave, preferring death to life, wishing that he could cease to be.

The stripping was not yet over. Bereft of his children he had said, "The Lord gave, and the Lord hath taken away; blessed be the name of the Lord." That was a declaration resulting from a sense of his relationship to Deity. In his lamentation that also was weakened, and by the time we come to his answer to Eliphaz, he cried out to God, "Why hast Thou set me as a mark for Thee?" He had lost his sense of relationship to Deity as a gracious relationship.

Yet one step further. After the loss of health, and the partnership of love in faith, he said, "Shall we receive good at the hand of God, and shall we not receive evil?" In that question there is manifest a conviction of the government of God over good and evil. When we come to his answer to Eliphaz, all the questions he asked show that he doubted, if not the fact of God's government, certainly the justice of it. He had lost his final anchorage.

Thus we see him, stripped of wealth; acquaintances; children; health; the partnership of love in faith; friends; his sense of the greatness of his own personality; his sense of intimate relationship to God; and his sense of the government of God over good and evil. All the things that men lean upon are gone. We now stand watching the naked spirit of the man. What was left to him? God was left, and Job never denied Him. Self was left, and he could not escape. Between God and himself there seemed to be no place of meeting, no reconciliation. God and self were absolute certainties, but he was in circumstances so full of agony, that there seemed to be no place of rest, and no possibility of relief.

In the course of his controversy with his friends, he occasionally uttered cries out of the very depths of his experience. Intensely interesting are his answers to his friends, full of satire and thunder and tremendous invective poured upon the men who were misinterpreting him. Notwithstanding this the speeches of Job are finally not so much an answer to these men, as the wail of his own soul; and the deepest things of all were spoken to the God he could not find, of the self that he could not understand, out of the midst of anguish and conflict which had no explanation. Let us attempt to gather up these profoundest utterances.

I find the first in the ninth chapter. The words were spoken in the course of an answer to Bildad.

> " How can man be just with God ?
> If He be pleased to contend with him,
> He cannot answer Him one of a thousand   . .
> For He is not a man, as I am, that I should
>   answer Him,
> That we should come together in judgment.
> There is no daysman betwixt us,
> That might lay his hand upon us both."

That is not an answer to Eliphaz, Bildad, or Zophar. It is the cry of a smitten soul. " How can man be just with God?" does not mean, How can a man be justified by God? but rather, How can a man argue his case with God, how can a man contend with God? There is still manifest his conviction of the existence of God, and his certainty of himself, but he enquires, How am I to find my way to God? And if He asks me questions, How am I to answer Him one of a thousand? Then he exclaims in complaint,

> " There is no daysman betwixt us,
> That might lay his hand upon us both."

Said this man in effect, If I should find my way to God, I could not argue with Him. Oh, that there were some one in the universe who could bring us together; who could put his hand on God, and on me; who could represent God to me, and me to God.

The next word occurs in the course of an answer to Zophar. The opening words of that answer were,

> " Man that is born of a woman
> Is of few days, and full of trouble."

Having made this general affirmation, he continued,

> " For there is hope of a tree, if it be cut down, that it
>   will sprout again,
> And that the tender branch thereof will not cease.
>
> Though the root thereof wax old in the earth,
> And the stock thereof die in the ground ;
> Yet through the scent of water it will bud,
> And put forth boughs like a plant.
> But man dieth, and wasteth away :
> Yea, man giveth up the ghost, and where is he ? "

That was a wail of hopeless despair, in which he declared that a tree has a better chance than a man. But continuing he exclaimed,

> " If a man die, shall he live again ?
> All the days of my warfare would I wait,
> Till my release should come.
> Thou shouldest call, and I would answer Thee :
> Thou wouldest have a desire to the work of Thine
>   hands."

That is as though Job had said, If I could but believe that a man could live again, I would bear all the conflict and would wait. This was hardly the expression of a hope ; it was only a sigh. Yet there was in it a gleam of light in the midst of the terrible darkness. He could not find a daysman able to put his hand on God and on himself. He declared there was nothing for him but death. A tree had a chance, but a man had not. Suddenly there flamed across his spirit a wonder, an enquiry, which came out of his essential nature. It was an affirmation of his consciousness of the need for more time and space for the realization of life than life itself seemed to afford.

A little later he exclaimed,

> " O earth, cover not thou my blood,
> And let my cry have no resting place.
> Even now, behold, my witness is in heaven,
> And He that voucheth for me is on high.
> My friends scorn me ;
> But mine eye poureth out tears unto God ;
> That He would maintain the right of a man with God,
> And of a son of man with his neighbour ! "

Notice carefully the marvel of this word. Job was passing into deeper darkness, and yet suddenly uttered this most remarkable word. It was the cry of his spirit ; it was prayer. It revealed a profound conviction.

> " Even now, behold, my witness is in heaven,
> And He that voucheth for me is on high."

This was an affirmation of his belief in the existence of God, and of the fact that He was in heaven, on high, that is, enthroned. He believed in God, but thought of Him as at a distance. Upon the basis of this conviction he expressed his desire that God would maintain the right of a man with God, and a son of man with his neighbour. He had said but a little while before, There is no daysman who can put his hand upon God and upon me. Now he declared that absolutely the only way for his case to be argued with God would be for God to argue it with Himself, " That He would maintain the right of a man with God." The passionate cry of his spirit was that God would become an Advocate with Himself on behalf of a man who had lost everything, and was conscious of his need.

A step further, and he uttered even more remarkable words.

> " I know that my Redeemer liveth,
> And that He shall stand up at the last upon the earth :
> And after my skin hath been thus destroyed,
> Yet from my flesh shall I see God :
> Whom I shall see for myself."

I would change the word "Redeemer" here to Vindicator; not that Redeemer is wrong but that our use of it does not accurately convey the thought of the Hebrew word, Goel. The business of the Goel was always that of vindication, when the one to be vindicated was unable to vindicate himself. The vindication might be by ransom or revenge.

Now said Job, "I know that my Goel liveth," that is my present conviction; "and that He shall stand up at the last"—not, in the latter day, but at the end of this conflict. This was the language of the court of justice. Job was making appeal for vindication, and affirmed his conviction that his Vindicator would stand up at the end upon the dust, that is, as a prevailing Advocate. On the basis of this conviction he declared,

> "And after my skin hath been thus destroyed,
> Yet from my flesh shall I see God."

A question arises here as to whether "from" in this sentence means, in my flesh, or, apart from my flesh. It certainly may mean either. Dr. Davidson gives an illustration from *King Lear*. When one of his daughters said that it was necessary for her to write a letter "from my home," the context shows that she meant when she was away from home. He holds therefore that Job meant, When I have done with my flesh, I shall see God in my spiritual life. I do not so understand it. Whereas the context in *King Lear* may demonstrate the fact that by "from my home" his daughter meant when she was away from home, the phrase itself might certainly have meant that she wrote when she was at home; and I personally believe that Job used the word in this sense. It was a tremendous affirmation coming up out of his spiritual nature, that even though his flesh seemed to be in process of destruction, yet from it, that is as still being in it, he would see God. It is quite true that he immediately added, "My reins are consumed within me," thus revealing the fact that he passed again into consciousness of the darkness about him. Nevertheless the affirmation was in itself a flash of light out of his essential spiritual nature. I do not suggest that Job could have interpreted it in the full evangelical sense in which we understand it to-day.

Still later he cried,

> "Oh, that I knew where I might find Him,
> That I might come even to His seat!
> I would order my cause before Him,
> And fill my mouth with arguments."

When he said this, his confidence was overshadowed; he was again in the region of despair; he declared the hopelessness of the search; and yet faith in God was tenacious, and he longed to find Him, and stand before His judgment seat.

Yet again he cried,

> "Oh, that I had one to hear me!
> (Lo, here is my signature, let the Almighty answer me;)
> And that I had the indictment which mine adversary
>   hath written!"

The word "adversary" here was a legal term, indicating an opponent in the case to be tried. He thus challenged God to indict him, and in pride declared that if such an indictment were written he would carry it upon his shoulders, and bind it unto him as a crown, going as a prince into the presence of God.

Then followed a long period of silence so far as Job was concerned. Elihu spoke, but Job did not answer him. Suddenly, in the process of the speech of Elihu, Jehovah spoke. God challenged him to attend, and then made pass before him visions of His power in the material universe, in His dealings with animate and inanimate creation. In answer to this theophany occurred the next word of Job,

> "Behold, I am of small account;
>   what shall I answer Thee?
> I lay mine hand upon my mouth.
> Once have I spoken, and I will not answer;
> Yea twice, but I will proceed no further."

These words were the outcome of the awakening of his naked spirit to the sense of the power of God. God had said no word to him about sin. God had uttered not a sentence about his sorrow. He had not spoken a sentence in explanation of the mysteries that had enshrouded him. Rather He made His glory pass before him, He put the universe in relationship to Himself, and made Job spectator. Job answered the unveiling by exclaiming, I am nothing. The word "vile" in our present use of it is a palpable mistranslation. Job meant, I do not count, I have been answering and arguing, I will say no more.

Then there was a second unveiling of Jehovah, in which with great tenderness and gentle satire

He challenged Job to take the seat of government in the universe, giving two illustrations of His purpose and power, those namely of behemoth and leviathan. Then Job exclaimed, "I abhor myself, and repent."

Let us group these words. We see this man stripped of everything, but left with the certainties of God, himself, and conflict. Out of these circumstances of intense and utter spiritual loneliness he asked for a daysman, for intermediation between himself and God; suggested the ultimate problem, "If a man die, shall he live again?"; uttered a prayer to God that He would argue with Himself about a man; then broke out into a great expression of confidence from the depths of his nature, "I know that my Vindicator liveth." This was almost immediately forgotten, and he proceeded in his quest, "Oh, that I knew where I might find Him." He challenged God to come out of hiding, and to write his indictment. Then suddenly he was brought into a sense of the presence of God in the universe, and said, "I am of small account," I will say no more. At last, without a word about sin or salvation, but only as the result of the unveiling of the power and glory of God, he abased himself and said, "I repent."

Have these cries of a human spirit ever been answered? The question is important, for if it were possible for us to pass into similar circumstances, these are the things we should say. When all the things upon which men depend are taken away, these are the essential cries of humanity in its alienation and distance from God. First there is the need of a daysman who can put his hand on God and on man. That Daysman has appeared, and we have felt the touch of his hand. "If a man die, shall he live again?" That is the surging, agonized cry of this materialized age. We treat it often with shocking flippancy, but this is only an attempt to hide the agony. We have the answer, He hath "brought life and incorruption to light through the Gospel." Job said, Would that God would argue my case with Himself. Jesus came to declare that God has argued with Himself the case of man. Then in beautiful sequence comes the affirmation, "I know that my Redeemer liveth." We take up Job's language with fuller, richer meaning. Job demanded that he should find his way to God as Judge. God hath appointed One Who shall judge the world, and every man can come to that Throne, and argue his case in the presence of Christ. Job asked that his indictment might be written. That is a most popular challenge to-day. Men are everywhere asking that God will write their indictment, and prove them sinners. The answer of God to that challenge is to be found in the revelation of His law in the ethic of Jesus. In the presence of the revealed glory of God, Job exclaimed, "I am of small account." The answer of Jesus to that consciousness is that He first agrees therewith, and demands that man shall deny himself in order to find himself. He then declares that no man is of small account, but in the estimate of God he is worth the stoop and suffering and dying to save him. Finally Job said, "I repent in dust and ashes." Jesus gives repentance unto life, and lifts out of the dust and ashes into the dignity and glory of partnership with Himself.

In Job we see a soul stripped naked; and hear the language of challenge, of need, and of enquiry. I turn to the New Testament and I find One Who answers the challenge, meets the need, and replies to the enquiry.

Tear up your New Testament, and fling it to the winds; crucify the Christ of God, and let there be no resurrection; and the book of Job still lives, the unanswered agony of a soul.

Retain the New Testament, and the agony becomes an anthem, and the despair merges into ultimate victory.

Psalms

THE PERMANENT VALUES	THE LIVING MESSAGE

The revelations of the truth about worship.
I. The conception of God that produces worship.
  A. *Jehovah.*
    1. Essential being.
    2. The becoming One.
  B. *Elohim.*
    1. Essential might.
    2. Operating in power.
  C. *Adonahy.*
    1. Essential lordship.
    2. Sovereignty.
II. The attitudes of man in worship.
  A. Submission—answer to sovereignty.
    1. Reverence.
    2. Obedience.
  B. Trust—answer to might.
    1. Honesty.
    2. Courage.
  C. Joy—answer to grace.
    1. Penitence.
    2. Adoration.
III. The activities of worship.
  A. God calling man to worship by revelation.
  B. Man responding to God's approach.
    1. Laying bare of the soul.
    2. Receiving God's gifts.
    3. Offering praise to God.
  C. God, true and faithful, dealing in love.
	The message of the
	  Psalter—Ps. 66.
	I. Worship God.
	  A. Know Him.
	  B. Reckon with Him.
	  C. Make all circum-
	    stances opportunities
	    of worship.
	II. The New Testament
	  summary—Phil. 4:4-7.

THE Psalter is a collection of sacred Hebrew poems, intended for use in worship. There can be no chronological arrangement of these psalms. It is perfectly evident, as Eusebius long ago pointed out, that the collection has been carefully edited, and the psalms grouped on the principle of affinity.

The individual psalms are natural expressions by many authors at various times under differing circumstances of their consciousness of God. The message of the book in its entirety has to do with the subject of worship.

The Hebrew word translated worship literally means prostration. It is used to indicate that prostration which recognizes the supremacy of the One before Whom the worshipper bows, and therefore indicates the attitude of submission in the presence of supremacy. As a matter of fact, the word itself does not often occur in the Psalter. As indicating the attitude of man in the presence of God, it is found fifteen times only in the one hundred and fifty psalms. It occurs in other places as indicating the attitude of man in the presence of angels, and as indicating the attitude of one man in the presence of another.

In the grouping of passages in which the word does occur as setting forth the attitude of the soul in the presence of God, there are certain matters full of suggestiveness. Even though it is impossible to deal fully with each passage, seeing it in its setting, and so gathering its full significance, I propose to read the fifteen passages in which the word occurs.

" In Thy fear will I worship towards Thy holy temple."—v. 7.

" All the ends of the earth shall remember and turn unto the Lord :
And all the kindreds of the nations shall worship before Thee."—xxii. 27.

" All the fat ones of the earth shall eat and worship :
All they that go down to the dust shall bow before Him."—xxii. 29.

" Give unto the Lord the glory due unto His name ;
Worship the Lord in the beauty of holiness."—xxix. 2.

" He is Thy Lord ; and worship thou Him."—xlv. 11.

" All the earth shall worship Thee,
And shall sing unto Thee."—lxvi. 3.

" Yea, all kings shall fall down before Him :
All nations shall serve Him."—lxxii. 11.

" All nations whom Thou hast made shall come and worship before Thee, O Lord ;
And they shall glorify Thy name."—lxxxvi. 9.

" O come, let us worship and bow down :
Let us kneel before the Lord our Maker."—xcv. 6.

" O worship the Lord in the beauty of holiness."—xcvi. 9.

" Worship Him, all ye gods."—xcvii. 7.

" Exalt ye the Lord our God,
And worship at His footstool :
Exalt ye the Lord our God,
And worship at His holy hill."—xcix. 5, 9.

" We will go into His tabernacles :
We will worship at His footstool."—cxxxii. 7.

" I will worship towards Thy holy temple."—cxxxviii. 2.

I am perfectly aware that the reading of these passages seems to have very little coherence or consistency, and very little helpfulness. I do not suggest for a moment that there is any immediate connection between the passages. I have merely selected them because in them the actual word worship occurs. There are, however, two or three deductions to be made, even from such simple reading. Throughout the whole of these the worship referred to is that of a Person Who is described sometimes as Jehovah, sometimes as God, and sometimes as Lord.

The worshippers are individuals, kings, nations, all the earth.

There is a centre of worship, sometimes spoken of as the temple, sometimes as the holy hill.

Finally there are certain attitudes indicated— those of fear, of holiness, and of song. I might confine myself to that statement, and dwell upon each of the points as suggested, but I am desirous of taking a still wider outlook upon this wonderful collection.

Before doing so, let me ask you to remember the marvellously constant use made of this book of psalms in the life of faith for thousands of years. I recently came across this very interesting passage by Tholuck. " What a record it would be if one could write it down—all the spiritual experiences, the disclosures of the heart, the combats and the conflicts which men in the course of the ages have connected with the words of the psalms. What a history, if we could discover the place the book has occupied in the inner life of the heroes of the Kingdom of God." It would be impossible for any one to write such a record as Tholuck there suggests, because the uses that have been made of these psalms throughout the centuries have been so varied.

Now, why is it that this book has been so perpetually used? First, because it is a collection of simple, honest, human experiences. I very much question if there be any circumstance possible to human life but that some psalm exactly expresses the experience thereof. The Psalter contains anthems of prosperity and dirges of adversity. It has major songs which celebrate holiness, the experience that comes when men are led to the heights and live above the snow line. It has minor songs bewailing sin, the experience that comes when men have wilfully, persistently sinned and sunk to the depths. Songs of hope, the experience when, in circumstances of difficulty, gleams of the coming day are seen upon the distant horizon. Songs of despair, the experience in hours of darkness, when there seems to be no glimmer of light. I repeat, it is impossible to think of any human circumstances which do not find expression in this book.

But a mere collection of expressions of human experiences would hardly be worth while, for the profounder an experience is, the more capable is a man of expressing it. Perhaps the first impression made by that statement is one of doubt. Think of it. It is in the moment of profound experience that a man speaks freely. " Out of the abundance of the heart the mouth speaketh," not out of its emptiness ! Whether it be of wisdom or of folly, of sin or of triumph, it is in the moment when the heart is fullest that man speaks most easily. It is quite true that he will often, under such circumstances, say things that he will wish he had not said, but he speaks freely. There was a day when King Saul told the absolute truth about himself, " I have played the fool !" No one could have persuaded him to say that in the day when experience was superficial; but when he was in the depths, the consciousness of all his unutterable folly broke upon him, and he uttered all the truth. I repeat, therefore, that a man does not want another to write for him expressions of experience. We have not touched the deepest fact in the book of psalms when we say that it is intensely human. The deepest thing is that it is a collection of songs in which human experiences are brought into the presence of God. They show how man feels and thinks and speaks and acts when he is conscious of God. That is why the psalms live to-day.

The permanent values of the Psalter, then, are its revelations of truth about worship. First it reveals the conception of God that produces worship; secondly, it reveals the attitude of man in worship; and finally, it reveals the activities of worship, initially on the part of God, responsively on the part of man, and finally on the part of God.

The Psalter reveals the conception of God, which produces worship. This conception is manifest in the names by which He is referred to. Of these the three that stand out supremely are Jehovah, Elohim and Adonahy. These reveal a conception of God which, wherever held, compels worship. The name Jehovah stands forevermore as suggestive of the essential Being of God, and of the fact that He becomes in grace all that His people need. That name occurs more often than any other. All these singers, through different times and climes and circumstances, of different temperaments, worshipped in the presence of Jehovah. The first thought is that of His essential Being. It is never questioned, never argued, but taken for granted.

Perhaps the chief exposition of the fact that He is, and of what He is, is found in the one hundred and thirty-ninth psalm, with its stupendous setting forth of the fact of the existence of God, and of all that fact connotes of His presence and knowledge, and of the impossibility of human escape therefrom.

If I were asked which of the psalms most perfectly sets forth the fact that God is the becoming One, I should answer the twenty-third, which opens with the declaration, "Jehovah is my Shepherd," and then celebrates His sufficiency for the needs of man in all the circumstances of time, until in the eternal habitation the soul is perfectly satisfied in Him. The first conception of God suggested by the prevalence of the name Jehovah is that of the essential One Who becomes what His people need.

The second conception is suggested by the great name Elohim, which we translate God, that intensive plural which does not necessarily signify number, but something so infinite that no singular can express it. This word suggests the essential might of God and the fact that He operates in power. His might is not only potential, it is also kinetic; not merely might, but might exercised. That is the perpetual reason of awe in the soul of man in the presence of God.

Perhaps psalm sixty-eight most perfectly sets forth the essential might of God, and psalm forty-six the fact of its activity.

The third title is not so frequently used, but the principle revealed by it is present from first to last. Adonahy means Lord in the simplest sense of the word. It is suggestive of the sovereignty of God. This is the abiding conviction of all the singers. It is, perhaps, most perfectly set forth in psalm eighty-six, in which the first word is Jehovah, immediately followed by the title Adonahy, and throughout which the soul is prostrate in the presence of the sovereign God.

The threefold revelation of God is that of His essential Being, which becomes in grace whatever man needs; His essential might, which operates in power on behalf of man; and His essential Lordship, which undertakes the government of the affairs of man. That is the conception of God which produces worship. Wherever an individual soul, or a king in official capacity, or a nation or kindred or race, or the whole world comes to that conception, the inevitable result is worship.

Pass now to the second matter, that of the attitude of man in worship. That attitude is threefold—submission, trust, joy. This threefold attitude is the answer to the threefold revelation. The final revelation is that of supremacy suggested by the title Adonahy. Submission is the answer of man to supremacy. The name Elohim suggests the might of God. Trust is the answer of man to God's might. The name Jehovah reveals that God becomes what His people need, which is but another way to declare the fact of the grace of God. Joy is the answer of the soul to grace.

The notes of submission are those of reverence and obedience; reverence in the outward form, and which expresses itself ultimately in obedience, is the attitude of submission. The notes of trust are honesty and courage. Perfect honesty is manifest in courage, and based on confidence in God. That is the attitude of trust. The notes of joy are penitence and adoration. Man reaches the highest joy when he finds the contrite heart. It is out of the penitent and broken heart that the sweetest music comes, and the highest note in the anthem of praise is reached. This does not apply to the songs of angels which we do not know, and shall never sing. We shall listen to them, but shall sing such songs as angels cannot sing.

Finally, as to the activities of worship as revealed throughout the book of psalms. The first activity is not of man but of God. Worship is always the outcome of something exterior to the worshipper. God unveiled Himself before those singers of the olden days, surprising them in the day of darkness with a great light, breaking upon them in the midst of sorrow with new joy, as in the case of Job, when his heart was broken, passing before him in the splendour of His glory. By such unveiling He compels worship. I take the Psalter, and read it at any point, and discover something of God's activity, constraining man to worship. The first note of a psalm is that of praise. You follow the singer, and enquire why he sings, and the answer is always of something that God is, that God has wrought, of some way in which God has revealed Himself. The first activity in worship is always that of God's self-revelation.

Then follow the activities of man. In answer to the approach of God in love, man lays bare his soul. The thirty-second psalm gives the story of how a man failed in worship, and of how he was restored to worship. It opens with an exclamation, "Oh, the blessedness of transgression forgiven," and proceeds to declare that man blessed in whose spirit there is no guile—that is, no deceit, no cloking. The psalmist then tells of days when it was different.

"When I kept silence, my bones waxed old
Through my roaring all the day long.
For day and night Thy hand was heavy upon me:
My moisture was changed as with the drought of summer."

Then he turned back to God:

"I acknowledged my sin unto Thee, and mine iniquity have I not hid."

That is the soul baring itself in the presence of God. The song was the outcome of the answer of God. "Thou forgavest the iniquity of my sin." There was no song while he was keeping silence in an attempt to hide his sin. The activities of man in worship are the laying bare of the soul, the reception of gifts, and ultimately the offering of praise.

The final activity of worship is that of God, Who is true and faithful in His dealing with the worshipping soul, becoming to that soul whatever is needed.

The supreme message of the Psalter is, Worship God. Make all circumstances opportunities of worship. Are you in sorrow? Worship! Are you in joy? Worship! Are you in darkness? Worship! Are you in the light? Worship!

I turn to my New Testament, and find the message of the Psalter: "Rejoice in the Lord alway: again I will say, Rejoice." "In everything by prayer and supplication with thanksgiving let your requests be made known unto God. And the peace of God, which passeth all understanding, shall guard your hearts and your thoughts in Christ Jesus."

Proverbs

THE PERMANENT VALUES	THE LIVING MESSAGE

I. **The fundamental declaration**—1:7.
A. The presupposition—God the all-wise. (This fact expressed in all His works and ways.)
B. The deduction—man must fear the Lord.
II. **The argument in illustration.**
A. The scheme.
  1. Home—1:8, 9.
  2. Friendships—1:10-19.
  3. The world beyond—1:20—9:18.
B. Consideration.
  1. The first sphere—home, father and mother.
  2. The second sphere—companions.
  3. The third sphere—the city, symbolizing life.
    a. The first call—warnings and promise.
    b. The call from home—2-7. "My son."
    c. The second call—8.
    d. A contrast—9.
III. **The final applications.**
A. First collection of proverbs—statements.
B. Second collection of proverbs—pictures.
C. Words of Agur and oracles of Lemuel.
	I. **Precepts**—3:1-10.
	The law of wisdom.
	II. **Practice**—8:32-36.
	The life of wisdom.
	III. **Power**—James 1:5.
	The Lord of wisdom.

THE book of Proverbs is essentially didactic, and consequently its content constitutes its message. There are certain peculiarities about the books of Job, Proverbs, and Ecclesiastes. While it is true that the peculiarly Hebrew titles of God are found in them, yet all the references to the law and ritual, the sacrifices and ceremony with which the other Old Testament books abound, are absent from these. While preëminently religious, they are yet primarily philosophic. They are the only three books of the wisdom literature of the Hebrew people in the Bible. The meaning of wisdom as applied to these writings is exactly what is intended to-day by the common use of the word philosophy. That common use is not strictly warranted by the real meaning of the word. Philosophy does not mean wisdom, but the love of wisdom. A philosopher is not necessarily a wise man. He is a lover of wisdom—that is, one seeking after wisdom.

There is a distinct difference between the Hebrew philosophy revealed in these books and all others. It starts with an affirmation. They begin with a question. All philosophies other than that of the Hebrew people result from investigation in order to the answering of Pilate's question, "What is truth?" I do not suggest that that is an improper method, but it must be recognized that the Hebrew philosophy begins by affirming God. Hebrew philosophers believed that there could be no discovery of ultimate truth save upon the basis of revelation, and the revelation with which they began was that of the existence of God.

The book of Proverbs is generally thought of as though it were merely a collection of wise sayings, lacking anything like system or order.

87

As a matter of fact, there is no book in the Old Testament more systematic than this. A reference to our analysis of its content will demonstrate the accuracy of this assertion. The first verse constitutes a title page, "The proverbs of Solomon the son of David, king of Israel." The next six verses are occupied with the preface, in which the purpose of the book and the method of the writer are clearly stated. The preface ends with the fundamental affirmation of the Hebrew philosophy,

"The fear of the Lord is the beginning of knowledge :
But the foolish despise wisdom and instruction."

The book itself falls into three parts ; first, a series of discourses in defense and application of the fundamental affirmation ; secondly, a series of proverbs collected and arranged by Solomon himself, and lastly, a posthumous collection of Solomon's Proverbs, made by the men of Hezekiah's day. All this is followed by an appendix containing the words of Agur and the oracles of Lemuel.

In dealing with the permanent values of other books, we have been conscious of very much local colour. In this book this is reduced almost to the vanishing point. It is a singularly living book. There are great passages of it which may be read in the heart of any of the great cities of to-day with perfect application to the existing conditions. Therefore, whereas in dealing with other books it has been necessary to search for the underlying principle, here that principle is plainly stated. In other cases we have borrowed from other books some outstanding statement of principle, in order to see how the book under consideration illustrated that principle. In this case we find in the book itself both the statement of its permanent value, and the actual words of its living message.

The two permanent values of the book, therefore, are its fundamental declaration and its argument of illustration.

The fundamental declaration is contained in the seventh verse of the first chapter. The presupposition and consequent deduction of this declaration constitute the deepest note in the Hebrew wisdom or philosophy. The presupposition is that God is all-wise ; that in the final meaning of the word, wisdom can only be postulated of God. This conception is perpetually present in the arguments of Job, in the remarkable and contrastive method of the book of Ecclesiastes, and in the systematic order of the book of Proverbs. Moreover, it is taken for granted and constantly insisted upon that the wisdom of God expresses itself in all His works and in all His ways. The Hebrew philosophers believed that all natural phenomena constituted a revelation of the Divine Wisdom. Wherever they looked, at the land or the sea, at the earth or the heavens, they saw God. That philosophy on the human side accounted for the magnificent declaration with which the first book in the Bible opens : "In the beginning God created." So they ever thought of wisdom as final in God.

From this fundamental conviction a clear and definite deduction was inevitable ; if wisdom is perfect in God, wisdom in man consists in the fear of the Lord. A man is wise in the measure in which he apprehends and fears God. Fear in the sense in which it is certainly used in this fundamental declaration does not mean a cowardly, servile dread which strives to hide from God. There are two kinds of fear possible in regard to God. There is the fear lest He should hurt me. There is the fear lest I should hurt Him. The first is selfish, and produces no fruit of righteousness. The last is the fear of love, which produces holiness of character and righteousness of conduct. This fear of the Lord is emotional recognition of God. Do not let us be afraid of the word emotional. The emotional side of man's nature is as much a creation of God as is the intellectual. The emotional fear of God, then, is the answer of the soul in wonder in the presence of infinite Wisdom. That is preceded by intellectual apprehension of God, and consummated in volitional submission to His will.

These Hebrew philosophers did not believe that by such intellectual apprehension, emotional exercise, and volitional submission, man achieved the ultimate Wisdom. The declaration is rather that in that fear, man comes into the condition for being wise. "The fear of the Lord is the *beginning* of wisdom." No man can begin to be wise until his life is in proper relation to the ultimate Wisdom. No man can become wise save as there is in him the fear of the Lord. It is a great word, mystical and philosophical. There is never anything mighty or practical that does not grow out of the mystical and philosophical. It is equally true that everything profoundly mystical and philosophical issues in that which is mighty and practical.

We now turn to the arguments in illustration. Beginning with the eighth verse of the first chapter, all that remains of the book is of practical value and of present application as a permanent value and a present message. There is no single proverb in either of the two collections, the antithetical proverbs of the first, or the pictorial proverbs of the second, which has not a present value and a living message. For the purpose of this study we shall confine ourselves to the discourses of the first division of the book.

In these discourses the philosophy deals first with the child, then with the youth, and finally with the man. The whole world for the child is its home. The first movement outward is made in the finding of a friend, a companion. The boy finds his chum, the girl another girl to whom she can tell her secrets. Finally the youth passes out into the wonderland of the life of the city.

The first circle is that of the home. There wisdom must be learned. The next circle is that of friendship, companionship formed outside the home. There wisdom must be applied. Finally there come " the street . . . the broad places . . . the chief places of concourse . . . the entering in of the gates—the city." In the midst of the rush, and hurry, and hurly-burly of life wisdom must be obeyed.

The fundamental proposition is, " The fear of the Lord is the beginning of wisdom." In these discourses that declaration is applied to practical life. We begin in the home.

" My son, hear the instruction of thy father,
And forsake not the law of thy mother :
For they shall be a chaplet of grace unto thy head,
And chains about thy neck."

That is a beautiful picture of wisdom—the fear of the Lord taught to children at home. The subject of the responsibility of father and mother is not dealt with here, but it is taken for granted, and set upon the highest plane. The children are to hear the instruction of their father, and forsake not the law of their mother, in order that they may live in the fear of the Lord. Children are not able to grasp the thought of the Infinite.

For them God is incarnate in father and mother. That is the meaning of fatherhood and motherhood. I say that with all care. God created man in His own image—male and female created He them. Both are needed to reveal God. Jesus expressed the fact of motherhood in God, when He said : " How often would I have gathered thy children together, even as a hen gathereth her chickens under her wings." We need not be anxious to teach our children theology. Let us live in the fear of the Lord, and presently, by the ladder of their perfect confidence in us, they will climb to that apprehension of, and faith in God, which will be the rock of their strength to the end of time. Wisdom for children is contained in the instruction of father, and the law of mother.

The day must come when the child, in the realization of its own life, moves out into the wider circles of experience. The command to obey parents is not of force to the end of life. There are two very distinct words in the Bible about the duty of children to parents. *Obedience* is for the days of childhood. *Honour* is forever. There will come a day when the child has no longer to obey. It must begin to make its own choices, guided at first by parental council, but ultimately quite alone. When the child enters this second sphere, Wisdom is particularly careful to give instruction :

" My son, if sinners entice thee,
Consent thou not."

Then follows a list of friendships which are not to be made. The principles may thus be stated. Those who seek to enter into comradeship upon the basis of selfish interest, and by unscrupulous methods, are to be refused. All not excluded by that negative description are included. The glory and beauty of friendship is recognized by the very warnings uttered against those who are not true friends. There is no more important hour in the life of youth or maiden than that in which they begin to choose their companions. If that wisdom, which begins in the fear of the Lord, master the life, then such choices will be made as will contribute to strength of character.

At last there comes the day when the youth passes out into the street, the broad place, the chief place of concourse, at the gates, into the city itself. To him:

> " Wisdom crieth aloud in the street ;
> She uttereth her voice in the broad places ;
> She crieth in the chief place of concourse ;
> At the entering in of the gates,
> In the city, she uttereth her words."

The first word of wisdom to the youth going out from home, and beyond his first circle of friend-ships, into the wide world with its bustle and turmoil is a word of solemn warning against the evil of the way of those who have no fear of the Lord, who do not live in right relationship with Him, and a word of gracious promise :

> ' Whoso hearkeneth unto me shall dwell securely,
> And shall be quiet without fear of evil."

Wisdom does not call the youth back from the street and the place of concourse, and the crowds and busy life ; but warns him of the fate of those who enter those circumstances in forgetfulness of God, and declares that if he hearken to her, and live in the fear of the Lord, he will be quiet and safe, even in the turmoil of the city.

If the youth do not learn wisdom from father and mother, how terrible the start in the city is. He does not understand the voice of wisdom ; he cannot hear it. We must teach our children the language of wisdom before they pass out into the hurly-burly of life, or there they may fail to detect it. One, taught by father and mother, who has made his first friendships upon the basis of that instruction, passing into the city, hears and under-stands the cry of wisdom as through the ruin and failure she warns him, and declares that he shall be quiet and safe if he will be true to that fear of the Lord which is the beginning of wisdom. Let those who live in the villages, from which young lives are ever pouring into the cities, see to it that they are instructed in the fear of the Lord. If they come, having learned wisdom in the home, and having practiced it in the choosing of their first companions, all hell cannot ruin them. I am no more afraid for the young man who comes into London with the fear of God in his heart, than I am if he stays in the village. When I see young people entering the city from professing Christian homes, who yet have never been in-structed, and do not know the secrets of strength, then I tremble.

Then follows a series of discourses, all begin-ning with the words " My son." These constitute the voice of home sounding in the soul of the youth who has departed into the midst of life's hurry and bustle. The father tells how his father had taught him, and how he had been saved by the teaching, and had proved it true in the self-same rush of life. Then exhortation follows exhortation against impurity, against indolence, against bad companionships, against adultery.

Finally, I see the young man not merely facing the excitement of the city, but climbing towards high position ; and wisdom comes to him again in the most wonderful appeal the Bible utters, except that of the Voice which speaks the very language of humanity when at last Wisdom is incarnate.

The discourses close with a contrast most vivid and most remarkable. Wisdom and folly are each personified as a woman ; the first as a woman of virtue and beauty and glory, and the second as a woman of vice and ugliness and shame. In that superlative contrast there is figuratively set before young life the value and victory of wisdom, and the disaster and defeat of folly ; in other words, the wisdom of the fear of the Lord, and the folly of forgetfulness of God.

The living message is to be discovered in the permanent value. It finds its complete expres-sion in words as fresh as the day in which we live, though they come to us from the long gone centuries.

The precepts are stated thus :

> " My son, forget not my law ;
> But let thine heart keep my commandments :
> For length of days, and years of life,
> And peace, shall they add to thee.
> Let not mercy and truth forsake thee :
> Bind them about thy neck ;
> Write them upon the table of thine heart :
> So shalt thou find favour and good understanding
> In the sight of God and man."

The practice is enjoined thus :

> " Trust in the Lord with all thine heart,
> And lean not upon thine own understanding :
> In all thy ways acknowledge Him,
> And He shall direct thy paths.
> Be not wise in thine own eyes ;
> Fear the Lord, and depart from evil :
> It shall be health to thy navel,
> And marrow to thy bones.
>
> Honour the Lord with thy substance,
> And with the firstfruits of all thine increase :
> So shall thy barns be filled with plenty,
> And thy fats shall overflow with new wine."

That is not out of date. I remember well the date when I first left home for school. The last thing my father said to me was this : I want to give you a motto for life. " In all thy ways acknowledge Him, And He shall direct thy paths." One cannot give any boy a better motto. That is the beginning of wisdom. It is the qualification for becoming wise. A man in right relationship to God holds the key of all secrets.

I turn to the New Testament for the final words : " If any of you lacketh wisdom, let him ask of God, Who giveth to all liberally and upbraideth not." The word " wisdom " in that passage is the exact equivalent of the Old Testament word. There are different words translated " wisdom " both in the Old and New Testaments, but the Hebrew word in Proverbs is translated in the Septuagint by that actual word of which James makes use. The Hebrew philosophy is illuminated by the Christian conception in the writing of James. A little later, in his letter, he described the " wisdom that is from above " as "first pure, then peaceable, gentle, easy to be intreated, full of mercy and good fruits, without variance, without hypocrisy."

The selfsame word is used by Paul in the crowning epistle of his system. Concerning the Christ of God, he affirms : " In Whom are all the treasures of wisdom and knowledge hidden." And again concerning the Church, he declares : " And in Him ye are made full."

Thus to-day we begin according to the ancient philosophy : " The fear of the Lord is the beginning of wisdom " ; but the light about us is brighter than it was in the olden time. God has been manifest in flesh. By that unveiling we have had a revelation of God's wisdom ; and now for all time—at home, in our friendships, and in the midst of the city's rush and hurry—we listen for the voice of the Son of God ; and following the track of His footsteps, we come into the ultimate Wisdom slowly, for we also are ofttimes fools and blind, but surely, for He is forever the All-wise and the perfectly patient One.

Ecclesiastes

THE PERMANENT VALUES	THE LIVING MESSAGE

I. **The revelation of folly.**
  A. An oblique outlook at the universe—1:4—2:26.
  B. A misconception of God—3, 4.
    1. Government of forces.
    2. Abandonment of people—Jehovah absent.
  C. A religion of fear and fatalism—5, 6.
  D. An attitude of cynical indifference—7, 8.
  E. A narrow outlook—self-shadowed. ⎫
  F. A false earnestness.　　　　　　⎬ 9—11:8.
  G. A hopeless pessimism.　　　　　⎭
II. **The statement of wisdom.**
  A. The true order—11:9, 10.
  B. The true beginning—12:1, 12.
  C. The true wisdom—12:13, 14.
	I. **A principle recognized.**
	  A. Conviction affects character through conduct.
	  B. Conduct untrue to conviction is disaster.
	  C. Conduct guided by conviction is fulfillment.
	II. **An application.**
	  A. To dethrone God is to lose the key of life.
	  B. To enthrone God is to enter into life.

THE book of Ecclesiastes is the third and last of the wisdom books of the Old Testament. Its ultimate message is that of the book of Proverbs, which is epitomized in the words :—

> "Trust in the Lord with all thine heart,
> And lean not upon thine own understanding:
> In all thy ways acknowledge Him,
> And He shall direct thy paths."

In the last chapter and the closing verse of the book of Ecclesiastes, these words occur :

> "Fear God, and keep His commandments ; for this is the whole of man."

The word "duty" in our version is italicized, and we do well to omit it. It has no existence in the Hebrew text. The whole of man, then, is to "fear God, and keep His commandments." That expresses the same philosophy as that of Proverbs, though in different words.

What then is the difference between these two books? In Proverbs wisdom is first defined, and then her voice is heard throughout.

In Ecclesiastes we have something quite different. Wisdom is still essentially the same. In God it is His ultimate knowledge. In man,

therefore, it is the result of right relationship to God. While in Proverbs the way of wisdom is described, in Ecclesiastes the results of disobedience are set forth. In this book we have the revelation of the experience of a man who failed to fear the Lord, and therefore lost the key to the ultimate knowledge and wisdom. In the study of this book we must be clear in our own mind as to the difference between the time when it was written, and the time when the writer passed through the experiences he describes.

Ecclesiastes is not a diary. It is, as we saw when we studied its content, a sermon ; that is, one set discourse. The text is first given ; the introduction is in proper place ; and then the main body of the discourse proceeds in regular sequence to mass the evidence to the truth of the proposition of the text.

The attitude of the preacher must be understood, or we shall miss the value of the book. Through all his experiences he never lost his intellectual conviction of the existence of God. He was neither infidel nor agnostic. Unless a man profoundly believe in the existence of God, he will never say " Vanity of vanities, all is vanity " when he is trying to live without God. There is a deadly satisfaction possible to a man if he can once rid himself' of his belief in the existence of God. It is deadly because it is similar to the satisfaction resulting from the use of an opiate. All the restlessness of humanity is cause for thankfulness in that it reveals the underlying sense of God. All the sob and agony of Ecclesiastes is the outcome of the fact that the man whose experience it describes never questioned the existence of God.

Notwithstanding all this, the answering attitude of fear described in the book of Proverbs was absent. He believed in God, but lacked the fear which is the beginning of wisdom. He did not trust in Jehovah with all his heart. He did lean upon his own understanding. Believing in the existence of God, he did not in all his ways acknowledge Him, and consequently his paths lacked direction, and he wandered over trackless deserts in an agony of desire without satisfaction. The book of Ecclesiastes, therefore, is a mirror in which we see what life becomes when it is lived without submission to intellectual conviction.

The permanent values of the book are two. The first is that of the revelation of the vanity of life unyielded to God; and the second is that of a brief statement of what true wisdom is.

The revelation of the vanity of a godless life is sevenfold. In studying the preacher's account of his own experiences, we observe in him an oblique outlook upon the universe, a misconception of God, a religion of fear and fatalism, an attitude of cynical indifference, a narrow conception of life, a false earnestness and hopeless pessimism.

He had an oblique outlook upon the universe. This is the euphemistic method of expressing the truth. A friend of mine, discussing with me the brilliant articles which appeared in the *Spectator* in former days from the pen of Hutton, declared that while they still are full of fascination, as revelations of the times in which they were written, they are of no use to-day. When I asked him how he accounted for it, he bluntly replied, " Hutton squinted at everything." Not perfectly catching his meaning, he explained by saying that Hutton saw only one aspect of things, and, therefore, while his articles appealed to men who lived in the midst of the circumstances with

which he dealt, at the distance of a quarter of a century they are valueless. The book of Ecclesiastes gives us the picture of the universe, which results from this kind of outlook. This man saw its machinery, but not its motive. He looked intently, and discovered things the scientific accuracy of which it has taken centuries to discover—such as the fact that the winds move in circuits; that rivers rising in the mountains flow to the sea and return again. When he declared that all was vanity, he was oppressed with the constant grind of the machinery of the universe, and that because he had no communion with the Master Spirit controlling the machinery, or, as we have said, had no consciousness of the motive. If one having no knowledge of machinery should be placed in the midst of the flying spindles and turning wheels of a Lancashire cotton mill, he would in all probability be oppressed by the monotonous movement; but if that machinery is understood from the standpoint of the counting-house where the masters of the movement are directing, in order to the completion of the fabric which is to serve the purposes of countless multitudes, he would discover the music of the machinery. The outlook of the man whose life is not one of fellowship with God is oblique, and the result must inevitably be that of depression.

This outlook resulted in a misconception of God. Neglecting the primary matter of personal dealing with God, he looked out upon the world; and observing its natural phenomena and its social conditions, attempted to discover God through them, and thus came to his misconception. His observation did not allow him to deny the Divine government of the universe, but he only saw it as the government of forces, and so God became to him merely the presiding genius maintaining the movement of the machinery without any high purpose. Not recognizing that God has dealings with man in the highest things of his life, failing to discover the issue towards which all things are working, looking merely at them in their motion, he came to the conclusion that there was no advantage in wickedness or in goodness. All things happened to all men in the same way, whether they were wicked or good. His conception of God is clearly evidenced in the fact that the name Jehovah is never found in the book. Elohim, the word which indicates majesty and might, is the only one he made use of. He had no conception such as that indicated by the word Jehovah, which suggests the fact that God draws near in grace to human life, becoming to each individual what it needs for its perfecting.

As the result of this misconception of God, this man's religion was a religion of fear and fatalism. He tried everything—knowledge, mirth and licentiousness. He had considered the mechanism of the universe; he had observed the social oppression existing on every hand; then he declared his religious position. "Keep thy foot when thou goest to the house of God." It is perfectly true that there is an application of that word which we often make, and which is necessary and proper, that, namely, of insisting upon the necessity for reverence in the hour and the place of worship. It is perfectly certain, however, that the writer meant a great deal more than that. Having put God out of practical account in personal life, and having therefore come to a false conception concerning Him, the only thought of worship which remained to him was that of fear in a slavish sense. It was not that he was afraid of hurting God, but rather fear lest God should hurt him. His only idea, then, of religion was that, in the presence of the relentless might of God, it was wise to be careful. The whole truth is revealed in his sense of the distance of God; "God is in heaven, thou upon earth."

The outcome of all this was that he at last adopted an attitude of cynical indifference. He declared that it was best never to be amazed at anything. He urged men not to be troubled by the conditions of life existing around them. His whole philosophy may be expressed in the terms of advice with which we are familiar in our own day. Do not be surprised at anything; never be anxious; and above everything, do not be extremists. Notice well the calculating cynicism of the advice, "Be not righteous over-much. . . . Be not over-much wicked." Strike the happy medium, and let things alone. It was the attitude of cultivated indifference to conditions which have troubled, and it resulted from the fact that life was not considered in its personal, direct, immediate relationship to God.

The inevitable result was that his outlook was narrow. Wherever he looked he saw the shadow of his own personality. He had no vision of anything beyond the present world. Consequently

he dreaded death for the simple reason that it ended life. He considered that beyond death he would not be able to remember the things he had left behind. His conception of life was narrowed by geographical boundaries, and the limitations of the calendar.

Contentment with such a conception was impossible, and the outcome was false earnestness. This is expressed in the words, "Whatsoever thy hand findeth to do, do it with thy might; for there is no work, nor device, nor knowledge, nor wisdom, in the grave, whither thou goest." Again we have a quotation which we constantly make use of in an entirely different way from that intended by the writer, neither is it wholly unjustified. If there be the larger outlook on life, it is well that we do with our might whatever we find to do; but in the case of this man it was the last advice of pessimism. In view of the fact that there was nothing beyond the present life, he decided that the best thing possible was to make the most of the present life, to put all the forces of life into present realization.

The ultimate consequence of the process was that of the hopeless pessimism expressed in the text, "Vanity of vanities, all is vanity."

Here, then, is the permanent value of the book. It reveals the fact that if a man put God out of count in the actuality of his conduct, no matter how accurate his intellectual conviction may be, these things inevitably follow. His outlook upon the universe is oblique; he comes to a misconception of God; his religion becomes that of fear and fatalism; he presently assumes an attitude of cynical indifference; his conception of life is narrow; into the activities of the near things he puts deadly and disastrous earnestness; until at last, weary of everything, he exclaims: "Vanity of vanities, all is vanity."

The second supreme value of the book is its statement of what true wisdom is. "This is the end of the matter; all hath been heard; fear God, and keep His commandments; for this is the whole of man." The section which culminates in this declaration commences: "Rejoice, O young man, in thy youth; and let thy heart cheer thee in the days of thy youth, and walk in the ways of thine heart, and in the sight of thine eyes: but know thou, that for all these things God will bring thee into judgment." This passage again has received interpretation which is startlingly out of harmony with its simplest intention. In my study I have an old Encyclopædia of Sermonic Literature, and it is interesting to note the titles of sermons preached on this text, all of them more that thirty years ago. One will suffice as illustration: The Ironical Permission. As a matter of fact, there is no irony whatever in the text. It is a plain call to a young man to rejoice in his youth. The final declaration, "For all these things God will bring thee into judgment," is not intended to fill the heart with terror, but rather to indicate the true line of wisdom. God intends the young man to rejoice, and to enter into the world of hope and joy, but he must ever remember that all these capacities of his being must not be abused, because God will require account of the way in which His gifts have been used. The intention is exactly the same as that contained in the words of Proverbs:

> "Trust in the Lord with all thine heart,
> And lean not upon thine own understanding.
> In all Thy ways acknowledge Him,
> And He shall direct thy paths."

Finally, in the words of Ecclesiastes, already quoted: "This is the end of the matter; all hath been heard; fear God, and keep His commandments." To forget God is to enter into life, and to fail of all its profoundest value, until the heart cries out, "Vanity of vanities, all is vanity." To "fear God, and keep His commandments" is to enter into life, and to live in all the fullest sense of the word.

What, then, is the living message of this book? Surely it is declared when the permanent value is discovered. Yet let me attempt to state it briefly in other words. The first note of the message is that conviction affects character through conduct. We cannot escape from that, whether we be Christian or not. It is an eternal principle. Conduct untrue to conviction is destructive. Conduct guided by conviction is constructive. Conviction of God yielded to by the conduct of obedience produces the character of contentment and of strength. The same conviction disregarded in conduct issues in character of discontent and weakness.

In the book of Proverbs I find the white light, indicating the direction of wisdom.

In the book of Ecclesiastes I have the red light, revealing the way of vanity.

To dethrone God is to lose the key of life. Man may try knowledge, he may turn to mirth, he may employ wealth, he may—to use the thought of the writer, and the language of this century—see life; but if he attempt to enter into these things without God, he has lost the key, and the innermost shrines he cannot discover.

On the other hand, if in all his ways he acknowledge God, count Him, enthrone Him; then answering his intellectual conviction, he will find the key of life, and knowledge will become power, mirth a perpetual refreshment, wealth a means of helpfulness, and in all fullness he will see life.

These Old Testament teachings are all fulfilled in the New Testament. The whole philosophy is expressed in the words of Jesus: "This is life eternal, that they should know Thee the only true God, and Him Whom Thou didst send, even Jesus Christ." To know and obey Christ, and so to know and obey God, is to find all the doors of life open:

> "In Thy presence is fullness of joy;
> In Thy right hand there are pleasures forever-
> more."

Whatever may be the circumstances of the passing hours, wealth or poverty, adversity or prosperity, sunshine or shadow; out of all, the true values are obtained if God is enthroned. If not, then whatever path be chosen or course pursued, the ultimate language of experience will be: "Vanity of vanities, all is vanity."

Song of Songs

THE PERMANENT VALUES	THE LIVING MESSAGE

I. The revelation of the true nature of human love.
  A. The foundations of love; mutual satisfaction—2:2, 3.
    1. Complementary.
    2. Exclusive.
  B. The strength of love; indestructible—8:6, 7; an unquenchable flame.
  C. The methods of love.
    1. Male—irresistible, intense, and protective.
    2. Female—yielding, answering, and trusting.
  D. The experience of love.
    1. Rest.
    2. Joy.
    3. Courage.
II. The unveiling of religious experience.
  A. The vindication of this value.
    1. The Old Testament.
      a. Chaldee Targum.
      b. Psalm 45.
      c. Hosea, Isaiah, Jeremiah, and Ezekiel.
    2. The New Testament—Eph. 5:25-32.
  B. The application.
    1. The foundations of love.
    2. The strength of love.
    3. The methods of love.
    4. The experience of love.
	I. "The Greatest is love."
	  A. In human interrelationships.
	  B. In the ultimate of human life, which is religion.
	II. Therefore:
	  A. Sanctify your human love by the ultimate.
	  B. Interpret your religious life in terms of human love.
	    1. Passion.
	    2. Abandonment.
	    3. Fidelity.

THERE is no book in the Old Testament more easy to deal with in regard to its message than the Song of Songs, if we accept one very simple canon of interpretation. That is to be found in our lecture on the content of the book. Let me, therefore, repeat the words of one brief paragraph therefrom :

" The songs should be treated first as simple and yet sublime songs of human affection. When they are thus understood, reverently the thoughts may be lifted into the higher value of setting forth the joys of the communion between the spirit of man and the Spirit of God, and ultimately between the Church and Christ."

To take this view of the Song of Solomon is to recognize the supremacy of love. Human life finds its highest fulfillment in the love of man and woman. The supreme thing in religion is love between the soul and God. The highest realization of that supreme experience of love between God and the soul is created by Christ. In Him, God came near to man in order to woo him. In Him, man came to know God and to love Him. Therefore I can sing the songs of Solomon, as did the mystics, as setting forth the relationship between Christ and His bride.

Still to my amazement I hear the Bridegroom singing :

" As a lily among thorns,
So is my love among the daughters."

Still I hear the bride replying :

" I sat down under his shadow with great delight,
And his fruit was sweet to my taste.
He brought me to the banqueting house,
And his banner over me was love."

Still I hear the mystic language both of bride and bridegroom as each of the other declares, " My beloved is mine."

In the first place, this was undoubtedly an earthly love-song, but it was very pure and very beautiful. There are men and women who would find indecencies in heaven—if they ever got there—but they would take them in their own corrupt souls. To those who live lives of simple purity, these songs are full of beauty, as they utter the language of human love; and finally, in spiritual experience, they express the relation of such as have been wooed by God in Christ, and thus have come to know and love Him.

The permanent values of the Song are two. It is, first, a revelation of the true nature of human love. It is, secondly, an unveiling of the highest religious experience.

The mode of expression is peculiarly Eastern. There are no neutral tints. My artist friends must be patient with me if I declare myself Philistine enough to believe that neutral tints are evidences of a decadent age. This Song of Solomon is magnificent in its gorgeous colours, in its high figures of speech, in the prodigality of its protestations. If there be no mystical value in the book, it is yet full of human interest. It is only in the atmosphere created by such flaming colour, superlative utterance, and overwhelming audacity, that it is possible ultimately to appreciate the strength of love. The cool, calculating, mechanical man who dislikes this book has never been in love, and probably never will be.

Beginning, then, with this acceptance of the book as a collection of human love-songs, I find that it reveals much concerning the nature of love which is of supreme importance. The foundation of love is laid bare. The strength of love is revealed. The methods of love are indicated. The experience of love is described.

Through all the words which Solomon and the Shulammite utter, each to the other, there breathes the spirit of mutual satisfaction. In that the very foundation of love is laid bare. Those standing without may be unable to see the reason why each finds perfect rest in the other. That inability does not alter the fact. And that fact is the fundamental one in love. Joseph Cook, of Boston, in his second lecture on " Infidel Attack on the Family," declared that a supreme affection is the only natural basis of marriage, and that supreme affection can only exist between two. In all the songs of bride and bridegroom throughout this book that supreme affection is manifest. In this fact they illuminate the original Divine purpose of love between man and woman as the basis of marriage. As we have said, the fact is evident through all the songs. One or two brief quotations by way of illustration will suffice.

" As a lily among thorns,
So is my love among the daughters."

That is the language of a man in love.

" As the apple tree among the trees of the wood,
So is my beloved among the sons."

That is the answer of the woman's love. The whole passage finely illustrates the meaning of supreme affection between two. In each case love is absolutely exclusive. Each sees the other as the only one. By the side of the lily, to the spirit of the man, all others are as thorns. To the vision of the woman one tree is supreme in glory and beauty, while all the rest are massed as "the trees of the wood." This kind of love is not born amid the feverish excitement of a London season. Neither does it result from inane trifling with the subject of love and marriage. Love at its highest is supreme affection between two. Love at its deepest is the unreasoned but absolute mutual satisfaction of one woman and one man in each other.

The strength of love is fully revealed throughout the songs. One passage will suffice by way of illustration :

" Set me as a seal upon thine heart, as a seal upon thine
    arm :
For love is strong as death ;
Jealousy is cruel as the grave :
The flashes thereof are flashes of fire,
A very flame of the Lord.
Many waters cannot quench love,
Neither can the floods drown it :
If a man would give all the substance of his house for
    love,
He would utterly be contemned."

No exposition is needed of this passage, so clear and forceful is it in its setting forth of the overwhelming and all-victorious strength of true love. In Paul's classic description of love there is one simple statement into which all this teaching is concentrated, so that it flashes with the lustre of diamonds :—

" Love never faileth."

That supreme and all-inclusive truth of the strength of love is illustrated throughout the whole of these songs.

The methods of love are revealed, as through the idyllic nature of the book the story of the wooing and betrothal, the marriage and the after life is told. Inspired by love, Solomon is irresistible, and to the strength of that appeal of love the Shulammite yields, not weakly, but with a strength that is only overcome by the supremacy of love. In every sentence that falls from his lips, Solomon reveals the intensity of his devotion, to the appeal of which the Shulammite answers with intensity more quiet but none the less strong. Finally, in all his attitude, Solomon is overshadowing and protective, and the Shulammite rests in his shadow with great delight, in perfect security.

The experience of love is that of rest, joy, and courage. Each finds in the other the place of that perfect content which is of the essence of rest, and which cannot be disturbed by storm or tempest. In the fullness of love there is abiding gladness, which fills the heart with songs, and flings its light upon all circumstances, so that the grayest day is illumined, and the roughest sackcloth is transfigured into the glory of the purple. In the union of the strength of the love of each there is courage, which enables both to face all circumstances without faltering, and side by side to win every contested field, or even out of defeat to gather values which are of the essence of victory.

If this, then, is only a human love song, would to God that those who know its strength would sing it in the highways and byways, to recall men and women from superficial and frivolous thinking about love, to a true conception of its height and depth and beauty.

Three times the singer breaks in upon the songs of the bride and bridegroom, and always with the same words :

" I adjure you, O daughters of Jerusalem,
By the roes, and by the hinds of the field,
That ye stir not up, nor awaken love
Until it please."

Thus suddenly, in the midst of the music, there is a pause, and the voice of the singer is heard in interpretation and warning. The method is not that of melody or of harmony, but rather that of recitative, in which at the end of the marriage, between the wooing and the betrothal, and in the midst of the united life the revealing caution is uttered. I would that the interrupting charge might be inscribed in letters of fire, and hung in every hall where young people assemble. In the presence of the glory of love it warns them not to trifle with the most sacred thing in life. Thus, as a song of human love only, it is chief of all the songs of human life, in very deed the Song of Songs.

It is when we thus see the beauty of it in its first application that we discover how wondrously it flashes its light upon the vaster spaces, and inevitably becomes the unveiling of religious experience at its highest and best. I do not hesitate to affirm that I believe this was the ultimate intention of the writer. It is an interesting fact that the Chaldee Targum contains a Jewish commentary on the book, the title of which reads : " The songs and hymns which Solomon, the prophet-king of Israel, delivered by the spirit of prophecy before Jehovah, the Lord of the whole earth." That title being, as we have said, not Christian but Jewish, is most suggestive. It describes Solomon, not as a king merely, but as a prophet-king, and justly affirms that the songs and hymns were delivered by the spirit of prophecy, and, moreover, that they were delivered before Jehovah, the Lord of the whole earth. If Solomon wrote of human love, he nevertheless sang before Jehovah. The undoubted thought of that ancient title is that the songs had a spiritual significance.

This interpretation is warranted, moreover, by the fact that the writers of the Old Testament dealt with the relationship between God and His ancient people as that between husband and wife. In the psalm which bears the title " A song of loves," in which the writer declares that he speaks of the things which he has made touching the king, both the king in his glory and the queen in her beauty are described. The whole of the prophecy of Hosea is based upon this great conception, and in some of the greatest passages in the writings of Isaiah, Jeremiah, and Ezekiel, the same illustration is used.

If we pass from the Old Testament Scriptures

to those of the New, we find in the crowning letter of Paul's system a passage in which, in order to state the marriage relationship on the highest plane, the apostle applies the same thought to the relation between Christ and His Church :—

" Husbands, love your wives, even as Christ also loved the Church, and gave Himself up for it ; that He might sanctify it, having cleansed it by the washing of water with the Word, that He might present the Church to Himself a glorious Church, not having spot or wrinkle or any such thing ; but that it should be holy and without blemish. Even so ought husbands also to love their own wives as their own bodies. He that loveth his own wife loveth himself : for no man ever hated his own flesh ; but nourisheth and cherisheth it, even as Christ also the Church · because we are members of His body. . . . This mystery is great : but I speak in regard of Christ and of the Church."

Thus the Hebrew writers used the figure to indicate the relation between God and His people ; and the great exponent of Christian truth shows how the ideal is perfectly realized in the relation between Christ and His Church.

If then we are justified in discovering in these songs language which may be used as setting forth the relationship between Christ and His people, we may take the revelations of human love which they convey, and use them as both revealing and expressing the perfections of that communion. The foundation of the love existing between Christ and His own is that of mutual satisfaction. As to our satisfaction in Him nothing need be written. We constantly give expression to the truth :

> " Thou, O Christ, art all I want,
> More than all in Thee I find."

The thought that He finds satisfaction in us is one which must fill us with perennial astonishment, but it is none the less true. Even if to-day we fail to see the glory of His perfected work in us, it is nevertheless true that in His redeemed at last He shall see of the travail of His soul, and be satisfied. That mutual satisfaction is the very foundation of love. Let each express it in individual language. I am satisfied in Him, and He is satisfied in me ; not in me as I now am, but in that which He will make me, in that which I shall be, when His work is perfected in me.

Of the strength of the love nothing finer can be said than by quotation of the actual words of the song :

> " Love is strong as death. . . .
> Many waters cannot quench love,
> Neither can the floods drown it."

As to His love for us, the Cross is the literal and actual proof of these words. As for us, in proportion as we yield ourselves to the constraint of His love, it becomes true that

> " Many waters cannot quench love,
> Neither can the floods drown it."

The methods of love suggested in the song perfectly interpret the methods of Christ with us, and our methods with Him. All who know Him are conscious of the irresistible nature of His love. It was and is to that we yield ourselves as we sing :

> " Nay, but I yield, I yield,
> I can hold out no more ;
> I sink, by dying love compelled,
> And own Thee Conqueror."

Moreover, of the intensity of His love it is impossible to speak ; but in its approach, in its constant method, we are forever conscious of it. Our love to Him has the same note of intensity in proportion as we yield in whole-hearted abandonment to the appeal of His. His love of us is ever that of the overshadowing and protective One. All the words of the song only find their perfect fulfillment in those who know and trust Him, and are able to say :

> " I sat down under his shadow with great delight. . . .
> He brought me to the banqueting house,
> And his banner over me was love."

Finally, in this mutual love of Christ and His people, there is the same threefold experience of rest, joy, and courage. Zephaniah, in the sweetest song of the Old Testament, which sets forth the love of God for His people, declared :

> " He will rejoice over thee with joy ;
> He will rest in His love,
> He will joy over thee with singing."

Thus, as we let this song sing to us in all its purity and strength, the story of human love on its highest level, it inevitably lifts us on wings into a more perfect understanding of the relationship between Christ and His own.

If these be the permanent values, what is the living message of this book? This may be stated in few words. The book declares to-day the truth embodied in the word of Paul: "The greatest of these is love." Love is the greatest fact in all human interrelationships. It is the greatest experience in the spiritual realm. It is religion. That surely was the meaning of our Lord's words, when He said: "Thou shalt love the Lord thy God with all thy heart, and with all thy soul, and with all thy mind. This is the great and first commandment. And a second like unto it is this, Thou shalt love thy neighbour as thyself."

The final living message of the book is twofold. First, human love should ever be sanctified by the thoughts of the ultimate love which it illustrates. All things on earth have relationships stretching out into the infinite and eternal. There should be—and, indeed, there can be—no perfect human love which does not harmonize with the spiritual and the Divine.

Secondly, we must attempt to interpret our religious life in the terms of our human love. Its terms are those of passion, abandonment, and fidelity, the burning flame which pours life right out in service, and keeps it true. If we may but come to such realization of our fellowship with the Lord as to express our love to Him on this wise, what a change will be wrought.

Thus we admit that the Song of Solomon is an Eastern love song, and if no more than that, it is full of beauty, and full of value; but because it is so perfectly a human love song, and because human love is offspring of the Divine love, the song reaches out and carries us with it to higher heights, forever helping us to understand the final experiences of the soul in religion, those of the love of God for us, and our love for God.

Isaiah

THE PERMANENT VALUES	THE LIVING MESSAGE

I. Government.
  A. The principles.
    1. Holiness—the inspiration.
    2. Righteousness—the activity.
    3. Justice—the method.
  B. The methods.
    1. Revelation.
    2. Explanation.
    3. Application.
  C. The characteristics.
    1. Patience.
    2. Persistence.
    3. Power.
II. Grace.
  A. The principle of the principles.
    1. Human sin violates the principles.
    2. The cross in the experience of God expresses His unutterable sorrow.
  B. The method of the methods.
    1. Human salvation depends upon submission to the method.
    2. The cross in the activity of God expresses His unsearchable grace.
  C. The character of the characteristics.
    1. Human destiny is determined by response to the characteristics.
    2. The cross in its effect on man expresses the unquenchable love of God.
	I. Fundamentals.
	  A. Submission to government.
	  B. Salvation by grace.
	II. The interrelation.
	  A. To government for grace.
	  B. In grace for government.

THE section of the Divine library containing the prophetic writings speaks with no uncertain sound to our own age.

We begin with the prophecy of Isaiah. Its message concerns the Throne, and was spoken to the nation.

Isaiah, in common with all the prophets, had practically nothing to say to men about individual relationship to God. Of course he never lost sight of the importance of individual life in order to the strength of national life; but he was preëminently dealing with the nation as a nation.

The content of the first section of the book reveals the fact that, in the economy of God, judgment ever proceeds to peace. It is important to recognize that judgment beyond this life is not in view. The prophet deals with judgment here and now. Let no one misunderstand this statement. I am not denying the fact of judgment beyond this life, but only pointing out that such judgment is not that to which the prophet refers in this book. It is rather the judgment of God in this world proceeding to the establishment of peace in this world.

So also in the final section of the book, which teaches that peace is ever based on righteousness, the application of the teaching is to a peace experienced in this world, upon the basis of righteousness established in this world. The prophet's outlook is never upon the life that lies beyond.

The permanent value of the book then is that it reveals the abiding Throne of God; and the principles of its activity in the affairs of men. The living message of the book is immediately dependent upon this revelation. As we stand in the light of the unveiled Throne, we are brought to an understanding of man's relation to that Throne; not merely a revelation of what his relation ought to be, but a revelation of what it is, for no man can escape the government of God either in this life or in that which is to come.

If I were asked to choose from this prophecy the two chapters which are supreme, because they fling their light upon all the rest, I should choose the sixth and the fifty-third, which respectively bring us into the presence of the Throne; and reveal to us the suffering of the Servant of God in Whom the authority of the Throne is vested.

The vision of the Throne was given to Isaiah in the year in which King Uzziah died. He had lived in the consciousness of that Throne before, but when the earthly throne became vacant, there came to him a new unveiling of the Throne which is never vacant. All the life of Isaiah had been lived in the reign of Uzziah. He had never known another king. Those of us who lived all the first part of our lives in the reign of Victoria can a little understand the prophet's experience. I well remember that there came a strange and almost weird sense of emptiness into my life when I saw on the placards that Victoria had passed away. I had never known any other sovereign on the throne, and it was with a strange sense of loss that I thought of the nation bereft of its queen. So Isaiah must have felt at the death of Uzziah. Then God gave him a special vision of the Throne that is always filled. That vision lifted his ministry on to a higher plane, and its central note and perpetual message became that of the unveiled Throne.

Concerning that Throne there are two great facts which this prophecy presents to us. First, that of government, and secondly, that of grace. These are evident, and the statement savours of the commonplace; but Isaiah was preëminently the prophet of the commonplace. That

was the complaint which the men of his day made against him. In words full of contempt they enquired, " Whom will he teach knowledge? and whom will he make to understand the message? them that are weaned from the milk, and drawn from the breasts? For it is precept upon precept, precept upon precept; line upon line, line upon line; here a little, there a little." All this was the language of satirical contempt. The prophet's answer was, in effect, a declaration of the fact that they needed this very teaching and this method, and their failure resulted from their forgetfulness of the simplest first facts of their national existence.

This in itself creates the pertinence of the message of this book to our own age. There is nothing we need more than a restatement of the first principles of life; and these are those of the Throne of God in its government and grace.

The study of the book reveals the principles, methods, and characteristics of government; and the principle, method, and character of grace. This phrasing in itself suggests that while the supreme teaching is that of the government of God, the profoundest revelation is that such government is inspired and unified by His grace. From first to last we hear from the Throne the thunderings of authority, and also the tender dominant note of love. If I were asked to select from the New Testament some one passage which would give expression to the inclusive revelation of the prophecy of Isaiah, I should quote from the revelation of John, " A throne . . . and . . . in the midst of the throne . . . a Lamb." In the sixth chapter of the prophecy we see the throne; in the fifty-third, the Lamb.

First, then, as to government. The first reading of the book of Isaiah would inevitably leave upon the mind the impression of government rather than that of grace. By that I do not intend to suggest that grace is a secondary matter. It will certainly be admitted that the deepest meaning of any book which is really worth reading is not discovered at the first. It is equally true that that profounder meaning can only be reached by the reception of the first impression, and the investigation which such an impression compels. I repeat then, that the stately imagery, the finished rhetoric, and the overwhelming splendour of this prophecy must necessarily impress the mind in the first place with the fact of government.

As we have indicated, a consideration of the teaching of this book concerning the Divine government reveals its principles, its methods, its characteristics.

As to the principles, three words will cover the ground : holiness, righteousness, and justice ; holiness being the inspiration, righteousness the activity, and justice the result. It may be objected that we have omitted mercy. As a matter of fact, in the economy of God, justice and mercy are synonymous terms. Their separation is a violation of the true moral order. When justice and mercy meet together, and righteousness and peace kiss each other, it may be a surprising thing to those who have had long acquaintance with injustice, but the meeting in each case is really the restoration of a lost harmony. In the midst of the chaos of social conditions today, absolute justice is the mercy for which the world waits. All who know what it is to rejoice in the mercy of God which has brought salvation, know also that their rejoicing is based upon the fact that mercy acts in justice. God is " just, and the Justifier of him that hath faith in Jesus."

The revelation of holiness in the book of Isaiah is fundamental. The expression, " The Holy One of Israel " is almost peculiar to this book. The song of the seraphim as they worshipped in the presence of the King Who occupied the uplifted Throne celebrated the profoundest fact of His being, " Holy, holy, holy, is Jehovah of hosts." That holiness is the ceaseless inspiration of His government. The word holiness was not peculiar to the Hebrew people. It obtained in the language of all forms of idolatry, but it did not suggest in them what it does in Isaiah's use of it. Its root significance is that of separation, distance. Isaiah's conception of God was one which revealed the deepest significance of this fact of separation, that, namely, of the essential, unquestioned purity of God. This is proved by the effect the consciousness produced in the mind of the prophet which drew from him the cry, " I am a man of unclean lips." Holiness then, as purity, is the inspiration of the Divine government.

Therefore the activity of that government is always that of righteousness. All conduct is the outcome of character, and where the character is holy, the conduct is righteous. Because God is holy, He does righteously.

The inevitable result is that of justice. In all the dealings of God, both with His own people and with the surrounding nations there is clearly manifest a fine and poetic justice. In the great impeachment of the nation contained in the first chapter this fact is really involved in words which do not at first seem to suggest it. Jehovah appealed to His people, " Come now, and let us reason together," and thereby claimed that His dealing with them was that of justice. The prophet described the people as bruised and broken from the crown of the head to the sole of the foot by the chastisements of Jehovah, and cried to them, " Why will ye be still stricken, that ye revolt more and more ? "

The reason of their chastisement was their revolt, and therefore their chastisement resulted not from arbitrary, capricious punishment, but from the necessity of eternal justice. If they could but have been brought to such consciousness of this fact as would have resulted in the ending of their revolt, the chastisement would have been removed, and healing would have followed. That was the significance of the Divine call, " Come now, and let us reason together."

Thus the principles of government are seen to be those of holiness as inspiration, righteousness as activity, and justice as result.

Turning to the consideration of the methods of the Divine government, we find them to be those of revelation, explanation, and application. The complaint of the prophet against the chosen people was, as we have seen, that they had been disobedient. Disobedience is only possible where there is knowledge of law, and knowledge of law involves revelation. The nation had been created by revelation. God had unveiled Himself to them through all their history, and made known His will by words and by messengers. Throughout the whole of his ministry Isaiah kept this fact of the Divine method before the mind of those to whom he spoke. The study of this book has, as one of its supreme values, the presentation of the Servant of God, first in dim, shadowy, mysterious outline ; finally in clear and accurate manifestation. So remarkably is this true that if we study the portraiture of the Servant of Jehovah as we have it in the prophecy of

Isaiah, and then that which we find in the Gospel stories, we find they coincide line for line, glory for glory, beauty for beauty. God's first method of government is that of revealing Himself to men by voices, by visions; and ultimately in the one inclusive manifestation of that Servant Who is the final Speech of God.

His method is not only that of revelation, it is also that of explanation. It is impossible to study the messages of this book without being impressed with the fact that God is ever at infinite pains to explain to men what He is doing with them either in punishment or in healing. He comes to the level of man in order that there may be no misconception of His purpose. It is quite conceivable that it may be declared that this is exactly what God does not do to-day. He seems strangely silent, and there is no immediate explanation of His meaning or of His method. As a matter of fact, He is working and explaining, but men are neither looking for Him nor listening to Him. Perhaps an illustration from another of the prophets may help us at this point. When Habakkuk was filled with trouble because it seemed to him that God was silent and inactive, God said to him in effect, I am at work, but if I told you what I am doing you would not believe it. When God declared that He was girding Cyrus, and using him for the accomplishment of His purpose, the prophet was more than ever astonished. All of which suggests that God is always at work, and, moreover, makes known His ways to such as listen. As well as by His acts, God is directly speaking to men and explaining to them His purposes in the daily newspapers, but they do not dream of seeking His messages therein. We do not read our newspapers from that high standpoint. We read them rather from the midst of dust, and the dust gets in our eyes and on their pages. Thus, all the while we do not see the flaming letters of God's revelation for looking at the lying letters of men's printing. In those days Isaiah was explaining the method of God, and yet men declared that he had nothing to teach them.

The final fact in the method of God is that of application. He is seen as actively interfering. One illustration of this will suffice. It is that of the word spoken to Cyrus, a man outside the covenant, "I have called thee. . . . I will gird thee, though thou hast not known Me."

This is a clear instance of this supreme truth that God has in no sense abandoned the world; but that for the fulfillment of His purpose, He takes hold of men and makes them all, if unconsciously, yet definitely, contribute to its carrying out. He makes the wrath of men to praise Him, and the remainder He restrains.

Finally, we come to the characteristics of the Divine government as revealed in this prophecy. The first is that of patience. God ever gives His people opportunity to return to loyalty. The second is that of persistence. He never makes terms with sin by condoning it, excusing it, or signing a truce with it. The third is that of power. He is forevermore revealed as irresistibly moving forward towards the accomplishment of His will. All these characteristics are revealed most forcefully in the description involved in the great passage, "Who among us shall dwell with the devouring fire? who among us shall dwell with everlasting burnings?" A study of these enquiries in the light of their context will show that to the mind of the prophet, God, full of patience, was persistent and powerful; and he saw the cities of sin, and the foes of right, and the enemies of God, being consumed in the fire of His presence, even in the hour when they imagined they were strong. To the clear vision of this man, God was everywhere as a fire, irresistible, searching, burning, destroying, even though men were unconscious of the fact.

Turning from this consideration of the revelation of government, to seek for that of grace, we find it everywhere. It is the principle of the principles, the method of the methods, the character of the characteristics. All the principles with which we have dealt in the consideration of the government of God are but the manifestations of this one inclusive principle. The supreme reason of the Divine holiness is the Divine love. The supreme inspiration of the Divine righteousness is the Divine love. The supreme certainty of the Divine justice is the Divine love. As we carefully study the prophecy and listen to the complaints of Jehovah, while they reverberate in thunder, they thrill with the tenderness of tears. In the first impeachment we find the words, "I have nourished and brought up children, and they have rebelled against Me." "They have rebelled against Me," that is the word of thunder. "I have nourished and brought up children." In that there is the tenderness of tears. It is the wail of the heart of the Father. It is the revelation of the Cross in the experience of God, the language of unutterable sorrow. May I dare to illustrate by quotation of a word from literature on an infinitely lower level ?

" How sharper than a serpent's tooth it is
To have a thankless child."

God's use of the word " children " is eloquent of the deepest fact in all the processes of His government. As I behold the activity of the Throne, whether in its inspiration of holiness, its activity of righteousness, or its result of justice, I discover that which lies deeper and makes necessary all this, the grace of God, the love of God. It is when this is most clearly seen that sin is known to be most damnable, because in the light of this revelation we understand that sin causes sorrow to the heart of God. That declaration cannot be contradicted in the light of New Testament teaching. One of the supreme injunctions to the saints is "Grieve not the Holy Spirit," and it is well that we remind ourselves of that which has been so often pointed out, that the literal and more expressive translation of that passage is Cause not sorrow to the Spirit of God. Thus, at the very beginning, before the awful thunder of the Throne is heard, or at least with its first reverberation, we hear the tone of infinite grace and infinite love.

Not only is grace the principle of the principles, it is also the method of the methods. Grace is the cause of revelation, the reason of explanation, and the perpetual motive of application. On the uplifted Throne is the One Whose worship in the songs of the seraphim causes the very foundations of the temple to shake ; but He is One Who hears the sigh of the sinning soul above the music of the seraphim, and the knowledge of the deepest fact of His being causes one of the flaming ones to cease his singing that he may catch the live coal from the altar, and swiftly pass with it to touch the lips of the sinning man in order to their cleaning. Thus, all the methods of His government are the result of the method of His grace.

Finally, grace is the character of the characteristics. The characteristics of government are those of patience, persistence, and power ; and these result from the essential character of love.

Grace is the reason of patience, the inspiration of persistence, and the passion of power. Human salvation must result from response to that love which first expresses itself in a veritable sob of anguish in the presence of sin, and then through suffering which cannot be measured makes possible the return and renewal of the sinner. If one is tempted to suggest that I am reading into this prophecy of Isaiah the revelation of the New Testament, I would reply, I am but retaining in the prophecy its own fifty-third chapter. In the New Testament itself there is no passage more full of flashing and revealing light concerning the grace of God than that wonderful chapter.

In this book, then, I see the Throne high lifted, and know that it is the Throne of active and determined government ; but I also know that the inspiration of its government is love.

The living message of this book to our own age is that submission to the government of God is the one sufficient condition for the fulfillment of all human life, whether it be social, national or racial. It declares, moreover, that the only hope of the restoration of man, bruised and broken by sin, is centred in the grace of God.

The message of the book, therefore, is finally that of the revelation of the interrelation between government and grace. It makes it impossible for us to separate these, or to consider them as though they were opposed to each other. In order to reap the benefits of the grace of God, it is necessary to submit to His government. In order to submit to the government of God, we must be prepared to receive the benefits of His grace. Grace is not an activity of God whereby He vacates His Throne. All the riches of grace are at our disposal as we kiss the sceptre and bow to the Throne.

Having been brought by grace into right relationship to government, through submission to government in order to the reception of the gifts of grace, we live henceforth within that government in the power of that grace. We submit to His government and enter into His grace. We stand in His grace in order to obey His government.

The revelation of this book is that of the Throne of God. It matters not where we open it, whether we read the message of fiery denunciation, or the song of the coming deliverance ;

whether we hear the chariot wheels of swift and awful judgment, or listen to the song that heralds the dawning of the day of restoration; in every case, message or song comes from the Throne. The Presence occupying the Throne cannot be defined, but in the midst is a Lamb as it had been slain. "He was wounded for our transgressions, He was bruised for our iniquities: the chastisement of our peace was upon Him."

Jeremiah

THE PERMANENT VALUES	THE LIVING MESSAGE

I. Jehovah's judgment of sin—denunciation.
  A. The impeachment—2:8, 19, 35.
  B. The process—failing kings and policies.
  C. Jeremiah, Jehovah's spokesman—alone, unheeded, persecuted, but persistent.
II. Jehovah's suffering for sin—lamentation.
  A. The man of His appointing shrinking.
  B. The man of His making identified with the sorrow—the interpretation in Jesus.
  C. Jeremiah, Jehovah's spokesman—shrinking, sorrowful, in profoundest fellowship with God.
III. Jehovah's victory over sin—sustentation.
  A. The activity of supremacy (see Isa. 63:1-7)—the house of the potter.
  B. The prophecies of hope.
    1. Uttered in prison.
    2. Through trouble in triumph.
    3. The days of the branch.
  C. Jeremiah, Jehovah's spokesman—uttering out of the midst of sin and sorrow, the songs of sure victory.
	I. Sin is sure destruction.
	  A. No policy can out-manoeuver God.
	  B. National rebellion is national ruin.
	II. The heart of God is wounded by sin.
	  A. Judgment is His strange act.
	  B. He weeps over the doom sin brings.
	III. The victory is with God.
	  A. He will make it again.
	  B. His branch is appointed.

THERE is no prophetic book concerning which it is more necessary that we have in mind the times and the man if we are to discover its permanent value and its living message.

These general facts are indicated in the opening sentences of our lecture upon the content of the book, "Jeremiah was Jehovah's spokesman in days of darkness and disaster." That is a very brief, but all-inclusive sentence reminding us of the times in which these words were uttered, and revealing the authority of the man who uttered them. The times were days of darkness and disaster. The man was Jehovah's spokesman. Let us then remind ourselves of the times which in a sentence are described as days of darkness and disaster. Jeremiah exercised his prophetic ministry in Judah about a century after Isaiah had delivered his last message. The Northern

kingdom of Israel had passed away, and the whole attention is centred upon Judah. Two nations affected her at the time; on the south, Egypt, and on the east, Assyria. During the time that Jeremiah exercised his ministry Judah was attempting either to play these off one against the other, or was hesitating as to which she should make an alliance with, in order to protect herself from the enmity of the other. A recognition of these facts will enable us to understand the reason of the terrible condition in which she found herself. Her vision of God was dimmed, if she had not lost it altogether. Her hope lay not in Him, her one and only King, but in her ability either to stir up strife between these two nations, or to secure the aid of one against the other. Her internal condition was equally terrible. Isaiah had delivered his great messages in Hezekiah's reign. Immediately succeeding Hezekiah Manasseh came to the throne. Notwithstanding the fact that there was a place of repentance found for him, his reign was characterized by reaction from the influence of Hezekiah ; he set up altars and idolatry even in the courts of the house of the Lord. The nation sank lower and lower. The brief reign of Amon was a failure. Then followed the period of Josiah. When he had been upon the throne for twelve or thirteen years Jeremiah commenced his ministry, which lasted at least forty-six years, being exercised through the reigns of Josiah, Jehoahaz, Jehoiakim, Jehoiachin and Zedekiah, and during the early part of the exile. It is but to name these kings to be reminded of the darkness of the days. The national movement was downward, the people sinking ever lower. The reform under Josiah was entirely upon the surface of things so far as the people were concerned. There was no vital change wrought in their character. Jehoahaz reigned for thirteen months in the midst of evil of every description. Under Jehoiakim, evil became even more widespread, and deeper. Jehoiachin reigned briefly and was deposed. Then came Zedekiah, a man meaning well, but preëminently weak, and the vassal of another nation. Never for one single moment during the forty or more years of his ministry did Jeremiah arrest the downward progress of the people ; never by anything he said, never by anything he suffered, never by anything he did was he able to check that deterioration. The description of the darkness of the times has thus been given by Dr. Moorehead :

"It was Jeremiah's lot to prophesy at a time when all things in Judah were rushing down to the final and mournful catastrophe ; when political excitement was at its height ; when the worst passions swayed the various parties, and the most fatal counsels prevailed ; . . . to . . . see his own people, whom he loved with the tenderness of a woman, plunge over the precipice into the wide, weltering ruin."

No words could more graphically portray the times. The prophesying of other men always seems to have produced periods of reformation. Even if Isaiah had at last to say, "Who hath believed our report? and to whom hath the arm of the Lord been revealed?" his influence was nevertheless manifest in Hezekiah, and in the reformation under him. Jeremiah, on the other hand, watched the ruin of his people, saw them rush headlong to the final calamity, constantly uttering the word of God to them out of a heart filled with despair.

Then also we must look at Jeremiah himself. It is not carelessly that I have described him as the spokesman of Jehovah. It is quite impossible to lay any great emphasis on the full meaning of his name simply because no one knows exactly what its real significance was. There is, however, one quantity included in it concerning which there can be no question. It has been suggested that the name means Jehovah appointed. Hengstenberg affirmed that it signified Jehovah throws, the idea being that of God throwing and overthrowing, Jeremiah being the instrument of His activity. It has also been declared that the name means Jehovah exalts. Yet again there are those who maintain, and I personally incline to this view, that the name signified Jehovah founded. Without laying undue emphasis upon that, however, it is noticeable that every suggestion relates the man to Jehovah, whether the thought be appointed, or throws, exalts, or founded. Moreover, that declaration is made in the opening chapter of the prophecy :

"Now the word of Jehovah came unto me, saying, Before I formed thee in the belly I knew thee, and before thou camest forth out of the womb I sanctified thee; I have appointed thee a prophet unto the nations."

That is a distinct declaration that he was foreordained to the ministry exercised. To that declaration Jeremiah replied, "Ah, Lord God ! behold, I cannot speak, for I am a child," and continuing his story the prophet declares :

"Say not, I am a child : for to whomsoever I shall send thee thou shalt go, and whatsoever I shall command thee thou shalt speak. Be not afraid because of them : for I am with thee to deliver thee, saith Jehovah. Then Jehovah put forth His hand, and touched my mouth ; and Jehovah said unto me, Behold, I have put My words in thy mouth ; see, I have this day set thee over the nations and over the kingdoms, to pluck up and to break down, and to destroy and to overthrow ; to build, and to plant."

Thus it is evident that he was foreordained, perfectly equipped, and Divinely appointed to that long, forlorn ministry which he so heroically and graciously fulfilled.

We may also look at the man as to his personal character, for there is no prophet who has given us so clear a revelation of himself as Jeremiah, and yet there was no other who shrank from publicity as he did. Because his message was of the very bone and fibre and sinew of him, because he entered both into the life of his people and into that of Jehovah, and because he spoke to them in such disastrous circumstances, the picture of the man is clearly stamped upon the page of his prophecy. There are three things apparent, his simplicity, his sensitiveness, and his strength. His absolute simplicity manifested itself when the command first came to him, "Ah, Lord God! Behold I cannot speak: for I am a child." He never lost the child heart and the child nature. His sensitiveness is seen in the way in which he shrank from his work. Even in hours of sacred fellowship with Jehovah he protested against having to deliver the messages of judgment. He felt all the pain of the judgments falling upon his people. He was, moreover, a man of absolute and overwhelming strength. If his nature was so simple that he had to say, "I am a child"; if his sensitiveness of soul was such that he constantly shrank from delivering his messages, his strength was such that he spoke every word that God gave him to speak.

No prophet in the long line was more like Christ than Jeremiah. He was a fit instrument for uttering the truth of the throne in days when its government was rejected and its grace neglected. It is most necessary in days when government is rejected and grace neglected that the voice of the Throne should be heard. Jeremiah was the fitting spokesman of that Throne. Chosen and known before his birth, equipped by the touch of God upon his lips, in his simple nature he was a perfect instrument through whom God was able to speak; in the sensitiveness of his heart he was a revelation to men of the love of God; and in the strength that dared he was able to coöperate with God.

All this brings us to an understanding of the permanent value of the book. It is the revelation of God in the midst of an age of unutterable failure. That revelation is threefold.

First, it is that of Jehovah's judgment of sin. Jeremiah saw in all the destruction, and devastation, and sweeping ruin, God's activity revealing God's attitude towards sin. Secondly it is that of Jehovah's suffering for sin. In the story of Jeremiah's shrinking and pain and tears we have a picture of a man in such perfect fellowship with God, that through him God was able to reveal His own suffering in the presence of sin. Thirdly, it is that of Jehovah's victory over sin. In Jeremiah's moral and hopeful triumph over sin even in prison, we have evidence of the certainty of God's ultimate victory.

First, then, this book reveals through the ministry of Jeremiah, God's judgment of sin. In the second chapter is recorded the prophet's impeachment of the nation. Let us recall some of his statements. A graphic picture of the degradation of those in authority is found in the eighth verse:

" The priests said not, Where is Jehovah? and they that handle the law knew Me not: the rulers also transgressed against Me, and the prophets prophesied by Baal, and walked after things that do not profit."

In the nineteenth verse the prophet declares the relation between wickedness and judgment:

"Thine own wickedness shall correct thee, and thy backslidings shall reprove thee: know therefore and see that it is an evil thing and bitter, that thou hast forsaken Jehovah thy God, and that My fear is not in thee, saith the Lord, Jehovah of hosts."

In the thirty-fifth verse the most sinful of all sins is revealed:

" Yet thou saidst, I am innocent; surely His anger is turned away from me. Behold, I will enter into judgment with thee, because thou sayest, I have not sinned."

Thus the message of Jeremiah to his own people was one which persistently declared that their ruin was the result of their sin. Politicians would have attributed the national trouble to the difficulty of their position, having Egypt on the south and Assyria on the east. The prophet declared that the reason was in themselves. They had forgotten God, and were discussing policy and arrangement, instead of putting away sin.

Then observe the process of Divine judgment as Jeremiah explained it. We read the history merely and say, What an unfortunate succession of kings; how singularly these people failed to produce statesmen who were able to cope with the political situation. This lonely figure, observing the race to ruin, said, The failure of your kings and the failure of your policy prove that the hand of God is upon you in judgment. It is He Who breaks down the power of your king.   It is He Who will bring to nought your intrigue with Egypt, and hand your city over to the Assyrian who is already at your gates.   He declared that the process of judgment was that of the direct action of God. Jeremiah stood, Jehovah's spokesman, alone, unheeded, persecuted, but insistent ; and events moved on and vindicated him, as Jehovah crushed and broke, and cast away the people who had sinned against Him.

I would to God a voice like that of Jeremiah might be heard to-day, calling men back to recognition of the fact that all ruin and loss and national decay are due first to the fact that we forget God, and then to the fact that God lifts up or breaks down according to whether or not a nation is living in right relationship to Himself.

This figure of Jeremiah is full of majestic force.   Though he spoke so long ago, his voice is a living voice to-day.   The things he said during those years of hopeless ministry have application to all nations through all time.   The root sin of national life is forgetfulness of God, and consequent rebellion against Him.   The failure of kings and politicians, the matters of which we speak as the misfortunes of the age, are evidences that God has not abandoned the Throne of supremacy.

I look again and see, through this man's suffering, a revelation of the most overwhelming and astonishing description ; that namely of Jehovah's suffering for sin.   Do not let us forget the beginning of this story, those words we have already read, " Before I formed thee . . . I knew thee."   Jeremiah was formed by God according to a pattern of Divine foreknowledge. This man of God's formation and appointment is seen shrinking, not from the delivery of the message, but because of the pain he saw coming to his own people.   He cried out in his anguish,

" Oh, that my head were waters, and mine eyes a fountain of tears, that I might weep day and night for the slain of the daughter of my people ! "

The prophet's agony created his need of being strengthened whenever he received the messages of Jehovah.   In the central lamentation he identified himself with the sufferings of his people, expressing all the sorrows that he had described in the earlier sections, as though they were his own.   We have read this prophecy very carelessly if we have simply seen in it the sorrows of a man, " Oh, that my head were waters, and mine eyes a fountain of tears, that I might weep day and night for the slain of the daughter of my people."   Can we find anything to match that ? We have already done so.   We have travelled through the centuries until we have stood upon the slopes of Olivet with a Man more lonely than Jeremiah, and have seen Him looking at Jerusalem, and have heard Him pronounce its doom, weeping as He did so.   That is the fulfillment of the prophecy of Jeremiah.   The stern denunciation that doomed Jerusalem was uttered in a voice choked with emotion, while the eyes were suffused with tears, as they saw the fire that soon was to destroy it.

The interpretation of Jeremiah's suffering is to be found in the suffering of Jesus, and the interpretation of the suffering of Jesus is to be found in the suffering of God.   Jeremiah stood as Jehovah's spokesman, shrinking and sorrowful, because he entered into the profoundest fellowship with God.

A wonderful revelation is this.   Stern denunciation of sin continued through all the processes of ruin, no truce with it, no excuse for it even though such denunciation resulted in stripes, brutality, and the dungeon ; never flinching, never excusing, never condoning ; yet all the while the message accompanied by the flow of tears and uttered in tones of anguish.

Once again, there is revealed in this prophecy the fact of Jehovah's victory over sin.   There is no figure in the Bible that sets forth the sovereignty of God so uncompromisingly as that of the potter and the clay.

" O house of Israel, cannot I do with you as this potter ? saith the Lord.   Behold, as the clay in the potter's hand, so are ye in Mine hand, O house of Israel "

How we have trembled in the presence of those words.   The potter moulds the clay as he pleases, and the clay cannot object.   It has no right to object.   That is the doctrine of absolute sovereignty.   It cannot fail to make the heart tremble ; but let us carefully note the use Jeremiah makes of this figure.   In words full of beauty he declares the ultimate activity of sovereignty.

" When the vessel that he made of the clay was marred in the hand of the potter, he made it again another vessel, as seemed good to the potter to make it."

If there were nothing but the figure of the potter with its awe-inspiring revelation of sovereignty, I should be broken and crushed with hopelessness, but there is more. There is the declaration of the ultimate activity of sovereignty, " he made it again." That was the great message of Jeremiah. Think of him as he watched the people he loved rushing to ruin, feeling all the time in his heart the very anguish of God in the presence of the disaster ; and then uttering this high word which seemed as though it never could be fulfilled, " He made it again another vessel."

Then come to the central chapters of the book and listen to him in the darkest day, the day in which he was in the innermost dungeon. It was then that he wrote the prophecies of hope contained in chapters thirty to thirty-three. When he spoke of Jacob's trouble he declared it was trouble that proceeded to triumph. He believed that ultimately God would work out the purpose of His love and the purpose of His grace. In this aspect also, therefore, Jeremiah stood the spokesman of Jehovah, and out of the midst of sorrow and sin gave utterance to the songs of certain victory.

The permanent values of this book constitute its living message. I utter that in briefest sentences. First, it teaches us that sin is its own destruction. No policy can outmanœuver God. National rebellion is national ruin. Sin carries within itself the force of its own punishment and its own retribution. Secondly, it affirms that the heart of God is wounded by sin. Judgment is His strange act. He weeps over the doom of a city. Finally it declares that the ultimate victory is with God, " He made it again." The Branch is appointed. The King-Priest has come.

We are to learn that God must punish sin, that the most awful fact of sin is that it wounds God ; and finally, that if we will but have it so, if we will but turn to Him and listen to His call, He overrules by cancelling, and breaking the power of sin, makes again the vessel marred in the hand of the potter.

Ezekiel

THE PERMANENT VALUES	THE LIVING MESSAGE

I. **The vision of God.**
  A. The embodied attributes.
    1. The face of a lion—supremacy.
    2. The face of an ox—service.
    3. The face of a man—manifestation.
    4. The face of an eagle—mystery.
  B. The wheels of procedure.
  C. The Spirit of life.
  D. The atmosphere of flashing light and fire.
II. **The bearing on circumstances.**
  A. These all present in reprobation and restoration.
    1. Supremacy—the authority claimed.
    2. Service—the actual working through pain.
    3. Manifestation—the ceaseless purpose—"That ye may know."
    4. Mystery—the reticence.
      a. Of the first vision.
      b. Of the last statement—"The Lord is there."
  B. Progressively revealed.
    1. Supremacy—judgment.
    2. Service—"The Shepherd" and "The Valley of Bones."
    3. Manifestation—the new order.
    4. Mystery—the last word.
III. **Such a vision of God the reason of hope—in its light:**
  A. Sin was most sinful.
  B. Judgment was most sure.
  C. Victory was most certain.
	I. **For a comprehensive outlook it is necessary to pass beyond principles and practice, to the Person.** (The incarnation is God's answer to that need.)
	II. **Having that answer, we must know the Person.**
	  A. "Acquaint now thyself with Him, and be at peace."
	  B. "That I may know Him...."
	III. **That knowledge will produce the song of hope.**
	  A. We shall see the sin.
	  B. We shall proclaim the judgment.
	  C. We shall rejoice in hope.

OF the prophet Ezekiel it has been said that "he was the prolongation of the voice of Jeremiah"; and it is certainly true that no one can study carefully the prophecies of these two men without discovering the influence of Jeremiah upon Ezekiel. It is evident throughout that in his life, in his outlook and in his conceptions Ezekiel had been affected by the prophetic message of Jeremiah. This is perfectly natural when we remember the circumstances in which Ezekiel exercised his ministry. He commenced that ministry in the fifth year of the captivity, and in the verse which chronicles this fact for us in the opening of the book, a reference is made to "the thirtieth year." It is almost certain that the reference is to his age. He was a priest, and in harmony with the Mosaic economy, at that age he should have entered upon his priestly work; but there was no temple, and therefore no official work for the priest; and he was called to exercise a prophetic ministry. If, then, that ministry was commenced in the thirtieth year of his age, and the fifth year of the captivity, it is at once evident that during the first twenty-five years of his life, Jeremiah was prophesying. From his earliest childhood, and through the formative and impressionable years of youth and young manhood, he was familiar with the ministry of this lonely man. Familiarity with his prophecy shows that his outlook on the corruption of his people, on the judgments of God, and his vision of light upon the Eastern sky which predicted the dawn of a brighter day, was practically identical with those of Jeremiah. His dealing with prevalent corruption was as severe as was that of Jeremiah, and his messages of judgment were equally stern. He never melted to tears as did Jeremiah, but his vision of the ultimate deliverance of the people by the triumph of Jehovah was even clearer. His vision was characterized by penetration, and perhaps the word *through* best describes the quality of the prophecy. His messages were addressed, in the first place, to the exiles on the banks of the River Chebar ; and yet it is evident that *through* them he spoke to all Israel. Morever, he distinctly affirms, in the course of his prophecy, that the application of the truths he enunciated is to all men, so that he not only spoke *through* the exiles to Israel, but *through* Israel to men of all nationalities and of all times. He saw the prevailing conditions, the ruin of his people, the obstinacy and rebellion even among the exiles in the midst of whom he lived, but *through* all these he saw the eternal verities as to their foundations and as to their principles.

It was George Herbert who sang :

" A man that looks on glass,
On it may stay his eye ;
Or if he pleaseth through it pass,
And thus the heaven espy."

Ezekiel saw the glass, but he saw through it. Accurately observing the temporal, he as surely perceived beyond it the eternal. He was sensitively conscious of the material, but supremely conscious of the spiritual. In all probability Jeremiah's prophecies of hope were the inspiration of Ezekiel's, but it may be that the absence of tears and lamentation in the messages of Ezekiel was due to the fact that his vision of God, and His processes, and His ultimate victory was clearer than that of Jeremiah. His recognition of the reprobation of his people was acute, and yet he foretold the certainty of their restoration with a note of profoundest assurance, and an outlook of more spacious sweep than any other prophet of the illustrious line.

The permanent value of the prophecy is that of its revelation of the reason of this man's hope.

Jeremiah was not without hope. Moreover, the messages in which he gave expression to his hope were uttered in days when he himself was in prison. Therein is a proof of the strength of his hope. Nevertheless, at other times his messages seem altogether devoid of that element. In the prophecy of Ezekiel the note of hope rings clear and jubilant throughout. We would fain discover the secret of this superabounding and jubilant confidence. The present outlook in some senses is dark enough, and we would fain discover the secret of rejoicing in hope even on the darkest day. It is an arresting fact that a man in more hopeless condition, in some senses, than that in which Jeremiah lived, being himself a captive by the River Chebar, among a band of exiles the most obstinate and rebellious, seeing that his people were reprobate, cast away, was nevertheless full of hope, and of the certainty of ultimate restoration

The secret is revealed at the beginning of his book. That which filled his heart with hope, and made him able to sing the song of coming victory on the darkest day, was his vision of Jehovah. The peculiar quality of that vision was that of manifestation. At first sight that statement hardly seems as though it could possibly be correct. The first impression made by the account which he gives of the vision he beheld is that of mystery rather than of manifestation. While recognizing the mystery, a quite simple examination of the prophet's description must inevitably leave upon the mind the sense of manifestation. The key-word to the vision is the word likeness. Likeness means that which reveals something else. The root idea of the Hebrew word is comparison. Its suggestion is exactly that of the Greek word which we translate parable. I do not say the root significance is the same, but the suggestion is identical. A parable is something placed by the side of, in order to explanation. It is a picture intended to interpret something, which apart from it might not be clearly understood. That is the key-note to the vision. It was a likeness, a similitude, a parable, a picture. He did not see what no man has seen, but he saw visions of Jehovah in the form of a likeness. It is not necessary for us to describe the visions save in the broadest outline. What Ezekiel saw began on the earth but it did not end there. If for the sake of contemplation we may temporarily forget the stately and wonderful language of Ezekiel and see the vision in barest, almost rudest, outline, we shall be helped to discover the truth it suggested. On the earth the central vision was that of four living ones, surrounded by wheels moving in every direction, the whole existing in an atmosphere, and actuated by an energy which the prophet described as spirit. The vision did not end there. Above the firmament he saw a throne, and on the throne a Man. The things on the earth were the manifestations of that which was above the firmament, and beyond the possibility of comprehension apart from such manifestation. The supreme and central verity upon which Ezekiel looked is to be discovered by examination, not of the wheels which suggest procedure, not of the Spirit which suggests energy, but of the living ones. I do not say that the other things are unnecessary, but it is not our business now to deal with them, and their wonderful and infinite suggestiveness. At the centre were the four living ones, and they constituted a revelation or manifestation of the infinite mystery of the Being Who occupied the throne above the firmament. This vision, and its bearing on the circumstances in the midst of which Ezekiel lived, constituted the reason of his hope. This vision therefore creates the permanent value of the book and its living message.

Let us retrace our steps in order that we may see the relation of this book to those which have preceded it, so far as their permanent values are concerned. The permanent values of Isaiah are its revelation of the throne, and the fundamental principles of government and grace. The permanent values of Jeremiah are its revelation of the activities of Jehovah, His judgment on sin, His suffering for sin, and His victory over sin. The permanent value of Ezekiel is its unveiling of the essential facts in the nature of God.

The central symbolism on the earth was that of the four living creatures, each one of which faced in four directions, each face suggesting a different idea by the differing symbolism of a man, a lion, an ox, and an eagle. Moreover, these four were so placed at the four corners of a square that the face of a man looked every way, the face of a lion looked every way, the face of an ox looked every way, and the face of an eagle looked every way. Thus in the unity of the four the same truths were suggested as in the unity of

each. Each had four faces, and the whole square had the same fourfold revelation.

Now we may enquire as to the suggestiveness of this ancient symbolism. It has been affirmed that it was borrowed from Babylon or Nineveh, or from both. Personally I have no quarrel with that contention. The making of an idol on the part of man originated in an attempt, however crude, however base, however mean, to embody thought about Deity. The very highest results of this process were reached in those pagan civilizations outside the economy of Israel; the highest result, that is, of man's attempt to understand, apart from the light of direct revelation. Here is the difference between all such religions, and that of Israel. The religion of Israel was not the result of man's attempt to understand, but of God's direct revelation. His method of revelation was constantly that of seizing upon an element of truth in a false system, redeeming it, purifying it, and making it a medium of revelation. As another illustration of the principle, the ark of the covenant may be cited. It has been affirmed that Moses was influenced by things he had seen in Egypt, and it is perfectly true that in certain systems of religion in Egypt at the centre of a ritual was an ark; and thus it is seen that there was an element of truth in the thinking of men. The final difference, however, between the sacred arks of Egypt, and the ark of the covenant, consisted first in what they contained, and secondly and preëminently, in what men were taught concerning them.

This symbolism of Ezekiel's vision may have been Babylonish or Assyrian. Admitting that, let us enquire of what these visions were symbols. For the moment I am perfectly content to enquire of Babylon, or to ask Nineveh, and I shall attempt to state the answer in terms of the abstract. The lion was the symbol of supremacy. The ox was the symbol of service. The man was the symbol of manifestation. The eagle was the symbol of mystery. Supremacy suggested kingship, and the lion was the symbol of the king. Service suggested sacrifice, and the ox was the symbol of the servant. Manifestation suggested the unveiling of life at its best, and man was the symbol of man. Mystery suggested the unfathomable, and the eagle was the symbol of Deity.

It has often been affirmed that Ezekiel was a

man saturated with pagan ideas, and that by the River Chebar he passed through a certain psychological experience as the result of which he came to imagine that the familiar symbols he saw engraven on heathen temples were visions of God. There is an element of truth in the statement; the fact being that God took hold of the symbolism in the midst of which His captive people lived, and made use of it for revealing to the prophet the comprehensive truth that in His Being, supremacy and service, manifestation and mystery, are merged in awe-inspiring unity. If in the prophecies of Isaiah we saw the Throne and its fundamental principles, and in those of Jeremiah we discovered the activities of the One Who occupies the throne; in those of Ezekiel we have the unveiling of the nature of God.

Ezekiel was also conscious of the Throne and the principles of the Divine government; he distinguished clearly the activities of God; but his supreme vision was that of God Himself. He saw Him manifest in the midst of the strange revolving wheels of procedure, and the resistless energy which he spoke of as the spirit. There was revealed to him the embodiment of the essential attributes of Deity, unqualified supremacy and sacrificial service; manifestation in the highest form of life, and infinite, unfathomable, and finally indefinable mystery. The deep secret of Ezekiel's hope was more than a consciousness of the Throne and the principles of government, more than the conviction of the actual activities of Jehovah, it was acquaintance with God Himself.

I know that at this point I join issue with a great many expositors who declare that the vision of Isaiah was greater than that of Ezekiel. I am compelled to say I cannot accept that view. If it is necessary to speak of degrees, and measurements, then here is the greatest vision of all, for in it there is unveiled the very nature of God. The issue of this is described in the last book of the Divine library, for the very same symbolism is used in describing the figures surrounding the throne. The seer of Patmos observed the four living creatures, and his description of them exactly coincides with the vision of Ezekiel.

This finally compels our recollection of the inspired presentation of the Son of God in the Gospels. In Matthew He is presented in His supremacy as King; in Mark in His sacrificial service as Servant; in Luke in His perfect manifestation as Man; in John in His infinite and fathomless mystery as God. When we have seen the four we have seen the One. Finally, as Ezekiel in the older vision looked above the firmament and saw the Throne, and on the Throne the likeness of a Man; we look to-day beyond the firmament, and exactly the same vision meets the eye of faith. Thus this man in the distant past, without knowing perfectly how in the economy of God the manifestation would be wrought out in the mystery of the Incarnation, did nevertheless see the essential, vital, eternal facts concerning God; that He is supreme; that He bends in service to the point of sacrifice; that He in Himself is all that man is, for man is in His likeness; and that He in Himself is more than man is, in the infinite mystery of Deity. In view of this vision I no longer wonder that Ezekiel was the prophet of hope.

Mark the bearing of this vision of God upon all the circumstances in the midst of which he found himself. In the great body of his prophecy he described the results of reprobation in the devastation of the people, declaring the reason of reprobation to be the sin of the people, and affirming the righteousness of reprobation. Looking through all this he saw restoration proceeding through judgment, until there broke upon his vision the glory of that last temple, which has never yet been built; and the final word of his prophecy is the declaration which sets forth the ultimate glory thereof, "The Lord is there." Throughout the whole of that prophetic movement the facts of the Divine nature are seen as he describes the processes of God. The supremacy of Jehovah is manifest whether in reprobation or in restoration. The service of Jehovah is the one story, as God is described as dealing with His people in order to remake them. The manifestation of Jehovah is perpetually revealed as to His purpose in the almost monotonous repetition of the refrain, "That ye may know Jehovah." The mystery of God is the supreme truth. Mark the fine reticence of the first vision. There is no description of essential Deity. When we have gazed upon the living creatures, watched the whirling wheels, been conscious of the all-pervasive spirit, lifted our eyes above the firmament and seen the Throne and on the Throne a Man, we are made supremely conscious of the fact that the ultimate truth is undiscovered, and the essential Being is invisible. Again, when we come to the last sentence of the prophecy, so simple that any child can remember it, "The Lord is there," mark the reverent reticence of it. We have looked upon the temple. We have been conscious of things missing which were found in the temple of Solomon. We have observed the presence of things not found in that temple. We have been made conscious of mystic movement; and have seen the glorious outflowing of a gracious river which - brings life wherever it comes, but we have never seen God. The only reference he makes to the actual presence of God in the temple is in that simple word already twice quoted, "The Lord is there."

It is not only true that these essential facts of the nature of God are all recognized throughout the processes of reprobation and restoration; it is also true that there is a progressive revelation. In the early part of the prophecy which deals with judgment, the overwhelming sense of God is that of His supremacy. In the movement in which the false shepherds are denounced, and the true shepherd character portrayed, Jehovah is revealed as Himself the Shepherd of His people, Who thus fulfills the true function of kingship.

Later in the course of the prophecy we have that weird and amazing spectacle of the valley of dry bones. We hear the moving of the wind over the bones, and then watch them as they come together and are clothed with sinew and flesh and skin, until presently they stand a living army; and as we watch, we learn how God stoops, King though He be, to serve in order to save. Still further, in the new order, the new law of life, and in the new consciousness of God, we see the full manifestation of life at its highest and best, not in an individual merely, but in a remade race, gathered around the central fact of worship. Until finally, we come to the last word, and all the great unveiling enfolds itself and announces that which cannot finally be known, but in the presence of which the exercise of worship is the only fitting activity of the soul.

In the light of this vision, sin was even more sinful, judgment was even more sure, but the victory was absolutely certain. So that in the midst of a handful of exiles, stubborn and rebellious, Ezekiel saw through to the ultimate because he knew God, not only as to the principles of His government, not merely as to the activities thereof, but as to Himself.

If these be the permanent values of the book, its living message may be briefly stated.

In order to a true and comprehensive outlook we need to pass beyond the principles of the Divine government, beyond the practice thereof, to the very presence of God. If we think simply of the principles we shall see them violated on every hand. If we simply contemplate the activities of Jehovah, though we worship in the presence of them, admitting the righteousness of His judgments on sin, being overwhelmed by the fact of His sorrow on account of sin, believing that at last He will gain the victory; the postponement of that victory is so terrible an experience as to be almost unbearable; but if we can be brought into actual consciousness of His nature we shall sing on the darkest day, because over all the gloom of the present we shall detect the glory of the coming victory. In order to abiding hope and abounding joy, we must pass beyond the principles and the practice, to the Person.

In order that we may do so, God is manifest in flesh. This is life eternal that we may know Him, and Jesus Christ Whom He has sent. Eliphaz said to Job, "Acquaint now thyself with Him, and be at peace." Paul expressed the deepest desire of his heart in the words, "That I may know Him, and the power of His resurrection, and the fellowship of His sufferings." It is a great thing to watch the goings of God in the world; it is a beneficent thing to know the principles of His government; but if the heart would find refuge and perpetual song, it must become familiar with God Himself.

Finally, then, the book declares that the knowledge of God is the perennial well-spring of joy and the inspiration of hope. To know Him is to see sin and hate it, to proclaim judgment fearlessly; but it is also to "rejoice in the hope of the glory of God."

Daniel

THE PERMANENT VALUES	THE LIVING MESSAGE

I. The government of the Lord God in the immediate (the historic night) Dan. 2:20-22.
  A. The fact of the government.
    1. Nebuchadnezzar.
      a. "The Lord gave Jehoiakim into his hand."
      b. The dream.
      c. The image.
    2. Belshazzar—the writing on the wall.
    3. Darius—the decree and the lions.
  B. The instrument of revelation.
    1. Separation—the king's meat.
    2. Inspiration—understanding of the mind of God.
    3. Adoration—the worship of God.
  C. The revealing facts.
    1. God's wisdom revealed through His own.
    2. God's might manifest in His care of His own.
II. The government of the Lord God in its processes to the end (the prophetic light).
  A. The Colossus.
    1. The head of gold—Babylon.
    2. The bust of silver—Medo-Persia.
    3. The belly of brass—Greece.
    4. The legs of iron—Rome.
      a. Division.
      b. Deterioration.
      c. The stone.
      d. Destruction.
  B. The visions; history unveiling character—beasts.
    1. The wisdom of God—knowing.
    2. The might of God—overruling.
	I. The revealed principles.
	  A. The wisdom and might of God.
	  B. His actual government.
	    1. Setting up and casting down.
	    2. Guiding evil to development and destruction.
	    3. Preserving good.
	II. The hidden things— Dan. 12:9, 10; Acts 1:7.
	III. The perpetual responsibility of His own.
	  A. Separation.
	  B. Inspiration.
	  C. Adoration.

THE book of Daniel falls into two parts. The first six chapters are historic, and the last six are prophetic. By that I do not intend to suggest that there is nothing of prophecy in the first six chapters, nor that there is no recognition of history in the last six ; but that the main note of the content of the first six is historic, and the principal value of the content of the last six is prophetic. These two parts are intimately related to each other, and in our study of the content of this book we have attempted to suggest the relation by the titles of the two divisions. In the first we have the historic night, and in the second the prophetic light. This distinction needs to be maintained when we turn to the consideration of the message of the book.

If of any book among these prophetic writings the description of Peter, "a lamp shining in a dark place," is peculiarly true, it is so of this one.

The historic section of the book gives a picture of the world when the national testimony of the Hebrew people was lost even more completely than in the time of Ezekiel. During many of the years Ezekiel was in captivity, Jeremiah was exercising his ministry in Jerusalem, and it is evident that his ministry influenced that of Ezekiel.

When we come to the book of Daniel we can discover no such general influence. The kings of the chosen people are only referred to in passing. The testimony of the people as a nation was wholly at an end. We see the great world powers of the time in the light shed on them by the ministry of Daniel, a most remarkable man in every way, a man who, loyal to the God of his fathers, nevertheless rose to positions of prominence in three empires; and who in the midst of circumstances, difficult and dangerous as were those of a Gentile court at that time, remained loyal to Jehovah. The prophetic section of the book gives us a picture of the working out of the Divine purpose through all human history.

In attempting to discover the permanent value and the living message of this book, we are aided by the fact that such value lies deeper than the immediate application of any one of its parts, and its living message is independent of any particular method of interpretation.

I desire first of all to set this book in relation to those which have preceded it. We have considered the message of Isaiah, the message of Jeremiah, and that of Ezekiel, and we shall now find that there is intimate relationship between these three and the message of Daniel.

There is an old division of these prophetic books into major and minor with which we are all familiar. We speak of Isaiah, Jeremiah and Ezekiel as the major prophets, and of the twelve, beginning with Hosea and ending with Malachi, as the minor prophets. There has been doubt in the minds of some as to whether Daniel should be reckoned among the major or the minor. There is a sense in which that division is in itself false and misleading. I refer especially to the designation of the twelve as the minor prophets. They are minor in no sense save that of bulk; indeed, that was the meaning of the word in its first application to them. For many reasons it would be an excellent thing if we could abandon the use of the words.

Nevertheless, there is an element of value in the division between the four and the twelve. They constitute two sections. The principle of the division is not chronological. I presume we are all agreed now that Hosea's prophecy was earlier than that of any of the four to which I have already made reference. There is a division, and I believe it is a spiritual one. When we seek for the permanent values and the living messages, we find in these first four a unifying revelation. Speaking broadly, I should be inclined to say that the permanent value of the four is that of the unveiling of the King, while the permanent value of the twelve is that of the unveiling of the Kingdom. I recognize that to make a division like that, and leave it as though it were final, would be most unsatisfactory. Both the Kingdom and the King are seen in the four; both the King and the Kingdom are discovered in the twelve; and yet undoubtedly there is this distinction, that the supreme and overwhelming revelation of Isaiah, Jeremiah, Ezekiel and Daniel is that of the King Himself, while the particular and special revelation of the twelve is that of the conditions within the Kingdom which occupied the attention of the prophetic voices as they declared the word of the King. Therefore, for the purpose of a general examination, I should always speak of the major prophets as revealing the King, and of the minor prophets as revealing the Kingdom. I have no difficulty, therefore, with Daniel, but deliberately place him with the first three. To use the word already referred to, I number him with the major prophets.

Let us go back, then, in order that we may place Daniel in relation to the messages already considered, for in his prophecy we have the completion of the revelation.

Isaiah began his ministry in the reign of Uzziah, one of the most prosperous as to material things in the whole history of Judah. It was in the year of his death that the prophet saw that new vision which lifted the whole of his subsequent ministry on to a higher plane. Jeremiah was the prophet of failure, exercising his ministry during the reign of the last of the kings of Judah. Ezekiel delivered his messages not to the people as a nation, but to a handful of exiles in captivity. Daniel personally delivered no messages to the chosen people themselves, but he exercised a ministry of remarkable force in the midst of the great world powers.

In the prophecy of Isaiah we saw the Throne. His supreme revelation is that of the uplifted, established Throne of Jehovah.   He declares two facts concerning it, the fact of its exercise of government, and the fact of its method of grace. These constitute the permanent value and living message of Isaiah.   As we said in our consideration of the content of the book, the two great passages in which this continuous purpose finds clearest expression are the sixth chapter, which gives an account of his vision, and the fifty-third, which thrills with the message of the grace of God.

In the prophecy of Jeremiah we have a vision of the activity of Jehovah.   That activity is threefold: that of judgment of sin, suffering for sin, and victory over sin.

Ezekiel strikes a deeper note as he presents the Person of Jehovah, and unveils four facts concerning that Person, those, namely, of supremacy and service, of manifestation and mystery.

Turning to the book of Daniel, we find none of these things dealt with, though all are recognized.   The supreme revelation of the book is that of the persistent government of God Almighty over the whole earth towards the fulfillment of the purpose of His grace.   In that sentence I express what I hold to be the permanent value of this book.   Let me state it more carefully and in slightly altered phrasing.   In Daniel we have the revelation of the power and wisdom of the Lord God in the government of the world to the end of the days.

Throughout the whole of this book, with one notable exception, God is described as Adonahy Elohim: Adonahy, supreme or sovereign Lord; Elohim, Mighty God.   The name of Jehovah is only to be found in one chapter—the ninth. Therein we have Daniel presented to us burdened with the failure of his people, and crying out in intercession for them.   In that great intercessory prayer the name Jehovah occurs seven times.   The nation to which God revealed Himself as the Becoming One was scattered and peeled, its testimony broken, its influence departed.   One man in whom all the principles of God's intention for the nation were preserved, and who was mastered by those principles, spoke for God, lived for God, and worked for God in three empires, but never spoke of God to those Gentile kings by the great name Jehovah.   He always referred to Him by the titles Adonahy Elohim.

When, as a result of his study of the writings of Jeremiah, and his consciousness of the passing of time, Daniel came to the conclusion that the seventy years were running out, his heart became burdened for his own people, and as he interceded for them, the old gracious name was used, Jehovah my God, Jehovah our God.

That in itself is an interesting fact in the study of this book.   Its main value, however, is that it affords a revelation of the power and wisdom of the Lord God in the government of the world unto the end of the days.   These words, "the end of the days," are the last made use of in the book, Daniel being told to wait, and being promised that he should stand in his lot at the end of the days.

Thus we discover the unifying principle of the major prophets.   In the first of them we find the principles of government; in the second, the practice of government; in the third, the Person of the Governor; and in the last, the persistence of His government.

In the light of this unity of the four, the permanent values of Daniel are the more clearly apprehended.   In the first part of the book we see the government of the Lord God in the immediate circumstances in the midst of which Daniel lived.   In the second we see the government of the Lord God in its processes to the end.   In the second chapter, verses twenty to twenty-two, this declaration is found: " Blessed be the name of God forever and ever: for wisdom and might are His: and He changeth the times and the seasons: He removeth kings, and setteth up kings: He giveth wisdom unto the wise, and knowledge to them that know understanding: He revealeth the deep and secret things: He knoweth what is in darkness, and the light dwelleth with Him."   That passage affords the key to the revelation of the book.   Indeed, its permanent value is contained therein.   Take the first of these divisions, the government of the Lord God in the immediate.   It gives the account of the victory of Nebuchadnezzar over Jehoiakim in these words: " The Lord gave Jehoiakim into his hand."   It is not only recognition, but definite declaration of the fact that Jehoiakim passed into captivity by the act of God.   If this were human history, rather than inspired story, we should read that Nebuchadnezzar defeated Jehoiakim, and took him prisoner.   That would be perfectly true, but it would not be the profoundest truth, nor the truth that this book was written to reveal. The writer was looking beyond secondary matters to primary ones, and he therefore declared, "The Lord gave Jehoiakim into his hand."

The next story is that of the strange, weird vision of the colossus with its head of gold, its breasts of silver, its belly and sides of brass, its legs of iron, and its feet a mixture of iron and brittle clay. The interpretation of the vision could not be discovered by the magicians, and Daniel was enabled both to recall the dream and give its interpretation. However we may interpret the vision as to detail, however far we may wander from the simple interpretation of Daniel himself, or however closely we may adhere thereto, the master thought of it is that of God reigning over the affairs of men; and through all the processes of deterioration or destruction, moving towards the final victory of the establishment of the true order amongst men. It is supremely a vision of the reigning, governing God.

When Daniel interpreted the vision of the colossus, he said to Nebuchadnezzar, "Thou art the head of gold," and indicated the fact that his appointment was made by the God of heaven.

When the effect of the vision had passed away, and the king made an image of gold, and commanded that men should worship it, a handful of men refused to bend the knee, and consequently were cast into the fiery furnace, but passed through it unscathed and unharmed. The words of Nebuchadnezzar following this deliverance prove that by its means he had discovered the fact of the government of God.

We pass from the reign of Nebuchadnezzar to that of Belshazzar; and imagination can fill in the details of his court—its luxury, its licentiousness, its lust. In the midst of a drunken carousal the mystic handwriting was seen upon the wall: "Mene, Mene, Tekel, Upharsin." This was the handwriting of God, and revealed most clearly the great truth for which this book stands, that God weighs kingdoms in balances, rejects kings from kingship by His own will, and sets up or flings down according to the purpose of His own government.

The last of the series of stories is that of how Darius flung Daniel into the den of lions at the bidding of his courtiers, and then in the early morning enquired: "O Daniel, servant of the living God, is thy God, Whom thou servest continually, able to deliver thee?" Daniel answered the enquiry in a word which affirms both the power and activity of God: "O king, live forever. My God hath sent His angel, and hath shut the lions' mouths."

These stories reveal the instruments through whom God made the fact of His government known, to Nebuchadnezzar, Belshazzar, and Darius, and through them to others. As we turn to look at these instruments we discover three things concerning them. First of all, their separation from all the things in the midst of which they lived which were contrary to the will of God. Secondly, their inspiration; they lived in fellowship with God, and thus came to an understanding of the mind of God, and were enabled to interpret it to kings without fear or faltering. Thirdly, their personal adoration of God as they worshipped Him, and Him alone, and that persistently. The interest centres in Daniel, who lived in the midst of things contrary to the will of God, but in separation from them; and in such close fellowship with God that it was possible for him to receive the interpretation of visions, and in such reverent and adoring worship as refused to be hindered by any form of opposition. That man became the instrument in the darkness through whom God was able to flash His light upon kings, and make courts feel the spell of His power.

Through Daniel and those associated with him, certain facts of the Divine government were forced upon the recognition of these kings. They saw His wisdom revealed through His own, in their ability to interpret. They saw His might manifest in His care of His own. Thus, standing back from this great book in order to observe it in general outline, while leaving the details, interesting and valuable as they are, we see God enthroned high above the thrones of men, governing in infinite wisdom and irresistible might.

Halting for one brief glance at the second part of the book, we see the government of the Lord God in its processes to the end. It is at this point that we find ourselves in the midst of widely differing interpretations. Notwithstanding these, there are broad truths, suggested by the vision of the image, upon which we are all agreed. The words of the prophecy itself declare that the head of gold referred to Babylon, that the bust of silver referred to the Medo-Persian empire which followed Babylon, and interpreting the symbolism of the vision by the facts of history, the belly of brass must have referred to the Grecian power which succeeded the Medo-Persian, and the legs of iron to the Roman Empire. Beyond that we see division and deterioration, until a new movement from without changes the whole course of history; a stone cut from the mountain smites the deteriorated feet of the image, and the whole falls to the ground. It is evident that much of this vision was prophetic. Daniel lived in the midst of some of the circumstances referred to. The image itself was a revelation of God's knowledge of the processes of the world powers, and pre-eminently a revelation of the fact that He remains enthroned above every empire as it comes and goes; and, moreover, that its rise and fall is under His government. Beyond the vision of the image we have those of the beasts, the difference between them being that whereas in the colossus we have the symbolism of external manifestation, in the beasts we have that of inward character. Dr. Scofield draws attention to the significance of the fact that the national symbols of the world powers to-day are all birds or beasts of prey.

I take this book, then, with its mystic passages and its strange figures; with its days, and dates, and dating, its times, half times, times missing, and times found; caring very little about these things for the moment, I see that its living message to this age is that of the wisdom and might of God; of the fact of His actual government, setting up and casting down, guiding evil on the one side to its full development and its ultimate destruction and on the other, preserving good to its full development and final victory. The vision is that of the overruling God, in wisdom knowing, and in might working; of kings reigning and passing, of dynasties and empires rising and falling, while God, enthroned above them, overrules their movements.

Looking through the visions of this book at the government of God, there are two things impressed upon the mind. The first is that God is guiding evil to full development, in order to final destruction. The second is that He is overruling good to full development in order to ultimate victory. There is untold value in the fact that both these movements are revealed. Sometimes we are told that the days in which we live are the most wonderful that the world has ever seen, that the world is getting better every day; on the other hand, there are those who affirm that we are in the midst of dreadful days, that the world is getting worse every day.

What shall we do with these opposing views? The message of this book is that we shall only discover the truth as we believe both of them. Evil is to-day worse than it ever was—more subtle, more devilish, and more refined, and therefore more dangerous and more damnable. On the other hand, good is more abounding than ever before. Men to-day have fuller revelation than they had, and are growing towards fuller realization.

If these two things be true, it follows that sooner or later there must be a crisis, a final conflict between the two forces. That is exactly what this book and the whole Bible teach. The Scriptures never suggest that these two processes will end by the reconciliation of good and evil, or by the weakening of good until there is nothing but evil, or the weakening of evil until there is nothing but good. The crisis will come when the stone cut without hands smites the image, and it breaks and crumbles, and the new kingdom of goodness fills the world.

If that be the main part of the living message of the book, there is another which must not be neglected. Daniel said, "I heard, but I understood not: then said I, O my lord, what shall be the issue of these things? And he said, Go thy way, Daniel: for the words are shut up and sealed till the time of the end. Many shall purify themselves, and make themselves white, and be refined; but the wicked shall do wickedly; and none of the wicked shall understand: but they that be wise shall understand."

It would be a great blessing if all students of the book would be as honest as the author: "I heard, but I understood not." Two things are certain as to the process. First, "Many shall purify themselves, and make themselves white and be refined"; secondly, "the wicked shall do wickedly."

It is impossible to construct an almanac on the

basis of that revelation. If we would have the New Testament message which exactly coincides with this, we turn to the last words of our Lord. The disciples had asked Him : " Lord, dost Thou at this time restore the kingdom to Israel ? " And He replied : " It is not for you to know times and seasons, which the Father hath set within His own authority. But ye shall receive power."

It is not our business to make a calendar. If we attempt to set these things in chronological order, we shall find a great gap, a space for which we cannot account, an unmeasured period. This at least is evident that we are living to-day in that unmeasured period.

What, then, is the last word of this message?

If we believe that God still reigns and rules in might and wisdom, if we believe that we cannot fix the date for the realization of His purpose by human calendars, wherein lies our responsibility ?

It is that of this handful of exiles of long ago. Separation from all the things that are unlike God in the world in the midst of which we live ; fellowship with God, which will enable us to declare Him to the age in which we live, so that it shall be compelled to recognition of Him ; and finally, such adoration of Him as must express itself in worship always, in spite of all difficulties ; such worship as refuses to bow the knee to any god save our one Lord God Almighty, as He has been revealed to us in Jesus Christ.

Hosea

THE PERMANENT VALUES	THE LIVING MESSAGE
I. **A revelation of the deepest nature of sin—infidelity to love.** A. God revealed as love by His actions. B. God acting in love towards His people. C. They received the gifts of love. D. They played traitor to the Giver. E. This sin against the clearest light. II. **A revelation of the inevitable activity of judgment.** A. Necessary result of sin. B. Man has no right to expect escape. C. God has no alternative when sin is persistent. III. **A revelation of the unconquerable force of love—**love's triumph lies through suffering. A. Love is unconquerable. B. Love suffers when sinned against. C. Love gathers the result of sin and bears it. D. Love expiates sin by suffering. E. Love pardons when it is submitted to.	I. **Sin.** (The notes of the failure of the church those of the failure of Israel.) A. Spiritual adultery. B. The harlotry of worldliness. C. The result. 1. Testimony silenced. 2. Name of God profaned. II. **Judgment.** A. Of moth and rust—the church speaks no authoritative word. B. Of the young lion. III. **Love.** A. Jehovah's constant love. B. The certainty of Christ's second advent and final victory.

THE book of Hosea pulsates with power. The ministry of this man combined intellectual and emotional forces in a remarkable way. These forces are discoverable acting in partnership, in all the messages he delivered. From the first chapter to the last we are conscious of them. The book thrills with emotion, and flames with light, from beginning to end.

Hosea came to clear vision through deep feeling. He passed to yet deeper feeling by reason of the clarity of his vision. He saw to the heart of the great subjects of which he treated, and he did so because in his training for the prophetic ministry his own heart was wrung with anguish. He who has much to teach must suffer much; and he alone can speak of the deepest things in the economy of God who has sooner or later entered into fellowship with the suffering of God. Hosea passed into fellowship with that suffering through his own suffering, and out of that fellowship in suffering spoke to his age. That, I think, is the key to all that is so appealing and powerful in this wonderful prophecy.

The book has three permanent values. They are its unveilings of sin, of judgment, and of love. In these pages we have first a revelation of what sin is at its deepest and its worst; secondly, we have a revelation of the nature of judgment, and of its inevitable activity as the result of sin; and finally, we have a revelation of the unconquerable force of love.

Hosea, while dealing incidentally and quite definitely with certain forms of sin, was yet more concerned with its deeper notes. He saw to the very heart of it, saw it at its worst, and understood the awful fact about it which makes it so appalling.

In order that we may understand this, we must remember that he was speaking to the chosen people of God. It is often debated whether there are degrees of sin. In some senses, No. In other senses, Yes. When a man chooses in his own life as between the little and the great in the matter of sin, he is doing that for which he has no warrant in the Scriptures of Truth. On the other hand, when we compare as between the sin of one man, and the sin of another, the sin of the one may be less than that of the other. The difference is caused by light. The measure of light creates the degree of sin. In proportion as men have light their sin becomes the more sinful. That is the perpetual principle revealed through all the Scriptures. We refer to it when dealing with some of the great problems of the peoples of the world, we declare that men will be judged according to the light they have had. That principle lies at the foundation of the prophesying of Hosea. His messages teach us that sin reaches its deepest and most awful activity and manifestation when it is sin against light, and when it is sin against such light as reveals the fact of love. . Sin against love is the most heinous sin of all. The people chosen of God to be His own people, upon whom He had lavished His love, had turned their backs upon Him, and were spending the very gifts of love in lewdness; and the prophet adopted the most tragic and awful illustration, as he declared that the sin of Israel in her infidelity to love was that of spiritual adultery; and that yet more heinous sin, more terrible even than spiritual adultery, the sin of prostitution for hire.

I can quite believe that in this age when we are afraid to handle things as they ought to be handled, there are those who dislike the prophecy of Hosea. Nevertheless its message is a living one, and needs emphatic statement. He declared to the people of God that the relation existing between them and God was most perfectly symbolized in the sacred relationship of marriage; and therefore that their sin against God was that of infidelity, unfaithfulness to love. The prophet learned the truth through the tragic and awful experience of his own domestic life. He entered

into fellowship with God when his own heart was broken, when there came to him the unutterable and most appalling sorrow that can befall the spirit of man. What the sin of Israel meant to God, Hosea learned by the tragedy in his own home and in his own heart; and with fierce, hot anger he denounced kings, priests, and people alike. Thus while he dealt with the incidental manifestations of sin, the real message of the prophet had to do with the central sin of infidelity to the covenant based upon love. This book, therefore, brings us to the consciousness that the deepest and most awful thing in the realm of sin is that of doing despite to love.

Then as to judgment. The prophet with determined insistence emphasized the fact that judgment is the necessary result of sin. He declared that judgment must fall upon the sinning people in awful force and completeness, and positively affirmed that they had no right to expect pardon. In the last section of the prophecy, dealing with the love of Jehovah, the movement declaring that love falls into three parts; the love of Jehovah in the light of past love; the love of Jehovah in the light of present and continued love; and the love of Jehovah in the light of future love. In our analysis we show how that great love-song of Jehovah is interrupted by the prophet's interpolations. We speak of them as constituting a minor obligato accompaniment. In those interpolations the prophet traced the history of the people downward, and the last word of them was one in which he declared there was no hope. That is to say, the prophet looked on the sin, and saw it inevitably working out to judgment; and he wrote his message in letters of fire, as undoubtedly he delivered it in words that burned the men who listened. Such sin has no right to expect mercy.

The man who sees most deeply into the heart of sin, and knows it at its worst, is the man who sees most clearly how inevitable judgment is; and how, therefore, man has no right to expect anything other than judgment.

Yet the greatest revelation of the book is that of love. In the midst of his own overwhelming sorrow, God called Hosea, and commanded him to seek again the sinning Gomer, and to bring her back into the wilderness of seclusion for a while, but ultimately into the place of love and privilege at his own side.

As through her infidelity Hosea entered into understanding of the sinfulness of sin; so by God's command to him and his obedience thereto, he entered into understanding of how God loves even in spite of sin.

These, then, are the three matters which stand out upon the page of this prophecy. It reveals sin as to what it is; it reveals judgment as inevitable and necessary; and it reveals love amazingly. These essential principles have present application, and constitute the living message of the book. I am profoundly convinced that we need that these words should be rediscovered and respoken in every successive age. The common consciousness of the Christian Church to-day is weak on all these fundamental matters. It is weak concerning the love of God, because it has failed to understand the meaning of its own sin, and the consequent necessity for, and inevitability of judgment. I repeat, we supremely need that the message of this book concerning sin, judgment, and love, should be reconsidered.

Hosea teaches us that the most heinous and damnable sin of which man is capable is that of infidelity to love. This is the sin of all such as have been brought into right relationship with God; and then, violating love's covenant, have committed—let us use the word which we fain would not use, which is yet stamped upon the pages of this prophecy—spiritual adultery. Compared with that, the animalism and brutality, and consequent corruption of heathen nations is as nothing. Hosea's message concerning sin leaves no conclusion other than that it were infinitely better never to have had the light, never to have known love, than having had the light to disobey it, and having known love to wound it by infidelity.

Such sinning generates the form of judgment which follows it. If this book teaches one thing clearly on the subject of judgment, it is that judgment is never the stroke of God inflicted upon man apart from man's sin. It is the outworking of the seed of sin to harvest. Judgment lies potentially in the act of sin. Infidelity to love can lead nowhere save to the unutterable darkness of pollution. No surface repentance, which is a device to escape punishment, can be acceptable to God. "O Ephraim, what shall I do unto thee? O Judah, what shall I do unto thee? for your goodness is as a morning cloud." The

penalties of apostasy are as irrevocable as are the laws of purity. If a man walk in the ways of purity, the harvest of blessing must follow; but if a man shall sin against love, the penalty must fall.

Yet the permanent message is of love. Though the pathway of love's triumph lies through suffering, of which no man can ever know the measure; though the cost of the restoration of the faithless lover be that of the bearing of judgment by the faithful lover, still love moves right onward, singing ever the song of the victory that is to be. We must never forget how this book of Hosea ends. Ephraim says at last, "What have I to do any more with idols?" When that word is uttered, the victory of love is won. The process of judgment was certain, and so clear was Hosea about this, that he declared without any hesitation that the generation to which he spoke would never come to ultimate triumph; but beyond the process, indeed through it, he saw the ultimate triumph of love.

These, as I understand them, constitute the living message of the book. To emphasize either of the thoughts apart from the rest is to minimize the value of the whole. Each must be pondered, and so far as the book has a message to our age, it is one concerning sin, judgment, and love.

I maintain that this message of Hosea cannot be applied to the nation, to our own nation for instance, because it is so peculiarly a message delivered to men and women who had the perfect light, that is, to the people of God. Moreover, this message was not delivered to any one tribe. Although Ephraim is often referred to, it is as the dominant tribe, and the whole nation is involved. It is a message, therefore, to the peculiar people of God. Consequently no application of its teaching can be fair except an application to Christendom, I might say an application of its teaching to the Church, if by the Church we mean all that organization of Christianity which exists in the world to-day. I am, however, increasingly inclined to differentiate between Christendom and the Church, increasingly inclined to believe that the Church of God consists of those known only to God, rather than of that of which we speak as the Churches or the Church. A great many people who seem to be outside all Churches are in the Church of

God. Consequently the message of this book is a message to Christendom.

The first note has to do with sin. The causes of the Church's failure are those of the failure of Israel of old, spiritual adultery, spiritual harlotry, and that self-centred life which is their outcome. These are the sins which lie at the root of the Church's weakness at the present hour.

Spiritual adultery is evidenced by the paganism which has become admixed with the things of God. It is supremely manifest in the Roman Church and the Greek Church, but is found in all other communities in the degree in which they are of the habit and spirit of these churches. The things which result from the Church's alliance with the world demonstrate her adultery, and are due to her infidelity to love; her failure to remember that she is espoused to the Lord Christ as His bride, and ought to be devoted to Him and to Him alone. The harlotry of worldliness is manifest in every direction. Thousands who name the name of Christ are taking possessions which have been bestowed by God, and are spending them in the pursuit of unworthy ambitions and pleasures. Those by covenant related to Christ are inflaming themselves with carnality under every green tree. Through these things the testimony of light and love which the Church should bear to the nation is failing, and the name of God is being profaned among the heathen.

The judgment of God is already upon the guilty, upon whom His love is set. Hosea dealing with judgment made use of three figures. He spoke of the judgment of the moth, then of that of the young lion, and finally of that most fearful form, the withdrawal of God from His people, so that they are left desolate, without testimony and without power. The judgment of the moth and rottenness is that of the insidious weakening of the strength of His people. That judgment is evidently upon us to-day. It is manifested in the failure of the hosts of God. The Church of God as a whole is unable to speak any authoritative word in the councils of the nations. Indeed the judgment of the moth and rottenness is so prevalent, that often, instead of helping the nation, the Church hinders it. The Church is mourning the dearth of conversions within her own borders, wondering at the depletion in her theological schools, and lamenting the indifference of the world to her testi-

mony. Like Ephraim she turns to Egypt and to Assyria for help, adopts worldly methods for raising money, desecrates the temples of God with bazaars, and attempts to attract the indifferent multitude by sensational methods and spectacular displays. The judgment of God is upon us. It is not coming, it is here. It is first manifest in the weakening of the spiritual forces of the Church, and in her inability to fulfil her mission in the world.

Let us remember, and quite solemnly, that beyond the method of the moth and rottenness is the method of the young lion, the fiercer anger of God; and beyond the method of the young lion is that of the withdrawal of God from His own people. It is just as certain that God will cast off the organized Church, as that He cast off Israel, unless she return to Him through the penitence of the wilderness, to the fullness of the fellowship of His love. I am not now dealing with eternal issues. Israel will yet be restored, and God will surely accomplish His purpose in and through the Church. But so far as we are concerned, unless we repent in dust and ashes of our harlotry and adultery, we shall be abandoned from service, the solemn word will surely be uttered, "Thou canst be no longer steward."

Yet it is ours to make application of the last of these great truths. Over all the failure, heartbreaking and desolating though it be, there still sounds the music of the love of Jehovah. Though Ephraim be a cake not turned, flaccid as dough on one side, and burned to a cinder on the other, utterly useless and contemptible, we may still hear the great cry out of the heart of God, "How shall I give thee up, Ephraim?"

The only comfort that comes to the heart in the days of the failure of the Church is that the music of the love of Jehovah is still sounding, and the soul is filled with the assurance that He has not exhausted all His methods. Another crisis is coming. The present dispensation was ushered in by the crisis of the first Advent, and a new dispensation will be ushered in by the crisis of the second Advent; and beyond that, and through it He will realize the triumph of love. "I will redeem; I will bring back." At the coming of Christ, love will triumph through judgment, and over judgment. Love must at last accomplish its purpose.

But Hosea had to tell the men and women to

whom he spoke that the triumph was postponed, and that they could never share in its ultimate fulfillment, save in the case of such individuals as by return to God would discover the real meaning of His love for them.

I am not prepared to make that declaration. I do not know that it is so. Of times and seasons I have no right to speak; they are not within my knowledge or understanding. I do say that the Church needs supremely to remember that the highest, most wonderful, and most inspiring figure of her relationship to God is that which declares she is the bride of Christ.

If that be once recognized, the sinfulness of spiritual adultery and harlotry with the forces which are opposed to Him will be realized.

We need to remember that when the Church is guilty of these sins it is inevitable that the judgment of God should rest upon her.

We may also remember that He loves her yet; and as the members of His body, His flesh, His bones, turn back to Him in loyalty of spirit, He will receive them in the fullness of His love, and the great word may be spoken of all such, "I will heal their backsliding."

Joel

THE PERMANENT VALUES	THE LIVING MESSAGE

I. The illustration of principles.
A. The principles.
  1. Government.
    a. Jehovah enthroned.
    b. Presiding in patience.
    c. Pressing all forces into His service.
    d. Finally asserting Himself.
  2. Grace.
    a. The inspiration of government.
    b. The restraint on judgment.
    c. The issue of government.
B. The illustrations.
  1. Of government.
    a. The locust plague—the act of God.
    b. The imminent judgment—2:11.
    c. The final movements—the day of Jehovah.
  2. Of grace.
    a. The call to repentance presupposes it.
    b. The declaration announces it—2:12.
    c. The patience and the purposes declare it.
II. The revelation of a plan.
A. Immediate.
  1. Judgment.
  2. The promise of deliverance.
B. Afterwards—the poured-out Spirit.
C. The day of the Lord.
  1. Restoration of Judah and Jerusalem.
  2. The finding of Israel.
  3. The judgment of the nations.
  4. Restoration of Israel.
  5. Supremacy of Judah.
	I. The principles.
	A. The day of the Lord always present and always coming. (This is the day of the Lord. It is also to come!)
	B. Through all we are to rejoice in and proclaim grace.
	C. Ever insisting on the conditions.
	II. The plan.
	A. We must recognize our place.
	B. We must proclaim the fullness of the Spirit.
	C. We must urge men to call on the name of the Lord.

TAKING it for granted that we are familiar with the contents of the book of Joel, in order to the discovery of its permanent values we need to remind ourselves of the threefold vision of the prophet.

In the first place we have his vision of the things that were nearest to him, the circumstances in the midst of which he and the men to whom he spoke were living. An actual plague of locusts had swept over the land, and the first part of his message was delivered in view of the desolation resulting from that plague.

The second vision was that of judgment of a more serious character threatening the people, that, namely, of the coming of an army which he described, using the locust plague for purposes of illustration.

The third vision was that of things beyond his own day and generation.

Joel looked around and saw the results of the locust plague. He looked ahead and saw the new judgment coming upon his people. Then climbing to a yet higher height he saw the things of the far distances. In each case he recognized the activity of Jehovah, and spoke of "the day of the Lord." The locust plague was "the day of the Lord." The swift judgment coming upon his people would be "the day of the Lord." The far distant vision was also that of "the day of the Lord."

The whole prophecy is the result of a vision in perspective of the highway of Jehovah through the centuries; while the burden of the book is expressed in the phrase, "the day of the Lord." Whether the prophet looked at the things in the midst of which he lived, or whether he looked at the judgment which was imminent, or whether he looked to the final activites, he saw "the day of the Lord." To him that day had always come, and was always coming. It was the burden of his prophesying.

The permanent values of the book are first, its illustration of the principles of the Divine govern ment; and secondly, its revelation of the plan of God in the ages.

Its illustration of the principles of Divine government. I use these words quite carefully. I do not say its declaration of the principles, because those are to be found in the prophecy of Isaiah, in which, after the vision of the established throne, its active principles of government and grace are declared. In this book of Joel those principles are illustrated.

First as to the activity of the throne in government. From first to last we are made conscious of the enthroned Jehovah. Whatever were the signs of the times, whatever the defection of the people, whatever the perils threatening them, the one main impression made upon the mind is that of Jehovah enthroned, presiding in patience over all the processes through which His people pass ; pressing into His service all forces, the forces of nature, the locusts; human forces, the coming army ; and finally asserting Himself in absolute and unqualified victory. Every day to this man was "the day of the Lord." The final "day of the Lord" is postponed, but it is absolutely certain. That will be the day of His established victory. The long-sightedness of this prophet is evident when we remember that the things he described at the close have not yet taken place. He saw the near things, the sin of his people, and the locust plague; the imminent things, the coming of judgment, and the restoration following it ; the far things, the day of the Spirit in

which we are living, and the things beyond.

Yet even this prophecy does not give the final things ; but only the beginning, the ushering in of that last dispensation of God when He will have won His victory and taken to Himself the reins of government, and demolished all other authority and power. The Kingdom of the Son which lies beyond the millennium is not in view in this prophecy.

As we read this book then, the first impression made upon the mind is that of the throne of God, and of God ever active in government.

The second fact illustrated is that at the heart of government is grace. Grace is the inspiration of government. It is seen acting as a restraint upon judgment, so that the locust plague was the occasion of the prophet's appeal to his people to repent ; so that his declaration of the judgment which he affirmed to be imminent opened the way for him to make the appeal of God to the people to return to Him, and rend their hearts rather than their garments. When we come to the ultimate triumph it is not that of a conqueror who rejoices that he has broken and crushed, but that of a conqueror who rejoices that he gives peace, and honour, and deliverance, and beauty. Looking at the issue of government we understand its inspiration. That issue is beneficent, glorious, and beautiful, and by these things we are assured that its inspiration is the tender grace of the heart of God. Through all the processes of necessary judgment leading to the establishment of His Kingdom ; the locust plague, the coming army, the final conflict, there is evident the restraint of grace, because grace inspires the process, and is the ultimate triumph towards which everything is moving.

Let us observe how these principles of government and grace are illustrated. Of the locust plague men would say, This is a sore misfortune. No one could foresee it, or prevent it. It has swept over the country, and so devastated everything, that no drunkard can obtain wine, that there are no offerings for the temple, that the people throughout the land are lacking bread. It is a terrible devastation, but no one could prevent it ! Then the prophet delivered his message, that the plague had come by the will and act of God. The age was forgetting God, and Joel stood in the midst of the devastation and declared that the things of which men spoke as simple happenings in the course of nature, were as a matter of fact the immediate and direct acts of God in judgment. He insisted upon the fact of the Divine government as he declared that the day of devastation and the plague was "the day of the Lord." He called the old men and the drunkards, the possessors of the land, and all the people to observe the destruction, and to recognize that it resulted from the immediate action of God. This he declared also concerning the judgment which was about to come. In his graphic description of the destroying army he said, "The Lord uttereth His voice before His army," thus calling them to recognize the invading foe as acting under the government of God. When we come to the final movement no argument is needed. It is most certainly a prophecy of the going forth of God, turning the captivity of Judah and Jerusalem, seeking and finding His scattered people, breaking the power of the nations that have oppressed them, restoring Israel, and raising Judah to the place of supremacy.

Thus whether Joel looked at the near, the imminent, or the distant, he insisted upon the presence and activity of God.

With equal clearness he illustrated the fact of the Divine grace. The call to repentance in the first place presupposes the grace of the Divine heart. The declaration of the second is perfectly clear, "Yet even now, saith the Lord, turn ye unto Me with all your heart, and with fasting, and with weeping, and with mourning: and rend your heart, and not your garments, and turn unto the Lord your God: for He is gracious and full of compassion, slow to anger, and plenteous in mercy, and repenteth Him of the evil." That is to say, He will change His mind concerning judgment, when men rend their hearts and not their garments, and turn back to Him. He is slow to anger. He halts the march of His wrath in order that men may repent.

When we come to the final movement, the grace is as clearly manifest. "I will show wonders in the heavens and in the earth, blood, and fire, and pillars of smoke." That is the description of the great and terrible day of the Lord; but even then His grace will wait and act, "for in Mount Zion and in Jerusalem there shall be those that escape, as the Lord hath said, and among the remnant these whom the Lord doth call."

Thus throughout the prophecy, in the things that are near, in the things that are imminent, and in the things of the final movement of God, the two facts plainly evident are those of the Divine government and the Divine grace. These constitute the first permanent value of the book.

Now as to the second; we have in this book the revelation of a plan. Looking forward Joel saw beyond the circumstances in the midst of which he lived, and beyond those immediately following, another day of the Lord; but ere its dawning a period undated and unmeasured, yet full of gracious and wonderful blessing.

"It shall come to pass afterwards, that I will pour out My Spirit." We are not able to say that we do not know where to place that period, because we have the New Testament in our hands, and therein the clearly spoken word of the apostle on the day of Pentecost, "This is that which hath been spoken by the prophet Joel." We know now what it was that Joel saw in dim outline, which he could not perfectly describe, yet which he did so accurately describe. He saw the glorious outpouring somewhere in the distance. He was unable definitely to place it; and referred to its distance by that indefinite word "afterwards." We know that it lay at least five centuries away from the day in which he uttered his prophecy.

The vision was most remarkable as that of a Hebrew prophet, because it foretold the outpouring of the Spirit upon all flesh, not merely upon Israel, not only upon the elect, but upon all flesh.

He saw, moreover, that this outpouring of the Spirit and its results were to be irrespective of caste; not merely upon the favoured, kings, princes, priests, and rulers, but also upon bondslaves.

Joel saw the strange and wonderful age in the distance. We are living in that age. There is no single statement in the Bible which enables us to say how long it will last, not a single note to enable us to measure it.

Beyond the age of the Spirit he saw other activities of the Divine government. Looking towards them he said, "I will show wonders in the heavens and in the earth, blood, and fire, and pillars of smoke. The sun shall be turned into darkness, and the moon into blood, before the great and terrible day of the Lord come." These are not the signs of the age of the Spirit.

They will indicate its close, and initiate a new age which is that of the final day of the Lord. During the period of these signs "it shall come to pass that whosoever shall call on the name of the Lord shall be delivered"; delivered, that is, from "the great and terrible day of the Lord." Thus we see the plan of the ages. Joel saw that the age in which he lived continued to a certain point, and its characteristics would be those of sin, of judgment, and of repentance. Then he saw that day of the Lord moving on towards another day of the Lord, in which the characteristics of government and grace would be even more marked. Afterwards he saw something new, the Spirit poured upon all flesh, a quiet hush descending everywhere; no longer the old manifestations, but a new order of prophesying, dreaming of dreams, seeing of visions, and breaking down of caste so that slaves also would be among the prophets. Then signs in the heavens and in the earth, and beyond these, "the great and terrible day of the Lord."

As to that great day the prophetic word was far more definite. His words concerning the age of the Spirit were to him full of mystery, but to us are clear. Beyond that age of the Spirit his vision was clearer, and he gave a definite description of what would happen. Judah and Jerusalem are to be delivered from captivity and from scattering among the nations. God will search among the nations for the lost and scattered Israel, and gather them together; He will judge the nations, and the basis of His judgment will be that of their attitude towards Israel. Israel will be restored to privilege and power; and the supremacy of Judah will be established in the midst of the restored order.

None of these things have yet been fulfilled. As surely as they were written, they will be fulfilled. Place Joel as late as we may, allow the latest scholar to have his way, and declare that he spoke only four centuries before Christ; it is still enough if we admit that so long before the Pentecostal miracle this man saw it, to warrant us in saying that none has the right to deny that the things which our eyes have not seen will be seen. So surely as Joel wrote, God will act, and in his brief writing we have a remarkable unveiling of the plan of the ages.

The living message results from these permanent values. From them we learn that "the day of the Lord" is always present and always coming.

> "Who would sit down and sigh for a lost age of gold
> While the Lord of all ages is here?"

There are those who deny that there ever will be a "day of the Lord" in which He will act in judgment. On the other hand there are those who are ever looking towards the future "day of the Lord," forgetting that this also is the "day of the Lord."

God is active at this hour. If that be denied, if it be true that God is doing nothing, then the outlook is indeed hopeless. This is "the day of the Lord," but it is not the final day. There is a sense in which this is man's day. It is an age of remarkable progress. Inventions are multiplied. Human culture has reached a level never before attained. Progress, inventions, culture are making man imagine that he is independent of God. There is a wide-spread tendency to the deification of human reason and human ability. It is peculiarly the age in which humanity is acting as though there were no God, or as though it were entirely independent of Him. The results are disastrous to all that is highest and best in human life. All our progress and inventions and culture leave us infinitely less than the highest, noblest and best possibilities of our being. But this is also "the day of the Lord"; and the activities in the midst of which we find ourselves, if our eyes are but anointed to see, are activities bathed in the fire of His presence. Let no man think he escapes God because he denies Him. To go back to the prophecy of Isaiah, "Who among us shall dwell with the devouring fire? Who among us shall dwell with everlasting burnings?" Isaiah saw the city and people of his age existing in fire. The everlasting burnings are not postponed. We live in the midst of them. I cannot tell how much Isaiah knew of what we call modern science. It is, however, perfectly evident that its teachings were apprehended by him in the spiritual realm. Modern science has revealed to us the fact that there is a slowly burning fire everywhere in nature. We leave iron in the dews of the night, and in the morning declare it rusted. Scientists tell us rust is the evidence of the slowly burning fire. In the autumn we watch the leaves turning to gold and vermilion, and this also is the work of the same fire. Isaiah recognizing such a fire in the spiritual realm asked Who can dwell in it? and answered his own enquiry, "He that walketh righteously, and speaketh uprightly." Everything else it destroys. London is wrapped in the fire of God's nearness. This is the day of God. The throne of judgment is erected now.

That, however, is not all; there is the final judgment throne. Every age will repeat the process until the last, in which He will finally deal with the sinning earth, in order that through the last fire baptism He may realize all the purpose upon which His heart is set. Yet thank God, there is committed to us also the ministry of reconciliation. Through all the movements there are evidences of His grace, and it is ours to rejoice in, and proclaim that grace, always insisting upon the only conditions upon which grace can operate, "Rend your heart and not your garments."

The final word of the living message is this. We are to remember where we are in the plan of the ages. We are in the midst of the age of the outpoured Spirit. The message we have to deliver to men is that of the possibility of the fullness of the life of the Spirit. Our business is to urge men to call on the name of the Lord, and thus to be saved from the judgment of His immediate day; from the judgment of His imminent day; from the judgment of His final day.

Let it be ours, who know anything of what it is to have received the Spirit, to hand over to that indwelling One all the keys of all the chambers of the being, that He may fill us, and use us as the instruments of both the government and the grace of God.

Amos

THE PERMANENT VALUES	THE LIVING MESSAGE

I. The philosophy of the divine government illustrated in the nations.
  A. The fact—assumed and applied.
  B. The method.
    1. Divine knowledge of national interrelationship.
    2. Light creates responsibility.
    3. The divine patience.
  C. The aim—establishment of highest conditions.
 	
II. The practice of the divine government illustrated in Israel.
  A. Privilege and its issue.
  B. The sins of the privileged.
  C. The judgment of the privileged.
 	
III. The promises of the divine government accomplished by Jehovah—9:11-15.
  A. Preliminary restoration—11-13.
    1. "I will."
    2. "That they may."
  B. Progressive restoration—14.
    1. "I will."
    2. "They shall."
  C. Permanent restoration—15.
    1. "I will."
    2. "They shall."
	I. To the nations.
	  A. The national sins which God punishes.
	    1. Cruelty—sin of Samaria.
	    2. Slave trade—sin of Philistia.
	    3. Slave agents in spite of covenant—sin of Phoenicia.
	    4. Determined and revengeful unforgiveness—sin of Edom.
	    5. Cruelty based on cupidity—sin of Ammon.
	    6. Violent and vindictive hatred—sin of Moab.
	    7. Jehovah's laws despised—sin of Judah.
	    8. Corruption and oppression—sin of Israel.
	  B. Peoples chosen to be depository of truth must be righteous.
	  C. No escape from doom but by way of penitence.
	  D. Yet let the hearts of the loyal be established.
	
	II. To the holy nation.
	  A. No countenance to national sins.
	  B. Rejoicing in the final victory which is assured.

THE prophecy of Amos is unique in that it differs in some ways from the others in the Divine library. It is peculiar in that the prophet himself was neither a prophet, nor the son of a prophet. These terms, however, must be understood technically. When he declared "I was no prophet; neither was I a prophet's son," he meant that he was not recognized as a prophet, nor had he been to one of the schools of the prophets. In the language of our own day, he was a layman, and an untrained man withal. The prophecy is preëminently peculiar in the matter of outlook. There is a most significant omission from this book. Amos never used the phrase so common in other writings, "the God of Israel." His outlook was a far wider one. It is only as we recognize this fact that we can appreciate the real value of the book.

According to Amos, Jehovah roars over Zion, and utters His voice over Jerusalem, but the things He has to say are said to Damascus, Gaza, Tyre, Edom, Ammon, Moab, Judah, and Israel. As we read these messages of Jehovah we are impressed by the fact that there is no peculiar and startling gap between the first six and the last two. It is one continuous message beginning with the word of Jehovah to Damascus and ending with His word to Israel. Amos spoke as one who saw God to be not the God of Israel and Judah only, but also the God of Damascus, Gaza, Tyre, Edom, Ammon and Moab.

In this prophecy, therefore, God is seen as detached, and yet directing; detached from the prophetic order, and yet directing through a man who became in the fullest, finest sense of the word a prophet; detached from every nation, and yet directing all, governing the affairs of each.

The permanent values of the book are three. First it gives us the philosophy of the Divine government in the comprehensiveness of its outlook. Secondly it reveals the practice of the Divine government in that while the prophet was careful to begin with the distant nations in order to show that the principles of government are the same in all nations, his supreme illustration is that of the application to Israel. Finally, in a brief and yet suggestive paragraph with which the book closes, we have the promise of the Divine government.

First, then, as to the philosophy. The fact of Divine government is recognized. Amos never affirmed it, never argued it, but from the first chapter to the last assumed it, and applied it. The supreme atmosphere of the book is that of the government of God. That fact being recognized, we discover in the method of the prophet a revelation of the method of God's government. Amos reveals the standard of the requirement, the principle of the administration, and the patience of the method of God.

As to the standard of requirement; all the denunciations of the nations are denunciations called forth by the fact that they have harmed other nations. The charge against Syria was that of cruelty; against Philistia, that of her slave trade; against Phœnicia, that she had acted as slave agent in spite of a covenant made in which she promised not to do so; against Edom, that of determined and revengeful unforgiveness; against Ammon, that of cruelty based upon cupidity; against Moab, that of violent and vindictive hatred; against Judah, the only case in which the description recognizes the relation of the people to God Himself, the charge was dismissed in a brief word as that of having been guilty of despising the laws of God. Finally, in the case of Israel the charge was that she had become corrupt, and had oppressed the poor and needy within her own borders. Thus it will be seen that the denunciations of the nations were due to their having violated the rights of humanity; and thus it is evident that the standard of God's requirement in His government of the nations is that of their attitude towards other nations.

Then we have the principle of government revealed. We see that principle as we watch the method. The severest words of denunciation were reserved for Israel. The judgment described as falling upon her was far more terrible than that upon either of the other nations. It is impossible to read these messages without discovering that the principle of government is that light creates responsibility, and the nations are judged by God according to the light they have received. National privilege spells national responsibility. If light be refused, then judgment is far severer than when light has been lacking.

Finally, we have the patience of the method of God. As we read these messages we notice how each one begins. " For three . . . yea, for four." This is a figurative way of declaring that God does not act immediately in judgment, but that He waits in order to give every nation the chance of repentance.

We have thus in this book not merely the revelation of the requirements, and of the standard, and of the patience of the government of God; but through these things we clearly see the aim of God in government. If cruelty makes Him angry, it is because His heart is set upon kindness. If oppression stirs up His wrath, it is because His purpose for man is that he should live in peace. If the sorrows inflicted upon man by man call down His judgment, it is because the one great desire of His heart for humanity is that of its well-being and happiness. His government always moves towards the establishment of the best and highest conditions. God is angry with everything that mars; strife, cruelty, war, oppression, because these are against the aim of His government. In the closing paragraph in which the prophet looks on to the day of ultimate restoration of the chosen people, his words are full of suggestiveness. " I will bring again the captivity of My people Israel, and they shall build the waste cities, and inhabit them; and they shall plant vineyards, and drink the wine thereof; they shall also make gardens, and eat the fruit of them. And I will plant them upon their land, and they shall no more be plucked up out of their land which I have given them, saith the Lord." The profits are to go to the toilers. That is a picture of the perfect order ultimately to be established in the world; all oppression, wrong, and fruitless toil forever done away. Thus whether we consider the charges the prophet made against the nations concerning their sin against God, or whether we look at that last chapter, we see that the aim of God's government is that of the establishment of conditions in the midst of which it shall be possible for humanity to realize its true life, and live in the full enjoyment thereof. That is the first permanent value of the book.

The second value is found in an examination of the practice of the Divine government as it is specially illustrated in the case of the nation of Israel. The prophet declared " Hear this word that Jehovah hath spoken against you, O children of Israel, against the whole family which I brought up out of the land of Egypt, saying, You only have I known of all the families of the earth : therefore I will visit upon you all your iniquities." No people had ever had the light which had been granted to Israel. No people had ever been brought into such intimate relationship with God as they had. The prophet moreover declared that God had definitely revealed His mind to them through the prophets, " Surely the Lord God will do nothing, but He revealeth His secret unto His servants the prophets." In these two passages Amos insisted upon the privileges of these people.

Now let us consider what he said concerning the sins of the privileged people. When he came to deal definitely and specifically with these sins, he did so by describing the luxury and wantonness of the women. " Hear this word, ye kine of Bashan, that are in the mountain of Samaria, which oppress the poor, which crush the needy, which say unto their lords, Bring, and let us drink." Isaiah in his sternest denunciation of the people recognized the same corrupting influence, and in satire more biting, and irony more bitter, denounced the sin of the women. John Ruskin attempted to teach his age the same lesson. He declared, and it has often been smiled at as a superlative statement impossible of belief, that in the day when a sanctified and pure womanhood demands that war shall cease, war must cease. It is a superlative statement, but careful consideration will make contradiction of it very difficult.

Thus when the prophet began to deal with the sin of the privileged people, he recognized the awful as well as the sublime influence of womanhood. In his view the sin of the privileged people had its most fearful manifestation in its degraded womanhood.

He then showed that these people had sinned in that they had violated holy associations. In a word full of irony he said, " come to Bethel to transgress." Think of what Bethel stood for, to these people, and so understand the force of his message.

He further showed that their sin had been that they had not yielded to chastisement. That is the value of the phrase running through one section of his prophecy, " Yet have ye not returned unto Me." In spite of blasting, and mildew, and all the other methods of chastisement, they had persisted in their sin. His final word about the sin of the people was that of a denunciation of their false confidence. He spoke to two parties in Israel. First to the people who were always talking about " the day of the Lord " and sighing for it. These he told that they did not know " the day of the Lord," for it would be to them a day of vengeance, of punishment, of judgment. Secondly to the people who never sighed for " the day of the Lord," and were " at ease in Zion," the indifferent people.

All this is the most graphic setting forth of the sins of a privileged people. We do not see such sin in all its darkness until we recognize the greatness of the privilege of the sinning people. They were the family God had known as He had known no other. God had done nothing among them but that He had revealed His secret to the prophets. They had received immediate revelation throughout their history, yet they were guilty of the sins of wanton womanhood ; of the violation of holy associations ; of refusal to submit to chastisement ; of professed desire for a day of judgment which would be to them a day of fire, and of tempest, and storm ; and of indifference to that day.

The prophet then pronounced the judgment which would fall upon the privileged people in five visions, of the locusts, of the fire, of the plumb-line, of the basket of summer fruit; and then all symbolism failing, of the active Jehovah coming by the way of the altar of judgment. In these visions judgment is seen determined upon, temporarily restrained, and finally executed. This message of the activity of the Divine government must have caused great astonishment to the men who listened to it. Jeroboam was on the throne of Israel. It was a day of material prosperity in which the people were saying in effect, See how God loves us, how great is our prosperity! Suddenly this herdman from Tekoa appeared, and first declared that of them Jehovah had said, "You only have I known of all the families of the earth." So far, in all probability, they listened to him with preëminent satisfaction. They were the privileged people. God had done everything for them.

The moment of astonishment came when the prophet continued, " *Therefore* I will visit upon you all your iniquities." Because their light had been clear, their judgment was to be profound. The measure of their privilege was the measure of their responsibility. According to their failure to respond to responsibility in the days of privilege, must be the depth of the ruin and degradation which would inevitably befall them.

Finally, as permanent value we find the promise of the Divine government. It is specially to be noted that the phrase "in that day," connects the closing promise of restoration with all that has preceded it. The day referred to is the day of judgment, the day of denunciation. "In that day will I raise up the tabernacle of David that is fallen, and close up the breaches thereof; and I will raise up his ruins, and I will build it as in the days of old." That is the promise of government. We have seen the philosophy of it. We have seen the illustration of it in practice. In the last paragraph we find the promise of its persistence. Through all the processes we have gleams of the ultimate restoration, and at last it is definitely promised.

First preliminary restoration is promised, " I will raise up the tabernacle of David that is fallen, and close up the breaches thereof; and I will raise up his ruins, and I will build it as in the days of old." Then progressive restoration is promised, "I will bring again the captivity of My people Israel, and they shall build the waste

cities." Finally permanent restoration is promised, "I will plant them, . . . and they shall no more be plucked up."

In this prophecy of Amos, then, we see the governing of God. We discover His standard of government, His principle of government, His patience in government. The practice is illustrated in the case of the people who had more light than any other nation, and gleaming through all the processes is the light of the ultimate victory.

The living message of this book is preeminently applicable to national life. The first note is that Jehovah still holds the balances of even justice, and that He is against all the things which He was against in the days of Amos. We speak of the changes of the centuries. God never changes. We say that the old order changeth. The Divine order never changes. The Divine methods change, the Divine dispensations change, but the underlying principles of the attitude of God towards man never change. Cruelty is as hateful to God on the Congo as it was in Syria.

This book teaches secondly that the people chosen to be the despository of truth have the greatest responsibility. When we make our boast in the Divine calling of the Anglo-Saxon peoples, let us also howl for our sins, and cry aloud and spare not against our corrupting of the covenant.

The sins with which the prophet charged Israel were those of injustice, avarice, oppression, immorality, profanity, blasphemy, and sacrilege; seven deadly sins. If Israel was guilty of them, so are we. Moreover, we are in danger of doing exactly what Israel did in the reign of Jeroboam. We speak of the prosperity which God has given us. We point to the greatness of our empire as evidence of the Divine approval, and all the while God is judging us for our sins. Only as we turn from them in profound repentance can we live. God has not changed. There can be no escape from doom but by the way of penitence. We are not yet independent of God, our inventions, our policies, our armaments notwithstanding.

Yet let the hearts of the loyal be encouraged. Not for utter destruction does He destroy a nation, but for restoration and fulfillment of promise.

If we have made application of the message of Amos to national life, and particularly to our own nation, there is a yet closer, more searching application. There is a holy nation. The Church of Christ is in very deed an elect race. She is assuredly a royal priesthood. Most certainly she is a people for God's own possession. But she is also a holy nation. In the economy of God the Church is the Christian nation, and there is none other. In the light of that fact the Church needs carefully to ponder the solemnity of the message of Amos.

The measure of light is the measure of responsibility. The measure in which that responsibility is not fulfilled, is the measure of the unutterable degradation which must come as God visits in judgment. The holy nation, above all, must give no countenance to the sins which are hateful to Jehovah. Oppression, avarice, blasphemy, impurity, must not be named among the saints, because the light in which the holy nation lives is the most perfect light of all. Let her above all others rejoice in the assurance of that final victory of which she is most perfectly assured, having had through her Lord " the word of prophecy made more sure." Therefore in the measure in which any of the sins denounced have power in the lives of the saints let their repentance be profound, and their return to Him Whose will is good, and perfect, and acceptable, be complete.

Obadiah

THE PERMANENT VALUES	THE LIVING MESSAGE
The unveiling of animalism—the revelation of Edom, which is Esau.	I. Inclusive—"The kingdom shall be Jehovah's."
I. The essential evil—pride.	A. It is His.
A. Godlessness.	B. It is being made His.
1. No spiritual conception.	C. It shall be His.
2. Simple animalism.	II. The application.
B. Defiance—"Who shall bring me down?"	A. The restoration and perfection of Jacob.
1. Self-deification—"Mount high as eagles."	B. The reprobation and destruction of Esau.
2. Self-protection—"Nest among stars."	III. The profane can be made sacred.
II. The supreme manifestation—violence.	
A. Opposition to all Jacob represented.	
1. Faith.	
2. A spiritual ideal.	
B. Manifestation.	
1. Passive.	
a. Day of disaster—looking.	
b. Day of destruction—rejoicing.	
c. Day of distress—speaking proudly.	
2. Active.	
a. Day of calamity—entering into the gates.	
(1) Looking on affliction.	
(2) Laying hands on substance.	
b. Day of distress—cutting off escape and delivering up.	
III. The inevitable issue—retribution.	
A. By act of the denied Jehovah.	
B. By cooperation of events.	
C. By poetic justice—"As thou hast done, it shall be."	
IV. The last word—"The Kingdom shall be Jehovah's."	

THIS prophecy occupies only one page in our Bible, and is characterized by the absence of many things with which we are familiar in the Old Testament Scriptures. Indeed, the first impression made upon the mind by the reading of this very brief prophecy is that it has very little in the nature of a message to this age. We may lay it down, however, as a principle always to be observed and acted upon, that those passages or books of Scripture which seem to have least in them need the most careful attention, and invariably yield the most remarkable results. Isidore, in his allegories of the Sacred Scriptures, said of this book: "Among all the prophets, he is the briefest in number of words; in the grace of mysteries he is their equal." That is most certainly true. The book contains one set message. The identity of the prophet and the historic setting are matters of minor importance. The message is quite independent of either.

The peculiar value of this one brief page is that the antagonism between Jacob and Esau is brought into clearer view than in any other of the prophetic writings. Edom was descended from Esau, and Israel from Jacob. The antagonism between them is patent throughout the Bible. In the book of Genesis occurs a simple and yet most suggestive declaration: "The children struggled together within her." From that hint of the consciousness of Rebekah, the story of the antagonism continues. It finds its fullest expression in the declaration, " I loved Jacob; but Esau I hated." In regard to that statement we must remember that God's love of Jacob and His hatred of Esau were not the causes from which their characters resulted, but the inevitable results of what they were in character. When we come to the New Testament these two antagonistic principles are still seen, and they are at last remarkably focussed in two persons.

The ultimate issue of all Jacob represented—I am not now referring to his meanness, his failure, to that which gave God so much trouble with him; but to the underlying principle and aspiration and spiritual conception for which he stood —is manifested in a person, and that Person is Jesus of Nazareth. He is the final fruitage after the flesh of those principles embodied in Abraham, expressed through Isaac and Jacob, and preserved in the nation.

The ultimate issue of all that Esau represented is also focussed in a person. The king of the Jews at the time of the death of Jesus was an Edomite. Herod was of the race of Esau. To him Jesus never spoke. He once sent him a message thus: "Go and say to that fox, Behold, I cast out devils and perform cures to-day and to-morrow, and the third day I am perfected," a most remarkable revelation of the antagonism between the two ideals. The words sound harsh and strange from the lips of Jesus, but they afford a startling revelation of the whole truth concerning Esau. The background of the picture presented to us by Obadiah is Jacob; the foreground is Esau. Jacob and those descended from him are seen passing through suffering, which is of the nature of chastisement, to ultimate restoration. Esau is seen proud, rebellious, defiant, moving towards ultimate destruction. The permanent value of this book is that of its interpretation of Esau. It brings out, in one single page of the Divine library, into clear relief and vivid outline the meaning of that word already quoted, " Jacob I loved; Esau I hated." To quote again from one of the fathers of the Church, this book historically tells the story of the destruction of Edom, and allegorically sets forth the destruction of the flesh.

Edom is Esau enlarged into national life. In the book of Obadiah we discover the essential evil in Esau, the supreme manifestation of that evil, and the inevitable issue thereof. Finally we find that the stern, hard word of prophecy ends with a gleam of hope even for "the mount of Esau."

Let us summarize these matters before considering them in detail. The essential evil of Esau was pride. The supreme manifestation of that evil was violence, wrong done to others. The inevitable issue thereof was retribution. The last word in the book is the sum total of all prophetic utterance: "Saviours shall come up on mount Zion to judge the mount of Esau; and the kingdom shall be Jehovah's."

The essential evil is graphically set forth in the words: "The pride of thine heart hath deceived thee, O thou that dwellest in the clefts of the rock, whose habitation is high; that saith in his heart, Who shall bring me down to the ground?" "The pride of thine heart hath deceived thee" is the revealing word. The result of that pride of heart was expressed in Edom's defiance: "O thou that dwellest in the clefts of the rock, whose habitation is high; that saith in his heart, Who shall bring me down to the ground?" We at once recognize that this is an actual geographical description of the place of the Edomite nation, those rocky fastnesses in which they lived, and in the seclusion and strength of which they seemed able to defy all invasion, and did indeed for long years successfully defy all attempts to dislodge them. They dwelt literally in the clefts of the rock in a district which gained the name of Petra because of its rocky nature. Hemmed in by rocks, they occupied a tract of land which was considered impregnable.

The difficulty of dealing with the declaration, " The pride of thine heart hath deceived thee," is due to the fact that we have lost our sense of proportion when we deal with sin. There has been so much dealing with specific sins that we have ceased to tremble when essential sin is described. If we speak of drunkenness, of lust, of theft, of lying, men pause for a moment awed by the consciousness of the sinfulness of such things. Yet, as a matter of fact, these are none other than the necessary, natural outcome of something far more deadly. In this sentence the sin of sins is named, "The pride of thine heart hath deceived thee." Pride of heart is that attitude of life which declares its ability to do without God. I am not prepared to say the Edomites had no gods, for I think there are evidences that they had; but the nation springing from Esau imagined that it was independent of God.

The New Testament flashes its light upon the whole history of Esau and the Edomites in a graphic and appalling description of Esau, "that profane person, Esau." Superficial thinking associates the word with indecorous and lewd speech. It has a profounder significance. A profane person is a person *against the temple*. A profane person is one who has no spiritual conception, who sets no value on a birthright, and will sell it for red pottage. A profane person has no consciousness of the eternal, no commerce with the spiritual, is proud of animal ability, and acts as though independent of God. Profanity never prays, never worships, never speaks of spiritual intercourse, has no traffic with the eternities, no commerce with heaven.

Then notice the words, "Though thou mount on high as the eagle, and though thy nest be set among the stars." That is God's description of Edom. The eagle in Eastern symbolism is always a type of Deity. It is as though the prophet's message to Edom was, Thou having dethroned God, hast deified thyself, and made thyself to be thine own and only god. The setting of the nest among the stars high up in the rocky fastnesses is a figure of self-protection. Thus, the description is graphic portraiture.

If that be the essential evil, notice carefully what is the supreme manifestation thereof. It is that of violence; that of wrong done to others, and of rejoicing in the presence of their suffering. "For the violence done to thy brother Jacob . . . in the day that thou stoodest on the other side, in the day that strangers carried away his substance, and foreigners entered into his gates, and cast lots upon Jerusalem, even thou wast as one of them." The Edomites had looked upon the suffering of the people of God, and had been complacent in the presence of it; more, had rejoiced over it; and yet more, had taken a definite part in it. This was the supreme manifestation of the evil, and it was caused by the fact that there was in the heart of Esau opposition to all that Jacob represented. Jacob represented faith in God. He stood for a spiritual ideal. Perhaps I should more accurately express the fact if I said that Jacob stumbled after a spiritual ideal. The supreme matter is that he saw it. In the deepest of his nature he desired it. He set his face towards it notwithstanding all his failure. There was in Jacob a principle upon which God could work for the accomplishment of His purpose. In spite of all his blundering he believed in God, he believed in the spiritual.

That ideal Esau hated. When the day of Jacob's calamity came, when Jacob was being scourged, chastised, Edom was glad; and crossed over and entered into the gate, and joined in unholy opposition, and snatched the substance from his brother.

The inevitable issue of such hatred is retribution. Use any other word which seems more accurately to fit the case—punishment, judgment, if you so will—only remember that judgment has many meanings and many applications, and that judgment as definite punishment even to destruction, is the thought here. Edom said, "Who shall bring me down to the ground?" and Jehovah replied, "Though thou mount on high as the eagle, and though thy nest be among the stars, I will bring thee down. . . . Shall I not in that day . . . destroy the wise men out of Edom, and understanding out of the mount of Esau? And thy mighty men, O Teman, shall be dismayed." The God without Whom Edom declares it is able to live successfully, is the God Who visits Edom with destruction. Though Edom climb as high as the stars and build its nests, and mount as the eagle in self-deification; the God above and around, from Whom he cannot escape, will bring him down, and prove to him the unutterable folly of his animalism, and the heinousness of his pride.

God will do this by overruling the policies and arrangements Edom can make: "The men of thy confederacy have brought thee on thy way, even to the border: the men that were at peace with thee have deceived thee, and prevailed against thee; they that eat thy bread lay a snare under thee." By the coöperation of the very forces in which Edom takes pride, God is working for Edom's destruction. Edom declares: I can do without God. I will be confederate with other men, will enter into political arrangements with them, and international treaties shall exist between us, and thus I shall be safe. God replies: I will bring thee to the dust, and I will do it through the men in whom you are putting your trust. The very forces on which you depend are working together with Me, not for your making, but for your destruction.

The judgment of God upon Edom is poetic justice: " As thou hast done, it shall be done unto thee." The New Testament states it thus: " Be not deceived; God is not mocked: for whatsoever a man soweth, that shall he also reap. For he that soweth unto his own flesh shall of the flesh reap corruption." That is the story of Esau, sowing to the flesh, answering the passions of the flesh, doing this in opposition to Jacob, and rejoicing over Jacob's trouble. In the end the flesh itself becomes the weapon of Edom's destruction. " As thou hast done, it shall be done unto thee."

We now come to the last word of this prophecy, " The captivity of this host of the children of Israel, which are among the Canaanites, shall possess even unto Zarephath ; and the captivity of Jerusalem, which is in Sepharad, shall possess the cities of the South. And saviours shall come up on mount Zion to judge the mount of Esau ; and the kingdom shall be Jehovah's." The last word is the final one of all prophecy, " The kingdom shall be Jehovah's." The preliminary movement is that of the deliverance of the despised Jacob. He is led through all the suffering towards the realization of the Divine purpose, and as a result saviours appear on mount Zion to judge the mount of Esau. I have already said we must be careful to remember that judgment has many meanings and various applications. Judgment may mean administration towards righteousness. I do not hesitate to say that in this last word the truth is expressed that, by the way of Jacob's redemption, restoration, and realization of the Divine purpose, there is hope for Esau.

The final word then is one concerning that day in which all conflict will end, all factions pass out of sight, and all racial divisions disappear,

" The kingdom shall be Jehovah's." The Seer of Patmos saw the ultimate, and described it in the words, " Fallen, fallen is Babylon the great. . . . The kingdom of the world is become the kingdom of our Lord and of His Christ."

Inclusively the living message is to be found in this last sentence, " The kingdom shall be Jehovah's." The conflict between animalism and spirituality still continues, but " the kingdom shall be Jehovah's." In spite of all difficulty, persecution, and opposition, Jacob will become Israel, and Esau will have judgment by the way of saviours. Restoration and perfection for Jacob ; retribution and destruction for Esau. These are certain. Yet the profane may become sacred, for saviours appear upon the mount of Zion.

The living message of this book is to individuals also, for all its principles are operating in human life. What sort of man am I? Am I profane as was Esau, or am I like Jacob? I do not think there are any other types. Even those of us who believe in God, who in the deepest of us have faith and real desire to fulfill the purpose of God, are Jacobs. He has to take us to the Jabbok, and cripple us in order to crown us. He has to be patient with us ; and He is patient, or we had been lost. The God Who chastises us and leads us through trouble is set upon doing us good at the latter end: and all the discipline and trouble, pain and punishment, are in order that at last we may realize our own deepest purpose, and satisfy His heart.

Are we profane, doing without God? We may be wonderfully successful materially ; we may mount up as eagles ; we may be our own gods, acting independently of heaven, of the spiritual world, and building our nests among the stars ; but already God is bringing us down. Our very confederacy with flesh is working our ruin.

The profane man can be made sacred, and if we will but recognize that " the kingdom shall be Jehovah's," and will but kiss His sceptre and bow to His control, and bend our proud necks in worship, and our knees in prayer, yielding ourselves to His revealed Saviour King, then He will make again the vessels, and we also may become His chosen. If not, all our boasting and all our building cannot secure our salvation.

Jonah

THE PERMANENT VALUES	THE LIVING MESSAGE
I. The revelation of Jehovah. A. Jehovah and Nineveh. 　1. His attitude--pity—4:11. 　2. His activity. 　　a. The message sent—against its wickedness. 　　b. The repentance of God—produced by Nineveh's repentance. B. Jehovah and Jonah. 　1. His need of a messenger. 　2. His persistence and patience. 　　a. For delivery of His message. 　　b. For fellowship of His messenger. **II. The revelation of the responsibility of representation.** A. The positive statement. 　1. To represent—he only sends those to represent Him who know Him—4:2. 　2. Therefore to obey. 　　a. His purpose rather than their desire. 　　b. Satisfaction in that purpose. B. The negative revelation. 　1. The underlying reason of failure—hatred of Nineveh. 　2. The resultant manifestation—estrangement from God.	Everything of value in this book is embodied and emphasized in Jesus, and to us. **I. Jehovah and the cities—Jesus and Jerusalem.** **II. Jehovah and His people.** A. Jesus needs us. B. Jesus sends us. **III. Our failure.** A. Not ignorance of God. B. Hatred of our brother. 　1. The foreigner. 　2. The pariah. **IV. How shall we overcome?** A. Not by forcing love to them. B. But by obedience to God, which issues in love to man.

THE book of Jonah is peculiar among the prophetic writings in that it contains no message delivered to the people of God by the prophet whose name it bears. The book is a story, and the story is the message. It was not written for Nineveh. It was written for Israel, using that word in its narrower application to the Northern kingdom, yet recognizing that the moral values of the book have their application to the whole nation.

In order, then, to discover the message of the book, we must seek for the outstanding facts in the story. In doing this it is of the utmost importance that we distinguish between the incidental and the essential. The incidental things are the ship, the storm, the whale, the gourd, the wind, and Nineveh. I need only pause here long enough to say that the incidental things are not necessarily things existing only in the imagination. These things are incidental because they were the instruments in the hand of the master Workman. The essential matters of the book are the transactions between Jehovah and Jonah. It is when the attention is fixed upon these, and all the other things are seen as incidental, that we begin to find the permanent value of the book, and to discover its living message.

Thus to concentrate the attention upon the essential persons is to find that the book is supremely the one of missionary teaching in the

Old Testament. Whereas a missionary purpose is to be found in the whole history of the Hebrew people, this one brief book in the prophetic section does more clearly set forth that missionary purpose, both as to its source and its method, than any other book in the whole of the Old Testament library. It reveals the attitudes and activities of God towards the nations, and towards His own for the sake of the nations. It rebukes the failure of those who should represent Him. It recalls to worship those who have neglected that responsibility of representation. We may hold different opinions as to when and by whom the book was written, but we cannot read it in the way indicated without seeing that its first intention was that of rebuking the exclusiveness of the chosen people of God. Whether Jonah wrote it himself or not, it purports to be the story of events in his life, and there can be no reasonable doubt that the Jonah referred to is the one named in the book of Kings as exercising his ministry in the reign of Jeroboam II. If we recall the prevailing conditions during that period we had two things of the most strangely contradictory character. Israel was attempting to form alliances with the nations around her, and at the same time was more exclusive religiously than she had ever been. She had come to hold the idea that the religion of Jehovah was hers only, that God had made her His peculiar people and cared nothing for others, and that the only attitude of God towards the people outside the covenant was that of hostility. The whole of the Hebrew contempt for, and antagonism to, surrounding nations is focussed in the picture of Jonah. The whole of the Divine attitude towards the surrounding nations, the Divine pity, the Divine patience, the Divine power, is revealed as we see Jehovah dealing with Jonah. Thus there are two permanent values. First, the revelation of the attitude of Jehovah; and secondly, the revelation of the responsibilities of such as represent Him.

We do not find the deepest note concerning Jehovah until we arrive at the end of the book. The story begins with a command to Jonah to arise and go to Nineveh, and cry against it. When we follow the story through, and come to the last words, we touch the deepest note: "Thou hast had pity on the gourd, for the which thou hast not laboured, neither madest it grow; which came up in a night, and perished in a night: and should not I have pity on Nineveh, that great city; wherein are more than sixscore thousand persons that cannot discern between their right hand and their left hand; and also much cattle?"

"*Should not I have pity on Nineveh?*" Here we touch the fundamental truth of the whole book. Everything else is the outcome of it. The command to Jonah to go to Nineveh, the patient persistence with which God compelled him to obedience, are alike the outcome of what is declared in that brief sentence. The relation of this book of Jonah to the books we have already considered is full of interest. It completes a remarkable triptych presenting three pictures of Jehovah. In Amos His sovereignty over the nations is revealed. In Obadiah He is revealed as the God of judgment. In Jonah the supreme revelation is that He is a God of mercy, a God of pity.

The word pity is significant. The Hebrew word literally means cover. Should not I cover Nineveh? The thought perfectly harmonizes with the revelation of God suggested in the words which Jesus uttered over Jerusalem: "How often would I have gathered thy children together, even as a hen gathereth her chickens under her wings, and ye would not." The idea is that of covering them, and so shielding them from danger. Should not I cover Nineveh, brood over it, protect it, feel its sorrows in My own heart, shield it from destroying forces? In that word we have His attitude towards sinning cities. That is the source of missionary endeavour in all the centuries, "Should not I have pity?"

Out of that attitude all the activities of Jehovah proceed. I think if I took up this book of Jonah, and read it for the first time, I should inevitably misread it, because I should put into the first command to Jonah an emphasis wholly of anger in the presence of the wickedness and abounding iniquity of Nineveh; but I cannot so read it after I have read, "Should not I have pity on Nineveh?" Not that the standard of holiness is lowered, not that Jonah was sent to it with any other message than that of judgment against its sin; but that I have now discovered that God's anger with sin is born of His pity for the sinner.

When Nineveh repented, God repented, and

repented because He cannot change. The Hebrew word here has more in it than the suggestion of change of mind. It suggests a sob, a sigh, a breathing of agony. Yet it does also suggest change, and therefore what He said He would do, He did it not. In the moment when Nineveh turned from its evil to Him, He straightway changed His purpose of judgment. Nineveh fulfilled its responsibility by obedience to Him; and His attitude was changed because He cannot deny Himself, He cannot be untrue to the central fact of His nature. Whenever we read that God repented, and we study the context, we shall find such statement either followed or preceded by a declaration of the cause, and the cause is always man's repentance. So that when a man turns from or repents of his wickedness, God turns from His purpose of judgment, which in itself was love-inspired.

In further examination of the essential things, we notice God's need of a messenger. "How shall they hear without a preacher?" is the enquiry of the New Testament, and in that enquiry, as in this story, there is manifest a great principle of supreme importance. Out of that grows the explanation of His persistent patience to secure the fellowship of His messenger, "The word of the Lord came to Jonah the second time." The man who had failed at first had a second opportunity of fulfilling the purpose of God in Nineveh; and beyond that, there is a third time, a third time of attempt to bring this man into sympathy with the purpose of God in mercy. The methods were of the gourd provided and withered, and the conversation between Jehovah and His messenger. There was tender satire in the question of God as the margin renders it, "Art thou greatly angry?" Jonah replied, "I do well to be angry even unto death." Again God asked the same question, and continued: "Thou hast had pity on the gourd, for the which thou hast not laboured, neither madest it grow; which came up in a night, and perished in a night: and should not I have pity on Nineveh?" Thus God appealed to Jonah, persuading him to fellowship in love. The story ends with the picture of this man still in rebellion, still angry. If he wrote the book, then I claim God won his victory and brought him into sympathy with Himself, for the story told reveals his folly and his failure.

What, then, is the revelation of this book as to the responsibility of those who represent God? Forgive me if I first state it in the most obvious and apparently unnecessary way. The responsibility of those who represent Jehovah is that they represent Him. Now what was the trouble with Jonah? Why, when sent to Nineveh, did he find a ship and attempt to reach Tarshish? Why, when commanded by Jehovah to deliver a message, did he attempt to escape by resigning his position as a prophet? Why, after the remarkable interposition and deliverance which came to him, and after he had delivered his message, did he sit in hot anger and rebellion against God? I think the answer we should be inclined to give at first is that he did not know God. That, however, is not true, for it is written that when Nineveh was spared, "It displeased Jonah exceedingly, and he was angry. And he prayed unto the Lord, and said, I pray Thee, O Lord, was not this my saying, when I was yet in my country? Therefore I hasted to flee unto Tarshish: for I knew that Thou art a gracious God, and full of compassion, slow to anger, and plenteous in mercy, and repentest Thee of the evil." Therein is revealed the tragedy of this book. The flight to Tarshish and the hot rebellion were expressions of something much more serious. The things Jonah knew of Jehovah are the great truths contained in the most wonderful words in the Old Testament, words in which God had unveiled Himself to His servant long before, "a God full of compassion and gracious, slow to anger, and plenteous in mercy and truth." Jonah knew all this, and that is why he did not go. Now we are finding the reason of his anger. It was not caused by ignorance of God, but by hatred of Nineveh. He did not want Nineveh to be spared. On the human plane I understand him perfectly. Nineveh was guilty of cruelty and abominations for which one hundred years later another prophet uttered her doom. She was merciless and cruel, and Jonah was in rebellion against her being spared. God only sends those to represent Him who know Him. The responsibility, therefore, of those who are called to represent God, is that of obedience. His purpose, rather than their desire, must be the master passion of their heart. Their predjudice must be overruled by the purposes of God, governed by them, and submitted to them.   The result of failure in this is estrangement between the messenger and God.

What, then, is the living message of this book? We have had this word of prophecy made more sure in that all its suggestiveness has been embodied for us in the Person and the mission of One Whom we call Lord and Master.   Everything of value in this book is embodied and emphasized in the Lord Jesus Christ.   Therefore its teaching comes to us with even greater force, because with greater light than that with which it came to ancient Israel.   That final word, which reveals the fount out of which all this story springs, the word which announces the pity of the Divine heart, flames for us in new light in the picture of Jesus Christ in His attitude towards Jerusalem.   Do not let us, however, make that picture of Christ weeping over Jerusalem the picture of something in the past ; it is the picture of His attitude at this moment towards this city, and towards all the cities of the earth.   Think of all the cities, the habitations of cruelty, places where humanity is manifesting its most awful corruption, and then remember that God pities them all.   However we may fail towards our own or other cities or lands, God has pity on them.   Do we care for the plant that comes up and perishes ?   Then God says, " Should not I have pity on Nineveh?"   We shall never be missionary enthusiasts until we come into fellowship with that pity.   Once we do so, we shall find the corrective to all our halting.   When He beheld the city He wept over it.   That is a revelation of the eternal fact in the nature of God.

All the picture of Jehovah in His dealing with Jonah is fulfilled for us also in the New Testament revelation.   If the Lord Christ pities men, in order to send His messages to them, He needs us.   God always needs a man to stand in the gap.   The Word must be incarnate before it becomes powerful.   We scatter our Bibles far over the world, and thank God that we do so, but the ordained method of reaching men is to send the Bible with a man.   It is by the human voice, the actual living messenger, that the Word of God is made powerful.   Christ still needs messengers to the cities, and He still sends us.   There is no man, woman, or little child who really belongs to Christ, who does not share the responsibility : " Arise, go to Nineveh, that great city, and cry against it ; for their wickedness is come up

before Me."   That command comes out of infinite pity and infinite love.   Why cry against Nineveh's wickedness?   Because it is damning Nineveh ; because God would save Nineveh ; because God's act of destruction is forever a strange act.   The act that comes out of His heart is the act of construction, salvation, and love.   Therefore cry against the wickedness that blights and spoils.

Before we criticize Jonah let us turn the light on ourselves.   How far have we obeyed ?   There are facts in the story of Jonah which show that there was much of nobility about him, even in the moment of disobedience.   When he went out from the presence of the Lord, he went down to Joppa and found a ship waiting (it is remarkable how accommodating circumstances seem to be sometimes when we are trying to escape responsibility), then he paid his own fare.   There is a fine touch of honesty about that.   We have not always been so honest.   Do not forget, however, that if we are really commanded by God, the fortuitous concurrence of circumstances, Joppa, the ship, and the fine independence of paying our own fare, will not ensure our reaching Tarshish.   The hand of God is still upon us, and we thank Him that it is so.

The secret of the Church's comparative failure in missionary enterprise is not that we do not know God and His compassion.   We do know Him.   His love has been commended to us. We have felt its warmth, its fire.   We know its victories in our own lives.   Why, then, do we halt ?   For exactly the same reason which halted Jonah.   Because we hate Nineveh.   The Church does not want to see the world saved, does not want to see the heathen nations brought to Christ. She still speaks of her work as *foreign* missionary work ; still describes men of other nationalities and other climates and other colours as *natives*, as *foreigners;* still adopts the attitude of supercilious indifference to them.

If that statement seems too severe, come nearer home.   Why does not the Church reach the outcast people in London and save them ?   Because the Church does not like the outcast people, does not want them saved.   We write of the pariahs of India in pity, but the submerged outside our own doors we prefer to keep outside.   In how many pews in the average church would the outcast be welcome if he or she appeared on Sunday next? Do we really want them? Are we ready to coöperate with God?

How shall we overcome this difficulty? Not by trying to love them. Never was a more absurd thing said by any man than that he would try to love some one. It is impossible. We cannot try to love these people. What, then, shall we do? Fall in line with the command of our Lord and what we know of Him, and do what He bids. Such obedience will create love even for those whom we cannot compel ourselves to love. There are a great many people in this city of whom we think with revulsion. We do not want to get near them. We are not really anxious they should be saved. We have never stretched out a hand to help them. Let us begin to do it, not out of love for them, but out of love for the Lord. As surely as we do, we shall find beneath the rough surface gems with lustre as wonderful as any we have discovered in any walk of life. We shall find that they also are lovable.

The whole lesson of the book of Jonah is that of the sin of exclusivism, the sin of imagining that if we have received light, it is for ourselves alone. Let us away to Nineveh because God commands it, whether the going falls in with our prejudices or not; and as we go we shall come into new fellowship with Him, and find a new comradeship with humanity, and withal hasten the coming of the day of His perfect victory.

Micah

THE PERMANENT VALUES	THE LIVING MESSAGE

I. The unmasking of false authority—3:11.
  A. Civil rulers—judge for reward—3:2.
    1. Character—hate good, love evil.
    2. Conduct—spoilation of the people.
  B. Spiritual rulers—teach for hire.
    1. Their claim—they lean upon the Lord.
    2. Their corruption—the corrupted motive.
  C. Moral rulers—divine for money—3:5.
    1. Their influence—they make my people err.
    2. Their methods.
      a. Fed—they cry peace.
      b. Unfed—they make war.
II. The unveiling of true authority.
  A. The coming One.
    1. From human obscurity.
    2. From everlasting.
  B. His administration.
    1. He shall stand.
    2. He shall feed.
  C. The issue.
    1. Positive—this man shall be peace.
    2. Negative—destruction of all false methods—v. 10-14.
	I. The test of all authority is in its motive—civil, spiritual or moral selfishness is evil.
	II. The strength of authority.
	  A. The strength of Jehovah.
	  B. The majesty of the name of Jehovah.
	III. The hope.
	  A. The One who came to lay foundations.
	  B. He will come to complete the work.
	IV. The duty.
	  A. To obey.
	  B. To enforce.
	  C. To wait.

THE position this book occupies in the Divine library maintains an interesting sequence. I do not suggest that the placing of these books is inspired. In the Septuagint the arrangement is entirely different. I do, however, say quite seriously that I am a Churchman, believing in the Catholic Church, and believing in the Catholic Church as an instrument of God. As I study my Bible I am more and more convinced that there is a reason for the order in which the books are placed. We have seen in our last two or three lectures that there has been an evident sequence of thought. Let us call to mind the three immediately preceding this one. In Amos the burden was that of the Divine government of nations, and of national accountability. In Obadiah it was that of Divine government proceeding to judgment against sin. In Jonah it was that of the Divine government proceeding in mercy in answer to repentance.

In Micah we have a picture of the administration of that government in the affairs of men. The nations are addressed. There is, of course, a sense in which this prophecy was not to the nations outside; but they are in view; and as we read, we find that the prophet's method was that of calling upon the nations to observe God's method with His own people. He recognized that the chosen people were created in order that through them the fact of the sovereignty of God might be made manifest to the nations. Therefore he called upon those nations to observe the judgment of the chosen people.

When God has chosen a nation or called a man, the truth of His government is made real through the nation or through the man, either by failure or by success. If the nation be obedient, there follows the revelation to other nations of the grace and tenderness of the Divine government in the realization of life at its highest and best; such realization resulting from such obedience. Had Israel fulfilled the purpose of God in the midst of the nations they would have seen in her prosperity, in her blessing, how good and gracious a thing the government of God is. Israel failed to bear that testimony to the nations. Then is there no message for them through her history? Micah shows that in the judgment of God upon the failing people a truth of vast importance is proclaimed to the surrounding nations. Therefore he makes his appeal to them, summons them to see the judgment of God upon the people who failed, in order that they may learn something of the meaning of His government.

The fundamental conception of this book in common with all the prophetic writings is that of the sovereignty of Jehovah. Micah was familiar with the condition of the people resulting from the misrule of Ahaz. He was first, and last, and always, conscious of, and confident in, the throne and the government of God. He was undoubtedly during a large part of his prophetic ministry contemporary with Isaiah, and their conceptions are strikingly similar. There is, however, a distinct difference between them, and in the difference we discover the peculiar value of this book. Isaiah saw the uplifted throne of Jehovah; and all through his wonderful ministry, whether in the prophecies of judgment proceeding to peace, or in those of peace proceeding to judgment, he dealt with men and affairs as having immediate relation to that throne.

Micah recognizes the place of delegated authority in the economy of God, and he spoke to princes, priests, and prophets as to the representatives of the Divine authority. "The powers that be are ordained of God," declared the Christian apostle, and so also taught the Hebrew prophet; and that conception of God's sovereignty as delegated and exercised through appointed rulers is discoverable throughout the prophecy. He traced the sin and corruption, the sighing and crying, the agony and tears of the people, to the misrule of the men in authority.

The permanent values of this prophecy of Micah then are two; first, the unmasking and denunciation of false rulers; and, secondly, the unveiling and proclamation of the true Ruler. In each case the authority is seen not in the abstract, but in the concrete. False authority is seen in the princes, priests, and prophets, by whom Micah was surrounded; true authority in the One, Whose advent he saw in an hour of exalted and holy vision, and of Whom he spoke remarkable words which are evidently Messianic.

Let us first consider what this prophecy teaches concerning false authority. It is completely unmasked in one brief statement, " The heads thereof judge for reward, and the priests thereof teach for hire, and the prophets thereof divine for money." In these words Micah named the three sections of rulers; civil, the princes; spiritual, the priests; and moral, the prophets. He showed wherein lay the secret of failure to rule in each case. and consequently the secret of the corruption of the people over whom they ruled. There is more satire in his last description than in the first two, for in that he was dealing with men of his own order, whom he understood more perfectly than he did either princes or priests. When speaking of the princes he used a word which characterized their proper activity; they judge, but they do it for reward. When he spoke of the priests he used a word which characterized their responsibility; they teach, but they do it for hire. When he came to deal with the prophets he used a word which did not characterize their responsibility, but which revealed what they were really doing. The prophets were not prophesying, they were divining. The Hebrew word here translated divining is one which indicates the activity which God had forbidden, that of sorcery and witchcraft. He thus employed a word which showed how deep their sin was. They divined for money.

Take each of these for brief examination. "The heads thereof judge for reward." In the earlier part of the chapter we find more particularly what that means. The prophet described their proper function, "Hear, I pray you, ye heads of Jacob, and rulers of the house of Israel: is it not for you to know judgment?" Then he described their character, "who hate the good, and love the evil." Finally, he described their conduct, "who pluck off their skin from off them, and their flesh from off their bones; who also eat the flesh of My people; and they flay their skin from off them, and break their bones: yea, they chop them in pieces, as for the pot, and as flesh within the caldron." The men who ought to know judgment, and exercise judgment, and rule over the people, are men who hate the good and love the evil, and the result is the spoliation of the people. "The heads thereof judge for reward." They are men who take bribes, men who can be bought, men who make it impossible for the poor and oppressed to find judgment and justice. A corrupt ruler is one who exercises the office to which he is appointed, not impartially, and not as the representative of the throne of eternal judgment, but for reward. There is no need that we should dwell upon the heinousness of that sin. Men, whether Christian or not, know theoretically how dastardly a thing it is for a judge to receive a bribe.

"The priests thereof teach for hire." The priests are the spiritual rulers, and one is almost startled to find the word Micah used of them, they teach. We have so far wandered from the Old Testament idea of priesthood as to imagine that teaching is not a part of its work. So far as the relation of the priest to man is concerned, this is the principal part of his work. So far as his relation to God is concerned he had to carry out the ceremonial instruction and sacrifices. But towards men the priest was a teacher. Moses in his final message had declared, " Thou shalt come unto the priests the Levites . . . and thou shalt enquire; and they shall shew thee the sentence of judgment, and thou shalt do according to the tenor of the sentence, which they shall shew thee from that place which the Lord shall choose; and thou shalt observe to do all that they shall teach thee; according to the tenor of the law which they shall teach thee, thou shalt do: thou shalt not turn aside from the sentence." When Micah denounced the priests he evidently had in mind that ancient provision in the economy of God. The true function, the spiritual function of the ancient priesthood was that of knowing the will of God and interpreting it to men. The work of the priest was that of bringing to bear upon material things the light and force of spiritual things. That is the meaning of teaching. The false priest holds out his hand for hire, and so corrupts the people.

Then we have the last description, " the prophets thereof divine for money." The true word descriptive of the prophetic work should have been proclaim. The prophets stood for the moral standards of the people. Of these men Micah declared, they " bite with their teeth and cry, Peace; and whoso putteth not into their mouths, they even prepare war against him." That is to say, the prophets were prepared to say certain things to the people on certain conditions. If the people would feed them they would say, Peace; if they would not, then the prophets would denounce them.

Thus in this brief description we have the most complete unmasking of false authority. Wherever we find distressed and suffering people the cause is to be discovered finally in the rulers. " The powers that be are ordained of God." If the powers that be are out of harmony with God, if they love evil and hate good, if they are mastered by pure selfishness, the people pass into the place of suffering and corruption. I care not whether the system of human government be autocracy, limited monarchy, or republicanism, we still find these orders referred to by Micah; there are the civil rulers, kings, princes or presidents; the spiritual rulers, the priests, men who stand among the people to tell them the things of the eternal world; the moral rulers, the prophets, the men who interpret to their age the standards of right. These are the leaders of men. Whatever may be the form of human government, men are still under the threefold rule of civil, spiritual and moral authority. When the civil rulers enrich themselves out of their office, the result is a demoralized people. When the spiritual rulers are seeking hire, the people are corrupted, and desolation ensues. When the moral rulers are seeking for money, the people are degraded. False authority is authority exercised on behalf of the men who exercise it. When the reason why a man rules is that he may get gain out of his ruling, the people suffer. The right to rule is the right of a self-emptied life, the right of a life that has no thought of its own aggrandizement or enrichment. That is the life that rises to a position of true power in the economy of God. When men in positions of authority in the spiritual, civil, or moral realms work for reward, hire, money, the people become demoralized, and corruption is the issue.

Through the mists, beyond the immediate,

Micah saw the coming Ruler. He saw Him coming out of human obscurity, " Thou, Bethlehem Ephratah, which art little to be among the thousands of Judah, out of thee shall One come forth unto Me that is to be ruler in Israel." The prophet, borne along through the centuries, carried away from the immediate surroundings in the midst of which he found himself, sick at heart of the false rule under which he lived and under which the people groaned and suffered, saw in the distance the one true Ruler to Whom Jehovah delegated His authority. Micah did not perhaps perfectly understand the things he saw, or the things he wrote upon the page of his prophecy, which we must date at least six or seven hundred years before Christ ; but they are the facts chronicled in the gospel story. He saw One coming out of human obscurity, out of Bethlehem Ephratah ; and yet not finally from Bethlehem, but from everlasting.

He then described the administration of the coming One in the words, " He shall stand, and shall feed His flock in the strength of the Lord." The false rulers, civil, spiritual, moral, were self-centred men who governed in their own interest and not in the interest of the people ; seeking for reward, hire, money. The true ruler will stand inflexible and invincible in authority, feeding His flock in the strength of Jehovah. The true Ruler will represent Jehovah and act in His strength.

Micah finally described the effect of the rule of the true Ruler, in one simple statement. " This Man shall be our peace." That is the positive issue. The prophet saw, moreover, in the establishment of the true rule, the destruction of all the things in which the people had put their confidence when they were under false rule ; horses, chariots, cities, strongholds, witchcraft, images, the Asherim.

The strength of a nation is never in its horses and chariots. The safety of a nation does not consist in its adoption of a two-power standard. The strength of a nation is not in its cities and strongholds, fortifications and armaments, soothsaying and witchcraft. The strength of a nation is in its Ruler.

The permanent values constitute the living message. The test of authority is its motive. If the motive of civil authority is the aggrandizement of the ruler ; if the motive of spiritual authority is the creation of power on behalf of the priest ; if the motive of moral authority is the enrichment of the prophet, then all such authority is false in itself, and pernicious in its effect.

The strength of authority is in recognition of Jehovah. We have seen it perfectly realized in the One to Whom Micah looked on, Who came from Bethlehem Ephratah, out of everlasting into time, to lay the broad foundations of the ultimate Kingdom. He will come again to complete His work, and we shall never see perfect government, authority, rule, by civil, spiritual, or moral rulers, until that hour in which He Who came shall come again, for the completion of His work.

Our duty is to obey Him. for our eyes have seen Him and our hearts know Him. We must enforce His ideals by our living and by our teaching. With loins girt about, and lamps burning, we must wait for the flaming of the glory of His advent feet ; and we must watch, not gloomily, but with sunlight in the heart, and confidence in the life, knowing that at last He will abolish chariots and horses, cities, strongholds, and all the things of the dust in which men put their confidence ; and establish the Kingdom of God in the eternal strength of righteousness.

Nahum

THE PERMANENT VALUES	THE LIVING MESSAGE

An explanation of the anger of God.
I. The prophet's vision of God.
  A. The general impression—the seven words—1:2, 3.
    1. Jealous.
    2. Vengeance.
    3. Wrath.
    4. Anger.
    5. Indignation.
    6. Fierceness.
    7. Fury.
  B. The careful exposition.
    1. The threefold description—1:2.
      a. The Lord—passion and action.
      b. The Lord—action out of passion.
      c. The Lord—discrimination.
    2. The threefold exposition—1:3-8.
      a. The Lord—slow.
      b. The Lord—irresistible.
      c. The Lord—salvation/destruction.
II. The prophet's vision of the vengeance of God.
  A. The reason—why?
    1. Pride—a Godward sin—1:11.
    2. Cruelty—a manward sin—3:1 ff.
  B. The principle—when?
    1. Godward—after patience.
    2. Manward—cup of iniquity so full that man agrees.
  C. The method—how?
    1. Destruction of the corrupt.
    2. Opportunity in interest of others.
	I. Concerning God.
	  A. To believe in His love is to be sure of His wrath.
	  B. His wrath must be interpreted by His love.
	II. Concerning man.
	  A. The sins against which the wrath of God proceeds.
	    1. Pride.
	    2. Cruelty.
	    3. Impenitence.
	  B. The conditions of safety—"Them that put their trust in Him."

IT is impossible to read the book of the prophet Nahum without an almost overwhelming sense of solemnity. The story it has to tell is that of the utter and irrevocable destruction of a great city and a great people. It was first uttered by the prophet Nahum as a prophecy. It is all the more solemn to-day because it has become history. When Nahum delivered his message, Judah was in grave peril, by reason of the cruel oppression threatened by Assyria. His name was suggestive to those who heard it, signifying "full of exceeding comfort." To people in such condition he uttered this start-

ling and remarkable prediction, that Nineveh, the cruel, the terrible, the mighty, though proud and defiant, should be utterly destroyed.

To-day the traveller finds his way to the ancient site, and discovers that in the interval which has elapsed since the uttering of the prophecy, armies have positively marched over the site of Nineveh, ignorant of the fact that beneath the dust on which they trod lay the ruins of a great city. The ruins are now being laid bare, and tablets and inscriptions have been discovered which show that the book which was prophetic when its message was delivered has become a page of actual history. The descriptions of the destruction of the city are no longer predictions; they are accounts of things which have actually happened. I repeat, this fact adds solemnity to the book.

The message of the prophet Nahum is closely compacted together. It is clear in statement, logical in argument, definite in its declarations. The writer describes his message as a vision. It is a vision, first, of Jehovah; secondly, of Jehovah in anger; and, thirdly, of Jehovah acting in anger. The permanent value of the book is that it sets before the mind as no other book in the Old Testament does, indeed as no other book in the Divine library does, the picture of the wrath of God.

The vision is, first, a vision of Jehovah. After writing the prefatory word, "The book of the vision of Nahum the Elkoshite," the prophet immediately began to describe the vision:

"Jehovah is a jealous God and avengeth; Jehovah avengeth and is full of wrath; Jehovah taketh vengeance on His adversaries, and He reserveth wrath for His enemies."

It is a vision of Jehovah, and of Jehovah acting in His wrath. The tendency of the day is either to deny or to shrink entirely from any reference to that aspect of truth concerning God. Therefore one comes to this book with an added sense of solemnity, and with a very sincere and earnest desire to discover what this prophet teaches on so startling a theme as that of the anger of God. In order to do this we must consider two aspects of the one great vision which this book contains; first, the prophet's vision of God; and secondly, the prophet's vision of the vengeance of God.

The prophet's vision of God. The Hebrew prophets constantly delivered messages to men under the constraint of some revelation of God. Isaiah had gazed upon the throne, and discovered the fundamental principles of government and grace. Jeremiah had seen Jehovah, and had watched His activities in the midst of perpetual, willful failure on the part of his own people. Ezekiel, the exile by the banks of the River Chebar, had seen the mystic unveiling of God in the strange imagery of living ones, amid wheels, and the pervasive energy of the Spirit. Nahum also saw Jehovah, and the revelation is one which overawes the spirit.

In the first passage of the prophecy the prophet makes use of no less than seven different and distinct words to describe the one overwhelming and awe-inspiring fact of the anger of God. Let us cite the words: "Jealous—vengeance — wrath — anger — indignation—fierceness —fury." The massing of these words in so brief a passage is full of suggestiveness, subduing the spirit, and compelling one to most careful examination. Let us take each in turn.

"*Jealous.*" The Hebrew word was derived from a root, the underlying thought of which is that of intensity. We might accurately express it by our word "zealous." It is a word which suggests an attitude of the emotional nature. The Hebrew word, like our English word, if carefully considered, presupposes love. We need not be afraid of interpreting the real suggestiveness of this word by the word "jealous" in our ordinary speech. It grows out of the thought of love. It is an attitude of the emotional nature. It describes the wrath of God subjectively, that is, as to what He feels within Himself, and thus helps us to find the deepest fact in His anger. There is a jealousy which is mean petty, self-centred. That is not the suggestion of this word.

"*Avengeth.*" Here we have the quite simple idea of definite punishment; only we must remember that punishment is retribution, and never retaliation in the economy of God. Vengeance on the part of man constantly means retaliation. Vengeance on the part of God always means retribution. If the word "jealous" presupposes the emotional nature, and indicates the subjective fact, the word "vengeance" presupposes the volitional nature, and indicates the objective aspect of the same fact.

"*Wrath.*" Here we have perhaps the strangest thought of all. The Hebrew word comes from another word which means to cross over. This particular word was perpetually used by the Hebrew people to indicate the other side of Jordan, and almost invariably referred to the eastern side thereof. Consequently this word "wrath" suggests a change in the Divine attitude. Judgment is "His strange act." God willeth not the death of a sinner, but in certain conditions, discoverable in the prophecy of Nahum, God inflicts the death penalty on a sinner. In wrath He has crossed over necessarily, and the resulting attitude is the opposite of tenderness, healing, and compassion.

"*Anger . . . indignation.*" We take these two words together, for they are both pictorial. Of anger the root thought is hard breathing. Of indignation the suggestion is of that formidable and terrible aspect of anger which accompanies hard breathing, foaming at the mouth. They are pictorial words, which startle and alarm us when used of God. The prophet employs them to indicate the outward expression of essential anger.

"*Fierceness . . . fury.*" Again we take two words. "Fierceness" means burning. "Fury" means heat. They are words adding intensity to every other word employed, and thought suggested.

This is only a grouping of words. It is impossible, however, to read the paragraph containing them without recognizing that Nahum saw God angry. Every Hebrew word found in the Bible suggesting anger is packed into the compass of that brief and awful description. Nahum saw God jealous and exercising vengeance: saw Him in wrath, having crossed over from that attitude with which the prophets were familiar; saw Him with all the expressions of wrath, anger, indignation; saw Him in vengeance, fierce in its burning, white hot in its intensity.

This, however, is not merely a piece of rhetoric, in which a man under the sway of some personal feeling of vengeance attributes to God the things that are in his own heart. It is a most careful and remarkable description of the anger of God. The paragraph falls into two portions. We have first a threefold description of the anger of God. We have next an exposition of that threefold description. The great name, unuttered by the Hebrew, appearing upon the page as the tetragrammaton YHVH, occurs three times in the second verse. It occurs again three times in the following six verses. This is a systematic arrangement. In the first case we have proclamation. In the second case we have explanation. We must put the explanation over against the proclamation if we would understand what Nahum teaches concerning the anger of God.

First examine the proclamation. "Jehovah is a jealous God and avengeth." In that declaration the prophet tells us that passion preceded action.

"Jehovah avengeth and is full of wrath." In the second declaration the prophet makes the same statement, but in the other order. He tells us of action growing out of passion.

"Jehovah taketh vengeance on His adversaries, and He reserveth wrath for His enemies." In that statement the prophet declares that the wrath of God as passion and action is characterized by discrimination, and is never capricious or careless.

That verse is a general proclamation of the fact that out of passion grows action, but that action out of passion is always governed by principle. I believe it was Pusey who declared that in the case of man, wrath becomes his master and drives him; in the case of God He is always Master of His wrath and uses it. It is a most important distinction.

Now let us turn to the explanation, taking in each case the proclamation in immediate connection with the explanation.

"Jehovah is a jealous God and avengeth."
"Jehovah is slow to anger, and great in power, and will by no means clear the guilty."
"Jehovah avengeth and is full of wrath."
"Jehovah hath His way in the whirlwind and in the storm, and the clouds are the dust of His feet. He rebuketh the sea and maketh it dry, and drieth up all the rivers: Bashan languisheth, and Carmel, and the flower of Lebanon languisheth. The mountains quake at Him, and the hills melt; and the earth is upheaved at His presence, yea, the world, and all that dwell therein. Who can stand before His indignation? and who can abide in the fierceness of His anger? His fury is poured out like fire, and the rocks are broken asunder by Him."
"Jehovah taketh vengeance on His adversaries, and He reserveth wrath for His enemies."
"Jehovah is good, a stronghold in the day of trouble; and He knoweth them that put their trust in Him. But with an overrunning flood He will make a full end of the place thereof, and will pursue His enemies into darkness."

That simple reading of proclamation and explanation in relation in each case gives a result which may thus be tabulated.

Jehovah's wrath is a passion born of love, which proceeds to action.
Jehovah is slow to anger.
Jehovah's wrath is an activity which proceeds out of the passion of His love.
Jehovah is irresistible in anger.
Jehovah's anger is discriminative.
Jehovah's anger is not for those who put their trust in Him, but for His enemies.

Do not let us imagine when we think of the anger of God that it is anything like the hot, passionate, blind, foolish blundering of a man in a temper. He is slow to anger; yet, having once crossed over in the presence of things which demand the new attitude of vengeance, He is irresistible as the hurricane that beats the sea into fury, or the simoom that sweeps the land with desolation. Nevertheless, He is forever discriminative; a stronghold to such as put their trust in Him, while of His enemies He makes a full end.

We turn now to the prophet's vision of the vengeance of God. We look for Nineveh to-day, and find that the prophecy has been fulfilled to the letter. There are three questions I propose to ask in the presence of this unveiling of the vengeance of God. They are such questions as a child might ask.

> Why does God act in vengeance?
> When does God act in vengeance?
> How does God act in vengeance?

The answers to these questions are given in this prophecy and reveal the reason of the Divine judgment; the principle of the Divine judgment; and the method of the Divine judgment.

Why does God act in judgment? The answer reveals the reason. That is stated in two passages which we will put into close connection.

"There is one goeth forth out of thee, that imagineth evil against the Lord, that counselleth wickedness."
"Hear, I pray you, ye heads of Jacob, and rulers of the house of Israel: is it not for you to know judgment? who hate the good, and love the evil; who pluck off their skin from off them, and their flesh from off their bones; who also eat the flesh of My people; and they flay their skin from off them, and break their bones: yea, they chop them in pieces, as for the pot, and as flesh within the caldron."

The reference in the first passage is to the sin of Sennacherib described in Isaiah, the sin in which the fundamental sin of Assyria had its manifestation. It was that of the pride which dared God. As to the second passage, it describes the sin of Assyria as manifested towards man, that of oppression and cruelty.

Thus, there are two sins calling for the anger of God: the Godward sin of pride and rebellion, expressed finally by Sennacherib as he went forth and challenged God; the manward sin of cruelty and oppression. These two are interrelated. We never find one without the other. A people proud and lifted up in rebellion against God is a people cruel in its treatment of men. The interrelation is inevitable and invariable. Jesus summarized all the law in the words,

"Thou shalt love the Lord thy God with all thy heart, and with all thy soul, and with all thy mind. . . . Thou shalt love thy neighbour as thyself." The man who says he loves God, yet hates his neighbour, is a liar. That description is not mine. It is the description of the apostle of love, the man who laid his head upon the bosom of the Christ, and listened to the beating of His heart. So that when I am asked what Nahum teaches concerning the reason of God's vengeance, the reply is that God acts in vengeance in the interest of others. He smites out of the love which is in His heart for those who are oppressed and stricken.

Let us take our second question. When does God become a God of wrath towards a nation or towards a man? The answer to this question reveals the principle of the Divine judgment. God destroyed Nineveh after long patience. One hundred years before He had sent a reluctant prophet to foretell its doom. Nineveh repented, but afterwards repented of its repentance. Now at last, Jehovah becomes a God that avengeth. When God proceeds in judgment, man, observing from the standpoint of essential right, is in absolute agreement with Him. "Thy shepherds slumber, O king of Assyria: thy worthies are at rest: thy people are scattered upon the mountains, and there is none to gather them. There is no assuaging of thy hurt; thy wound is grievous; all that hear the bruit of thee clap the hands over thee; for upon whom hath not thy wickedness passed continually?" When the ruin of Nineveh came, the story of it came as an evangel to the nations, because of Assyria's cruelty and oppression. When God proceeded in judgment, men who loved righteousness and saw things in their true relation to the eternities agreed in the necessity for His vengeance.

Our last question is, How does God act in vengeance? The answer reveals the method. That answer is discovered in Nineveh as she is to-day. In the hour of her ruin, natural forces and the enmity of men coöperated to bring about the result. Deodorus Seculus had prophesied that the ancient capital would never be captured until her river turned against her. The actual history tells how in the day when she was hemmed in by enemies, suddenly the river swept in, and by the great gap it made in her walls, the enemy entered. The materialist will speak of the way in which Nineveh *happened* to be destroyed. The men of spiritual vision know that through natural forces and the opposing army, God moved forward and blotted out a people with whom He had long had patience.

What is the living message of Nahum to our own age? It is first a message concerning God, which I propose to state in the briefest sentences. To believe in His love is to be sure of His wrath. In the hour in which you can persuade me that God is never angry, you persuade me that He cannot love. We are often asked to-day to interpret the Divine from the standpoint of the human. I am quite willing, for the moment, to adopt the method. Can you look at sin, wrong, oppression, and never be moved? If so, it is because you are incapable of love. Have you no care about China and the oppression of her people? Have you really no interest in the Congo atrocities? Have you no care for the wronged multitudes of your own city? As a Christian worker, have you never longed to lay violent hands upon some devil incarnate who has wronged a woman? Then you have no love in your nature. If it be true that God cannot burn, smite, destroy in vengeance, then He is a God incapable of love. To believe in His love is to be sure of His wrath.

Nahum teaches, moreover, that His wrath must always be interpreted by His love. Let us beware how we commit blasphemy in thinking of God as petulantly angry, selfishly ill-tempered. Behind the wrath is the infinite mystery of His love. His activity in vengeance in the last, the final analysis, proves the depth of His love.

The message is also one concerning man. Nahum reveals the sins against which the wrath of God proceeds. I do but name them. Whether they are national, social, or individual the same truth applies. The sins against which God acts in vengeance are the pride that neglects Him; the cruelty that is exercised towards our fellow men; the impenitence which persists, in spite of the slowness of His anger; or that most awful repentance, which is repentance of repentance, in the exercise of which man turns back to the sin he professed to have abandoned.

There is one final note in the message. It is that of the absolute justice of God, for His wrath is forevermore discriminative. "Jehovah is good, a stronghold in the day of trouble; and He knoweth them that put their trust in Him. But with an overrunning flood He will make a full end of the place thereof, and will pursue His enemies into darkness."

Habakkuk

THE PERMANENT VALUES	THE LIVING MESSAGE
Crystallized in one clear statement—2:4.	**I. Of Habakkuk's experience.**
I. The declaration itself.	A. The problems recognized.
A. The actual text (see translations).	B. The attitude adopted.
B. The contrast.	C. The answer vouchsafed.
1. On the one side.	**II. Of the principle.**
a. The manifest—"conceited."	A. Recognizing it.
b. The hidden—"the crooked soul."	B. Applying it.
2. On the other side.	**III. The personal word.**
a. The manifest—righteousness.	A. Application to personal life.
b. The hidden—faith.	B. Application to service.
C. The affirmation.	**IV. The central word—"wait."**
1. Positive—"the just shall live!"	
2. Negative—of the conceited, nothing is said.	
a. Faith the principle of life in spite of all appearances.	
b. Pride destructive in spite of all appearances.	
II. The illustrations.	
A. Of the self-consuming nature of life which is self-centered—2:6-19.	
1. Its manifestations.	
2. Its retribution.	
B. Of the triumphant experience of life which is God-centered—2:20—3.	
1. The vision of God.	
2. The reward of faith.	

THE method of this book is peculiar. While it constituted a message to the people of God, its method was not that of direct address. This is seen at once if we put it into contrast with that of Hosea. In the prophecy of Hosea we have the notes, or general outlines, of a public ministry extending over more than half a century; and in all there are the elements of public address, of messages delivered to men. These are absent from the book of Habakkuk. Like the book of Jonah, it tells the story of a personal experience.

The book of Jonah gives the account of a man's failure to sympathize with God, and therefore of his failure to sympathize with Nineveh. The book of Habakkuk is the story of a believer's conflict of faith, and of the ultimate triumph of faith.

The very character of the book makes it easier than usual to discover its permanent value. That is crystallized in one definite statement which lies at its heart:

" Behold, his soul is puffed up, it is not upright in him: but the just shall live by his faith."

This statement in itself suggests difficulty rather than declaration. Therefore, in order to understand it, we need the whole background of the prophet's experience. That background of experience may, for the purpose of this study, be stated by the repetition of a brief paragraph from my previous lecture on the content of the book:

" In this book we have a man of faith asking questions and receiving answers. A comparison of i. 2 with iii. 19 will give an indication of the true value of the book. Opening in mystery and questioning, it closes in certainty and affirmation. The contrast is startling. The first is almost a wail of despair, and the last is a shout of confidence. From the affirmation of faith's agnosticism we come to the affirmation of agnosticism's faith."

That is the story of Habakkuk. At the beginning, a man who believes in God is heard declaring his agnosticism, "How long shall I cry, and Thou wilt not hear? I cry out unto Thee of violence, and Thou wilt not save" : or to give the more literal and forceful translation, " I cry, Violence, and Thou wilt not save." That is faith's agnosticism, belief's problem. Every man of faith faces a similar problem sooner or later.

Faith is the underlying principle of the life, but it is bewildered by the circumstances, and it says so. In answer to its challenge it receives a declaration, and so is confirmed. The story of Habakkuk is that of a movement from the experience of doubt and questioning, to that of certainty and praise, and the doorway between the two is found in the statement already quoted. All the first part of the book leads to that door. All the latter part of the book proceeds from that door into ever widening experience.

Habakkuk does not end with a wail; he ends with a song. He does not end with enquiry; he ends with affirmation. He begins by saying, There is violence and cruelty, and God does nothing. He ends by saying :

> " For though the fig tree shall not blossom,
> Neither shall fruit be in the vines ;
> The labour of the olive shall fail,
> And the fields shall yield no meat ;
> The flock shall be cut off from the fold,
> And there shall be no herd in the stalls :
> Yet I will rejoice in the Lord,
> I will joy in the God of my salvation."

I want to discover the secret of this change, and I do so in the central statement, which reveals the contrasted principles or motives of false and true life.

Let us first examine the declaration itself. We recognize at once that there have been difficulties in translating this particular verse. We are familiar with the reading of the Revised Version. Let us take four other translations in order that we may recognize the difficulty, and yet see that while there is difficulty, there is agreement also in certain fundamental matters, which are the matters of supreme importance.

George Adam Smith translates thus :—

" Lo, swollen ! Not level is his soul within him ; but the righteous shall live by his faithfulness."

Pusey translates thus :

" Lo, swollen is it, not upright is his soul in him. The righteous by his faith he shall live."

Henderson translates thus :

" Behold the proud ! His soul is not right within him ; but the righteous shall live by his faith."

Joseph Bryant Rotherham translates thus :

" Lo ! as for the conceited one, crooked is his soul within him ; but one who is righteous by his faithfulness shall live."

So far as I have any right to make a distinction, I infinitely prefer this last translation. The difficulty of expressing the thought of one language in another is very great, it being almost impossible to carry over the light and shade of suggestion. I like this translation of Rotherham, because it seems to me to convey the more delicate tones of the original, better than others.

The differences are those of the words swollen, proud, conceited one. Yet as we think of the peculiar quality and value of these different words, we also discover the identity of suggestion. Again there is the difference between the expressions " By faith " and " By faithfulness." I have no doubt whatever that the word which is an actual translation of the original is not *faith*, but *faithfulness;* yet that necessarily includes the idea of faith. It is to that fundamental idea those would draw attention who have translated the Hebrew word by our word faith ; while the use of the word faithfulness suggests rather the result of the operation of faith on the character and conduct of the man of faith. The word faithfulness means, quite literally, fullness of faith. It may be affirmed that faithfulness means fidelity. And so it does ; but what is fidelity other than fullness of faith ? Fidelity is a word which expresses the outward result of the inward grace, which is fullness of faith. The Hebrew word carries both thoughts. The inward grace, the master principle, is fullness of faith ; and the outward manifestation, the obedient practice, is fidelity.

It is patent, therefore, that all these translations are in perfect agreement in the way in which they put two attitudes of life into contrast. An examination of the different terminology by which the one attitude of life is described, reveals the same attitude in each case. So also if with equal carefulness we examine the words which describe the other attitude, we discover that the attitude is always the same.

Let us now observe the contrast. On the one side we have certain manifest things, and a hidden secret. On the other side we have also certain manifest things, and a hidden secret.

As to the first. The words conceited, swollen, or proud indicate the external manifestation. What, then, is the hidden secret? That of the soul not upright, not right, not level, crooked. The outward manifestation is conceit; the hidden secret is crookedness of soul.

As to the second. Here also is the outward manifestation of righteousness, and the hidden secret of fullness of faith. One need not dwell here a single moment, for the statement is perfectly simple. Goodness is always simple. It is evil which is complex. It is much more difficult to discover the devil than God, to define evil than goodness. It is always more difficult to deal with a crooked thing than with a straight thing. Suffer me a parable. Supposing I had in my possession, but out of your sight, two sticks. If I said to you, I have a straight stick and a crooked stick, which can you imagine best? Your answer would inevitably be, the straight one, for a straight stick is a straight stick; but a crooked stick may be crooked in a hundred different ways. All of which is but to remind us of the complexity of evil and the simplicity of goodness.

So far we have not considered the declaration itself. We have been dealing with terms only, the instruments through which the light is to flash. What, then, is the central affirmation? "My righteous one shall live by his faith." I am convinced that we have been in danger of putting too much emphasis upon the thoughts suggested by the words "*righteous*" and "*faith*." Or perhaps it would be more correct to say that we have put too little emphasis upon the positive and flaming affirmation, "He shall *live*." In this connection notice the remarkable contrast of silence. Of the conceited soul nothing is said. He is puffed up, his soul is crooked within him. What does he do? Nothing. Does he not live? No.

Now carefully observe the application of all this to the problem of Habakkuk. He looked around, and saw everything crooked, unlike God, proud; the wicked flourishing like a green bay tree; violence rampant! What was God doing? The righteous were oppressed, broken; hardly any of them were left; they were dying out.

Poor pessimistic soul! What does the text say? "Behold, swollen is he; crooked is his soul within him." Anything else? Nothing about the apparently flourishing wicked, but something about the fainting righteous. "My righteous one shall live."

The result of that declaration for Habakkuk was that his agnosticism merged into song. Faith is the principle of life in spite of all appearances. Pride is destructive in spite of all appearances. These godless men and affairs seem to be so high and so proud; these enterprises, which are in rebellion against eternity, seem so mighty, and encased in armour so strong that we cannot overcome them. Look again. "My righteous one"—poor, despised, in difficulty, hardly daring to lift his head—"shall live." The principle of faith is the principle of life. Anything that is not of faith is crooked and swollen; leave it alone. It will pass and perish.

What is God doing? He is presiding over His own law, watching it work out to its ultimate conclusion, holding everything in His grasp; and, in spite of the appearance of the moment, surely, if as men count time, slowly, crushing all that which is crooked in its soul and swollen in its pride, and lifting into life all the things which are of faith.

Then the prophet turns to affirmation! The illustrations that follow flash their light back upon this central declaration.

He first describes the swollen and the proud, their pride and their passing, the manifestations of the self-centred life, and the retribution that inevitably follows such life. All the things of pride and self-seeking pass before the vision—ambition, covetousness, violence, insolence, idolatry —and the prophet shows that every one involves its own nemesis and judgment. Those who have been crushed under the rule of the swollen, revolt; and he is spoiled. When the swollen would come into possession of the cities he has coveted; the very walls talk, the very beams thunder out judgment. There is no possession granted to greed. Violence issues in self-destruction. Insolence made men drunk, and laughed at them when they were drunk; in turn the proud himself is made drunk, and becomes the shame of all who gaze upon him. The keen satire of Habakkuk is poured upon idolatry, as he declares of idols there is no breath in them; to pray to them is to be unanswered; to be in agony is to find no helper. The self-centred life—ambitious, covetous, idolatrous—seems to rise higher and still higher; but the prophet has heard the secret, and he knows that pride-destroying forces are already working the destruction of the proud.

Then he illustrates the life of faith. There is first the vision of God coming from Teman. Then he traces, as I think, the whole history of the Hebrew people through the great file-leaders of faith—Abraham, Moses, Joshua. At last he trembles as he watches God's judgment. He who had thought God was doing nothing to punish evil, now prays that in the midst of wrath He will remember mercy. He who had imagined that God had forsaken the faithful, and left them to their fate, at last breaks out into the great psalm with which the book ends.

The living message is perfectly patent. Faith has still its problems. The outlook is often dark and desolating enough. The message of this book is first that we cannot and ought not to judge by the appearances of the hour, but by the word of God, which is at once His oath and covenant.

When we have to confront these problems, let us take up Habakkuk's attitude. Habakkuk might have started out as a lecturer on the inconsistencies of the doctrine of the supposed government of God. Instead of that he told God of his perplexity. He poured out his heart in the presence of God. He said, I cry Violence! and You do nothing. Oh, the comfort of the fact that we may say anything to God. There is a hymn we sometimes sing, and I wonder if we really mean it: "I tell Him all my doubts and griefs and fears." The trouble is that we talk of our doubts to our neighbours instead of telling them to Him. The best place to speak of the secret problem is the Secret Place. Let us take time to listen to God that He may explain Himself to us. Some one says God does not speak to men to-day as He did of old. I will give you a truer statement: Men do not listen to-day as they listened of old. If men will listen, God will speak.

Let us believe the truth of this central principle, and apply it. Let us who name His name, and profess to be men of faith, put the measurements of this verse upon all the problems that confront us in this world. To do so would be to find ease from a great deal of pain, to be saved from a vast amount of suffering. We should not so often be degrading Christianity by discussing in the newspaper columns our own inability and weakness. There are vested interests—high, proud, swollen things—lifting themselves against God; but they do not live. The life element is to be found in the man who has faith in God. There is life in none other.

Is there not a personal word of application here? Has this book anything to say to me? "The swollen is crooked in soul, but My righteous one shall live by his faith." In the compass of my own life, that life which none can know but God and myself in its inner and deepest things, how does that verse appeal? Does it rebuke me for crookedness of soul, or vindicate me for the trust that means triumph?

Did I say that my own life none can know save God and myself? That is true, yet it is always manifest sooner or later in the external things. If I am crooked in soul, men will find it out by my conceit. Every secret sin sooner or later flames through the windows of the soul, burns upon the cheek, blasts the external. That matter is too solemn to illustrate in public; it is for consideration in the inner chamber, and when the door is shut.

What is the final word of this message for us? "Though the vision tarry, wait for it." Does that seem an easy thing to do? I ask the question, and would give you time to think. Have you never discovered that waiting is the hardest of all work? "Wait." It is a great word. How shall I wait? On the watch-tower, telling God everything, and listening to God. When Habakkuk looked at his circumstances he was perplexed. When he waited for God and listened to God, he sang.

Zephaniah

THE PERMANENT VALUES	THE LIVING MESSAGE

Its revelation of the day of the Lord.
I. The content.
    A. The direct act of God—1:12b.
    B. Supernatural—1:14-16.
II. The extent.
    A. Judgment upon sin.
        1. Luxury and indifference—1:12—the last stages.
        2. The evil spirit—3:2.
        3. The results—3:3, 4.
    B. The whole extent: princes, judges, prophets, and priests.
        1. Man, and all he has polluted.
        2. National life and history, as well as immediate sins swept away.
        3. Chaos consumed.
III. The intent.
    A. The enthronement of Jehovah—3:17.
    B. The new order—vindication of the trusting.
        1. Songs instead of sorrow.
        2. Service instead of selfishness.
        3. Solidarity instead of scattering.
	I. The joy of the assurance—"We rejoice in hope of the glory of God."
	II. The responsibility of the assurance—II Peter 3.
	    A. "Holy living and godliness"—11.
	    B. "Looking for and hastening"—12.
	    C. "Give diligence"—14.
	    D. "Beware"—17.
	    E. "Grow"—18.

THE key to the book of Zephaniah is the phrase "the day of the Lord." The phrase is not peculiar to Zephaniah. Most of the prophets make use of it in the course of their prophesying. In our study of the permanent value and living message of the prophecy of Joel we noticed that Joel used it five times in the course of his brief message, and by his use of it we found that the phrase stands for a perpetual method in that activity of God which moves ever forward until at last it accomplishes all His purpose in the affairs of men. To him the locust plague was "the day of the Lord"; the threatened invasion would be "the day of the Lord"; that ultimate procedure whereby God will establish His rule in the world will be "the day of the Lord."

Zephaniah used this phrase more frequently than any other prophet. It was his burden.

Consequently we find, as we should expect, in his prophecy a fuller explanation of the meaning of the phrase than in any other of the Old Testament writings. The explanation of the phrase is the permanent value of this book of Zephaniah.

Wherever we find this phrase in any of the prophets or in the New Testament, it invariably suggests a contrast. Each prophet who uses it does so in a certain set of circumstances, in order to put such circumstances into contrast with that which he describes as "the day of the Lord." The contrast is always that between the day of man and the day of Jehovah.

Zephaniah uttered his prophecy in the time of Josiah. A remarkable thing which has puzzled expositors is that Zephaniah, whose prophecy opens with the declaration,

"The word of the Lord which came unto Zephaniah, the son of Cushi, the son of Gedaliah, the son of Amariah, the son of Hezekiah, in the days of Josiah the son of Amon, king of Judah,"

never referred to the reform under Josiah. The days of Josiah stand out, when we study the history of the people, as days of reform. I think the explanation is simple. The reform under Josiah, so far as it affected the nation at all, was a reform brought about by the popularity of the king, and not by heart repentance. Huldah the prophetess had declared that this would be so. Zephaniah took no account of the reform, knowing as he did that the hearts of the people were still in rebellion and in sin. Amid circumstances of rebellion, sin, and corruption, he spoke of "the day of the Lord."

The day of man is the day of Jehovah's patience. "The day of the Lord" is the day of man's judgment. Wherever this phrase occurs, it refers to God's judgment, in order to the establishment of His Kingdom. To Joel the locust plague was "the day of the Lord," because it was a day of judgment; the coming armies constituted "the day of the Lord" because their coming was the coming of God's judgment upon a sinning people. The ultimate "day of the Lord," according to Peter, is the day in which "the elements shall be dissolved with fervent heat, and the earth and the works that are therein shall be burned up." The day of man is the day of God's patience. "The day of the Lord" is the day when patience has had her perfect work on the part of God, and He takes up the sword of judgment.

The permanent value of this book, then, is its unveiling of "the day of the Lord." One of the most significant things about the book is that it is impossible to deal with it from the standpoint of a calendar or almanac. It cannot be placed historically beyond the introductory words. As one reads it, the nations seemed to have ceased to be; all are involved in one sweeping hurricane of judgment. History seems to be forgotten. "I will utterly consume all things from off the face of the ground" is the first word. It is a picture of devastation, and kings as instruments of judgment are no longer to be found here. No longer through mediation is God dealing in judgment, but directly, absolutely, and finally. The prophecy reveals the meaning of "the day of the Lord" in its broad processes, and in its detailed application.

There are three things revealed in the reading of the book. Let us indicate them by three simple and related words. First, the content of "the day of the Lord." Secondly, the extent of "the day of the Lord." Finally, the intent of "the day of the Lord."

According to this prophecy, what is the content of "the day of the Lord"? That can only be answered by a repetition of certain declarations of the book. The first of these follows immediately after the first verse:

"I will utterly consume all things from off the face of the ground, saith the Lord. I will consume man and beast; I will consume the fowls of the heaven, and the fishes of the sea, and the stumbling-blocks with the wicked; and I will cut off man from off the face of the ground, saith the Lord."

This is a declaration that God will visit this earth in direct and positive judgment, using the word judgment not now in that broader sense, in which we often use it as indicating administration, but in the narrower sense of vengeance, punishment. The prophet then proceeds to declare that this will be so in spite of unbelief:

"And it shall come to pass at that time, that I will search Jerusalem with candles; and I will punish the men that are settled on their lees, that say in their heart, The Lord will not do good, neither will He do evil."

Men are saying that God is neither doing good, nor will He visit men with judgment and scattering. Zephaniah affirms that He will act in human history suddenly, swiftly, and irrevocably in judgment.

That is also the teaching of Peter in his second letter. It is to be observed also that Peter insists upon it that God will act in spite of unbelief.

Again the prophet declares that this "day of the Lord" will be not merely a day as other days have been when God presses into His service the armies of men. It will be entirely supernatural:

"The great day of the Lord is near, it is near and hasteth greatly, even the voice of the day of the Lord; the mighty man crieth there bitterly. That day is a day of wrath, a day of trouble and distress, a day of wasteness and desolation, a day of darkness and gloominess, a day of clouds and thick darkness, a day of the trumpet and alarm, against the fenced cities, and against the high battlements. And I will bring distress upon men, that they shall walk like blind men, because they have sinned against the Lord."

All these terms, descriptive of the day, suggest

that the judgment will be supernatural. The indefiniteness of the terms creates a sense of the terribleness of the judgment.

That, then, is the message of Zephaniah. There is a day when God will come to judge the earth, when He will interfere in human history and end it ; a day in which God will come Himself directly, supernaturally, immediately into the presence of human affairs, and that to judgment. The men of Zephaniah's day said, " The Lord will not do good, neither will He do evil." The men of Peter's day said, " Where is the promise of His coming ? For, from the day that the fathers fell asleep, all things continue as they were from the beginning of the creation." The men of our own day are saying exactly the same thing, that God will never interfere in judgment in this way. The declaration of this book is that there is a day of Jehovah, a day in the history of humanity, when His patience will be at an end, and when He will bring to pass His act, His strange act, of judgment.

This prophecy also declares the extent of that activity. Judgment is to be discriminative. It will be judgment upon sin. Let us repeat the words already quoted, and ponder them :

" And it shall come to pass at that time, that I will search Jerusalem with candles ; and I will punish the men that are settled on their lees, that say in their heart, The Lord will not do good, neither will He do evil."

The last stages of sin are luxury and indifference. " Men that are settled on their lees " ; that is luxury. Men who say, " The Lord will not do good, neither will He do evil " ; that is indifference. There is the constantly recurring application of " the day of the Lord " in history. The history of the decline and fall of the Roman Empire shows that the last stages of sin before judgment fell in Rome were luxury and indifference. The final stage of sin in the history of man upon which the wrath of God will fall will be characterized by the same things.

What is the secret of luxury and indifference ?

" Woe to her that is rebellious and polluted, to the oppressing city ! She obeyed not the voice ; she received not correction ; she trusted not in the Lord ; she drew not near to her God."

Opinions differ as to whether the prophet in these words referred to Jerusalem or to Nineveh. For our purpose, whether Jerusalem, Nineveh,

Rome, or London matters nothing. This is the spirit upon which judgment falls. The last stage of sin is that of luxury and indifference, and the spirit which issues in such a condition is that of disobedience to the voice of God, refusal to receive His correction, failure to put trust in Him, and distance from Him.

The result of such a spirit in the life of the city is that —

" Her princes in the midst of her are roaring lions ; her judges are evening wolves ; they leave nothing till the morrow. Her prophets are light and treacherous persons : her priests have profaned the sanctuary, they have done violence to the law."

The extent of the judgment is that man and all he has polluted are swept away.

It has been said that this prophecy of Zephaniah is peculiarly desert and barren—no life, no flower, no fruit, none of the beauties of nature ; nothing but a world swept by a simoom. If this is so, what is the reason of it ? Look at the conditions described. Men settled on their lees in luxury, denying the interference of God. A city that did not obey the voice, received not correction, did not trust in the Lord, did not draw near to God. Men and city materialized, self-centred, luxurious ; the rulers, princes, judges, prophets, and priests alike corrupt. The whole condition may be expressed in the one word—chaos. What, then, is the story of " the day of the Lord " ? That of chaos consumed, disorder disorganized, evil conditions destroyed, until the whole city appears before the eyes of the astonished prophet as a simoom-swept landscape with never a blade of grass.

What is it all for ? What is the intent of this terrible activity ? Read to the end :

" Sing, O daughter of Zion ; shout, O Israel ; be glad and rejoice with all the heart, O daughter of Jerusalem. The Lord hath taken away thy judgments, He hath cast out thine enemy : The King of Israel, even the Lord, is in the midst of thee : thou shalt not fear evil any more. In that day it shall be said to Jerusalem, Fear thou not : O Zion, let not thine hands be slack. The Lord thy God is in the midst of thee, a mighty One Who will save : He will rejoice over thee with joy, He will rest in His love, He will joy over thee with singing."

A modern expositor has said that it is perfectly patent that this last chapter was not written by Zephaniah, because the contrast is too great between the picture of the awful, sweeping, irrevocable judgment, and that of the restoration. No one can imagine, he declares, that the same man wrote both. All of which is the result of the expositor's blindness. The last picture is that of the enthroned Jehovah, the picture of a new order; songs instead of sorrow, service instead of selfishness, solidarity instead of scattering. That is the intent of judgment. Its content, God's immediate, supernatural visitation of the earth to destroy; its extent, sin and its last issues of pollution—man and everything he has spoiled; the intent, the established throne and the new order, in which God and His Kingdom sing over each other. The very contrast demonstrates the unity of authorship. There was a man whose name was John. We describe him to-day as the apostle of love; Jesus described him in the early days as the son of thunder. In his writings two words are of constant recurrence—*commandments* and *love*. It is the man who sees most clearly the fierceness of God's wrath against sin, who sees most clearly through all the processes to the restoration, and therefore sings his song. If I seek the supreme example of this principle of the " day of the Lord," I come again to the Man of Nazareth, and listen to the word He uttered when from the slopes of the mountain He looked at the city of His love. Was there ever such merging of fire and tenderness, of severity and goodness, as in His words, "O Jerusalem, Jerusalem, which killeth the prophets, and stoneth them that are sent unto her! How often would I have gathered thy children together, even as a hen gathereth her chickens under her wings, and ye would not! Behold, your house is left unto you desolate." Zephaniah will write of "the day of the Lord" as a day of swift, fiery judgment upon a sinning earth, but he will end with the song that tells of Jehovah's singing.

What is the living message of this book? Zephaniah teaches that it is ours to rejoice in the hope of the glory of God. He called the men of his own day to sing for joy because of " the day of the Lord," because " the day of the

Lord " is the day of destruction of the things that destroy, because " the day of the Lord " will be the beginning of a new era when songs shall take the place of sighs, and service shall take the place of selfishness, and solidarity shall take the place of scattering. Surely Charles Kingsley had been reading Zephaniah when he wrote " The Day of the Lord " : —

> " The Day of the Lord is at hand, at hand !
>   Its storms roll up the sky :
> The nations sleep starving on heaps of gold :
>   All dreamers toss and sigh.
> The night is darkest before the morn ;
> When the pain is sorest the child is born,
> And the Day of the Lord at hand."

Mark the note of triumph in the next verses :

> " Gather you, gather you, hounds of hell —
>   Famine, and Plague, and War ;
> Idleness, Bigotry, Cant and Misrule,
>   Gather, and fall in the snare !
> Hireling and Mammonite, Bigot and Knave,
> Crawl to the battlefield, sneak to your grave,
> In the Day of the Lord at hand."
> " Who would sit down and sigh for a lost age of gold
>   While the Lord of all ages is here ?
> True hearts will leap up at the trumpet of God,
>   And those who can suffer can dare.
> Each old age of gold was an iron age too,
> And the meekest of saints may find stern work to do
> In the Day of the Lord at hand."

That is sentimental and useless joy which finds its reason in the thought of escape. We need to-day a renewal of the passion that delights in judgment which ends the things of wrong and evil, and brings new birth to the whole creation.

> " Who would sit down and sigh for a lost age of gold
>   While the Lord of all ages is here ? "

The living message may be expressed in the words of Peter :

> " Seeing that these things are thus all to be dissolved, what manner of persons ought ye to be in all holy living and godliness, looking for and earnestly desiring the coming of the day of God."
> " Give diligence that ye may be found in peace."
> " Beware lest, being carried away with the error of the wicked, ye fall from your own stedfastness."
> " Seeing that ye look for these things . . . grow in the grace and knowledge of our Lord and Saviour Jesus Christ."

Haggai

THE PERMANENT VALUES	THE LIVING MESSAGE

I. A revelation of the peculiar perils of an age of adversity.
  A. A false content—they looked at their conditions only.
  B. A false discontent—they looked at their building in the light of the past.
  C. A false expectation—they looked at their adversity in the light of their building.
  D. A false fear—they looked at their position in the light of the nations.
II. A declaration of the duty of men of faith in such an age.
  A. The corrective of false content.
    1. The duty—"build."
    2. The dynamic—"I am with you" (1:13).
  B. The corrective of false discontent.
    1. The duty—"be strong . . . and work."
    2. The dynamic—"I am with you" (2:4).
  C. The corrective of false expectation.
    1. The duty—"Ask a Torah."
    2. The dynamic—"I will bless" (2:19).
  D. The corrective of false fear.
    1. The duty—patience.
    2. The dynamic.
      a. I will shake, overthrow, destroy, and overthrow.
      b. I will take and make.
	I. The wickedness of waiting for psychic moments and set times—the essence of rebellion.
	II. The folly of attempting to interpret the present in the terms of the past—a better thing is always at hand.
	III. The paralysis of expecting immediate results.
	  A. The necessity for patience.
	  B. The certainty of God.

HAGGAI stands first in the last group of the prophetic books. In common with Zechariah and Malachi it is post-exilic. In considering the messages of these three books we find ourselves in new circumstances and in a new atmosphere. The history of the people was at once full of glory and full of shame. It is easy to imagine how they felt as they thought of the ancient glory of the nation. Some amongst them would be filled with shame as they came back to their own city and their own country, and found themselves without national constitution and without power, tributary to the Gentiles. Their circumstances were those of difficulty and discouragement. Their hopes were of the most shadowy and uncertain kind.

These three men prophesied in the midst of such circumstances. Haggai had one burden upon his heart, that of leading the people to build the temple. Zechariah helped him in the delivery of that message, and then produced his great apocalypse. Malachi uttered the final mourning and warning to the ancient people of God.

Let us consider a little more particularly the circumstances in which Haggai delivered his message. About sixteen years earlier the people had returned to their own land under Zerubbabel, and had begun to build the temple a year later. They had laid the foundations, and perhaps the first course of stones, when the work of building was abandoned through Samaritan opposition,

For fifteen years nothing more was done. Then Haggai delivered his message and exercised his ministry. He dealt with the immediate. He was a man of faith, whose one business was that of persuading the people to do one thing. The greater part of his ministry consisted not of public preaching but of private application thereof. He delivered four brief messages, and succeeded in persuading the people to build. His first message was delivered, and they commenced. Then a difficulty arose and they halted. He immediately delivered his second message, and they resumed the work. After a while another difficulty arose, and again they halted. He delivered his third message, and on the same day his fourth and last; and the work was completed.

The permanent value of this book is twofold. First, it is a revelation of the peculiar perils of an age of adversity; and secondly, it is a declaration of the duty of the man of faith in such an age. Haggai helps us to see the perils of the hour when everything looks dark; and to understand the duty of the man of faith in such an hour, and in the presence of such perils.

There are four perils indicated in the prophecy, and the four addresses deal with them respectively. First, the peril of a false content. Secondly, the peril of a false discontent. Thirdly, the peril of a false expectation. Finally, the peril of a false fear.

First, a false content. As these people looked at the conditions in the midst of which they found themselves they said,

"It is not the time . . . for the Lord's house to be built."

Secondly, a false discontent. After the work had commenced they looked at their building in the light of the olden days, and they said,

"Who is left among you that saw this house in its former glory? and how do ye see it now? is it not in your eyes as nothing?"

Thirdly, a false expectation. When the building had proceeded further they expected immediate material results from their moral reformation.

Finally, a false fear. They were filled with fear of the nations by whom they were surrounded.

The first peril is that of a false content. These people were waiting for the psychic moment in which to begin to build the house of God. They said, The set time is not yet come. They expected some manifestation of Divine readiness to help them. On that side of their life which had to do with God, they were waiting; but they were busy building their own houses. They were only psychologists in the matter of religion. They were preëminently practical when they had to do with the places in which they themselves had to live.

The next peril is that of a false discontent. When in obedience to the prophet they began to build, they looked at their building in the light of the past, and their outlook was entirely material. They compared the poverty of the material erection with the glory of the ancient temple of which they had heard, and which some of them had seen. The old men amongst them, in childhood's days had gazed upon the glory of the past temple, and they put this new temple in its material poverty, into comparison with the one of old and its material glory. The result was that they were filled with discontent, and broke out into lamentation. That was a note of false discontent.

The third peril is that of a false expectation. They looked at their adversity in the light of their building. They said, We have begun to obey, and the weeks have passed away and grown into months, and yet there is no sign of better conditions. It was autumn when we began to build, and now it is winter, and there is no improvement. Haggai taught them that it was an unwarranted expectation in view of the appalling penetration of evil resulting from their sin.

Finally, they looked at the surrounding nations, saw their strength and the solidarity of the opposition, and were filled with a false fear.

In each case the prophet sought to counteract the perils by declaring an immediate duty, and revealing an available dynamic.

For the correction of their false content, he declared that their immediate duty was to build. As dynamic, he gave them the inspiration of the Divine declaration, "I am with you, saith the Lord." The people said, The time has not yet come to build. The prophet affirmed, The set time has come, because Jehovah is with us.

For the correction of the false discontent the prophet declared that their duty was to "be strong . . . and work." Again as dynamic, he gave them the inspiration of the Divine word, "I am with you, saith the Lord of hosts."

For the correction of false expectation the prophet bade them "Ask the priests concerning a law"; and there follows the account of the opinion given by the priests, evidently in answer to the appeal. This needs to be considered carefully. They were to ask not *the law*, but for *a law*. In order to understand this passage we must go back to Deuteronomy. There will be found instructions given to the people that in any case of difficulty, the priest was to declare a law, that is, declare the principle involved in the difficulty. Here Haggai framed the enquiry of the people in the words,

"If one bear holy flesh in the skirt of his garment, and with his skirt do touch bread, or pottage, or wine, or oil, or any meat, shall it become holy? And the priests answered and said, No."

That was the statement of the law or principle, and the prophet applied it thus. The pollution of nature which had resulted from their sin could not be immediately set right by their reformation and return. The lesson he drew from this declaration was that of patience. There must be return and obedience; but not eager anxiety for immediate material results. There must be return and obedience, although there seemed to be no immediate benefit accruing therefrom.

In spiritual revival there should be freedom from anxiety about material results. That is the principle. There will be material results, but the inspiration for patient waiting is found in the words, "From this day will I bless you." The material blessing that will follow will not be created by obedience, but will be given as a gracious act on the part of God. The people said in effect: We are giving God obedience, we are building; but He is giving us nothing in return. The lesson they had to learn was that obedience must be without bargaining. Yet the prophet did not leave them with that stern application of the principle; he gave them this word out of the heart of God, "From this day will I bless you." The blessing must come from God. Men must never imagine that by their return and obedience they have a right to blessing.

For the correction of false fear the prophet laid down the duty of patience, and uttered for their inspiration the great promises of Jehovah. The consciousness of the people concerning the strength of the enemies about them is revealed in the references to those enemies in the promise of deliverance; "the throne of the kingdoms . . . the strength of the kingdoms . . . the nations . . . the chariots, and those that ride in them . . . the horses and their riders." These were the forces of which the remnant were conscious. Wherever they lifted their eyes they saw the strength of the kingdoms; chariots and them that ride in them; horses and their riders; massed military powers! There was no hope of deliverance. All these things filled them with dull despair. There seemed to be no chance of their ever regaining national constitution and power. The corrective of the prophet was that of his utterance of the word of Jehovah, "I will shake . . . I will overthrow . . . I will destroy . . . I will overthrow." By that activity of Jehovah there would issue the degradation of the strength they feared, and the disintegration of the forces which held them prisoners.

Let us put the perils and the corrective teaching side by side.

The people were content to let the temple remain unbuilt, saying, The set time has not yet come. The prophet bade them arise and build, knowing that the set time had come, because God was with them, knowing that

"God is on the field when He
Is most invisible."

The people were filled with discontent as they compared the house as they saw it in the course of building with the glory of the previous house. The prophet called them to be strong and to work, because God was with them; and therefore the glory of the latter house would be greater than that of the former, because the method of God is always progressive. The former glory was material, but to the latter house would come the fulfillment of all things foreshadowed in the former.

The people expected immediate material benefit as the result of their moral reformation. No, said the prophet, you do not know the meaning of sin, how deep its pollution goes, how all nature is affected by it. There must be patient waiting for God from Whom the blessing will come as a gift of grace, and not as a result created by human amendment.

The people were looking at enemies, at thrones,

at chariots, and horses, at the military multitudes, and consequently they were filled with fear. The prophet called them to cease looking at the foes and to look to God Who would break the power of the surrounding nations.

The living message of the book is patent. It teaches first the wickedness of waiting—waiting for the psychic moment, for the set time—is of the essence of rebellion when immediate duty calls. God's windows wait man's opening.

"Bring ye the whole tithe into the storehouse, that there may be meat in Mine House, and prove Me now herewith, saith the Lord of hosts, if I will not open you the windows of heaven."

Those windows are never opened in response to sighing and crying. In that hour in which we bring the whole tithe into the storehouse, the windows will be opened and the blessing will come. "Now is the accepted time, now is the day of salvation" is a word of constant application, and constitutes the true answer to man's declaration that the set time has not come.

The next peril is that of lamenting the past ; desiring an experience to-day like that of the past. In Wales men to-day are desiring to go back to the experiences of the revival. Christian men are sighing after the experiences of '59. Some sigh for a return to apostolic times, to that peculiar manifestation of the Spirit, necessary in the first stage of the Church's history, but unnecessary to-day. It is impossible to unlock the present with the rusty key of the past. The attempt to crowd the Spirit of God to-day into the manifestation of the past is of the nature of sacrilege. It is utterest folly to attempt to interpret the present in the terms of the past. There is always a better thing at hand than anything the past has seen ; better, that is, for to-day, for the present time. Many of the ecclesiastical quarrels of the Christian Church are due to attempts to live in the past, and the consequent failure to recognize the living presence of the Spirit of God, and the fact that in one age He must use one method and in another age an entirely different one. In the gift of the Spirit we have the charm and value of perpetually changing methods. The simplicity, the commonplace, the dullness of the present hour, may be of the very essence of God's method. Let us get to work. The word of God to us also is, " Be strong . . . and work."

Again, we need to be reminded that there is a grave peril in expecting immediate material results. Those who serve in spiritual things in a world permeated with the virus of sin need great patience. That was a wonderful vision of Isaiah in which he saw that the poison of human sin had permeated the very earth, and that the only way in which God could get it out was by burning, smiting, and destruction. We must be content to do our best work with perhaps but little result that can be tabulated.

Finally, we need the message of this book for the correction of our fear. Do we not still hear men of faith saying, Those that are against us are mighty and strong? What we supremely need is a new vision of God, a new understanding of the fact that He will overthrow the thrones, and the kingdoms, and break their strength, and finally set up His government in the earth.

We may summarize the whole message of Haggai in one brief word of his second prophecy, " Be strong . . . and work." If we do that, we may leave the issues with God ; but we have no right to leave the issues with God unless we work. The initial sin was that of waiting for the psychic moment. When we are strong and work, then we may be, and shall be delivered from all anxiety about the ultimate, knowing that He will bless, and accomplish, and perfect. It should be the highest honour of life, its crowning glory, and its chief joy in the midst of the ages, to have done one day's work with God.

"Yet will I live my life,
    Dim though its mystery be,
Not wholly lost to sense, nor yet
    Absorbed in what I see.

"For me—to have made one soul
    The better for my birth :
To have added but one flower
    To the garden of the earth :

"To have struck one blow for truth
    In the daily fight with lies :
To have done one deed of right
    In the face of calumnies :

"To have sown in the souls of men
    One thought that will not die—
To have been a link in the chain of life :
    Shall be immortality."

Zechariah

THE PERMANENT VALUES	THE LIVING MESSAGE

I. **Its fundamental revelation of the pervasive power and persistent purpose of Jehovah.**
  A. The suggestive title—"the Lord of Hosts."
    1. Its history and meaning.
      a. History.
        (1) Born with the monarchy—I Sam. 1:3 and 11.
        (2) Not prevalent during the period.
        (3) The prophetic name.
      b. Meaning—sovereignty.
        (1) Stars.
        (2) Angels.
        (3) Israel.
    2. Its introductory grouping—1:3.
      a. The will made known—1:6.
      b. The way provided—3:8.
      c. The work accomplished—4:6.
  B. The pervasive power.
    1. The visions.
    2. The oracles.
  C. The persistent purpose.
    1. The principle illustrated by the visions.
    2. The principle illustrated by the oracles.
II. **The resultant revelation of the true attitude and activity of His people under all circumstances.** Key words: *hearken, return, see,* and *obey.*
  A. The attitude (7, 8).
    1. Look back, and know your sin.
    2. Look on, and see God's purpose.
  B. The activity.
    1. Build the house.
    2. Abolish the human fasts.
    3. Keep the divine feasts.
	I. **A revelation of the secret of strength—** "while we look . . ." (II Cor. 4:17).
	  A. The secret of strength is vision.
	  B. The proof of vision is strength.
	II. **An appeal to be strong—**Heb. 12:12, 13.

THIS is the second of the three prophetic books which are undoubtedly post-exilic; consisting as they do of messages delivered to the people after their return from captivity. The relation of Zechariah to Haggai we recognized in our study of the latter book. The atmosphere is the same. The people to whom Zechariah delivered his message were looking back, and were conscious of a history which was at once glorious and shameful. The history of God's dealing with them was full of glory. The history of their dealing with God was full of shame. The immediate outlook was one of difficulty and discouragement. The hope of the nation was practically extinguished. Hemmed in by opposing forces, without national constitution or power, it certainly must have seemed to that feeble remnant that there was very little hope in the future. The peculiar value of the teaching of Zechariah was that it was calculated to inspire hope in the heart of the discouraged people.

The first message of Zechariah was delivered between two messages of Haggai, so that the first phase of his ministry was one of actual and immediate coöperation with Haggai. In that first message the one burden upon the heart of the prophet was that of urging the people to obey the message of his co-worker, and to build the house of God. Following the first simple message, we have the visions of the prophet; not easy of exposition, but flaming with light, singing in hope, and resonant in confidence. Finally, we have those messages in which, in language as stately as any to be found in the prophetic books, and with somewhat more of detail, there is presented the portrait of the great Deliverer-King, Who through suffering comes to crowning. The principal value of such message was that of filling the heart with hope, even in the days of darkness and of hopelessness.

The burden of Zechariah was that of the pervasive power and the persistent purpose of Jehovah. The book has been accurately described as the apocalypse of the Old Testament. An apocalypse is the removal of something that hides; an unveiling.

Zechariah was the great unveiler, the man through whose message the people were enabled to see things which, while actual, were nevertheless obscured by the prevalent conditions of adversity.

Our observation is limited to the sight of the eyes and the hearing of the ears. The peculiar peril of the day of adversity is that therein men are in danger of seeing only the things that are near. The apocalypse provides visions and voices; visions through the near to the distant, voices from the distant calling to the near. These men were looking at the near; Zechariah bade them look through to the things beyond. They were looking at the narrow circumstances; Zechariah called them to the wider circumstances of the Divine government and activity.

The permanent values of Zechariah then are: first, its fundamental revelation of the pervasive power and persistent purpose of Jehovah; and secondly, its resultant revelation of the true attitude and activity of the people of God in all circumstances.

As to the first of these permanent values, let us look at the opening paragraph,

" In the eighth month, in the second year of Darius, came the word of the Lord unto Zechariah the son of Berechiah, the son of Iddo, the prophet, saying, The Lord hath been sore displeased with your fathers. Therefore say thou unto them, Thus saith Jehovah of hosts: Return unto Me, saith Jehovah of hosts, and I will return unto you, saith Jehovah of hosts."

His one inclusive appeal is contained in the words,

" Thus saith Jehovah of hosts: Return unto Me, saith Jehovah of hosts, and I will return unto you, saith Jehovah of hosts."

Everything which follows is by way of application and illustration.

Notice first very carefully the suggestive title thrice repeated, "Jehovah of hosts," as to its history and its meaning. Think of its history. You cannot find it in Genesis; it does not occur in Exodus; it is absent from Leviticus; it is to be discovered neither in Numbers nor Deuteronomy. You never find it in the Pentateuch. You may go still further and you will not find it in the book of Joshua or the book of Judges. Then you come to the first book of Samuel, which is the book of transition from the Theocratic to the monarchic form of government, the story of how these people turned from God to a human government. In that book the title first occurs. The phrase was born with the monarchy. On the human side, as Perowne suggests, it was the result of the people's new thought of massed and marshalled armies. We are principally interested in the significance it gathered in the process of the years. In the historic books it very rarely occurs; but in the prophetic literature it is the constantly recurring title of Jehovah. Isaiah repeatedly employed it. Jeremiah used it more often than did Isaiah. Zechariah used it more frequently than any other prophet. Fifty-three times at least does this majestic and wonderful title appear upon the pages of this brief prophecy of fourteen chapters. In order to an understanding of the suggestiveness of the title we should need a careful examination of the prophetic use of it; not merely a study of the actual words, but of the place in which we find them in our Bible. Let three very simple thoughts suffice. The word hosts is used of stars, of angels, of the nation of Israel, of the armies of other nations. The significance of this fact is that whatever the title meant when it was first employed, it came ultimately to mean that Jehovah is sovereign Lord and Master of the universe. In the prophetic use of it is suggested, not the sovereignty of Jehovah in the abstract merely, but that sovereignty in activity. The prophet saw Jehovah marshalling all hosts—of stars, of angels, and of men. Zechariah lived in a day when Israel had lost its army, its power, and its organization ; and he constantly spoke of Jehovah of hosts, thus reminding the people of the abiding and active sovereignty of Jehovah. The threefold use of the title in the opening paragraph of Zechariah speaks of that fact of sovereignty to the conditions in the midst of which the people found themselves.

" Thus saith Jehovah of hosts."

The declaration first suggests that the will of God is made known to His people. That is further illustrated by what follows.

" Be ye not as your fathers, unto whom the former prophets cried, saying, Thus saith Jehovah of hosts, Return ye now from your evil doings : but they did not hear, nor hearken unto Me, saith Jehovah."

The main value of that reference to the past is its insistence upon the fact that God has spoken His will to His people. That is His perpetual method. He speaks. He makes known His will. The prophet insists upon it that He continues that method. That is the first part of the prophetic burden.

" Return unto Me."

That is the second value of the prophetic message. Jehovah calls His people back, and provides a way for their return. In the subsequent vision of Joshua, the high priest, confronted by Satan the adversary, the title is linked to the great announcement.

" Thus saith Jehovah of hosts . . . Hear now, O Joshua the high priest, thou and thy fellows that sit before thee ; for they are men which are a sign : for, behold, I will bring forth My Servant the Branch."

Thus the way back to God is provided.

" I will return unto you."

That is the third value of the message. Jehovah promises to return to His people, and He accomplishes the work which makes this return possible.

" Not by might, nor by power, but by My Spirit, saith Jehovah of hosts."

The power necessary for the restoration of order will be provided by the coming of God to His people, by His Holy Spirit.

These are only the key-phrases, but around them the whole system of the prophet's thinking was grouped. His conviction was threefold ; Jehovah reveals His will ; Jehovah calls men back to Himself, and provides the way for their coming ; Jehovah promises that if they will return, He will return to them, and He does so in the power and might of His own Holy Spirit. I am not prepared for one single moment to affirm that Zechariah apprehended the great doctrine of the Trinity, or those of our evangelical faith ; but all are to be found potentially in his words. Jehovah of hosts speaks ; it is the perpetual method of God with men, that of making known His will. Jehovah of hosts calls men to return ; and in the mystery of that Branch—Whose nature is dealt with later on in the prophecy, and Whose history is written in the last movement—He makes the way of return. Jehovah of hosts declares that if men will return to Him, He will return to them, and this He does by the coming of the Spirit. All this teaching was inclusively an unveiling first, of the pervasive power of God ; and secondly, of the persistent purpose of God.

The pervasive power of Jehovah is illustrated by the visions and by the oracles. This is seen when we take each one in separation, and allow it to make its own impression upon the mind. In every case certain conditions are described, and side by side with the conditions, facts are declared which the average man cannot see.

The first vision is that of the shady place ; and also of the Watcher, the angel of Jehovah. The people were conscious of the shady place ; but they were not conscious of the Watcher. He was unveiled.

The second vision is that of the opposing forces and the weapons being formed against the people of God ; and also of the forces for the destruction of the opposing forces. The people were conscious of the weapons formed against them ; but not of the forces for the destruction of those weapons. These were unveiled.

The third vision is that of a city, and a young man so interested therein that he desired to measure it ; and also of the fact that the new city had no walls, for two reasons ; first, because it is too great to be included by walls, and secondly, because it does not need the defense of walls by reason of the defense of Jehovah.

The people were conscious of the city and of its imperfections, but they were not conscious of the splendour of the city that is to be. This was unveiled.

The fourth vision is that of the adversary; and also of the Advocate. The people were conscious of the adversary; but they were not conscious of the Advocate. He was unveiled.

The fifth vision is that of responsibility, the candlestick and the light shining in the dark places; and also a vision of resource, the oil and the perpetual supply. The people were conscious of the responsibility, but not of the resource. That was unveiled.

The sixth vision is that of the presence of evil; and also of the practice and application of law. The people were conscious of the presence of evil; but not of the administration of law. That was unveiled.

The seventh vision is that of the pollution of commerce; and also of the restriction of the area of its influence. The people were conscious of the pollution, but not of the restriction. That was unveiled.

The eighth vision is that of the need of administration; and also of the spirit of government, the horsemen from the mountains of brass riding through the world for the establishment of order. The people were conscious of the need of administration; but were not conscious of the spirit of government. That was unveiled.

Thus, under all circumstances, the prophet was conscious of the presence and activity of Jehovah of hosts. Jehovah the becoming One, the One Who becomes exactly what His people need in any and every hour of need. Are they in the shady place? He is the Watcher. Are weapons being formed against them? He is the destructive force that breaks the weapons. Is the new city being built? He is its defense. Is the adversary unmasked? He is the Advocate. Is the responsibility heavy? He is sufficient resource. Is evil present everywhere? He gives the law to which evil must bow. Is commerce polluted? He restricts the area. Is there need of administration? He sends forth riders upon horses from mountains of brass. This man in the midst of the difficulty, disappointment, and desolation of his day, saw Jehovah everywhere.

The oracles teach the same lesson. The anointed King is rejected, but the book does not end with that story. The rejected King is enthroned by the pervasive power of Jehovah.

The persistent purpose of Jehovah is illustrated by the same visions and oracles. This is seen when they are considered, not in separation, but in sequence. Here I am compelled to touch upon controversial ground in the matter of interpretation. I hold that the vision of the myrtle trees is the vision of the present hour, so far as Israel is concerned, and that all the succeeding visions are yet unfulfilled. Israel has been in the shady place for over two millenniums. During all the period the Watcher is with her. Beyond the day of adversity, the day of trouble, will come the hour when Israel's enemies will be defeated. Then Jerusalem will be rebuilt. Israel, as the servant of God, will be cleansed from filthiness. Then she will fulfill her function in the world as the great light-bearer. Under those conditions the law will go forth from Jerusalem for the government of the world. Then Babylon will be held in check. Finally the Kingdom of Heaven will be established on earth, when the riders upon horses will proceed from the mountains of brass, and in the power of the Spirit encompass the world.

All this reveals the persistent purpose of Jehovah, whereby, in spite of human failure, and all opposition of men or demons, He moves on towards the final goal.

The same principle is illustrated by the oracles. The Advent of rejection prepares for the Advent of coronation. The Advent of coronation perfects the Advent of rejection.

This prophecy, then, reveals the true attitude and activity of the people of God in days of darkness and of difficulty.

" Thus saith Jehovah of hosts."

What is the attitude of the people of God in the presence of that declaration? That of attention.

"Return unto Me, saith Jehovah of hosts, and I will return unto you, saith Jehovah of hosts."

What is the attitude of the people of God in the presence of that promise? To believe it, obey it, and work in the power of it.

The great burden of the prophet to the men of his own age was that they were to build the house of God even though it was a day of darkness and disappointment; that they were to abolish their fasts by removing the cause for them, to have done with them by getting rid of the sin which occasioned them.

However diversified our opinions may be as to the interpretation of the details of this book, its spirit speaks with no uncertain sound.

There can be no mistaking its living message. If the final charge of Haggai is " Be strong . . . and work," the supreme message of Zechariah is its revelation of the secret of strength.

When Paul was feeling the difficulties and discouragements of the Christian ministry, he wrote,

" We faint not ; but though our outward man is decaying, yet our inward man is renewed day by day.   For our light affliction, which is for the moment, worketh for us more and more exceedingly an eternal weight of glory ; while we look not at the things which are seen, but at the things which are not seen : for the things which are seen are temporal ; but the things which are not seen are eternal."

That is the message of Zechariah in New Testament terms.

"While we look not at the things which are seen." Haggai said, " Be strong . . . and work." Zechariah said, You will only be strong as you see the things that are not seen, the heavenly visions, and hear the things that are never heard, the heavenly voices. While we look at, and while we listen to the unseen things and the unheard things, we do our best work.

The proof of vision is strength. You tell me these days are dark days. So they are. But let us look not only at the things seen, but also at the things unseen. See the shady place if you will, but see also the angel of Jehovah watching. See clearly the horns that are being prepared for the destruction of the purposes of God, but see also the smiths that will destroy the horns. See the unseen. The secret of strength is vision.

The proof of vision is strength. If men declare that they see these things and believe these things, and still do nothing, I cannot believe what they declare. Their sight is borrowed sight. They have been looking at a picture and not at the living fact. The man who sees the unseen is the man who grips the seen and masters it. The man who is conscious through all the appalling defeat of the hour, of the immediate, pervasive presence and power of God, is the man who gets hold of the piece of desolation nearest to him, and wrestles with it until it blossoms like the rose. The demonstration of vision is the strength with which men take hold of the difficulty of the present hour. I turn once again to the New Testament for the word which reveals the thought that was in the heart of the prophet, and which inspired him as he saw the visions fulfilled.

" Wherefore lift up the hands that hang down, and the palsied knees ; and make straight paths for your feet, that that which is lame be not turned out of the way, but rather be healed."

I am very much afraid that there are those who think it to be a sign of true sanctification to have hands hanging down, and palsied knees ; that the measure of sanctification is the measure of pessimism; that the measure in which men are really spiritual is the measure in which they waste their breath deploring the difficulties of the hour.

Though there be darkness to-day, if we see Jehovah, know His Presence, and fall in line with His power, it is ours to be sure of the consummation, and to hasten it. To see God here and now, and to fall in line with Him, is to be perfectly certain that presently when the Rejected is the Crowned, we shall share in the triumph, as we have shared in the travail.

Malachi

THE PERMANENT VALUES	THE LIVING MESSAGE

I. A revelation of the unfailing love of Jehovah.
  A. The constancy of love.
    1. The opening statement—1:2a.
    2. The persistence.
  B. The consciousness of love.
  C. The courage of love.
II. A revelation of human failure.
  A. The secret—failure of all motives other than love to maintain true relationships to God.
  B. The manifestation—the death of love issuing in callousness.
  C. The issue of failure—the worthlessness of form without power.
III. A revelation of the secrets of strength in an age of failure.
  A. Values "the name" thought upon
  B. Occupation—fellowship.
  C. Hope—the coming One.
	I. The present position of Christendom portrayed—the difference between the church and Christendom.
	II. The final message is the same—the coming One, as a sun.
	  A. Healing.
	  B. Burning.
	III. Our attitude towards that last word is the supreme test of our position.

THIS is the last of the prophetic utterances before the coming of the Messiah. There can be no doubt that the message of Malachi must be interpreted in the light of the work of Nehemiah. While it is true that in the book of Nehemiah, Malachi is never mentioned, it is quite evident that the conditions revealed in that book were practically the same as those with which Malachi had to deal. Let us turn back to the book of Nehemiah in order that we may compare three passages therefrom with three from Malachi.

Nehemiah xiii. 29.

"Remember them, O my God, because they have defiled the priesthood, and the covenant of the priesthood, and the Levites."

Malachi ii. 8.

"Ye are turned aside out of the way; ye have caused many to stumble in the law; ye have corrupted the covenant of Levi, saith Jehovah of hosts."

Nehemiah xiii. 23–25.

"In those days also saw I the Jews that had married women of Ashdod, of Ammon, and of Moab: and their children spake half in the speech of Ashdod, and could not speak in the Jews' language, but according to the language of each people. And I contended with them, and cursed them, and smote certain of them, and plucked off their hair, and made them swear by God, saying, Ye shall not give your daughters unto their sons, nor take their daughters for your sons, or for yourselves."

Malachi ii. 11, 12.

"Judah hath dealt treacherously, and an abomination is committed in Israel and in Jerusalem; for Judah hath profaned the holiness of the Lord which He loveth, and hath married the daughter of a strange God. The Lord will cut off to the man that doeth this him that waketh and him that answereth, out of the tents of Jacob, and him that offereth an offering unto the Lord of hosts."

Nehemiah xiii. 10, 11a.

"I perceived that the portions of the Levites had not been given them; so that the Levites and the singers that did the work, were fled every one to his field. Then contended I with the rulers, and said, Why is the house of God forsaken?"

Malachi iii. 8–10.

"Will a man rob God? yet ye rob Me. But ye say, Wherein have we robbed Thee? In tithes and offerings. Ye are cursed with the curse; for ye rob Me, even this whole nation. Bring ye the whole tithe into the storehouse, that there may be meat in Mine house, and prove Me now herewith, saith Jehovah of hosts, if I will not open the windows of heaven, and pour you out a blessing, that there shall not be room enough to receive it."

The reading of these passages is quite sufficient to show that the general conditions described at the close of the book of Nehemiah were identical with the conditions to which Malachi's message was addressed. Nehemiah deplored the defiled and corrupted priesthood. Malachi's central charge was that the priesthood had corrupted the covenant. Nehemiah dealt with the mixed marriages and the evil resulting therefrom. Malachi's message was directed against the same evil which was cursing the people. Nehemiah charged the people with neglecting to bring the tithe into the storehouse and so making it necessary for the Levites to turn from the service of the house of God to earn their own living upon the soil. Malachi uttered a complaint in the presence of the same neglect, there being a deeper spiritual note in his word, in that he recognized the spiritual failure involved in the material which Nehemiah deplored, and against which he made his protest. Most probably as Malachi is not mentioned by Ezra or Nehemiah, he followed closely, but was not contemporary with these men. He found the conditions described on the last page of inspired history aggravated rather than removed when he began to exercise his ministry.

It is very important that we should get into the atmosphere of this prophecy; and the condition of things generally will be best understood by going back over the history of about a hundred years. About 536 B. C. there had been a return from Babylon under Zerubbabel. A year later the foundation of the temple was laid. The work was soon abandoned. Fifteen years later Haggai and Zechariah delivered their messages, and as a result the building of the temple was resumed. Four or five years later the temple was finished, in the year 575 B. C. In 458, Ezra went up to Jerusalem with a letter from Artaxerxes. In 445 Nehemiah went up to Jerusalem, and accomplished his work. Thus the coming of Nehemiah to Jerusalem was about ninety years subsequent to the return from Babylon. Malachi prophesied in all probability about one hundred years later than that return, and so about ten years later than the period of Nehemiah.

It would seem as though the special evils which Ezra and Nehemiah set themselves to combat still existed, side by side with correct outward observance. The people are seen restored to Jerusalem, their temple built, the services of the temple observed, both special fasts and feasts, and regular seasons of worship.

The condition of the people is revealed by a question repeated seven times in the course of the book.

> " Wherein hast Thou loved us? "
> " Wherein have we despised Thy name? "
> " Wherein have we polluted Thee? "
> " Wherein have we wearied Him? "
> " Wherein shall we return? "
> " Wherein have we robbed Thee? "
> " Wherein have we spoken against Thee? "

Malachi charged the people with seven sins, and in reply they said " Wherein? " They did not admit that they had failed, as he declared they had.

The prophecy reveals a sensitive God, and a stultified people. Malachi declared the sensitiveness of Jehovah, and charged the people with lack of sensitiveness, hardness, callousness. The people were not conscious of their own shortcoming. They imagined they were perfectly satisfying the Divine heart, and fulfilling the Divine requirement. The book presents the picture of a people having a form, while they are devoid of power; fulfilling all the external requirements of religion, but being utterly without the internal experience; maintaining the sacramental symbols, while destitute of the spiritual grace of which those symbols should be the sign. It should be remembered that this message was delivered not to Judah, and not to Israel, if by Israel we mean the Northern kingdom. The burden of the word of the Lord was to Israel. Malachi spoke not to the ten tribes or to the two; not to the North, or to the South, as in separation from each other, but to the whole nation. When these people had returned from Babylon under Zerubbabel, and when later another contingent had returned in the time of Ezra and Nehemiah, the returning remnants were made up of members of all the tribes.

In the last book of the inspired history of these people, the book of Nehemiah, we saw them without a king, without a priest, and without prophet; and moreover, without any Messianic hope. To people in that condition Malachi delivered his message. As the book of Nehemiah was the last page of inspired history, the book of Malachi is the last page of inspired Hebrew prophecy.

This book is different from those of Haggai and Zechariah. The first business of Haggai was that of inspiring the people to be strong and build the house of God. It was local, practical, immediate, important. The business of Zechariah was that of inspiring the people to the selfsame activity; but also that of leading them to look at things unseen. The master thought of Malachi is that of fellowship with God. He had to deal with a people whose glorious history was that of their fellowship with Jehovah, whose shameful history was that of their infidelity to that fellowship. If that be recognized, we shall find the threefold permanent value of this book.

It is first, a revelation of the unfailing love of Jehovah. It is secondly, a revelation of human infidelity. It is finally, a revelation of the secrets of strength in an age of failure. Let us take these in order.

First, its revelation of the unfailing love of Jehovah. If we read this prophecy, listening for the master tone of it, we shall find it to be that of love, the love of God. Its opening words are almost startling,

"The burden of the word of Jehovah to Israel by Malachi. I have loved you, saith Jehovah."

That is the whole burden. "I have loved you, saith Jehovah." Our translation does not quite convey all the forcefulness of the thought. The tense employed is not exactly the Hebrew tense, nor have we any tense that exactly answers the Hebrew. I do no violence to the declaration that fell from the lips of Malachi if I render it thus, I have loved you, I do love you, I will love you, saith Jehovah. It is a declaration of the continuity of His love. That is the opening statement; the burden of the book is that of the constancy of the love of God. God sent that message to His people, when the nation was without king, priest, or prophet, when the nation consisted of a remnant satisfied with formality and lacking power, when the spokesmen of the nation answered the prophet by denying his charges, so callous had they become. There was to be no other voice until the herald should announce the Advent of the King. The last message of Isaiah's thunder had died away. Jeremiah's lamentations were almost forgotten.

Malachi, the last prophet, came declaring, "I have loved you, saith Jehovah," and right through the prophecy that is the master note of the music. It rises high above all the other notes. Whether we listen to the thunders of judgment, or to the plaintive complaint, we hear the great love-song of Jehovah. Malachi charged the people with profanity, sacrilege, greed, indifference; he charged them with perversion of the moral order, calling good evil and evil good; he charged them with robbing God in that they did not bring the whole tithe to His altars; he charged them also with blasphemy, in that they said, There is no value in serving God. These charges reveal in every case the consciousness of love in the presence of sin. It is love that is wounded. The book, therefore, is a revelation of the constancy of love, the consciousness of love, and the courage of love.

The chief sinfulness of form without power is that it hurts the heart of God. The one master note of the message which God sends to every age of failure is that which affirms the constancy of His love.

Then, in contrast, we have the revelation of human failure. This prophecy teaches that all motives other than love fail to produce maintenance of true relationship to love. It is possible to attend the temple, bend the knee, and make an offering regularly, but unless there is love in the heart there is no communion with God. To go to the temple merely as a matter of duty is to blaspheme. To carry offerings to the house of God simply because it is commanded, is to be guilty of sacrilege. There is only one motive sufficiently strong to maintain the relation between the heart of God and the heart of man, and that is love. When these people lost their love for Jehovah, all their religious observances became as tinkling brass and a clanging cymbal, noise without music.

The death of love issues in callousness. Think how surprising a thing it is, that when the last prophet came with his message, "I have loved you, saith Jehovah," the people answered, "Wherein hast Thou loved us?" That is the inspiration of all sin, and when we consider it, and wonder at it, we have no astonishment at all the other charges which Malachi brought against these people. The hour in which we cease to love God is the hour in which we begin to wonder whether God loves us. Then form is robbed of power, and form without power is not only useless, it is paralysis, blight, mildew; and when the matchless music of the Divine love is declared by the messenger of love, the formal religionists will say "Wherein?"

There is yet another value in this book. It reveals the secrets of strength in an age of failure.

"Then they that feared the Lord spake one with another: and the Lord hearkened, and heard, and a book of remembrance was written before Him, for them that feared the Lord, and that thought upon His name."

Here are revealed the secrets of strength in an age of failure; they "thought upon His name." The Hebrew word translated *thought* is elsewhere translated *regard*. When Paul wrote "If there be any virtue, and if there be any praise, *think* on these things" he used the same Greek word which in the Septuagint version is employed here, they "thought upon His name." Thus the Hebrew word, illuminated by the Greek word, helps us to understand what otherwise might appear a shallow statement. The Greek word means to take an inventory; they "thought upon His name," that is, they took an inventory of the wealth they had in His name, Jehovah Jireh. Jehovah-nissi. Jehovah-Shalom. Jehovah Tsidkenu. Jehovah Shammah. These people had nothing left to think of, other than the name. The grandeur of their nation was perished. The prophetic voices were silent. The priests had corrupted the covenant. The kings had passed away. All about them was formality devoid of power. But there was left them the real value of life. It was the name. They thought upon His name. "The name of the Lord is a strong tower; the righteous runneth into it and is set on high." When the king has failed, the priest is corrupted, and the prophet is silent; when the national power has declined and we are bewailing the failure of our age, then let us think on the name, take an inventory in the name, count it as our wealth, take time to go over our wealth in order to discover how rich we are.

Then again they "spake one with another." The word *often* is omitted in the Revised Version; but sometimes it is possible to say less and so to say more. The speaking together may be repeated, but when we say they spoke often we admit times of silence. That is not what the prophet said. He described constant, continuous, unbroken fellowship with each other, based on thought centred upon the name of Jehovah.

This is followed by another unveiling, "The Lord hearkened, and heard." Both these words are pictorial. "Hearkened" is a word suggesting the action of a horse at the sound of its master's voice, the pricking of the ears. It is only a figure of speech. The horse is arrested by the voice it knows. "They spake one with another, and the Lord hearkened." "Heard" means bending over patiently listening that no syllable may be missed. When His people spake one with another—not when they spoke to Him—Jehovah hearkened, and heard. They thought on His name and talked to each other thereof, and He hearkened and heard. God always attends to the conversation of those who are bound together by their loyalty to His name, and their consciousness of the wealth of their possessions in Him. Two or three of His people never meet together to speak of the deep things of His name and all the name means to them, but that He hearkens and hears.

The final secret is that of hope in the coming One; in the dawning of that new day which is to have two effects.

"The day cometh, it burneth as a furnace; and all the proud, and all that work wickedness, shall be stubble: and the day that cometh shall burn them up. . . . But unto you that fear My name shall the Sun of righteousness arise with healing in His wings."

That is not two days, but one. When that day comes, and the Sun arises, it will burn or it will heal. It will burn the plant that has no roots and no river resources; but it will heal the tree planted by the river.

The present position of Christendom is vividly portrayed by Malachi. Let us draw a very sharp line of distinction between the Church and Christendom. The terms are not synonymous. The Church consists of those who are His own. Christendom is the external appearance in every form. Christendom is characterized by formality devoid of power. Formality is not peculiar to one section of the Church. The form may not be the same. It may be stately ritual, or it may be of the simplest. Formality is the result of a conception that religion consists in external observance. To that condition the message of Malachi is: The day is coming which will be a day of healing, or a day of burning according to the condition of those who come to its dawning.

What is our attitude towards that day? That is the supreme test of our position. As the last word of the Old Testament economy was a word declaring the coming of that day, so also is the last word of the New Testament economy. The attitude of men towards that day determines their ultimate relation thereto, and their ultimate destiny. Let us live, putting all our trust in the name, in holy and unbroken fellowship with each other around our possessions therein, waiting for the daybreak, that so we may not be ashamed from Him at His coming.

Matthew

THE ESSENTIAL MESSAGE	THE APPLICATION

I. **The central teaching**—"the Kingdom of Heaven is at hand."
  A. Proclamation of the Kingdom.
    1. The fundamental conception.
      a. The Kingship of God—sovereignty.
      b. The Kingship of God—sphere.
    2. The special revelation.
      a. The King revealed.
      b. The Kingdom revealed.
  B. Interpretation of the Kingdom.
    1. Its principle, righteousness—the words of the King.
    2. Its practice, peace—the words of the King.
    3. Its purpose, joy—the will of the King.
  C. Administration of the Kingdom.
    1. By the King as King—His person.
    2. By the King as Prophet—His propaganda.
    3. By the King as Priest—His passion.
II. **The abiding appeal**—"repent."
  A. The fundamental meaning—consideration.
  B. The inevitable sequence—conviction.
  C. The resulting activity—conversion.
	I. **To the church.**
	  A. She is "the holy nation."
	    1. Submitted to Christ.
	    2. Realizing the Kingdom.
	    3. Manifesting it to the world.
	  B. Repent.
	    1. Submit.
	    2. Realize.
	    3. Manifest.
	II. **To the world.**
	  A. Under the sovereignty of God—yet in anarchy.
	  B. Repent.
	    1. Conception.
	    2. Conduct.
	    3. Character.

IN seeking for the messages of the books of the New Testament it is necessary to remember the difference between these books and those of the Old Testament. In those we sought amid local conditions and colouring for permanent values, which permanent values create the living and abiding message. In every book of the Old Testament we had to do with an incomplete revelation, for the Old Testament itself does not constitute a complete revelation. It is a library of expectation and of hope.

When we turn to the New Testament we still find ourselves amid local conditions, but we have no longer to deal with an incomplete revelation. We have now to consider the literature of that Christ Who is the final speech of God to the world. The writer of the letter to the Hebrews affirms that " God, having of old time spoken unto the fathers in the prophets by divers portions and in divers manners, hath at the end of these days spoken unto us in His Son." That message of the Son is God's final message to man. It is for us now to ask what is the essential message of each book, and what is its abiding appeal.

The four gospel narratives constitute the foundation literature of Christianity in that they present the Person of Christ, record His teaching, and give an account of His work on earth in the days of His flesh.

When we turn to the Gospel according to Matthew we find in it the final teaching on the subject with which it deals.

What then is the essential message of Matthew, and what its abiding appeal ? Here we are not left to anything in the nature of speculation. The essential message and the abiding appeal are contained in one brief declaration.

That declaration is twice uttered. It was first made by the voice of the herald who foretold the coming of the King ; it was repeated by the King Himself when He commenced His ministry ; " Repent ye, for the Kingdom of heaven is at hand." That is the voice of the herald, and the word of the King. The essential message then is " the Kingdom of heaven is at hand " and the abiding appeal is " Repent ye."

I recognize that there is a sense in which both the message of the herald and that of the King had immediate and local application. This word was spoken by John the Baptist peculiarly to the Hebrew people. When Jesus commenced His ministry He did so as the Jewish Messiah, and His word was consequently peculiarly to the people of the ancient covenant. While that is admitted it must not be forgotten that in the economy of God the Hebrew people existed not for themselves but for the world at large. This cannot be too often repeated if we are to understand that economy of God, in the case of His people Israel, and as to His perpetual method. Consequently the word of the herald and the word of the King constitute the one great message of this Gospel. This is not the final message of Christ ; not that He has changed or altered this by a hair's breadth, but He has a great deal more than this to say. The message of Matthew is not the final Christian message, for just as we need the four Gospels for the presentation of Christ, so we need the four messages for the delivery of the Christian message to the world at the present hour.

First then let us examine the essential message, " The Kingdom of heaven is at hand." Both the herald and the King uttered first the words of appeal, " Repent ye," but that appeal gained its force from the declaration which immediately followed it, " The Kingdom of heaven is at hand." That is the central teaching of the whole Gospel, and in examining it we shall discover three values. It is first the gospel of the proclamation of the Kingdom. It is secondly the gospel of the interpretation of the Kingdom. It is thirdly the gospel of the administration of the Kingdom. It proclaims the fact, explains the meaning, and describes the method of administration.

The abiding appeal of the Gospel is that of its call to repentance in the light of its teaching concerning the Kingdom.

The one theme of the book is that of the Kingdom. The word Kingdom occurs fifty times in the course of the story. There are different phrases of which it forms a part. The one most often recurring is that of " The Kingdom of heaven." This is peculiar to this Gospel according to Matthew, and occurs two-and-thirty times. The phrase " The Kingdom of God " occurs four times. The phrase " The Kingdom," which evidently has reference to the same idea, occurs eight times. The phrase " Thy Kingdom " when the reference is to God Himself is found once, and once when the reference is to Jesus. The phrase " His Kingdom " occurs twice with reference to the Son of Man, and once with reference to God. The last occurrence of the word is in the phrase " My Father's Kingdom."

That is a somewhat mechanical paragraph, but it serves to show that the word Kingdom is stamped upon the page from first to last. As this Gospel presents the King, its message is that of the Kingdom.

This word has two values which are complementary to each other, and both of which we need to recognize. These values may be expressed by the two words Kingship and Kingdom, in the way in which we make use of them to-day in our general conversation. The word Kingship emphasizes the fact that God is King. The word Kingdom refers to the realm over which He reigns. When we speak of the Kingdom of God we most often think only of the latter value, that, namely, of the realm over which He reigns. The fact that He is King is the fundamental message of this book.

Of the phrases to which we have referred " The Kingdom of God " is the greatest, because it at once insists upon the fact that God is King and refers to the realm over which He rules. There are occasions when it is evidently limited by the context, but considered alone it is certainly the greatest of these phrases, being the most spacious in its suggestiveness.

The phrase " The Kingdom of heaven," which as we have said is only used by Matthew, demands our special attention in any consideration of the message of the Gospel. In order to understand it, it is necessary that we should find out what it meant to the men who first heard it. Now it is an interesting fact that Christ never explained the phrase, neither did His forerunner. Simply because all who heard it were perfectly familiar with the one idea for which it stood. In the book of Exodus, which deals with the founding of the nation, we find the declaration " Ye shall be unto Me a kingdom of priests, and an holy nation," and there we discover the idea which the phrase "the Kingdom of heaven" suggested to the Hebrew. The peculiarity of the nation consisted in the fact that it was a Theocracy, a people with no king other than God Himself. It was a nation under the Kingship of God. It was a holy nation, a kingdom of priests, the Kingdom of heaven. When therefore these people heard John the Baptist and Jesus say " Repent ye, for the Kingdom of heaven is at hand " they understood them to mean that they were not living in accord with the underlying principle of their national life, and that it was necessary for them to repent in order to the restoration of the lost ideal.

The simple meaning of the phrase then is that it refers to the establishment in the world of the heavenly order, the submission of every king to God, the overturning of all save that which results from the recognition of the abiding throne of God. The Kingdom of heaven is the establishment of the Divine order on earth, the supremacy of the will of God in the affairs of men. The teaching of this Gospel then is that the only hope of humanity is in the establishment of the Kingdom of heaven, and that this can only be secured by submission to the throne of God. When men talk about the Kingdom of heaven as though it could be set up by human action, by the parliaments of men, or by a godless social propaganda, they are proving their blindness; and when they attempt the enterprise they are attempting to build without a foundation. The Kingdom of heaven is the reign of God over humanity. This Gospel proclaims that fact.

In the second place this Gospel interprets the Kingdom. It does infinitely more than assert the fact of the Divine Kingship, it explains the order of the Divine Kingdom. It contains a proclamation of the principle of the Kingdom, an explanation of the practice of the Kingdom, and a revelation of the ultimate purpose of the Kingdom. These things may be expressed in three words by quotation from the letter to the Romans in which the apostle declares, "The Kingdom of God is not eating and drinking, but righteousness and peace and joy in the Holy Ghost." Righteousness is the principle, peace the practice, and joy the purpose, of the Divine Kingdom. The words of the King constitute the law of the Kingdom, and proclaim the principle of righteousness. The works of the King exhibit the powers of the Kingdom which operate towards the practice of peace. The will of the King is revealed in the opening word of the Manifesto, " Blessed,"—or perhaps Happy, for happiness is the ultimate purpose of the Kingdom.

Thus the interpretation of the Kingdom is best expressed in the words of the apostle to the Gentiles. The master principle is righteousness, the practice is peace, and its purpose is joy.

Finally, this Gospel reveals the method of the administration of the Kingdom. In the key words to the analysis of the book this method is suggested. In the first division we have the presentation of the Person, and it is that of a King. In the second division we have the Propaganda, in which the King is revealed as Prophet. In the third division we have the Passion, in which He is seen as Priest. He is at once King, Priest, Prophet. The Old Testament asks for this Person. In the law, consisting of the first five books, it demands the Priest. In its historic section it seeks for the King. In its prophetic books it reveals the need of the Prophet. The Gospel of Matthew shows how the whole expectation of the old economy is fulfilled through One Who is Priest and Prophet and King. Through that threefold ministry, the Kingdom of God is to be established, and in no other way. The Gospel presents the One Who as King has all authority; Who as Prophet utters the final words of truth; Who as Priest deals with sin in such a way as to make possible the redemption and renewal of man, and through man of the whole creation. Thus the administration of the Kingdom is accomplished by the King Who is also Prophet and Priest.

In the light of that central teaching we turn to the consideration of the abiding appeal of this Gospel which is expressed in the one word " Repent."

It is necessary that we should first consider the fundamental meaning of this word. We are all familiar with the long continued controversy between the Roman and Protestant theologians as to the nature of repentance. This controversy arises out of the fact that two distinct words in the Greek New Testament are translated in our versions " Repent." One of these lays emphasis upon a change of mental attitude ; the other is burdened with a sense of sorrow. Into that discussion we need not enter here. The particular word made use of by the forerunner and by the King is the one which quite literally means, Think again. The fundamental meaning then of the appeal of this book is that it calls men to consideration.

Such consideration will have as its inevitable sequence, conviction of sin, and a consequent sense of sorrow. While it is perfectly true that the sense of sin and the sense of sorrow are not suggested by the word, they are involved, for it is impossible for any man honestly to consider his life in the light of what this Gospel reveals without coming to consciousness of his own sin, and sooner or later to the sense of sorrow.

There is, however, yet another and further result involved—that namely of the activity of conversion which will follow. Conversion in itself is not regeneration. Regeneration is the act of God Conversion is the act of man. Conversion is that turning round from rebellion to submission which results from the conviction of sin which follows repentance as reconsideration. Thus the threefold fact suggested by the word may be expressed as a sequence by the use of these three words, Consideration, Conviction, Conversion.

It must, however, be remembered that this word " Repent " loses its force if it be removed from its immediate connection with the central teaching contained in the words " The Kingdom of heaven is at hand." It is possible for a man to think again, and for his second thinking to be as false as the first. Therefore the Gospel says to man, Behold the King, understand the Kingdom, and think again in the light of these facts. Repentance here then means the submission of the life to the standards of the Kingdom and to the throne of the King. It is possible for men to repent without moral or spiritual result. They can think again, and depart from the old secularism to the new theosophy without being any nearer to realization or establishment of the Kingdom of God. This Gospel proclaims the King, interprets the Kingdom as righteousness, peace and joy ; shows that the Kingdom is administered by One Who is perfect King, perfect

Prophet, perfect Priest. It then appeals to men in the presence of these facts to repent.

To obey its appeal is inevitably to be brought to a consciousness of sin as coming short of the glory of God, and such consciousness invariably results in sorrow for sin. Repentance has its final value in that turning round, from sin and towards God, which Paul described, when writing to the Thessalonian Christians, in the words, " ye turned unto God from idols."

While therefore the great appeal of this Gospel is Repent, it is useless to take that word and preach it save in connection with the central teaching of the Kingship of God revealed to men in Jesus, and of the Kingdom of God opened to men through the work of Jesus.

There is a twofold application of the message of this book to our own age. Its first application is to the Church because the Church is now the holy nation, the Theocracy, whose function it is to realize and to manifest the principles and practice and purpose of the Kingdom of God. At Cæsarea Philippi Jesus said to Peter, " I will give unto thee the keys of the Kingdom " He also declared to the disciples after instructing them in the mysteries of the Kingdom, that every scribe instructed to the Kingdom of heaven " is like unto a man that is a householder, which bringeth forth out of his treasure things new and old." The world to-day can only understand the meaning of the Kingship and Kingdom of God through the Church. The first application of the message of this Gospel must therefore be to the Church, and this because she is responsible for manifestation.

The measure in which she is failing to reveal these things to the world is the measure in which she should obey its call to repentance. Her membership consists of those who are submitted to Christ, who realize in their own lives the fact of His Kingship and who therefore through their transformed lives manifest to others the grace and glory of His reign. The measure of the failure to reveal is the measure of the failure to obey. To Ephesus, fallen from first love, the word of the King was, " Repent, and do the first works." That is still His word to those who name His name, but fail to reveal Him to others

The message of Matthew to the world can only be delivered through the Church. Its first note must be that of insistence upon the abiding Kingship of God. No man can escape from that Kingship. It is possible for men to live within the Kingdom of God in such wrong relation to it that it becomes a scorching, destructive fire instead of a beneficent and healing force. God reigns to the uttermost bound of the universe. Nothing escapes His authority. It is our business to proclaim to men the established fact of the Kingdom of God, and the fact that He has anointed His well beloved Son as King over the whole earth.

In the light of that fact, men who are in rebellion against the Divine government are to hear as the first note of the Gospel the word " Repent."

Mark

THE ESSENTIAL MESSAGE	THE APPLICATION

I. The central teaching—1:14, 15.
 A. The nature of the service—creation of a gospel.
 B. The law of the service.
   1. Sympathy.
   2. Suffering.
   3. Sacrifice.
 C. The result of the service.
   1. The gospel.
     a. The person—cf. 1:1.
     b. The resurrection—16:15.
   2. The opportunity of salvation.
 II. The abiding appeal.
 A. The perpetual preliminary—"repent."
 B. The essential call—"believe in."
	I. To the church.
	 A. The law of its life—abiding confidence in the servant of God.
	 B. The law of its service—abiding confidence in the gospel.
	 II. To the world.
	 A. The gospel.
	   1. A perfect Servant.
	   2. A perfect service.
	   3. A perfect salvation.
	 B. The condition.
	   1. Repent—activity of mind in the presence of sin.
	   2. Believe—activity of mind in the presence of the Saviour.

THE Gospel according to Mark presents Jesus as the Servant of God. Whereas in Matthew He is seen in the purple of His royalty, in Mark He appears girded for service.

The inclusive message of the book is found in ch. i. 14, 15 —

"Now after that John was delivered up, Jesus came into Galilee preaching the gospel of God, and saying, The time is fulfilled, and the Kingdom of God is at hand : repent ye, and believe in the gospel."

As in the first Gospel the inclusive message is contained in the words which record the message which Jesus delivered as He commenced His preaching, so in the same place, in the same relation, we find the message of this Gospel of Mark.

Another verse, central to the Gospel, gives its content in brief outline —

"The Son of Man came not to be ministered unto, but to minister, and to give His life a ransom for many."

That covers the whole Gospel: the first division, Sanctification, "The Son of Man came" ; the second division, Service, " not to be ministered unto, but to minister " ; the last division, Sacrifice, "and to give His life a ransom for many."

What then, is the message of that life, of that service, and of that sacrifice ?

We shall follow exactly the same method as we adopted in dealing with the message of Matthew ; inquiring first what is the essential message, and then noticing the application of that message.

In dealing with the essential message we shall attempt first to state the central teaching, and then to consider its abiding appeal.

We have said that this Gospel presents the Servant of God. When we turn from the study of its content in order to listen to its message, we must pause first to inquire in what sense it is true that Jesus was Servant of God. There are senses in which He never can be described in that way Indeed, there is only one sense in which the Son of God can be spoken of as the Servant of God. By nature He is Son of God. By nature He is equal with God ; but for certain purposes, and in

183

certain relationships, He became Servant of God.

This Gospel, standing as it does in the midst of revelation, is intimately related to the prophecies of the past, and has close relationship to the apostolic writings which follow. Isaiah was the prophet of the Servant of God; and Paul was the apostle who most clearly wrote of the Kenosis, or self-emptying, whereby the Son of God became the Servant of God. We have in this Gospel the real portraiture of that Servant. It reveals first, the nature of His service; secondly, the law of His service; and finally, the result of His service.

First then, as to the nature of His service. The introductory word of the Gospel is, "The beginning of the gospel of Jesus Christ, the Son of God." The final command of the Servant of God is, "Go ye into all the kosmos, and herald the gospel to the whole creation."

The Son of God became the Servant of God in order to create a gospel, to provide good news for men. The Servant of God is the Saviour of men. In order to provide salvation for them. He, Who was equal with God, became Servant; and in no other relationship can He be thus described. Wherever in the ancient prophetic writings, or in this Gospel, or in the subsequent apostolic writings, our Lord is referred to under this title of Servant of God, the subject under consideration is that of salvation. Mark commences with citation from the prophecy of Isaiah which is preëminently the prophecy of the Servant of God. The prophet's picture of that Servant was that of One Who comes to accomplish the Divine purpose of salvation. As we study the book we see the growing portrait of Him, line added to line, beauty to beauty, until we reach the mystic teaching of the fifty-third chapter, in which the Servant of God is seen, wounded for our transgressions, bruised for our iniquities, the chastisement of our peace laid upon Him. Thus He is seen fulfilling His service and accomplishing the purpose of God, that of providing a way whereby it is possible, immediately after the record of suffering, to sing the song of redemption, and to tell the story of great and gracious restoration.

Thus at the heart of the prophetic fore-vision of the Servant of God is the picture of the passion through which He is able to provide pardon, purity, peace, and power for humanity.

In the writings of Paul we may confine our attention to one passage in the Philippian letter. The injunction of that passage is, "Have this mind in you, which was also in Christ Jesus." All that follows is argument, but the argument is greater than the injunction. Charging the Philippian Christians to have the mind of Christ, the mind of graciousness, of humility, of love, Paul argued for obedience by showing what that mind really was. In studying the matchless passage we must keep our mind on the Person referred to, Who, in the essential fact of His personality, is the same throughout. This Person is first declared to be One Who, being in the form of God, did not count it a prize to be on an equality with God. It is next affirmed that this same Person emptied Himself. We must remember here that the Person is still the same. He did not empty Himself of Himself. That doctrine of the Kenosis which declares that the Son of God laid aside His Deity is not warranted by New Testament teaching. He emptied Himself as He became Man. That emptying consisted in His taking the form of a Servant. The form chosen was that of Man. Thus He laid aside one form of manifestation and took another. The form laid aside was that of sovereign Deity. The form taken was that of subservient humanity. The form alone changed; the essential Being remained the same.

For what purpose then did He thus empty Himself and take the form of a Servant? In what sense can He be spoken of as Servant?

In order to find the answer to these inquiries let us follow the descending scale. "Being made in the likeness of men; and being found in fashion as a man, He humbled Himself, becoming obedient even unto death, yea, the death of the Cross." That is why He became a Servant, and that is the sense in which He was a Servant. He is revealed in this passage as one Person, emptying Himself of one form of manifestation and taking another for the purpose of the Cross, and the purpose of the Cross is that of the salvation of man.

Thus Isaiah when he presents the great Servant shows that the central meaning of His mission is that of salvation through sacrifice; and Paul in language still more definite even though more mysterious, language which shows a deeper insight into the infinite mystery, presents this same Son of God, equal with God in His nature, partner of His throne, becoming a Servant for the Cross and for salvation. There is no sense in which the Son of God is Servant of God, save that He became such to create a gospel by providing salvation for man who is without salvation, and fast bound in sin and nature's night.

When Jesus began His ministry in Galilee He struck the key-note thereof in the words " The time is fulfilled." I remember hearing Mr. Johnston Ross say that there are some texts in the Bible of which none but an Eastern can appreciate the full meaning. Such a text is this word of Jesus, full of profound significance. " The time is fulfilled." It is the language of One Who in circumstances of lowliness, about to make His home in despised Galilee of the Gentiles, recognized the fact that the ministry He was about to exercise was the fulfillment of eternal purpose. The hour had struck, the time was filled to the full. The statement referred to all the economy which ended with the prophecy of John the Baptist. The last voice of prophecy had been heard, and all that the prophet uttered, together with all that the prophets preceding him had said, was fulfilled. Seers had for ages been looking towards the dawn of a new age, the coming of the Servant-Son, the advent of One Who would be Son by nature, and Servant for the accomplishment of the purpose of salvation and restoration.

When Jesus commenced His ministry He said, " The time is fulfilled." The Kingdom of God is near. God Himself is near. He is here in the form of a Servant, bending toward the Cross, in order that in the mystery of that " death-grapple in the darkness 'twixt old systems and the Word," He may conquer that which has spoiled, ascend the throne of empire, restore the lost and ruined order, and establish the Kingdom of God in all its grace and glory.

Thus the nature of the service is that of providing a gospel of salvation ; and that fact is indicated in the opening words, ' The beginning of the Gospel " ; after which the Person is described by names and titles which perfectly reveal Him. Jesus is the familiar name of His humanity ; Christ is the title of His Servanthood ; the Son of God is the designation of His nature.

In the second place let us observe what this book teaches concerning the law of His service. This may be expressed in three words intimately related to each other ; sympathy, suffering, sacrifice.

The Servant of God was in sympathy with man even in his sin ; not in sympathy with his sin, but in sympathy with the sinner. If this Gospel be carefully considered—indeed if the four of them be examined—no single word of severity can be found which this Servant of God uttered to sinning men and women. His severity was reserved for hypocrisy, and that because it wrought ruin in the lives of others. For the woman taken in the very act of sin ; for men steeped in sin, and held in contempt by the religious teachers of their day ; He had nothing but tenderness, sympathy, and infinite compassion.

Oh, that all of us who name His name might learn the lesson of this Gospel in that respect ! Salvation results from sympathy ; sympathy means suffering ; and suffering is only dynamic when it becomes sacrifice. If we say to men, Be warmed, and do not clothe them, there is no sympathy in such speech, neither is there any value in it. Let these men be warmed and clothed at cost, that is sacrifice. Whether we make application in the material or spiritual realm the principle is the same. I think that is what the apostle meant in his Galatian letter when he uttered the injunction which seems so commonplace in comparison with the argument which is so profound, " Bear ye one another's burdens, and so fulfill the law of Christ." I do not understand the apostle to mean that we should obey the law that Christ enunciated, but rather that which He Himself obeyed. The law of Christ's life was that of bearing the burdens of others. That is the whole story of the service of the Servant of God. The master law of His life in the presence of human sin and sorrow was that of the bearing of burdens—" Behold, the Lamb of God, which taketh away the sin of the world." He took our sins and bare them. The law of His service then was that of sympathy, suffering, and sacrifice.

What then was the result of His service ? Its nature was the creation of a gospel ; its law was the bearing of burdens ; its result is found in the gospel created. The Servant is introduced as " Jesus Christ, the Son of God " ; and the last words recorded by Mark as falling from His lips by way of command, are " Go ye into all the kosmos, and herald the gospel to the whole creation."

What did He mean by the Gospel? We have no right to speculate on the matter. The answer is found in the context, which, when we examine, we find that He presenced Himself in the midst of His disciples after the resurrection, and they were filled with doubt and fear. He rebuked their unbelief, and then said, Go, and preach the good news to the whole creation; that is, He commanded them to tell the good news of the resurrection. The good news then is that of the risen Christ. The resurrection is the demonstration of the fact that the Servant has accomplished His work, that He has provided salvation, that He is master over the forces that wreck and ruin and spoil. The result of His service is the provision of that gospel.

If that be the central teaching, what is the abiding appeal? The answer is found in the words of our Lord at the commencement of His ministry, " Repent ye, and believe in the gospel." "Repent ye" is the abiding preliminary. No man is ever ready to believe in the Gospel until he has obeyed the first word. That, however, is not the supreme appeal of this Gospel. The supreme appeal is contained in the words " Believe in the gospel." I know it is unsafe to base a great doctrine on a preposition; but nevertheless there is wonderful value and instruction in the prepositions made use of by the writers of the New Testament. " Believe *in* the gospel," not into it. Whenever the preposition *eis* is used with the accusative it suggests motion into. The preposition *en* used here has quite another significance. It signifies neither motion into, nor nearness to, but rest at the centre of. Jesus said, " Believe in the gospel." The Gospel is the sphere of rest; have confidence in this gospel, put your trust in it, having ventured into it, rest in it. That is the abiding appeal.

What is the application of this message to the Church of God? There is first the application to the life of the Church. This word " Believe ' reveals the law of the Church's life. That life is continued and developed as she has abiding confidence in the Gospel of the Servant of God, abiding confidence in its message of pardon and power. Again, the message has yet another emphasis in its application to the Church. Not only is belief in the Gospel the law of the Church's life, it is also the law of her service. When we lose our confidence in this Gospel,

then our service becomes weak. If we doubt the Gospel of the Servant of God, then we have no Gospel for the man who is fast bound in sin and nature's night. It is in the proportion that we believe in it, are sure of it, know it, that we are able to help our day and generation. The inter-relation between life and service is of the closest. We cannot believe in this Gospel as the result of intellectual argument. We can only believe in it as the result of experience. It is only as we believe into the One it presents and find His power to save, that we believe in it when we are in the presence of other men.

What does this book say to me personally? It first calls me to believe in this Gospel, to rest in it for my life, for pardon and for power. It also calls me to rest in it for my service. The word gospel occurs eight times in the book, and a study of the passages will show the true relation of the Christian to Christ in the matter of service. It is a study for which we cannot take time here, but I suggest it as full of interest and value.

Once again, what is the message of this book to the world? What is its message to London, East End and West End, to rich and poor, to high and low, to man as man, to humanity as humanity? It tells the story, announces the good news, of the perfect Servant of God, of His perfected service, and of His perfecting salvation. Get men to read this book, help them to understand it, interpret it to them. Sit down by the side of men mastered by sin, and read them this book. Say to them, Behold God's Servant, God's Son become Servant in order to get near to you, to help you, to lift you. Through that perfect Servant's perfected service there is perfecting salvation for you. That is preaching the Gospel.

If that be the essential message of the book to the world, its appeal is first, Repent. That is the necessary activity of the mind in the presence of sin. Its final appeal is, Believe. That is the activity of the mind in the presence of the Saviour.

This Gospel according to Mark begins where that according to Matthew ends. Matthew said, " Repent ye, for the Kingdom of heaven is at hand." As I read his story I see the King and know my own failure; I become conscious that this personality of mine is territory belonging to the King, but waste, spoiled, wilderness without blossom.

I take up the Gospel according to Mark, and it says, Behold the Servant of God. He is the Saviour of men. I believe into Him. I believe in His Gospel. I risk eternity and my soul upon Him, and thus I am restored to the possibility of the garden, and of all fruitfulness.

Luke

THE ESSENTIAL MESSAGE	THE APPLICATION

I. **The central teaching.**
  A. The presentation of the Saviour—"The Son of Man."
    1. The racial first-born.
      a. The fact.
        (1) The Hebrew merged in humanity.
        (2) Humanity springing from God.
      b. The method.
        (1) Immaculate conception.
        (2) The sinless man.
    2. The representative brother.
      a. The negation of distinctions.
      b. The realization of essentials.
    3. The redeeming kinsman.
      a. The right.
      b. The accomplishment.
  B. The proclamation of salvation—"To seek and to save that which is lost."
    1. Through redemption—regeneration.
    2. Through regeneration—relationship.
    3. Through relationship—realization.
II. **The abiding appeal.**
  A. The attraction of the personality.
    1. The identity.
    2. The distance.
    3. The sympathy.
  B. The terms of discipleship.
    1. Negation of old relationships and choice of new—14:26.
    2. Acceptance of law of new relationships—14:27.
    3. Renunciation of all in order to the reception of all—14:33.
	I. **To the church—** "witnesses."
	  A. In the power of relationship with the Son of Man.
	    1. Fulfillment of terms—redemption.
	    2. Realization of results—fellowship.
	    3. Demonstration of truth—manifestation.
	  B. For the sake of the lost.
	    1. Revelation.
	    2. Conviction.
	    3. Persuasion.
	II. **To the world—**"The Son of Man came to seek and to save that which was lost."

THIS third Gospel presents Jesus of Nazareth to us in the grace and glory of His perfect Manhood.

Its essential message is crystallized in the declaration of the Lord Himself in answer to the persistent criticism of the Pharisees; "The Son of Man came to seek and to save that which was lost."

The message of this Gospel is not a simple message. The more carefully we study this book the more are we impressed with its profundity, with the wonder and spaciousness of the thing it has to say to us concerning Christ. It first presents the Saviour, the Son of Man; it secondly, and consequently, proclaims the possibility of salvation for the sons of men.

Let us then first consider the Saviour that this book presents to us. There are three things to be noted. Luke is careful, in his introductory section, to show us the nature of this Person. He presents to us the racial First-born; the *second* man; the *last* Adam. The first man appears upon the page of the Old Testament, and he fails. The second Man appears upon the page of the New Testament, and He realizes all the Divine intention for humanity. The first Adam, the head of the race, from whom the race has proceeded, is presented to us in the Old Testament. The last Adam, the Head of a new race, is presented in the New Testament. There will be no other. The ultimate, the final race, is to spring from this second Man, Who is the last Adam.

He is then presented as the representative Brother, not Brother of the race that is fallen, but Brother of the race that is to be made—a distinction which we need to make very carefully. There is a sense in which He took on Him the very nature of Adam ; but He did not share his sinful nature, although eventually He bore his sin in the mystery of His dying. We look first of all, not at the Saviour Who in the mystery of His passion wrought out human redemption ; we look at a Man, the second Man, the last Adam, the racial First-born, and therefore the representative Brother of all such as are to follow, of all such as are to spring from Him, as surely as the race sprang from Adam.

Finally, and let us mark the sequence, He is presented as the redeeming Kinsman, or, to borrow the old Hebrew word, the *Goel*.

The experimental process is in the reverse order. We come to the redeeming Kinsman ; and receiving the redemption which the Kinsman provides, enter into fellowship with the representative Brother ; until at last we are made perfect partakers of that life which makes us one with the racial First-born.

In presenting the First-born of the new race, Luke is careful to show how the Hebrew was merged in humanity, and how humanity sprang from Deity. That is the suggestiveness of the genealogy which he gives. Notice the difference between that of Matthew and that of Luke. Matthew, who was presenting the King, was careful to set Him in relation to David, as of the royal line, and to Abraham, as of the Hebrew people. Luke sweeps back through everything that is purely Hebrew, until he comes to the fountainhead of humanity, Adam ; of whom, in a word that would astonish us if we were not so perfectly familiar with it, he says, "the Son of God." Thus he presents Jesus as human, of our very nature, human as we are human, but he puts Him even in that nature into immediate relationship with God.

Luke then tells us the mystery of how this second Man came into human life. He declares that the conception of this Man was immaculate. The Roman dogma of the immaculate conception has nothing to do with the phrase in the sense in which I use it. That dogma was promulgated in 1854, and was never held before. There had been long arguments from the twelfth century, not as to the sinlessness of Jesus, but as to the sinlessness of Mary, which is a very different thing. When the Roman speaks of the immaculate conception, he means that Mary was sinless in being, because sinless in the mystery of conception, which is the Roman theologians' way of attempting to account for the sinlessness of Jesus. To say the least that is but to put the difficulty one stage further back, namely, to the mother of Mary, and then to fail to solve it. With fine delicacy of touch Luke declared that in the mystery of the conception of this new Man there was a process by which He was sinlessly conceived—"That which is to be born shall be called holy." In the mystery of that Divine activity of the overshadowing of the Virgin, she was cleansed from all sin, so that the Man Who appears before us is immaculately conceived, and therefore is a sinless Man.

In the Biblical account of creation we have an ascending scale. Day one ; light and darkness, day and night. Day two ; the dividing of waters. Day three ; land, and vegetable life. Day four ; signs and seasons, days and years. Day five ; sentient life. Then what ? Man, the result of all the upward processes from chaos and darkness, the crowning glory of all that which constitutes the lower side of his being. But how ? Mark this most carefully ; there was now a new activity, not part of the process that had preceded, but distinct from it ; God "breathed into his breathing places the breath of lives," and man appeared. The processes did not create man, they only contributed towards the material fact of his human nature. Human nature is not animal nature. All the processes did but produce the temporary tabernacle, that which is to pass and perish. The Divine inbreathing produced the man.

The next picture is that of an assault upon man by the powers of darkness, of man yielding to those powers, and of his consequent descent or fall. The process runs on through history. From that man sprang the race, inheriting and sharing the results of that man's loss of the sceptre, because of his rebellion against the throne of God.

Now behold the second Man, the last Adam. As the first man was, as to his material nature, taken out of the dust through the processes of ascent, and then by the final act of Divine breathing was made man, who never had been man before, and never could be man but by that mystery; so now in the fullness of time God again took hold of dust, only beginning this time not away back where we cannot trace the workings, but beginning at the point where He ended before. This second Man was taken out of humanity, inheriting all its essential qualities, but distinct from it; like in all things to His brethren, unlike all those from whom He is taken, because of immaculate conception, and therefore sinless. This is a new beginning, a new start in the history of the race. From that moment I read on, and the Gospel reveals this Man as the First-born of the race, as the representative Brother of the whole family.

When we look at this Man we see the negation of all distinctions. I quote from Paul in the Galatian letter for the sake of conciseness and brevity: "There can be neither Jew nor Greek, there can be neither bond nor free, there can be no male and female: for ye all are one in Christ Jesus.' Mark the divisions. How is humanity divided to-day? By race, by caste, and by sex. In Christ there is neither race, nor caste, nor sex. Think in the presence of Paul's word of this Man presented in the Gospel, and see how He represents every type, every class, every possibility, every phase. Jesus was not a poet. You cannot place Him in the Poets' Corner; but more poetry has come out of the things He said than from any other fountainhead in the history of literature. Jesus was no philosopher. He enunciated no system of philosophy; yet the great philosophies all owe something to His inspiration and suggestion. Jesus was not a Man of science; but all scientific investigation has had its chance as the result of His opening the way and making possible the investigations of the centuries. The Easterner is at home in the presence of Christ with all his mystic dreaming; and so also is the Westerner, with his ceaseless, practical, determined endeavour. Whatever the type or class may be, both men

and women find in Him the inspiration of noblest things, the crown and glory of all that which is peculiar to them. There He stands upon the page of the Gospel, the Representative Brother. Whether men dwell North, South, East or West, they touch Him and feel the answering thrill of His Brotherhood. He is the Head of the race, and therefore the Representative Brother.

If in Him I find the negation of distinctions, in Him I also find the realization of the essentials of human nature as I know it.

Finally, He is the redeeming Kinsman. What was the right of the *Goel*, according to Hebrew law and practice? Nearness of kin was the fundamental right. It was the next-of-kin that must redeem his brother. So He came, the next-of-kin to humanity. But the redeemer must accept responsibility. He came accepting responsibility. The redeemer must overcome those who are against his brother. He overcame all the forces against humanity. The redeemer must create the opportunity for his brother's reinstatement; the work of the *Goel* was the redemption of the person and the inheritance. All these things are fulfilled in this Man. Luke the Greek, writing to Theophilus the Greek, declared that in this Man he had found the fulfillment of the Greek ideal: being and birth, childhood and confirmation, development and anointing; physical, mental, spiritual perfection. In the next section he showed how this perfect Being was perfected, demonstrated perfect through processes of temptation, teaching, and transfiguration. That was the filling to the full of the Greek ideal. They never saw any further than the possibility of perfecting the individual.

The final section of the Gospel, the greatest section of all, shows that this Man not only fulfilled the Greek ideal of personal perfection, but He broke it into a thousand fragments, seeing it was too small to hold Him, as He turned His back upon His personal rights, that He might die and liberate His life, and so make it dynamic for others.

This Gospel of Luke says, Behold the Man; the racial First-born; the representative Brother; the redeeming Kinsman. So it presents the Saviour.

Then it makes proclamation of salvation. "The Son of man"; that is the Saviour presented; "Came to seek and to save that which was lost " ; that is salvation proclaimed.

Through His redemption, He regenerates men who have fallen ; and through that regeneration, He brings them into living relationship with Himself as the new Head of the new race ; and through that relationship with Himself, makes them members of the new race. That is salvation.

He came " to seek and to save that which was lost." By the mystery of His death He put sin away, and liberated His life, placing it at the disposal of those who have lost their own. When they receive His life, it is His life they live. Through regeneration He brings them into living relationship with Himself. By that relationship He makes possible their realization of the same nature. Christ is more than human. Every Christian becomes more than human. Christians are made " partakers of the Divine nature."

What then is the abiding appeal of this Gospel ? Its first note is that of the attraction of the Personality. First because of the identity between men and Himself. His familiarity with men was born of His conception of the dignity of humanity. If we feel that there are people we hold in contempt, it is because we have a low estimate of humanity.

People were attracted to Christ also by the sense of distance. They said, He is so near us, and yet is so different. He sits down to eat with us, and yet all the while He is saying things we have never heard before.

The final reason of His attractiveness was that of His sympathy Give that Gospel of Luke to some man who has never read it, who is an honest man ; let him sit down and read it, and I venture to affirm he will feel the same charm that men of old felt, the humanness of this Man, the identity with our own life, His distance from it, and the tender sympathy breathing through everything He does and says. That is the first appeal of this Gospel.

The appeal is more than that. It is not only the attraction of Personality. It is that of the terms of discipleship. It is in this Gospel that I find the passage which I never read without trembling. Just before the parable of lost things occur the most severe and appalling words that ever fell from His lips, " If any man cometh unto Me, and hateth not his own father and mother, and wife, and children, and brethren, and sisters,

yea, and his own life also, he cannot be My disciple. Whosoever doth not bear his own cross, and come after me, cannot be My disciple . . . Whosoever he be of you that renounceth not all that he hath, he cannot be My disciple." That is the appeal of the Gospel.

These three conditions correspond to the three facts we have considered. Racial First-born, He says to men, You must sever connection with the old race entirely if you are coming after Me ; if there is any love in your heart for father, mother, wife, child, brother, sister, which is going to interfere with your loyalty to Me, you must crucify it. I am the First-born of a new race, and you must come after Me by severing your connection with the old race.

Representative Brother of the new race, He says that we must accept the new responsibility. If you are coming after Me you must take up the cross ! You cannot find your way into the brotherhood with all its benefits, if you are not fulfilling the conditions.

Redeeming Kinsman, He declares that He can only redeem us, as we give up everything for Him. If you are going to have the benefit of redemption, you must renounce all that you have ! There must be mutual sacrifice. It is upon the plane, where He is stripped of dignity, and I am stripped of everything, that we meet.

That is the appeal of the Gospel according to Luke. The attraction of Personality and the terms of discipleship.

In a word, let me make the twofold application. I find the application to the Church in the words of the risen Lord, " Ye shall be My witnesses." In the power of the relationship with the Son of Man, I am to become His witness, His defense, His evidence ! His witness, fulfilling the terms we have considered. His witness, realizing the results of the fulfillment of those terms in actual fellowship with Himself. His witness, demonstrating His power because I who was ruined am now redeemed, I who had lost my sense of the infinite and my love of the pure have been brought into fellowship with God, and have purity as the passion of my heart.

Then, because He came to seek and to save the lost, this Gospel calls the Church into fellowship with Him for the sake of the lost ; by revelation of what He is able to do in our transformed lives, by conviction so produced in the minds of those who observe, and then by persuasion of such as are convinced towards the selfsame Saviour.

What is the message of this Gospel to the world? Carry it to the ends of the earth, let it speak its own truth to the men who are lost, and it tells them of a Kinsman Who, to borrow the old Hebrew figure, is able to discharge their debt, destroy their enemies, make possible the redemption of their persons and the redemption of their inheritance, as offspring of God.

Behold the Man, but do not try to place Him on a level with yourself. He is intimately near; all the essential things of my humanity are in Him! He is infinitely far; all the incidentals of my sin and pollution are not in Him! Because of His purity, in the mystery of His death, He is the Son of man seeking and saving the lost.

John

THE ESSENTIAL MESSAGE	THE APPLICATION

I. The central teaching—God.
A. Full of grace.
  1. The fact: love
    a. Love is the divine consciousness.
    b. Love is the inspiration of the divine activity.
    c. Love is the law of the divine government.
  2. The illustrations—works.
    a. Water to wine—the joy of life—marriage.
    b. Nobleman's son—family life.
    c. Bethesda man—sin and suffering.
    d. Feeding five thousand—the support of life.
    e. Walking on sea—the succour of life.
    f. Blind man—the light of life.
    g. Lazarus—redemption.
  3. The equal fullness of truth—passion governed by principle.
B. Full of truth.
  1. The fact: light
    a. Light is the divine consciousness.
    b. Light is the inspiration of the divine activity.
    c. Light is the law of the divine government.
  2. The illustrations—words.
    a. "I am the Bread of Life"—sustenance by holiness.
    b. "I am the Light of the World"—illumination by holiness.
    c. "I am the Door"—safety by holiness.
    d. "I am the Good Shepherd"—supply by holiness.
    e. "I am the Resurrection and the Life"—triumph by holiness.
    f. "I am the Way, the Truth, and the Life"—progress by holiness.
    g. "I am the Vine"—fellowship by holiness.
  3. The equal fullness of grace—principle suffused with passion.
II. The abiding appeal.
A. The call to worship:
  1. The tabernacle—the flesh.
  2. The glory—full of grace and truth.
B. The call to service—"As the Father hath sent Me . . ."
	I. To the church.
	A. Intellectual—give the Lord Jesus Christ His true place.
	B. Spiritual—believing, you have life.
	  1. Grace—love the motive.
	  2. Truth—light the method.
	II. To the world.
	A. No man hath seen God.
	B. The only-born hath declared Him, to the satisfaction of:
	  1. The intellect.
	  2. The conscience.
	  3. The heart.

IT is sometimes affirmed that the synoptic Gospels are simple and easy of understanding, and that the Gospel according to John is profound, full of mystery, and difficult of interpretation. There is a sense in which all this is true. There is another sense in which the first three are books of mystery, while the last is the book of revelation, of unveiling. In John we find the solution of the mysteries of which we are inevitably conscious in studying Matthew, Mark, and Luke.

The Gospel according to Matthew presents Jesus as King, and it is impossible to read it without being brought to consciousness of His authority, even though we may not yield thereto. We are convinced of His kingliness, but are unable to account for that tone of authority which distinguishes His teaching from that of all others. In the Gospel according to Mark we find the picture of the Servant of God, eager, full of ceaseless activity, accomplishing His service and crowning it by sacrifice. We cannot read it, however, without feeling that there are depths to the consecration, and sublimities in the sacrifice, for which we cannot account. In the Gospel according to Luke we find a Man of our own humanity, but are conscious that while He is in many senses near, in others He is far away, and the contemplation fills us with awe and wonder.

These three stories demand another, or else they remain full of beauty, but inexplicable, for the Person presented as King, as Servant, as Man, possesses in all these aspects some qualities or quantities which lack explanation. In the Gospel according to John we find the answer to the riddle, the solution of the enigma, the unveiling of the mystery. This Gospel is as certainly an apocalypse as is the book which bears that name. This is unveiling. Here we meet exactly the same King we met and crowned in Matthew; the same Servant we saw and trusted in Mark; the same Man we observed and longed to be like in Luke. It is indeed the same Person; the same face, the same love-lit eyes and awful purity; the same regal authority; the same unobtrusive humility. Sometimes I think in reading this Gospel that I feel the touch of the flesh of Jesus more really than in Matthew, Mark, or Luke; yet from the first and sublime words with which it opens, to the simple and wonderful declarations with which it closes, I know that I am in the presence of an unveiled Person. The mystery of Matthew, Mark, and Luke is solved for me when I read John. This Gospel accounts for that note of authority which sounded in the Manifesto, and which breathed in power through the invitation, "Come unto Me all ye that labour . . . and I will give you rest." When I see Him in the Gospel of John I understand the secret of His sublime service. Here I have the explanation of the spaciousness and wonder of His humanity. In this Gospel the Person comes not from Abraham through the royal line of David; not from Nazareth; without genealogy; not from Adam, without a

father; but from eternity and from God, as the Only-born of God.

The essential message of this Gospel is found in the closing declaration of the prologue. "No man hath seen God at any time; the only begotten Son, which is in the bosom of the Father, He hath declared Him." First, a recognition of limitation and need, "No man hath seen God at any time"; then the essential affirmation, "God only-born which is in the bosom of the Father, He hath declared Him." There is diversity of opinion concerning the actual form of the phrase translated in our English versions, "only begotten Son," resulting from the fact that the manuscripts are not in agreement. It is difficult, therefore, to be dogmatic. I do not think the meaning is materially changed whichever form we take, as either phrase suggests the same thought of relationship between the Son and the Father.

This "only begotten Son," or "God only-born of the Father," has declared God. The Greek word translated declared is that from which we have obtained our word exegesis, and means the leading-out of something that is hidden, in order that it may be seen. The Son, therefore, is declared to be—I use the word, knowing the difficulty of it—the exegesis of God; that is, the interpretation of God, the explanation of God. That is also the teaching of the principal statement of the prologue. "In the beginning was the Word, and the Word was with God, and the Word was God. . . . And the Word became flesh, and dwelt among us (and we beheld His glory, glory as of the only begotten from the Father), full of grace and truth." That is the value of this book. It presents the Person Who is the exegesis of God, that is, the manifestation of God.

Consequently the central teaching of the book is that it reveals the truth about God. If we would know the truth concerning His nature, we must study this Gospel. If we would know the laws which govern His activity, we discover them here. All that man needs to know about God is contained in this Gospel according to John. It is the final document of revealed religion concerning God. It is the story of the Son as the Revealer of the Father; the presentation of the One Who unveiled the face of God, Who told us the deepest secrets about His nature, Who revealed to men the laws of His activity.

> " Would we see God's brightest glory,
> We must look in Jesu's face."

Man is forever attempting to represent God in some way. That is the meaning of all idolatry, and of every idol. In the intention of those who made it, the golden calf was a like-ness of God; for when they erected it they worshipped Jehovah. The golden calf was the golden ox, the symbol of service and sacrifice, and these people were attempting to express certain truths in some way which would appeal to the senses. Their action was the result of hunger for manifestation. God had said, " Thou shalt not make unto thee a graven image, nor the likeness of any form that is in heaven above, or that is in the earth beneath, or that is in the water under the earth; thou shalt not bow down thyself unto them, nor serve them," be-cause that which man makes as a likeness of God can only libel God. The highest forms of man's attempts to give expression to the facts concerning the nature of God consist in the pro-jection of human personality into immensity. The trouble with all false religion is that man has projected himself into immensity with all his faults and failure, and the deity so imagined is a magnified sinner, and men worshipping that, become more and more like that which they have made.

Man is ever seeking a manifestation, and the incarnation was God's answer to that need of humanity. He came into human nature, and through the Manhood of Jesus manifested Him-self, in order that men seeking for manifestation which should enable them to know Him might find it. He was of our humanity, not by will or act of humanity, as we have seen in Matthew, and in Luke; but by the overshadowing and mystery of the Divine power, and by the activity of His own Holy Spirit, grasping our humanity, grafting Himself upon it in order that man seek-ing for manifestation might find One Who is at once of his own nature and of the nature of God. In the Gospel of John we look at Jesus, but at the same moment we see God. In the tears of Jesus we see the tears of God. In the pain of Jesus we see the passion of God. That is the value of this book, and that is why it is not easy to deal with. We touch and handle a Man; He is

the Word of life; a word cannot be touched, and life cannot be handled; yet through this Man we do touch and handle life, age-abiding life, for in Him the Word is become flesh. To use the daring declaration of Charles Wesley, " God is contracted to a span " in order that men may see Him.

What then is the central teaching of this book concerning God? What do we know of God through Jesus? In the prologue we have a comprehensive answer which is dealt with more particularly, subsequently by illustration, " We beheld His glory, glory as of the only begotten from the Father, full of grace and truth." When we have uttered those two words, grace and truth, we have uttered all the truth about God. In the subsequent part of the book these words are illustrated; but the inclusive fact of grace may be revealed in a threefold affirmation concerning love. Love is the Divine consciousness. Love is the inspiration of the Divine activity. Love is the law of the Divine government. The result is grace.

Love is the Divine consciousness. When we speak of our own mind we speak of conscious-ness and subconsciousness. The fact of sub-consciousness results from our finite and limited nature. With God there is no subconsciousness. He has perfect consciousness, and that is love. If it would be right to speak of God in the terms which we use about ourselves we might ask, What is the experience, the consciousness of God underlying all His action? There can be but one answer, and that is Love. That is the profoundest truth.

Therefore all the activity of God is love in-spired, and the law of His government is love. That is the truth which is revealed concerning God through His Son.

For illustration of that we may take out of the mass of material the great signs. Sign is John's word for the wonders of Jesus. He never speaks of a parable. The word parable as we find it in the other Gospels does not occur in this one. We do find it in our English versions, but the margin suggests proverb, which is perhaps a more insufficient translation than parable. The Greek word of which John makes use would be better translated in our language, allegory, for it has a much wider meaning than parable. The miracles which John records are chosen with evident intention of teaching larger truths ; they are signs. Every one is an activity of love. The first was that of turning the water into wine. Right on the threshold of the revelation of God, this Man went to a marriage feast and ministered to the joy of life. The next sign was the restoration of the nobleman's son to health. Love recognized the sorrow in the family circle through sickness, and the fact that death was threatening ; and acted to end the sorrow by healing the sickness, and defeating death. The next sign was that of the healing of the man in the Bethesda porches. Love suffering in the presence of sin, as seen in its result, acted for the sake of the sinner. Love entered into suffering, and breaking the power of sin ended it, and so gave deliverance to the sinner. The next sign was that of the feeding of the five thousand. Love, recognizing man's need of actual support, provided it. The next sign was that of the walking on the sea. Love, coming to troubled souls, tempest-tossed, bewildered, walking in infinite dignity over the waters that threatened to engulf them, and through the wind which impeded their progress, coming on board produced a great calm. The next sign was that of the blind man. Love opened his eyes and, claiming to be the Light of the world, gave spiritual teaching. Love is the illumination of all life. The last sign was the raising of Lazarus. Love groaned in spirit and was troubled and wept ; and in that groaning we hear the distress of God, in those tears we behold the grief of Deity. Love was troubled in the presence of death, and through the mystery of its own trouble and pain broke the bands of death.

There is equal fullness of truth wherever we look upon the fullness of grace. Love breathes through every one of the signs, but light shines also. Grace is there, but so also is truth. There was no shadow, no duplicity, no turning aside from the master principle of holiness which rests at the heart of the universe, no deflection from the straight line of righteousness. Love and light, grace and truth, passion governed by principle.

What we have said of grace when interpreting it as love, we can with equal accuracy affirm of truth when interpreting it as light. Light is the Divine consciousness. Light is the inspiration of the Divine activity. Light is the law of the Divine government. As we took the great works to illustrate grace we may take the outstanding words to illustrate truth.

"I am the Bread of life " ; sustenance by holiness.

"I am the Light of the world " ; illumination by holiness.

"I am the Door " ; safety by holiness.

"I am the good Shepherd " ; supply by holiness.

"I am the Resurrection and the Life " ; triumph by holiness.

"I am the Way, the Truth, and the Life " ; progress by holiness.

"I am the Vine " ; fellowship and identity with holiness.

From out of the resplendent glory of the revelation of God in the bush, burnt but not consumed, Moses heard the Divine affirmation, " I AM " ; and then, as though there could be no unveiling, the declaration turned back upon itself in majestic mystery, and ended with the affirmation " THAT I AM."

"The law was given by Moses; grace and truth came by Jesus Christ." He took up the same great revealing name " I am," and linking it to simple symbols, enabled men to understand in fuller measure the being of God. In connection with the communication of the name to Moses the supreme fact insisted upon was that of the holiness of Jehovah, as he had been commanded " Put off thy shoes from off thy feet, for the place whereon thou standest is holy ground " ; that same fact of holiness is always present in the use of the title by Christ, and as we have seen, He revealed the relation of holiness to all the facts of life already suggested.

When we study these words revealing the truth, the light, we must not forget the equal fullness of grace. As when speaking of grace we insisted upon the equal fullness of truth, so while we are conscious of the awful purity of holiness in the shining of the light, we are nevertheless conscious that the light is suffused by a great love. If when considering grace we declared that therein we saw passion governed by principle, in this consideration of truth we may declare with equal accuracy that we have principle suffused with passion. John saw in the Man upon Whom he looked grace and truth, and thus saw the glory of the Father.

The abiding appeal of this is first that of the call to worship. "The Word became flesh and tabernacled among us," that is, pitched His tent among us. John, a Hebrew, used language which would be perfectly familiar to his own people. He was thinking of the tabernacle in the wilderness, the tent pitched in the midst of the people, the centre of their life, and the appointed place of their worship, and he said, "The Word . . . pitched His tent among us." His flesh became the tent; but as in the ancient tabernacle the central fact was the glory of the Shekinah, so in this new tent of the flesh of the Man of Nazareth, the central fact was the glory of the Only begotten of the Father, full of grace and truth. When the tabernacle was finished according to pattern, the glory of the Lord filled it, and it became the place of worship. In the new covenant we find the fulfillment of the olden symbolism. The Word is incarnate and through the eyes of the Son of man we see the light of God; and in His voice we hear the accents of the love of God; in Him we see God full of grace and truth, and the unveiling cries to us, "O worship the Lord in the beauty of holiness."

The appeal is a call to service as well as a call to worship. The tabernacle being erected, the nation was completed by worship, and so prepared for witness. When we stand in the presence of this Man and see through the veil of His flesh Divine "the light that were else too bright for the feebleness of a sinner's sight" we worship, and we are also compelled to serve. When Isaiah beheld the temple full of the glory of the Lord, and cried out because of the uncleanness of his lips, and when the seraph had cleansed those lips with the live coal from off the altar, then the voice of God was heard, "Whom shall I send, and who will go for Us?" the answer of the prophet was immediate, "Here am I; send me." When we stand in the presence of this unveiling and see the glory of God in this tabernacle; when we worship in response to that revelation, then we hear out of the tabernacle the word "As the Father hath sent Me, even so send I you," and we shall be ready individually to respond, "Here am I; send me."

There is intellectual and spiritual application of this message of John to the Church of God. The intellectual application is that the Church must give to the Lord Jesus Christ His true place, and His true place is that which is here revealed. In this Gospel we see Him perfectly, finally. To speak of Him as Jesus of Nazareth only is to degrade Him, and the moment we do so we fail to find God, and sooner or later our conception of God will be false. There will be denial of essential truth, and excuse made for sin. There will be denial of essential grace, and all the springs of service will be dried up. It is only when the Church of God sees this Man at the centre of her life, and He is recognized as being the tabernacle in which essential God is resident for purpose of revelation that she can realize her own life, or fulfill her service.

The spiritual application is that in believing we have life, and that such life will manifest itself in grace and truth. Grace will be the motive, and truth the method of all our acts. The proportion in which we have seen and believed and become what He would make us, is the proportion in which we manifest His life in grace and truth.

There is an application of this message of John to the wider world. "No man hath seen God at any time," yet man needs God, and subconsciously is aware of his need, and is groping after a god, trying to find a centre for his worship, something to which he can bow himself down. All the result of such groping is deeper darkness and more disastrous failure. Let man take the Person of this Gospel and consider Him well, and he will find God to the satisfaction of his intellect, to the satisfaction of his conscience, to the satisfaction of his heart.

The final appeal is to the will of man. This God satisfies my intellect, my emotion, and appeals to my will. I can still rebel. This Man stood in the midst of His own age and said, "Ye will not come to Me, that ye may have life." May that lament of Jesus not be true of us, but may we come to Him, and find our life, as we find our God.

Acts

THE ESSENTIAL MESSAGE	THE APPLICATION

I. **The central teaching**—concerning the church.
  A. The abiding principles.
    1. Origin—created by the Son.
    2. Nature—"many Sons unto glory."
    3. Function—the work of the Son.
  B. The revealed perils.
    1. Prejudice—the grip of the past.
      a. Judaism.
      b. Lack of confidence in the Spirit.
    2. Passion—the power of the flesh.
      a. Carnality.
      b. Lack of yielding to the Spirit.
    3. Pride—the lure of the world.
      a. Apostasy.
      b. Lack of obedience to the Spirit.
II. **The abiding appeal.**
  A. The master passion of the church is that of the glory of God.
    1. The unveiling of Himself.
    2. The establishment of His kingdom.
  B. The inclusive principle of the church is that of loyalty to the Lord.
    1. Realization of His life.
    2. Prosecution of His work.
  C. The sufficient power of the church is that of the Holy Spirit.
    1. Likeness to the Lord for the revelation of God.
    2. Direction in His work for the glory of God.
	I. **To the church.**
	  A. A question of motive—the glory of God.
	  B. A question of method—the work of the Son by the Spirit.
	II. **To the world.** (This book, as a book, has no application to the world.)

THIS book is of great importance to the students of the New Testament. It is the link of continuity, binding together into one great whole the historic records of the life of our Lord, and the didactic and devotional writings of the apostolic period. In the gospel narratives, as the writer of this book reminds us, we have the story of beginnings ; the beginnings of the doing and teaching of Jesus ; and this is the only historic record upon which we can depend, as to those events which immediately followed His death and resurrection and ascension.

Turning to the other part of the New Testament, I find constant references to churches.

The word church has no full and final explanation in the four gospel stories. Thirteen of the pamphlets in that which remains of the New Testament were written by a man whose name was Paul. He is never mentioned in the four Gospels. In order to understand the continuity of the story commenced in the Gospels we need this book. In order to an interpretation of all that follows in the great didactic and devotional writings we need this book. It is the link between the first four books and all that remains, binding them together. It is the bridge over which we cross from the story of the beginning of the doing and teaching of Jesus, to those writings which are the result of the fulfillment of the promise He made to His people that, after He had left them as to bodily presence, they should have full and spacious teaching for all life and service. He said that it was better for them that He should go away. He declared that when He went away the Spirit should be given, Who would bring to their remembrance the things He had said to them, guide them into all truth, and teach them concerning things to come. In the epistles and devotional literature we have the fulfillment of these promises in interpretations of the Christ, and in teaching concerning things to come. How the promise was fulfilled we find in the book of the Acts of the Apostles, in the account of the coming of the Spirit, and in the record of that Spirit's ministry in and through the disciples of Jesus.

In our study of the content we laid great emphasis upon the one word "began"; and in our analysis of the book we devoted a section of the first division to one verse, because the light from it flashes back upon the story of the Gospel, and forward upon the story of this book, and upon all the writings that follow.

That word "began" gives the true value to the gospel story, showing that it is not the account of consummated work, but the story of the initiation of work. It also flings its light upon the book of the Acts of the Apostles, suggesting that it is the story of the things He continued to do and to teach. One Christ is presented to our view both in the Gospels and in the Acts. In the Gospels we see Him in limited, localized, and straitened circumstances; the limitation, localization, and straitening necessary in order to completion of the initial, preparatory work. In Acts we see the same Christ, no longer limited, no longer localized, no longer straitened; the unlimited nature of His work, the universal application of His power, and the unstraitened operation thereof, all resulting from the mystery of the things He began to do and to teach in circumstances of localized limitation.

Now when we begin to seek for the message, there is another word upon which we must lay equal emphasis. It is the first word of the second verse; "until the day in which He was received up, after that He had given commandment through the Holy Ghost unto the apostles whom He had chosen." In the former treatise we have the account of the things He began to do until. That word "until" carries over the force of the word "began" into the new book. In the first book we have the things He began to do and to teach until He was received up. In the book of the Acts we have the things He began to do after He was received up. This book is also the story of beginnings. Nothing is finished. That quality creates its value. When we discover it, and remember it, and depend upon it, we are very near to the discovery of its message. It is not the story of a completed movement. It is the story of all He began to do after He was received up. He has never ceased the doing until now. The work is going forward. He is still doing. He is still teaching. The risen, ascended Lord is the living centre of His Church.

The beginnings of Divine activities are always ideally and potentially perfect; but they are always actually and effectively imperfect. I turn to the first book of the Bible and read, "In the beginning God created." That was the beginning of Divine activity in creation. In the Gospel of John I read, "In the beginning was the Word, and the Word was with God, and the Word was God"; and that declaration prepares the way for the teaching concerning the beginning of the Divine activity of redemption in human history when the Word became flesh. The third new beginning is in this book of the Acts of the Apostles. The beginning in creation; the beginning of the new departure in incarnation; the beginning of the new departure in the Church; these are the three great beginnings of Divine activity which our Bible reveals to us, and in each case we see beginnings ideally and potentially perfect; and actually and effectively imperfect.

As we look at the creation as it is revealed in the poetic, majestic, true story of Genesis, it is ideally, potentially perfect. The morning stars sang together over that first creation, and I think I know the burden of their song; The whole earth is full of the glory of God. In the midst of the earth is man, made as the psalmist long afterwards sang, "but little lower than God," crowned with glory and honour that he might have dominion over the whole creation. That is creation ideally, potentially perfect! But actually, effectively it is imperfect, in that it is waiting for development. The perfect earth needs cultivation, development ; needs that man, its king, shall discover its secrets and obey its laws, in order to the discovery of its hidden mysteries and wonders. Man to-day is standing in the presence of the wonders and hidden forces of the earth saying: We have but scratched the surface, and have hardly begun to understand the depths. But all the forces and all the glories and all the beauties were resident in the earth on that morning flushed with beauty when the sons of God sang together over creation. The Divine beginnings are always ideally, potentially perfect ; and actually, effectively imperfect.

If with profounder reverence we look upon the mystery of the incarnation we find the same facts. Mark the perfection of it ; " We beheld His glory, glory as of the only begotten from the Father, full of grace and truth." That was the beginning, ideally, potentially perfect ; but actually and effectively the beginning was imperfect. The life must be consummated ; and the death must be accomplished. The beginning of the Divine activity was perfect, ideally and potentially, " It was the good pleasure of the Father that in Him should all the fullness dwell . . . in Him dwelleth all the fullness of the Godhead bodily." But there was work to be done ; through the processes of passion, death, and resurrection the work must be accomplished ; actually and effectively the beginning of the incarnation was imperfect.

Now we come to the beginning described in the book of the Acts. " Having received of the Father the promise of the Holy Ghost, He hath poured forth this, which ye see and hear." That statement is full of suggestiveness. That was the new beginning ; the dawn of a new day ; as wonderful a thing, a more wonderful thing, than the dawn of creation long ago.

It was a new beginning, ideally and potentially perfect. The risen and ascended Lord, in His own Person, by virtue of the victory of the purity of His life, and the passion of His death, had received the plenitude of the Spirit of God as a deposit for all for whom He lived and died. This gift He poured out upon His waiting disciples, and in the upper room there was the dawn of a new creation, the break of a new day, the initiation of a new movement.

It was a new beginning, actually and effectively imperfect. These waiting men in the upper room received the Holy Spirit, but they had to learn the law of the Spirit, to discover the method of the guidance of the Spirit ; through long processes they had to learn the meaning of the power that had come to them through Christ. This book gives us the picture of the new beginnings. That is its value. A note of warning is immediately necessary. We must not go back to the Acts of the Apostles and try to imitate the incidentals. We must go back to it to discover its essentials, and these essentials are not nineteen centuries away from us ; they are with us perpetually. This book then is of supreme value because it reveals the principles and the perils of the age of Pentecost. These constitute the message of the book, and create its abiding appeal.

The central teaching of this book concerns the Christian Church, and deals with fundamental matters. Through the incidentals we see the essentials.

First, it is a revelation of the abiding principles of the Church of God. For purposes of conciseness and brevity I want to group these under three heads ; the origin of the Church of God ; the nature of the Church of God ; the function of the Church of God. The revelation is all the more wonderful, and all the more valuable, and all the more perpetual, because it is not formulated. I know that some would be far more comfortable if they could have a book with a formulated system of Church government ; but spiritual intelligence thanks God for atmosphere.

As to origin, the Christian Church is the creation of the Son. He prepared, during the three years of His public ministry, a little group of men and women ; stored their minds with truth, which they did not then understand ; impressed upon them the fact of His personality, which they did not then apprehend. Then He left them, prepared for something larger and greater, yet unable to move forward until they should be " clothed with power from on high."

Then having risen from the dead and ascended to the right hand of the Father, He received the fullness of the Holy Spirit and poured it out ; " There came from heaven a sound as of the rushing of a mighty wind, and it filled all the house where they were sitting. And there appeared unto them tongues parting asunder, like as of fire ; and it sat upon each one of them.

And they were all filled with the Holy Ghost."
That is the Christian Church; created by His
humiliation, by the perfection of His human life,
by the mystery of His passion, by His victory
over sin and death and all the enemies of the
race, by His triumphant resurrection, by His
ascension, by the Spirit bestowed as the result of
His own accomplished victory. When He
poured the Spirit out upon that handful of
people, the Church was born. The Church
consists then of all those men and women who
are made one Spirit with the Lord, who share
His very life by the coming of the Spirit, who
are united to Him, no longer upon the basis of
human sentiment, no longer by the limitation of
geographical situation, but because the one
Spirit of God that fills the risen Man in glory,
perfectly fills men and women who trust Him in
the world. The unity of the Church is not
ecclesiastical; it is not based upon uniformity.
I could hold a brief for Presbyterianism, Episco-
palianism, or any other form of ecclesiastical
polity upon the basis of this book. The underlying unity of the Church is that of the baptism
by the Spirit into union with the risen Lord of
all such as believe on Him. Thus is created and
constituted the Church.

As to nature, the Church is of one life with the
risen Lord. In the Gospel accorded to Luke,
we saw Jesus as the racial First-born, the second
Man, the last Adam, the Head of the new race;
the representative Brother of all such as are in
the new race; the Goel, or redeeming Kinsman.
In this book we see the race springing from the
racial First-born; the brotherhood resulting from
the representative Brother; the redeemed kinsmen resulting from the redeeming Kinsman.
The Church is the fulfillment of that which He
uttered prophetically when His mother after the
flesh, in anxiety because He was overworking,
came to persuade Him to go home; " Who is
My mother? and who are My brethren? . .
Whosoever shall do the will of My Father which
is in heaven, he is My brother, and sister, and
mother." That was a great prophetic word,
into the meaning of which the little band of
disciples could not enter at the time, declaring
that there is an affinity nearer and dearer than
that of flesh and blood. We behold in the Acts
of the Apostles that new race; very foolish, very
feeble, very faulty, but brothers of the Lord,

kinsmen of the Kinsman Redeemer. Christ is
repeating Himself in redeemed men and women.
That is the nature of the Church. Through
nineteen centuries she has been upon her march,
growing ever, faulty, failing, trembling, but her
life is ever His life.

As to function, the Church is the instrument
of the risen Lord for carrying on His doing and
His teaching. He came to perfect and bring to
glory many sons; every son incorporated in the
family by the communication of the life of the
Son carries on that work. Life in the Spirit is
the life of Christ communicated by the Spirit.
Therefore it is life like the life of Christ; and
consequently it is life for Christ. That is the
story of the men revealed in this book. Its
greatest interest centres in Paul and his missionary journeyings. In all kinds of peril he
pressed forward, the regions beyond his perpetual watchword. That is the function of the
Church. The life of Christ repeated in the
power of the Spirit. So she marches, enlarg-
ing the opportunity of Christ, by multiplying the
members of His holy and sacred body.

Life in the Spirit is also light in the Spirit.
The Spirit chooses persons, indicates places,
initiates practices. Choosing persons; Saul of
Tarsus to the Gentiles; Philip the deacon to go
to Samaria; nameless men, " Men of Cyprus
and Cyrene, to Antioch, preaching the Lord
Jesus." Indicating places; the strategic centres,
Jerusalem, the city of Judaism; Antioch, the
gateway to the Gentiles; Corinth, the market
of Greece; Ephesus, the centre of pro-consular
Asia; Rome, the metropolis of the world. The
centres occupied, and so the villages and ham-
lets evangelized. Initiating practices; we cannot
read the Acts of the Apostles without seeing that
where the Spirit of God is, there is liberty. The
moment men try to cramp the Church's operations within rules and regulations they cripple
and spoil her.

Not only life and light in the Spirit; but also
and supremely, love in the Spirit. Love of the
Lord, that is the master passion of this Church;
and out of it grows love of the brethren, and
love of the whole world. That is the function
of the Church, life, light, and love, in the Spirit;
or in other words, Christ's work continued.

The revealed perils may be grouped under
three heads. There is first the peril of preju-

dice; the grip of the past, Judaism. It is manifest all the way through. The bondage of the past is always the result of lack of confidence in the Spirit in the present. How these things continue! There is no need to make application. How constantly the Church of God is hindered in her work because the grip of prejudice is upon her. " As it was in the beginning, is now, and ever shall be." That is not a Biblical quotation. The Spirit of God forevermore will break down traditions by doing new things.

Another peril is the mastery of Christian men and women by unholy passion. That was a peril of the Church at the beginning. It is a peril of the Church to-day. If prejudice is the result of lack of confidence in the Spirit; unholy passion is the result of lack of yielding to the Spirit.

The final peril is pride; the pride of the eye, the vainglory of life, the lure of the present world. Demas forsook Paul. Demas is a type. This results from lack of obedience to the Spirit; or lack of attention to the Spirit's teaching; or both. When we cease to listen to the Spirit's interpretation of the spiritual and eternal things, then the lure of the present world is upon us.

The abiding appeal of this book consists in the fact that it teaches us that the master passion of the Church must be that of the glory of God. She goes, as her Master went, to unveil God to the world, and to establish the Kingdom of God upon the earth. That must be the master passion of the Church. It is not that of the amelioration of human suffering. God is glorified by the amelioration of human suffering; but our passion is that of the glory of God. It is not the bettering of human conditions. The best conditions of human life are in the purpose of God for humanity; but we are to seek them because they are in harmony with the will of God. The great discourses of the Acts of the Apostles were all delivered to the outside world, except the one Paul addressed to the elders of Ephesus. Read those discourses, and find that their purpose was always the glory of God.

The inclusive principle of the Church's ac-tivity is that of loyalty to the Lord Christ, Whose passion is that of the glory of God. The Church is to prove that loyalty by realization of His life and prosecution of His work.

Finally, the sufficient power of the Church is that of the Holy Spirit; sufficient for the life of likeness to the Lord in order to the revelation of God; sufficient for direction in work for the glory of God.

What then does this pamphlet say to the Church of God to-day? It institutes investigation along two lines. It asks the Church first, what is the *motive* of all its activity? It asks secondly, what is the *method* of all its activity?

The motive of the Church ought to be the glory of God, nothing less, nothing more, nothing else; and that means devotion to the Lord Jesus Christ. The method of the Church ought to be the work of the Son, seeking and saving the lost by the Holy Spirit; and that means fellowship in the cross and resurrection and ascension of Christ.

This book, as a book, has no application to the world. Only as the Spirit-filled race continues the ministry revealed here will like results follow in the world. It is not by this book I make my appeal to the world; but it is by the Church living and serving according to the pattern revealed in this book that she makes her appeal to the world. It is only thus that similar effects in the world will be produced; the arrest of cities; the adding to the Lord of men and women; the abandonment of idols. When the Church is true to the principles revealed in this book she will arrest the attention of cities again; she will always be adding men and women to the Lord; in the wake of her triumphant march idols will be destroyed.

When we are in this succession we shall set forth the God, ignorantly worshipped by the Athenians; we shall proclaim the evangel to the uttermost part of the earth; we shall win territory for the King; and hasten the coming of His final victory.

Romans

THE ESSENTIAL MESSAGE	THE APPLICATION

I. The central teaching.
  A. The awful helplessness of the sinful race.
    1. The light of nature—failure.
    2. The light of revelation—failure.
  B. The absolute perfection of the divine salvation.
    1. The provision in Christ, the Son of God.
      a. Manifestation.
      b. Propitiation.
    2. The relation to God.
      a. The activity of His love in holiness.
      b. The vindication of His holiness by love.
    3. The provision for man.
      a. Justification.
      b. Sanctification.
      c. Glorification.
    4 The relation to creation.
      a. The restoration of its King.
      b. The realization of its possibilities.
II. The abiding appeal.
  A. The revelation of the true sanctions and final standards of life—the divine throne and government.
  B. The call to faith as the faculty to apprehend the unseen.
    1. The divine provision for sight—"the Son of God. . . ."
    2. The call for faith in all that which the manifestation declares.
  C. The call to dedication, the attitude which is the only evidence of faith.
	I. To the church.
	  A. The ultimate value—the glory of God.
	  B. The supreme responsibility—communication to others.
	  C. The personal necessity—full realization in character and conduct.
	II. To the world.
	  A. "All have sinned"—3:23.
	  B. God "the justifier of him that hath faith in Jesus"—3:26.

IN this letter we are dealing with one of the greatest writings of the New Testament; greatest, that is, in its setting forth of the foundation facts of our most holy faith. It was Martin Luther who said of it, "It is the chief part of the New Testament and the perfect gospel"; Coleridge the poet declared it to be "the most profound work in existence"; and Godet described it as "the cathedral of the Christian faith."

In order to a clear and sharp apprehension of the message of this letter, we need to recognize the assumptions of the writer, for these constitute the sanctions of his teaching. In the back-ground of this letter there is evident a definite cosmology; and an equally definite conception of history.

The cosmology and history are those of the Old Testament. If we have lost the book of Genesis, and the history of the Old Testament, this is a foolish and meaningless document.

First, there is on the part of the writer a very clear recognition of the one God. He never attempts to demonstrate the existence of God; nor does he argue for the unity of Deity; he takes these things for granted; and in many references we find evidences of this fact.

Moreover he assumes that this God is in

character holy and just. Again he never argues for either of these things; but takes them both for granted. He argues of other matters, assuming this twofold fact of the holiness and justice of God. If this man, living in the midst of sin, iniquity, and difficulty is conscious of the problem of human redemption, that problem is as to how God can be just and the Justifier.

It is further taken for granted that this one God, Who is holy and just, is the Creator, Sustainer, and Governor of the universe. He never admits for a single moment in the process of his argument concerning human salvation, that any part of the universe has escaped or can escape the government of God. He never admits that man can escape from the government of God. He does admit that man may give himself up to material wrong-doing, mental depravity, and spiritual death; but he affirms that if man does give himself up to these things, then God gives him up to the issues of them; and thus he reveals the supreme fact, that even a sinning man is still held in the grip of the Divine government; and shows that if a man will not submit to the infinite love and mercy of God by falling into line with the provision of His grace, that man must endure the unutterable penalty of his sin.

Man by nature, by first creation, by Divine intention, by the possibilities and potentialities of his own being, stands in the universe, subject to the throne of God, and reigning over all the creation beneath him.

Creation then, according to the cosmology of Paul, is subject to man, beneath his control, dependent upon him for realization and fulfillment of its hidden potentialities; and consequently sharing man's experiences. If man be noble, the nobility in creation is manifested. If man be debased, creation is debased. If man shall through sin groan and travail in pain, the whole creation groaneth and travaileth in pain beneath him. If man shall be manifested in the midst of creation as the son of God, the sighing and groaning of creation shall cease, and it shall be lifted to the level of the man who is over it. Such, in brief, is the cosmology behind the letter; this man's conception of things as they are, as to origin, nature, and government.

Now observe history as this man sees it. It is interesting how very few references there are in the writings of Paul to what we call profane history, to events that stand out upon the page of human history. Human history is set entirely in the light of the Divine. History for Paul begins with Adam, the first man, the head of the race. That man is seen in rebellion against the Throne, —disobedient, is Paul's word. One man's disobedience produces one result in human history; the dethronement of God from the actuality of human consciousness, the degradation of man immediately following the dethronement of God, and the consequent degradation and spoiling of all creation beneath him. Paul did not look upon all the groaning and pain of creation as a process that was tending to upward development. The first man disobeying loses his sceptre because he ceases to bow to the sceptre of God; losing his sceptre, the kingdom beneath him suffers, he is unable to realize it, unable to lead out its hidden potentialities into fulfillment. Creation groans and travails in pain because its king has lost his sceptre, because he has ceased to kiss the sceptre of God, or to bow to His throne.

After long centuries, Paul recognizes another point of departure; a man, Abraham, and a people, called out into separation from all that order of things which has resulted from the sin of the first man; and this man and this people called out for the sake of all the rest, that by the life of faith, which is a life of submission to the throne of God, they might reveal to men the breadth, the beauty, and the beneficence of the Divine government. And again there follows the story of failure; failure of faith and consequently failure of testimony. The next point of departure is that of the advent of a second Man, the last Adam, the Head of a new race; with the result of the enthronement of God in human consciousness and in human life. This restoration of man to the image and likeness of God results ultimately in the restoration of the whole creation.

One man failing and falling, the whole creation failing and falling with him; groaning, travailing, sighing, sobbing. One Man victorious and realizing, and by the mystery of death bringing every man into fellowship with Himself; and creation by the manifestation of the sons of God restored to the true order of the universe. In the midst of darkness and sorrow and sin, Paul sings, " Let us rejoice in hope of the glory of God."

Upon these assumptions Paul bases the arguments of his teaching; and they constitute the sanctions of his system of human salvation. That teaching has to do specially and definitely with the gospel of the second Man, the last Adam. It is the statement in order and sequence of the method by which God, Who has never vacated His throne, never given up the reins of government, comes into the midst of all the failure resulting from the sin of the first man, in order to restore, and heal, and realize His own high and gracious purpose.

This letter is not a tract to be put into the hands of the sinning man in order that, believing what it says, he may be saved. It is rather a treatise to be put into the hands of Christian men in order that they may understand the method of their salvation.

The central teaching is first that of the awful helplessness of the sinful race; and secondly that of the absolute perfection of the Divine salvation. There is no book in the New Testament, there is no book in the Bible, that so fearlessly looks into the abysmal depth of the degradation resulting from human sin. Read the third chapter of this book, and read no more, and you will say that it is the most pessimistic page of literature upon which your eyes ever rested. Read that which immediately follows it, and follow the argument to the end, and you will say that it is the most optimistic poem to which your ears ever listened. These are the two qualities of this book. A straight, fearless, daring look at the human heart, and at human sin; and then a clear look at the Divine heart, and the perfection of the Divine salvation. Ruin and redemption; these were the words of our fathers; we use them much less than they did, and the loss is ours. Absolute ruin and helplessness, that is the apostolic outlook upon man; plenteous redemption and perfect salvation, that is the apostolic outlook upon God.

In dealing with the ruin and helplessness of the human race, Paul divides that race into two parts. He speaks of the Gentiles, who have had the light of nature; and he speaks of the Jews, who have had the light of revelation.

In dealing with the Gentile he does not admit that God has left men anywhere without light. Those who have had the light of nature have at least had the opportunity of discovering two things about God, His wisdom and His Divinity.

These are the things which men will always find in nature, and never anything beyond. It is a remarkable fact that this apostolic declaration harmonizes with the most recent findings of men of science who have turned away from revelation. Huxley, Darwin, Tyndall, Spencer, and Bayne, all admitted the evidences of force and intelligence in nature. The admission was most forcibly put by Bayne when he declared that the varied phenomena of nature revealed the activity of a double-faced somewhat; double-faced in that it had these two qualities of force and intelligence, working in harmony. That is exactly what Paul says. The men who walk in the light of nature can and will discover the Divine wisdom and power; that is, force and intelligence. The apostle then described the state of those who had the light of nature, in character and conduct. Let me take out some of the descriptive phrases: " vain reasonings . . . senseless hearts . . . fools; . . . vile passions . . . unseemliness . . . reprobate mind; . . . unrighteousness, wickedness, covetousness, maliciousness; envy, murder, strife, deceit, malignity; whisperers, backbiters, . . . insolent, haughty, boastful, inventors of evil things, disobedient to parents, without understanding, covenant-breakers, without natural affection, unmerciful." If any are inclined to make a protest against that description as being unfair, let them walk through the streets of London, where men have turned from the light of revelation, and turned from the faith of Christianity, and are walking only in the light of nature; and they will find that this is still an accurate description.

The writer then turns to those who have had the light of revelation. The Jew, judging the Gentile, called him heathen. Now what does Paul say of the men who have had the light of revelation? He declares that they do the same things. Read again the dark and awful list of the things done by men who have the light of nature. Men who have the light of revelation do the same things; and worse, because they have named the name of God, and profess to be teachers, the name of God is blasphemed among the heathen through them.

Therefore Paul expressed his conviction of the appalling helplessness and hopelessness of humanity; " There is none righteous, no, not one "; " All have sinned, and fall short of the glory of

God." It is the most terrible indictment of humanity that was ever penned. Thank God there is something more in the letter than that.

The second message is that of the absolute perfection of the Divine salvation provided in Christ the Son of God. Paul introduces Christ in the very first page of the letter, declaring that He was Son of David according to the flesh; and that He "was declared to be the Son of God with power according to the spirit of holiness, by the resurrection of the dead." I never can quote that passage without desiring to anglicize the Greek word which is there translated "declared to be"; "Who was *horizoned* the Son of God with power, according to the spirit of holiness, by the resurrection of the dead." He appeared on the horizon as the Son of God by the resurrection. We must start the Roman letter there; for unless we do so, we have lost the key. The Person presented to men, upon Whom they may believe; the Person from Whom comes the new life, creating the members of the new race; the Person Who is the second Man, the last Adam, the First-born of the new creation; is the Son of God; and He was declared to be the Son of God, horizoned as the Son of God, by the resurrection. Deny the resurrection, and we may tear up the Roman letter. Admit the resurrection, then at once the Jesus of the gospel stories is the Son of God, demonstrated such, definitely revealed as such, so that there can be no doubt about it.

Two words tell the story of the office of this Person: Manifestation, and Propitiation. The righteousness manifested in Him is righteousness at the disposal of every man through the mystery of propitiation wrought out in His death. That is the perfection of salvation. In that Person there is righteousness at the disposal of every man, because in Him there is propitiation for every soul that believeth.

The relation of this salvation to God is that it results from the activity of His love in holiness; and is the vindication of His holiness by the activity of His love.

The result to man is threefold; that of justification, sanctification, and glorification.

Justification; that is infinitely more than human forgiveness can ever be, infinitely more than a promise to pass over, and never mention again, the sin committed; justification is the reinstatement of the soul of man in such relationship and actual fellowship with God, as that soul would have occupied had there never been any sin, had there never been any guilt.

Sanctification; all the forces of the life of the Son of God, Head of the new race, are communicated to the members of the new race, so that they may live as He lived; growing up into Him in all things which is the Head.

Glorification; man resuming finally his true place in the universe of God, lifts again, to the place from which it has fallen, groaning, sighing, sobbing creation.

The relation therefore of creation to the work of salvation is that of the restoration of its king, the manifestation of the sons of God, and the realization of its possibilities.

Paul looks at human history and sees two or three outstanding facts; the original creation, and man; man rebelling and falling, and following that fall, the fall and sob of creation; the new daybreak, when the Head of the new race stands horizoned by resurrection; all men believing in Him, receiving righteousness, not merely imputed but imparted also; and he watches the process on and ever on, until the groaning creation ceases its groaning, and its sob and its sigh merge into the song of a great triumph. That is the march of history.

If that be the central teaching of the letter, what is its abiding appeal? It first recalls men to the true sanctions and the final standards of human life, those of the Divine throne and government. This book calls men to measure themselves no longer by the standards of their own aspirations or ideals, but by the standards of Divine requirement.

If any man will obey the call which demands that he shall abandon the standards of his own age, the measurements of his own imagination, the ideals of his own heart; and presenting himself to the throne of God, accept the purposes of God, what is the result? It is always the same. Every mouth must be stopped; all the world must become guilty before God. If we measure ourselves as among ourselves many of us will find a good deal to satisfy ourselves in the exercise. If we measure ourselves by our own ideals and aspirations we shall not be quite so satisfied, but we shall think that we are doing fairly well. But if we have done with false measurements, and stand in the light of the Throne of holiness and purity, and are measured there, we shall lay our hand upon our lip as surely as did the leper, and cry unclean, unclean; guilty before God.

This letter calls men to the exercise of the only faculty which can apprehend the unseen; that is the faculty of faith. That is what submission to the throne of God means; it is remitting all the life to the unseen; and the only faculty which can do that is faith. God in great grace has stooped to the human level and has presented Himself to the human mind, in order that faith may repose upon that manifestation, and make connection with the infinite forces that lie behind the manifestation. That is the meaning of the incarnation. By incarnation God did not come any nearer to humanity, but He came into observation. He was as near to humanity before the mystery of the appearing in Judæa, as then and since. But He then came into visibility. He has given men a vision in the Son of God, horizoned by resurrection. This letter says belief in Him, faith in Him, the Son of God, is the starting-point of the new life. If you ask me to discuss the reason, I reply that it is not upon the basis of reason that man finds his way into life. This is God's appointment, God's provision; that when a man shall rest upon this Jesus, believe into Him, venture everything on Him, risk eternity and heaven upon Him, then by that act of faith, that man takes hold of all the forces of the spiritual and unseen, and receives in answer the value and dynamic of righteousness.

This letter calls men also to the attitude which alone is evidence of faith, that of dedication, " I beseech you therefore, brethren, by the mercies of God, to present your bodies." If a man shall say he have faith, and there be no works giving evidence of his faith, then his declaration that he has faith is not true. Faith in the death of Jesus is expressed in consent to die to everything that caused His death. Do I trust in His death for my salvation? Then I am to show my trust by reckoning myself to be dead to the things that caused His death. If I simply consent to trust in His death, and there be no corresponding consent to death in my own life,

then my profession of consenting is blasphemy and impertinence. Faith in the life of the Son of God is to be expressed in the habits of the life of that same Lord Whom we trust. We are to present our bodies as alive from the dead; and it is in the activities of life, harmonizing with the life of Jesus, that we give evidence of our faith.

The present application of this letter to the Church of God is that the ultimate value of the salvation which God has provided is the glory of God; and the supreme responsibility resting upon those who share this life is that of communicating to other people the great evangel.

On the first page he writes it, " I am debtor . . . I am ready . . . I am not ashamed of the gospel." Do we feel we are in debt to every man we meet, that he may know our salvation and share it? That is the great responsibility, and in it is involved that of the personal necessity for the full realization in character and conduct of all God has provided for us, not merely that we should be beautiful in character; but in order that through our conformity to our Lord, men may see Him and be attracted to Him. In order that men may share the virtue of His dying, He calls us to fellowship with His sufferings. Do we rejoice in the plenteous salvation? Then let us remember that it lays upon us these tremendous responsibilities.

What does this letter say to the men and women who are outside, who are still living as members of the lost race? Two things, First, all have sinned, all are guilty. Then what? God is "just and the Justifier of him that hath faith in Jesus." Come with all your weakness and pollution, your inability, the awful helplessness of your own nature; and put your confidence in this Christ; and He will blot out your sins through the mystery of the shedding of His blood; and by the gift of His life communicated, He will negative the poison, quench the fires, break the chains; and lifting you into fellowship with Himself, make you a channel through whom His virtue shall flow to creation for its healing and its lifting.

I Corinthians

THE ESSENTIAL MESSAGE	THE TWOFOLD APPLICATION

I. **The central teaching.**
  A. The causes of failure.
    1. The spirit of the city had invaded the church.
      a. Religious licence.
      b. Moral laxity.
      c. Social disorder.
    2. The failure of the church to realize its own life.
      a. The word of the cross.
      b. The purity of the Christ.
      c. The law of His love.
  B. The secrets of success.
    1. The realization by the church of its own life.
      a. The organism—one Lord, one Spirit, one God.
      b. The law—love.
      c. The supernatural secret—the resurrection of Christ.
    2. The Spirit of the church invading the city.
      a. Proclaiming the Lord.
      b. Rebuking immorality.
      c. Cancelling selfishness.
II. **The abiding appeal.**
  A. To a recognition of responsibility.
  B. To a complete separation in order to a fulfillment of responsibility.
  C. To a fulfillment of her own powers.
	I. **To the church.**
	  A. The influence of a church is the influence of her members.
	  B. The conflict between the city and the church.
	  C. Certain questions.
	    1. What is our influence?
	    2. Is there a conflict?
	    3. If not, why not?
	II. **To the world.**
	  A. The church is against the city as it is, in order to make the city what it ought to be.
	  B. Our central message is that of the resurrection.

IN attempting to discover the message of this letter a phrase in the introduction, "The church of God which is at Corinth," is of great value. It immediately suggests the theme of the letter, because in it two pictures are presented to the mind; first, that of the church of God, and secondly that of the city of Corinth; the church of God being a community sharing the life of God, governed by the will of God, co-operating in the work of God; Corinth being a city of the world, ignorant of God, self-governed, antagonistic to the purposes of God. The two pictures stand opposite each other in striking and vivid contrast.

Of course the phrase "The church of God" here had reference not to the whole Catholic Church, but to the local church in the city of Corinth. Nevertheless, because the local church is a microcosm of the Catholic Church, each local church embodying the principles and methods of the whole Church, being an assembly of men and women united in the bonds of the life of the Lord Christ, the very fact of their churchmanship consisting in their relation to Him and in the real presence in the midst of them of this Christ, the things said of the Church are most evidently true of the church at Corinth. It consisted of a community of people sharing the life of God, made partakers of the Divine nature ; a community of people therefore governed by God ; a theocracy, a holy nation ; and consequently a people in fellowship with Him, in coöperation with Him in Corinth for the accomplishment of His work. All that is included in the first picture suggested by the phrase " The church of God which is at Corinth."

The city of Corinth was at the time a centre of learning and luxury. The name Corinth was a synonym for profligacy and vice. There was a proverb extant, " They live as they live at Corinth," which suggested life in lust, lasciviousness, and luxury. Corinth as a city was ignorant of the one true God, and entirely self-governed. Individual life in Corinth was self-centred, and consequently social life was self-governed. Therefore, unconsciously perhaps, but quite definitely, Corinth was a city antagonistic to God. It is impossible to have two things more entirely opposed brought close together into one brief phrase, than these two facts of the church of God, and the city of Corinth.

The atmosphere of this letter is that of Paul's conception of the responsibilities of the church for the city. In the Acts of the Apostles we have the account of the presence of this man in Athens in one brief declaration, " While he waited for them at Athens, his spirit was provoked within him, as he beheld the city full of idols." He left Athens and came to Corinth, and during that visit the foundations of the church were laid. Now, after some years had passed, he wrote a letter to the church there, and evidently his conception of the responsibility of the church concerning the city harmonizes with his own consciousness when in the city of Athens. At the commencement of the letter in the fundamental proposition he said, "God is faithful, through Whom ye were called into the fellowship of His Son Jesus Christ our Lord," and in these words we at once discover his conception of the responsibility of the church for the city. The word "fellowship" means a great deal more than privilege ; it includes responsibility. Fellowship with Jesus Christ does not merely mean that all His resources are at our disposal ; it means that all our resources are, or ought to be, at His disposal. The church in Corinth was in fellowship with Jesus Christ. All the resources of Christ were at her disposal,

and all the resources of the church were properly at the disposal of Christ, and that in order to the accomplishment in Corinth of the work of God. Three sentences at the portal of the Roman letter indicate the apostolic sense of responsibility, " I am debtor . . . I am ready . . . I am not ashamed." Whereas in that case the note is personal, that sense, multiplied, reveals the apostolic conception of the responsibility of the church of God in any given city. The church of God in Corinth is in debt to Corinth, because the truth which the church holds as a deposit and has realized in her own life, is the very truth that Corinth needs. When Paul said, "I am ready to preach the gospel to you also that are in Rome," he expressed the true attitude of the church in every city. The church should be ready to declare to the city in its godlessness and its resulting lust, lasciviousness, and luxury, the same great evangel. When he said, "I am not ashamed of the gospel," he indicated what should be the attitude of the church in the midst of the city. This whole letter to the Corinthian church was written out of this overwhelming sense of the responsibility of the church for the city in which it exists.

The church at Corinth had failed to discharge its debt to Corinth ; failed in readiness to declare the evangel ; failed in courage and conviction concerning her own gospel. That was the trouble which filled the heart of the apostle. It was not merely that the church was in itself carnal ; it was rather that the carnal church in Corinth was unable to deliver the spiritual message to Corinth.

In this letter we discover the causes of the church's failure and the secret of her success. In dealing with the content we divided the letter into two sections: Corrective—of the carnalities ; Constructive—of the spiritualities. The carnalities prevented the church bearing spiritual witness in Corinth ; the spiritualities were for the correction of the carnalities, that the church might be enabled to deliver her message.

In dealing with the central teaching of the letter we notice first the causes of failure, and secondly the secrets of success.

Now, again if we fix our attention upon the two thoughts suggested by the phrases the church of God and the city of Corinth ; if imaginatively we look back through the centuries to Corinth, and see the church of God in the centre of its life, we shall understand the causes of the failure of the church there.

The first cause was that the spirit of the city had invaded the church. Every evil thing with which Paul dealt in his letter was an evil thing which had come into the church from the city. There was first religious licence; secondly. moral laxity; and thirdly, social disorder.

Look at Corinth alone and it will be seen full of religious licence. Intellectually, it was the centre of divers opinions, for the hour was one of intellectual strife, and in that strife the city was finding amusement. It was an hour of superb rhetoric and eloquence; "Corinthian words" was another of the phrases of the times, a synonym for rhetoric. In the schools of Corinth men were debating, and rejoicing in the wisdom of words; all sorts of opinions were rife, and men were gathered into small sections defending those varied opinions. The city of Corinth religiously was characterized by diversities, differences; great dialectical skill; an infinite variety of opinions; perpetual arguments in the schools, and among the religious leaders. That was the spirit of the city. That spirit had invaded the church. Men and women within the fellowship had caught the intellectual restlessness of the religious life of the city, with the result that some said, We are of Paul, others, We are of Apollos, others, We are of Cephas; while yet others said, We are of Christ. The diversities of opinions expressed within the church were the results of the differing emphases in the preaching of these men, Paul, Apollos, and Cephas. All this was due to the invasion of the church by the intellectual restlessness of the outside world.

The city was also characterized by moral laxity. The effect of the diffusion of devotion was the lowering of the moral standard. For example, the nature of the worship of Aphrodite is a story too vile for telling in the assembly of the saints. That moral laxity had invaded the church. Many of these Christian people were lax in their own moral life, and there was one case so flagrant and so terrible, that Paul declared that those outside the church would have been ashamed of it.

Finally, in the city self was supreme; there was no conscious responsibility for others. Each

was for himself, and selfishnesss was the basis of all endeavour, the method of all government. This spirit also had invaded the church, and relative obligations were unrecognized.

Beneath all this there was something profounder. These were really effects, rather than causes. While Paul saw and corrected disorder in detail in the early part of this letter—and indeed throughout it, for even in the constructive part he perpetually returned to correction—he did so consistently by showing that the reason of the disorder was that the church had forgotten the central, unifying word of the Cross.

She had been invaded by the spirit of division from the city, and had created her own sects out of divisions and differences concerning doctrine, because she failed to respond to the word of the Cross in her own life. She had been invaded by the moral laxity of the city, because seeing that she had not lived according to the word of the Cross, neither had she lived in the power of the resurrection, which is the power of the infinite purity of Christ. The church had been invaded by the selfishness of the ideals of the city, because unyielded to the Cross; and devoid of the power of the resurrection, she had failed to be impulsed by the abiding law of love.

The two central truths which this letter teaches are first that the church fails to fulfill her function in the city when she is invaded by the spirit of the city; secondly, that the church allows the spirit of the city to invade her when she is untrue to the central facts of her own life, when she does not realize in actual experience what she is potentially in the economy of God.

These facts account for the perpetual method of the apostolic writers and teachers; that method which Paul adopted when in effect more than once in the course of his writings he said, You are saints, be saints; you have put off the old man, put off the old man; you have put on the new man, put on the new man; be what you are; realize your own life; be true to the great word of the Cross by which you have become redeemed, ransomed people; let the word which is in you, dwell in you richly.

Here are laid bare the secrets of the Church's failure whenever the Church fails to deliver the message of God to the age. This is the secret of her failure through the centuries. The measure of failure on the part of the Church is the measure in which she has allowed herself to be influenced by the spirit of the age, because she has been untrue to the facts of her own life. We are sometimes told to-day that what the Church supremely needs is that she should catch the spirit of the age. A thousand times no. What the Church supremely needs is to correct the spirit of the age. The church in Corinth catching the spirit of Corinth became anæmic, weak, and failed to deliver the message of God to Corinth. The church of God in London, invaded by the spirit of London, the materialism, militarism, sordidness, and selfishness of London, is too weak to save London.

When the Church of God is invaded by the spirit of the age or of the city, it is because the forces equal to repelling the invasion of that destructive spirit are neglected. The Church of God needs no new visitation of power from God. She needs the realization of the power she already has, the appropriation of the forces already resident within her.

The word of the Cross, the Corinthians had heard it, they knew it; the purity of Christ had touched them in regenerative miracle; the love of God was already shed abroad in their hearts; but they had not abandoned themselves to the claim of the word of the Cross; they had not yielded themselves in entirety to the impulse of His purity; they had not responded to the clamant cry of the love of Christ. The forces of their own preservation being weakened within themselves, the spirit of the city swept in, and the church in Corinth failed because she was invaded by the spirit of the city which she ought to have saved.

Thus we learn what are the secrets of success. The church can only be successful in fulfilling her function in the city by realization of her own life in Christ, that life which is revealed as an organism; one Lord, she shares the life of her Lord; one Spirit, she is under the government of that Spirit Who communicates gifts severally as He will, blessing each member of the body in order to the fulfillment of the function of the whole body; one God, she makes His glory the supreme and ultimate fact. The realization of these facts is the secret of success. Let the Church of God share the life of the Lord, obey the government of the Spirit, and seek the glory of God; and by that separation from the city,

she prepares herself for the work of helping and lifting the city.

The law of the Church is the law of love, severest of sentinels as it watches the activity of men, mightiest of all motives as it impels life and service. At the centre of the classic passage on love which we know so well by letter is the declaration " Love never faileth." That is the law of the Church's life.

The supernatural secret of the Church is that of resurrection. The Church of God is a community of people related to the historic resurrection of Christ, and to the coming resurrection of the saints. Between these the Church must fulfill her function in immediate relation to both. Her life is life won out of death, and communicated by the resurrection of Christ. Her life is life tending to consummation and perfection in the resurrection of the saints at the second Advent. The Church is supernatural, mystical, separated in the very nature of her life from all the men of the age. The secret of the fulfillment by the church of her function in the city is her realization of these facts. She is an organism; she has one law, that of love; the supernatural secret of her life is that of resurrection.

The exercise of function is that of the Spirit of the church invading the city. If the Church's failure is due to the fact that the spirit of the city has invaded the church; the Church's success is due to the fact that the Spirit of the church invades the city, proclaiming the Lordship of Christ based upon His resurrection; rebuking the immorality of the city by the revelation of His purity; cancelling the selfishness of the city by her own example, and by insistence that all men shall have granted to them an opportunity to live.

The Church of God always fails when she becomes conformed to the methods, maxims, and manners of the city. The Church of God always succeeds when, true to the supernatural nature of her life, she stands in perfect separation from the city. Only thus is she able to touch and help the city.

Consequently the abiding appeal of the letter is patent. It calls the Church of God in every age to recognition of responsibility concerning the city. The church is responsible for the religious life of the city, for the moral standards of the city, for the social order of the city.

If you can persuade me that we have no responsibilities, that the Church exists merely for the conserving of the life of her own members, then I will leave the Church, and join with others who have a keener sense of moral and religious responsibility; but it is impossible to persuade me to that conclusion in the light of New Testament teaching. The Church is responsible for the religious life of the city, for the affirmation and revelation of God therein. There never was a time when the fulfillment of that function was more necessary than now. We are no longer face to face with old-fashioned antagonism. A time there was when blatant infidelity had its halls in all our great towns, and in them made attack upon the very idea of the existence of God. There may be such halls of assembly still; but they lurk in hidden corners. The infidelity of the hour is the infidelity of indifference; and the business of the Church is to arrest the indifferent, to arouse the conscience, to affirm God, to compel men to the consideration of the infinite, eternal, and abiding things.

The religious effect must first be produced. Then resulting from it there must be the erection of moral standards. The Church is to deny that there can be lasting and final morality unless it is homed in spirituality of conception. In the teaching of the Lord Jesus Christ there was always the closest connection between spiritual conception and moral standard; so with the Church, she is to stand in every age affirming that the only sufficient moral standard is that of right relationship to God and eternity.

Consequently the Church is responsible for the social order of the city. She cannot, if she be true to her own life, be silent and careless while there are in the city men, women, and little children without the opportunity of finding and worshipping God, living and working in such conditions that culture of the essential spiritual life is impossible.

The call of this letter in the second place is a call to complete separation in order to the fulfillment of responsibility. Separation, first, from all licence in religious thinking. There is a toleration which is of the very essence of destruction. If we admit for a single moment that all these differing opinions outside the Church concerning matters of religion may lead ultimately to true

religion, apart from the word of the Cross, that will presently make us untrue ourselves to the word of the Cross, which word declares all men guilty, and all human wisdom foolishness, and demands that men shall find their way into true wisdom and true life through, and only through, the surrender of the life to the Lord Christ.

We are called also to complete separation from all laxity in dealing with immorality. While the outside world is declaring to-day, for instance, that it is time we faced again the problem of the marriage relationship and made easier divorce laws, it is for the Church of God to abide in the name of Christ by the great ideal of the Bible, and whatever personal suffering may be entailed, insist upon it that men and women must be true to the marriage relationship in the interests of the family and the national life. That is only a passing illustration of the principle. The Church must never give countenance to the lax conceptions of morality which abound in the life of the city. The Church must be free from carelessness about social iniquities.

This letter calls us supremely therefore to the fulfillment of the powers of our own being; the life of the Lord in the Spirit; love supreme; the power of the resurrection, His resurrection from among the dead operating in victory in our own lives, our coming resurrection at the second Advent flashing like a beacon light upon all the pathway and calling us to purity.

The application of this great appeal to the Church of God may thus be stated. The influence of the Church is the influence of her members. The sum total of the membership in any church is the sum total of that church's influence. Thus ultimately the great truth about the Church is reduced to the point of personal application. Each one in the measure of personality is responsible for the influence of the church in the city.

There is a perpetual conflict between the city and the church; the city that is godless and the church which is God-centred. By way of application let one question be asked and answered alone. What is our influence in the life of the city? Is there any conflict between the Church of God and the city? If not, is it not because the spirit of the city has invaded the church until it has become difficult to discover where the city ends and the church begins; sometimes almost impossible to distinguish between the man actuated by the godlessness of the city, and the man who, calling himself by the name of Christ, is yet not living the life God-centred and God-governed.

In some senses this letter has no message to the world. Inferentially it declares that the church is against the city as it is, in order to make the city what it ought to be. The Church lifts her voice in protest against iniquity in the city or nation, because her business is to make the city and the nation what God would have them be. Our central message to the world, according to the teaching of this letter, is that of the resurrection of the Lord. That resurrection unifies religious truth. Every doctrine is centred therein. That resurrection is the standard of morality, for in that stupendous mystery God did accept the Man of Nazareth as the type and pattern of humanity. That resurrection is the declaration of power at the disposal of all men, for in the mystery of His resurrection the Lord placed His life at the disposal of others.

Inclusively and finally, the appeal of the letter to the Church is contained in the actual words of the apostle, " Be ye steadfast, unmovable, always abounding in the work of the Lord."

II Corinthians

THE ESSENTIAL MESSAGE	THE APPLICATION

I. The central teaching.
  A. The ministry within the church.
    1. Its authority—divine appointment.
    2. Its message.
      a. The word.
      b. The unveiled glory.
    3. Its resources.
      a. The comfort of God.
      b. Visions and revelations.
      c. The prayers of the saints.
    4. Its experiences.
      a. Tribulation.
      b. Hope.
      c. Triumph.
    5. Its aim—the perfecting of the saints.
  B. The ministry of the church.
    1. Its equipment.
      a. Obedience to the Word.
      b. Separation from the world.
      c. Conformity to the will.
    2. Its exercise.
      a. Discipline to restoration.
      b. "No occasion of stumbling."
      c. The grace of giving.
II. The abiding appeal.
  A. To the ministry within.
    1. Loyalty to the message of the world of reconciliation.
    2. Absolute rest is the sufficiency of God.
    3. Acceptance of the principle of the cross.
    4. The relationship of the minister to the people.
  B. To the church as to its own ministry.
    1. "Be ye reconciled to God."
    2. "Receive not the grace of God in vain."
	I. To the church.
	  A. A recognition of the sacredness of the ministry.
	    1. By the ministers.
	    2. By the church.
	  B. An acceptance of the responsibilities of reconciliation and grace.
	    1. Purity—discipline in love.
	    2. Unity—the collection for the saints.
	    3. Testimony—to the world.
	
	II. To the world.
	  A. ". . . that the life also of Jesus may be manifested in our mortal flesh."
	  B. "We are witnesses."

IT is quite evident that the second letter to the Corinthians is a sequel to the first. There is a marked difference between the two. The first is systematic; corrective and constructive. The second seems to be characterized by lack of system; it is largely personal, and emotional; it throbs with a sense of anguish, and yet perpetually rises to the height of great and gracious song. The matters dealt with were of an immediate and local kind. The writer was suffering from personal misunderstanding, resulting from personal misinterpretation; and evidently wrote to set himself right with those who had misunderstood him because of this misinterpretation. The letter was also concerned with a certain collection which was being made; and with the apostle's proposal to visit Corinth.

All this is not to undervalue this letter, for it is impossible to read it without feeling that in some senses, perhaps a little difficult to explain, there

214

is in it a note and a quality of intense spirituality almost beyond that of the first letter. This note of intense spirituality results from the fact that the matter of his own personal misunderstanding and misinterpretation ; the matter of the collection in Corinth on behalf of the poor saints in Jerusalem ; and the matter of his proposal to visit them, and his reasons for not visiting them when they expected he would ; are all set in the light of the great Christian conceptions.

The essential message of this letter is discovered as we recognize these great conceptions. We find in it the recognition and revelation of certain truths that are of vital importance to the Christian Church.

In our consideration of the message of the first letter we found that the spirit of the city had invaded the Church ; and by that invasion the Church had become unfitted for fulfilling its true functions of ministry in the city. The message of the letter, therefore, was one of warning against the perils of the city to the Church ; and one calling the Church to fulfill its function in the city.

In this second letter we have the same two pictures. Again Paul wrote to the Church of God in the city of Corinth. As in his first letter he called the Church to fulfillment of its ministry in the city ; in his second he dealt with the ministry within the Church, by which the Church is to be perfected, in order to the fulfillment of its ministry in the city. This is peculiarly, therefore, the letter of the ministry, taking that word in its fullest sense. Whenever ministry is dealt with in the New Testament, the ultimate thought is not that of the ministry of the men we call ministers to-day, but that of the ministry of the whole Church. That is not to undervalue the sacredness of the ministerial calling within the Church ; but to reveal its deepest meaning. Within the Church there are ministers, created by gifts bestowed by the Holy Ghost ; and the business of such ministers is that of the perfecting of the saints, in order that the Church may fulfill its ministry in the city.

With that key to the situation, I understand the passion in the heart of Paul ; the reason of his trouble, the reason of his tears, the reason of his anxiety. He knew that the Church at Corinth was failing to understand the true function of the ministers of Jesus Christ, and was failing to obey the teaching of those ministers ; and therefore was failing to fulfill its own ministry in Corinth. He was not fighting for official recognition. He was not angry because some did not think as highly of him as of Apollos or Cephas.

In this letter then we have a picture, for all time, of what the ministry within the Church is ; and of what the ministry of the whole Church ought to be. Therefore the central teaching has to do, first, with the ministry within the Church ; and secondly, with the ministry of the Church ; principally with the ministry within, for the ministry of the Church had been dealt with in the first letter, and appears here again only incidentally, though quite clearly.

Dealing first then with the ministry within the Church : we notice in the first place the apostle's teaching concerning the authority thereof, in his opening words ; " Paul, an apostle of Christ Jesus through the will of God, and Timothy our brother." Carefully notice how he brings into association with himself a man who is not an apostle. He had to fight for his own apostleship as against the misunderstanding and misinterpretation even of some who were apostles ; but Timothy was not an apostle ; he was an evangelist certainly, and in all probability ultimately a pastor and teacher. Thus two men were associated in the writing of the letter, and presently Paul referred to Silvanus, and also to Titus. All these were in the ministry by Divine appointment. That is the New Testament conception of the authority of the Christian ministry. I am not now discussing the methods by which the Church of God recognizes the gift bestowed, prepares for the exercise of it, and solemnly ordains to work within the Church. All these are necessary and important matters, but the form which these arrangements of the Church may take is of minor importance. The supreme value of this letter, in the matter of the authority of the Christian ministry, is its revelation of the fact that a man is in the ministry, whether it be as apostle, prophet, evangelist, or pastor or teacher, by the appointment of God. That fact creates his authority, and consequently the authority he exercises must be the authority of the One Who appoints him, and the authority of the One Who appoints him is always the authority of His Word spoken. The authority of Jesus was the authority of His teaching. The multitudes heard Him utter His Manifesto, and they were astonished because He taught as One having authority. It was the authority of inherent and essential truth which captured them. The authority of God is always the authority of His Word, the authority of essential Truth. The authority of the minister is not the authority of an office conferred; it is the authority of the Word that is committed to him to preach; that great and sacred deposit which he holds on trust for the Church, and by exposition of which he perfects the Church for its work of ministry.

This leads us naturally to what this letter teaches concerning the message of the minister. The apostle says, " We are not as the many, corrupting the Word of God: but as of sincerity, but as of God, in the sight of God, speak we in Christ"; and later, " Therefore seeing we have this ministry, even as we obtained mercy, we faint not: but we have renounced the hidden things of shame, not walking in craftiness, nor handling the Word of God deceitfully; but by the manifestation of the truth commending ourselves to every man's conscience in the sight of God." The message then of the apostle, prophet, evangelist, pastor, and teacher, is the Word of God, which must not be corrupted, not handled deceitfully.

Between these essential declarations, the supreme glory of the Word to be preached is revealed; it is that of the unveiled glory. There was a ministration of death in the case of Moses. The ministration of life and the Spirit came through Jesus Christ. The apostle claimed that the same results follow the preaching of the Word by Christian ministers of the Word as followed the ministry of the Lord Himself. Therefore that Word is the burden of the message of every Christian minister. The difference between the apostle, the prophet, the evangelist, and the pastor and teacher, is not a difference of message, but a difference of emphasis and application. Whether the work be apostolic, pioneer work, in exposition of the doctrine; or prophetic, which makes application of the truth of God to the age; or evangelistic, which repeats the message, and woos men to allegiance to Christ; or pastoral and didactic, which feeds and instructs the flock; the message is always the Word of God, the Word of this unveiled glory in the face of Jesus Christ, the Word of Spirit and life.

Next in order we have in this letter a revelation of the resources of the Christian minister. Of these there are three, and the first is dealt with at length in the first chapter; it is that of the comfort of God. This becomes more wonderful as, reading on through the letter, we see the experiences through which the apostle had passed, and what he had proved of that comfort in circumstances of testing and trouble and trial. The first resource of the Christian minister is always that of the comfort of God.

As we get to the end of the letter, we find him making his boast in visions and revelations; that is, in the fact of personal, first-hand, direct, immediate speech of God to his own soul. It is to be observed that these visions and revelations were not for publication. In all probability fourteen years had passed before he made any reference to these visions and revelations; and then he declared they were not lawful to be uttered; but they completely captured his life, and kept it bent in the true direction, so that there was no possibility of doubt or fear. I believe that men still have visions and revelations; but I am always suspicious that a man who is anxious to talk of visions is suffering from nightmare. The true vision and revelation cannot be talked about. Even when at last, compelled by the misunderstanding of this Corinthian Church, to refer to them, the apostle apologized, saying: You have compelled me, I am bound to boast now. He could not, however, explain the experience. I may have been in the body or out of it, I know not, God knows; I saw things and heard things that I cannot tell.

Let any man in the ministry feel that there is something lacking, unless in the hour of lonely communion with God there flame before him such visions, that he never can tell, but which, abiding with him, create the note of his confidence and authority, and inspire his determination to prosecute the work of his ministry to the end.

The final resource of the minister is that of the prayers of the saints; and the apostle declared that, not only by this exceeding comfort of God, and not only by visions and revelations; but also by the prayers of the saints had he been delivered. The value of such prayers cannot be overestimated; and those who are in the ministry know them to be among the most powerful and prevailing sources of strength.

Again the letter is a remarkable revelation of the experiences of the Christian ministry. These are described in three notable passages which are so graphic that they need little exposition. Let us read them.

"We have this treasure in earthen vessels, that the exceeding greatness of the power may be of God, and not from ourselves; we are pressed on every side, yet not straitened; perplexed, yet not unto despair; pursued, yet not forsaken; smitten down, yet not destroyed; always bearing about in the body the dying of Jesus, that the life also of Jesus may be manifested in our body."

"In everything commending ourselves, as ministers of God, in much patience, in afflictions, in necessities, in distresses, in stripes, in imprisonments, in tumults, in labours, in watchings, in fastings; in pureness, in knowledge, in long-suffering, in kindness, in the Holy Ghost, in love unfeigned, in the word of truth, in the power of God; by the armour of righteousness on the right hand and on the left, by glory and dishonour, by evil report and good report; as deceivers, and yet true; as unknown, and yet well known; as dying, and behold, we live; as chastened, and not killed; as sorrowful, yet alway rejoicing; as poor, yet making many rich; as having nothing, and yet possessing all things."

"I take pleasure in weaknesses, in injuries, in necessities, in persecutions, in distresses, for Christ's sake; for when I am weak, then am I strong."

These are the experiences of the Christian ministry. There is experience of tribulation. That is a subject not perhaps to be dealt with in detail in the great assembly; yet one which we all need to face. Is it not true that the Word of God only becomes truly quick and powerful, full of solace and help, when spoken by such as have suffered? I say this, not that any should seek the pathway of suffering, but that the man to whom is committed the preaching of the Word, and who is in the midst of buffeting and bruising and suffering, may know that by such processes the Word of God from his lips will become quick and powerful. I had a young friend who was brought to God, through His good grace, by my ministry. He devoted himself to the ministry. I never heard him preach until his college days were over. Then his sermon was wonderful, brilliant, sparkling in eloquence. When it was over and we were in the private seclusion of home, I asked my wife what she thought of the sermon. Her reply was: It was wonderful; but it will be better when he has had some trouble. I never heard him again until he had stood by the side of a grave, and his heart had been smitten; and oh, the difference! It is through tribulation that the Word of God becomes powerful. I think I would hardly dare to write that, but it may be that some brother in the ministry may read this, who is in trouble. God help you, my brother! It is by the pressure on the earthen vessel that the light flames through. It is by the hour of sorrow that we become instruments able to convey to the people of God the message that heals and helps.

Tribulation is not all of the experience of the minister of the Word. He has an experience of hope; of perfect confidence; there is always a song in his heart if he preach the Word of God; and he has also an experience of triumph, for He leadeth us everywhere in triumph.

With the aim of the Christian minister we need not tarry, having already seen in another connection that it is that of the perfecting of the saints, unto the work of ministering. We are only successful in the measure in which the result of our ministry is the larger ministry of the Church in the city.

Neither need we stay to consider at any length the ministry of the Church, that having been the burden of the first letter. We need only stay to remind ourselves of our responsibilities as to equipment and exercise.

The Church's equipment for its ministry is that of obedience to the Word which is preached; separation from the world which is to be saved; and conformity to the will of the Lord which is revealed.

The Church is to exercise its ministry by seeing to it that it puts no occasion of stumbling in the way of the Word; by seeing to it that it is living a life of reconciliation to God; by seeing to it that it does not receive the grace of God in vain.

Or to summarize the whole suggestiveness of this letter in this respect, the Church of God fulfills its ministry when it incarnates the truth to which it listens. The responsibility of the Church towards the minister is not that of obedience to an official; but of obedience to the Word of God which he proclaims.

The abiding appeal of the letter is patent. It appeals to those of us who are in the ministry within the Church, to be loyal to the message of the Word of reconciliation. "All things are of God, Who reconciled us to Himself through Christ, and gave unto us the ministry of reconciliation; to wit, that God was in Christ reconciling the world unto Himself." That is the all-inclusive harmony of the evangel. It has many notes, many tones, many emphases, many applications; but that is our message; and this letter calls us to be faithful to it.

It calls us also to absolute rest in the sufficiency of God, and to acceptance of the principle of the Cross. "We have this treasure in earthen vessels," and the measure in which the treasure in the earthen vessel is communicated to those who need it is the measure of the pressure on the vessel. The sacrificial note must be in the life of the preacher, or his preaching is in vain.

Finally, this letter teaches us that the true relationship of the minister to his people is first that of disinterested independence; and secondly, that of dependent interest.

The final appeal of this letter is to the Church as to its own ministry; and that is crystallized in the words, " Be ye reconciled to God." The measure in which the Church is composed of men and women who are living the life of reconciliation, is the measure in which the Church is declaring the evangel of reconciliation to the world. Are we reconciled to God? Fundamentally, as to standing, if we are Christian men and women we are reconciled; but experimentally, as to state, are we reconciled? Is there controversy between us and God, something that breaks in upon the experience of reconciliation? By that controversy we are rendered unable to proclaim the evangel of reconciliation in the city. The Church reconciled experimentally, living in fellowship with God, is the Church that preaches the gospel of reconciliation. Therefore the final word of appeal is, " Receive not the grace of God in vain."

There is a twofold application needed at the present hour. First to the Church. The Church needs a return to recognition of the sacredness of the ministry. I use the word ministry now in its more restricted sense. There has been an appalling tendency amongst us to degrade and forget the sanctity of the office of the minister of the Word of God. We serve tables altogether too much; and are unable to give ourselves to the proper ministry of the Word. We allow ourselves all too constantly to be deflected from the main line of our endeavour; and find that we have been so busy doing excellent nothings that we have been able to do nothing excellently.

The minister of the Word needs to get back to the fact that his burden is the Word, and his business is to preach it. His toil is to know it, and he cannot trifle with it without degrading the sacredness of his office. Oh, for the tears and the travail of Paul! As I look at him, my soul is often ashamed, because I seem to lack the brands of Jesus.

There must be return to recognition of the sanctity of the ministerial position by the Church itself. She must come to understand that those whom God has appointed to this ministry have a responsibility to Him, and that the Church has a tremendous responsibility of obedience, not to the minister as an official, but to the Word of which he is the messenger, the expositor.

There must therefore be acceptation of the responsibilities of reconciliation and of grace. There must be discipline of the sinning brother, but there must be his restoration after he has repented. There must be recognition of unity, and if the poor saints in Jerusalem are suffering for lack of material things, then the grace of giving must be exercised by the wealthy church at Corinth, and she must give, not as though the giving were a charitable addition to her activities, but out of a heart of love.

Is there any application of this letter to the world? None; save that if the Church of God, and the ministry within the Church, are not true to the ideals, they had better hide this letter from the world; because if the worldly man shall read this letter, and then look for the marks and the signs, what an appalling disaster if he do not find them!

So may we all in this ministry learn its secrets, obey its call, and fulfil the purposes of our Lord.

Galatians

THE ESSENTIAL MESSAGE	THE APPLICATION

I. **The central teaching**—a proclamation.
  A. Life—the root; the supply of the spirit—3:5.
    1. The way of life is faith.
    2. Nothing else necessary to salvation.
    3. To add is to deny faith and to destroy life.
  B. Law—the culture; the lust of the spirit—v. 17.
    1. Liberty is not licence.
    2. It is capture and constraint by the spirit.
    3. Ability to obey.
  C. Love—the fruit; the triumph of the spirit—v. 22.
    1. The mastery of love—fruit.
    2. The mastery of selfishness impossible—works.
    3. Results—works issue from ritualism; fruit results from life.
 	
II. **The abiding appeal**—a protest.
  A. The preachers of another gospel—accursed 1:8-9.
    1. Anathema (Cf. I Cor. 16:22).
    2. That is the condition—suicide.
    3. Let those loyal to the one gospel agree.
  B. The receivers of another message—severed from Christ—v. 4.
    1. To trust in ceremony is to deny Christ.
    2. To deny Christ is to be severed from Christ.
    3. To be severed from Christ is to fall from grace.
  C. The practicers of resulting deeds excluded from Kingdom of God—v. 21.
    1. The works of the flesh.
      a. Sensual.
      b. Spiritual.
      c. Social.
    2. Resulting from lack of life.
    3. Resulting in exclusion.
	I. **To the church.**
	  A. To superimpose on faith any rite or ceremony or observance as necessary to salvation is to sever from Christ; both in the case of the individual and the church.
	  B. Those guilty of so doing are anathema; whether individuals, councils, or churches.
	
	II. **To the world.**
	  A. The way of life.
	    1. Faith in Christ.
	    2. Any other way is the way of death.
	  B. To believe in Him is to need no other; it is deliverance from all bondage.

I T is impossible to read this letter without being impressed by the severity of its note. It is evident that the writer was dealing with matters which, from his standpoint at least, were of vital importance. The letter is vibrant with passion, and yet consistent with principle. From the introductory sentences to the final words, it is quite evident that the apostle was profoundly moved; but it is equally evident that he never allowed emotion to carry him away from the line of a clearly defined system of thought and teaching. Whereas, as our analysis of the content reveals, personal matters largely enter into the letter, yet the supreme concern of the writer is for truth, and its bearing upon human life, in view of the perils which threaten men when truth is in any way violated or changed. There is an entirely different note running through this letter to that which characterized the Corinthian letters. This also is corrective; but as we turn over from the Corinthian letters we find a tone entirely different. Note the omissions from the salutation. Paul makes no reference to their standing in Christ. There is no single word of commenda-

219

tion. These two things mark this letter as peculiar from all others in the Pauline writings to the churches. The introduction is almost prosaic, "the churches in Galatia," not "them that are sanctified in Christ Jesus, called saints," and such rich phrases as mark the beginnings of other letters; no word of thankfulness for their state. After a few brief words of introduction, he commences, "I marvel," and immediately he proceeds to deal with them in terms of great severity.

Notice the specially declamatory passage of this letter in chapter one, and mark the severity of it ;—

"I marvel that ye are so quickly removing from Him that called you in the grace of Christ unto a different gospel; which is not another gospel: only there are some that trouble you, and would pervert the gospel of Christ. But though we, or an angel from heaven, should preach unto you any gospel other than that which we preached unto you, let him be anathema. As we have said before, so say I now again, If any man preacheth unto you any gospel other than that which ye received, let him be anathema."

Turn to another declamatory passage, in the third chapter, and again note the intense severity ;—

"O foolish Galatians, who did bewitch you, before whose eyes Jesus Christ was openly set forth crucified? This only would I learn from you, Received ye the Spirit by the works of the law, or by the hearing of faith? Are ye so foolish? Having begun in the Spirit, are ye now perfected in the flesh? Did ye suffer so many things in vain? if it be indeed in vain He therefore that supplieth to you the Spirit, and worketh miracles among you, doeth he it by the works of the law, or by the hearing of faith?"

Turn over yet once more to chapter four, and the same severe note is found ;—

"Howbeit at that time, not knowing God, ye were in bondage to them which by nature are no gods: but now that ye have come to know God, or rather to be known of God, how turn ye back again to the weak and beggarly rudiments, whereunto ye desire to be in bondage over again? Ye observe days, and months, and seasons, and years. I am afraid of you, lest by

any means I have bestowed labour upon you in vain."

Or take the one tender outburst of the letter :

"My little children, of whom I am again in travail until Christ be formed in you, yea, I could wish to be present with you now, and to change my voice; for I am perplexed about you."

This passage thrills with the pain of a troubled heart; concern fills the mind of the writer.

I lay emphasis at such length upon these matters in order that we may come with solemnity to the letter, in our attempt to discover its message. Evidently the matter of which the apostle wrote was, in his estimation, of supreme importance. He was not writing to people who had failed in behaviour. The peril was of the gravest; the foundations were threatened, and consequently the whole superstructure was in danger.

This letter has been called the Magna Charta of the early Church. It is the Manifesto of Christian liberty, explaining the nature of that liberty, applying the laws of that liberty, and cursing the enemies of that liberty. It is of perpetual value from that standpoint, and more than once in the history of the Christian Church this little pamphlet has sounded the clarion call of return to freedom. Take one flaming illustration of the truth of what I now declare. This was Luther's letter, the letter that found him, and revealed to him the true meaning of Christianity, and made him the flaming prophet of liberty, breaking the chains of cruel oppression from the captive people of God. Godet says with reference to Luther and this letter, "This was the pebble from the brook with which, like another David, he went forth to meet the papal giant and smite him in the forehead." Whenever the Church of God bends to a bondage which results from denial of the foundation principles of her life, we find in this letter to the Galatians the corrective for such apostasy.

In seeking for the message we must begin at the right point. We are perhaps a little prone to be occupied only with the denunciations which the letter contains. As a matter of fact, the profoundest value of this letter is not to be discovered in the denunciations. The profoundest value of the letter is discovered in its enunciations. To discover these is not to weaken the denunciations, but to understand their force. We read the declamatory passages; they must be read, and ought to be read; but we must understand what Paul meant when he said, "If any man preacheth unto you any gospel other than that which ye received, let him be anathema"; we ought to understand what he meant when he declared that to produce works of the flesh which result from ritualism is to be excluded from the Kingdom of God. We do not understand the force of the denunciations save as we are conscious of the enunciations of truth which lie behind them. The truths constitute the dynamic. The teaching causes the explosion. We are often more occupied with the explosion than with the dynamic when we read this letter; more interested in the way in which Paul dealt with Peter when he came to Antioch, than with the reason of Paul's so dealing with Peter. If I am to discover and interpret in any sense intelligently the message of this letter I am compelled to lay my emphasis, not principally upon the denunciation, but upon the enunciation of principle; not upon the protest, but upon the proclamation that lies behind the protest.

The essential message of this letter has to do then with liberty. Its central teaching is a proclamation or enunciation of truth, concerning liberty. Its abiding appeal is a protest or denunciation of everything which contradicts that truth.

First, then, as to the central teaching. In the proclamation of Galatians the epistle to the Romans is found in essence. Here we have in unified form, in germ and potentiality, the great doctrines which are elaborated and systematically stated in the larger epistle. It is perfectly evident that this letter was written in the light, and under the impulse, of that great controversy which broke out at Antioch after the first missionary journey, and which resulted in the Council at Jerusalem. The apostle, in correcting error, did not go into any detailed statement of truth; but the truth is recognized.

The proclamation of this letter may be gathered round three words—life, law, love; and the teaching is condensed in three principal statements.

The fact of Life is recognized in the words,

"He therefore that supplieth to you the Spirit." That is not to take a text out of its context; it is rather to discover within a text the supreme thought which inspired the teaching. The whole paragraph gives the apostolic conception of Christianity. Life is supplied in the supply of the Spirit. That is the root of Christianity in individual experience.

The fact of Law is recognized in the words, "The flesh lusteth against the Spirit, and the Spirit against the flesh; for these are contrary the one to the other; that ye may not do the things that ye would." The doctrine involved is that the Christian life is not a life of licence; it is under law, but it is a new law, that of the lust of the Spirit. I retain the word lust, using it in its true sense of desire. As the root principle of the Christian life is the supply of the Spirit, the culture of this life is the result of obedience to the lust of the Spirit.

The fact of Love is recognized in the words, "The fruit of the Spirit is love." That is the final word, fruit, the triumph of the Spirit.

In these statements we have the doctrine of this letter revealed. Christianity is a life; its root principle is the supply of the Spirit. No man is a Christian unless he have the Spirit of God. But Christianity does not set a man free to go where he likes, or to do what he pleases. There is a law for the culture of the life received, and it is that of the lust of the Spirit within the man; the Spirit desiring in him, correcting his desires. As man yields to the lust of the Spirit, he is master over the lust of the flesh. The outcome of such life, yielded to such law, will be love, which is the fruit, the triumph of the Spirit.

Let us pass over that ground again for it is fundamental. First, as to Life. Life is received by receiving the supply of the Spirit. The Spirit is received in answer to the exercise of faith. That is the master thought of the letter. The deduction from that is that nothing other than faith is necessary to salvation. Therefore to affirm that men must be circumcised or baptized in order to salvation is to proclaim the most deadly heresies that can possibly be taught. To superadd anything to faith is to destroy the foundations of Christianity. Life is by faith.

Secondly, as to Law. Liberty is not licence. When a man has life by faith he is thereby set free from all other bondage. He is set free from the bondage of the flesh, because he has the power that masters it and brings it into subjection. He is set free from the bondage of rites and ceremonies, because he has found life apart from rite, and without ceremony ; and he is henceforward, so far as 'life is concerned, independent of all ceremony and of every rite. He is set free from bondage by life; but that liberty is not licence. The liberty of this life is that of the capture and constraint of the spirit of man, by the Spirit of God. The capture of the spirit of man by the Spirit of God means that man is made able to obey, and no man was made able to obey by circumcision or by baptism. Man is made able to obey when that life becomes law, and he yields to it. The lust of the Spirit within is the law of the new-found life.

Finally, as to Love. The fruit of this life, obedient to this law, is love ; the whole life under the dominion of love, bondage to self is therefore no longer possible. When we read the fifth chapter, whatever wider application we may make of it, we must be true to the first line of its argument. I know there are more spacious applications of these Bible truths than were made by the writers. They dealt with great principles, the ultimate applications of which are far wider than the one the writers indicated at the moment. But when we read of "the works of the flesh," and "the fruit of the Spirit," we must remember that the passage is part of one great argument. "The works of the flesh" are things which result from a religion which is not a religion of faith unto life. Works of the flesh are the activities of godless and irreligious men ; but primarily, in the apostolic argument, the phrase refers to things resulting from the observance of rites and ceremonies as though such observance constituted religion. Works of the flesh are things which result from ritualism which becomes an evasion of righteousness.

Here we touch the real reason of the vehemence of the apostle's anger. Superadd to faith anything else, as necessary to salvation, and inevitably the outcome is that faith is neglected. The moment we make anything other than faith supreme, we establish a rite—whether it be this, that, or the other, I care nothing—and men will say, If we fulfill this rite, then are we religious, and religion will be divorced from morality, religion will have lost the inspiration of righteous-

ness. That is what is wrong with all false religion. That is the supreme difference between Christianity and every other religion. All the great systems of religion have rites, and ceremonies, and creeds, but no life. Consequently there is not the remotest connection between religion and morality. That is what the apostle saw was the supreme danger of these Judaizing teachers. They were adding to faith, which is the only way into life, with the inevitable result that presently men would say, We have observed this rite, now we can do what we like. All forms of sensuality and spiritual sin result from the tragedy of superadding something to the one law of faith.

Therefore the abiding appeal of this letter is of the nature of a protest. Its first note is a denunciation of the preachers of another gospel ;— "If any man preacheth unto you any gospel other than that which ye received, let him be anathema." That is not an episcopal curse; it is not an apostolic malediction. It is the statement of the case as it is. "Let him be anathema." The word anathema, which means accursed, occurs in only one other passage in the New Testament, in the letter of Paul to the Corinthians, "If any man loveth not the Lord, let him be anathema." That is not a curse pronounced as by ecclesiastical authority; it is a declaration of truth concerning the condition of any man who loves not the Lord Jesus Christ; he is anathema ; therefore let him be anathema. And so with the use of the word in this letter ;— "If any man preacheth unto you any gospel other than that which ye received, let him be anathema" ; the man who preaches another gospel, by such preaching substitutes the false which issues finally in the works of the flesh, for the true which issues in the fruit of the Spirit.

Not only the preacher, but the receiver of the other gospel is severed from Christ. To trust in ceremony is to deny Christ ; and to deny Christ is to be severed from Christ ; and to be severed from Christ is to fall from grace. To add to faith in Christ as the foundation of religious life, either rite or ceremony, as necessary to salvation, is to deny Christ and to be severed from Christ, and fallen from grace.

I am not dealing with rites and ceremonies save as rites and ceremonies are made essential to salvation. Baptism has its place in the Christian Church. The observance of the Lord's Supper has its place in the Christian Church. The assembling of men and women for worship has its place in the Christian Church. But to make baptism, or the Lord's Supper, or the assembling, necessary to salvation, is to deny Christ.

There is only one way in which a man can be a Christian, and it is the way of honestly and sincerely saying,

> " Nothing in my hand I bring,
> Simply to Thy Cross I cling."

If I come to the Cross and say, By that and by my baptism I will become a Christian, I deny Christ.

The last note of the appeal is the solemn declaration that the practicers of the deeds resulting from a false gospel, the deeds of the flesh, are excluded from the Kingdom of God. With what great and grave sense of responsibility the apostle wrote these words.

These were the terrible possibilities which Paul saw. These were the things that made his words vibrant with passion. His profound understanding of the peril of the Christian Church, through the influence of Judaizing teachers, called forth this letter.

In a closing word let us make a twofold application of the teaching of the letter. This Galatian letter warns the Church that to superimpose upon men any rite or ceremony or observance, as necessary to salvation, is to sever from Christ both in the case of the individual and in the case of the Church. I care not what the Church may be as to ecclesiastical conviction. I have less and less concern for such things. I am growingly convinced that ecclesiastical matters are not essential matters. There is room for every form of Church government within the economy of the Spirit of God. I decline controversy over ecclesiastical convictions. But whatever Church adds to faith in Christ, any rite or ceremony or observance of any kind, as essential to salvation, that Church is severed from Christ.

We need to get back to these fundamental documents, to these tremendous revelations of the apostolic writings ; to the sense of the importance of things, which, if we are not very careful, we are allowing to appear as though they were unimportant. You began in the Spirit, will you attempt to gain perfection by the flesh ? That is the great question of the letter. We need to-day to understand that in our preaching and in our teaching, and in order to strength of Church life for the accomplishment of the Divine purpose in the world, the one condition of salvation is that of faith in Christ, and the reception of life from Christ ; not because of our observance of rite or ceremony, but simply and solely and wholly by His great unmerited grace in response to faith. That is fundamental to personal Christianity and to Church life. Those guilty of superimposing upon faith any rite or ceremony or observance, as necessary to salvation, are anathema ; whether they be individuals, or councils, or churches.

If I am emphatic about this, it is because the letter is emphatic about it. Where there is faith unto life, the life becomes a law, and there result no works of the flesh, neither sensual things, fornications, uncleanness, and lasciviousness; nor spiritual things, idolatry, sorcery, and the like.

The freedom of the Church is not political. It is spiritual or nothing. The only freedom that comes from absolute unbending loyalty to the will of God is bondage to the law of life, interpreted by the Spirit of God. Let us make our protest, and let it be vehement, against all bondage; but let us see to it that behind the denunciation is the enunciation of principle. It is only as we live in the power of that dynamic, that we shall be strong enough to burst all bonds, and fling off all yokes, and live in the spaciousness of spiritual freedom. May we learn the lesson and live the life.

Ephesians

THE ESSENTIAL MESSAGE	THE APPLICATION
I. **The central teaching**—"The saints . . . in Christ Jesus."	I. **To the church.**
A. The eternal character of the church.	A. The measure of the church's power to help this world is the measure of her other-worldiness.
1. The conception—the plan of God from eternity.	
2. The construction—the power of God in time.	
3. The consummation—the purpose of God to eternity.	B. The test of the other-worldliness of the church is the measure of her influence in this world.
B. The temporal conduct of the church.	
1. The construction—conformity to the unity.	
2. The confession—sanctification of all life.	
3. The conflict—to stand, to withstand, to stand.	II. **To the world.**
II. **The abiding appeal**—"Walk worthily. . . ."	A. The church of God is the instrument of God for the establishment of His Kingdom.
A. According to the eternal plan—"Grow up into Him . . . the increase of the body."	
B. Appropriating the eternal power—"Understand the will of the Lord . . . filled with the Spirit."	B. The way into the church is through the one Lord, one faith, one baptism.
C. Approaching the eternal purpose—"Against" . . . "The whole armour of God."	

THIS letter leads us to the high places of vision, and to awe-inspiring sublimities; it leads us there, and then leaves us in amazed and wondering adoration in the presence of the truths revealed. There is a sense in which an attempt to declare its message is easy. There is a sense in which it is difficult. It is easy because the whole letter is a message. It is difficult because the letter is a message, and therefore, having studied the content we have already heard the message. Yet with the consciousness of that content in our minds, we may reverently inquire what is its essential message, and what its persistent application.

Let us then consider, first, in broad outline the essential message, as to its central teaching, and its abiding appeal; and secondly, give attention to its application.

We are immediately arrested by the fact that there are no salutations in this letter, in the ordinary sense of the word; and as we proceed through the argument we are impressed by the fact that there is very little local colouring. It stands alone, a great message of truth. It is quite evident that more than one particular church was in the mind of the apostle. Even if he wrote it to one, it is a message preëmi-nently to the whole Church, the Catholic Church of Jesus Christ.

The teaching of this letter has to do entirely with the Church. It is the final word of the New Testament concerning the Church. It is the last exposition of the words of Jesus Christ at Cæsarea Philippi, " Upon this rock I will build My Church ; and the gates of Hades shall not prevail against it. I will give unto thee the keys of the Kingdom." In that declaration we have the full and final truth concerning the Church. For its exposition we need the whole of the Petrine and Pauline teachings; but especially the Pauline, because Paul was the steward of the mystery of the Church. In this letter, then, we have the last exposition of the meaning of Christ. To study it in the light of that statement at Cæsarea Philippi is at once to discover the connections. The Lord said. "I will build My Church," and the figure of building is here employed by the apostle. The Lord said, "The gates of Hades shall not prevail against it," and the apostle deals with the conflict very fully. Finally the Lord said, "I will give unto thee the keys of the Kingdom"; that is, the standards of moral and ethical interpretation; and in the heart of this letter we find the application of the ethic of Jesus, to all the details of every-day life.

The central teaching of this whole letter is suggested by words taken from its opening address, "The saints . .   in Christ Jesus," as they describe the composition of the Church of God.

The phrase "in Christ Jesus" following the words "the saints" indicates the unification of the units into the unity of the Church. The word "saints" suggests diversities, differences; the phrase, "in Christ Jesus," reveals the fact that all are one; and thus there breaks upon the mind the vision of the whole Church, that Church being Christ and all those who are united to Him.

The central teaching deals with the Church, and falls into two parts; that first, of the eternal character of the Church; and that secondly, of the temporal conduct of the Church.

And first as to the eternal character of the Church, the letter teaches us three things as it deals with the conception, construction, and consummation thereof; showing that it was in the plan of God from eternity, is being realized by the power of God in time, and will fulfill the purpose of God in eternity.

The conception of the Church comes up out of the past eternity. It is almost impossible to use such words with absolute accuracy. I have spoken of eternity past; there is a sense in which that is a contradiction in terms. Eternity is eternity; it is an ever-present now. With God there is neither past nor future. His is age-abiding life; a great and infinite mystery which our finite minds cannot fully grasp. Consequently we are bound to think of these things by the dimensions with which we are familiar, and we speak, therefore, of the past, present, and future. A fine attempt to give expression to these truths is found in Hebrew literature in the declaration, "From everlasting to everlasting Thou art God." If we translate the Hebrew word rendered "everlasting" in our versions, according to its first significance, the statement will read, "From the vanishing-point to the vanishing-point Thou art God." That is to say, the writer was conscious that there is a limit to human understanding, and a limit to the stretch and sweep of the human mind, both backward and forward. There is a vanishing-point. Some men have seen further than others because they have climbed higher than others; but there always has been, and still is, a vanishing-point. We find it in Genesis, as we step out of the unseen into the seen; "In the beginning," that is the vanishing-point. John climbed far higher up the mount than Moses, and he also said, "In the beginning," but his "beginning" was further back than that of Moses, for Moses referred to the period immediately preceding creation; but John referred to the essential fact of eternity, that timeless, limitless fact ere time or creation in any form existed.

To-day we are looking on. How far can we see? As far as the second Advent? Yes, and beyond it. To the millennial reign? Much further! To the Kingdom of the Son? Yes, and beyond. To the generation, that is to the new birth, of the age of the ages. There again we come to the vanishing-point. "From the vanishing-point to the vanishing-point, Thou art God."

Turning our thoughts back again to what we thus speak of as eternity past, this letter teaches us that the plan of the Church was formulated there; it is eternal. It comes up out of these vast distances, out of the eternities, the ages that we cannot comprehend, and of which the utmost we can say is that they are beyond the vanishing-point.

May God deliver us from taking so great, so stupendous and sublime and far-reaching a vision of the wisdom which transcends our finite theory, in order to formulate a doctrine that God has chosen a few people to be saved and left the rest to be damned. That is an unwarranted deduction.

The plan of the Church existed in the mind of God from eternity. He predestined the Church that it should be conformed to the image of His Son. Paul peered into the deep things, the infinite mysteries, until somewhere back in those past eternities he saw in the mind of God, the Son of His love, the archetypal pattern of all perfection, and he declared that He predestined men and women that they should be conformed to that likeness. The Church then is not an experiment in human history. It is part of the plan of God. Let no member of the Church be anxious as to whether it is going to be destroyed or not. Let us not be filled with panic because the Church of God is being criticized by men who know neither the Church nor God. It is eternal because it is the conception, the plan of God, from eternity.

It is eternal in another sense. If the conception is the plan of God from eternity, the construction is by the power of God operating in time; that is eternal power; it is power coming from eternity past, and continuing to eternity future. The power which, operating in Christ, raised Him from the dead, is the power by which He builds His Church. In Christ, men and women are quickened, raised, and seated in the heavenlies. That is the operation of the power of God in time, and that is the whole story of the construction of the Church.

And finally the Church is eternal in yet another sense. The consummation is eternal, for the Church is to serve the purpose of God in the coming eternity. Through the Church in its union with Jesus Christ there will be revealed to the ages to come "the exceeding riches of His grace"; and there will be unveiled before the angels "the manifold wisdom of God."

That is the first note of the central teaching of this letter. The Church of God is eternal. Its conception in the past eternity was the plan of God. Its construction in time is by the power of God. Its consummation in the coming eternity will be for the fulfillment of the purposes of God. Are we of this Church? Then we were in the heart and mind and plan of God in the ages gone; we are to fulfill the purposes of God in the ages to come; and the plan of the past, and

the purpose of the future, are linked by the power of the present; for plan, and power, purpose are alike eternal.

From these stupendous declarations the apostle turned to the subject of the temporal conduct of the Church. When that great vision has broken upon the life, and its virtue has empowered it, what will be the result in conduct? With the winds of the past eternity blowing across her, and the light of the coming eternity streaming upon her path, what manner of people will the members of this Church be?

The apostle describes that conduct as having relation to the construction of the Church; as constituting a confession before the world; and as being a conflict against all opposing forces.

Concerning the construction of the Church, he appeals to the members thereof; "I therefore . . . beseech you to walk worthily of the calling wherewith ye were called." This he shows they will do by "giving diligence to keep the unity of the Spirit in the bond of peace." This is followed by a picture of the Church, being built up, growing up, "in all things into Him." The first responsibility of churchmanship then is the maintenance of the Spirit of unity. Can such a word be uttered without shame, without a sense of disappointment and of failure?

In the next place the apostle shows that the Church is to make a great confession in time concerning God; the mind of God, the purpose of God, the will of God. This she will do by the sanctification of life. Not by creeds written or recited; but by life, true to the heavenly standard and the eternal measurement in the details of every-day experience; husbands and wives, parents and children, masters and servants. The sanctification of all life in the power of the heavenly conception is the confession which the Church makes to the world.

The result of such a confession must inevitably be that of conflict with the forces which are opposed to the purpose of God. The Church must be armed, and at war with these forces. In that conflict she is to stand, to withstand, and having done all, to stand.

Once again, if that be the picture of the temporal conduct of the Church, we cannot fail to notice how it coincides with the word of Christ at Cæsarea Philippi. He declared, "I will build My Church." The first responsibility of the Church is that she obtain and maintain the view of the unity of that Church and "grow up in all things into Him, which is the Head, even Christ . . . unto the building up of itself in love." Building according to the pattern is our first responsibility.

His final word was, "I will give unto thee the keys," that is, the insignia of the office of ethical teaching. The Church is to fulfill that responsibility by the sanctification of life.

Between that first proclamation and that final commission He said "the gates of Hades shall not prevail against it." In order to fulfill the responsibility suggested by that declaration the Church must obey the apostolic injunction: "Put on the whole armour of God, that ye may be able to stand against the wiles of the devil . . . take up the whole armour of God, that ye may be able to withstand in the evil day, and, having done all, to stand."

The Church of God is eternal in character; the plan of God in the past; the power of God to-day; the purpose of God in the future. Therefore in temporal conduct she must coöperate with God in His building by growing up into the Head; deliver the message of God's purity and holiness to the world by her sanctified life; fight the foes of God by putting on the whole armour of God.

If the central teaching of this letter is unified in that opening phrase, "The saints in Christ Jesus," its abiding appeal is focussed in the injunction, "Walk worthily of the vocation."

First, the members of the Church are to walk according to the eternal plan, to behave in time according to God's purpose from eternity. He predestined us that we should be conformed to the image of His Son. We are therefore to "grow up in all things into Him, which is the Head, even Christ." That is the standard. The measure in which we are living in holiness and in love, is the measure in which we are conforming to the eternal plan. We are not to be holy because decency demands it; we are not to be righteous because the policeman may arrest us if we are not; these are not our motives. We are to walk according to the eternal plan, remembering that our individual life was in the thought of God, and of it He has revealed the pattern in His Son, and He calls us to be true to the plan that has come up out of the past eternity by conforming to that pattern.

If we are to walk according to the eternal plan we must do it by appropriating the eternal power. When we read this letter we are amazed at its height, and the glory of its suggestion, and we are inclined to say, Who is sufficient for these things? Then we come to the great word in which the apostle says, "Now unto Him that is able to do exceeding abundantly above all that we ask or think, according to the power that worketh in us." Am I a Christian man? Then I am such because I share the life of Christ, and if I share the life of Christ, I have resident within me power enough to make me all that God meant me to be from eternity. The eternal power is within the Christly soul, and we walk worthily as we appropriate it, and make use of it, understanding what the will of the Lord is, being filled with the Spirit, that so we may walk in harmony with the will of God.

The appeal of the letter is finally that we walk not only according to the eternal plan, not only appropriating the eternal power, but approaching the eternal purpose.

That walk will mean a fight against the forces that are attempting to hinder us, spiritual antagonisms, intelligences from the upper spaces who occupy lower places, who inhabit the heavenlies where the saints walk, that they may attack them. The devil's masterstroke to-day is that he has so largely succeeded in hiding himself, while still hard at work. It is quite time the saints awoke to recognition of these principalities and powers. They are manifested in many ways. We read of spiritualistic séances and bureaus; and the tragic thing is that the Church of God is laughing at these things, and saying there is no reality in these doings. It is certain that messages from the spirit-world are being actually received by men to-day; but they are messages of demons. If we are living the age-abiding life, if the plan of our life comes out of eternity, and its purpose runs into eternity, then false spirits will impede our progress, and attempt to seduce us from loyalty to the one Spirit of God; "Our wrestling is not against flesh and blood, but against the principalities, against the powers, against the world-rulers of this darkness, against the spiritual hosts of wickedness in the heavenly places." We are to keep our eye upon the consummation, and "put on the panoply of God," and fight.

So may we walk worthily of the vocation,

according to the eternal plan, appropriating the eternal power, and approaching the eternal purpose. Such is the abiding appeal of the letter.

Finally let us briefly make an application of the message of this letter to our own age.

Its message to the Church is, first, that the measure of her power to help this world is the measure of her other-worldliness. I use that phrase because it is being used as a term of reproach. There are men who tell us that the Church has been other-worldly, and therefore has failed. The measure in which she has failed is the measure in which she has ceased to be other-worldly. The darkest day in the history of the Church was the day when Constantine patronized her. Then she ceased to be other-worldly, and instead of leaning wholly and solely upon God, and upon the presence of the Spirit of God, she leaned on the arm of flesh, and by doing so lost her power. That is going far back, but we may make a present application. The measure of the Church's power to help the world is still the measure of her other-worldliness. Only as the Church remembers her heavenly, her Divine calling, can she set up the standards of life, and supply the sufficient dynamic thereof.

This letter further teaches that the test of the Church's other-worldliness is the measure of her influence in this world. If she is so other-worldly that she has no care for the condition of this world; if she is so other-worldly that she is unconscious of its sigh and sob and sorrow; if she does not care anything about the slums, then she is other-worldly, but the world she is of is the other world of the devil, which is selfish and un-Christlike. That is the tragic mistake we have too often made. We have sung songs of heaven, and have forgotten this poor sinning, suffering earth; and so have demonstrated our ignorance of heaven, for it is in heaven that earth's sorrows are most keenly felt, and it is upon the heart of God that earth's wrongs lie most heavily. The measure in which the Church of God is other-worldly in the true sense is the measure in which she is putting her life against the sins and sorrows of the world, to sympathize, to shepherd, and to save. It is not possible to do that unless we are other-worldly. Unless we can bring into the slums of London the light and life of the city of God, we had better leave it alone; it will only degrade us, and we shall not help it. Socialism that begins by telling men that man is in process of evolution, and that sin is an incident, is a cruel lie; such socialism was born in the pit. But the socialism that sees the city of God, the Kingdom of God established in the world, and then lives in the midst of human sorrow and sin to bring to it redemption by blood, and regeneration by life, is the socialism of Christianity.

I take up this epistle to the Ephesians and climb the heights and scale the mountains and gaze upon the far-flung splendours of the eternal vision; and then I climb down and live at home, and in my relation to wife and child, to servant and master, my confession is to be made. The Church of God can never help God when she ceases to be other-worldly. When she is other-worldly she helps the world; and cannot avoid doing so.

This letter declares to the world that the Church of God is the instrument of God for the establishment of His Kingdom; and it teaches that if any man would help to the establishment of His Kingdom, there is one way into the Church; he may enter through the one Lord, by one faith, and one baptism.

While this plan comes out of eternity, while this purpose lies in the distant eternity, and while this power is operating in time, there is no man or woman who may not come into the plan and into the purpose by coming into contact with the power. One Lord, the Lord Christ; Child of the eternities; Master of the ages; the Glory of the coming eternity. One faith; the simple abandonment of the needy soul who says:

> " Just as I am, without one plea,
> But that Thy blood was shed for me,
> And that Thou bid'st me come to Thee,
> O Lamb of God, I come."

One baptism; the baptism of the Holy Ghost, whereby that trusting soul is made a member of Christ, a member of the Church; and enters the plan of the eternities, and travels towards the purpose of the eternities, by appropriating the power of the eternities.

Philippians

THE ESSENTIAL MESSAGE	THE APPLICATION

I. **The central teaching**—the mind of Christ.
A. Of Christ Jesus.
  1. The mental attitude—"Counted it not a prize. . . ."
  2. The consequent activity—"Emptied Himself. . . ."
  3. The resultant crowning—"God highly exalted Him."
B. Of the saints in Christ Jesus.
  1. The mental attitude.
    a. Love abounding more and more.
    b. Sincere and void of offence.
  2. The consequent activity.
    a. Manner of life worthy of the gospel.
    b. Children of God blameless . . . harmless.
  3. The resultant crowning.
    a. Present victory over circumstances.
    b. Ultimate realization of divine purpose.
II. **The abiding appeal**—"Have this mind in you."
A. The resource—"To me to live is Christ."
B. The responsibility—"Work out. . . ."
C. The rules.
  1. Rejoice in the Lord.
  2. Forbearance towards men.
  3. The life of prayer.
  4. The life of thought.
	I. **To the church.** (The measure of the church's authority is the measure of her conformity to the mind of Christ.)
	A. That mind is love.
	B. Its consciousness is joy.
	C. Its expression is sacrifice.
	II. **To the individual believer**—the mastery of Christ.
	A. Individual capture by Christ.
	B. The one desire for others.

THE Philippian letter is a revelation of the Christian mind. It is largely without system, and extremely difficult to analyze. Who can analyze a love-letter, and that is what this letter is, which Paul wrote to his children at Philippi ; and whereas in the deepest fact of his spiritual love this great apostle had no favourites, in the affections of his emotional nature, his children at Philippi were certainly his chiefly loved children. He had come to Philippi in answer to the call of the man of Macedonia. When, crossing over the Ægean Sea, he reached that city and began his work by the riverside, there almost immediately followed that wonderful experience in the prison. With feet fast in the stocks through the brutality of the jailer, at midnight Paul and Silas had sung praises to God.

This letter to these Philippian Christians was written in prison, and it seems to me as I read that Philippi was always to Paul the place of prison and the place of song. These children at Philippi were near and dear to his heart. They ministered to his need, as he says, once and again ; and the letter which he wrote to them from prison is a letter brimming over with love.

If there be no definite system in the letter, some of the profoundest and most wonderful things that ever came from his pen are to be found therein. That marvellous and matchless passage describing the whole mission of the Son of God, from His Self-emptying, through all the experience of His sorrows, back to the throne of heavenly empire, is in this letter. That autobiographical passage is here also, in which Paul gives us the story of his own life in brief sentences, every one of which is full of light and full of colour; so that if we want to know the truth about Paul we turn to this wonderful piece of self-revelation.

The supreme value of the letter is that of its revelation of the true Christian consciousness. Notice the recurrence of the word *mind*, or of cognate words. "To be thus *minded*" i. 7; "Be of the same *mind*" ii. 2; "Lowliness of *mind*" ii. 3; "Have this *mind*" ii. 5; "Let us . . . be thus *minded*" iii. 15; "Who *mind* earthly things" iii 19; "Of the same *mind*" iv. 2; "Your *mind* of me" iv. 10;—though our translation, neither Authorized nor Revised, shows the fact, when the apostle spoke of their care for him he used the same word, *mind.* That of course is a grouping of phrases with no apparent connection; and there are some senses in which there is no connection between them. Our only purpose in thus grouping them is that we may notice how the word repeats itself. The fact that these words do not form a key to the analysis is all the more remarkable. They are incidental words arising out of an attitude of mind, and revealing that attitude, as the apostle wrote from his prison-house to his children at Philippi. In every chapter, and in every division, the word is to be found.

The Greek word so translated is one which signifies consciousness, either as the cognitive faculties, or as impression made on the mind. In the Thessalonian letter, we find an analysis of personality by this same apostle,—spirit, soul, and body. Spirit is the essential fact in a man's life; the body is the probationary dwelling-place of the spirit, the instrument through which the spirit communicates with others, and receives communications from others; the soul, or mind is the consciousness; and it is fleshly, or spiritual, according to whether the flesh or the spirit is dominant in the life.

The central teaching of this letter is suggested by the phrase "the mind of Christ." It reveals the mind of Christ. First the mind of Christ personally; and secondly the mind of Christ in the saints. The supreme appeal of the letter is that of the apostle's injunction, "Have this mind in you, which was also in Christ Jesus." Thus if we are to understand the message of the letter we must first discover what it reveals to us of the mind of Christ Himself; then what it reveals to us of the mind of Christian men and women. The appeal of the letter will then be seen to be patent, and necessary; "Have this mind in you, which was also in Christ Jesus."

When we attempt to examine this unveiled mind of our Lord, we are at once brought into the presence of light and glory that surprise, and arrest us, in adoring wonder. The gospel stories tell us of His words and His works, reveal to us His character, and the influence produced upon men by that character; but when we want to see the mind of Christ we turn to the Philippian letter. Herein is revealed that conception, that consciousness, of the Christ of God which lay behind all His words and works, inspiring them.

In the contemplation we first discover His mental attitude, that which caused everything else; then we see the activity springing out of that attitude; and finally we see the victory and crowning following that activity.

The attitude of mind is described in these words; "Being in the form of God, counted it not a prize to be on an equality with God." That is the mind of Christ Then follows a statement of the activity resulting from that attitude of mind; "emptied Himself, taking the form of a servant, being made in the likeness of men; and being found in fashion as a man, He humbled Himself, becoming obedient even unto death, yea, the death of the Cross." Finally the issue of the activity is declared; "Wherefore also God highly exalted Him, and gave unto Him the name which is above every name; that in the name of Jesus every knee should bow, of things in heaven and things on earth and things under the earth, and that every tongue should confess that Jesus Christ is Lord, to the glory of God the Father."

The crowning of Christ proceeded from the activity of Christ. The activity of Christ was the result of the mind of Christ. To know the mind of Christ then we must observe His activity. First He emptied Himself. To understand that we must watch the steps that follow. Every sentence tells of a downward movement. He emptied Himself in the infinite heights; and took the form of a Servant in the universe in which He had been Sovereign. He might have taken the form of the highest Servant in the universe, angel, archangel, seraph, or cherub;

but He was made a little lower than the angels, and was made in the likeness of men. He might have come into human life at its highest and best, in the midst of ease and comfort; but "being found in fashion as a man, He humbled Himself, becoming obedient even unto death." As a man He might have died, surrounded by those who loved Him, ministering to Him to the last, and helping Him through the hour of weakness; but He died the death of the Cross.

Whence sprang such activity? The first words tell the story, "Being in the form of God, counted it not a prize to be on an equality with God." That is the mind of Christ; it is the mind of lowliness; it is the mind of pure and absolute love. "Love vaunteth not itself." The thirteenth chapter of Corinthians in its description of love is but the description of the mind of the Master. Though in the form of God, of the nature of God, on an equality with God, He had no conception of such a position as to make Him value the position for the sake of the position. When there was a race to be redeemed, the position must be laid aside in order that the Person of such mind might stoop to unutterable depths in order to lift out of ruin those who had been involved therein. That is the mind of Christ.

I am quite well aware that these words of mine are of the poorest, for what expositor can help men to understand this thing? We can only understand it when we have done listening to men and reading books, and when we sit in solemn loneliness in the presence of the unveiled glory of the mind of Christ. I take up this little New Testament, every book of it precious, every page of it invaluable, every pamphlet having some message; but not from Matthew to Revelation have I anywhere else such an unveiling of the mind of Christ, as I have in this one short paragraph, over which we have passed with almost rude footsteps in our attempt to understand it.

This letter reveals also the mind of the saints who are in Christ Jesus. We will take the same three divisions; the mental attitude, the consequent activity, and the resultant crowning; for as these are the great things revealed concerning the mind of Christ, all its preciousness, its values, its virtues, its victories, are at the disposal of the children of God. Even though we descend from the height of ineffable glory and splendour to the level of our own halting and failing experience, nevertheless we find that the true mind of the saint is the mind of the Lord.

What then is the true mental attitude of the Christian man? At the beginning of the letter, Paul prayed for his Philippian children that their "love may abound yet more and more," not emotionally merely, and certainly not ignorantly, but "in knowledge and all discernment." Then he prayed that they "may be sincere and void of offence." I lift my eyes amazed, to the wonder and glory of the mind of Christ; and with all reverence, for one is almost reluctant to do this, I say that His love is the revelation of our love. Being in the form of God He did not count such relation a prize to be snatched at for Himself and His own enrichment, though it was already His. That is love abounding, love sincere, love void of offence. That mental attitude of Christ is to be the mental attitude of the saints. Consequently the saint will be mastered by love, and therefore, although we are so far from the heights we must take the measurement of the heights, for whatever position of privilege the child of God occupies within the economy of God, it must not be held as a prize to be snatched at for self-glorification. That is the mind of Christ.

Had Paul the mind of Christ? I affirm that he had. We see it supremely manifest when he wrote these words, "I say the truth in Christ, I lie not, my conscience bearing witness with me in the Holy Ghost, that I have great sorrow and unceasing pain in my heart. For I could wish that I myself were anathema from Christ for my brethren's sake, my kinsmen according to the flesh." That is the mind of Christ; the mind of the man made one with Christ. He had written immediately before, Nothing can separate me from the love of God which is in Christ Jesus; but he did not count that as a prize to be snatched at for his own enrichment, but could wish that he were anathema from Christ for his brethren's sake. That is the mind of Christ.

What then is the consequent activity? Following still the method of examination afforded by the unveiling of the mind of Christ, I take two of Paul's descriptions; "Let your manner of life be worthy of the gospel of Christ"; and "blameless and harmless, children of God without blemish in the midst of a crooked and perverse generation, among whom ye are seen as lights in the world." That is the activity growing out of the mind. The manner of life worthy of the Gospel is that of holiness, purity, truth; but these words do not touch the deepest note. The life must be worthy of the Gospel. The Gospel is the good news of God's grace bringing salvation to all men. Life is worthy of that when it suffers to carry that news, when it enters into travail and pain in order to bring men under the sound of it, and under the power of it, that they may be saved by it. That is the manner of life worthy of the Gospel. It is not merely rectitude of conduct or of character, it is not merely personal; the manner of life worthy of the Gospel is life driven by the Gospel in order to make it known, to proclaim it. That is the activity resulting from the mind.

Again, Children of God, blameless and harmless; blameless, that is the relationship to God; harmless, that is the consequent relationship to men. Once again I lift my eyes to the splendour of the unveiled activity of Jesus resulting from His mental attitude, and I see Him emptying Himself, taking the form of a servant, made in the likeness of man, humbling Himself, becoming obedient to death, the death of the Cross. That is the meaning of life worthy of the Gospel; that is the Son of God blameless and harmless. The mind that was in Christ is to be in the saint; and the mind that was in Christ being in the saint, is to produce in the saint the activity which was produced in Christ. How much do we know about emptying ourselves? How much do we know about humbling ourselves, about being obedient unto death, even the death of the Cross?

Looking thus at the mind of the saints, let us observe, not only the attitude, and the consequent activity, but also the resultant crowning. Of Christ it is said, "Wherefore also God highly exalted Him, and gave unto Him the name which is above every name." So also with the saint. Whenever we find this mind and this activity resulting, we find triumph. This whole letter is a triumph; triumph over circumstances calculated to make Paul feel he was being defeated; the intrepid missionary, the pioneer evangelist; the regions beyond, the perpetual watchword of his strong endeavour; was now in prison and everything was against him; circumstances were combining to crush him. Nothing of the kind. He sang in prison in Philippi long ago; he will sing in a letter to Philippi out of the Roman prison now; that is triumph over circumstances. That is not seen in this letter only, but also in all the letters. This man never called himself a prisoner of anybody save Jesus Christ, he said he was His prisoner; he did not consent to refer to Nero; Nero was out of sight entirely. He had no thought for the jailer by his side, except one of compassion and endeavour to bring him into that bondage to Christ which meant real liberty. He did once say in human weakness, "Remember my bonds"; but he also said that his bonds "have fallen out rather unto the progress of the gospel." Where there is the mind of love, and the consequent activity of self-emptying service, there is perpetual and glorious triumph over circumstances. Any man can sing when he escapes from prison; but this man sang in prison. God has highly exalted Paul and given him a throne of power because of the activity growing out of the mind of love. He triumphed over all circumstances and lifted his eyes, not doubtingly, but courageously, to the ultimate realization of the Divine purpose, so that he said in this same letter, "Not that I have already obtained, or am already made perfect:

. . but one thing I do, forgetting the things which are behind, and stretching forward to the things which are before, I press on towards the goal"; that goal is the hour in which He "shall fashion anew the body of our humiliation, that it may be conformed to the body of His glory." The mind of Christ in the saint is the mind of royalty, of authority, of power.

In the light of that attempt to understand this unveiling of the mind of Christ, we hear the abiding appeal, "Have this mind in you." If that is the abiding appeal, think what this letter teaches us concerning the resources, responsibilities, and rules of the Christian life.

What are the resources? Why should I use the plural form? I will give you the whole story in one little word, "To me to live is Christ." "Have this mind in you." How can I? By imitating it? Surely not. By endeavouring to cultivate it? Certainly not. How then? By entering into the meaning of that

"To me to live is Christ." This man said, I only have one life, and that is Christ. As he said in another epistle, "That life which I now live in the flesh I live in faith, the faith which is in the Son of God, Who loved me, and gave Himself up for me." "To me to live is Christ."

Christ's vision; Christ's virtue. This man saw God as Christ saw God. This man saw man as Christ saw man. This man saw ruin as Christ saw ruin. This man saw God's purpose as Christ saw God's purpose. Christ's outlook, Christ's vision! But more, Christ's virtue, Christ's strength, Christ's ability in the presence of the difficulty. These are the resources. If we would have the mind of Christ, we must have the life of Christ, not by imitation, not by cultivation, but by identification. That is the secret of having the mind of Christ.

What is our responsibility if we have this life and so have this mind? "Work out your own salvation with fear and trembling; for it is God which worketh in you." Our business is to work out what God works in. The apostle shows us how to work out, not in immediate teaching, but in illustration, the illustration of his own life in the autobiographical chapter. How did he work out the salvation which God wrought in him? First by keeping clearly before him the vision of the ultimate. With that vision of the ultimate before him what were his attitudes? Towards the past, abandonment; "I count not myself yet to have apprehended: but one thing I do, *forgetting the things which are behind*, and stretching forward." Towards the present, effort: "I press on towards the goal." "I press," the Greek word so translated might be rendered I persecute, for the word is exactly the same as that used of this same man when he was persecuting the Christians. The significance of this is that it shows us that into this business of pressing towards the goal Paul put all the passion and fervour which, in the olden days, he had employed in his determined effort to stamp out the name of Jesus Christ. That is the kind of loyalty we need. Why is it that when a man steps over the line and finds Christ he so often leaves his passion, a good deal of his common sense, and much of his business ability behind him? When Christ arrests a man, He wants the whole man, every part of him, every ability he has. Our responsibility is that of absolute dedication and unfailing endeavour.

What are the rules? At the end of the letter we find them. First, "Rejoice in the Lord." Is that a rule? I maintain that it is. Paul does not speak of joy as a privilege but as a duty. It is our duty to rejoice; we ought to sing, we ought to be glad. We owe it to our Lord to go through the streets of London on a foggy day with a smiling face. We ought to be the most cheerful people in the world. There ought to be in our very attitude the manifestation of perennial gladness. That is the rule, and Paul knew that all down the centuries there would be people who would forget, so he added "again I will say, Rejoice."

The other rules all follow; "Let your forbearance be known unto all men"; "In nothing be anxious; but in everything by prayer and supplication with thanksgiving let your requests be made known unto God"; "Think on these things."

The application of this message to the Church to-day is that the measure of the Church's authority is the measure of her conformity to the mind of Christ. The Church of God is authoritative in proportion as the Church of God has the mind of Christ. We depend on all sorts of things to give us authority. The mind of Christ is the only thing that makes us truly royal. Of the mind of Christ the essence is love, the consciousness is joy, the expression is sacrifice. Let the Church of God be mastered by love, filled with singing and with joy, perpetually serving, and she rises to a throne of power and authority in this, and in every age.

If that be the application of the message to the Church, what is the application to the individual? The supreme thing is that we should be wholly, absolutely mastered by Christ, that we should be captives of the Lord. That is the ideal. The ideal of the Son should be our only ideal. The resources of His power should be all we ask in order to fulfilment of the ideal. The certainty of His ultimate victory, in us and everywhere, should be the inspiration of our unceasing, undying song. The present joy of life should be that of constant and immediate comradeship with Him. If I can once learn this secret I shall learn how to sing, and how to smile; how to love, and how to serve.

Colossians

THE ESSENTIAL MESSAGE	THE APPLICATION

I. **The central teaching**—2:9, 10a.
  A. The fullness of the Godhead in Christ.
    1. Creation—the origin of life.
    2. Resurrection—the mastery of death.
    3. Peace—the reconciliation of all.
  B. The filling of the saints in Christ.
    1. Restored to their place in creation—kingship.
    2. Restored to their relation to God—subjection.
    3. Restored to their fellowship with God—cooperation.
 	
II. **The abiding appeal**—2:6.
  A. False philosophy—"Take heed . . ." (2:8).
    1. The tradition of men—speculation.
    2. The rudiments of the world—materialism.
  B. False mediation—"Let no man . . ." (2:16-18).
    1. Ceremonialism.
    2. Spiritualism.
  C. False confidence—"Why . . ." (2:20-23).
    1. Submission to human opinion.
    2. Ascetic practices.
	I. **To the church.**
	  A. The matter of supreme import to the church of Christ for her life and service is that of her doctrine of Christ.
	  B. To hold fast the Head as He is revealed in this letter will make impossible the failures here also revealed.
	
	II. **To the individual.**
	  A. A Christless philosophy ends in animalism.
	  B. A religion of added intermediation despoils of the prize.
	  C. Asceticism is of no value against the flesh.

WE must necessarily remind ourselves of the connection between this letter and that to the Ephesians. They have been spoken of as twin epistles, and that is a perfectly accurate description with regard to the positive doctrines with which they deal. They are complementary the one to the other, so much so that it is almost impossible to study one without studying the other. As in the Ephesian letter, the theme is that of the glory of the Church in her relation with Christ; in the Colossian letter, the theme is that of the glory of Christ as at the disposal of the Church. In the Ephesian letter we are led to the supreme height, from which it is possible to view the Church in its eternal character, and so to understand what its immediate conduct ought to be. In the Colossian letter the resources of the Church are revealed, and they are all centred in Christ.

While that is true there are differences between the two letters. I propose to refer to one of them only, by way of introduction. This letter to the Colossians cannot be read without a sense of argument, of conflict, of dangers, and of difficulties. All that was absent from the Ephesian letter; it was constructive, preëminently a document of teaching. By that I do not mean to say that the Colossian letter is not constructive; it is distinctly so, but we shall miss the complete message unless we recognize that it is corrective also. Through the letter we have a vision of the Church at Colossæ, and are made conscious of the perils threatening it in the very subtle and insidious dangers which the apostle most evidently had in mind as he wrote. I am not proposing to deal with these in detail, for I do not think an explanation of the dangers constitutes the living message of the letter. We shall, however, be compelled to recognize them, because one vital value of the letter is that it is a corrective for certain perils which threatened the Church at Colossæ, and which threaten the Church to-day. We may forget the local colouring, we may recognize that some of the matters dealt with have passed away; but the essential doctrines abide; and the perils still abide, and can only be corrected by these selfsame doctrines.

Let us first consider the essential message of the letter, as to its central teaching, and as to its abiding appeal.

The whole teaching of the Colossian letter is gathered up in the few brief words, "In Him dwelleth all the fullness of the Godhead bodily; and in Him ye are made full." (Col. ii. 9, 10.) That is a composite sentence, having within it two supreme declarations. The first declaration is that "In Him dwelleth all the fullness of the Godhead bodily;" and the second is that "In Him ye are made full."

The fullness of the Godhead is in Christ; that is the Christian doctrine of the Person of the Lord Jesus Christ. The saints are filled in Christ; that is the Christian doctrine of saintship. The facts are correlative and may thus be stated, The fullness of the Godhead is in Christ; The filling of the saints is in Christ; making a distinction between *fullness* and *filling*. The fullness of the Godhead is an eternal fact, and the apostle made use of, what I would term for the moment, the ever-present tense, when he wrote that the fullness of the Godhead bodily, not dwelt, or will dwell, but dwelleth. That is the constant present tense of essential Deity. God knows nothing of the limitation of time. When the apostle referred to the saints he used another word, filling. The fullness dwells in Him; but the saints are made full. He is not made full, He is full. The saints are not full, they are made full. Thus we have in two brief sentences the whole of the Christian doctrine with regard to Christ, and with regard to the Church of Christ. Consequently, the central teaching of the letter has to do with the fullness of the Godhead in Christ, and with the filling of the saints in Him.

In dealing with the first of these facts it is a matter, somewhat technical, yet full of interest, that the Greek word here translated "*Godhead*" occurs nowhere else in the New Testament. The

word rendered Divinity in the Roman letter is radically different, and signifies an attribute of Deity which may be discovered in nature. This word refers not to an attribute, but to the essential fact of Deity. According to Augustine, Thayer also agreeing, the Latin Fathers had to create a word to convey the thought of the Greek word. The Latin word *Divinitas* did not meet the suggestiveness of the Greek word, and they made the word *Deitas*. That is a distinctively Christian word, unknown prior to Christianity. This word Deity best conveys the thought of the word translated Godhead.

That is a distinction which we must be very careful to make. It is not enough to say that Christ was Divine, to affirm belief in the Divinity of Christ. There is a sense in which every man is Divine; but it cannot be said of every man that he is Deity. Divinity is an attribute of Deity. Deity is the essential, peculiar, lonely nature of God. That is the thought of the word used here. Here then we have the statement of the supreme fact concerning Christ, that the fullness, the pleroma of essential Godhead, dwelt in Him corporeally, that is in bodily manifestation.

In the context we have some phases of this fullness dealt with. The relation of Christ to creation is declared in the words, "The First-born of all creation; for in Him were all things created . . . all things have been created through Him; . . . and He is before all things, and in Him all things consist." Christ is the Creator and Sustainer of the universal order.

The relation of Christ to Redemption is revealed in the declaration that He is not only First-born of all creation, but "First-born from the dead." Resurrection presupposes death. Death is due to sin. Between the original creation and the resurrection there was the tragedy of sin and its issue of death. In resurrection He was Victor over these. The result is peace, reconciliation between all that had been separated as the result of sin.

Thus with clear vision the writer looked back as far as human eyes can look, through all the processes of the things in the midst of which he found himself; he traced the material order back until he reached the beginning, and there he found Christ, the First-born of creation.

Again he looked and beheld the tragedy of

evil, of sin, the rivers of darkness and of death sweeping through the centuries; until he saw death's power broken, the resurrection, life won out of death, and there again found Christ, God coming into the midst of human sin and human wrong, the First-born from among the dead.

Then he looked on, and where his gaze ended I cannot see, but his vision was that of an ultimate reconciliation of things on earth and things in heaven; and the Reconciler is this same Christ, Who is behind creation, and Who caused it to be; Who came into human history and broke the power of death. He is the Reconciler, having made peace through the blood of His Cross. These all are the activities of Deity and not of humanity. Humanity did not create, did not break the power of death, cannot produce peace and reconciliation where there is war and strife.

Having thus described the activities of Christ, he declared that "in Him dwelleth all the pleroma of the Godhead bodily," all the fullness of Deity; creating, rising out of death in triumph, reconciling to the utmost bound of the heavens. That is Paul's Christ. That is the Christ of the Christian Church.

The second part of the central teaching is; "In Him ye are made full." In days when I am discouraged and very fearful by reason of my own frailty, and my own near-sightedness, I come back and read this statement, and then I break into song in celebration of this Christ of mine. I am made full in Him. There is nothing I need which is not to be found in Him.

Let us interpret the making full of the saint by the pleroma of the Saviour. Let us explain the filling of the human by the fullness of Deity We will do so by the illustrations which the apostle used. This Christ is the Origin of creation, the Creator. We are made full in Him. That means that we are restored to our true place in the creation. It means that in Christ man regains his sceptre and his crown. Out of that fact grows part of our missionary responsibility. "Go ye into all the cosmos"; not merely travel over the earth, that is not all; but go into the cosmos, into the creation, crying, groaning, sobbing, agonized creation; go into it and preach the evangel of that risen Christ, Who is Lord and Master, and the Redeemer of all creation. Every true Christian is restored to the

place of dignity and rule in the creation of God. I know we do not realize it. I know we are too often busy hunting among rubbish heaps, attracted by the glitter of straws. But the fact remains that in this sense we are made full in Him. He is the Creator and Sustainer of the universe, of mountains and hills; of beasts, birds, and flowers; and we are made full in Him. We come into relation with all the kingdom of nature, in Christ, as we never can come into relationship with it, save under His dominion and power. The animals will have a better time if we live in Him. Flowers will become more beautiful under our touch if He energize it. All the glory and beauty of the cultivation of flowers has resulted from missionary enterprise. Nature runs riot in her beauty in the wilderness, where the foot of man comes not, and the hand of man does not touch; all the delicate and fine results of cultivation have come after the evangel to the creation. We are made full in Him, so that we are restored to our proper place in the creation. I begin there because Paul began there; but that, glorious as it is, is the lowest thought of all.

Let us take a step further. We are made full in Him, in our restored relationship to God by the way of His resurrection. By His resurrection the very life of God is communicated to the spirit of man, so that he takes his right place as subject to God, bending before Him, not by the breaking of his will, but by the capture and constraint of the will, by the indwelling grace of the life of Christ. Thus we are made full in Him.

That leads us to the final fact, we are restored to fellowship with God in Him. Fellowship does not merely mean that we receive from God; it also means that which to me is more and more amazing, indeed the most amazing fact of all, that we can give to God in service. I think every day I live, the thing about the grace of God which amazes me most, is not that He loves me, not that He saves me, but that He calls me to be a fellow-worker with Himself. Christ has made it possible for me to be a worker together with God. I can help Him to bring in His Kingdom, to establish His righteousness, to hasten the day of His ultimate victory.

We are made full in Him; for it is in Christ that we are restored to our true place in creation; in Christ that we are restored to our true relation to God; in Christ that we are restored to that fellowship with God which means coöperation in all His purposes.

These are the central teachings of this letter, stated in broadest, barest outlines; the doctrine of the fullness of Christ; and the doctrine of the fullness of the saint in Him.

The abiding appeal is threefold.

"Take heed lest there shall be any one that maketh spoil of you through his philosophy and vain deceit, after the tradition of men, after the rudiments of the world, and not after Christ" (ii. 8).

"Let no man therefore judge you in meat, or in drink, or in respect of a feast day" (ii. 16). "Let no man rob you of your prize by a voluntary humility and worshipping of the angels" (ii. 18).

"If ye died with Christ from the rudiments of the world, why, as though living in the world, do ye subject yourselves to ordinances? Handle not, nor taste, nor touch (all which things are to perish with the using), after the precepts and doctrines of men? Which things have indeed a show of wisdom in will-worship, and humility. and severity to the body; but are not of any value against the indulgence of the flesh. If then ye were raised together with Christ, seek the things that are above" (ii. 20—iii. 1).

It will at once be recognized that this threefold appeal is entirely dependent upon the great doctrines of the letter; that it is the necessary sequence and corollary of the provision made in Christ. The first note is a warning against false philosophy, the second is a warning against false mediation; and the third is a warning against false confidence.

The warning against a false philosophy; "Take heed lest there shall be any one that maketh spoil of you through his philosophy and vain deceit." The warning against false mediation; "Let no man therefore judge you in meat, or in drink, or in respect of a feast day, or a new moon, or a Sabbath day," and "Let no man rob you of your prize by a voluntary humility and worshipping of the angels"; the mediation of ceremonialism, and the mediation of angel worship or symbolism in any form. The warning against false confidence; Why do you submit yourselves to ordinances and to severity to the body? These things are of no value against indulgence of things of the flesh. "Set your mind on the things that are above."

This false philosophy Paul summarized with a masterly hand as the tradition of men, the rudiments of the world; the tradition of men, speculation; the rudiments of the world, materialism. This philosophy is the result of human guessing; a philosophy which puts God out of His universe, and attempts to account for everything within the limitation of the material. Such false philosophy is to be corrected by recognition of the fact that Christ is the solution of the problem of the universe. There is no other solution. Beware of the philosophy which is vain deceit, which comes from the tradition of men; beware of it, because it is only speculation; because it is bounded by the cosmos, by the rudiments of the world, by elementary things, things having a beginning; you may call them atoms or electrons or anything you will, but if you attempt to account for the world by the world, then your philosophy is a philosophy of vain deceit. This is to be corrected by recognition of the fact that God through Christ is at the back of all æons and electrons. That is a philosophy characterized by dignity, by majesty. The vision of Christ as the First-born of creation, the Upholder of creation, gives a true view of the universe.

The next appeal is a warning against the false mediation of ceremonialism. Men will judge us in the matter of what we eat and drink, and as to whether we observe feasts, and new moons, and Sabbath days. They are shadows all; and we are to have done with them, because we have Christ, Who is the substance.

There is another false mediation, that of the worshipping of angels, a voluntary worshipping and humility which is of the essence of pride. With all this also we are to have done, by recognition of the fact that we need no intermediary, because we have access to the Lord Himself, direct, immediate communication with the Lord of all angels, the Master of all spirits. We are not to suffer ceremony or angel to come between us and Christ.

The final note of appeal is a warning against false confidences. The first is that of slavery to human opinion. If we have died with Christ from the rudiments of the world, we are not as though living, to subject ourselves to ordinances of men, which have no value against the indulgence of the flesh, and which are only matters of human opinion. Of such ordinances Paul gives an illustration in the words, " Handle not, nor taste, nor touch." I constantly hear Christian people saying that the Bible says, " Handle not, nor taste, nor touch." As a matter of fact the Bible teaches us that we are not to obey those who lay such restrictions upon us; and that, not in order that we may have licence to play with evil things, but because we are to take our commands from our living Lord, and not to allow anybody to interfere between us and Himself.

Another false confidence is that in ascetic practice. Severity to the body Paul dismisses as of no value against indulgence of the flesh. It is possible to wear a hair shirt and be sensual. It is possible to lacerate the body with whips and scourges and think indecently while we do it. We are risen with Christ; therefore we are to seek the upper things, to set our minds on the upper things ; to have a true view of our Lord, to see Him Lord of creation, Master of death, Reconciler of the universe ; and then by living union with Him, we shall need none of these things which never yet made men spiritual. All the fullness of the Godhead is in Christ, and we are made full in Him !

A final word as to the application of these things to the Church of God to-day. The matter of supreme importance to the Church, for her life and service, is that of her doctrine of Christ. I know that is hardly the view of current philosophy. We are being told that it does not matter what a man thinks, it matters what a man is. Yes ; but let us not forget that as a man thinks, so is he. The supreme matter for the Christian Church is what she thinks of Christ. It is not enough that our conceptions should be Christocentric. The supreme question is, Who is the Christ at the centre ? We may be Christocentric, and yet not be Christian in the New Testament sense of the word. If the Christ at the centre be the Christ, Who is the First-born of creation, the First-born from the dead, in Whom is all the pleroma of Deity ; then our position is Christian according to the New Testament.

To hold fast the Head as He is revealed in this letter will make impossible all the failures which are here revealed. To hold fast this Christ will make it impossible to accept a philosophy of the universe which is the result of speculation, and which begins and ends in the material. We cannot be New Testament Christians without believing that every blade of grass flashes with the glory of God in Christ. We cannot be New Testament Christians without seeing tokens of His majesty and His infinite glory in the delicate beauty of the pencilling of the flowers, and in the rolling rhythmic order of the system of the stars. The New Testament Christian cannot consent to any solution of the riddle of the universe which shuts out God and Christ.

This doctrine of Christ will as certainly put an end to all false mediation and false confidence. The New Testament Christian cannot be content with the mediation of ceremonialism in any form. The New Testament Christian will waste no time listening to the muttering of witches in the hope of discovering some secret of the spirit world, when it is possible to hold direct and immediate communication, in street and city, in the railway train, as well as in the sanctuary, with the Lord of angels, and the Master of all spiritual realms.

A Christless philosophy ends in animalism. Beware of it. A religion of added intermediation robs of the prize of religion. Beware of it. Asceticism is of no value against the flesh. Beware of it.

> " Christ ! I am Christ's ! and let the name suffice you,
>   *Ay, for me too He greatly hath sufficed:*
>   Christ is the end, for Christ was the beginning,
>   Christ the beginning, for the end is Christ."

Whether we look up or down ; back or on ; to depth, height, length or breadth, we still see Christ, and all the pleroma of Deity resident within Him is our fullness ; so that in Him, for to-day, for to-morrow, and forever, we are filled to the full.

I Thessalonians

THE ESSENTIAL MESSAGE	THE APPLICATION

I. **The central teaching**—the relation of the second advent to Christian experience.
  A. The final argument producing faith—1:9, 10.
    1. To God from idols—to order from disorder.
    2. The completion of the mission of the Son.
  B. The abiding confidence inspiring labour—2:19.
    1. To serve a living and true God—by faith in suffering.
    2. The final rewards—those won at His coming.
  C. The ultimate victory creating patience—3:13.
    1. Personal—the certainty of perfection.
    2. Relative—with God and the world.
II. **The abiding appeal**—the response of Christian obedience to the second advent.
  A. In life—sanctification—4.
    1. Personal purity.
    2. Love of the brethren.
    3. Honesty in the world.
  B. In view of death.
    1. The comfort of the bereaved.
    2. The joy of the living.
  C. In view of judgment.
    1. Sons of day.
    2. Appointed to salvation.
	I. **To the church.**
	  A. The light that failed.
	    1. Unbelief—idols.
	    2. Indolence—strife.
	    3. Impatience—sin.
	  B. The light obscured.
	    1. Knowing without doing.
	    2. Waiting without work.
	    3. Singing without suffering.
	  C. The light shining.
	    1. The passion for the kingdom.
	    2. The service of love.
	    3. The optimism of hope.
	II. **To the individual.**
	  A. Spirit.
	  B. Soul.
	  C. Body.
	    1. Waiting.
	    2. Serving.

THIS letter thrills with conflicting emotions. On the one hand there are evidences of the apostle's unbounded joy and satisfaction in the work accomplished at Thessalonica. On the other hand there are equally clear evidences of his concern for the Thessalonian Christians in view of the circumstances of peril in which they lived.

The letter differs from any we have already considered; not because it was written at an earlier period in the ministry of the apostle; but because the need calling for it was different. I draw attention to this, because it has been said that this was one of the first of Paul's letters, and that when he wrote the later ones he had entirely departed from some of the positions he held when he wrote this one.

All Paul's letters were written with some very definite, immediate, and local purpose. Paul did not sit down intending to write a system of theology, or to write letters for the Catholic Church; but he nevertheless did both these things in the purpose and economy of the inspiring Spirit of God, though quite unconsciously to himself at the time. He wrote to the people whom he named, and on some subject of immediate importance to them.

In all the letters we have considered so far, some great doctrine of the faith, or duty of the Church has been discussed. Here there is no definite teaching of that kind. This is not a letter stating a great doctrine of the faith. This is not a letter insisting upon some special duty of the Church. In two verses only do we find anything in the nature of definite teaching which is new; "The Lord Himself shall descend from heaven, with a shout, with the voice of the archangel, and with the trump of God: and the dead in Christ shall rise first: then we that are alive, that are left, shall together with them be caught up in the clouds, to meet the Lord in the air: and so shall we ever be with the Lord" (iv. 16, 17).

In that brief paragraph we have the only passage which is of the nature of positive statement. And let us be careful even in regard to this. It is not an announcement of the fact of the second Advent. It does declare the fact, but that is not the purpose of the statement of the apostle. Neither is it a defence of the truth of the second Advent. It becomes a defence, for it is an apostolic and inspired declaration; but that is not its purpose. It is rather a simple statement of the order of events at the Advent, made for the comfort of bereaved Christians. It must be taken in connection with that which has preceded it, beginning at the thirteenth verse; "We would not have you ignorant, brethren, concerning them that fall asleep."

Having written this the apostle gave the order of events, showing that at the second Advent of Jesus those that have fallen on sleep will take precedence of those that remain. That is the purpose of the declaration. Thus, the only positive statement of truth in this letter is, after all, an incidental part of the argument.

It is nevertheless patent, alike to the casual and most critical student of this letter that the fact of the second Advent of Jesus was paramount in the mind of the writer from beginning to end Its glory gleams on every page and shines through every argument, and was the supreme matter in all that he had to say to these Thessalonian Christians.

Let us attempt to discover the reason of this. Paul's work in Thessalonica had been characterized by the most remarkable spiritual awakening, and that in spite of peculiarly vindictive opposition and persecution, the history of which is found in the Acts of the Apostles. He came to Thessalonica and for three Sabbaths he spoke in the synagogue; then he turned to the Gentiles, and there was a marvellous awakening, followed by most vicious opposition, so that Paul was compelled to escape from Thessalonica, to Berea, to Athens, and finally to Corinth. At Corinth he was joined by Timothy, whom he had left behind, and from whom he learned of the state of his Thessalonian converts. Only a few months elapsed between his first coming to Thessalonica and the writing of this letter.

These Thessalonian Christians were firm in their loyalty to the gospel which had been declared unto them; but they were enduring suffering, persecution, and affliction for the sake of the Kingdom of God. To these people Paul wrote; and the letter therefore was one intended to comfort those who were suffering for their loyalty to that King Jesus, for preaching Whom, the apostle had been sent away. What more natural then than that His Advent of vindication and victory should be uppermost in his thought? He could best comfort them by reminding them that the unseen King to Whom they were loyal would again be manifested, and would vindicate their loyalty in the grace and glory of His second Advent.

The essential message of this letter, therefore, is that of the relation of the second Advent to Christian experience. The letter does not deal doctrinally with the Advent; it takes the fact for granted, and applies it.

It does take the fact for granted. No man can read this letter without seeing that when Paul wrote it he believed that as surely as Jesus had been seen in this world, He would be seen again; that as certainly as He had once appeared, He would appear again; that as certainly as there had been a coming to suffering, there would be a coming to sovereignty. To go back to the brief paragraph already quoted; the simplest honest reading of it can leave no doubt that the apostle referred to an actual coming of the same Jesus Who had already come. That is the force of the introductory phrase, "the Lord Himself." Why the introduction of that word " Himself" unless it be to emphasize the fact of the personal Advent of Jesus? No comment is needed. Of course, it might be pertinent for us to discuss the question whether Paul was right or wrong. My business, however, is simply to emphasize what Paul said and meant. There are those who say that he was mistaken. In that view there is necessarily involved the question of the inspiration and authority of these letters. Our attitude is that of belief in their inspiration and authority.

The teaching of Paul was in harmony with that of the Lord; "Whosoever shall be ashamed of Me and of My words, of him shall the Son of man be ashamed, when He cometh in His own glory, and the glory of the Father, and of the holy angels." "The Lord Himself shall descend from heaven, with a shout, with the voice of the archangel, and with the trump of God; and the dead in Christ shall rise first; then we that are alive, that are left, shall together with them be caught up in the clouds, to meet the Lord in the air; and so shall we ever be with the Lord." Thus Paul reaffirmed Christ's definite declaration.

The central teaching of this letter then is that of the relation of the second Advent to Christian experience. This fact of the coming of Jesus is the final argument, producing faith. This fact of the second Advent of Jesus is the abiding confidence, inspiring labour. This fact of the coming of Jesus is the ultimate victory, creating patience. In the introduction to this letter the apostle declared that he remembered without ceasing their work of faith, their labour of love, and their patience of hope. These are the facts of Christian experience. The work of faith is that act of faith by which men become Christians. Said Jesus, "This is the *work* of God, that ye *believe* on Him Whom He hath sent." That work of faith is followed necessarily and inevitably by the labour of love. That labour of love is maintained through all circumstances by the patience of hope. These are the three attitudes of the Christian life.

Let us carefully notice how the first three chapters end. The first ends with the words "to wait for His Son from heaven, Whom He raised from the dead, even Jesus, which delivereth us from the wrath to come." The second ends, "What is our hope, or joy, or crown of glorying? Are not even ye, before our Lord Jesus at His coming? For ye are our glory and our joy." The third ends, "To the end He may stablish your hearts unblameable in holiness before our God and Father, at the coming of our Lord Jesus with all His saints."

These are all references to the Advent. The first indicates that which I have named as the first fact, the relation of the Advent to Christian experience in its beginning. The final argument producing faith is that of the coming of Jesus. They turned from idols to God to serve God and

to wait for His Son. The last argument producing faith was the declaration that the One Who had come was coming again. They were to wait for Him. Think of the actual circumstances of these Thessalonians; they were living in the midst of idols that could be seen; their Lord was unseen. They were men who had been brought up in the midst of idolatry, worshipping things seen and handled, which appealed to the senses; and they turned to an unseen God. What was the last argument persuading them to do this? The fact that He would yet again be manifested; and that at His Advent there would be the vindication of faith in sight. When they turned to God from idols, they turned towards a restored order, from the disorder in the midst of which they were living; towards the establishment of the Kingdom, from the anarchy in the midst of which they had been living, from the anarchy of idolatry to the Government of God. When they did that, they did it, determining to wait for the Son. Faith acted not only upon the declaration that He has come, but that He is coming again. Faith is a venture which trusts in the first coming, and waits for the second. Thus the second Advent is the final argument producing faith.

Then, as in the power of faith they turned to their labour of love, the second Advent became their abiding confidence, inspiring that labour. They turned "to serve a living and true God." When they turned to the unseen God, having heard the declaration that the Son should be revealed again, determining to wait for the Son, they turned to serve this living and true God. The reward of service will be received when the Son returns. In order to comfort these Thessalonian Christians in the midst of their suffering, Paul spoke of his own experience; "What is our hope, or joy, or crown of glorying? Are not even ye, before our Lord Jesus at His coming?" The reward of Christian service is, in its finality and completion, postponed until the second Advent. There is a sense in which rewards come in the act of service. In the Corinthian letter the apostle deals with that phase of the truth, "Be ye steadfast, unmovable, always abounding in the work of the Lord, forasmuch as ye know that your labour is not in vain in the Lord." The reward of service is in the service, in the immediate success of service; but the great reward, the ultimate gladness, will be when those whom we have led to Christ by patience and by perserverance and persistence, in the midst of toil and travail, are presented faultless at His coming.

As I watch this apostle on his journeys, the intrepid missionary, pressing ever on to the regions beyond, suffering perils by land and sea, from enemies and false brethren; glowing in his heart forevermore, as the inspiration of his labour of love, is that glad hour when those who are won for Christ will be presented faultless in the glory of the second Advent.

Finally, the Christian experience is made up not only of the work of faith and the labour of love, but also of the patience of hope. The ultimate victory, creating the patience, is to be won at the second Advent. "To the end He may stablish your hearts . . . before our God and Father, at the coming of our Lord Jesus with all His saints." That conviction of the heart produces patience. Patience in this matter of personal salvation, with ourselves; not with ourselves as severed from Him, or as apart from Him; not with ourselves as disloyal to Christ. But even when loyal to Christ we are disappointed. If we are satisfied with ourselves it is an evil thing for us spiritually. How dissatisfied with ourselves we become whenever we think of ourselves; but at His coming He will stablish us, unblameable in holiness. Not for a moment is this to be an excuse for carelessness in Christian life, but on the contrary it is to be a perpetual inspiration, driving us towards approximation to that final perfection, lest, as John says, we be ashamed from Him at His coming. We shall be patient with ourselves if we are loyal, in proportion as our hearts are resting in the glory of the Advent. We know that then we shall be perfected.

Then also this conviction will give us patience with God. We have all experienced hours in which, because of our frailty, we have been inclined to be impatient with God; impatient with God about the world. If we have ever come very near the world's agony, there have been moments when it has seemed as though God were doing nothing. But when we see this fact of the second Advent, and know that by a crisis in the future, as definite as the crisis in the past, God will consummate the thing that to-day is being prepared for by processes, then the heart is patient with God, and with all conditions.

Here suffer a word of personal testimony. If you take away from me the doctrine of the second Advent of Christ, which is to be a crisis in human history as definite as the first, I am the most pessimistic of men. If you tell me that the work of the missionary is to convert the world by preaching, I am hopeless indeed! But when I realize that the work of missions is to evangelize the world by the preaching of the Gospel for a witness; and that beyond the Advent there will be a new age in which human history will be perfected; then I wait with patience for the crisis which is to come, and serve, as God helps me, in order to hasten that coming, the coming of our Lord Himself.

Thus the central teaching of the letter is of the second Advent in relation to the whole fact of Christian experience. It is the last argument producing faith. How can I turn to God? He Who came is coming! Then I will trust and wait. The fact of that Advent is the abiding confidence which inspires labour. Then shall I know the real result of my toil, and that makes me quite careless about present statistics and figures. Then the sheaves of the harvest will be garnered; the statistics of God will be published. Then the heart will know its final joy, when in the presence of Christ we see men, women, and little children, whom we have tried to help and win for Him. The fact of that coming produces the patience which is the very strength of life, for then we shall be perfected and the ways of God vindicated.

The abiding appeal of this letter is that we should respond to this great truth of the second coming of our Lord. How are we to respond?

First in our own life, by sanctification. The life of sanctification is the true response to the doctrine of the second Advent. The life of sanctification is that of personal purity; love of the brethren; and honesty in the world. That is response to the doctrine.

If we believe that He may in any day disturb us in our work, or in any night wake us from our sleep by His own voice, how pure we shall desire our personal life to be, that we may be ready; how we shall love the brethren, lest He should come and find us quarrelling; how honestly we shall live before the world.

What is the response to this fact in the presence of death? First there is comfort for the bereaved. "If we believe that Jesus died and rose again, even so them that are fallen asleep in Jesus will God bring with Him." Then, what rapture and gladness, what uniting of severed friendships when partings are no more. Oh, the comfort of it. "Comfort one another with these words." This is the transfiguration of death, the abolition of death.

If there come what men call death to the child of God, then the child of God will lay down his head and sleep, knowing that when the Lord shall come, he will be awakened before those who are left; that he will be changed first, that in their transfiguration there may be perfect re-union. Yet we wait not for death, but for Him.

In view of the judgment that lies beyond death what is the response to this truth? The Advent is not a question of times and seasons; would God the Church believed that! It is the study of this Advent in connection with calendars and almanacs that has brought the whole subject into disrepute. There is a Day of God of which the ancient prophets spoke, which will be a Day of Judgment; but we are not appointed to judgment but to salvation and to deliverance from the disasters of that day.

It is my own personal and strong conviction that this truth of the second Advent is the light that has failed in the history of the Christian Church. I am sometimes inclined to think that I am a very lonely man as an expositor to-day in the view I take of the second Advent. I believe that the results of the loss of this doctrine to the Church are: unbelief, and return to idols; indolence, which issues in strife; and impatience, which issues in sin; the opposites of the great things which Paul describes, as the work of faith, the labour of love, and the patience of hope.

The measure in which this great doctrine becomes vital and real is the measure of faith, the measure of labour, the measure of patience.

If this is the light that failed, it is also a light which was given again, and then strangely obscured during the nineteenth century. God raised up certain men of vision, and restored this great truth; but the most amazing wonder and calamity is that they have so largely obscured the light by making it the one and only fact for which they have cared anything; waiting without working; singing about the Advent, without suffering in order to hasten its coming; treating the Advent as though it were a method by which God would gather them away to everlasting rest, while He let the rest of the world drift to darkness and death. That is a lie. It is a more terrible heresy than to forget the Advent. Belief in the second Advent of Jesus should be the inspiration of all things that are of service and sacrifice.

Paul ended his letter by the prayer, "The God of peace Himself sanctify you wholly; and may your spirit and soul and body be preserved entire, without blame at the coming of our Lord Jesus Christ. Faithful is He that calleth you, Who will also do it." The sanctification of the spirit, soul, and body, consists in that waiting for Jesus which is the waiting of unceasing service; not in gazing at the stars, not in attempting to decipher hieroglyphics, not in fatuous endeavours to fix a date.

With that music of the second Advent in our souls, with the assurance in our hearts that He Who came will come; we will wait and watch, while we love and labour. Thus waiting, the time will soon pass, and we shall see Him and be like Him.

II Thessalonians

THE ESSENTIAL MESSAGE	THE APPLICATION

I. **The central teaching**—the truth about the day of the Lord.
  A. A distinction concerning the parousia.
    1. "Our gathering together unto Him"—see I Thess. 4:16, 17.
    2. "The day of the Lord"—see II Thess. 2.
  B. The day of the Lord.
    1. The present facts.
      a. "The mystery of lawlessness . . ."
      b. "That . . . one . . . He . . . restraineth."
    2. The crisis.
      a. "He [that restraineth] taken away."
      b. Man of sin—son of perdition; lawless one; apocalypse; parousia.
    3. The ultimate.
      a. Epiphany of parousia.
      b. Destruction of lawless one.
II. **The abiding appeal.**
  A. A call to courage—the heart comforted, established.
    1. In word.
    2. In work.
  B. A call to conduct.
    1. Work and thus wait.
    2. Wait and thus work.
	I. **To the church.**
	  A. Interpretation of the times.
	    1. Lawlessness.
	    2. Restraint.
	  B. The coming crisis—the unveilings.
	    1. The man of sin.
	    2. The Lord Jesus.
	  C. The church the instrument of restraint.
	    1. Salt.
	    2. Light.
	II. **To the individual.**
	  A. The responsibility for restraint.
	  B. The principle against lawlessness.
	  C. The secret of courage—the day of the Lord.

THE second letter to the Thessalonians was a sequel to the first; but the purpose was different. The purpose of the first letter was comfort, while that of the second was correction.

To understand this letter it is important that we should recognize the circumstances of these Thessalonian Christians at the time when Paul wrote. Of these, we have no historical picture. The Book of the Acts tells the story of the founding of the church, and of the departure of the apostle; but gives no account of the subsequent history of the church. From these letters we may learn the condition of affairs in Thessalonica so far as these Christians were concerned.

We must bear in mind the conditions referred to in our last study. They are distinctly described in the beginning of this letter;

" We ourselves glory in you in the churches of God for your patience and faith in all your persecutions and in the afflictions which ye endure; which is a manifest token of the righteous judgment of God; to the end that ye may be counted worthy of the Kingdom of God, for which ye also suffer " (i. 4, 5).

These people were enduring persecutions and afflictions, and the apostle recognized the reason of the persecution and affliction; they suffered for the Kingdom of God. These experiences of trial had called forth the first letter, and they had not changed when this second was written.

In this, however, new conditions are clearly

revealed. These arose in all probability from a misreading of the first letter, accentuated perhaps by the arrival in Thessalonica of spurious letters, purporting to be from Paul himself, but in reality sent by some one else ; and also from the teaching of certain people in Thessalonica.

The new conditions are seen in the first two verses of the second chapter ;

"Now we beseech you, brethren, touching the coming of our Lord Jesus Christ, and our gathering together unto Him ; to the end that ye be not quickly shaken from your mind, nor yet be troubled, either by spirit, or by word, or by epistle as from us, as that the day of the Lord is now present."

They were in danger of being *shaken from their mind*. That phrase is an attempt at literalness in translation, which it is not easy to improve upon, and yet it hardly conveys the idea of the text. Dr. Findlay's translation is very graphic because more literal ; he renders it " shaken out of your wits." These Thessalonian Christians were alarmed, perturbed ; and the apostolic word was a protest against that attitude of mind ; because such mental disturbance produced another condition which is described in verse eleven of chapter three ;

" We hear of some that walk among you disorderly, that work not at all, but are busybodies."

In these two references we have a description of the new conditions. In the midst of their trials they were suffering from mental disturbance, which resulted in disorderly conduct. Their mental disturbance was caused by the fact that they were expecting the immediate manifestation of Jesus in judgment to set up the Kingdom of God. The result was disorderly conduct. A great many abandoned their toil, gave up work in order to wait ; yet they had to live, and consequently they were eating at other people's charges ; and they became busybodies. In Paul's actual statement there is a play upon words, as though he should say, you are busy about everything except your own business.

Thus it is seen that the conditions obtaining when he wrote his first letter were still continued ; they were in affliction and persecution for the sake of the Kingdom of God. But now there was this added trouble, they were mentally disturbed, by his first letter partly, and by letters received " as from us " ; they were expecting that the day of the Lord was close at hand, that He would immediately manifest Himself in judgment to set up the Kingdom ; and the result of it was that very many of them had given up their daily callings, and had become busybodies. Paul had written his first letter dealing with the fact of the second Advent in order to comfort them. Now he heard from Thessalonica, that many of them were giving up work, and waiting for the coming of the Day of the Lord and the establishment of the Kingdom. This second letter was written in order to correct that false view.

It may be said therefore that Paul wrote this letter for two purposes. First, to correct a false view of the Advent ; and secondly, to correct alse conduct arising out of such a false view. In these two purposes of the apostle we discover the essential message of this letter, its living, lasting, and immediate teaching ; and in that part in which he corrected the false conduct, we discover the abiding appeal.

The central teaching of this letter is that of its setting forth of the Christian position concerning *the day of the Lord*. Students of Holy Scripture will at once recognize that phrase. So far as we are able by internal evidence to date the writings of the Old Testament we believe that the prophecy of Joel must be placed at a very early period, and therefore that he was the first to make use of it. From that time the phrase constantly recurs in the writings of the prophets. When we come to the New Testament the idea and the phrase are still present. In this letter the apostle explained to these Thessalonian Christians the relation of the Day of the Lord to the New Testament covenant, and the New Testament economy.

The importance of this teaching cannot be overestimated. The old phrase of the Hebrew prophets and the New Testament writers obtains until now. We are constantly using it in our common speech. Yet while the phrase is Scriptural and valuable, we very often use it in entire ignorance of its meaning according to Scripture. Consequently difficult and mystical as this subject may seem to be, we have no right to pass it idly over. It is most important that we should know what Holy Scripture says to us concerning " the Day of the Lord " and its relation to the Christian covenant.

There are two things we need specially to notice in considering this teaching ; first the careful distinction which the apostle made ; and secondly, his definite teaching concerning the Day of the Lord.

First then as to the distinction. He had written to them telling them that " the Lord Himself shall descend from heaven, with a shout, with the voice of the archangel, and with the trump of God." He had written in such a way as to fasten their attention upon that Advent as the hope of Christian souls. He now wrote to them to tell them that " the day of the Lord " was not near, that it could not come until certain things had happened. Now the question is, did Paul in his second letter contradict the teaching of the first? Some expositors say, yes ; that when Paul wrote his first letter he said one thing, and that when he wrote his second letter he modified his state- ment in the direction of actual change of teaching.

Now let us carefully observe the distinction which he made, a distinction which has given rise to the view that the second letter contradicted the first. The whole burden of the first letter is this ; He is coming again ; wait for Him. The whole burden of the second letter is this, He cannot come yet ; continue your work. Here is the ap- parent contradiction. As a matter of fact there is no contradiction.

The first chapter of the letter is largely intro- ductory. When we come to the second chapter we find this distinction made ;

" We beseech you, brethren, touching the com- ing of our Lord Jesus Christ, and *our gathering together unto Him ;* to the end that ye be not quickly shaken from your mind, nor yet be troubled, either by spirit, or by word, or by epistle as from us, as that *the day of the Lord* is now present ; let no man beguile you in any wise : for it will not be, except the falling away come first, and the man of sin be revealed."

The distinction there between " our gathering together unto Him," and " the day of the Lord " is patent. The whole purpose of the paragraph is to show the difference between the two.

In the first place let us carefully notice the Greek word Parousia. That word simply means presence ; it does mean the actual, positive, per- sonal Presence. We shall see that the same word is used about the antichrist ; the man of sin is to have a parousia. It is a word always

used with reference to the second Advent, and suggests that it is to be personal as was the first, as definite, as positive, as visible. No man can make his appeal to the authority of Scrip- ture without believing that He Who came is coming. We may differ as to the details ; but the fact that Jesus is to come again, as surely as He came, the New Testament most certainly teaches. Parousia is the word used to describe that Coming. That Coming, that Presence, was the theme of his first letter to these people. At the close of every great section therein that word occurs. It is as though he now said : I wrote to you about the Presence ; I want to say some- thing else about it, I desire to make a dis- tinction.

That distinction is not between the Parousia and the " Day of the Lord " ; but between " our gathering together unto Him " and " the Day of the Lord." The trouble in the Thessalonian church resulted from confusion between two aspects of the Parousia, or Presence of Jesus ; those namely of " our gathering together unto Him " and " the day of the Lord."

They had received his first letter, in which he had said ;

" The Lord Himself shall descend from heaven, with a shout, with the voice of an archangel, and with the trump of God : and the dead in Christ shall rise first : then we that are alive, that are left, shall together with them be caught up in the clouds, to meet the Lord in the air : and so shall we ever be with the Lord."

That is a description of " our gathering to- gether unto Him " at His Parousia or Coming.

He now wrote to tell them they were not to be troubled and disturbed as though " the Day of the Lord " were at hand.

Thus he revealed the fact that there is a distinction to be made when considering the Parousia or Coming of the Lord, between " our gathering together unto Him," and " the day of the Lord." The apostle desired to teach these Christians that their relation to the Parousia was that of people waiting to be gathered unto Him ; and that " the day of the Lord " was not that in which they were personally interested, so far as their habits of life were concerned.

Nevertheless it is an interesting subject ; and one full of importance. Therefore he proceeded with care to deal with the subject.

He first declared that before "the day of the Lord" comes, there will be apostasy and a revelation of the man of sin; and then clearly described the man of sin, and the method of his manifestation;

"He that opposeth and exalteth himself against all that is called God or that is worshipped; so that he sitteth in the temple of God, setting himself forth as God. Remember ye not that, when I was yet with you, I told you these things? And now ye know that which restraineth, to the end that he may be revealed in his season. For the mystery of lawlessness doth already work; only there is one that restraineth now, until he be taken out of the way. And then shall be revealed the lawless one, whom the Lord Jesus shall slay with the breath of His mouth, and bring to nought by the manifestation of His coming; even he, whose coming is according to the workings of Satan with all power and signs and lying wonders."

In that paragraph there are three matters we need specially to notice; first, the description of existing conditions; secondly, the declaration that there will be a crisis; and thirdly, the teaching concerning the ultimate day of the Lord.

First as to the present facts. The apostle mentions two; first, the fact that the "mystery of lawlessness doth already work"; and secondly, the fact that there is "One that restraineth."

I am perfectly well aware of how many interpretations there have been of this passage. Everything depends upon the view held of the person here referred to. There are three descriptions; "lawless one," "son of perdition," "man of sin." The history of the interpretation of this passage is the history of the Christian Church for almost nineteen hundred years. Early Christians believed that the power that hindered the manifestation of the antichrist was the Roman Empire. Then there came a time when Christians believed that the power that prevented was the State. Views as to the man of sin have changed in the same way. There are those even to-day who say that the spirit of antichrist is Romanism and that the ultimate man of sin will be the Pope of Rome. And some believe that the State, organized under the government of God, is the restraining force. My own view is that they are all right, and that they are all wrong. They are all right in that they all discover the working of the mystery of lawlessness; but they are wrong in that they have not apprehended the fullness of the apostolic teaching. "The mystery of lawlessness" is one of the most remarkable of Bible phrases as a definition of sin; I cannot say of evil, because evil is not only the actual moral wrong, but all that results from it, of pain and suffering. Lawlessness is the root trouble with human life individually, socially, nationally, and racially. The apostle spoke of it "as the mystery of lawlessness," and he used that word mystery as he did in all his letters. A mystery according to the Greek philosopher was something that could only be known to an inner circle of initiated, and hardly known to them. A mystery, according to Paul, was something that no man could discover, but which God reveals. The "mystery of lawlessness" is that hidden, subtle, underlying force, ruining, blighting, spoiling humanity and creation. That lawlessness has been revealed. Jesus Christ came not only to reveal God and man, but the Devil also, by dragging him out of darkness into light that man might see him. The mystery underneath; the root of all humanity's maladies and diseases; the hidden spring of poison from which the polluting rivers flow; is lawlessness. This, the apostle declared, is already at work.

But he declared also that there is a restraining power opposing it, so that it cannot come to full manifestation; "there is one that restraineth" and I believe that he referred to the Church of God, as created by and indwelt by the Holy Spirit of God. As all these great truths are found in germ and potentiality in the teaching of Jesus, let us go back to the Manifesto of the King. He said to His disciples: "Ye are the salt of the earth . . . ye are the light of the world." What is the effect of salt? It is aseptic. What is the effect of light? It is illuminative. Lawlessness is corruption; it is darkness. The Church is salt, to prevent the spread of corruption; it is light flashing upon the darkness, so that lawlessness is hindered from full victory, and the men of lawlessness cannot accomplish all their dastardly works. That is true of the Church of God and the Spirit of God in the world at this present moment. Lawlessness is working; it is an attitude of heart, of mind, of will. If the Church of God, the whole company of new-born souls, were lifted out of the world, and taken right away, what would be the result? Lawlessness would have its full manifestation. The thing that saves London from unutterable corruption, and from the deepest darkness is the presence in it of the Holy Spirit of God through Christian men and women. That then is the present condition of affairs. The mystery of lawlessness working, but the Holy Spirit through the Church restraining.

The second matter to be observed is the apostle's declaration that there will presently come a crisis. It will come when He that restraineth is taken away, that is when the Spirit is withdrawn. When will the Spirit be withdrawn? When the Church of God is withdrawn, and never until then. "I will pray the Father, and He shall give you another Comforter, that He may be with you forever." When will the Church be withdrawn? At "our gathering together unto Him" at His coming. When He that restraineth is withdrawn, the man of sin, the son of perdition, the lawless one, will have his apocalypse, his parousia. The apostle teaches with great distinctness that at last lawlessness will have its final manifestation in some one person, a despot far worse than any the world has ever yet seen; and yet one characterized, not by the old-fashioned brutality of the beast, but by the oppression and cruelty of culture and refinement. If you would know the character of that one, the man of sin, we have the revelation in Paul's description; "He that opposeth and exalteth himself against all that is called God or that is worshipped." He will be entirely godless, but of so remarkable a character as to persuade men that he is himself divine.

The final matter is that of the ultimate fact which will bring the Day of the Lord. At last, all evil focussed in a person and manifested; there will be an epiphany of the parousia of the Lord—that is a very remarkable phrase; not His parousia merely; that includes the whole fact of the Advent. There will be first of all that aspect of the coming which will result in the gathering together of His own to Himself; when that happens, that which restrains being taken away, lawlessness will come to its head, and will have its manifestation in a person. Then the parousia, the presence of Christ in which His own have been gathered to Him, will become an epiphany; a flaming, shining glory; destroying the man of sin, and setting up that Kingdom on the earth which is the Kingdom of the iron rod; the rule of perfect, inflexible justice; the reign of the One Who does not judge by the seeing of the eyes or the hearing of the ears, but with righteous judgment.

How often as we look at human life, or see its portrayal in literature, we feel that this is what the world supremely needs. Then for the first time the world will come to the realization of the breadth, beauty, and beneficence of the will of God. I have no hope in kings, or parliaments, or policy, for the ultimate establishment of the Kingdom. Only by the presence of the Christ, returning with the saints He has gathered to Himself, shall be set up and established His Kingdom in the world. The manifestation of the presence will be for the destruction of the lawless one, and the establishment of the Kingdom.

The abiding appeal of this letter is first a call to courage. Paul said: Do not let your mind be disturbed, do not be shaken out of your wits. Let your heart be comforted and established. Courage is always an affair of the heart. Comforted is from the same root as the word which is used for the Holy Spirit; a word of great strength, which suggests a sense of peace and quietness. Let your heart be comforted and established.

It is also a call to conduct. Get on with your work! Wait and work! The man who gives up the fulfillment of his daily vocation to wait for Christ is doing exactly what some of these Thessalonian Christians had been doing. The work to which the apostle referred is the practical, commonplace work of every-day life; that actual work by which a man supplies the necessities of his physical life.

So let us wait, with calm and steady hearts, knowing that there will be a gathering together to Him; and afterwards, an epiphany of the presence, when lawlessness having come to manifestation in a person, will be smitten to its death, and the Kingdom of God will be established.

The application of this letter to the Christian Church is in its interpretation of our own times; these are days of lawlessness, and, thank God, of restraint also. The gravest peril that we have to confront is not that of socialism, nor that of feudalism; it is rather that of a growing spirit of rebellion against all government; lawlessness. It is abroad everywhere. The gravest menace to our national life is that of the man who leaves out God, mocks at authority, and vaunts his own independence. Wherever you find him, the mark of the beast is on him. It is well that the Church should realize this.

But let the Church remember that there is One that restraineth; the mighty grip of God is on all the forces which seem to be making for lawlessness, restraining them until He be ready that they shall manifest themselves. The crisis is coming, it will be for the world, first the unveiling of the man of sin; and then the unveiling and apocalypse of the Lord Jesus. Our hearts are to be firm and steady in absolute assurance that in that last unveiling it is not the Lord Jesus Christ, but the man of sin, who will be destroyed. Only let us also remember that in the interim the Church is the instrument of restraint. She is salt, and she is light, by the indwelling and power of the Holy Spirit.

What is the application to the individual? The measure in which I share the life of the Christ is the measure in which I am exercising restraint. Let each Christian ask then: How far am I by influence of speech and work restraining lawlessness? And then let us remember that the measure in which we restrain lawlessness in the world is the measure in which there is no lawlessness in our own hearts.

I Timothy

THE ESSENTIAL MESSAGE	THE APPLICATION

I. **The central teaching.**
A. The true function of the church—the proclamation of the truth in the world.
  1. The instrument—church; pillar; ground—3:15, 16.
  2. The truth—the mystery of godliness—3:15, 16.
B. The true function of the minister—the exposition of truth in the church.
  1. By teaching and exhortation.
  2. By example.
II. **The abiding appeal.**
A. To the church. (The instrument fitted for the fulfillment of function.)
  1. Her gospel unchanged.
  2. Her worship unceasing.
  3. Her ministry unfailing.
B. To the minister. (The instrument fitted for the fulfillment of function.)
  1. Loyalty to truth.
  2. Consistent in behaviour.
  3. Personal life.
	I. **To the church**—the things that hinder.
	A. False doctrine.
	B. Failure in prayer.
	C. False government.
	II. **To the minister**—the things that hinder.
	A. Failure in doctrine.
	B. Failure in duty.
	C. Failure in diligence.

THIS letter is the first of three; which while separated from each other in that they were written at different times and to two persons, are yet correlated in that they deal with one subject, that of the relation between the minister and the Church. They were all written to men occupying positions of responsibility in regard to churches of Jesus Christ; Timothy in Ephesus, and Titus in Crete.

The doctrine of the Church, and the fundamental doctrine concerning the ministry, we find in other of Paul's writings which we have already considered; and the things therein taught must be borne in mind as we come to these letters which, while so largely personal, are yet full of relative values. We find in our study of the New Testament that sometimes the Church is spoken of, sometimes the churches, sometimes a church. That is to say, the word is used in reference to the whole Church, the complete Church. It is also used of local churches. Whereas it is perfectly true that there is one Church of God; it is equally true that there was the church at Ephesus, the church at Corinth, and so on. In that sense therefore we use the word "churches"; not that these churches are divided each from the other; but that the whole Church is divided by locality, by circumstances, by geographical distances, into churches. In the New Testament it is evident that every local church was a microcosm of the catholic Church, and all the great fundamental doctrines concerning the catholic Church are equally applicable to the local church. Timothy was in oversight of the church at Ephesus; Titus was fulfilling a special work in connection with the church in Crete; and these letters were written to these men, holding positions of spiritual responsibility for very definite and specific purposes, and their theme is that of the inter-relation of the minister

The first part of 1 Timothy deals with the charge of the minister, that over which he has care, the church. The second part is the apostolic charge to the minister concerning his consequent responsibility. In these three letters then the great theme is that of the church and the minister. The first letter to Timothy is general and fundamental; the letter to Titus deals particularly with the method by which the minister is to set the church in order; and in the second letter of Timothy the particular subject is that of the minister's personal responsibility.

Having thus recognized the inter-relationships of these letters we may now turn our attention to the first.

The central teaching of this first letter to Timothy is that of its revelation of the true function of the church; and the true function of the minister.

The true function of the church is the proclamation of Truth in the world. The true function of the minister is that of the exposition of Truth in the Church. The one function for which the Church exists is that of the proclamation of Truth in the world. The one function for which the ministry is created is that of the exposition of Truth within the Church. That is the exact thought underlying Paul's teaching in the Ephesian letter concerning the catholic Church. In that letter, when we turn from the discussion of the Church's predestination, edification, and vocation, to the application of the truth in detail, we find Paul writing "I therefore, the prisoner in the Lord, beseech you to walk worthily of the calling wherewith ye were called"; and in close connection declaring that when Jesus ascended and received gifts, "He gave some to be apostles; and some, prophets; and some, evangelists; and some, pastors and teachers; for the perfecting of the saints, unto the work of ministering"; that is to say that the saints are to fulfill the ministry, and men qualified by gifts are to perfect the saints for the fulfillment of that ministry. The ministry of the Church is that of the proclamation of the truth of God in the world. The ministry created by gifts bestowed is that of perfecting the saints. The saints are to be perfected by the truth. The one function of the ministry then is the exposition in the Church of the truth which the Church is to proclaim to the world.

That is the central teaching of this letter in application to the local church.

The true function of the Church then is that of the declaration of the Truth to the world.

"That thou mayest know how men ought to behave themselves in the house of God, which is the church of the living God, the pillar and ground of the truth. And without controversy great is the mystery of godliness; He Who was manifested in the flesh, justified in the spirit, seen of angels, preached among the nations, believed on in the world, received up in glory."

There we reach the central light of the epistle concerning the true function of the Church. The Church is an instrument; it is "the pillar and ground of the truth"; it is that upon which the truth is to be displayed; it is that upon which the truth is to be so raised up that men may see it. This is in perfect agreement with the teaching of our Lord.

"Ye are the light of the world. A city set on a hill cannot be hid. Neither do men light a lamp, and put it under the bushel, but on the stand; and it shineth unto all that are in the house. Even so let your light shine before men, that they may see your good works, and glorify your Father which is in heaven."

The value of the Church in the world is that of the Truth which the Church reveals, proclaims; that Truth is light, which flashes upon the darkness, rebuking it, dissipating it, making it easy for men who are stumbling to find their way.

The apostle immediately, comprehensively, and most marvellously described the Truth in the words "without controversy great is the mystery of godliness."

The word which most simply conveys the meaning of the Greek work here translated "godliness" is the old word *piety*. It has largely dropped out of use in recent years, and for some reasons we are not sorry, for it was very much abused. Yet that is the real thought

---

[1] A glance at our analysis of contents will show an inter-relation between these letters which is remarkable and interesting.

In 1 Timothy, there are two divisions A and B. In 2 Timothy, the theme of B in 1 Timothy is elaborated in three divisions, A, B, C, which cover the same ground as III., II., I. of B in 1 Timothy.

In Titus the theme of A in 1 Timothy is elaborated; the application is different, but the general conceptions are the same. See "The Analyzed Bible," Vol. iii., p. 248, and on.

of godliness, and if we use it, as did our fathers, to describe religion in life, relationship to God in the actualities of every-day life, we have the true thought of godliness.

Where is this piety? Where is this life of relationship to God to be seen? The answer to such inquiries is to be found in the fact that the apostle immediately passed from the abstract ideal of godliness to a concrete and positive Person in Whom the idea was perfectly revealed; "He Who was manifested in the flesh." For poetic beauty of expression Humphrey's translation of this passage in the Cambridge Bible is very fine;

> " Who in flesh was manifested,
> Pure in spirit was attested;
> By angel's vision witnessèd,
> Among the nations heralded;
> By faith accepted here,
> Received in glory there ! "

According to that setting of the passage, the three couplets suggest the central facts in the life and work of Jesus; the first the life-story; the second the angels desiring to look into the mystery, and the nations hearing the ministry; the third the victory among men by faith, and the ascension.

Though it is poetic and beautiful, I do not think that it reveals the deepest values of the passage.

Rotherham thus translates;

> " Who was made manifest in flesh,
> Was declared righteous in spirit,
> Was made visible unto messengers;
> Was proclaimed among nations,
> Was believed on in (the) world,
> Was taken up in glory."

So far as I have any right to express an opinion, I do not hesitate to say that I consider that to be a most accurate, and beautiful translation. It covers far more than the life-story of Jesus when He was in the world, including the whole mystery of godliness manifested, beginning with the life-story, and ending with the second Advent.

The first line deals with the whole fact of the human life; "Who in flesh was manifested." The second line, "Was declared righteous in spirit," refers to the resurrection from the dead, for it was by the resurrection from the dead that He was "declared to be the Son of God with

power, according to the spirit of holiness." The third line, "Was made visible unto messengers," needs to be carefully noticed. The Greek word is sometimes translated "angels," and sometimes "messengers"; and here I believe Rotherham is quite right in translating it *messengers*. The messengers were not angels in our general sense, but those who saw Him after resurrection, and who became the first apostles of the new movement. The immediate result of that manifestation to the messengers is declared in the fourth line "Was proclaimed among nations"; and the spiritual result in the fifth "Was believed on in (the) world." These two facts of proclamation and belief are going forward now. The last line, "Was taken up in glory," refers to the Ascension of our Lord, and ultimately to that hour when, completed in His saints, His whole body perfected at the second Advent, Christ and His Church as an eternal unit pass into the heavens.

The great mystery of godliness then, according to this earliest hymn of the Church, is that of the manifestation of godliness in the flesh of the Son of Man; the declaration of His righteousness by resurrection; that risen One made visible to messengers, who proclaim the resurrection which is the foundation truth of Christianity; the proclamation issuing in the belief which brings men into living union with the manifested One; and ultimately, the complete manifestation in the Church in her union with Christ.

Thus the true function of the Church of God in the world is that of the proclamation of godliness; the Christ, and all those associated with Him, manifesting to the world the true life of piety, of religion, of godliness.

The true function of the minister then is that of the exposition of Truth in the Church. This is to be done by teaching, by exhortation, and by example.

The word is full of solemnity, one that always searches the heart of those who are called to the ministry of the Word. It is not by orthodoxy of intellectual comprehension merely that this work can be done. It is only as Truth is incarnate in the life of the teacher that the teacher has the power to prepare others to reveal the Truth. The responsibility of the Church in regard to the ministry is that it shall incarnate the Truth taught, in order that it may fulfill its function in the world as the pillar and ground of the Truth, that from which the glory and light of the Truth flashes upon the darkness of the world.

The abiding appeal to the Church is that the instrument must be fitted for the fulfillment of the function. The supreme matter of importance in the life of the Church is that she shall be an instrument able to proclaim the Truth. First her gospel must be an unchanged gospel. There must be no turning aside to false knowledge and heresies, such as Gnosticism and others that were then creeping in; no turning aside from the one doctrine of godliness manifested in flesh; the great faith once delivered to the saints in the Person of Christ, and multiplied in exposition through all these who share His life. The Church must be true to her gospel.

Secondly her worship must be unceasing; hence that whole section which deals so wonderfully with the subject of prayer.

Finally she must be responsive to the authority of a faithful ministry.

In order to be an instrument fulfilling her true function the Church needs a gospel unchanged, worship unceasing, and an unfailing ministry.

The responsibility of the minister may be described in the same way. The instrument must be fitted for the fulfillment of function. That fitness on the part of the minister consists of unswerving loyalty to truth; consistent behaviour, that is behaviour towards others in harmony with the truth proclaimed; and realization of godliness in personal life; that is personal life harmonious with the truth, mastered by the truth, responsive to the truth.

There is an immediate application of this message to the Church of God, and I choose to make it, having thus seen the positive teaching, by a negative statement. Let the Church beware of the things that hinder. They are false doctrines; failure in prayer: false government. False doctrine is any doctrine that denies the essential truths focussed in the apostolic statement. When the Church relaxes her hold upon any vital part of the essential truth of the New Testament, she is weakening her testimony. Failure of prayer is so patent a secret of failure that it only needs to be stated. False government is government by men who lack the

godly character. Both bishops and deacons must be men of true Christian character. We have been too eager to seek men for other reasons than for the highest; and to put them in charge of the affairs of the Christian Church. Those in oversight should be men full of faith and the Holy Ghost, men whose lives are transformed by the great doctrines for which the Church stands. Oversight must be in fulfillment of the truth, by incarnation of the truth; or what hope is there that the Church will rise to the fulfillment of her function in the world?

The application to the minister is that he is warned against failure in doctrine; failure in duty; and failure in diligence. No man can be in the ministry of Jesus Christ and fulfill the ideals of this letter to Timothy without putting into the business of his ministry, the business of his study, the business of his exposition, the business of his life, all the forces of his being.

Our sources of strength are sufficient. Truth itself, if known and responded to, will make us free from all the things that hinder us in the fulfillment of our service. Let those who teach the Word of God, whether in the larger assembly, or in the smaller circle, remember that teaching is only valuable and dynamic in the measure in which it is given, not by intellectual processes merely, but by volitional obedience and the changed life that results. How often we need to remind ourselves of the word of Emerson, "I cannot hear what you say for listening to what you are." Let us solemnly remember it in the presence of God. However orthodox the thing we say, however godly the method of our presentation of the truth, unless the life harmonizes, it is not only true that the things said will have no effect, it is true that the things said become a blasphemy and an impertinence.

The Church of God in the world to-day has as her function the proclamation of the truth of godliness. Those who teach the Word of God have as their responsibility that they give such exposition of the truth in teaching and life that the Church shall be equipped for her great work. May He Who has honoured us with the sacred responsibility fit us for the fulfillment of the duty.

II Timothy

THE ESSENTIAL MESSAGE	THE APPLICATION

I. **The central teaching**—the true minister of Jesus Christ.
  A. His perfect equipment—gifts and grace.
  B. His prevailing methods.
    1. Construction.
    2. Character.
  C. His supreme work.
    1. Know the writings.
    2. Preach the word.
II. **The abiding appeal**—"Fulfill thy ministry." (4:5)
  A. As to equipment.
    1. Gift—"Stir up the gift."
    2. Grace—"Be strengthened in the grace."
  B. As to methods.
    1. Construction—"Give diligence. . . ."
    2. Character—"Flee . . . follow."
  C. As to work.
    1. The writings—"Abide."
    2. The preaching—"Instant. . . ."
	I. **To the church.**
	  A. The preaching of the word as the corrective to abounding perils.
	  B. The importance of the ministry.
	  C. Recognition.
	    1. Of gift and grace in choosing.
	    2. Of time and teaching in work.
	II. **To the minister.**
	  A. The safety of the deposit.
	  B. The trusteeship of the deposit.
	  C. The fidelity to the deposit, because of:
	    1. Christ's appearing.
	    2. Formalism.
	    3. Paul's departure.

IN our consideration of this letter, in order to discover its main teaching, the central teaching of the first letter is assumed. That letter teaches us that the true function of the Christian Church is the proclamation of the Truth in the world, and that the true function of the Christian minister is that of the exposition of the Truth in the Church.

Between the writing of the first letter and this one, some period had elapsed. Paul, who was in prison when he wrote the great epistles, had been liberated when he wrote the first letter to Timothy; but was again in prison before he wrote this second one; and there is practically no question that this is the last writing that ever came from his pen.

The reason of the writing of this second letter to Timothy was that of the perils threatening the church, which were likely to prevent the church fulfilling its function as the pillar and ground of the truth. These perils he described in the words:

"Know this, that in the last days grievous times shall come. For men shall be lovers of self, lovers of money, boastful, haughty, railers, disobedient to parents, unthankful, unholy, without natural affection, implacable, slanderers, without self-control, fierce, no lovers of good, traitors, headstrong, puffed up, lovers of pleasure rather than lovers of God; holding a form of godliness, but having denied the power thereof."

That is a picture of what the apostle saw happening in the Church; it was being invaded by godlessness and worldliness. The Church is the pillar and ground of the Truth, and if the Church fails, then the Truth ceases to be proclaimed to the world; and that was the reason of the writing of this letter. The great missionary heart of Paul was troubled about the Church, because where the Church fails to give its testimony, the city abides in darkness. In view of these perils he wrote to Timothy, upon whom there necessarily rested grave responsibility.

The purpose of the letter then was that of preparing Timothy for the fulfillment of his responsibility for the Church, in order to the maintenance of its testimony ; and therefore it is preeminently a letter to those who are in the ministry of the Word.

The central teaching of this letter is that of its revelation of the true minister of Jesus Christ. The content is the message. The order is so systematic, the movement is so regular, the method is so logical, that any young man preparing for the ministry, or any man in the ministry, may read it as a letter to himself from this great apostle, and from God Himself by the Spirit through the apostle.

The letter gives us a perfect picture of the true minister of Jesus Christ, and that in three respects ; those namely of his perfect equipment ; of his prevailing methods ; and of his supreme work.

The perfect equipment of the Christian minister is revealed in two words, *gifts* and *grace*. In the old days when a candidate presented himself for the work of the ministry, the questions asked were : Has this young man gifts, and has he grace ? I am not sure that we always ask those questions to-day. Yet these are the supreme qualifications ; and no man can be a true minister of the Word in the Church, and no church can call a man to be a minister, and no college can make a man a minister if he lack these.

A man can become a minister of the Word only when a gift is bestowed upon him by the Head of the Church through the Holy Spirit. That is the supreme qualification. Roman Catholics speak of a vocation ; it is a great word. The vocation, according to the New Testament is received with the bestowment of the gift. The gift bestowed is the first qualification for the Christian ministry.

But grace also is necessary, with all that word means, of fellowship with Christ and with God, and the consequent approximation to the character of Christ and of God ; the appropriation of the very resources of Christ and of God, and these so reacting upon the character as to make it the character of light and life and love.

The gifts are described in the Ephesian letter :
" When He ascended on high, He led captivity captive, and gave gifts unto men. . . . He gave some to be apostles ; and some, prophets ; and some, evangelists ; and some, pastors and teachers."

The gift of the apostle is that of the first messenger, the pioneer, the missionary. The gift of the prophet is that of the ability to discover what the Word of God has to say, not so much to the individual as to the nation, the age. The gift of the evangelist enables a man to tell the story of Jesus with such wooing winsomeness that men are drawn towards Him, and are won for the Kingdom and the Church. The gift of the pastor and teacher enables a man to watch the flock and to feed them. A gift is in itself a Divine deposit, flaming in fire, burning in heat, driving in energy ; that is the first thing.

Beyond this there must be grace, that infinite resource of God at our disposal through Christ, which creates the tone of our preaching and the temper of our living, bringing all into harmony with the character of God.

The prevailing methods of the true Christian minister are those of construction and character. He is to aim at the development in holiness of those to whom he ministers ; and this by the guarding of his own character, so that it may express concretely the truth he preaches. These are the true methods. As to constructive work, he builds upon foundations, and watching the building, patiently corrects it where it is faulty, testing it ever by the Word.

" Every Scripture inspired of God is also profitable for teaching, for reproof, for correction, for instruction." The whole idea of that passage is that of character building. The first word refers to authoritative teaching, upon which a man can depend, upon which he can build. Reproof does not mean rebuke, it means proof over again. The Greek word is figurative and suggests the letting down of a plumb-line by the side of a building to test its straightness. Correction means pulling the thing that is out of line into the straight. Instruction means construction, that is carrying the building higher. That is the work of the Christian minister. All the gifts of the ministry of the Word tend to the building of character according to the will of God.

The supreme work of the Christian minister is twofold; first to know the writings; and then to preach and teach the Word. No man can exercise the Christian ministry, whatever be the nature of his gift, who does not abide in the Scriptures. His business is to preach the Word, not to destroy it, not to defend it, but to preach it.

The abiding appeal of this letter to the Christian minister is contained in the charge of the apostle, "Fulfill thy ministry." This is necessary as to equipment, methods, and work.

As to equipment, the first responsibility concerns the gift; and is declared in the words, "Stir up the gift of God which is in thee." To stir up is to set on fire, to fan to a flame. The gift received for the ministry is a thing of fire; we are to fan it to a flame; and not allow it to burn to an ember. Are we not all in danger of allowing the fire to die down? There is nothing the Christian minister has to guard against more earnestly than the danger that he should come to the hour when the Word of God ceases to move him. It is a subtle danger. We are always handling the Word, reading it, studying it; and unless we are careful, it will cease to surprise us, cease to amaze us; and the gift, whether of apostle, prophet, evangelist, or pastor, will become dull and dead.

The second responsibility as to equipment concerns the grace, and is revealed in the words: "Be strengthened in the grace that is in Christ Jesus." We must not neglect the means of grace, in the true full sense of the word. Let no minister imagine that he of all men can afford to neglect prayer and devotional study of his Bible, and that fellowship with God which, being neglected, the fire always burns dimly, the pulse beats slowly, and the Christian life is poorer than it ought to be. " Be strengthened in the grace." "Fulfill thy ministry."

As to methods, our responsibility for construction is declared in the simple and yet incisive charge, "Give diligence"; while our responsibility as to our own character, if we are to construct character in others, is declared in the words; "Flee youthful lusts, and follow after righteousness, faith, love, peace . . . foolish and ignorant questionings refuse." " Fulfill thy ministry."

As to work, we fulfill our responsibility as to the Scriptures when we abide in them; and as to the Church, by being instant in season and out of season.

All this is but the gathering out of sentences, the whole teaching of the letter being in mind. These are the revelations of the secrets of success in the Christian ministry.

This letter emphasizes the fact that the teaching of the Word is the corrective of all the perils that threaten the Church; just as the preaching of the Word, and the Word incarnate in the lives of the saints who constitute the Church, is the corrective of all the perils that threaten the city and the nation. In proportion as we really know this Word of God, all the things which sap the life of the Church and make her devoid of power are corrected. The Church must flourish by the preaching of the Word. Nothing will take its place. Whether it be a church, or an organization taking the name and responsibility of Christian work in the world, if it neglect the Word, it robs itself of power, and sooner or later the whole must crumble to pieces. The churches that have placed the preaching of the Word at the centre of their life, and have aimed at its embodiment in the lives of their members, are the churches which have truly served their day and generation.

Consequently the Church must recognize the importance of the ministry of the Word. I think a grave peril threatening us to-day is that the churches take so little interest in the men who go to our colleges. I think the hour must come when the colleges will have to say, We will accept no man for training unless he not only brings his minister's recommendation, but one also from a church which knows that he possesses a gift for the work of preaching. We take men too often before we are sure that they have the gift. We give such men training, and then are surprised that no church wants them. Let the Church take over this responsibility and understand how important and sacred a thing this ministry of the Word is. The Church should be able to say: We recognize this man has gift and grace, and because he has gift and grace he is called to the ministry; therefore we will see to it that he has time for preparation and training, in order that his gift may be realized and his ministry fulfilled.

The first note of application to the minister is one of comfort if he be indeed a minister of

Jesus Christ. If he have the gift and grace, then this letter brings him comfort, and it is comfort coming from the testimony of a man whose ministry of the Word was closing. This man, anxious about Timothy, and anxious that the Church should fulfill its function, anxious therefore that this young minister should be able to fulfill his function in order that the Church might fulfill her function in the world, said : " I know Him Whom I have believed, and I am persuaded that He is able to guard my deposit." That phrase, "my deposit," may mean something deposited with Him, or something deposited with me. The popular interpretation has been that He is able to take care of something we have given over to Him. I think the apostle meant that the Lord is able to take care of a deposit which He commits to us, the deposit of Truth. If I have gift and grace, I need waste no time guarding the truth or defending it. I am sorry for the man who thinks his business is to go about defending the Truth. The Lord is able to take care of that. The safety of the deposit is the fundamental word of comfort to the man who wants to preach the Word of God.

The responsibility of the minister is that of the trusteeship of the Word of God. I hold the Word of God as a trustee ; it is mine for others.

If I am called into this ministry and am given a gift, the gift means power to convey ; that is the peculiar quality that makes a man a minister. Consequently the Truth is a deposit which He is able to guard and of which I become the trustee. I am in debt to other men for all I know of the Truth, and I cannot get out of debt so long as there remains one single sphere of my influence, in which that has not been heard which has been entrusted to me.

The final application of this letter to the minister is that it calls him to fidelity to the trusteeship of the deposit, fidelity to the exercise of the gift in order that the Truth may be known to other men ; fidelity because of Christ's appearing presently ; because of the formalism that is growing within the Church ; and because gaps in the ranks are always occurring.

The appeal is a constant appeal. The apostles, prophets, evangelists, pastors and teachers fulfill their ministry and pass on ; but the Word abides, and the responsibility of those who follow in their train abides. When next we hear of some labourer fallen in the forefront, some teacher of the Word, let us say : So help us God, a little more faithfulness, a little more of passion, a little more of suffering, a little more of outpoured life, and the victory will be won.

Titus

THE ESSENTIAL MESSAGE	THE APPLICATION

I. The central teaching—the true church of Jesus Christ.
  A. The motive of its order.
    1. General—"The truth which is according to godliness"—1:1.
    2. Negative—"To convict the gainsayers"—1:9.
      a. Liars.
      b. Evil beasts.
      c. Slow bellies.
    3. Positive—"Instructing . . . live"—2:12.
      a. Soberly.
      b. Righteously.
      c. Godly.
  B. The method of its order.
    1. General—oversight; bishops—1:7.
    2. Passive—clear vision.
      a. Of truth.
      b. Of prevailing conditions.
      c. Of true method.
    3. Active—authority—2:15.
      a. "Speak"—enunciation of truth.
      b. "Exhort"—application to need.
      c. "Reprove"—insistence upon obedience.
  C. The might of its order—the facts and forces of the Epiphanies—2:11-14.
    1. "Grace hath appeared."
    2. "The . . . appearing of the glory."
II. The abiding appeal—the church true to Jesus Christ.
  A. The inclusive church responsibility—"To adorn the doctrine"—3:10. (See "trimmed," Matt. 25:7.)
  B. The individual Christian responsibility—"Careful to maintain good works"—3:8.
  C. The consequent responsibility of those in oversight—"To affirm confidently"—3:8.
	I. To the church.
	  A. The power of the church in the world is that of her revelation of truth.
	  B. All her overseers must be men themselves under the dominion of truth.
	II. To the overseers.
	  A. The power of the overseer is that of the truth to be revealed.
	  B. The measure of the success of oversight is the measure in which the church exercises the power of truth.

IN considering this letter we need again to remind ourselves of the inter-relation between the two letters to Timothy and this one to Titus.

In the first letter to Timothy we saw that the true function of the Church is that it should be the pillar and ground of the truth. In order that this function may be fulfilled, it is necessary that every local church should be properly organized.

As in the second letter to Timothy we saw the perfect equipment of the minister, his prevailing method, and his special work ; in this letter we see the true Church of Jesus Christ so far as her ecclesiastical order is concerned. It is a very remarkable thing that this letter has to do with a church of Jesus Christ in a most difficult place. Paul described the Cretans by quotation from one of their own poets as " liars, evil beasts, slow bellies." In this letter also the most startling and amazing thing as to the possibility of Christian life is said concerning those who are in this most difficult position, and of those who are in the most trying circumstances, the bond-slaves. The apostle declared that they were to "adorn the doctrine of God."

Thus in order to show the true spiritual power of the Church, and the possibility of the lowest exercising it, the most difficult soil was selected, the most difficult circumstances were employed; and of those in the midst of trying and impossible conditions of life the finest possibilities were postulated. Thus the Spirit of God teaches us that the Church of God can be the pillar and ground of the truth in the most dark, desolate, and difficult places of the earth; and that men and women whose circumstances are most trying and difficult, can fulfill the highest function of Christianity, that of "adorning the doctrine of God our Saviour in all things."

The central teaching of this letter is that of its revelation of the true Church of Jesus Christ; and its abiding appeal that the Church be true to Jesus Christ. The Church of Jesus Christ is revealed in its true order; as to motive, method, and might. We could appropriately write as a motto over this letter the words, "Let everything be done decently and in order."

The motive of church order is revealed in a phrase at the very beginning of the letter; "The truth which is according to godliness." That word "godliness" we found in the first letter to Timothy, "great is the mystery of *godliness*." That is the truth of which the Church is to be the pillar and ground. More than half our disputes within the one catholic Church are disputes about order; whereas if we were more occupied with the reason for order, there would be very much less division about it. The passion of the apostle when he sent Titus to Crete and wrote to him there, was a passion for the truth which is according to godliness, that godliness of which the mystery is great.

The motive of the order is further explained, first negatively as the apostle shows that the result of the setting in order of the church will be that of convicting the gainsayers. In that connection we have the threefold description of the Cretans already referred to, "Liars, evil beasts, slow bellies." These are the things of animalism; and the business of the church, by its revelation of truth, is to correct and convict the gainsayers, those who by their animalism speak against godliness.

Secondly, there is a positive value. That we find stated in the second chapter in the midst of the great passage on grace, in which the apostle declared that "the grace of God hath appeared, bringing salvation to all men, instructing us, to the intent that, denying ungodliness and worldly lusts, we should live soberly and righteously and godly in this present world." The Cretans were liars; Christians were to live soberly. The Cretans were evil beasts, sensual, animal, and fierce in their passions as against one another; Christians were to live righteously, that is, in right relationships with the world around them. The Cretans were slow bellies; Christians were to live godly.

That is the motive for setting the church in order. The saints who constitute it are to deny ungodliness and worldly lusts in their own lives, and so become God's negatory forces, in the midst of the cities in which they live and move and have their being. To set our church in order so that we may worship as we desire to worship, is to act from a low motive. That the church may be the pillar and ground of the Truth: upon which and from which shall flash the light of truth; in order that the forces of death and darkness and devilry may be rebuked; ought to be the motive behind all church organization.

The method of church order is that of oversight. Elders were to be appointed, and the apostle explains the office by the use of the word "bishop." A bishop is one in oversight, one who watches, one who sees clearly. I am not now discussing as to whether the bishop is to be a pastor of one flock, or whether there are to be two or three bishops for one flock or whether one bishop is to have a diocese. I do not believe that there is any final word in the New Testament as to ecclesiastical government. The matter of supreme importance is that we understand that the office of a bishop is that of oversight. Ruskin draws attention to this fact, and in his caustic way he asks whether the bishop is aware that down yonder alley Bill has been knocking Nancy's teeth out, and if not, he declares that he is not a bishop, though his mitre be as high as a steeple. The function of the office may be described as first, active ; and then, passive. The one placed in oversight by the Holy Spirit through the gift bestowed and through grace abounding, must have a clear vision of the truth of God of which the Church is to be the pillar and ground ; he must also have a clear vision of the prevailing conditions in the midst of which the Church is to flash and shine ; he must finally have a clear vision of the true method in oversight.

The bishop is to speak, exhort, reprove ; and these words are not idly chosen. He is to speak, that is, to enunciate truth. That is his first business, but it is not his last business. He is to exhort, that is, he is to apply the truth to local conditions. That is his second business, but it is not his last business. He is to reprove, that is, he is to insist upon obedience to the truth. That is the threefold activity of the man in oversight. He is placed in oversight by the Holy Spirit of God, or he has no claim to oversight. The method of the order of the Church is that of oversight by men appointed by the Spirit of God.

The might of the Church's order is revealed in that great passage already quoted, the recitation of which is always a revelation and interpretation. How does the passage open ? "The grace of God hath appeared." How does it end ? "The appearing of the glory." The facts and forces of the two epiphanies constitute the true strength of church government, and church order, and church service. "The grace of God hath appeared . . . looking for the appearing of the glory." I have sometimes said that if I were to build a new church I should like to call it the church of the two Epiphanies ; the epiphany of grace ; and the epiphany of glory. When was the first ? When He came. When will be the second ? When He comes. The first was the Advent of grace ; the second will be the Advent of glory. When we see the first Advent we see " Glory as of the only begotten from the Father." That was the Advent of grace. When we see the second Advent, we shall see the final unveiling of grace. The one catholic Church of God ; the assembly of believers by whatever human name it is called ; lives between the light of the first Advent and the light of the second ; the first Advent, which was the setting of the Sun in blood, and the second, which shall be the rising of the Sun in glory. Between these we live, and the forces of the first and the forces of the second, the dynamic that came from the Cross, the inspiration which comes from the Crowning, constitute the might of church order, both for the overseer and for the flock in order that the Church may be the pillar and ground of the Truth.

The abiding appeal of this letter is that the Church shall be true to Jesus Christ Who is the Truth. The inclusive church responsibility is to adorn the doctrine. The individual Christian responsibility is to be careful to maintain good works. The consequent responsibility of those in oversight is to affirm confidently these things.

The inclusive responsibility of the Christian Church is to adorn the doctrine. Paul says this of the bond-slave, a servant in the most difficult situation and condition of life, and certainly if such can adorn the doctrine all others can. The word translated "adorn" is *kosmeo*, and is derived from the Greek word *kosmos*, a word suggesting order and beauty. When our Lord spoke of the virgins wise and foolish, and declared that at midnight the cry went out, Behold the bridegroom cometh ; He said that they *trimmed* their lamps. "Trimmed" is the same word as here is translated "adorn." To trim the lamp was to snuff the wick. That is the way to adorn the doctrine. A wick is snuffed that the flame may burn the brighter ; and in proportion as that poor carbon of our life knows the principle of the Cross, which is the snuffing of the wick, we adorn the doctrine. It does seem so impossible to adorn the doctrine ; but it is not so. I once heard Dr. Watkinson illustrate this. He said : Here is a piece of music. I take it up and look at it. I notice that the marks upon the page are darker and thicker here, and more straggling there ; I am told it is a wonderful piece of music, but I cannot comprehend it. Presently some one comes and takes the piece of music, and plays it upon an instrument ; and so the player *adorns* the music. The player does not compose it, is quite unequal to composing it, but he plays it, interprets it, *adorns it*, to his fellow man who has no knowledge of it. That is the great business of the Christian Church, to adorn the doctrine. We cannot create the doctrine ; the doctrine is created ; but this great mystery of godliness the Church is to adorn by living it. That is the supreme responsibility of the Church.

The individual Christian responsibility is to carefully maintain good works. That phrase does not refer to charitable philanthropy. It does not mean doing meritorious things in order to win salvation. It means doing all good, true noble, beautiful things, out of the forces of salvation. Alone I cannot perfectly adorn the doctrine; but I can watch and be careful to maintain good works, and in that measure I contribute to the adorning of the doctrine. That is the individual responsibility.

The consequent responsibility of those in oversight; bishops, elders, those gifted and having grace, is that they affirm confidently. We do not help men and women to adorn the doctrine when we debate our doubts in their presence. We may have doubts; I suppose every man has them. I have them, doubts and difficulties, questionings, problems, but I never preach them. Let us wait until the light has become clearer if there be a subject on which we are in doubt, before we speak about it. We are to affirm confidently the essential, fundamental things of the Christian faith epitomised in that passage concerning the mystery of godliness.

Our general application may be briefly made. First this letter reveals to me the fact that the power of the Church in the world is that of her revelation of the truth of God. I dare not begin an exposition of that, yet ponder it well. The Church is not influential because she is able to manipulate the affairs of the State. The Church is powerful in the measure in which she is revealing the truth of God in her own life. That is the central truth of this letter. Concerning the Church this also is revealed, that all overseers must be men themselves under the dominion of the truth; and the principle of selecting a leader, a bishop, must be that of his mastery by the truth; and I am not now referring merely to those who preach; but to all those who hold office in the Christian Church. Trustees, managers, deacons, stewards, who have been appointed because of their wealth or social influence, are a hindrance and not a help. It is on the basis of spiritual life, resulting from mastery by the truth, that all must be placed in office in the Christian Church if she is to fulfill her function.

The application of the letter to overseers therefore is; first that the power of the overseer is that of the truth and not that of his office. No man has any real power because he holds office. The only power of the overseer is that of the truth he proclaims, and confidently affirms, until it captures and masters those who hear it. The measure of success in oversight therefore, is the measure in which the Church exercises the power of the truth. The test of success is not the crowd; but the souls transformed under the power of the Word who adorn the doctrine, and thus fulfill the holy function of being the pillar and ground of the truth.

Philemon

THE ESSENTIAL MESSAGE	THE APPLICATION

I. **The central teaching**—pictures of Christianity in its outworking.
A. Of individuals.
  1. Paul
    a. Triumph over circumstances in the fellowship of Christ—1, 9.
    b. Triumph over personal authority in the power of love—8, 9.
    c. Triumph over inclination in a passion for righteousness—13, 14.
  2. Onesimus—the change—11.
  3. Philemon—the principles—5-7:
    a. Love.
    b. Faith.
B. Of social relations.
  1. Paul and Philemon—"Love seeketh not its own"—14.
  2. Paul and Onesimus—"Love beareth all things"—17-19.
  3. Onesimus and Philemon—"Love suffereth long, and is kind."
    a. The slave to return—12.
    b. The master to receive him—16, 17, 21.
  4. The church—"Love never faileth"
    a. Interested—1, 2.
    b. Cooperative.
 	
II. **The abiding appeal**—the power of Christ in its inworking.
A. Ephesians—"Be filled with the Spirit"—v. 18.
B. Philippians—"Have this mind"—2:5.
C. Colossians—"Let the word of Christ . . ."—3:16.
	I. **To the individual.**
	A. Life in Christ changes every relationship.
	B. Our relationships to others test our relationship to Christ.
	
	II. **To the church.** (Social evils are to be changed by transformed lives.)

IN this letter as in the second and third letters of John, we have pictures and portraits which serve as illustrations.

The letters of the first imprisonment of Paul, in the order of their placing in our Bible, were those to the Ephesians, the Philippians, the Colossians, and Philemon. The value of the last consists in the fact that it is an illustration of the outworking into every-day life of the great doctrines dealt with in the other three. It is a page of pictures of Christianity in its outworking. They are all boldly drawn, in bare outline, yet full of beauty. We have first, pictures of individuals; Paul, Philemon, Onesimus. Secondly, pictures of social relationships; Paul and Philemon; Paul and Onesimus; Paul, Philemon, and Onesimus; and finally we have a picture of the Church. Thus in this one page of the New Testament we have at least seven pictures presented to the mind. Let us first look at these pictures in bare outline.

The first is that of Paul. Of course we have no biography, no autobiography; no detail about those minor matters of human life which we so perpetually emphasize when we tell the story of the lives of men; but the essential facts of his character are revealed in this letter all unconsciously by the writer.

First this letter reveals Paul as a man of triumph over circumstances in fellowship with Christ. He is seen secondly as a man triumphing over the right to exercise personal authority in the power of his love. He is also seen as a man triumphing over personal inclination in a great passion for righteousness. If there were no other revelation of Paul in the whole of the New Testament, this in itself reveals the transformation wrought in him, and manifested through him, as the result of his life in Christ, and consequent fellowship with Christ.

Paul was a prisoner in Rome, and by his imprisonment all his missionary journeyings were at an end; the burning passion of his heart to be out upon the highway of missionary endeavour, pressing ever on to the regions beyond, might have been quenched as he found himself held by the irksome chain of his imprisonment. That, however, is not the way in which Paul refers to his imprisonment. He describes himself as "Paul a prisoner of Christ Jesus." That is perfect triumph over circumstances in the power of fellowship with Christ. That is the first fact of the outworking of Christianity in individual experience. Fellowship with Christ gives the individual perfect triumph over circumstances. Paul was a prisoner not of Rome, not of the Roman emperor, but of Jesus Christ. He saw through all the secondary, incidental things, to the primary and fundamental fact, that, to the man abandoned to the will of his Lord, nothing can happen outside the good and perfect and acceptable will of God. How many of us really know what it is, in circumstances of limitation, when all our highest aspirations seem checked and thwarted, when our passion to work for God is not allowed to find vent and exercise, to sit down and write of ourselves as the prisoners of Christ Jesus? That is the privilege of all the saints, but it is only possible to those who are living in true fellowship with Jesus Christ.

The next note is that of triumph in the power of love over the right to exercise authority. Not that the authority of Paul was lessened; not that his appeal would fail to produce the effect he desired; but here was a man who had the right

to enjoin that which was befitting, but who said, I will not enjoin, command thee; I prefer to beseech thee for love's sake. That is the perfect victory of love in the life of a man; when he is able not to command, though his authority for so doing may be vested in Christ, but chooses rather to deal with others as God does, by beseeching in love. That is the Divine method; "As though God were intreating by us; we beseech you on behalf of Christ, be ye reconciled to God."

Then finally there was triumph over personal inclination in a passion for righteousness. Notice the two *I woulds* of Paul in verses thirteen and fourteen. "Whom *I would* fain have kept with me" is the "*I would*" of personal inclination. Onesimus was the child of his bonds, he would have ministered to him and made things easier for him, so that the apostle said, I would like to keep him with me. But the second "*I would*" is the revelation of his sacrifice of personal inclination, because he knew the other course to be right. It was a triumph over inclination in the passion for the right.

When I think of Paul I am usually impressed by the magnificence of his intellect sanctified by the indwelling Spirit; and by his tremendous devotion to his Lord; but here I see the profoundest things of his character. Christianity outworking through his experience was manifested as triumphing over circumstances in the fellowship of Christ, so that he could say I am the prisoner of Christ, while to all human seeming he was the prisoner of Rome; triumphing over the right to exercise personal authority on highest levels, in the power of love, so that rather than enjoin, he besought; triumphing over inclination to keep Onesimus to be useful to himself, in the passion which was in his heart for the doing of the right thing in all circumstances.

The next picture is more briefly drawn. It is of "Onesimus, who was aforetime unprofitable to thee, but now is profitable to thee and to me." There was a sanctified humour in Paul's play upon words here. It was Martin Luther who said, "We are all the Lord's Onesimi, we are all the Lord's profitable servants. How have we been made profitable to the Lord? We were unprofitable." This man, said Paul in effect, when he was with you, Philemon, bore a name to which he was not true; he is now Onesimus in reality, profitable to thee and to me.

The picture of Onesimus is that of the radical change which Christ works in the life of any man of whom He gains possession; the unprofitable becomes profitable. It is a perpetual picture of what Christ does with men. The waste, unprofitable material He makes valuable, profitable.

The last of these single pictures is that of Philemon; "Hearing of thy love, and of the faith which thou hast towards the Lord Jesus, and towards all the saints . . . for I had much joy and comfort in thy love, because the hearts of the saints have been refreshed through thee, brother."

Philemon was a man governed by two principles, faith and love. These were associated in his practical life. As to faith Paul said, "The faith which thou hast towards the Lord Jesus, and towards all the saints." Faith towards the Lord Jesus, and faith towards the saints. The preposition employed in each case is the same; and what is meant in one case is meant in the other. The fundamental principle in the life of the Christian man is faith towards the Lord Jesus, and towards the saints; and that faith towards the Lord Jesus and towards the saints is expressed in love; love works through faith.

The experimental order is revealed if we take the portraits in the other order. Beginning with that of Philemon, we see the principles of faith and love; glancing next at Onesimus, we see a man changed from unprofitable to profitable; finally, looking at Paul, we see the triumph of Christianity in its outworking in a threefold application.

Turning to the picture of social relationship we come first to that of Paul and Philemon. I should be inclined to write underneath the picture of these two men as I see them here, "Love seeketh not its own." The apostle wrote to his friend, "Without thy mind I would do nothing; that thy goodness should not be as of necessity, but of free will." That is very simple and very human; yet the very simplicity and humanness of it constitute its sublimity and beauty. In effect Paul said: I should like to have kept Onesimus, but I would not without thy mind. If I had kept Onesimus you would not have complained; but you would have been helpless, and your goodness would have been of necessity. I want your goodness to be manifested towards this man, of your own free will I am seeking the development of your Christian character at its highest, noblest, and best. I would have kept him; but I am seeking not only his blessing, and his restoration to favour; but your blessing, and the development of all that is highest and best in you. If you did a good thing of necessity, it would not be on the highest level; but if a good thing be done of your own free will, it is on the highest level. Thus in this beautiful, tender, gracious regard of Paul for Philemon is revealed the love which seeketh not its own.

The next picture is that of Paul and Onesimus. Beneath that I would write the words: "Love beareth all things." The Greek word translated *beareth* suggests a roof upon which the rain falling, the person standing underneath is protected. Love is a covering roof; sheltering the friend beneath. "If he hath wronged thee at all, or oweth thee aught, put that to mine account," wrote Paul. Onesimus the unprofitable runaway slave was the child of Paul's very heart, the child of his bonds; and Paul's love was the roof over Onesimus which protected him. Love beareth all things. That is the relationship which Christ creates between men.

The third picture of relationship is of that between Onesimus and Philemon. Here let us write the words "Love suffereth long, and is kind." What will Christianity do in this case? Onesimus was the runaway slave of Philemon. What will Christianity do with him? Send him back. The slave must return. What will Christianity do in the case of Philemon? It will prepare him to receive him as a brother; "No longer as a servant, but more than a servant, a brother beloved"; and as a partner, "if then thou countest me a partner, receive him as myself." Then followed that touch, which did not say the last thing, but pointed the way to it as the apostle wrote, "Having confidence in thine obedience I write unto thee, knowing that thou wilt do *even beyond what I say*." That something beyond was almost certainly the giving of his freedom to the slave. Christianity sent Onesimus back to fulfill the obligations of the law. Christianity taught Philemon to receive the slave kindly, and cancel the obligations of the law in the power of indwelling love.

Finally we have a picture of the church in the

house of Philemon. Its title may fittingly be "Love never faileth." Paul wrote to the church, because in the highest ideal of Christianity you cannot write to the individual without the church being interested and being brought into coöperation. The true fellowship in Christ Jesus is such that if one member suffers all suffer, and if one member rejoices all rejoice; when one member fulfills obligation and goes back to duty, all the members coöperate with him in his return; if one member fulfills the law of love and receives the runaway, all the members enter into the joy of heart that comes to the one. We have here then a picture of an ideal church in which the runaway slave is to be received on his return as a brother and a partner by all who share the common life, and walk in the common light, in the power of the common love.

If this be the central teaching of these pictures of Christianity in the outworking, what is their abiding appeal? I am constrained to say that it is not to be found stated in words in the epistle. The pictures themselves create the appeal. They appeal to all who look upon them and who share the life which produces these results, to yield themselves to that life entirely, absolutely.

In order to find the appeal of this letter stated in actual words I go back to the other epistles written in imprisonment. It has often been pointed out that some of the greatest things we have ever had for our spiritual instruction were written in prison. Paul never rendered greater service to the Church of God than in those days when he was shut up in prison. No others are more wonderful, more full of light and glory, more evidently the revelation of the Spirit of God to His servant, than the letters of the imprisonment. The apostle was thinking the Ephesian, Colossian, and Philippian letters, and while such thoughts filled his mind he wrote this letter to Philemon about a runaway slave. There was a time when some thought that this page should be left out of the New Testament because the subject was not worthy the dignity of an apostle; but thank God that in His overruling in the arrangement and selection and preservation of the writings which are essentially of the Spirit, Philemon is not left out. In this epistle we see the commonplaces of every-day life set in the atmosphere and power of the sublimest things of the eterni-

ties. Philemon is but a page of pictures resulting from Ephesians, Philippians, and Colossians.

I go then to these great epistles and take from them the central words of each in order to find the words of appeal. In Ephesians, that great unveiling of the glorious Church, "Be filled with the Spirit." In Philippians, that great unveiling of Christian character, "Have this mind in you, which was also in Christ Jesus." In Colossians, that great unveiling of the glory of Christ as at the disposal of the Church, "Let the word of Christ dwell in you richly." That is the threefold abiding appeal of the letter to Philemon.

How is it possible for me to live the life of faith and love? How is it possible for me, who have been most unprofitable, to be indeed a man profitable? How is it possible for me ever to know such triumph over circumstances as Paul manifested; such triumph over personal authority in the power of love; such triumph over personal inclination in the passion for righteousness?—How can I fulfill this life?

All the necessary resources are in Christ. Then the power of Christ must have full sway, and right of way in and through me; and my responsibilities are stated in the words of these great epistles, "Be filled with the Spirit," "Have this mind in you, which was also in Christ Jesus," "Let the word of Christ dwell in you richly."

What then are the applications of this brief letter? First as to the individual. This letter teaches me that life in Christ changes every relationship. All the relationships that might be suggested do not appear upon this page: but those which do appear have a bearing on all the rest. My son, my daughter, my father, my husband, my wife, my neighbour; all bear new relationship to me the moment I am a man in Christ. I bear a new relationship to them, and consequently they bear a new relationship to me. I have a new relationship to my servant if I am a man in Christ. I have a new relationship to my master if I am a man in Christ.

I learn also that our relationships to others test our relationship to Christ. Not by what I sing about my Lord, not by what I affirm of relationship to Christ, but by my relationship to other men, is my relationship to my Lord made manifest. Philemon angrily refusing to receive Onesimus would have contradicted all the profession he made of love for Jesus Christ. Onesimus refusing to return to Philemon would have rendered null and void all his profession of faith in Jesus Christ. Had Paul yielded to personal inclination he would by that act have proved a measure of disloyalty to Christ. It is the relationships I bear to other men which constitute the real test of my relationship to Christ.

If I am living in true fellowship with Him, letting His mind be in me by being filled with His Spirit, and having His word richly dwelling in me, my relationship to others will be changed; and my relationship to Christ will be revealed.

There is one word of application to the Church at large. From this letter one of the profoundest matters is learned; that social evils are to be ended by the transformation men, and in no other way. There is no protest here against slavery. There was a day when Christian teachers used this very letter in defence of slavery. We know full well that any such use was absolutely unwarranted. Onesimus was sent back to Philemon, but Philemon was charged to receive him in a new way. The supreme work of Christianity is to transform men, so that out of their transformed lives shall come the transformation of all social conditions, and the victories of righteousness and of love.

Hebrews

THE ESSENTIAL MESSAGE		THE APPLICATION
I. The central teaching. A. The perfection of the reve- lation through the Son. 　1. Superseding all others. 　　a. Angelic. 　　b. Human. 　　c. Ritualistic. 　2. Meeting all needs. 　　a. Prophetic. 　　b. Priestly. 　　c. Kingly. 　3. Ensuring all victories. 　　a. Individual. 　　b. Social. 　　c. Universal. B. The principle of life by faith—faith defined: 　1. Volitional surrender (in spite of appearances). 　2. Faith active. 　　a. Doing. 　　b. Suffering. 　　c. Waiting. 　3. Faith triumphant. 　　a. In the deed. 　　b. Over the suffering. 　　c. Ultimately with God. C. The peril of death through apostasy. 　1. Apostasy defined— disobedience (because of appearances). 　2. Apostasy active. 　　a. Doing. 　　b. Suffering. 　　c. Waiting. 　3. Apostasy hopeless. 　　a. In the deed. 　　b. Under the suffering. 　　c. Ultimately without God.	**II. The abiding appeal.** A. Warnings. 　1. As to speech of Son— 2:1a; "Lest": 　　a. Haply we drift (2:1). 　　b. Haply . . . falling 　　　. . . God (3:12). 　　c. Hardened (3:13). 　　d. Haply . . . rest 　　　. . . short (4:1). 　2. As to goal of God. 　　a. "Falleth short of grace" (12:15)—life. 　　b. "Root of bitterness" (12:15)—love. 　　c. "Profane person" (12:16)—light. B. Encouragements—"Let us." 　1. As to Son. 　　a. Prophet: "Fear"—4:1; "Give diligence"—4:11. 　　b. Priest: "Hold fast"— 4:14; "Draw near"—4:16. 　　c. King: "Press on"—6:1. 　2. As to saintship. 　　a. "Draw near"—10:22; "Hold fast"—10:23. 　　b. "Consider one another"—10:24. 　3. As to service. 　　a. Towards the goal: "Lay aside"; "Run"— 12:1; "Have grace"—12:28. 　　b. Suffering: "Go forth"—13:13; "Offer praise"—13:15.	**I. To the church.** A. The message assumes the biblical conception of God. (To deny this concep- tion is to destroy these conclusions.) 　1. Universal sovereignty. 　2. Knowable and revealing. B. The message depends upon the Christology of the writer—see 1:2, 3. (To deny this Chris- tology is to destroy these appeals.) **II. To the individual.** A. The power of faith. B. The peril of apostasy.

F OR inclusive value, suggestive teaching beauty of statement, perfection of system, perhaps there is no writing of the New Testament more wonderful than this letter to the Hebrews.

Its central teaching is threefold; first, the perfection of the revelation through the Son; sec-ondly, the principle of life by faith; thirdly, the peril of death through apostasy.

As to the first, the perfection of the revelation through the Son, there are three values of the revelation set forth; that it supersedes all others; that it meets all needs; and that it ensures all victories.

267

This letter does not reveal Christ to us in His personal glory as some others do; but it does show that through the Son, God has given us His most perfect revelation of Himself. God is the first word of the letter; it is the theme of the letter. It is God revealed; God at work; and God triumphing. As we take our way through this letter, we are following the pathway of God through human history to consummation. It begins where the first verse of Genesis begins; and ere it closes, we find ourselves upon the mount, amid all the hosts of glory, as we find them in the Apocalypse.

It teaches us first of all that the revelation through the Son supersedes all others; angelic, human, and ritualistic. It supersedes the angelic; for the Son is superior to angels. It supersedes the human, as represented by Moses and Joshua; for the Son is greater than the servants. It supersedes the ritualistic method, the method of the priest and the altar, the method of the temple and sacrifice, and all the things through which God did by picture and symbol speak to men of Himself; because when the Son came, there was fulfillment of all of which these were but the shadows. When the Son came to speak from God, angels were no longer required, human teachers and interpreters were set on one side, all ritualism was rendered unnecessary.

The revelation through the Son was sufficient to meet all human need. The first need of man is a prophet who shall utter the word of God as the standard for his life. He needs also a priest, whose mediation shall reconcile him to God. He needs finally a king who shall govern according to the will of God.

When the Son came He came as Prophet, Priest, and King, meeting all these needs; and this is clearly set forth in the argument of the writer. God speaks through the Son; and angels, and Moses, and Joshua are silent. So the prophetic need is met. Then He establishes a new covenant; and His priesthood is higher than that of Aaron, higher than the Levitical order, being of the order of Melchizedek. Thus the priestly need is met. Finally, He, as King, establishes the Kingdom of God in this world. So the kingly need is met.

Once again, the revelation through the Son ensures all victories. The individual is perfected through the Son. The old economy is abolished because it made nothing perfect. Social victory is realized through the Son; "Ye are come unto mount Zion, and unto the City of the living God, the heavenly Jerusalem." Finally, universal victory is made certain, for the ultimate glory is that triumph of God wherein He Who suffered shall find His perfect satisfaction.

All that, so far as we are concerned, may be said to be objective. Faith is revealed as the principle by which these things become subjective, part of our own experience. If there is one book of the Bible which more carefully than any other defines faith, it is this letter. It contains one passage in which faith is defined in so many words, but that is not the only definition of faith which it affords. Faith, according to the whole teaching of the writer, is volitional surrender, and obedience in spite of appearances. Faith is not merely intellectual conviction. Faith is the action of the will which follows intellectual conviction and harmonizes with intellectual conviction. That is the only faith that saves. Faith as a creed, apprehended by the intellect, never saves. If we carefully follow the argument of the writer, when he is dealing with the subject of the people who could not enter in because of unbelief, we discover that unbelief is described as disobedience. The men who triumphed by faith were men who did things because they believed, when all appearances made it seem as though their doing was the doing of unutterable folly. Think of the unutterable folly of any man turning his back on Ur of the Chaldees and going, no one knew whither, not even himself, because he believed God, and looked for a city. That is faith; volitional surrender and obedience in spite of appearances. That is how the letter to the Hebrews in its wider teaching defines faith.

Faith is not only defined, it is revealed at work. Faith is not merely a sentiment, an attitude of mind; it is energy that drives and accomplishes. These men did something. Faith also suffers, and the story of suffering is graphically told. And finally, faith waits, the most difficult thing that faith ever has to do; "These all died in faith, not having received the promises. . . . God having provided some better thing concerning us, that apart from us they should not be made perfect." And they are waiting still! The life of faith does not end when we die. The life of faith runs on into the paradise of God. There is no uncertainty in the waiting, no unhappiness, no misery; but they are waiting because the victory is not yet won, the work is not done, and God's Kingdom has not yet come. For us the most heavenly activity, and the most difficult activity of faith, is to wait. So long as I can work, even though I may suffer, it is not so difficult; but when I can no longer work, or suffer, and simply have to wait, that is the most trying activity of faith.

Finally, this letter gives us a picture of faith triumphant. It is triumphant in the deed. Go through the eleventh chapter again, and see how constantly those men did things, and how in the doing there was triumph. The things that they did are the things that have made the world what it is to-day, in so far as it harmonizes with the will of God. Faith suffers, but in the suffering it is triumphant. It makes sorrow the occasion for song. Finally faith is triumphant in its waiting, for it is in itself the assurance of things hoped for, the certainty of the ultimate accomplishment of the will of God.

The final note of the teaching of this letter reveals the peril of death through apostasy. Apostasy is defined here. It is the exact opposite of faith, and consists of disobedience because of appearances. Let the history interpret the teaching. The men of old said, The land is full of Anakim, and walled cities; these were appearances; because of them they disobeyed; that is apostasy; and so they failed to enter into rest.

Therein is revealed the whole truth about apostasy. Men are not apostate because the doctrine they hold is wrong. They are apostate when they hold the true doctrine, and refuse to obey it. Disobedience is the unbelief that hardens the spirit, and ends in death. Apostasy is active also, it will do things. Apostasy will suffer; and will wait. Let no man imagine that by apostasy he will escape from effort, or suffering, or waiting. The strain of effort, the actuality of suffering, the tragedy of waiting all continue; but mark the difference. As faith is always triumphant in deed, and over suffering, and ultimately with God; apostasy is always hopeless in the deed, in the suffering, and ultimately without God. The end of apostasy is

restlessness, just as surely as the end of faith is perfect rest.

In the light of this central teaching, let us hear the abiding appeal of the letter. The first note of that appeal is one of warning, and the application is introduced in every case by the use of the word " Lest." There are two groups of such warnings. The first deals with perils threatening us in view of the finality of the speech of the Son; and the second with perils confronting us in view of the ultimate victory of God.

The first group is found in the section of the letter specially dealing with the speech of the Son. God has spoken to us by the Son; we ought therefore to give most earnest heed to the things we have heard.

Take the four warnings;

" Lest haply we drift."

" Lest haply there shall be in any of you an evil heart of unbelief, in falling away from the living God."

" Lest any of you be hardened by the deceitfulness of sin."

" Lest haply, a promise being left of entering into his rest, any one of you should seem to come short of it."

That is a sequence. Lest we drift; that is the first thing; it is the picture of a vessel dragging its anchor and drifting. What next? " An evil heart of unbelief, in falling away from the living God." If I drift from the things the Son has said, I fall away from the living God Whom the Son reveals. With what result? I am " hardened by the deceitfulness of sin." With what issue? " A promise being left," I " come short of it." To avoid the first is to be saved from all the rest. To fail in the first is inevitably to pass through all the experience described in the rest. No storm is sweeping the sea; we are still close to the shore; but drifting just a little way. If by God's grace we recognize the drift, and hasten back, we shall not fall from the living God, we shall not become hardened, we shall not lose our rest.

The second group is found in the twelfth chapter;

" Follow after peace with all men, and the sanctification without which no man shall see the Lord: looking carefully lest there be any man that falleth short of the grace of God; lest any root of bitterness springing up trouble you, and thereby the many be defiled ; *lest* there be any fornicator, or profane person, as Esau, who for one mess of meat sold his own birthright."

These three warnings occur in that part of the letter which has to do peculiarly with the ultimate victory of God. In the eleventh chapter we pass through the hall of the heroes and heroines of faith in the past ; the last note is that which declares that the whole of them are not yet made perfect. Then in chapter twelve, we are brought face to face with our own experience in its relation to the ultimate victory of God.

The first warnings had to do with the revelation of the Father through the Son, and the notes were those of personal relationship ; Lest we drift, Lest we fall away from the living God, Lest we become hardened, Lest we lose our rest. But now there is something more important than our rest, our heaven. It is God's glory which is in view, the joy that was set before the Christ. We are responsible about that.

"Lest there be any man that falleth short of the grace of God." Falling short of the grace of God means being unable to run the race, or to coöperate with God in the work that makes His Kingdom come.

"Lest any root of bitterness, springing up . . the many be defiled" and therefore cannot run the race.

Lest there be a profane person who will turn his back upon the high, supernal glory of God for some mess of earthly pottage, and so fail to coöperate towards the consummation.

These warnings do touch personal salvation, but that is not the ultimate meaning of them. If we fail, we fail to coöperate with God for the bringing in of His Kingdom and His glory. Falling short of grace is falling short of life ; the root of bitterness is falling short of love ; the profane person is falling short of light. If we fall short of life, of love, and of light, we cannot run this race and be fellow-workers with God. These three warnings then have ultimately to do, not with the matter of personal salvation, but with the matter of our fitness for coöperation with God in order to the winning of His victory in the world. Thus, warnings greet us at the beginning of the letter, and confront us at its close.

The appeal of this letter is also one full of encouragement, and the notes are introduced by the words : "Let us." They fall into three groups ; words intended to encourage us in our relation to the Son through Whom the final speech has been uttered ; words to encourage us as to our own saintship ; and words to encourage us in our service.

Those referring to the Son touch upon His threefold work as Prophet, Priest, and King.

The first two are ;

"Let us fear therefore.

"Let us therefore give diligence."

We are to fear lest the promise being made we do not enter in. We are to be diligent "that no man fall after the same example of disobedience." Both these words of encouragement have to do with the prophetic work of Christ, the teaching of Christ. "The word of God is living, and active, and sharper than any two-edged sword, and piercing even to the dividing of soul and spirit." Let us fear lest we fail of the promise made in the Word, and let us be diligent in order that there be no disobedience to the Word.

The next two are ;

"Having then a great high Priest, Who hath passed through the heavens, Jesus the Son of God, let us hold fast our confession."

"Let us therefore draw near with boldness unto the throne of grace, that we may receive mercy, and may find grace to help us in time of need."

These words have to do with the priestly work of the Son, and need no exposition.

The last word is ;

"Wherefore let us cease to speak of the first principles of Christ, and press on unto perfection."

That is a picture of the ultimate victory of the King, Who will build the city, and establish the Kingdom ; and towards that victory we are to press on.

Then we come to words of encouragement concerning our saintship ;

"Let us draw near with a true heart in fullness of faith, having our hearts sprinkled from an evil conscience, and our body washed with pure water :

"Let us hold fast the confession of our hope that it waver not ; for He is faithful that promised :

"Let us consider one another to provoke unto love and good works."

As in the first group of five words we have encouragement as to the Son as Prophet, Priest,

and King; here we have words of encouragement as to the experience of saintship in the
present life, and they again need no exposition.

Finally, we have words of encouragement in
our service ;

"Let us also, seeing we are compassed about
with so great a cloud of witnesses, lay aside
every weight, and the sin which doth so easily
beset us ;

"Let us run with patience the race that is set
before us."

"Let us have grace."

In order to coöperate in the work which will
eventuate in the victory we are to lay aside all
that hinders, run with patience, and have grace.

"Let us therefore go forth unto Him without
the camp, bearing His reproach. . . . Let
us offer up a sacrifice of praise to God continually."

In such service we are to have fellowship with
Him in suffering ; and fellowship in praise.

The teaching of this letter assumes the Biblical
conception of God. Its first note is that of His
universal sovereignty. The God of the Bible is
not a Being within the universe, enslaved by it.

He is Sovereign. The God of the Bible moreover is knowable and revealing. He spake in
times past ; He has spoken in His Son. If we
deny these things we shall of course find no
teaching in the letter to the Hebrews. There can
be no meaning in it, apart from these fundamental
conceptions of God.

Again, the teaching depends upon the Christology of the writer. We have it set before us in
the early part of the letter. There is a sevenfold description of Christ, leaving no question as
to the position He occupied in the mind of the
writer. To deny the Christology of the writer is
to deny his appeals. If our Christ is not the
Christ of this writer, He is not superior to
angels, to Moses, to Joshua, to Aaron, to all that
magnificent ritualism which the writer knew so
well.

If this letter is to be of any value to us in the
Christian Church, we must be true to its conceptions of God and its presentation of Christ.

To the individual, the word of application is
that of its teaching as to the power of faith, and
the peril of apostasy.

James

THE ESSENTIAL MESSAGE	THE APPLICATION

I. The central teaching.
  A. Positive—faith in God produces life according to the will of God.
    1. Personal life.
      a. In trial—patience.
      b. In enticement—steadfastness.
      c. In religion—love.
    2. Relative life.
      a. In thought—no respect of persons.
      b. In speech—the silence of heavenly wisdom.
      c. In action—peace.
  B. Negative—life contrary to the will of God denies faith in God.
    1. Personal life.
      a. In trial—storm-tossed.
      b. In enticement—drawn away.
      c. In religion—unbridled.
    2. Relative life.
      a. In thought—respect of persons.
      b. In speech—set on fire of hell.
      c. In action—strife.
II. The abiding appeal.
  A. Prove your faith.
    1. Venture on it.
    2. Vindicate it.
  B. Perfect your patience.
    1. It comes by proving faith.
    2. It issues in perfect life.
	I. To the individual.
	  A. The life of faith is a life of peril.
	    1. It challenges the spirit of the age.
	    2. It denies the call of the flesh.
	    3. It provokes the enmity of the devil.
	  B. The life of faith is the life of power.
	    1. It is superior to the spirit of the age.
	    2. It triumphs over the claim of the flesh.
	    3. It causes the devil to flee.
	  C. Life lacking these signs is not the life of faith.
	II. To the church.
	  A. In the assembly faith kills class distinctions.
	  B. In the assembly faith makes strife impossible.
	  C. In the assembly faith is the principle of communion.

IN dealing with the content of this letter we indicated its theme by suggesting as a sub-title, Christ and His Ethic. Its burden is ethical, not doctrinal. Some of the fundamental truths of our most holy religion are hardly referred to from beginning to end. The writer was preëminently occupied with the practice of Christianity.

There are many parallelisms between the Manifesto of Jesus and this letter of James. Let us recall three passages in that Manifesto (Matthew v. 20 ; v. 48 ; vi. 1) ;

"I say unto you, that except your righteous-ness shall exceed the righteousness of the scribes and Pharisees, ye shall in no wise enter into the Kingdom of heaven."

" Ye therefore shall be perfect, as your heavenly Father is perfect."

" Take heed that ye do not your righteousness before men, to be seen of them : else ye have no reward with your Father which is in heaven."

I have taken these three because in some senses they are inclusive. In the first one, by way of introduction our Lord uttered the fundamental demand of His ethic ; " Except your righteousness shall exceed the righteousness of the scribes and

Pharisees, ye shall in no wise enter into the Kingdom of heaven." These words were spoken immediately before the actual enunciation of His laws.

In the second the King revealed the ultimate aim of His ethic ; " Ye therefore shall be perfect, as your heavenly Father is perfect."

Immediately following we have the King's revelation of the abiding principle of His ethic ; " Take heed that ye do not your righteousness before men, to be seen of them."

The fundamental demand was for righteousness exceeding the righteousness of the scribes and Pharisees, which was intellectually orthodox, but lacked the harmony of the corresponding life.

The ultimate aim was that of the perfecting of humanity in harmony with the character of God.

The abiding principle was that of doing everything as in the sight of God, and to be pleasing to Him, rather than in the sight of men, to be pleasing to them. In these three words then we have the master principle of the ethic of Jesus.

For the purpose of the present study and by way of introduction let us give a little closer attention to the word revealing the ultimate aim ; " Ye therefore shall be perfect, as your heavenly Father is perfect." With that in mind we turn at once to the letter of James, and within the first few sentences we find these words, " Let patience have its perfect work, that ye may be perfect and entire, lacking in nothing." The interpretation of the perfection which James enjoined must be discovered by an understanding of the perfection which Jesus demanded.

Before uttering His laws, Jesus had said that righteousness must exceed the righteousness of the scribes and Pharisees. Righteousness is not to be a thing of words, but of works ; not of creed, but of conduct ; not orthodoxy of doctrine, but fulfillment of duty. Perfection is righteousness according to the will of God, rather than according to the opinion of men.

That perfection, the perfection of righteousness which seeks to be pleasing to God, and makes that the one unending, unceasing, unbending aim of the life, can only result from faith in God. So that the root of righteousness is faith, and the fruit of faith is righteousness. That takes us back to that central enunciation of the master principle of life in the prophecy of

Habakkuk, " The just shall live by his faith." That word of Habakkuk reappears constantly in the teaching of Jesus. He consistently linked life to belief. One supreme illustration is found in a word recorded in the third chapter of John, " He that believeth on the Son hath eternal life." We must not be narrow in our interpretation of that great word. It has to do most certainly with the initial fact that a man believing on Jesus receives the gift of life ; but it has a much wider application. Life is the outcome of faith. " The just shall live by his faith," both as to the beginning, and as to the continued victories and manifestations. The proof of a man's belief in Christ is the manifestation of the Christ-life in that man's life.

Paul argued for the same principle and always in relation to Christ Himself. In Galatians he declared that there is no righteousness by law, and quoted the word of Habakkuk. In Romans he put the declaration into close connection with faith in the gospel of the Son of God. In Hebrews, he—or some one else—put the same quotation in relation to the second Advent of our Lord.

That principle is recognized by James. It was stated to the prophet ; the fulfillment of it was claimed by Christ in His own Person ; it was argued by the great apologist of the gospel, Paul ; it was illustrated by James. The theme of James was preëminently that of faith producing works. James did not argue against faith ; he argued for faith.

Recognizing this fact we turn to consider the essential message of the letter, and find that its central teaching has a positive and a negative emphasis. The positive teaching may be summarized thus ; Faith in God produces life according to the will of God; while the negative teaching is that life contrary to the will of God denies faith in God.

It may appear at first sight that the teaching of this letter is entirely negative, but the negative is only of value as we discover the positive behind it. It may be said that the negative is really the central teaching ; if a man say he has faith, let him show it by his works ; life contrary to the will of God denies faith in God ; if a man shall say he has faith, and his life is not life that springs out of faith, then his affirmation of faith is false. But it is at once evident that such a negative statement implies a positive truth. Consequently we have in this letter quite as surely the positive teaching that faith in God produces life according to the will of God.

The abiding appeal of the letter is twofold; first, prove your faith; secondly, perfect your patience. The two injunctions are intimately associated.

There is an application of the letter; first to the individual, and secondly to the Church.

Familiarity with the movement of the letter, with its content and line of argument, will show how James first of all declared that faith in God produces life according to the will of God; and that in two respects. He gave those to whom he wrote two pictures, one of personal life, and one of relative life; and in each case he illustrated the fact that where there is faith in God, the life harmonizes with the will of God, insisting that it must do so, that there can be no escape.

His first picture is one of individual life in circumstances of trial. He shows that where a man lives by faith in such circumstances his attitude is that of patience. Faith produces patience in trial. His next picture is one of individual life in the midst of enticement to evil. In such circumstances the man living by faith remains steadfast, and is victorious over every temptation. His final picture is one of individual life in the matter of religion. When there is faith in God, " Pure religion and undefiled before our God and Father is this, to visit the fatherless and widows in their affliction, and to keep himself unspotted from the world "; that is to say, religion is love. The one and only principle which enables a man to live this life harmonizing with the will of God is faith in God.

When a man of faith is in the midst of circumstances of trial and difficulty, his attitude is that of calm patience. We know how true this is when we test the matter by personal experience. When the child of God in circumstances of trial is impatient, it is always because confidence in God wavers. Faith failing, patience passes away. Christian souls living by faith in God in the midst of circumstances of trial are not callous, not hardened. They are conscious of the sweeping of the storm; but they are filled with quietness and patience. Faith in God is the only principle which can produce that patience in the

soul of any man or woman in circumstances of trial.

In dealing with the subject of enticement to evil, James gives us a wonderful definition of the genesis of sin. No man is lured towards evil by God. A man is drawn away, enticed of his own lust. By faith in God there is steadfastness, and refusal to answer the enticement. There is no other secret of victory over temptation to sin than that of faith in God. No man is safe to-day by reason of the fact that for ten, twenty, thirty, forty years he has been a Christian. Men are not safe one moment longer than they live by simple faith in God. It is perfect faith in God which gives perfect victory over enticement towards sin.

So also in the matter of the life of religion in the truest, deepest sense of the word. There is no more wonderful definition of religion in the New Testament than this; and it is only faith in God which inspires a man to give expression to his religion in acts of love and sympathy. Destroy faith in God, and by that act you destroy love towards man.

With regard to relative life, James shows what faith does for a man in these respects; in thought, in speech, in action.

In thought, by faith in God a man ceases to be a respecter of persons. As he looks upon his fellow men, if he have faith in God, he sees these men as they are related to God, and thus loses sight of the things that the man who lacks faith in God sees. If a man has no faith in God he is material in his outlook upon his fellow men, and expresses it by differentiating between rich and poor. The man who lives by faith in God sees every man as related to God. I have sometimes said in speaking of our Lord that which is not literally true, but which is true in spirit; that Jesus looked upon scribes and Pharisees and never saw their phylacteries; and looked at poor men and never saw their rags. That is not literally true, for He saw everything; but it is spiritually true that His mind was not affected by the incidentals, but by the essentials. We divide as between men, and hold them in differing approbation on the basis of the incidentals. By faith in God every man is seen to be a man The thought of every man as to his fellow man is determined by his faith in God, or his lack of such faith. Faith in God creates that attitude of mind towards our fellow men which may be described as having no respect of persons. " There is no respect of persons with God." The man who is living by faith shares the Divine attitude of mind towards men ; he is without respect of persons.

As to speech, we must look for the positive carefully. James is emphatic about the negative, the evil of the tongue. The paragraph which immediately follows is one that speaks of the heavenly wisdom that will not lie. The speech of the man who lives by faith in God is characterized by the silence of heavenly wisdom. Faith in God makes more for silence than for speech about our fellow men.

As to action ; faith in God brings peace as between man and man. Wars, strifes, enmities, these are never the outcome of faith in God. War in any kind never results from faith in God. When we come to the individual aspect, it is certain that strife as between man and man cannot be the outcome of faith in God.

The life of faith in God is a life that has no respect for persons ; and is characterized by that carefulness in speech which is most often manifested in the silence of heavenly wisdom, and by those activities which produce peace between man and man. That constitutes the positive teaching of this letter.

We turn now to the negative. Life contrary to the will of God denies faith in God.

Personal life in trial is storm-tossed, like the waves of the sea ; and such experience is proof of lack of faith in God. I say it very carefully because I know how it searches the heart, and yet I know it is true. When in hours of trial and suffering we murmur and complain, it is because we are failing in faith.

In the matter of enticement towards evil, a man is drawn away of his own lust, and enticed. If he yield, it is because he fails in faith towards God. It is a searching, practical word. We cannot attend to the message of this letter without feeling how very practical it is. Whenever we sin it is because our faith fails. Discussions as to whether it is necessary for the believer to sin or not are surely unnecessary. Whenever we listen to the clamant cry of lust, and answer it independently of the Divine will, it is because we fight in our own strength ; but it is finally because we fail to trust in God. No man need be

overcome by enticement towards evil, if he live by faith in God.

In regard to religion, one illustration is sufficient, that of the unbridled tongue. That is the expression of an attitude of mind which is the opposite of love. Whenever the tongue is unbridled, untamed, unmanaged, there is evidence of lack of faith in God.

The negative teaching concerning relative life is equally clear. Where there is no faith in God there is respect of persons. If we show a man into a back seat in the church because he wears shabby clothes, we are saying by that action that we have lost faith in God. We have no business to know whether he has on goodly apparel or not. It is quite as possible to have respect of persons in the opposite direction, as in the one which we most often condemn. It is as possible to hold in contempt the man who is well dressed as to hold in contempt the man in rags. Faith in God does not see the incidentals. It is always conscious of the essentials.

In speech, lack of faith means the tongue set on fire of hell. Is there a more startling and awful word than that in the whole of Scripture ? A tongue set on fire of hell is the result of lack of faith in God. Where there is faith in God there is the silence of heavenly wisdom. Where it is lacking the tongue is set on fire of hell. It is almost impossible to read this word without feeling that James had in mind the symbol of the tongue of fire. Speech is always inspired in hell or in heaven. It is always the expression of heavenly wisdom or an utterance inspired of hell. When the tongue is used to say things that are contrary to love and truth, it is because there is failure of faith in God. The master principle of true speech is that of faith in God.

As to action ; wars, strifes, fightings, are all the outcome of fleshly lusts, all the result of the fact that the life is not governed by the principle of faith in God. The forces that overcome and spoil individual life, and relative life, are all the result of the absence of the master principle of faith in God.

The abiding appeal of this letter is first, Prove your faith. "Count it all joy, my brethren, when ye fall into manifold temptations ; knowing that the proof of your faith worketh patience. And let patience have its perfect work, that ye may be perfect and entire, lacking in nothing."

In this connection, prove your faith means venture on it, put it to the test. So to prove faith is to vindicate it. Vindicate your faith by venturing on it. When you venture on it, it immediately produces a definite result, and that result proves, or demonstrates, your faith.

A man says, I have faith. Let him prove it. How shall he prove it? By argument? No, by venturing on it, by doing the things that are in harmony with faith in God. If a man says that he has faith, and does not venture on it, then no results are produced. If he do not thus prove it, he cannot prove it at all. If he do not put this principle of faith into active proof, he cannot demonstrate the fact that he has faith; he rather demonstrates the fact that he lacks faith. As we pass through this letter and read the things that are denounced as evil things, and then look at our own lives, and find these things existing, we know that the measure in which these things are present is the measure of our lack of faith. On the other hand the measure in which life perfectly harmonizing with the will of God is manifest in conduct, is the measure in which we are proving that we have faith. We prove the faith we have, and so we prove that we have faith. A man says, I have faith. I have no right to deny it; but I have the right to say: Prove your faith, put it to the test; live by faith homed in God, aiming at the perfection upon which the heart of God is set, and expect that by your faith in Him He will coöperate with you in that activity. He always does. In every victory won by faith there is the evidence of faith.

The second note of the appeal is, Perfect your patience. Patience comes by proving faith; and patience issues in perfect life. "Let patience have its perfect work, that ye may be perfect and entire." Notice the process. Faith is first. I believe the thing that God says. I will prove my faith by venturing on it, and doing the thing I could not do without it. In that deed I prove my faith to another man. In that victory won, patience fills my soul, I come to quietness and strength. When that patience, which is the outcome of faith, has completed its process, I shall be "perfect and entire, lacking in nothing."

Thus it is clear that James was not arguing against faith; he was arguing for it. He revealed the fact that faith is the one and only principle that is equal to that perfection of life, upon which the heart of the Lord is set.

The application of this letter to the individual is twofold. It teaches me first that the life of faith is a life of peril; and secondly, that the life of faith is a life of power.

The life of faith is a life of peril. We cannot live the life of faith in God without being immediately in great peril.

The life of faith challenges the spirit of the age. The spirit of the age is not in favour of faith; it never has been, it is not to-day. The spirit of the age is the spirit of life by sight, by wit, by wisdom, and by human cleverness. To live the life of faith is immediately to challenge the spirit of the age.

The life of faith denies the call of the flesh. The moment we begin the life of faith in God, we begin where Christ said we must, "If any man would come after Me, let him deny himself."

The life of faith provokes the enmity of the devil, because the life of faith is the only life that challenges the empire of sin. When a man begins to live by faith he inevitably therefore provokes the enmity of the devil. That is why the young Christian so often asks, How is it that since I gave myself to Christ I have been tempted as I have never been tempted before? Immediately a man is regenerated he becomes the object of the attack of all spiritual antagonisms. The life of faith is not a soft, dilettante life in which we sing hymns all the time. It is a life of conflict, demanding heroism and courage and definiteness. It is a life of peril.

" They climbed the steep ascent to heaven,
　Through peril, toil and pain,"

is always true of the saints.

But the life of faith is a life of power. If it challenge the spirit of the age, it is superior to the spirit of the age.

If the life of faith denies the call of the flesh, it triumphs over the claim of the flesh.

If the life of faith provokes the enmity of the devil, it causes the devil to flee. "Resist the devil, and he will flee from you." There is no other way in which you can compel him to flee.

Wherever a man is living by faith he is living the life of power. I suppose one would have to argue that in the case of many a man. Some one is saying, This is all theory. No, it is more ; it is experience. For that simple faith in God that obeys and ventures I am not an advocate merely. As a witness I declare that I have, and can, and do, overcome where else I were overcome. The life of faith is a life of peril ; but it is also a life of power.

The last word is an application of this teaching to the Church.

In the assembly of the saints faith kills class distinctions. A community of men and women living by faith in God is at the end of the distinctions which are of the world, the flesh, and the devil. Let every church then test its faith not by recitation of its creed, but by that inner atmosphere of true communism and fellowship. The life of faith destroys all class distinctions.

In the assembly of the saints faith makes strife impossible. In that aspect of the assembly which is local, or in that which is catholic, where there is strife there is lack of faith in God.

In the assembly of the saints faith is the principle of communion. If we would correct the things of difference and hatred that are amongst us, we need to say to our Lord and Master what one said to Him of old, " Lord, I believe ; help Thou mine unbelief."

I Peter

THE ESSENTIAL MESSAGE	THE APPLICATION

I. **The central teaching**—the sufficiency of grace.
A. The fountain and the river—1, 2.
   1. Grace, interpreted by 1:1.
   2. Multiplied, interpreted by the letter.
B. The secret of confidence.
   1. Foretold by prophets—1:10.
   2. Supplied by the advents—1:13.
C. The secret of conduct.
   1. Servants—2:19, 20: enduring wrong; enduring patiently.
   2. Husbands and wives—3:7: Joint heirs.
D. The secret of character.
   1. The resource for communion—4:10.
   2. The crown of humility—5:5.
E. The secret of courage—the guarantee of God—5:10.
F. Emmanuel's land—this is the true grace of glory—5:12.
II. **The abiding appeal**—"Stand ye fast therein."
A. The inclusive thought—In the country watered by the river. (Cf. 1:2, 5:12)
B. The application.
   1. When faith is tried.
   2. When circumstances are difficult.
   3. When suffering for conscience' sake.
   4. When assaulted by the adversary.
	I. **To the individual**—"For you . . . is the preciousness"—2:7.
	II. **To the church**—"Ye are . . . the excellencies of Him"—2:9.

THE final paragraph of the first letter of Peter is one of salutation, but in the midst of it occurs this statement: " I have written unto you, briefly, exhorting, and testifying, that this is the true grace of God; stand ye fast therein." This closing affirmation of the writer, inserted parenthetically, startles, demands attention, and compels a consideration of the message in the light of what it says.

In these words the apostle first described his method: " I have written unto you, briefly, *exhorting* and *testifying*." The word translated " exhorting " suggests all the qualities of the ministry of the Holy Spirit, coming from the same root and having the same values as the word Paraclete. In the word translated "testifying," we find the same values as in the word of Jesus describing the work of His disciples, *witnessing;* and the root from which the word comes is the same as that from which our word martyr is derived. The methods of the apostle then were those of *exhortation*, that is such teaching as was for instruction and encouragement; and *testimony*, that is, witness out of personal experience.

Then he declared his theme, " That this is the true grace of God." That is to say, the real subject of all his exhortation and testimony was the grace of God.

Finally, he made his last appeal in the words

"Stand ye fast therein"; that is in the grace of God, which had been the theme of his exhortation and testimony.

The central teaching of the letter then is that of the sufficiency of grace; while its abiding appeal is that we stand fast therein.

Now it must be admitted that this is a startling statement, for at first it does not seem that the grace of God has been the definite, specific theme of the letter. Let us therefore first read a selection of passages;

"According to the foreknowledge of God the Father, in sanctification of the Spirit, unto obedience and sprinkling of the blood of Jesus Christ; *Grace* to you and peace be multiplied" (i. 2).

"Concerning which salvation the prophets sought and searched diligently, who prophesied of the *grace* that should come unto you" (i. 10).

"Wherefore girding up the loins of your mind, be sober and set your hope perfectly on the *grace* that is to be brought unto you at the revelation of Jesus Christ" (i. 13).

Thus in the first chapter this great word *grace* occurs three times.

"For this is *acceptable*, if for conscience towards God a man endureth griefs, suffering wrongfully. For what glory is it, if, when ye sin, and are buffeted for it, ye shall take it patiently? but if, when ye do well, and suffer for it, ye shall take it patiently, this is *acceptable* with God" (ii. 19, 20).

In these verses we must substitute *"grace"* for "acceptable"; and thus we find it twice in the second chapter,

"Ye husbands, in like manner, dwell with your wives according to knowledge, giving honour unto the woman, as unto the weaker vessel, as being also joint-heirs of the *grace* of life" (iii. 7).

"According as each hath received a gift, ministering it among yourselves, as good stewards of the manifold *grace* of God" (iv. 10).

Thus we find the word once both in chapter three and chapter four.

"Likewise, ye younger, be subject unto the elder. Yea, all of you gird yourselves with humility, to serve one another: for God resisteth the proud, but giveth *grace* to the humble" (v. 5).

"And the God of all *grace*, Who called you

unto His eternal glory in Christ, after that ye have suffered a little while, shall Himself perfect, stablish, strengthen you" (v. 10).

"This is the true *grace* of God: stand ye fast therein" (v. 12).

Thus we find it three times in chapter five.

That very simple exercise at least reveals the fact that the word is found in every chapter of the letter.

In considering the content of this letter, we found that the thought is ever that of the establishment of Christian people, and the word grace is in every division. The first great statement of the letter is the expression of desire, "Grace to you and peace be multiplied"; the final declaration of the apostle is, "I have written unto you briefly, exhorting, and testifying that this is the true grace of God: stand ye fast therein"; and in every division the word appears not by some studied arrangement, but incidentally, naturally; it is the central word of the argument, and the appeal finds in it its value and force.

It is also remarkable that in every case the word grace occurs, not in the earlier part of the division dealing with doctrine, but in the application.

There is first the introduction, in which the writer introduced himself as the apostle, and described his readers as elect; but it was when he came to the explanation of the word elect, and breathed the desire of his heart that these people might come to practical experience of what it is to be elect, that he said "Grace to you and peace be multiplied."

The second occurrence is in the latter part of the first division; not in that section describing the life of faith, the statement of doctrine; but in that section in which doctrine is related to duty.

So also in the second division, the word is found; not in the first part dealing with the doctrine of holiness, but in the section dealing with the practice of holiness.

In the third division, the word occurs, not in the part dealing with the theory of victory, but in that showing the process of victory.

So also in the last case; not when the apostle was describing the life of conflict or the fellowship of conflict, but when he wanted men to understand the secret of strength for that conflict did he use the word.

All that may seem technical. It does, however, help us to realize that throughout the letter the fact of the grace of God was present to the mind of the writer; and it serves to explain his concluding word, "This is the true grace of God."

As we saw in studying the content, the main purpose of the letter is that of the establishment of such as were passing through suffering and difficulty and testing. The writer established his brethren by showing that all that was needed for strength was provided in the grace of God. Indeed, I should be inclined to say that, if we want a perfectly accurate sub-title for the message of this letter, we may quote from Paul, "My grace is sufficient for thee." That, as I understand it, is the living message of this letter.

In the essential message then the central teaching is that of the sufficiency of grace. That we may divide into six parts suggested by the passages to which we have referred.

First, The Fountain and the River. i. 2.

Secondly, The Secret of Confidence. i. 10, 13.

Thirdly, The Secret of Conduct. ii. 19, 20; iii. 7.

Fourthly, The Secret of Character. iv. 10; v. 5.

Fifthly, The Secret of Courage. v. 10.

Sixthly, Emmanuel's Land. v. 12.

The waters of the river, to quote the figurative language of Ezekiel, come by the way of the altar; that is the river of the living grace, the river of which Ezekiel declared, everything lives whithersoever it comes.

> " Grace is flowing like a river,
>   Millions there have been supplied,
>   Still it flows as full as ever
>   From the Saviour's wounded side."

Go farther back than that, and we find that the river proceeds from the very heart of God. "Grace unto you and peace be multiplied." "This is the true grace of God."

The central teaching of this letter is that of the sufficiency of grace. It opens not by a doctrinal statement or by argument; but with a great expression of the apostolic desire for those to whom he wrote, "Grace unto you and peace be multiplied."

Then it proceeds to show how forevermore grace is the secret of maintained confidence, the secret of triumphant conduct, the secret of holy character, the secret of victorious courage. It is grace

the whole way through, until at last the apostle wrote, "I have written unto you, briefly, exhorting, and testifying that this is the true grace of God. All that experience, the true Christian experience of triumph, is the experience of the Christian in Emmanuel's land. Do not forget that this is Emmanuel's land. Do not postpone Emmanuel's land to heaven; we are already in Emmanuel's land by grace;

> " I've reached the land of corn and wine,
>   And all its riches freely mine;
>   Here shines undimm'd one blissful day,
>   For all my night has passed away."

Only the man who lives in the land fertilized by the rivers of grace can sing that hymn, and understand its meaning.

In the opening passage the word "grace" must be interpreted by that which immediately precedes it. "To the elect . . . according to the foreknowledge of God the Father, in sanctification of the Spirit, unto obedience and sprinkling of the blood of Jesus Christ." In those words we see the great fundamental verities of our faith homed in the being of that one triune God who is Himself Father, Son, and Spirit. We must interpret "grace" by these phrases, and by these doctrines of the faith. " Grace unto you and peace be multiplied."

Recognizing the source whence this river springs, we see how it is the secret of confidence. Take the whole passage in the first chapter and let me summarize it thus. There are two things to notice in the operation of grace. First; it was foretold by the prophets, "Concerning which salvation the prophets sought and searched diligently." Secondly; it is supplied through the Advents of Jesus, "Set your hope perfectly on the grace that is to be brought unto you at the revelation of Jesus Christ." What were the prophets looking for? They were searching what time or what manner of time the Spirit testified when it testified the suffering of Christ and the glory which should follow; these are matters into which the very angels desire to look. The prophets foretold that grace. For the interpretation of that fact we need the four, and the twelve. Their theme was ever that of grace which was to come. It came by the suffering of Jesus, and assures the glories that follow His suffering, those glories which will have their full outshining at

His revelation. The two Advents are in view. Thus Peter shows that our secret of confidence is the certainty of that grace to which all the prophets bore testimony, and which became operative in human history and life through the work of Christ.

It is also the secret of conduct. This is illustrated in the simplest relation. In all the apostolic writings, the most radiant, beautiful things of the Christian life are spoken of as being exhibited where the world would be least likely to look for them. The grace, that is the glories and beauties flowing out as the result of this life communicated by Christ, is most radiantly revealed in the most trying and difficult circumstances. Servants, if you endure wrong patiently, this is grace. Conduct can have its most beautiful manifestation of the power of this grace in circumstances the most trying and most difficult. Conduct can be manifested most perfectly and beautifully, as Paul suggests, by that most sacred union between husband and wife, the most perfect revelation of the union between Jehovah and all trusting souls; for we are "joint-heirs of the grace of life"; and in the power of that grace we are to meet all the difficulties of every-day life, that our prayers be not cut off, or hindered. Servants whose masters are ungodly and unjust have a great opportunity to reveal the grace of God. That is the point you miss if we read "acceptable with God," when the word is the same, and we should read "This is grace with God." If to-day in some house of business, for Christ's sake men and women have suffered wrongfully, and patiently; God has there plucked the fairest flowers that have blossomed in London. This is grace with God. The commonplaces of home-life may be sanctified, glorified, and made to flame with the beauties of the grace of God. This is the true grace of God.

Yet again, grace is the secret of character. Peter urged those to whom he wrote to use "hospitality one to another without murmuring, according as each hath received a gift ministering it among yourselves, as good stewards of the manifold grace of God." What a strange and wonderful merging of the commonplace and the sublime according to the measurements of men. Hospitality, and the ministry of the Word in the assembly of the saints! The grace of God is the secret of such character. Or again, "All

of you gird yourselves with humility, to serve one another: for God resisteth the proud, but giveth grace to the humble." Grace is not only the source of hospitality and communion, it is the ground of humility. These are the things of high character. The Christian character is revealed in beauty in these commonplaces of life. What is at once the inspiration of character that is filled with hospitality and with love; and the ultimate crown of beauty upon that character! The humility that girds itself for service. The Greek word there will bear translation by a phrase; Gird yourself as with a slave's apron of humility. Peter was surely thinking of the day when Jesus took a towel and girded Himself and washed the disciples' feet. He was remembering that the towel, the sign and badge of slavery, was made by Jesus the insignia of nobility in His Kingdom. The secret of such character is the grace of God.

Then we come to the question of conflict. "Your adversary the devil, as a roaring lion, walketh about, seeking whom he may devour. . . . The God of all grace, Who called you unto His eternal glory in Chist, after that ye have suffered a little while, shall Himself perfect, stablish, strengthen you." Grace in the conflict is the guarantee of the glory which will be perfect, and of final victory over the forces of evil that are against us.

The inclusive thought of the abiding appeal is that we are to live in the country watered by the river of grace, and that the apostle expressed in the charge "Stand ye fast therein."

Go over the four thoughts again. When faith is tried, remember that in grace there is perfect resource which being appropriated will make us strong in the Lord, and in the power of His might.

When faith is trembling, let us come into new understanding of the sufficiency of this grace of God, and faith will triumph.

When circumstances are difficult—and do not let us be afraid of the simplest illustrations—in the place of service which is not appreciated when it ought to be, in all the constant difficulties of the home, if we would manifest that conduct which is in harmony with the will of God, the resources are in grace. When we fail, it is because we neglect the grace of God.

When suffering for conscience' sake, being

persecuted because we bear the Christian name, how shall we bear it, how shall we still manifest the Christian character? Only in the power of this grace.

When assaulted by the adversary who goeth about like a roaring lion seeking; how are we to overcome? Only by remembering that our God is the God of all grace; and that through suffering and the assault of the adversary, He will perfect that which concerneth us.

The abiding appeal I can venture to make in no other way than by using the great words, " For you therefore which believe is the preciousness." Link that very carefully with the teaching which goes before it; living stones coming to the living Stone, and the living Stone, " elect, precious." Then follows the declaration, " For you therefore which believe is the preciousness." When we come to Him He communicates to us those virtues which constitute His preciousness, and we become precious also. Preciousness is the result of having the elemental forces compacted together into consistent strength. Peter was an elemental man, lacking preciousness until Christ gave him His own nature, His own life; then he became precious. What is a precious stone? It is the embodiment of passion mastered by principle. That is the thought in the figurative language of one of the old prophets, "the stones of fire"; the diamond is a stone of fire; it is precious, solidified, mastered by principle. This is the great truth about grace. Grace communicates to us the preciousness of Christ; all that which in Him was precious to the heart of God, that which made Him the one supreme and lonely glory in the diadem of Deity, is made over to us.

If we take the individual stones that thus receive His preciousness, and build them into the whole assembly, what then? Then the description follows, " Ye are an elect race, a royal priesthood, a holy nation, a people for God's own possession, that ye may show forth the excellencies of Him Who called you out of darkness into His marvellous light." The preciousness of Christ being communicated to individuals, the whole company of such individuals will reveal the excellencies of God.

Grace is the secret of all establishment in the Christian life. It is the river that flowing through the desert makes it blossom as the rose until it becomes Emmanuel's land.

> " All the rivers of Thy grace I claim.
> Over every promise write my name.
>
> .   .   .   .   .
>
> Grace there is my every debt to pay,
> Blood to wash my every sin away,
> Power to keep me spotless day by day."

" This is the true grace of God : stand ye fast therein."

II Peter

THE ESSENTIAL MESSAGE	THE APPLICATION

I. The central teaching—responsibilities of grace.
  A. Resources creating responsibility.
    1. The power—1:3.
      a. Things for life according to His glory.
      b. Things for godliness according to His virtue.
    2. The coming—1:4 and 11.
      a. The final escape from corruption.
      b. Entrance into the eternal kingdom.
  B. Responsibilities created by resource.
    1. Appropriation of the resources.
      a. Remembrance.
      b. Response.
    2. Avoidance of the perils.
      a. Test the prophets.
      b. Holy living and godliness.
II. The abiding appeal—give diligence.
  A. In cooperation with the power—1:5.
    1. Faith appropriating power.
    2. Diligence developing character.
  B. In view of the coming—3:14.
    1. Faith looking for the coming.
    2. Diligence guarding character.
	I. To the individual.
	  A. Relation to the power—remembrance in order to diligence.
	  B. Relation to the coming—anticipation in order to realization.
	II. To the church.
	  A. Her only perils.
	    1. Denying the master—2:1.
	    2. Denying the coming—3:4.
	  B. The inter-relation of these—to deny Him is to deny His coming.
	  C. The issue of these.
	    1. Near-sightedness.
	    2. Lust.
	    3. Destruction.

THE main purpose of this second letter, like that of the first, is the establishment of believers in their faith and in their life. Both were undoubtedly written in fulfillment of the charge of the Lord Jesus to Peter: "When once thou hast turned again, stablish thy brethren."

The first letter was written to "the elect who are sojourners of the Dispersion in Pontus, Galatia, Cappadocia, Asia, and Bithynia"; and the opening words of the third chapter of the second epistle lead us to believe that it was written to the same people. In each case the method is the same, although the apostle was dealing with different difficulties. In the former, he dealt with perils threatening the spiritual life of the Church from without. In this, he dealt with perils threatening the spiritual life of the individual believer from within.

There is a sense in which this second letter touches a deeper note than the first. Perhaps it would be more accurate to say that it has a more searching effect; its note is deeper, in the sense that it deals with us personally, individually, whereas the first presented to us in a more general way the great and sublime truth of the sufficiency of that grace wherein we stand. Grace is sufficient; that was the theme of the first letter. That is still the message; but now it is insisted on that grace is only sufficient as its laws are obeyed. No man has any right to say God's grace is sufficient to keep him if he is breaking the laws of grace, and so putting himself in peril. God's grace is not sufficient to keep a man from falling who is not obedient to the law of that grace, and to the revealed will of God. The first letter began "Grace to you and peace be multiplied," and ended "Stand ye fast therein." The second letter begins, " Grace to you and peace be multiplied," and ends " Grow in the grace." The same beginning in each case reminds us of the fountainhead and the flowing river. The final word of the first is, " Stand ye fast therein," that is, live in Emmanuel's land, watered and fertilized by this great flowing river of grace. The last word of the second letter is " Grow in the grace," that is, being in the land, appropriate its resources and grow. It is not enough to abide, to stand fast; there must also be growth. In the first epistle the burden is that of the sufficiency of grace, and the consequent first responsibility of standing fast. In the second letter the burden is that of the responsibility which the fact of being in grace creates.

This must be clear. The great burden of the first letter is the sufficiency of grace; grace in every time of need; ending with the one note indicating responsibility, " Stand ye fast therein." The burden of the second letter takes for granted the burden of the first, that grace is sufficient, and sets forth the responsibility that rests upon those who are in grace, revealing two grave perils forever threatening the life of those in grace. While its burden is that of responsibility, and while it ends with the note which insists upon responsibility, " Ye therefore . . . grow in the grace"; the thought of this last word is also that of sufficiency, as it really means, being in the grace, grow; you are in the grace, God has put you in His grace, you are in the land watered by the river of His grace, therefore grow.

Let us then consider the essential message of this second letter as to its central teaching; and as to its abiding appeal.

The central teaching has to do with the responsibilities of grace; first, the resource creating the responsibilities, and secondly the responsibilities created by that resource.

After the introduction in the first two verses, the apostle wrote: " Seeing that His divine power hath granted unto us all things that pertain unto life and godliness, through the knowledge of Him that called us by His own glory and virtue." An interpretation of this letter must be sought in the light of the mount of transfiguration. If that be borne in mind, this declaration immediately becomes full of meaning. The central thought is that of Divine power. This power grants us " all the things that pertain to life and godliness, through the knowledge of Him that called us by His own glory and virtue." Put the things of grace which are there referred to, " glory and virtue,' against the things for which power is provided, " life and godliness," and it is at once seen that they are mutually explanatory. The Divine power being at our disposal, we have everything that is necessary for life, according to His glory; and for godliness, according to His virtue.

His glory these men had seen on the holy mount. What they saw was not the outshining of the Deity of our Lord, but the coming to final perfection of His humanity. Deity has never had that kind of outshining. Deity has no manifestation to the eyes of sense. When God hid Himself in flesh, then men saw God; the glory of Deity was revealed not in any splendour, but in the humanity of our Lord. That humanity came to its perfection on the holy mount. The story of the life of Jesus may be told thus; innocent in babyhood and childhood; holy in youth and manhood; coming to ultimate glory on the mount of transfiguration. There humanity was revealed at its highest and best.

It was glory, but it was also virtue; that is, it was not merely what life was in itself, inherently, in its perfection, but it was the fact that that life was filled with every excellency which made God declare, " This is My beloved Son, in Whom I am well pleased."

The word virtue here has not the meaning which it usually has when we make use of it. We recall the great passage in the first letter, " Ye are . . . that ye may show forth the *excellencies*," " the praises," as the Authorized Version has it. The word excellencies or praises is exactly the same word as virtue. Virtue refers there to that in Him which was excellent, that in Him which satisfied the heart of God.

His Divine power has given us all that we need, in order that life may come to the pattern of that glory; and that godliness may be the realization of that virtue. These are the resources of His power.

Then there are the resources of His coming. These are also referred to in the first chapter; " Whereby He hath granted unto us His precious and exceeding great promises; that through these ye may become partakers of the Divine nature, having escaped from the corruption that is in the world by lust." " For thus shall be richly supplied unto you the entrance into the eternal Kingdom of our Lord and Saviour Jesus Christ." " The eternal Kingdom " is an arresting phrase, and this is the only occasion in the New Testament in which it is used. In this letter the subject of the Second Advent is not dealt with as it is in some of the other writings of the New Testament. The main thought of the apostle is not that the Second Advent will mean the setting up of the Kingdom of God in this world, but that it will result in the perfecting of the saints. We should always draw a distinction between the Coming of the Lord and the Day of the Lord, that day of judgment ushering in the reign of righteousness. The apostle is here dealing with the value of the Coming to the saint. In that Coming we shall finally, perfectly escape from the corruption that is in the world by lust. In that Coming we shall enter into the age-abiding Kingdom of our Lord and Saviour Jesus Christ.

Here again is the resource provided for us in grace. If I stand in grace, I have power sufficient to conform my life to the perfect pattern of His life, so that it shall be well pleasing to God. If I stand in grace I stand in the light of the Parousia, the Presence, the Coming; which for the world will lead to His process of judgment establishing righteousness; but which for me, standing in grace, will be the hour when I finally escape from corruption. There is a sense in which every believer has already escaped in the economy and purpose of God; but in the hour of that Coming, that Advent at which scoffers are still scoffing, we shall finally escape from corruption. This corruptible must put on incorruption. Then shall be brought to pass the word that is written. That is the final outcome of our Christian life; and we lose a very great deal if we forget or neglect, as a part of the resources of grace, the presence or coming of our Lord.

What then are the responsibilities which these resources create? They can be expressed in two words; appropriation of the resources; and avoidance of the perils.

Two words will indicate the method of appropriation; first remembrance, and secondly, response. In proportion as we forget the beginning we are in danger of wandering from the pathway that leads to the end. It is an ill day in my Christian life when I do not remember my Lord's death, and that Cross from which I receive the benefit of my life. There is a great value in the Lord's command, " This do in remembrance of Me." When gathering about the table, one ot our first responsibilities is that there we remember the beginning of our Christian life by His atonement; and we must keep our life day by day set in relation to these things, the first things. But we are to remember not only the first things, but also the ultimate things. When I forget the ultimate, forget the Coming, then my life becomes careless. I am perfectly sure that Dr. Denny is right when he says in his volume on Thessalonians that the very bloom of the beauty of the Christian communion in the early days was that of their ever expecting the return of the Lord; and I believe he is perfectly right when he says that the measure in which the Church has lost that expectation is the measure in which the bloom of that beauty has been brushed from her character. By remembrance of these things, I appropriate them.

But infinitely more is needed. If I remember them only as an intellectual exercise, there is no value in that. I must respond to them. Remembering the Cross and what it means with regard to sin, I am to put sin away and yield myself to its inspiration for service. Remembering the Advent, His return, then " what manner of persons ought ye to be in all holy living and godliness, looking for and earnestly desiring the coming of the day of God ? " So, resources are to be appropriated by remembrance and response.

That necessarily involves the second thought, avoidance of the perils. The solemnity and searching power of the second chapter are great. There is no pity in the heart of this man for false prophets; for very love of truth, there cannot be. He warns against the false prophets; and in the next chapter he charges them that they " remember the words which were spoken before by the holy prophets." How are we to avoid the perils? By remembering the truth, the messages of the prophets, of the Lord Himself, of the apostles. We are to test prophecy by the established prophecies of essential truth.

We are to avoid the peril of evil living that grows out of listening to false prophets, by all holy living and godliness resulting from obedience to the holy prophets.

The abiding appeal of the letter is that we give diligence. This we do first by coöperation with the Power. "Adding on your part all diligence in your faith supply virtue; and in your virtue knowledge; and in your knowledge temperance; and in your temperance patience; and in your patience godliness; and in your godliness love of the brethren; and in your love of the brethren love." First faith appropriates power; then diligence develops the character which is potentially taken hold of by faith. Faith is the first thing. Faith appropriates the Divine power. The Divine power has put all things at my disposal, and faith appropriates that power. That is not enough. I am to give diligence to supply. That process is described through the flowering of faith, until the fruit is reached, which is love. The figure is that of the opening flower. The root principle is faith taking hold of the resources of power; then we see the flower open; until we get at last to the fruit, love. If we want to know what love is, we leave Peter and go to Paul, "The fruit of the Spirit is love, joy, peace, long-suffering, kindness, goodness, faithfulness, meekness, temperance." In order to that development from faith to love, cultivation is needed; self-cultivation, and diligence withal. It is perfectly true we grow; and it is perfectly true that not by effort can we grow, not by taking thought can we add one cubit to our stature even spiritually; but it is equally true that we are to be diligent in adding, not adding to, as though we got from somewhere else a new quality; but bringing out the thing that is already there; reaching down into the Divine power until all the petals of the perfect flower are unfolded, and until the fruit itself is formed, which is love.

The appeal of the letter goes farther. We are to give diligence, not only to coöperate with power, but also in view of the Coming. "Seeing that ye look for these things, give diligence that ye may be found in peace, without spot and blameless in His sight." Just as we saw faith appropriating power, now we see faith looking for the Coming. It is faith and nothing else that looks for the Coming. The scoffers are always present, saying: "Where is the promise of His coming?" As things have been, so they will remain. Faith looks up, and expects the fulfillment of the sure word of prophecy. Faith is certain that what God has spoken He will do. Faith does not attempt to explain away the prophecies of the Old Testament as though they had happened, when most evidently they have not happened. Faith looks and expects, and affirms that though there be no flush of dawn to the eyes of sense, He is coming, and the day is coming in which the elements shall melt away with fervent heat.

I speak out of my own experience. Unless I looked for that coming I would be of all men the most miserable, and the most hopeless. In this matter God is working as He always has worked, through processes leading to crises. Faith is looking for the coming, and it must give diligence that in the crisis we may be found in peace, without spot, and blameless in His sight.

That is the abiding appeal. Give diligence with regard to the power, to coöperate with it for the development of character. Give diligence with regard to the Coming, to look for it and to guard character so that at any moment—to quote from John for the illumination of Peter—we may not be ashamed from Him at His Coming.

The application of the letter to the individual is first that it reveals the law of relation to that Divine power which is at his disposal in Christ; remembrance in order to diligence, remembrance the inspiration of diligence. To forget is to become negligent; to remember is to be forever more diligent.

It also reveals the law of relation to the coming; anticipation in order to realization. If I really anticipate His coming, if I really live so that I may be ready when He comes—how the thought touches all life—if I really believe He may disturb me at my work, or worship, or play, then I shall work and worship and play so as not to be ashamed when He comes. If we have lost that, how much we have lost.

The application of this letter to the Church is first that it reveals her only perils. The first is that of denial of the Master. "There arose false prophets also among the people, as among you also there be false teachers, who shall privily bring in destructive heresies, denying even the

Master that bought them, bringing upon them-selves swift destruction." Denying the Master; His glory and His virtue, those essentials concerning Him which were revealed to Peter and the Church for all time upon the holy mount. Denying all that He is in Himself, denying that which was the central subject of the converse of the holy mount, the *exodos*, not death, but the fact that through death He would break a highway into life. The second peril is that of denying His coming; " In·the last days mockers shall come with mockery, walking after their own lusts, and saying, Where is the promise of His coming? for, from the day that the fathers fell asleep, all things continue as they were from the beginning of the creation." When the Church joins in the mockery of the mocker, and denies the prophetic utterance of the Scriptures, and the definite declarations of the Lord and His apostles, then she is in peril, for to lose the sense of His coming is to lose the most powerful force and inspiration for holy living.

The inter-relation of these perils is manifest. To deny Him in any sense is to deny His coming. To deny Him by making Him merely a moral exemplar is to doubt the saving value of His death, and to deny His resurrection; and to deny the resurrection is to deny His Second Advent.

The issue of such denial is near-sightedness, seeing only the things that are near. This issues in lust. And lust brings forth death.

The note of the letter is one of great solemnity, I had almost said severity; but it is the severity of a great love and a great desire for the strengthening of believers. Let us ever hear its great words to us; In remembrance, give diligence. Grace is sufficient; but we must discover and obey its laws, or it is valueless.

The Letters of John

THE ESSENTIAL MESSAGE	THE APPLICATION

I. **The central teaching**—the life of fellowship explained.
A. As to resources.
    1. Objective—the pattern provided.
      a. Of light—the sinless One—2:6.
      b. Of love—"He loved us"—4:10.
    2. Subjective—the power provided.
      a. For light—Begotten we see—2:20, 27.
      b. For love—Begotten we love—4:7.
B. As to realization.
    1. Its value to us—the fulfillment of life.
      a. The perfected being.
      b. The friendship of God.
    2. Its value to God—the fulfillment of purpose.
      a. Media of manifestation.
      b. Instruments of accomplishment.
II. **The abiding appeal**—the responsibilities of fellowship declared.
A. As to light.
    1. Its testing must be sought.
    2. Its revelation must be obeyed.
B. As to love.
    1. Its impulse must be yielded to.
    2. Its holiness must be maintained.
	I. **To the individual.** (Life must be tested by light and love.)
	II. **To the church.** (The law of its fellowship is that of life expressed in love tested by light.)
	A. "Believe not every spirit."
	B. "Look to yourselves."
	C. "Welcome such."

THE three letters of John are intimately related to each other. In the first we have teaching, and in the second and third, illustrations; but the message is one.

There is, moreover, a close relation between these letters and the Gospel according to John. Two statements, one in the Gospel, and one in the letters, in which the apostle declared the purpose of his writing in each case, reveal that relation.

The purpose for which the Gospel was written was that those reading it should believe that Jesus is the Christ, the Son of God, and that as a result of their belief, they might themselves enter into life. This the writer clearly declared in the words,

"These are written that ye may believe that Jesus is the Christ, the Son of God; and that be-lieving ye may have life in His name" (John xx. 31).

The purpose for which the letters were written was that those reading them, having already believed on the name of the Son of God, might have the means whereby to find assurance of their possession of eternal life. This with equal clearness John declared in the words,

"These things have I written unto you, that ye may know that ye have eternal life, even unto you that believe on the name of the Son of God" (1 John v. 13).

In the Gospel, then, we have the unveiling of eternal life in its manifestation in the Son of God; and the revelation of the fact that this life is, through Him, placed at the disposal of men through the mystery of His death, and the victory of His resurrection. When we read the

Gospel story, we know what eternal life really is, for it is clearly manifested in the Son of God; and further, we learn that we may share in that life by believing in His name. Thus the theme of the Gospel is that of eternal life; as it is revealed in the Son of God; and as the Son of God is able to communicate it to believing souls.

In the letters, the theme is still that of eternal life, only in these we see its manifestation in the children of God, that is, in those who through faith in the Son of God have received that life. So that the theme of the letters is that of eternal life, as it is revealed in the children of God, as they are under the mastery of the Son of God.

The theme of the Gospel and the letters is thus seen to be the same. It is that of age-abiding life, that is, life according to the will and purpose of God. In the Gospel we see one lonely figure, that of the Son of God, revealing and communicating eternal life. In the epistles we see the children of God, those whom the Son brings into this life, that is all such as believe on His name.

In the prologue of the Gospel, John wrote of the Son of God,

" In the beginning was the Word, and the Word was with God, and the Word was God. . . . And the Word became flesh, and dwelt among us . . . full of grace and truth" (John i. 1 and 14).

In the parenthesis of the fourteenth verse, John, in evident exultation of spirit, wrote,

"And we beheld His glory, glory as of the only begotten from the Father full of grace and truth," and in that brief and almost abrupt phrase, "full of grace and truth," he gave the distinguishing facts of the " glory."

When we turn to his letters, we find the same facts of grace and truth dominating his thought: the first of them illustrating the power of grace in the life of all those who believe in the Son of God, and the second and third insisting upon the importance of truth, by showing the necessity for loyalty thereto on the part of those who share the privileges of grace.

These letters, then, afford a teaching and a test. They teach us what eternal life is in the experience of the child of God; and they enable us therefore to test our life, and to know whether it is eternal life.

In dealing with the essential message we find that its central teaching is an explanation of the life of fellowship; while its abiding appeal is that of a declaration of the responsibilities of fellowship.

As we commence our reading of the first letter, the word *fellowship* is found, and it is the key-note of the three epistles, the master-thought of the writer being that eternal life is life in fellowship with God; we enter upon eternal life when we are brought into fellowship with God; we continue in eternal life as we abide in fellowship with God.

The explanation of the life of fellowship falls into two parts, the first dealing with resources, and the second with realization.

The resources of the life of fellowship are objectively presented in the pattern provided in the Son of God; and subjectively received in the power provided when we are begotten children of God.

The pattern of eternal life is given in Christ, and the writer dealt with it in its twofold aspect of light and of love.

When dealing with the subject of light, the apostle wrote,

" He that saith he abideth in Him ought himself to walk even as that One walked " (1 John ii. 6).

It is evident from that literal translation that as John wrote, he had before his vision the Lord and Master Whom he knew so intimately. If we desire an accurate interpretation of the phrase, "that One," we must go back to the Gospel to find it, for there we see the One upon Whom John was looking in spirit, and by faith, when he wrote the words. In that Gospel the Son of God is revealed, walking in light, and, therefore, as the sinless One, never consenting to darkness, never hiding from God, or attempting so to do; the One of Whom it was preëminently true that in His spirit there was no guile, no deceit. He is the pattern, therefore, of eternal life, as perfect conformity to light. In the measure in which we walk as He walked, we walk in light.

It must be remembered that this writing was for the children of God, that the Lord Jesus Christ is not presented as a pattern to men until they have yielded themselves to Him; for the perfection of His life is such that to present it as an ideal to be realized would be but to mock the impotence of unregenerate men. It is perfectly true that we may present Him as the great Ideal to men who have not yet received His gift of life; but in doing so we only succeed in discovering to them their inability to imitate the pattern, and so to reveal to them the necessity for the new birth. Having become His by the gift of life, we are called upon to live the life of fellowship with God, and our first resource is that of the pattern which He thus presents.

In dealing with the subject of love, the apostle wrote,

"Herein is love, not that we loved God, but that He loved us, and sent His Son to be the Propitiation for our sins" (1 John iv. 10).

In all the life of the Son of God thus sent by the Father there was a revelation of the attitude and activity of perfect love. No word ever passed His lips but that was love inspired. He wrought no deed but in answer to the demand of love. Thus in Him we see eternal life in the sinlessness of light, and the selflessness of love.

If, however, as we have already indicated, our resources in Christ are only objective, then we are left helpless indeed. The more carefully I contemplate the revelation of eternal life in Christ, the more impossible do I feel it to be to imitate the pattern given. Those who speak of imitating Jesus Christ, and seem to hope to realize the ideal in their own strength, have surely never seen Him in that marvellous wonder of perfect sinlessness and absolute love which John has presented to us in his Gospel. The pattern is not enough, and therefore in dealing with our resources, he shows that Christ is not merely objectively presented to us as from without, that we may gaze upon Him; but that by the communication of His own life to us He becomes a subjective, an actual power, working within our lives.

This is true both with regard to light and to love. The light only comes when comes the life, and the love only comes when comes the life. When a man is begotten of God, he sees, he becomes sensitive in the matter of sin, he knows exactly what he ought to do. Moreover, when a man is begotten of God, the first impulse of his new life is love, which drives him out upon the pathway of sacrificial service on behalf of other men.

The relation of life to light in the case of the children of God is revealed in two statements;

"Ye have an anointing from the Holy One, and ye know all things."

"And as for you, the anointing which ye received of Him abideth in you, and ye need not that any one teach you; but as His anointing teacheth you concerning all things, and is true, and is no lie, and even as it taught you, ye abide in Him" (1 John ii. 20 and 27).

While there are many values in these statements for the purpose of our present meditation we may summarize their teaching in this respect by saying that the child of God is never left in doubt by God as to the thing which is sinful, and the thing which is right. That statement may be challenged, but let it be carefully pondered in the light of Christian experience. There are times when we may be tempted to argue with ourselves that we are not sure; but in the deepest fact of our life in Christ we always know. As we have received His life, that life is always light, and though there may be moments when on some threshold between light and darkness we waver and wonder, that very uncertainty does but demonstrate the necessity for fleeing the danger, and pressing back into the clear light. The man begotten of God sees, and if we are conscious of the loss of a keen sense of sin, we may know that our life is at a low ebb.

The relation of life to love in the case of the children of God is revealed in the words;

"Every one that loveth is begotten of God, and knoweth God" (1 John iv. 7).

The man begotten of God loves. That is the very essence of Christianity. The first movement in the soul of a man born of God is a movement inspired by love and impelling to service. Let that be illustrated in the simplest possible way. Here is a man born again in some service, or, it may be, in the loneliness of his own home. Then immediately, and without any exception, he thinks of some one else whom he loves, and desires that such an one may share his joy; and is consequently impelled to go and tell that one the secret of his new-found life. There is no exception to this. The life of God is love, and the moment we share it, we love. We may quench love, be afraid to let it lead us to full expression, but all such action reacts upon life itself. The truth of infinite value is that the most loveless become love mastered as they are born of God.

These writings reveal not the resources of life alone, but also the values of its realization. These are twofold, the value to us, and the value to God.

The value of the life of fellowship to us is that of the realization of our own life, the perfection of our being, in friendship with God.

Some time ago I received a letter, in which the writer said, "How am I to find the secret that will admit me to the realization of all of which I am conscious? Life seems to me as though it ought to be made up of love and laughter, but I am afraid that this is an improper definition of life." In answer to that letter I said that such is life indeed, according to the will of God, and that life only becomes love and laughter as it is eternal life, or life in fellowship with God. It is self-evident that when I use the word laughter I am not referring to such laughter as the preacher described in the book of Ecclesiastes, when he wrote,

"For as the crackling of thorns under a pot, so is the laughter of the fool: this also is vanity" (vii. 6).

I refer rather to that exultant hilarity which results from full consciousness of life. When a man is born of God, he is made to realize what God meant when He first made man. That is eternal life.

That way of stating the fact may surprise a great many truly Christian people who seem to have an idea that eternal life changes a man into some other order of being. Let us ever carefully remember that what we are essentially, in our first creation, we are by the will and power of God. He creates each human being a member of the great commonwealth of humanity, necessary for the perfecting of the whole. We never come to a realization of these powers, or make our contribution to the larger whole, until we are living eternal life, that is, life in fellowship with God. The words of Jesus are most significant in this respect, in which He declares, "Whosoever loseth his life shall find it," that is, the very life he loses. He that loses his life for Christ's sake does not find a different life. He finds rather the key to his own life, which unlocks its secrets; and the power which enables him to realize its potentialities. The value of eternal life to us then is the perfecting of our personalities in friendship with God, according

to the will of God. Eternal life is true life, life as God intended it should be.

Realization of eternal life by the children of God is valuable to God Himself, in that He finds in every human being who lives in fellowship with Himself a medium through which He can manifest Himself, and an instrument through which He is able to accomplish His purposes. When a man begins to live the life eternal, God gains in him an opportunity to show Himself in the shop or the office where he works, in the circle of men and women among whom he moves.

The abiding appeal of these letters consists in their declaration of the responsibilities of the life of fellowship. These responsibilities are those of light and love.

With regard to light, the first responsibility is that its testing must be sought. It is not enough that I should say that light must be obeyed. Our first duty is to seek the light. We often say that we have no light on a given subject. Let it be remembered that if that is so, the fault is with us. We can have light if we will. That fact is most clearly taught by Paul in one of his letters, in which he said, "Awake, thou sleepest, and arise from the dead, and Christ shall shine upon thee." This does not merely mean once, at the beginning, but along the whole pathway of life. It is possible for us not to seek the light, not to want to have the light, not to desire its shining; and our first responsibility therefore is that we do seek the light. If indeed we bear His name and profess to live the life of fellowship, we have no right to undertake any business without seeking light, no right to enter upon any pleasure without desiring to know His will. There must be the testing of the life by light on the part of all those who are living in fellowship with God.

Then when the light shines, it must be obeyed wherever it leads, and at whatever cost.

Our responsibilities as to love are that its impulse must be yielded to, and its holiness must be maintained.

It is a matter for the most solemn consideration that we may destroy our capacity for love by not yielding to its impulse. There is a time in the earlier experiences of all Christian life when the soul is conscious of a great passion for lost men and women. It is possible to lose this. It is possible to continue the service, and yet to have lost the love. We lose the love impulse when we refuse to obey its suggestions. Love asks for some sacrificial service, and we listen to some calm, calculating, satanic voice, and caring for ourselves, we stifle love. If the life of God in the soul of a man is in its first movement an impulse of love, our first responsibility is that of obedience thereto. Love will lead us to the doing of such things that the world will be unable to understand. Judas will still inquire, "Why this waste?" If we listen to that criticism, and cease to respond to love, love will die. If we turn a deaf ear to such suggestions of Satan, and yielding ourselves to love, serve in answer to its impulse, love will deepen and intensify.

We are not only to yield to love; we are to guard its holiness. It is possible to be led astray from the activity of true love by yielding to a false charity. At the very centre of love is light. That is not true love which sacrifices principle. God has never acted in love at the expense of light. If I could be persuaded for one moment that God can be so loving as to pass lightly over sin, then I should feel that the government of the universe was insecure. The fact is otherwise. He loves with such intensity that He never can excuse sin. In all our love, therefore, we must see to it that the light is shining, and that holiness is maintained.

These letters have an immediate application to the individual and to the Church. That to the individual may thus be briefly stated. Life must be tested by light and by love. That is a word full of solemnity. We talk of our fellowship with God. How are we to prove to ourselves that we are really living in fellowship with Him? The test of the life is that of light and love. If the light is not shining clearly, or if shining, we are disobedient to it; if the love that once burned and inspired is no longer operative, then may God deliver us from mere satisfaction with the formulæ of orthodoxy, or correct intellectual apprehensions of the doctrines of grace.

As to the Church, the law of its fellowship is life, and as in the case of the individual, life must be tested by light and by love. We have no right to be so broad in our Church fellowship as to receive men who deny Christ as He is presented in the Gospel, and as He has accomplished His victories in the souls of men in the centuries of the Christian era. We may respect the convictions of these men, but there can be no fellowship with them in Church life, which does not weaken the testimony of the Church. It would be infinitely better that the fellowship of any Church should be smaller than that its numbers should be enlarged by the inclusion of those who fail to walk in light, or to respond to love.

It is a remarkable fact and not to be lightly passed over, that in these writings of John, who has become known preëminently as the apostle of love, we find the sternest words as to the necessity for loyalty to truth; and the Church of God needs to remember that fellowship with God necessitates separation from all who fail to fulfill the responsibilities of fellowship in light, or in love.

Jude

THE ESSENTIAL MESSAGE	THE APPLICATION

I. **The central teaching**—the peril of apostasy.
  A. Apostasy defined.
    1. Its character (verse 4).
    2. Its characteristics (verses 12, 16, 19).
  B. Illustrations of its nature and issue.
    1. Israel—unbelief; destruction.
    2. Angels—rebellion; kept in bonds.
    3. Sodom and Gomorrah—fornication; age-abiding fire.
    4. Cain—self-righteousness.
    5. Balaam—greed.
    6. Korah—presumption.
    Note: All these are contrary to faith.
II. **The abiding appeal.**
  A. The inclusive command (verse 3).
    1. Passionate and determined effort.
    2. The abandon and cautiousness of the athlete (verses 20-23).
  B. The exposition.
    1. Keep yourselves—building; praying; looking.
    2. "Some. . . ."
  C. The inspiration—the doxology.
	I. **To the church**—the faith for which we are to contend.
	  A. The system of truth.
	  B. That truth centered in a person.
	  C. That truth operating in grace.
	II. **To the individual**—the contending which defends the truth.
	  A. Constant loyalty.
	  B. Ceaseless caution.
	  C. Courageous confidence.

THIS letter is one of the briefest of the New Testament writings; but it is by no means unimportant. It is characterized by great and grave solemnity, making appeal to "them that are called, beloved in God the Father, and kept for Christ Jesus." It is catholic, and has perpetual application to the people of God.

Its purpose is evident. We have to spend no time in seeking to discover its message; it is in itself a definite message. Its solemnity is increased by the fact that the writer declares that whereas he had purposed writing on an entirely different subject, he turned aside from that original purpose, in view of the urgency of the need, as he saw it, for solemn warning.

Glancing at the early verses of the letter, let us notice first the reason for the writing; secondly, his own declared purpose in writing; and then, before turning to the statement of the message, let us notice the method he adopted in the writing.

The reason is declared in verse four; there were certain "ungodly men, turning the grace of our God into lasciviousness, and denying our only Master and Lord, Jesus Christ." When Jude was giving all diligence, that is, making careful preparation, to write a treatise on the subject of our common salvation, there was borne in upon his spirit the necessity for writing this letter, because there were certain men within the circle of the Church, who had crept in privily, and were being received and listened to, and whose influence was affecting the life of Christian people. They were "turning the grace of our Lord into lasciviousness, and denying our only Master and Lord, Jesus Christ."

Jude gave with equal clearness the purpose for which he wrote the letter in the words, " I was constrained to write unto you exhorting you to contend earnestly for the faith which was once for all delivered unto the saints."

The method of the letter is that of giving illustrations of apostasy, showing its nature and results ; and also instructions for fidelity.

Here again, in another way, and from another view-point, and with other emphasis, the great theme is that of the Hebrew letter, the two great values of which were the revelation of the perils of apostasy, of how death comes through apostasy ; and of the powers of faith, how the righteous man lives by his faith. The same two underlying thoughts are in this brief letter.

The central teaching of the letter is that of the peril of apostasy.

Apostasy is first defined as to its character and its characteristics. Secondly, illustrations of its nature and issue are given ; Israel, Angels, Sodom and Gomorrah, Cain, Balaam, Korah.

The abiding appeal consists of an inclusive command ; an exposition thereof ; and finally an inspirational Doxology.

The central teaching has to do with apostasy ; which is first defined.

When I speak of apostasy being defined, I am referring of course to apostasy within the Christian faith and fact. The illustrations are taken from the Scriptures and history of the Hebrew people ; consequently they touch the underlying principle, rather than the immediate fact of the apostasy of which Jude was afraid as he wrote this letter to Christian people.

Apostasy is not finally intellectual ; it is volitional ; but it is closely united with the intellectual. It may be very difficult for us to say whether apostasy from Christ, the denial of faith, the turning of the back upon the Lord Himself, begins with intellectual doubt, or moral declension. If I were asked personally for an opinion— which I shall only give as a personal opinion—I should be inclined to say that the very order in which Jude has stated it is a revelation of the order in which it happens. First some moral declension, some disobedience to the Lord Himself, some turning of the grace of God into lasciviousness, the outcome of which is some denial of the Lord and Master Himself. My own conviction is that heresy within the Church is almost invariably the outcome of disloyalty to the teaching of the Lord at some point in the life. When a man turns the grace of God into lasciviousness, when he consents to act upon the idea that because he stands in grace, therefore his conduct is of very little moment, he is apostatizing. That is the most terrible of all apostasies. There have been periods when that apostasy has been formulated into a definite doctrine ; the antinomian heresy declared that because a man is in Christ he cannot be lost. and therefore it matters little what his conduct may be, because nothing he can do can sever as between Christ and himself. That is apostasy in its worst form. No man can hold that doctrine without denying the Lord and Master. That is to deny everything for which He stood ; to deny the real meaning and purpose of His dying, to deny the whole purpose of His heart, as He came to destroy the works of the Devil, in order to make possible to man a life of purity, to save man not merely from the punishment of sin, but from sin itself. To continue in sin that grace may abound is to deny the perfection of His Person ; the passion of His heart that bore Him through the Cross ; and His purpose for the establishment of the Kingdom of God in righteousness and holiness through the whole world.

Doubt is not apostasy. I believe there are a great many who, passing through a period of honest doubt and difficulty and inquiry in the presence of the great mystery of our Lord's Person, do not apostatize because they remain true to the measure of light they have, and they do not turn the grace of God into lasciviousness. In other words, apostasy, according to this first definition and whole argument, is not intellectual mistake, but moral failure on the part of those who name the name of Christ.

In verses twelve, sixteen, and nineteen, we have the characteristics of apostasy ; they each begin with the same words. Perhaps there is no more forceful passage in the whole of the New Testament than that of verses twelve and thirteen. It is figurative but graphic. Reading it, one is conscious of the awfulness of apostasy. In verses sixteen and nineteen we have a description of those who apostatize, what they are in themselves, and what they do in the assemblies.

Between the declaration of the character of

apostasy and the description of its characteristics, we have a series of very startling illustrations. In Israel the form of apostasy was that of unbelief; and the issue of it was that they were destroyed. The nature of the apostasy of Angels was rebellion; they kept not their proper habitation, they moved out of their God-appointed orbit; choosing for themselves, they wandered out of bounds; and the issue was that they are kept in bonds. They wandered out of the bounds of His law, and therefore they are kept in bonds, reserved in darkness until the final day. Sodom and Gomorrah afford a startling illustration, in its recognition of the solemn fact that there light is given in some measure to every nation and man, and that men are judged by God according to the light they have. The apostasy of Sodom and Gomorrah consisted in their giving themselves over to all manner of lust and fornication. The issue was that of the age-abiding fire.

Then three persons are given as illustrations; Cain who was self-righteous; Balaam whose sin was greed; and Korah whose sin was presumption. All these are contrary to faith.

Go over the ground again. In the first illustration it is plainly stated, the sin of unbelief. The angels when they left their first estate, their proper habitation, did so as the result of unbelief. In the case of Sodom and Gomorrah it was failure of faith. The sensual life is the opposite of the life of faith. Sodom and Gomorrah, when they gave themselves to fornication, were answering the clamouring call of the carnal and sensual which is always a contradiction to faith. Cain's attitude was devoid of faith; his was the self-righteous attitude of life. Balaam's attitude was in contradiction to faith. In a sense Balaam had faith; he had belief intellectually. He failed in faith in that he did not obey. So also with Korah's presumption.

Where faith fails, morality fails. I pray you interpret that word morality in its widest sense, not as it is interpreted by the man in the street or by the magazine writer. The immorality of the angels was the denial of the government of God, and rebellion against it. Wherever you find it, immorality is denial of faith. Not the ending of intellectual conviction, that is not immorality. Immorality is refusal to obey the truth of which I am convinced, and that is also apostasy.

Where there is such apostasy, inevitably the judgment must fall. It is contained in germ within the apostasy. "My righteous one shall live by faith." If faith fail, God is not unfaithful; which does not mean that He will maintain the promise when the conditions are broken; but that He *cannot* maintain the promise when the conditions are broken.

Turning to the abiding appeal; we have first the inclusive statement. Jude wrote exhorting us to "contend earnestly for the faith." The one word translated "contend earnestly" occurs nowhere else. The root of the word is found in the New Testament in other applications; where it is said for instance that Epaphras strove in prayer, we have the same word, which might be rendered agonizes. Here the word is intensified by its context, consequently our translation is, "contend earnestly." There is not the slightest suggestion of argument. We are not asked to defend the faith by arguing for it. What then is the thought of the word? It is that of passionate and determined effort. The word really has in it the thought of the abandon and cautiousness of the athlete. "Contend earnestly for the faith." The apostle did not mean, Lecture on Christian evidences. That may be a perfectly proper thing to do in its place. He did not mean, Form a league for the defense of the Bible. He did not mean, Argue with every man you meet that these things are so. The final argument for faith in the world is not the argument of words, but the argument of life. What he meant was this: Put into the business of your defense of this great faith passionate and determined effort; let there be the abandon and cautiousness of the athlete.

In the closing verses we have the exposition of the way in which we are to obey the command to contend earnestly for the faith, "building up yourselves on your most holy faith, praying in the Holy Spirit, keep yourselves in the love of God, looking for the mercy of our Lord Jesus Christ unto eternal life." We are to keep ourselves in the love of God; not to put ourselves there; we are in the love of God; being there, we are to keep ourselves in that love; which again does not mean that we are to remain there, but seeing that we are there, we are to behave as we ought to behave. We are in that love; therefore we are to respond to it, obey it. How are we to do that? By building, praying, looking. "Building up yourselves on your most holy faith," that is by answering the claim of the faith we possess, carrying it into all the activities of our every-day life so that we become stronger and grow perpetually. " Praying in the Holy Spirit." If our personal effort is that of building; our perpetual consciousnes is that of dependence, praying. All this with the goal in view, "looking," the eye ever fixed upon the ultimate consummation, the glorious issue.

If we desire to contend for the faith that is how we are to do it. The profoundest argument, indeed the only argument in favour of faith, is life homed in the love of God, building itself up on faith, forever praying in the Holy Spirit, and forevermore looking for the mercy of our Lord unto age-abiding life. Find the man or woman, youth or maiden, boy or girl, professing faith in the Lord Jesus Christ, holding in that sense the faith of Christianity, who stays in the love of God, builds up the life upon faith, never undertaking any enterprise save as it is conditioned by the underlying facts of Christianity, living forevermore under the Holy Spirit, in dependence upon that Spirit's coöperation, looking ever for the ultimate perfecting; such an one is doing more for the defense of the faith than all wordy argument. The faith is contended for by the whole business of life, by consecration characterized by caution and courage; the putting out of our lives of all the things that are contrary to the will of the Lord and Master, refusing to turn the grace of God into lasciviousness; never denying, but forevermore affirming in life, the Lord and Master of us all.

There is something else. We cannot contend for the faith and keep ourselves, save as we help others. How are we to help them? " On some have mercy, who are in doubt ; and some save, snatching them out of the fire ; and on some have mercy with fear; hating even the garment spotted by the flesh."

Finally, what is the inspiration of this life in which we contend for the faith? " Now unto Him that is able to guard you—as with a garrison—from stumbling, and to set you before the presence of His glory without blemish in exceeding joy, to the only God our Saviour, through Jesus Christ our Lord, be glory, majesty domin-

ion, and power, before all time, and now, and forevermore." The inspiration is the certainty that the Master is able to guard us from stumbling, and at last to set us before the presence of God with exceeding joy and without blemish. But He cannot guard us from stumbling if we deny Him. He cannot guard us from stumbling if we are apostate, if we deliberately continue in unbelief as in the case of Israel; in speculative attempts to act on our own behalf as in the case of the angels ; in descent towards sensual things and fornication as in the case of Sodom and Gomorrah ; in self-righteous satisfaction even in our worship as in the case of Cain ; in greed as in the case of Balaam ; in presumption as in the case of Korah. If in any of these things we are guilty of apostasy, He cannot guard us from apostasy. If we are abiding in the love of God, building on faith, praying in the Spirit, looking for mercy, then all hell cannot make us stumble, because He is able to guard us as with a garrison from stumbling.

A final word by way of application. First to the Church. What is the faith for which we are to contend? The faith once for all delivered to the saints; that is, the whole system of truth. What is the system of truth? That truth is centred in a Person. That Person is the Person of these New Testament revelations ; the Person of the Gospels, the Acts, the Epistles. The Person is seen in the flesh in the first four pamphlets ; but is interpreted by the Spirit in the apostolic writings. That is the faith. It is that truth embodied in a Person, operating in grace and holiness, for which we are to contend.

Then to the individual. What is the contending which defends the faith? Constant loyalty to Christ; ceaseless caution in the presence of things contrary to His will; courage and confidence. By these things we shall indeed defend the faith. It is possible for a man to attempt to defend the faith by argument, and successfully by argument to state the facts of the faith, while instead of defending it, he is actually destroying it by his own life, by his own character. Faith, and contending for the faith by obedience to the claims of the faith will forevermore make apostasy impossible.

Revelation

THE ESSENTIAL MESSAGE	THE APPLICATION
I. **The central teaching**—unveiling. A. The unveiled Person—the Alpha and Omega. 　1. The identification. 　　a. The Lord God, the Almighty—1:8. 　　b. God dwelling with men—21:6. 　　c. The coming One—22:13. 　2. The vocation. 　　a. The Priest—cf. ver. 5. 　　b. The King—the established city. 　　c. The Prophet—cf. ver. 10. B. The unveiled power. 　1. Personal—inherent; acquired. 　2. Instrumental—all material forces; all spiritual forces. 　3. Effectual—destructive; constructive. C. The unveiled purpose. 　1. The ultimate. 　　a. God dwelling with men. 　　b. Men blessed in God. 　　c. God glorified in men. 　2. The progressive. 　　a. At war against sin. 　　b. The destruction of sin. 　　c. The patience of even justice. II. **The abiding appeal.** A. An opening word of courage—"Fear not." 　1. The vision producing fear—1:17a. 　2. The voice interpreting the vision—1:17b, 18. 　3. The vision inspiring courage—1:19. B. A closing word of caution—"I testify." 　1. No additions—speculative deductions. 　2. No subtractions—unbelieving denials.	I. **To the church.** A. This is preeminently a book for the friends of Jesus. B. To know it is to be saved from mistakes about: 　1. His Person. 　2. His power. 　3. His programme. II. **To the individual.** A. The new creation as revealing the meaning of life in Christ. B. The processes as revealing the principles of life in Christ.

IN attempting to discover the message of the book of Revelation, it is well that we should remember that differing interpretations of detail need not detain or trouble us, because its essential message is not interfered with, whatever view may be held as to how the book should be interpreted in such matters of detail.

There are at least four schools of interpretation of this wonderful book. I simply mention them in passing. They have been described as the Preterist, the Historic, the Futurist, and the Spiritual. The first affirms that in this book we have Jewish history to the fall of Jerusalem, and to the fall of pagan Rome set forth in symbolic form. The second interprets the book as giving an outline of events through the whole of the Christian era. The third treats the book as giving the events associated with the second Advent of our Lord. The fourth deals with the book as being entirely spiritual, declaring that therein in signs and by symbols we have the revelation of the principles of the perpetual conflict between good and evil until the winning of the final victory. I am not going to enter into discussion as between these views. I believe there is an element of truth in every one of them. I do not think either of them exhausts the truth. However full of mystery this book is, it is the only book in the Bible which opens with a distinct blessing promised to the man who reads it, and keeps its words. That fact at least should arouse our attention, and give us to see that we ought not to treat the book carelessly, or lightly, or pass it over. I admit quite freely the difficulty of interpretation in the matter of detail; and there is no book in the Bible which I have read so often, no book to which I have tried to give more patient and persistent attention. As I have said, all the views to which I have referred may be partially true. The present study, however, is not concerned with them.

The first word of the Greek document is the keyword to the message as well as to the content. That is the word Revelation, the Greek word *Apokalupsis*. We have anglicized that word and now speak of the Apocalypse. In the Greek there is no definite article. The book opens with the word *Apokalupsis*, which means quite literally uncovering, disclosure. A literal translation is not always a correct one; for we must always understand the use of the word as well as its root meaning. Quite literally this word apocalypse means uncovering; far more beautiful and therefore nearer the truth for us is our word unveiling. That is the first word of the book. It is the key to the content, and it is positively, and inclusively the key to the message. An interesting fact is that this is the only occurrence of the word in the whole book; it is not found again. The word does not often occur in the New Testament. Paul uses it, and so does Peter. This is the one and only place in the writings of John where this word is to be found. It is as though it were reserved for this book. I do not mean that John reserved it, for it is quite possible that this book was written before his letters. It may be that if I could have talked to John the aged, after he had written the last of his words for his beloved children, I should have found that he did not know that he had never used the word but once, and only there. These are very human documents so far as the men who wrote them were concerned. It

is in the recognition of the human that we come to the discovery of the Divine in the study of the Bible. While not now staying to enter into all that is involved, I believe that the Spirit presided over and led men in the arrangement of the Canon, as certainly as He presided over and led men in the writing of the books. I do not think the Spirit was withdrawn when the last inspired literature was given to the Church. I think the Spirit still presided over human choices until the Library was completely arranged. I repeat, therefore, that it is as though this word *Unveiling* were reserved for this book. We read the first word Unveiling; and it is as though the great doors swing open, and visions of glory appear, introduced by this word. We have been following from Genesis, through message after message, and at last we come to the final book in the library, and it opens with this word Unveiling. It is the ultimate book in the Bible; the final book in the Canon; and the attention is immediately centred upon a Person. It is "the unveiling of Jesus Christ, which God gave Him to show unto His servants, even the things which must shortly come to pass: and He sent and signified it by His angel unto His servant John." The Unveiling of Christ, the final truth about Christ is in this last book of the Bible. That is the key to its message.

Let us first consider the essential message. The central teaching is all suggested by the word Unveiling. This book is for the friends of Jesus. The proportion of our understanding of secret things is the proportion of our love for the Lord. There are too many things assumed here for the book to be apprehended by any save those who know the secret of the Lord.

First we have the unveiled Person; described as "The Alpha and the Omega"; a phrase which occurs three times, and only at the most remarkable situations. The message concerning Him is concerned with identification and vocation. The threefold use of that title identifies the Person; and shows the vocation of that Person in human history. Let us observe the three occasions.

It first occurs in the eighth verse of the first chapter. The "Even so, Amen" of verse seven is not the language of the one speaking before; it is the introduction to the affirmation of verse eight, and should be read in close connection with it, and is more forcible, I think, in the older form, "Yea, amen. I am the Alpha and the Omega, saith the Lord God, which is and which was and which is to come, the Almighty."

The next occurrence is in chapter twenty-one, verse six, "They are come to pass. I am the Alpha and the Omega, the beginning and the end."

The third is in chapter twenty-two, verses twelve and thirteen, "Behold, I come quickly; and My reward is with Me, to render to each man according as his work is. I am the Alpha and the Omega, the first and the last, the beginning and the end." That is the unveiling of the Person. The whole book is about that Person. Everything circles about that Person.

The first affirmation is characterized by simplicity; there is no ambiguity, there can be no mistake as to the meaning; "I am the Alpha and the Omega, saith the Lord God, which is and which was and which is to come, the Almighty." There is no verse in the Bible more explicit than that as a description of absolute and positive Deity. Thus in the first occurrence of the strange yet wonderfully symbolic and beautiful description, "the Alpha and the Omega," the first and the last, the beginning and the end, it is used of God Himself. He is described by the conceptions of the Old Testament, condensed into brief statements, "The Lord God, which is and which was and which is to come, the Almighty." All the titles of God in the Old Testament are represented in that description. The qualities of every Old Testament title for God are in that wonderful passage.

The next occurrence is in the chapter of the final triumph. The millennium is described in six verses in the twentieth chapter. Beyond it there is conflict, and a great assize, and then the Kingdom of the Son is established, which must not be confused with the thousand years. It is in that unmeasured period that the city of God, descending out of heaven, God dwells with men; and concerning that ultimate triumph the words are employed; "I am the Alpha and the Omega, the beginning and the end." The process began when the Word Who was with God, and was God, "became flesh and tabernacled among us (and we beheld His glory, glory as

of the only begotten from the Father), full of grace and truth." It will end with the ultimate victory. "Behold, the tabernacle of God is with men, and He shall dwell with them. . . . I am the Alpha and the Omega." That again is evidently the language of God.

The final occurrence is in the promise, "Behold, I come quickly; and My reward is with Me, to render to each man according as his work is." Who now is the speaker? The answer is immediately given; "I Jesus have sent Mine angel to testify unto you these things."

The first reference is patently to the God of the Old Testament, the Sovereign Lord, the Almighty God, the Becoming One, Who is and was and is to come, the Almighty. The last is linked to that simple declaration, "I Jesus have sent Mine angel to testify unto you these things." Thus the identification is complete. Jesus is Jehovah.

In these connections the Person is unveiled as to vocation. The first declaration was made in answer to an ascription of praise; "Unto Him that loveth us, and loosed us from our sins by His blood." The answer was "I am the Alpha and the Omega, saith the Lord God, which is and which was and which is to come, the Almighty." That reveals the Person as Priest.

The next was made in connection with the fall of Babylon. The ultimate victory is won; the Kingdom has come; then the word is again spoken, "I am the Alpha and the Omega, the beginning and the end." That reveals the Person as King as well as Priest.

At the close of the book when the solemn warning is given that the words of the prophecy are not to be sealed, that the great teaching is to be the open secret of all those who read it; then again the voice is heard, "I am the Alpha and the Omega, the first and the last, the beginning and the end." That reveals the Person as Prophet.

Thus the Person is Jehovah—Jesus, at once Priest, King, and Prophet. The whole of the Old Testament is answered. The Pentateuch sighs for a Priest, but never finds Him. The historic books cry for a King, but He does not appear. The prophetic books attempt in broken words to speak the Word, the abiding Truth;

but they were never harmonized, and final. The Old Testament says, Humanity needs a Priest, a King, and a Prophet. Here we have the Priest, the King, and the Prophet unveiled; and He is the Alpha and the Omega, the One from Whom all came, to Whom all proceeds, and through Whom the end is assured from the beginning. This One is the mystic, mighty, very God of Gods; and this One is Jesus. That is what this book teaches. No man can read it, and escape from the conviction that this is what the writer thought.

In the second place we have in this book the unveiled power of the Person; and it is revealed as personal, instrumental, and effectual.

The personal power is first inherent, and secondly acquired. He is, as we have seen, the essential Being; and we cannot read this book without feeling the awfulness of the power of God. We are made conscious of how terrible are the powers which are against God, in the figurative language which describes them as beasts, dragons. That is only the first impression. The final impression is that all these beasts and dragons are in the grip of God and cannot escape Him. That is a revelation of the inherent power of the unveiled Person. Then there is the acquired power; we see not the throne only, but also the Lamb in the midst of it, as it had been slain. That is power won out of some mystery of passion and pain and suffering. The book opens with the anthem of this acquired power, "Unto Him that loveth us, and loosed us from our sins by His blood."

The instrumental power of the unveiled Person is also unveiled. All elemental forces, earthquakes, lightnings, thunders; forces of the air; plagues; He makes use of. Spiritual forces also; angels, good and evil; all of them are under His command.

The effectual power of this One Person is seen to be both destructive and constructive. When we get rid of the idea that God can destroy, we get rid of the idea that God can construct. There must be destruction in order to construction in a world like this. The two activities are seen operating through all this book, and always through the same Person.

Thirdly we find the unveiled purpose, both ultimately and progressively.

The ultimate purpose of God is to dwell with men; man is to be blessed in God; God is to be glorified in man. We do not find in this revelation any reference to the highest glory of all. We must go to the Ephesian letter for that, and see the Church telling the wisdom of God to the ages to come. Here the glory is that of the Kingdom established in this world. This is the programme of God's final methods in the world. The ultimate note is that of the tabernacling of God with men; the city of God coming out of heaven; the realization of the Divine purpose on earth.

The progressive purpose of God is that He is at war against sin. He is destroying sin. I thank God for this book. Symbolic as it is, full of signs and wonders, the significance of which I have not yet been able to understand in detail; it nevertheless clearly presents this picture of God, the Alpha and the Omega, at war with sin; and it is as full of comfort as anything within the covers of the Divine Library. Persuade me for a single moment that God is going to make peace with sin, and I become the most hopeless man in the world. Let me see God with drawn sword fighting against sin; then I see a God of such infinite love, that I know that "though a wide compass first be fetched," the kingdom of the world shall become the Kingdom of this One.

The abiding appeal consists of an opening word of courage; and a closing word of caution.

When John was in Patmos he saw a vision of his Lord, a wonderful vision, symbolically revealing sublime things with which we are not going to deal in detail. When he saw that vision, he became as one dead; then there came to him the touch of the human hand, and the sound of the human voice, and the great "Fear not." "When I saw Him, I fell at His feet as one dead. And He laid His right hand upon me, saying, Fear not; I am the first and the last, and the Living One; and I was dead, and behold I am alive forevermore, and I have the keys of death and of Hades. Write therefore the things which thou sawest, and the things which are." If you take the "therefore" out of the verse you have lost much. The "therefore" links the command to write with the great "Fear not." Write *therefore* the things you have seen, the things that are, and the things which shall be; write these visions and fear not.

Because I have said, "Fear not," therefore

write. Write without fear. That is indeed a great word of courage to the man who writes the book, and to the man who reads the book. Be not afraid, because I am He that liveth, and I have the keys! Do you not feel that you could walk with Him through hell itself? Let us see the end of the whole matter. Let us watch the process of that righteous judgment that makes no peace with sin until it have established righteousness on the earth. Sin slew Him; but He slew sin. He was alive, and was dead; but is alive forevermore. The great "Fear not!" I hear it now, not only through the reading of the book, but above the clamour of the hour in which I live, amid the clash of arms, amid all the babel of earth's confused noises. "Fear not." This unveiled Person fills the vision. It is He that was dead but is alive forevermore. "Therefore will we not fear, though the earth do change, and though the mountains be moved in the heart of the seas."

Then there is a closing word of caution, "I testify." No additions must be made to this book, no subtractions from it. No additions; no speculative deductions. Take the things written and attempt to understand them; ponder them, but beware of speculative deductions. No subtractions; no unbelieving denials, no declaration that these things cannot be, because we cannot understand them. The Person as He is revealed; the power as it is unveiled; the purpose as it is declared; without addition or subtraction. That is the final caution of the book.

In making application of the message of this book first to the Church, I would say again what I have already said. This is preëminently a book for the friends of Jesus. To know it is to be saved from mistakes about His Person, about His power, about His programme.

No man who denies the absolute Deity of Jesus can accept this book, he must get rid of it.

No man who has any panic in his heart as to the issue can believe this book. There is no book in the Bible to which I turn more eagerly in hours of depression than to this, with all its mystery, all the details which I do not understand. I go back to it, to the throne, and to the Lamb as it had been slain; and my puzzled mind and troubled heart feel the healing virtue; and I hear the song, and am ready for another day's fighting, for I know that Jesus shall reign.

No man who reads this book expects that the world is going to be converted by gospel preaching without judgment. There must be a period of judgment. God will have the double harvest. There will be the harvest of evil; evil must work itself out to its final manifestation. It is not to be smothered. It is to be seen, not upon the housetop of the earthly city merely, but in the universe of God.

To the individual this book says, Behold the new creation; and by observing that understand the truth about thyself. If any man be in Christ, he is a new creation. Study well the beauty and the glory of life governed by this Person, and know the meaning of thy life in Christ. Study well the processes of life in the new creation, and understand the principles of thy life in Christ. Know that this new creation within thy experience can only come to its final perfecting, as God fights within thee against sin and slays it. The ultimate victory is not reached in a moment. Pardoned, justified, made nigh, we are, in a moment; but all the processes are necessary for the subjection of the territory, and the establishment of the Kingdom; thunder, earthquake, as well as the gentle and caressing touch of the dawning of the morning. Jesus Who is the Lamb in the midst of the throne is God; and in His presence is the place of worship; and in His power is the place of refuge.